Arctic Ocean

NORWAY
SWEDEN
FINLAND
DENMARK
ESTONIA
LATVIA
LITHUANIA
NETH.
Spy • Neander Valley
BEL. • Heidelberg (Mauer)
FRANCE POLAND BELARUS
SWITZERLAND CZECH REP.
Krapina • SLOVAKIA
Arago • HUNG. UKRAINE
ITALY MOLDOVA
Ceprano • Petralona ROMANIA
GREECE BULGARIA
Tighenif • Dmanisi
TUNISIA TURKEY GEORGIA
Amud • SYRIA ARMENIA AZERBAIJAN
ALGERIA Skhūl/Tabun • Shanidar
LIBYA LEBANON IRAQ
ISRAEL
JORDAN
EGYPT KUWAIT
BAHRAIN
QATAR
U.A.E.
SAUDI
ARABIA
OMAN

RUSSIA

KAZAKHSTAN

UZBEKISTAN
Teshik Tash •
KYRGYZSTAN
TURKMENISTAN TAJIKISTAN
IRAN AFGHANISTAN
PAKISTAN
NEPAL BHUTAN
INDIA
BANGLADESH
MYANMAR
(BURMA)

MONGOLIA

Jinniushan •
Zhoukoudian •
NORTH KOREA
Lantian • Dali •
CHINA Hexian •
Maba •

SOUTH KOREA
JAPAN

TAIWAN
HONG KONG (U.K.)
MACAU (Port.)

LAOS
THAILAND VIETNAM
CAMBODIA

NIGER
CHAD
SUDAN
Bahr el Ghazal •
ERITREA YEMEN
Hadar •
DJIBOUTI
Bodo • Middle Awash (Aramis; Bouri)
• Konso-Gardula
ETHIOPIA
Omo •
SOMALIA
UGANDA
Kanapoi • KENYA • East and West Turkana
• Olduvai/Laetoli

NIGERIA
BENIN
TOGO
CAMEROON
CENTRAL AFRICAN REP.
GUINEA
SAO TOME & PRINCIPE
GABON
CONGO
DEMOCRATIC REPUBLIC OF THE CONGO
RWANDA
BURUNDI
TANZANIA

SRI LANKA

MALDIVES

SEYCHELLES

PHILIPPINES

BRUNEI
MALAYSIA
Borneo
Sumatra SINGAPORE
INDONESIA

Sangiran • • Ngandong
• Trinil

Pacific Ocean

NORTHERN MARIANA ISLANDS (U.S.)

REPUBLIC OF THE MARSHALL ISLANDS

FEDERATED STATES OF MICRONESIA

PAPUA NEW GUINEA

SOLOMON ISLANDS

TUVALU

Indian Ocean

COMOROS IS.

ANGOLA
ZAMBIA
Broken Hill •
NAMIBIA ZIMBABWE
MALAWI
MADAGASCAR
MAURITIUS
MOZAMBIQUE

WALVIS BAY
(Status to be determined)
BOTSWANA
Makapansgat •
Taung • Sterkfontein/Swartkrans/Kromdraai
SWAZILAND
Florisbad • LESOTHO
SOUTH Border Cave
AFRICA
Klasies River Mouth •

AUSTRALIA

Lake Mungo •
• Kow Swamp

NEW CALEDONIA (Fr.)
VANUATU
FIJI
NEW ZEALAND

1. SLOVENIA
2. CROATIA
3. BOSNIA AND HERZEGOVINA
4. ALBANIA
5. MACEDONIA

ANTARCTICA

ARCTIC CIRCLE
80°N
60°N
40°N
TROPIC OF CANCER
20°N
EQUATOR 0°
20°S
TROPIC OF CAPRICORN
40°S
60°S
ANTARCTIC CIRCLE
80°S

20°E 40°E 60°E 80°E 100°E 120°E 140°E 160°E 180°

www.wadsworth.com

wadsworth.com is the World Wide Web site for Wadsworth and is your direct source to dozens of online resources.

At *wadsworth.com* you can find out about supplements, demonstration software, and student resources. You can also send email to many of our authors and preview new publications and exciting new technologies.

wadsworth.com
Changing the way the world learns®

FOURTH EDITION

ESSENTIALS OF Physical Anthropology

Robert Jurmain
San Jose State University

Harry Nelson
Emeritus, Foothill College

Lynn Kilgore
Colorado State University

Wenda Trevathan
New Mexico State University

Wadsworth
Thomson Learning™

Australia • Canada • Mexico • Singapore
Spain • United Kingdom • United States

Anthropology Editor:	Lin Marshall
Development Editor:	Robert Jucha
Assistant Editor:	Dee Dee Zobian
Editorial Assistant:	Analie Barnett
Marketing Manager:	Matthew Wright
Project Editors:	Jerilyn Emori, Lisa Weber
Print Buyer:	Karen Hunt
Permissions Editor:	Joohee Lee
Production Service:	Hespenheide Design
Text Designer:	Janet Bollow
Art Editor:	Hespenheide Design
Photo Researcher:	Hespenheide Design
Copy Editor:	Janet Greenblatt

Illustrators:	Alexander Productions, DLF Group, Hespenheide Design, Randy Miyake, Paragon 3, Sue Sellars, Cyndie Wooley
Cover Designer:	Hespenheide Design
Cover Image:	Reconstructed cranium of *Australopithecus garhi* from Bouri, Ethiopia. Approximate age 2.5 million years. © 1999 David L. Brill/ Atlanta *Background image:* Drawing by Leonardo da Vinci. © Windsor Castle, Royal Library/A.K.G., Berlin/SuperStock
Cover Printer:	Phoenix Color Corp.
Compositor:	Hespenheide Design
Printer:	Quebecor/World Book Services, Versailles

Library of Congress Cataloging-in-Publication Data
Essentials of physical anthropology / Robert Jurmain . . . [et al.].-4th ed.
   p. cm.
  Includes bibliographical references and index.
  ISBN 0-534-57816-0
  1. Physical anthropology. I. Jurmain, Robert.
GN60.N43 2000
599.9—dc21
00-028442

Wadsworth/Thomson Learning
10 Davis Drive
Belmont, CA 94002-3098
USA

For more information about our products, contact us: **Thomson Learning Academic Resource Center**
1-800-423-0563
http://www.wadsworth.com

International Headquarters
Thomson Learning
International Division
290 Harbor Drive, 2nd Floor
Stamford, CT 06902-7477
USA

UK/Europe/Middle East/South Africa
Thomson Learning
Berkshire House
168-173 High Holborn
London WC1V 7AA
United Kingdom

Asia
Thomson Learning
60 Albert Street, #15-01
Albert Complex
Singapore 189969

Canada
Nelson Thomson Learning
1120 Birchmount Road
Toronto, Ontario M1K 5G4
Canada

Brief Contents

Contents

CHAPTER 6

Primate Behavior   120

CHAPTER 7

Mammalian/Primate Evolutionary History   147

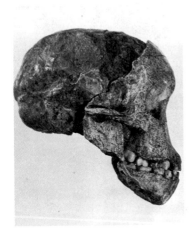

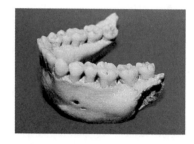

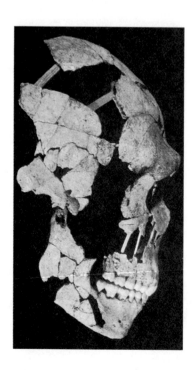

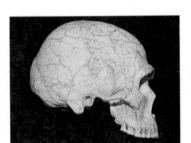

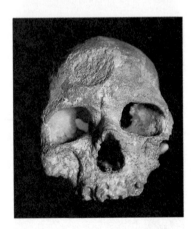

CHAPTER 11

Homo sapiens sapiens   271

CHAPTER 12

Microevolution in Modern Human Populations   297

CHAPTER 13

Human Variation and Adaptation   316

PHOTO ESSAY

Paleopathology: Injuries and Diseases of the Bone   340

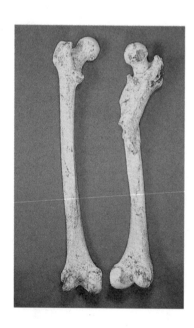

CHAPTER 14

The Anthropological Perspective on the Human Life Course   346

CHAPTER 15

Lessons from the Past, Lessons for the Future   368

Preface

Over the more than two decades that we have been preparing textbooks in physical anthropology, we have been guided by one major objective: To make physical anthropology accessible to introductory students. From our own teaching experience we have long recognized that introductory physical anthropology courses usually attract students coming from diverse educational backgrounds. Some students have had college courses in biology, while others had such a course in high school. But a significant portion of undergraduate students has not had any biology background prior to taking physical anthropology.

It is recognition of this wide diversity of student experiences and expertise that has shaped our approach to text content and organization. In order to make the material technically accurate and up-to-date, while at the same time engaging, we have organized the text to provide a step-by-step discussion of topics.

Since physical anthropology is a *biological science,* it is necessary to present background information concerning basic biological processes. These topics are oftentimes highly challenging for students with little prior background. Accordingly, we make every attempt to present *scientific* concepts using a minimum of jargon (and definitions of key terms appear both in a running glossary in the margins when they are first presented as well as at the back of the text).

Additionally, and most basic to our entire approach, the writing style is carefully designed to be clear and understandable, while not insulting the intelligence of college-level readers. Moreover, the text organization provides students various types of aids to promote comprehension (see section below). Fundamental to all these efforts is the authors' conviction that the best text is one written with the students' perspective always in mind.

Features

As mentioned, *Essentials of Physical Anthropology* contains a number of features designed to encourage student learning. In summary:

- **Chapter outlines** at the beginning of each chapter, list all major topics covered.
- A **running glossary** in the margins provides definitions of terms immediately adjacent to the text, when the term is *first* introduced. A full glossary is provided at the back of the book.
- **Line drawings** and **photographs,** most in full color, are carefully selected and placed to directly support discussion in the text.
- **Photo essays** introduce topics (e.g., Tools and Techniques of Physical Anthropology: Paleopathology) to stimulate student interest in contemporary applied research done by physical anthropologists.

- **Full bibliography** at the end and citation of complete sources throughout the text demonstrate to students how standard referencing is used in scientific/scholarly presentation and provide an example for students preparing their own research papers.
- The **concluding chapter,** "Lessons from the Past, Lessons for the Future," is unique to this text and challenges students to use an *evolutionary perspective* when considering contemporary issues such as population growth, global warming, habitat destruction, and loss of biodiversity.

Organization of the Fourth Edition

To those familiar with the third edition of *Essentials of Physical Anthropology,* the fourth edition contains two major organizational changes. First, rather than 16 chapters, the current edition has 15 (accomplished by combining two chapters on Plio-Pleistocene hominids into one comprehensive chapter, Chapter 8). Second, the materials on modern human variation and adaptation (formerly Chapters 5, 6, and 7) have been moved to the back of the book (Chapters 12, 13, and 14) where they precede our concluding chapter (Chapter 15, "Lessons from the Past, Lessons for the Future"). Moreover, all three of these chapters have been somewhat refocused as reflected in new chapter titles for each: Chapter 12 ("Microevolution in Modern Human Populations"); Chapter 13 ("Human Variation and Adaptation"); Chapter 14 ("The Anthropological Perspective on the Human Life Course"). Finally, so as to synthesize information more clearly with this new chapter order, Chapter 4 has been reorganized to integrate materials on heredity and evolution better (as reflected in a new chapter title, "Heredity and Evolution").

What's New in the Fourth Edition?

In order to stay abreast of new developments in physical anthropology, several updates have been incorporated into this edition. Chapter 4 includes expanded coverage of the Human Genome Project. We have also significantly updated the materials on fossil hominids, including recent discoveries of Plio-Pleistocene species (*Ardipithecus; Australopithecus garhi*) in Chapter 8; new discoveries of *Homo erectus* (or contemporaries) from Spain and Italy (Chapter 9); and recent finds of Neandertals or early modern *H. sapiens* from Portugal, France, and Croatia (Chapter 10). In addition, since many contemporary scholars recognize considerable complexity in the evolution of *Homo,* a new section in Chapter 10 presents varied interpretations and species designations (i.e., *H. rudolfensis, H. ergaster, H. heidelbergensis, H. neanderthalensis*).

The exciting new attempts to extract and sequence Neandertal DNA are also covered in Chapter 10. In fact, emerging molecular technologies utilized by physical anthropologists are covered in more depth; new materials reflecting this research have been added to the photo essays.

Chapter 14 expands the focus on infectious disease with an emphasis on HIV/AIDS. The discussion of infectious disease also deals with the role of cultural factors such as population growth, human-induced climate change, and overuse of antibiotics in the reemergence of some infectious diseases. Chapter 15 focuses more fully on the application of an explicit anthropological perspective to understand the human life course, and this more holistic interpretation is further integrated with discussions found throughout earlier chapters. Finally, we have added a new appendix (Appendix C, "Sexing and Aging the Skeleton"). This extensively illustrated new section is designed to provide students with an appreciation of some of the basic skeletal techniques used by osteologists and forensic anthropologists.

Multimedia Learning Aids

This edition also allows students easier access to multimedia learning aids. A major new addition is the systematic integration of links with the *Virtual Laboratories for Introductory Physical Anthropology* CD-ROM, Second Edition, prepared by John Kappelman of the University of Texas at Austin. In the margins throughout the text there are icons linking the concepts discussed in the book with specific virtual labs on the CD-ROM.

Archaeology is discussed in Virtual Lab 11 and includes many 3-D animations of stone tools.

Internet Exercises   Another expanded feature of the fourth edition is the addition of Internet exercises at the end of each chapter. Incorporating specific sites on the Internet, these exercises are designed to help students become more competent in using the Internet.

***InfoTrac College Edition* Exercises**   Also new to this edition are exercises utilizing the *InfoTrac® College Edition,* a comprehensive on-line library. Tracey O'Rourke of San Jose State University prepared both the Internet and InfoTrac exercises.

Acknowledgments

Over the years many friends and colleagues have assisted us with our books. For this edition we are especially grateful to the reviewers who so carefully commented on the manuscript and made such helpful suggestions:

Nancy Cordell
Tacoma Community College

Robert S. Corruccini
Southern Illinois University, Carbondale

Lawrence P. Greska
Case Western Reserve University

Anne Grauer
Loyola University, Chicago

Shawn Lehman
SUNY, Stony Brook

Karen Lupo
Washington State University

Elizabeth H. Peters
Florida State University

Susan Pfeiffer
University of Guelph

Meredith F. Small
Cornell University

Flora L. Price
Albuquerque T-VI, Community College

In addition, we thank the reviewers of the previous edition:

David H. Dye (University of Memphis), Mark J. Hartmann (University of Arkansas at Little Rock), Lynnette E. Leidy (University of Massachusetts), Deborah J. Overdorff (University of Texas at Austin), Anna Lucy Robinson (Lambton College, Ontario), Dianne Smith (Santa Rosa Junior College), and Ameeta S. Tiwana (DeAnza College).

We also wish to thank at Wadsworth Publishing Dee Dee Zobian, Assistant Editor; Lin Marshall, Anthropology Editor; Robert Jucha, Development Editor; Eve Howard, Publisher; and Susan Badger, President and CEO. Moreover, for their unflagging expertise and patience we are grateful to our copy editor, Janet Greenblatt, and our production coordinators, Gary Hespenheide and Patti Zeman.

For their assistance with the photo essays we are indebted to Art Aufderheide, Diane France, Susan and Kirk Jenkens, Don Johanson, Margaret Maples, Jim Moore, Anne Silver, Ruby Tilly, and the Photography Department, San Jose State University Instructional Resources Center.

To the many friends and colleagues who have generously provided photographs we are greatly appreciative: Art Aufderheide, Julie Bitnoff, C. K. Brain, Günter Bräuer, Desmond Clark, Raymond Dart, Henri DeLumley, Jean deRousseau, Denis Etler, Diane France, David Frayer, Kathleen Galvin, David Haring, Ellen Ingmanson, Fred Jacobs, Peter Jones, Arlene Kruse, Richard Leakey, Carol Lofton, Margaret Maples, Russ Mittermeier, Lorna Moore, John Oates, Bonnie Pedersen, Lorna Pierce, David Pilbeam, William Pratt, Ann Rademacher, Judith Regensteiner, Sastrohamijoyo Sartono, Wayne Savage, Eugenie Scott, Rose Sevick, Elwyn Simons, Meredith Small, Fred Smith, Judy Suchey, Li Tianyuan, Philip Tobias, Alan Walker, Milford Wolpoff, and Xinzhi Wu.

Robert Jurmain
Harry Nelson
Lynn Kilgore
Wenda Trevathan

Supplements

Supplements for Instructors

Instructor's Manual with Test Bank   Written by the text authors, the manual includes concept outlines, chapter overviews, learning objectives, and lecture suggestions. The Test Bank includes multiple choice and short answer/essay questions.

***ExamView* Computerized and Online Testing from Wadsworth/Thomson Learning**   Create, deliver, and customize tests and study guides (both print and online) in minutes with this easy-to-use assessment and tutorial system.

Wadsworth's Physical Anthropology Transparency Acetates   A set of four-color acetates is available to help prepare lecture presentations.

Slides   Color slides of art found in the text are available.

PowerPoint   Available free to adopters, this book-specific PowerPoint presentation can be viewed and downloaded from our Web site at http://anthropology.wadsworth.com/instructor/. A user name and password are available from your Wadsworth/Thomson Learning sales representative.

AnthroLink   AnthroLink CD-ROM is an easy-to-use presentation tool that permits instructors to integrate media from this CD-ROM digital library into their lecture presentations. AnthroLink contains hundreds of pieces of graphic art from Wadsworth anthropology textbooks, photographs, and short video segments as well as the software to edit, sequence, and present customized lectures which can be saved and even posted to the Web.

Wadsworth Anthropology Video Library   Qualified adopters may select full-length videos from an extensive library of offerings drawn from such excellent educational video sources such as *NOVA, Films for the Humanities and Sciences, The Disappearing World,* and *In Search of Human Origins.*

CNN Physical Anthropology Today Video Series, Volumes I, II, and III   The CNN *Physical Anthropology Today Videos* is an exclusive series jointly created by Wadsworth and CNN for the physical anthropology course. Each video in the series consists of approximately 45 minutes of footage originally broadcast on CNN within the last several years. The videos are broken into short two- to seven-minute segments, which are perfect for classroom use as lecture launchers, or to illustrate key anthropological concepts. An annotated table of contents accompanies each video with descriptions of the segments and suggestions for their possible use within the course.

Web-Based Resources

Anthropology Online: Wadsworth's Anthropology Resource Center   http:///anthropology.wadsworth.com At Wadsworth's Anthropology Resource Center, you will find surfing lessons (tips to find information on the Web), a career center, anthropology Web surfing links, InfoTrac, News, and an online forum.

At http://anthropology.wadsworth.com/texts/jurmain _essen.html you will find text-specific resources for *Essentials of Physical Anthropology,* Fourth Edition. Here you can access online quizzes, flashcards, Internet projects, hyper-contents, and more.

***InfoTrac* College Edition**   Ignite discussions or augment your lectures with the latest developments in anthropology. *InfoTrac College Edition* (available as a free option with this text) gives you and your students four months' free access to an easy-to-use online database of reliable, full-length articles (not abstracts) from hundreds of top academic journals and popular sources. Among the journals which are available 24 hours a day, seven days a week, *American Anthropologist, Current Anthropology, Evolution* and *Science.* Contact your Wadsworth/Thomson Learning representative for more information.

Supplements for Students

Virtual Laboratories for Physical Anthropology CD-ROM, Second Edition, by John Kappelman The new version of this Interactive CD-ROM provides students with a hands-on computer component for doing physical anthropology lab assignments at school or at home. It encourages students to actively participate in their physical anthropology lab or course through the taking of measurements and the plotting of data; it also tests their knowledge of important concepts. It contains full-color images, video clips, 3-D animations, sound, and more. In addition, students can link between the CD and Wadsworth Anthropology Resource Center to access additional online quizzes.

Study Guide Prepared by Denise Cucurny and Marcus Young Owl Chapter-by-chapter resources for the student, including learning objectives, fill-in-the-blank chapter outlines, key terms, and extensive opportunities for self-quizzing.

WebTutor This Web-based distance learning tool helps professors take the physical anthropology course beyond classroom boundaries to an interactive online, anywhere, anytime environment. Students access study tools, which correspond chapter by chapter and topic by topic with the book, including flashcards (with audio), online quizzes, and tutorials. Professors can use WebTutor's discussion forums and online communication tools to provide virtual office hours, post syllabi, set up threaded discussions, and track student progress on the quizzes. WebTutor is easily customizable to specific course needs.

Lab Manual and Workbook for Physical Anthropology, Fourth Edition, by Diane L. France, Colorado State University By emphasizing human osteology, forensic anthropology, anthropometry, primates, human evolution, and genetics, this lab manual provides students with hands-on lab assignments to help make the concepts of physical anthropology clearer. It contains short-answer questions, identification problems, and observation exercises.

ESSENTIALS OF
Physical Anthropology

CHAPTER
1

CONTENTS

Introduction

Introduction

One day, perhaps at the beginning of the rainy season some 3.7 million years ago, two or three individuals walked across a grassland savanna in what is now northern Tanzania. These individuals were early members of the taxonomic family **Hominidae,** the family that also includes ourselves, modern *Homo sapiens.* Fortunately for us (the living descendants of those distant travelers), a record of their passage on that long-forgotten day remains in the form of fossilized footprints, preserved in hardened volcanic deposits.

As chance would have it, shortly after heels and toes were pressed into the dampened soil and volcanic ash of the area, a volcano, some 12 miles distant, erupted. The ensuing ashfall blanketed everything on the ground surface, including the footprints of the **hominids** and those of numerous other species as well. In time, the ash layer hardened into a deposit that preserved a quite remarkable assortment of tracks and other materials that lay beneath it (Fig. 1–1).

These now-famous Laetoli prints indicate that two hominids, one smaller than the other, perhaps walked side by side, leaving parallel sets of tracks. But because the prints of the larger individual are obscured, possibly by those of a third, it is unclear how many actually made that journey so long ago. What is clear from the prints is that they were left by an animal that habitually walked **bipedally**

Hominidae
The taxonomic family to which humans belong; also includes other, now extinct, bipedal relatives.

Hominids
Members of the family Hominidae.

Bipedally
On two feet. Walking habitually on two legs is the single most distinctive feature of the Hominidae.

FIGURE 1–1

Early hominid footprints at Laetoli. The tracks to the left were made by one individual, while those to the right appear to have been formed by two individuals, the second stepping in the tracks of the first.

(on two feet). It is this critical feature that has led scientists to consider these ancient passersby as hominids.

In addition to the preserved footprints, scientists at Laetoli and elsewhere have discovered numerous fossilized skeletal remains of what most now call *Australopithecus afarensis*. These fossils and prints have volumes to say about the beings they represent, provided we can learn to interpret them.

What, then, have we actually gleaned from the meager evidence we possess of those creatures who beckon to us from an incomprehensibly distant past? Where did their journey take them that far-gone day, and why were they walking in that particular place? Were they foraging for food within the boundaries of their territory or were they going to a nearby water source? Did the two (or three) indeed travel together at all, or did they simply use the same route within a short period of time?

We could ask myriad questions about these individuals, but we will never be able to answer them all. They walked down a path into what became their future, and their immediate journey has long since ended. It remains for us to sort out what little we can know about them and the **species** they represent. In this sense, their greater journey continues.

From the footprints and from fossilized fragmentary skeletons, we know that these hominids walked in an upright posture. Thus, they were in many respects anatomically similar to ourselves, but their brains were only about one-third the size of ours. Although they may have used stones and sticks as tools, much as modern chimpanzees do, there is no current evidence to suggest they manufactured stone tools. In short, these early hominids were very much at the mercy of nature's whims. They certainly could not outrun most predators, and their lack of large projecting canine teeth rendered them relatively defenseless.

Chimpanzees often serve as living models for our early ancestors, but in fact, the earliest hominids occupied a different habitat, exploited different resources, and probably had more to fear from predators than do chimpanzees. However much we may be tempted to compare early hominids to living species, we must remind ourselves that there is no living form that adequately represents them. Just like every other living thing, they were unique.

On July 20, 1969, a television audience numbering in the hundreds of millions watched as two human beings stepped out of a spacecraft and onto the surface of the moon. To anyone born after that date, this event is taken more or less for granted, even though it has not been repeated often. But the significance of that first moonwalk cannot be overstated, for it represents humankind's presumed mastery over the natural forces that govern our presence on earth. For the first time ever, people actually walked upon the surface of a celestial body that (as far as we know) has never given birth to life.

As the astronauts gathered geological specimens and frolicked in near weightlessness, they left traces of their fleeting presence in the form of footprints in the lunar dust (Fig. 1–2). On the atmosphereless surface of the moon, where no rain falls and no wind blows, the footprints remain undisturbed to this day. They survive as mute testimony to a brief visit by a medium-sized, big-brained creature who presumed to challenge the very forces that created it.

We have uncovered the Laetoli footprints, and we question the nature of the animal who made them. Perhaps one day, creatures as yet unimagined will ponder the essence of the being that made the lunar footprints. What do you suppose they will think?

Species
A group of organisms that can interbreed to produce fertile offspring. Members of one species are reproductively isolated from members of all other species (i.e., they cannot mate with them to produce fertile offspring).

FIGURE 1–2
Human footprint left on the lunar surface during the Apollo mission.

Primate
A member of the mammalian order Primates (pronounced "pry-may-tees"), which includes prosimians, monkeys, apes, and humans.

We humans, who can barely comprehend a century, can only grasp at the enormity of 3.7 million years. We want to understand the essence of those creatures who traveled that day across the savanna. By what route did an insignificant but clever bipedal **primate** give rise to a species that would, in time, walk on the surface of a moon some 230,000 miles from earth? How did it come to be that in the relatively short (geologically speaking) span of fewer than 4 million years, an inconsequential savanna dweller evolved into the species that has developed the ability to dominate and destroy much of life on the planet?

How did it happen that *Homo sapiens*, a result of the same evolutionary forces that produced all other life on this planet, gained the power to control the flow of rivers and alter the very climate in which we live? As tropical animals, how were we able to leave the tropics and disperse over most of the earth's land surfaces, and how did we adjust to the varied local environmental conditions we encountered? How could our species, which numbered fewer than 1 billion individuals until the mid-nineteenth century, come to number 6 billion worldwide today and, as we now do, add another billion every 11 years?

These are some of the many questions that physical (biological) anthropologists attempt to answer, and these questions are largely the focus of the study of human evolution, variation, and adaptation. These issues, and many more, are the topics covered directly or indirectly in this textbook, for physical anthropology is, in part, human biology seen from an evolutionary perspective. However, physical anthropologists are not exclusively involved in the study of physiological systems and biological phenomena. When such topics are placed within the broader context of human evolution, another factor must also be considered: the role of **culture.**

Culture
All aspects of human adaptation, including technology, traditions, language, and social roles. Culture is learned and transmitted from one generation to the next by non-biological means.

Culture is an extremely important concept, not only as it pertains to modern human beings, but also in terms of its critical role in human evolution. It has been said that there are as many definitions of culture as there are people who attempt to define it. Quite simply, culture can be said to be the strategy by which humans adapt to the natural environment. In this sense, culture includes technologies that range from stone tools to computers; subsistence patterns ranging from hunting and gathering to agribusiness on a global scale; housing types, from thatched huts to skyscrapers; and clothing, from animal skins to high-tech synthetic fibers (Fig. 1–3). Because religion, values, social organization, language, kinship, marriage rules, gender roles, inheritance of property, and so on, are all aspects of culture, each culture shapes people's perceptions of the external environment, or world view, in particular ways that distinguish that culture from all others.

One fundamental point to remember is that culture is *learned* and not biologically determined. Culture is transmitted from generation to generation independent of biological factors (i.e., genes). For example, if a young girl of Vietnamese ancestry is raised in the United States by English-speaking parents, she will acquire English as her native language. She will eat Western foods with Western utensils and will wear Western clothes. In short, she will be a product of Western culture, because that is the culture she will have learned. We are all products of the culture in which we are socialized, and since most human behavior is learned, it clearly is also culturally patterned.

Evolution
A change in the genetic structure of a population. The term is also frequently used to refer to the appearance of a new species.

But as biological organisms, humans are subject to the same evolutionary forces as all other species. On hearing the term **evolution,** most people think of the appearance of new species. Certainly, new species formation is one consequence of evolution; however, biologists see evolution as an ongoing biological process with a precise genetic meaning. Quite simply, evolution is a change in the genetic

(a)

(b)

(c)

(d)

makeup of a population from one generation to the next. It is the accumulation of such changes, over considerable periods of time, that can result in the appearance of a new species. Thus, evolution can be defined and studied at two different levels. At one level there are genetic alterations *within* populations. Although this type of change may not lead to the development of new species, it frequently results in variation between populations with regard to the frequency of certain traits. Evolution at this level is referred to as *microevolution*. At the other level is genetic change sufficient to result in the appearance of a new species, a process sometimes termed *macroevolution* or speciation. Evolution as it occurs at both these levels will be addressed in this text.

FIGURE 1–3

(a) An early stone tool from East Africa. This artifact represents the oldest type of stone tools found anywhere. (b) Assortment of implements available today in a modern hardware store. (c) A Samburu woman building a simple, traditional dwelling of stems, plant fibers, and mud. (d) A modern high-rise apartment building, typical of industrialized cities.

Biocultural evolution
The mutual, interactive evolution of human biology and culture; the concept that biology makes culture possible and that developing culture further influences the direction of biological evolution; a basic concept in understanding the unique components of human evolution.

Anthropology
The field of inquiry that studies human culture and evolutionary aspects of human biology; includes cultural anthropology, archaeology, linguistics, and physical anthropology.

One critical point to remember is that the human predisposition to assimilate culture and to function within it is influenced by biological factors. In the course of human evolution, as you will see, the role of culture increasingly assumed an added importance. Over time, culture and biology interacted in such a way that humans are said to be the result of **biocultural evolution.** In this respect, humans are unique among biological organisms.

Biocultural interactions have resulted in such anatomical, biological, and behavioral changes as increased brain size, reorganization of neurological structures, decreased tooth size, and development of language in humans, to list a few, and they continue to be critical in changing disease patterns as well. As a contemporary example, rapid culture change (particularly in Africa) and changing social and sexual mores may have influenced evolutionary rates of HIV, the virus that causes AIDS. Certainly, these cultural factors influenced the spread of HIV throughout populations in both the developed and developing worlds.

The study of many of the biological aspects of humankind could certainly be the purview of human biologists, and it frequently is. However, particularly in the United States, when such research also considers the role of cultural factors, it is placed within the discipline of **anthropology.**

What Is Anthropology?

Stated ambitiously but simply, anthropology is the study of humankind. (The term *anthropology* is derived from the Greek words *anthropos,* meaning "human," and *logos,* meaning "word" or "study of.") Anthropologists are not the only scientists who study humans, and the goals of anthropology are shared by other disciplines within the social, behavioral, and biological sciences. For example, psychologists and psychiatrists investigate various aspects of human motivation and behavior while developing theories that have clinical significance. Historians focus on recorded events in the past, but since their research concerns documented occurrences, it is limited to, at most, a few thousand years. The main difference between anthropology and such related fields is that anthropology integrates the findings of many disciplines, including sociology, economics, history, psychology, and biology.

In the United States, anthropology comprises three main subfields: cultural, or social, anthropology; archaeology; and physical, or biological, anthropology. Additionally, some universities include linguistic anthropology as a fourth area. Each of these subdisciplines, in turn, is divided into more specialized areas of interest. Following is a brief discussion of the main subdisciplines of anthropology.

Cultural Anthropology

Cultural anthropology is the study of all aspects of human behavior. It could reasonably be argued that cultural anthropology began with the fourth century B.C. Greek philosopher Aristotle, or even earlier. But for practical purposes, the beginnings of cultural anthropology are found in the nineteenth century, when Europeans became increasingly aware of what they termed "primitive societies" in Africa and Asia. Likewise, in the New World, there was much interest in the vanishing cultures of Native Americans.

The interest in traditional societies led numerous early anthropologists to study and record lifeways that unfortunately are now mostly extinct. These studies produced many descriptive **ethnographies** that became the basis for subsequent comparisons between groups. Early ethnographies emphasized various phenomena, such as religion, ritual, myth, use of symbols, subsistence strategies, technology, gender roles, child-rearing practices, dietary preferences, taboos, medical practices, and how kinship was reckoned.

Ethnographic accounts, in turn, formed the basis for comparative studies of numerous cultures. Such *cross-cultural* studies, termed *ethnologies,* broadened the context within which cultural anthropologists studied human behavior. By examining the similarities and differences between diverse cultures, anthropologists have been able to formulate many theories about the fundamental aspects of human behavior.

The focus of cultural anthropology shifted over the course of the twentieth century. But traditional ethnographic techniques, wherein anthropologists spend months or years living in and studying various societies, are still employed, although the nature of the study groups may have changed. For example, in recent decades, ethnographic techniques have been applied to the study of diverse subcultures and their interactions with one another in contemporary metropolitan areas. The subfield of cultural anthropology that deals with issues of inner cities is appropriately called *urban anthropology.* Among the many issues addressed by urban anthropologists are the relationships between ethnic groups, those aspects of traditional cultures that are maintained by immigrant populations, poverty, labor relations, homelessness, access to health care, and problems facing the elderly.

Medical anthropology is the subfield of cultural anthropology that explores the relationship between various cultural attributes and health and disease. One area of interest is how different groups view disease processes and how these views affect treatment or the willingness to accept treatment. When a medical anthropologist focuses on the social dimensions of disease, physicians and physical anthropologists may also collaborate. Indeed, many medical anthropologists have received much of their training in physical anthropology.

Economic anthropologists are concerned with factors that influence the distribution of goods and resources within and between cultures. Areas of interest include such topics as division of labor (by gender and age), factors that influence who controls resources and wealth, and trade practices and regulations.

Many cultural anthropologists are involved in gender studies. Such studies may focus on gender norms, how such norms are learned, and the specific cultural factors that lead to individual development of gender identity. It is also valuable to explore the social consequences if gender norms are violated.

There is also increasing interest in the social aspects of development and aging. This field is particularly relevant in industrialized nations, where the proportion of elderly individuals is higher than ever before. As populations age, the needs of the elderly, particularly in the area of health care, become social issues that require more and more attention.

Many of the subfields of cultural anthropology (e.g., medical anthropology) have practical applications and are pursued by anthropologists working outside the university setting. This approach is aptly termed *applied anthropology.* While most applied anthropologists regard themselves as cultural anthropologists, the designation is also sometimes used to describe the activities of archaeologists and physical anthropologists. Indeed, the various fields of anthropology, as they are practiced in the United States, overlap to a considerable degree, which, after all, was the rationale for combining them under the umbrella of anthropology in the first place.

Ethnographies
Detailed descriptive studies of human societies. In cultural anthropology, an ethnography is traditionally the study of a non-Western society.

 Archaeology is discussed in Virtual Lab 11 and includes many 3-D animations of stone tools.

Artifacts
Objects or materials made or modified for use by hominids. The earliest artifacts tend to be tools made of stone or, occasionally, bone.

Material culture
The physical manifestations of human activities; includes tools, art, and structures. As the most durable aspects of culture, material remains make up the majority of archaeological evidence of past societies.

Archaeology

Archaeology is the study of earlier cultures and lifeways by anthropologists who specialize in the scientific recovery, analysis, and interpretation of the material remains of past societies. Although archaeology often deals with cultures that existed before the invention of writing (the period commonly known as *prehistory*), *historical archaeologists* also examine the evidence of later, complex civilizations that produced written records.

Archaeologists are concerned with culture, but their sources of information are not living people. Rather, archaeologists rely on the **artifacts** and other **material culture** left behind by earlier societies. Obviously, no one has ever excavated such aspects of culture as religious belief, spoken language, or a political system. However, archaeologists assume that the surviving evidence of human occupation reflects some of those important but less tangible features of the culture that created them. Therefore, the material remains of a given ancient society may inform us about the nature of that society.

The roots of modern archaeology are found in the fascination of nineteenth-century Europeans with the classical world (particularly Greece and Egypt). This interest was primarily manifested in the excavation (sometimes controlled, sometimes not) and removal of thousands of treasures and artifacts destined for the museums and private collections of wealthy Europeans.

New World archaeology has long focused on the pre-Columbian civilizations of Mexico and Central and South America (the Aztecs, Maya, and Inca). In North America, archaeological interest was sparked particularly by the large earthen burial mounds found throughout much of the southeast. In fact, Thomas Jefferson conducted one of the first controlled excavations of a burial mound on his Virginia plantation in 1784. Importantly, his goal was not simply the recovery of artifacts; he specifically wished to address the question of how the mound was constructed.

Today, archaeology is aimed at answering specific questions. Sites are not excavated simply because they exist or for the artifacts they may yield; excavation is conducted for the explicit purpose of gaining information about human behavior. Patterns of behavior are reflected in the dispersal of human settlements across a landscape and in the distribution of cultural remains within them. Through the identification of these patterns, archaeologists can elucidate the commonalities shared by many or all populations as well as those features that differ between groups. Research questions may focus on specific localities or peoples and attempt to identify, for example, various aspects of social organization, subsistence techniques, or the factors that led to the collapse of a civilization. Alternatively, inquiry may reflect an interest in broader issues relating to human culture in general, such as the development of agriculture or the rise of cities. But the design of most archaeological projects centers around questions that address a wide range of interests, both specific and broad.

Archaeology is a discipline that requires precise measurement, description, and excavation techniques, for it must be remembered that when a site is dug, it is also destroyed. Errors in excavation or recording result in the permanent loss or misinterpretation of valuable information. Therefore, contrary to what many people think, the science of archaeology is much more than simply digging up artifacts. Rather, archaeology is a multidisciplinary approach to the study of human behavior as evidenced by cultural remains.

For many projects, the specialized expertise of several disciplines is needed. Chemists, geologists, physicists, paleontologists, and physical anthropologists may all be called on. Even the sophisticated satellite technologies of NASA have been employed to locate archaeological sites.

In the United States, the greatest expansion in archaeology in recent years has been in the important area of *cultural resource management (CRM).* This applied approach arose from environmental legislation requiring the archaeological evaluation and even excavation of sites that may be threatened by construction and other forms of development. Many contract archaeologists (so called because their services are contracted out to developers, government agencies, municipalities, and the like) are affiliated with private archaeological consulting firms, state or federal agencies, or educational institutions. In fact, an estimated 40 percent of all archaeologists in the United States now fill such positions.

Archaeological techniques are used to identify and excavate not only remains of human cities and settlements, but also paleontological sites containing remains of extinct species, including everything from dinosaurs to early hominids. Together, prehistoric archaeology and physical anthropology form the core of a joint science called *paleoanthropology,* described shortly.

Linguistic Anthropology

Linguistic anthropology is the study of human speech and language, including the origins of language in general as well as specific languages. By examining similarities between contemporary languages, linguists have been able to trace historical ties between languages and groups of languages, thus facilitating the identification of language families and perhaps past relationships between human populations.

There is also much interest in the relationship between language and culture: how language reflects the way members of a society perceive phenomena and how the use of language shapes perceptions in different cultures. For instance, vocabulary provides important clues as to the importance of certain items and concepts in particular cultures. The most famous example is the use of some 50 terms for snow among the Inuit (Eskimos), reflecting their need to convey specific information about the properties of this form of frozen precipitation. (For that matter, downhill skiers also employ many more increasingly precise terms for snow than do nonskiers.)

Because the spontaneous acquisition and use of language is a uniquely human characteristic, it is a topic that holds considerable interest for linguistic anthropologists, who, along with specialists in other fields, study the process of language acquisition in infants. Since insights into the process may well have implications for the development of language skills in human evolution, as well as in growing children, it is also an important subject to physical anthropologists.

Physical Anthropology

Physical anthropology, as has already been stated, is the study of human biology within the framework of evolution, with an emphasis on the interaction between biology and culture. Physical anthropology is composed of several subdisciplines, or areas of specialization, the most significant of which are briefly described in the following paragraphs.

The place of physical anthropology within the discipline of anthropology is discussed in Virtual Lab 1, section I.

Introduction

The origins of physical anthropology are to be found in two principal areas of interest among nineteenth-century scholars. First, there was increasing concern among many scientists (at the time called *natural historians*) regarding the mechanisms by which modern species had come to be. In other words, increasing numbers of intellectuals were beginning to doubt the literal, biblical interpretation of creation. This does not mean that all natural historians had abandoned all religious explanations of natural occurrences. But scientific explanations emphasizing natural, rather than supernatural, phenomena were becoming increasingly popular in scientific circles. Although few scientists were actually prepared to believe that humans had evolved from earlier forms, discoveries of several Neandertal fossils in the 1800s began to raise questions regarding the origins and antiquity of the human species.

The sparks of interest in biological change over time were fueled into flames by the publication of Charles Darwin's *Origin of Species* in 1859. Today, **paleoanthropology,** or the study of human evolution, particularly as evidenced in the fossil record, is one of the major subfields of physical anthropology (Fig. 1–4). There are now thousands of specimens of human ancestors housed in museum and research collections. Taken together, these fossils cover a span of at least 4 million years of human prehistory, and although incomplete, they provide us with significantly more knowledge than was available even 15 years ago. It is the ultimate goal of paleoanthropological research to identify the various early hominid species, establish a chronological sequence of relationships among them, and gain insights into their adaptation and behavior. Only then will there emerge a clear picture of how and when humankind came into being.

Paleoanthropology
The interdisciplinary approach to the study of earlier hominids—their chronology, physical structure, archaeological remains, habitats, etc.

FIGURE 1–4
Paleoanthropological research at Hadar, Ethiopia, during a field season in 1993.

A second nineteenth-century interest that had direct relevance to anthropology was observable physical variation, as seen in skin color, body build, shape of the face, and so on. Enormous effort was aimed at describing and explaining differences between human populations. Although some endeavors were misguided, they gave birth to literally thousands of body measurements that could be used to compare people. Physical anthropologists use many of the techniques of **anthropometry** today, not only to study living groups (Fig. 1–5), but also to study skeletal remains from archaeological sites. Moreover, anthropometric techniques have considerable application in the design of everything from airplane cockpits to office furniture.

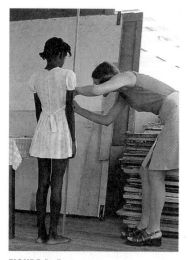

FIGURE 1–5

Dr. Eugenie Scott measures stature in a Garifuna (Black Carib) girl in Belize.

FIGURE 1–6

Researcher using a treadmill test to assess a subject's heart rate, blood pressure, and oxygen consumption.

Anthropologists today are concerned with human variation primarily because of its evolutionary significance. In other words, many traits that typify certain populations are seen as having evolved as biological **adaptations,** or adjustments, to local environmental conditions. Examining biological variation between and within populations of any species provides valuable information as to the mechanisms of genetic change in groups over time, which is precisely what the evolutionary process is all about.

Modern population studies also examine other important aspects of human variation, including how various groups respond physiologically to different kinds of environmentally induced stress (Fig. 1–6). Such stresses may include high altitude, cold, or heat.

Other physical anthropologists conduct nutritional studies, investigating the relationships between various dietary components, cultural practices, physiology, and certain aspects of health and disease. Closely related to the topic of nutrition are investigations of human fertility, growth, and development. These fields of inquiry are fundamental to studies of adaptation in modern human populations, and they can provide insights into hominid evolution as well.

It would be impossible to study evolutionary processes, and therefore adaptation, without a knowledge of genetic principles. For this reason and others, **genetics** is a crucial field for physical anthropologists. Modern physical anthropology would not exist as an evolutionary science were it not for advances in the understanding of genetic principles.

Not only does genetics allow us to explain how evolutionary processes work, but today's anthropologists use recently developed genetic technologies to investigate evolutionary distances between living primate species (including humans). Moreover, genetic techniques have been used (with much debate) to explain, among other things, the origins of modern *Homo sapiens*.

Primatology, the study of nonhuman primates, has become increasingly important since the late 1950s for several reasons. Behavioral studies, especially those conducted on groups in natural environments, have implications for numerous

Anthropometry
Measurement of human body parts. When osteologists measure skeletal elements, the term *osteometry* is often used.

Adaptations
Physiological and/or behavioral adjustments made by organisms in response to environmental circumstances. Adaptations may be short-term or long-term, and strictly defined, they are the results of evolutionary factors.

Genetics
The study of gene structure and action and the patterns of inheritance of traits. Genetic mechanisms are the underlying foundation for evolutionary change.

Primatology
The study of the biology and behavior of nonhuman primates (prosimians, monkeys, and apes).

scientific disciplines. Moreover, studies of nonhuman animal behavior have assumed a greater urgency in recent decades owing to concern over rapidly declining numbers of many species.

The behavioral study of any species provides a wealth of data pertaining to adaptation. Because nonhuman primates are our closest living relatives, the identification of underlying factors related to social behavior, communication, infant care, reproductive behavior, and so on, aids in developing a better understanding of the natural forces that have shaped so many aspects of modern human behavior.

Moreover, nonhuman primates are important to study in their own right, and this is particularly true today because the majority of primate species are threatened or seriously endangered. Only through study will scientists be able to recommend policies that can better ensure the survival of many nonhuman primates and thousands of other species as well.

Primate paleontology, the study of the primate fossil record, has implications not only for nonhuman primates but also for hominids. Virtually every year, fossil-bearing beds in North America, Africa, Asia, and Europe yield important new discoveries. Through the study of fossil primates, we are able to learn much about factors such as diet or locomotion in earlier forms. By comparisons with anatomically similar living species, primate paleontologists can make reasoned inferences regarding behavior in earlier groups as well. Moreover, we hope to be able to clarify evolutionary relationships between extinct and modern species, including ourselves.

Osteology, the study of the skeleton, is central to physical anthropology. Indeed, it is so important that when many people think of physical anthropology, the first thing that comes to mind is bones. The emphasis on osteology exists in part because of the concern with the analysis of fossil material. Certainly, a thorough knowledge of the structure and function of the skeleton is critical to the interpretation of fossil material.

Bone biology and physiology are of major importance to many other aspects of physical anthropology, in addition to paleontology. Many osteologists specialize in metric studies that emphasize various measurements of skeletal elements. This type of research is essential, for example, to the identification of stature and growth patterns in archaeological populations.

One subdiscipline of osteology is the study of disease and trauma in archaeologically derived skeletal populations. **Paleopathology** is a prominent subfield that investigates the incidence of trauma, certain infectious diseases (such as tuberculosis), nutritional deficiencies, and numerous other conditions that leave evidence in bone (Fig. 1–7). In this area of research, a precise knowledge of bone physiology and response to insult is required.

A field directly related to osteology and paleopathology is **forensic anthropology.** Technically, this is the application of anthropological (usually osteological and sometimes archaeological) techniques to the law. Forensic anthropologists are commonly called on to help identify skeletal remains in cases of disaster or other situations where a human body has been found.

Forensic anthropologists have been instrumental in a number of cases having important legal and historical consequences. They assisted medical examiners in 1993 with the identification of human remains at the Branch Davidian compound in Waco, Texas. They have also been prominent in the identification of remains of missing American soldiers in Southeast Asia and the skeletons of most of the Russian imperial family, executed in 1918 (see pp. 19–20).

Osteology
The study of skeletons. Human osteology often focuses on the interpretation of the skeletal remains of past groups. The same techniques are used in paleoanthropology to study early hominids.

Paleopathology
The branch of osteology that studies the traces of disease and injury in human skeletal (or, occasionally, mummified) remains.

Forensic anthropology
An applied anthropological approach dealing with legal matters. Forensic anthropologists work with coroners and others in the analysis and identification of human remains.

Anatomical studies constitute another important area of interest for physical anthropologists. In the living organism, bone and dental structures are intimately linked to the soft tissues that surround and act on them. Thus, a thorough knowledge of soft tissue anatomy is essential to the understanding of biomechanical relationships involved in movement. Such relationships are important to the development of conditions, such as arthritis, that are frequently encountered in paleopathology. Moreover, accurate assessment of the structure and function of limbs and other components in fossilized remains requires expertise in anatomical relationships. For these reasons, many physical anthropologists specialize in anatomical studies. In fact, several physical anthropologists hold professorships in anatomy departments at universities and medical schools.

Physical Anthropology and the Scientific Method

Science is a process of understanding phenomena through observation, generalization, and verification. By this we mean that there is an **empirical** approach to gaining information through the use of systematic and explicit techniques. Because physical anthropologists are engaged in scientific pursuits, they adhere to the principles of the **scientific method,** whereby a research problem is identified and information subsequently gathered to solve it.

The gathering of information is referred to as **data** collection, and when researchers use a rigorously controlled approach, they are able to describe precisely their techniques and results in a manner that facilitates comparisons with the work of others. For example, when scientists collect data on tooth size in hominid fossils, they must specify precisely which teeth are being measured, how they are being measured, and what the results of the measurements are (expressed numerically, or **quantitatively**). Subsequently, it is up to the investigators to draw conclusions as to the meaning and significance of their measurements. This body of information then becomes the basis of future studies, perhaps by other researchers, who can compare their own results with those already obtained. The eventual outcome of this type of inquiry may be the acceptance or rejection of certain proposed facts and explanations.

Once facts have been established, scientists attempt to explain them. First, a **hypothesis,** or provisional explanation of phenomena, is developed. But before a hypothesis can be accepted, it must be tested by means of data collection and analysis. Indeed, the testing of hypotheses with the possibility of proving them false is the very basis of the scientific method.

Scientific testing of hypotheses may take several years (or longer) and may involve researchers who were not involved with the original work. In subsequent studies, other investigators may attempt to obtain the original results, but such repetition may not occur. For example, repeated failures to duplicate the results of highly publicized cold fusion experiments led most scientists to question and ultimately reject the claims made in the original research. While it is easier to duplicate original studies conducted in laboratory settings, it is equally important to verify data collected outside tightly controlled situations. In the latter circumstance, results are tested relative to other, often larger samples. The predicted patterns will either be confirmed through such further research or be viewed as limited or even incorrect.

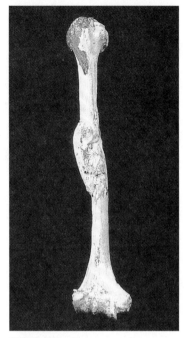

FIGURE 1–7

Healing fracture of a human humerus (upper arm bone).

Science
A body of knowledge gained through observation and experimentation; from the Latin *scientia,* meaning "knowledge."

Empirical
Relying on experiment or observation; from the Latin *empiricus,* meaning "experienced."

Scientific method
A research method whereby a problem is identified, a hypothesis (or hypothetical explanation) is stated, and that hypothesis is tested through the collection and analysis of data. If the hypothesis is verified, it becomes a theory.

Data (*sing.,* datum)
Facts from which conclusions can be drawn; scientific information.

Quantitatively (quantitative)
Pertaining to measurements of quantity and including such properties as size, number, and capacity. When data are quantified, they are expressed numerically and are capable of being tested statistically.

Hypothesis (*pl.,* hypotheses)
A provisional explanation of a phenomenon. Hypotheses require verification.

Scientific testing
The precise repetition of an experiment or expansion of observed data to provide verification; the procedure by which hypotheses and theories are verified, modified, or discarded.

Theory
A broad statement of scientific relationships or underlying principles that has been at least partially verified.

 A discussion of the scientific method can be found in Virtual Lab 3, section III.

 Exercises in which you formulate and test hypotheses with data that you collect are found in nearly all of the Virtual Lab exercises.

If a hypothesis cannot be falsified, it is accepted as a **theory.** There is a popular misconception that theories are nothing but hunches or unfounded explanations. But, in scientific terms, a theory is a statement of relationships that has a firm basis as demonstrated through testing and the accumulation of evidence. As such, theories not only help organize current knowledge, but they should also predict how new facts may fit into established patterns.

Use of the scientific method not only allows for the development and testing of hypotheses, but also permits various types of *bias* to be addressed and controlled. It is important to realize that bias occurs in all studies. Sources of bias include how the investigator was trained and by whom; what particular questions interest the researcher; what specific skills and talents he or she possesses; what earlier results (if any) have been established in this realm of study and by whom (e.g., the researcher, close colleagues, or those with rival approaches or even rival personalities); and what sources of data are available (e.g., accessible countries or museums) and thus what samples can be collected (at all or at least conveniently).

Trained scientists must be forever vigilant of various (and often personal) biases, and you should be, too. In addressing some issues in this book, we present views that we, the authors, might not personally favor. However, we include those views because scientists should not simply dismiss views or ideas of which they are skeptical. Similarly, you should be reluctant to accept or reject an idea based solely on your personal feelings or biases. Science is an approach—indeed, a *tool*—used to eliminate (or at least minimize) bias.

Application of the scientific method thus requires constant vigilance by all who practice it. The goal is not to establish "truth" in any absolute sense, but rather to generate ever more accurate and consistent depictions and explanations of phenomena in our universe. At its very heart, scientific methodology is an exercise in rational thought and critical thinking.

The Anthropological Perspective

Perhaps the most important benefit you will receive from this textbook—and this course—is a wider appreciation of the human experience. To understand human beings and how our species came to be, it is necessary to broaden our viewpoint, both through time and over space. All branches of anthropology fundamentally seek to do this in what we call the *anthropological perspective.*

Physical anthropologists, for example, are keenly interested in how humans differ from and are similar to other animals, especially nonhuman primates. For example, we have defined *hominids* as bipedal primates, but what are the major components of bipedal locomotion, and how do they differ from, say, those in a quadrupedal ape? To answer these questions, we would need to study human locomotion and compare it with the locomotion seen in various nonhuman primates. Moreover, in addition to observing how humans walk while wearing shoes, we also would be interested in their pattern of locomotion while walking barefoot. Indeed, it would probably be useful to look at the locomotion of people who have never worn shoes, and to obtain these data, we would probably have to leave our own culture and study other quite geographically distant groups.

Through such a wider perspective, we can begin to grasp the contemporary diversity of the human experience and, in so doing, understand more fully both human potentialities and human constraints. And by extending our breadth of knowledge it is easier to avoid the **ethnocentric** pitfalls inherent in a more limited view of humanity.

In addition to broadening perspectives over space (i.e., encompassing many cultures and ecological circumstances as well as nonhuman species), an anthropological perspective also extends our horizons *through time*. For example, in Chapter 14 we will discuss human nutrition. However, the vast majority of the kinds of foods currently eaten (coming from domesticated plants and animals) were unavailable prior to 10,000 years ago. Human physiological mechanisms for chewing and digesting foods nevertheless were already well established long before that date. These adaptive complexes go back many hundreds of thousands—perhaps even millions—of years. In addition to the obviously different diets prior to the development of agriculture (approximately 10,000 years ago), earlier hominids might well have differed from humans today in average body size, metabolism, and activity patterns. How, then, does the basic evolutionary "equipment" (i.e., physiology) inherited from our hominid forebears accommodate our modern diets? Clearly, the way to understand such processes is not just by looking at contemporary human responses, but also by placing them in the perspective of evolutionary development through time.

Indeed, most of the topics covered in this book—as most topics considered by all types of anthropologists—are addressed by using a broad application of the anthropological perspective. For physical anthropologists, such an approach usually means extending the perspective both over space as well as through considerable periods of time.

Ethnocentric
Viewing other cultures from the inherently biased perspective of one's own culture. Ethnocentrism usually results in cultures being seen as inferior to one's own.

Conclusion

From this brief overview, it can be seen that physical anthropology is the subdiscipline of anthropology that focuses on many varied aspects of the biological and behavioral nature of *Homo sapiens*. Humans are a product of the same forces that produced all life on earth. As such, we represent one contemporary component of a vast biological **continuum** at one point in time, and in this regard, we are not particularly unique. Stating that humans are part of a continuum does not imply that we are at the peak of development on that continuum. Depending on which criteria one uses, humans can be seen to exist at one end of the continuum or the other, or somewhere in between. But humans do not necessarily occupy a position of inherent superiority over other species.

There is, however, one dimension in which human beings are truly unique, and that is intellect. After all, humans are the only species, born of earth, to stir the lunar dust. Humans are the only species to develop language and complex culture as a means of buffering the challenges posed by nature, and by so doing, to eventually gain the power to shape the very destiny of the planet.

It has been said that humans created culture and that culture created humans. This statement is true to the extent that the increased brain size and reorganization of neurological structures that typify much of the course of human evolution would never have occurred if not for the complex interactions between biological and behavioral factors (i.e., biocultural evolution). In this sense, then, it is neither unreasonable nor presumptuous to say that we have created ourselves.

We hope that the ensuing pages will help you develop an increased understanding of the similarities we share with other biological organisms and also of

Continuum
A set of relationships in which all components fall along a single integrated spectrum. All life reflects a single *biological continuum*.

the processes that have shaped the traits that make us unique. We live in what may well be the most crucial period for our planet during the last 65 million years. We are members of the one species that, through the very agency of culture, has wrought such devastating changes in ecological systems that we must now alter our technologies or face potentially unspeakable consequences. In such a time, it is vital that we attempt to gain the best possible understanding of what it means to be human. We believe that the study of physical anthropology is one endeavor that aids in this attempt, and that is indeed the goal of this text.

SUMMARY

In this chapter, we have introduced the field of physical anthropology and have placed it within the overall context of anthropological studies. Anthropology as a major academic area within the social sciences also includes archaeology, cultural anthropology, and linguistic anthropology as its major subfields.

Physical anthropology itself includes aspects of human biology (emphasizing evolutionary perspectives), the study of nonhuman primates, and the hominid fossil record. Especially as applied to the study of early hominids (as incorporated within the interdisciplinary field of paleoanthropology), physical anthropologists work in close collaboration with many other scientists from the fields of archaeology, geology, chemistry, and so forth.

QUESTIONS FOR REVIEW

1. What is anthropology? What are the major subfields of anthropology?
2. How does physical anthropology differ from other disciplines that concern human biology?
3. What is meant by biocultural evolution, and why is it important in understanding human evolution?
4. What are some of the primary areas of research within physical anthropology? Give two or three examples of the types of research pursued by physical anthropologists.
5. What is meant by the term *hominid*? Be specific.
6. What fields, in addition to physical anthropology, contribute to paleoanthropology?
7. Define the term *science*.
8. What is the scientific method? How do you think it differs from other methods of explaining phenomena?
9. What is hypothesis testing?

SUGGESTED FURTHER READINGS

Ferraro, Gary, Wenda Trevathan, and Janet Levy. 1994. *Anthropology, an Applied Perspective.* St. Paul: West.

Spencer, Frank, ed. 1997. *A History of Physical Anthropology.* New York: Garland.

MULTIMEDIA RESOURCES

 Wadsworth Anthropology Resource Center

http://anthropology.wadsworth.com

Visit Anthropology Online to obtain current updates in the field, surfing tips, career information, and more. In addition, enrich your study efforts with text-specific study aids arranged by chapter.

InfoTrac College Edition

http://www.infotrac-college.com/wadsworth

1. Anthropology is a very broad discipline. Search InfroTrac College Edition for the subject *anthropology.* How many different topics are there? How many are related to biological or physical anthropology? Choose one subject not introduced in the text and read some of the articles about it. What makes this topic anthropological?

2. Now choose *forensic anthropology* and go to the periodical articles. Read one article, preferably one that concerns a specific case. What is the article about? What were the results of the forensic analysis? In general, what does a forensic anthropologist do? What sort of training is needed? Go through your college catalog and make a list of courses that you might take if you were interested in becoming a forensic anthropologist.

Internet Exercises

1. Begin by becoming familiar with the scope of anthropology on the Internet. Visit one of the many Internet search engines or indexes, such as Excite (**www.excite.com**) or Yahoo! (**www.yahoo.com**) and search for *anthropology.* How many sites did you find? Do these sites cover the range of anthropological subdisciplines? Visit a couple of them. What do they have in common?

2. Visit the major association of anthropologists in the United States, the American Anthropological Association. (If your search did not provide the link, try **http://www.aaanet.org.**) The American Anthropological Association represents anthropologists in all subdisciplines, and this site serves as a good indicator of the breadth of anthropology. Take time to explore the site thoroughly. Visit About AAA to learn more about the field and the association. Read "Careers in Anthropology." What could you do with a major in anthropology without going to graduate school?

PHOTO ESSAY

The Tools and Techniques of Physical Anthropology

Physical anthropologists are interested in the study of people, both living and dead. Except for some unusual circumstances, such as natural mummification (where some soft tissues are preserved), what is left of earlier populations are the hard tissues (bones and teeth).

One very common approach used by osteologists in the study of these hard tissues is to take precise measurements of the cranium and other elements of the skeleton. Several standard tools have been developed for this purpose.

Carefully defined landmarks have been established on the cranium, as well as on many of the long bones, to facilitate standardization of measurements. Practitioners of osteometric techniques can then make sure that the measurement device (calipers) is placed in exactly the proper location.

FIGURE 1

The osteometric board is used to measure the length of long bones, such as the human femur shown here.

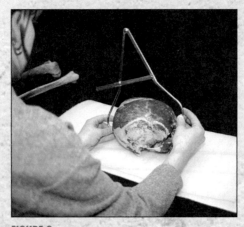

FIGURE 2

Spreading calipers are used for the three-dimensional surfaces of the cranial vault. Here they are being used to measure cranial length.

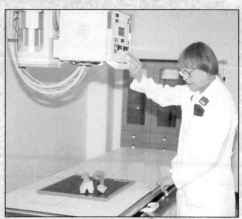

FIGURE 3

A standard X-ray machine at a university student health center being used to radiograph two human long bones (femur and tibia).

Physical anthropologists can observe many useful characteristics using simple tools. (This approach is called gross analysis.) However, specialized equipment can also provide data for variables that cannot be observed directly. Standard X-rays are most helpful in revealing subsurface bone modifications, such as those resulting from healed fractures. The techniques for taking, as well as reading, the X-rays are analogous to those developed for living patients. Indeed, skeletal biologists often work closely with medical colleagues to analyze and interpret the evidence of disease and trauma in bone.

Forensic anthropologists (physical anthropologists who specialize in the identification of skeletal remains of crime victims, or victims of mass fatalities) are sometimes asked to confirm the identities of historical figures. In 1992, a team of scientists led by the late Professor Bill Maples, used standard osteological techniques to identify the skeletons of members of the Russian Royal family, murdered in 1918. Positive identifications were made for Tsar Nicholas II, his wife, the tsarina Alexandra, and three of their daughters. A family physician and three servants were also identified. Missing were the remains of the tsarevich Alexis, heir to the throne, and his sister, Anastasia.

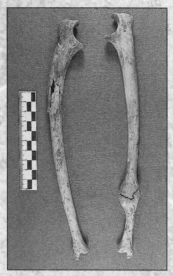

FIGURE 4

Left and right forearm bones (ulnae) from an adult female chimpanzee killed by other chimpanzees at Gombe National Park. The right ulna (on the right) has a partially healed fracture. The left ulna is shown for comparison. This animal (Madam Bee) was attacked several times, and it appears that an earlier fracture (as evidenced by the thickened portion of the shaft) was rebroken, presumably during the fatal attack.

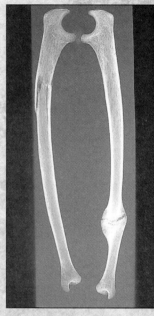

FIGURE 5

X-ray of the same two elements shown in Figure 4. The partially healed fracture is clearly visible.

FIGURE 6

The Russian royal family.

The Tools and Techniques of Physical Anthropology (continued)

To further confirm these identities, mitochondrial DNA (mtDNA) (see. p. 45), was extracted from the skeletons of Alexandra and her daughters, amplified through PCR techniques (see p. 76), and compared to mtDNA provided by Prince Philip, a maternal relative of Alexandra and husband of Queen Elizabeth of England. Mitochondrial DNA, taken from the tsar's skeleton and teeth, was compared to samples donated by distant living maternal relatives and the exhumed remains of his brother who died in 1899. In all cases, the results of the DNA analysis confirmed the initial results and clearly demonstrated the usefulness of mtDNA in skeletal identification.

Making exact replicas (casts) of specimens is another useful technique. By this method, it is possible to preserve precise three-dimensional models of rare specimens (e.g., fossils) or unusual diseases

FIGURE 7

Professor Bill Maples examining the cranium of Tsar Nicholas II. (Photo courtesy of Margaret Maples.)

FIGURE 8

Dr. Diane France pours casting mixture into a rubber mold. The mold for this cast was formed earlier around a human cranium. After the casting mixture sets, the mold is peeled away from the cast. The cast will then be finished by hand. The same mold can be used several times to make further identical replicas.

(pathologies). In addition, for forensic (legal) cases, where the human remains are eventually buried, the casts allow preservation of evidence. Finally, in cases where Native American remains are scheduled for reburial, retaining the replicas will serve as the best record of these individuals.

Physical anthropologists also focus on variation seen in living populations. A common technique used on human populations world-wide is blood typing. The best-known, and most widely reported, manifestation of blood type is the ABO system. (Note that there are many other "blood types" under the control of different genes.)

From data on blood type, the frequency of the genes responsible for each type can be calculated. These data then become the baseline for measuring and interpreting recent human evolution.

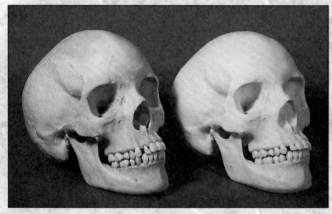

FIGURE 9
A completed cast of a human cranium. The original is on the left.

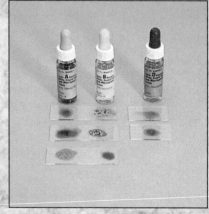

FIGURE 11
To determine an individual's blood type, a few drops of blood are treated with specific chemicals. Presence of A and B blood type, as well as Rh, can be detected by using commercially available chemicals. The glass slides below the blue- and yellow-labeled bottles show reactions for the ABO system. The blood on the top slide (at left) is type AB; the middle is type B; and the bottom is type A. The two samples to the right depict Rh-negative blood (top) and Rh-positive blood (bottom).

FIGURE 10
A blood sample is drawn.

21

The Tools and Techniques of Physical Anthropology (continued)

Physical anthropologists, working with other biomedical scientists, are also concerned with measuring health, nutrition, and physiological response to environmental stress in various populations. Treadmill tests, bicycle ergometer tests, and questionnaires are just a few of the tools used to measure functional capacity in healthy and diseased persons. In addition, these techniques can be used to assess human biological adaptation to different environments (e.g., high altitude) or to disease (e.g., coronary artery disease).

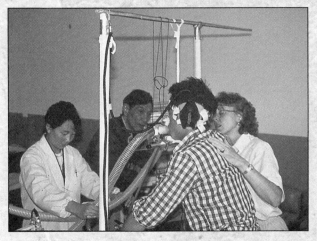

FIGURE 12

Brain blood flow, volume and frequency of breathing, oxygen consumption, and carbon dioxide production are being monitored in this Tibetan subject during exercise on a bicycle ergometer. These data are used to assess physiological response to reduced oxygen availability in indigenous residents of high-altitude regions.

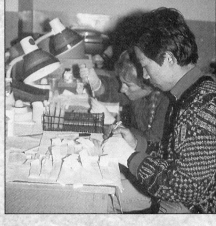

FIGURE 13

Dr. Jianguo Zhuang (foreground) and Dr. Stacy Zamudio (rear) are separating white blood cells from whole blood samples taken from Tibetan research subjects. The white blood cells provide DNA used to investigate genetic variation in populations residing at high altitude.

FIGURE 14

Dr. Kathleen Galvin measures upper arm circumference in a young Maasai boy in Tanzania. Note the scale she has used to record the boy's weight. To the right is an anthropometer, an instrument used to take a variety of body measurements, including, as in this example, height. These data (and others) were collected as part of a health and nutrition study of particular groups of Maasai cattle herders.

CHAPTER 2

The Development of Evolutionary Theory

CONTENTS

Introduction

The term **evolution** is sometimes charged with emotion. The concept is often controversial, particularly in the United States, because some religious views hold that evolutionary statements run counter to biblical teachings. In fact, as you are probably aware, there continues to be much opposition to the teaching of evolution in public schools.

Those who wish to denigrate evolution frequently insist that it is "only a theory" in an attempt to reduce its status to supposition. Actually, to refer to a concept as "theory" is to lend it support. As we noted in Chapter 1, theories are general hypotheses that have been tested and subjected to verification through accumulated evidence. Evolution *is* a theory, one that has increasingly been supported by a mounting body of genetic evidence. It is a theory that has stood the test of time, and today it stands as the most fundamental unifying force in biological science.

Because physical anthropology is concerned with all aspects of how humans came to be and how we adapt physiologically to the external environment, the details of the evolutionary process are crucial to the field. Moreover, given the central importance of evolution to physical anthropology, it is valuable to know how the mechanics of the process came to be discovered. Additionally, to appreciate the nature of the controversy that continues to surround the issue today, it is important to examine the basic evolutionary principles within the social and political context in which the theory emerged.

A Brief History of Evolutionary Thought

The individual most responsible for the elucidation of the evolutionary process was Charles Darwin. But while Darwin was formulating his theory of **natural selection,** his ideas were being duplicated by another English naturalist, Alfred Russel Wallace.

That natural selection, the single most important mechanism of evolutionary change, should be proposed at more or less the same time by *two* British men in the mid-nineteenth century may seem highly improbable. But actually, it is not all that surprising. Indeed, if Darwin and Wallace had not made their simultaneous discoveries, someone else would have done so in short order. That is to say, the groundwork had already been laid, and many within the scientific community were prepared to accept explanations of biological change that would have been unacceptable even 25 years before.

Like other human endeavors, scientific knowledge is usually gained through a series of small steps rather than giant leaps. Just as technological innovation is based on past achievements, scientific knowledge builds on previously developed theories. (One does not build a space shuttle without first having invented the airplane.) Given this stepwise aspect of scientific discovery, it is informative to examine the development of ideas that led Darwin and Wallace independently to develop the theory of evolution by natural selection.

Throughout the Middle Ages, one predominant component of the European **world view** was *stasis.* That is, all aspects of nature, including all forms of life and their relationships to one another, were fixed and unchanging. This view of natural phenomena was shaped in part by a feudal society that was very much a hierar-

Evolution
A change in the genetic structure of a population. The term is also frequently used to refer to the appearance of a new species.

Natural selection
The mechanism of evolutionary change first articulated by Charles Darwin. Refers to genetic change, or to changes in the frequencies of certain traits in populations due to differential reproductive success between individuals.

World view
General cultural orientation or perspective shared by members of a society.

chical arrangement supporting a rigid class system that had changed little for several centuries.

The world view of Europeans during the Middle Ages was also shaped by a powerful religious system. The teachings of Christianity were taken quite literally, and it was generally accepted that all life on earth had been created by God exactly as it existed in the present. This belief that life forms could not change eventually came to be known in European intellectual circles as **fixity of species.**

Accompanying the notion of fixity of species was the belief that all God's creations were arranged in a hierarchy that progressed from the simplest organisms to the most complex. At the top of this linear sequence were humans. This concept of a ranked order of living things is termed the *Great Chain of Being* and was first proposed in the fourth century B.C. by the Greek philosopher Aristotle. Although position within the chain was based on physical similarities between species, no evolutionary or biological relationships were implied. Moreover, "lower" forms could not move up the scale to become "superior" ones.

In addition, there was the common notion that the earth was "full" and that nothing new (such as species) could be added. Thus, it was believed that since the creation, no new species had appeared and none had disappeared, or become extinct. And since all of nature and the Great Chain of Being were created by God in a fixed state, change was inconceivable. Questioning the assumptions of fixity was ultimately seen as a challenge to God's perfection and could be considered heresy.

The plan of the entire universe was seen as the Grand Design—that is, God's design. In what is called the "argument from design," anatomical structures were viewed as planned to meet the purpose for which they were required. Wings, arms, eyes—all these structures were interpreted as neatly fitting the functions they performed, and nature was considered to be a deliberate plan of the Grand Designer.

The date the Grand Designer had completed his works was relatively recent—4004 B.C., according to Archbishop James Ussher (1581–1656), an Irish scholar who worked out the date of creation by analyzing the "begat" chapter of Genesis. The idea of a recent origin of the earth did not begin with Archbishop Ussher, but he was responsible for providing a precise and late date for it.

The prevailing notion of the earth's brief existence, together with fixity of species, provided a formidable obstacle to the development of evolutionary theory because evolution requires time. Thus, in addition to overcoming the concept of fixity of species, scientists needed a theory of immense geological time in order to formulate evolutionary principles. In fact, until these prior concepts of fixity and time were fundamentally altered, it would have been unlikely that the idea of natural selection could even have been conceived.

The Scientific Revolution

What, then, upset the medieval belief in a rigid universe of planets, stars, plants, and animals? How did the scientific method as we know it today develop and, with the help of Newton and Galileo in the seventeenth century, demonstrate a moving, not static, universe?

The discovery of the New World and circumnavigation of the globe in the fifteenth century overturned some very fundamental ideas about the planet. For one thing, the earth could no longer be perceived as flat. Also, as Europeans began to

Fixity of species
The notion that species, once created, can never change; an idea diametrically opposed to theories of biological evolution.

explore the New World, their awareness of biological diversity was greatly expanded through exposure to plants and animals previously unknown to them.

There were other attacks on the complacency of traditional beliefs. In 1514, a Polish mathematician named Copernicus challenged Aristotle's long-believed assertion that the earth, circled by the sun, moon, and stars, was the center of the universe. Copernicus removed the earth as the center of all things by proposing a *heliocentric* (sun-centered) solar system.

Copernicus' theory did not attract widespread attention at the time, but in the early 1600s, it was restated and further substantiated by an Italian mathematics professor, Galileo Galilei. Galileo came into direct confrontation with the Catholic Church over his publications, to the extent that he spent the last nine years of his life under house arrest. Even so, in intellectual circles, the universe had changed from one of fixity to one of motion, although most scholars still believed that change was impossible for living forms.

Scholars of the sixteenth and seventeenth centuries developed methods and theories that revolutionized scientific thought. The seventeenth century, in particular, was a beehive of scientific activity. The works of such individuals as Keppler, Descartes, and Newton established the laws of physics, motion, and gravity. Other achievements included the discovery of the circulation of blood and the development of numerous scientific instruments, including the telescope, barometer, and microscope. These technological advances permitted investigations of natural phenomena and opened up entire worlds for discoveries such as had never before been imagined.

Scientific achievement increasingly came to direct as well as reflect the changing views of Europeans. Investigations of stars, planets, animals, and plants came to be conducted without significant reference to the supernatural. In other words, nature was seen as a mechanism, functioning according to certain universal physical laws, and it was these laws that scientists were seeking. Yet, most scientists still insisted that a First Cause initiated the entire system. The argument from design was still defended, and support for it continued well into the nineteenth century and persists even today.

The Path to Natural Selection

Before early naturalists could begin to understand the forms of organic life, it was necessary to list and describe those forms. As attempts in this direction were made, scholars became increasingly impressed with the amount of biological diversity that confronted them.

John Ray By the sixteenth century, a keen interest in nature's variation had developed, and by the mid-1500s, there were a few descriptive works on plants, birds, fish, and mammals. But it was not until the seventeenth century that the concept of species was clearly defined by Englishman John Ray (1627–1705), an ordained minister trained at Cambridge University.

Ray was the first to recognize that groups of plants and animals could be distinguished from other groups by their ability to reproduce with one another and produce offspring. Such groups of reproductively isolated organisms were placed into a single category he called *species* (*pl.,* species). Thus, by the late 1600s, the bio-

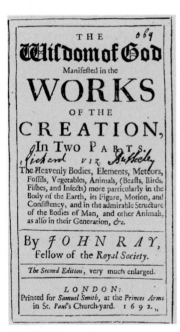

FIGURE 2–1

Title page from John Ray's publication showing God's plan in nature.

The species concept is presented in Virtual Lab 1, section II.

logical criterion of reproduction was used to define species much as it is today (Young, 1992), and upon its publication, the concept was enthusiastically received by the scientific community.

Ray also recognized that species frequently shared similarities with other species, and these he grouped together in a second level of classification he called the *genus* (*pl.*, genera). Ray was the first to use the labels *genus* and *species* in this manner, and they are the terms still in use today. But Ray was very much an adherent of fixity of species. His 1691 publication, *The Wisdom of God Manifested in the Works of Creation* (Fig. 2–1), was intended to demonstrate God's plan in nature, and in this work Ray stressed that nature was a deliberate outcome of a Grand Design.

Carolus Linnaeus   One of the leading naturalists of the eighteenth century was Carolus Linnaeus (1707–1778) of Sweden (Fig. 2–2). He is best known for developing a classification of plants and animals, the *Systema Naturae* (Systems of Nature), first published in 1735.

Linnaeus standardized Ray's more sporadic use of two names (genus and species) for organisms, thus firmly establishing the use of **binomial nomenclature.** Moreover, he added two more categories: class and order. Linnaeus' four-level system of classification became the basis for **taxonomy,** the system of classification still used today.

Another of Linnaeus' innovations was to include humans in his classification of animals, placing them in the genus *Homo* ("human") and species *sapiens* ("wise"). The inclusion of humans in this scheme was controversial because it defied contemporary thought that humans, made in God's image, should be considered separately and outside the animal kingdom.

Linnaeus was also a believer in fixity of species, although in later years, faced with mounting evidence to the contrary, he came to question this long-held assumption. Indeed, fixity of species was being challenged on many fronts, especially in France, where voices were being raised in favor of a universe based on change and, more to the point, in favor of biological relationships between similar forms based on descent from a common ancestor.

Comte de Buffon   Georges-Louis Leclerc (1707–1788), who was elevated to the rank of count under the name Buffon, was Keeper of the King's Gardens in Paris (Fig. 2–3). He believed neither in the perfection of nature nor in the idea that nature had a purpose, as declared by the argument from design, but he did recognize the dynamic relationship between the external environment and living forms. In his *Natural History,* first published in 1749, he repeatedly stressed the importance of change in the universe, and he underlined the changing nature of species.

Buffon believed that when groups of organisms migrated to new areas of the world, each group would subsequently be influenced by local climatic conditions and would gradually change as a result of adaptation to the environment. Buffon's recognition of the external environment as an agent of change in species was an important innovation. However, he rejected the idea that one species could give rise to another.

Erasmus Darwin   Erasmus Darwin (1731–1802) is today best known as Charles Darwin's grandfather (Fig. 2–4). However, during his life, this freethinking,

FIGURE 2–2
Linnaeus developed a classification system for plants and animals.

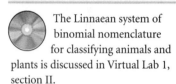
The Linnaean system of binomial nomenclature for classifying animals and plants is discussed in Virtual Lab 1, section II.

Binomial nomenclature
(*Binomial* means "two names.") In taxonomy, the convention established by Carolus Linnaeus whereby genus and species names are used to refer to species. For example, *Homo sapiens* refers to human beings.

Taxonomy
The branch of science concerned with the rules of classifying organisms on the basis of evolutionary relationships.

FIGURE 2–3
Buffon recognized the influence of the environment on life forms.

FIGURE 2–4

Erasmus Darwin, grandfather of Charles Darwin, believed in species change.

FIGURE 2–5

Lamarck believed that species change was influenced by environmental change. He is known for his theory of the inheritance of acquired characteristics.

high-living physician was well known in literary circles for his poetry and other writings. Chief among the latter was his *Zoonomia*, in which evolutionary concepts were expressed in verse.

More than 50 years before his grandson was to startle the world with his views on natural selection, Erasmus Darwin had expressed similar ideas and had even commented on *human* evolution. From letters and other sources, it is known that Charles Darwin had read and was fond of his grandfather's writings, but the degree to which the grandson's theories were influenced by the grandfather is not known.

Jean-Baptiste Lamarck   Neither Buffon nor Erasmus Darwin codified his beliefs into a comprehensive system that attempted to *explain* the evolutionary process. The first European scientist to do so was the French scholar Jean-Baptiste Pierre Antoine de Monet Chevalier de Lamarck (1744–1829). (Thankfully, most references to Lamarck use only his surname.)

Expanding beyond the views of Buffon, Lamarck (Fig. 2–5) attempted to *explain* evolution. He postulated a dynamic interaction between organic forms and the environment, such that organic forms could become altered in the face of changing environmental circumstances. Thus, as the environment changed, an animal's activity patterns would also change, resulting in increased or decreased use of certain body parts. As a result of this use or disuse, body parts became altered.

Physical alteration occurred as a function of perceived bodily "needs." If a particular part of the body felt a certain need, "fluids and forces" would be directed toward that point and the structure would be modified to satisfy the need. Because the modification would render the animal better suited to its habitat, the new trait would be passed on to offspring. This theory is known as the *inheritance of acquired characteristics,* or the *use-disuse* theory.

One of the most frequently given examples of Lamarck's theory is that of the giraffe, who, having stripped all the leaves from the lower branches of a tree (environmental change), strives to reach those leaves on upper branches. As vital forces progress to tissues of the neck, the neck increases slightly in length, thus enabling the giraffe to obtain more food. The longer neck is subsequently transmitted to offspring, with the eventual result that all giraffes have longer necks than did their predecessors (Fig. 2–6a). Thus, according to the theory of inheritance of acquired characteristics, *a trait acquired by an animal during its lifetime can be passed on to offspring.* Today we know this explanation to be inaccurate, for only those traits coded for by genetic information contained within sex cells (eggs and sperm) can be inherited (see Chapters 3 and 4).

Because Lamarck's explanation of species change was not genetically correct, his theories are frequently derided. Actually, Lamarck deserves much credit. He was the first to recognize and stress the importance of interactions between organisms and the environment in the evolutionary process. Moreover, Lamarck was one of the first to acknowledge the need for a distinct branch of science that dealt solely with living things (i.e., separate from geology). For this new science, Lamarck coined the term *biology,* and a central feature of this new science was the notion of evolutionary change.

Georges Cuvier   The most vehement opponent of Lamarck was a young colleague, Georges Cuvier (1769–1832). Cuvier (Fig. 2–7) specialized in vertebrate paleontology, and it was he who introduced the concept of extinction to explain the dis-

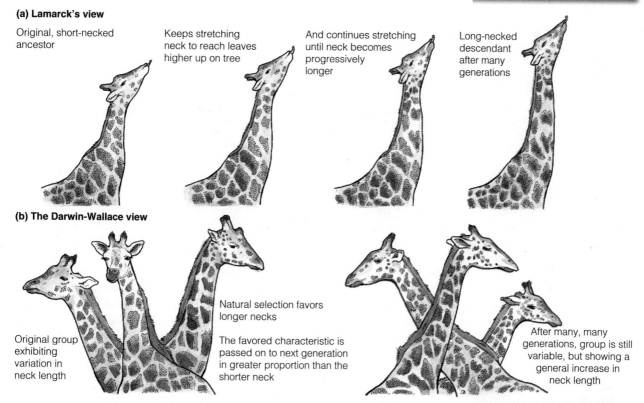

(a) Lamarck's view

Original, short-necked ancestor

Keeps stretching neck to reach leaves higher up on tree

And continues stretching until neck becomes progressively longer

Long-necked descendant after many generations

(b) The Darwin-Wallace view

Natural selection favors longer necks

The favored characteristic is passed on to next generation in greater proportion than the shorter neck

Original group exhibiting variation in neck length

After many, many generations, group is still variable, but showing a general increase in neck length

FIGURE 2–6

Contrasting ideas about the mechanism of evolution. (a) According to Lamarck's theory, acquired characteristics can be passed to subsequent generations. Thus, short-necked giraffes stretched their necks to reach higher into trees for food, and, according to Lamarck, this acquired trait was passed on to offspring, who were born with longer necks. (b) According to the Darwin-Wallace theory of natural selection, among giraffes there is variation in neck length. If having a longer neck provides an advantage for feeding, this trait will be passed on to a greater number of offspring, leading to an increase in the length of giraffe necks over many generations.

appearance of animals represented by fossils. Although a brilliant anatomist, Cuvier never grasped the dynamic concept of nature, and he adamantly insisted on the fixity of species. Just as the abundance of fossils in geological strata was becoming increasingly apparent, it also became more important to explain what they were. But rather than assume that similarities between certain fossil forms and living species indicated evolutionary relationships, Cuvier proposed a variation of a theory known as **catastrophism.**

Catastrophism held that the earth's geological features were the result of sudden, worldwide cataclysmic events, such as the Noah flood. Cuvier's version of catastrophism also postulated a series of regional disasters that destroyed most or all of the plant and animal life within a region but not worldwide. These areas of destruction were subsequently restocked with new forms that migrated in from neighboring, unaffected regions.

To be consistent with the fossil evidence, Cuvier also proposed that destroyed regions were repopulated by new organisms of a more modern appearance and that these forms were the result of more recent creation events. (The last of these

FIGURE 2–7

Cuvier explained the fossil record as the result of a succession of catastrophes followed by new creation events.

Catastrophism
The view that the earth's geological landscape is the result of violent cataclysmic events. This view was promoted by Cuvier, especially in opposition to Lamarck.

FIGURE 2–8

Lyell, the father of geology, stated the theory of uniformitarianism in his *Principles of Geology.*

Uniformitarianism
The theory that the earth's features are the result of long-term processes that continue to operate in the present as they did in the past. Elaborated on by Lyell, this theory opposed catastrophism and provided for immense geological time.

 See Virtual Lab 7, section I for a discussion of several geological methods for determining the age of the earth and the passage of time.

creations was said to be the one depicted in Genesis.) Thus, Cuvier's explanation of increased complexity over time avoided any notion of evolution, while still being able to account for the evidence of change as preserved in the fossil record.

Charles Lyell Charles Lyell (1797–1875), the son of Scottish landowners, is considered the founder of modern geology (Fig. 2–8). He was a barrister by training, a geologist by avocation, and for many years Charles Darwin's friend and mentor. Before he met Darwin in 1836, Lyell had earned wide popular acclaim as well as acceptance in Europe's most prestigious scientific circles, thanks to his highly praised *Principles of Geology,* first published in three volumes in 1830–1833.

In this immensely important work, Lyell argued that the geological processes observed in the present are the same as those that occurred in the past. This theory, which has come to be known as **uniformitarianism,** did not originate entirely with Lyell, but had been proposed by James Hutton in the late 1700s. Nevertheless, it was Lyell who demonstrated that such forces as wind, water erosion, local flooding, frost, the decomposition of vegetable matter, volcanoes, earthquakes, and glacial movements all had contributed in the past to produce the geological landscape that exists in the present. Moreover, the fact that these processes could still be observed in operation indicated that geological change continued to occur and that the forces that drove such change were consistent, or *uniform,* over time. In other words, although various aspects of the earth's surface (e.g., climate, flora, fauna, and land surfaces) are variable through time, the underlying *processes* that influence them are constant.

The theory of uniformitarianism flew in the face of Cuvier's catastrophism and did not go unopposed. Additionally, and every bit as controversially, Lyell emphasized the obvious: namely, that for such slow-acting forces to produce momentous change, the earth must indeed be far older than anyone had previously suspected.

By providing an immense time scale and thereby altering perceptions of the earth's history from a few thousand to many millions of years, Lyell changed the framework within which scientists viewed the geological past. Thus, the concept of "deep time" (Gould, 1987) remains as one of Lyell's most significant contributions to the discovery of evolutionary principles. The immensity of geological time permitted the necessary time depth for the inherently slow process of evolutionary change.

Thomas Malthus In 1798, Thomas Robert Malthus (1766–1834), an English clergyman and economist, wrote *An Essay on the Principle of Population,* which inspired both Charles Darwin and Alfred Wallace in their separate discoveries of the principle of natural selection (Fig. 2–9). In his essay, Malthus pointed out that if not kept in check by limited food supplies, human populations could double in size every 25 years. That is, population size increases exponentially while food supplies remain relatively stable.

Malthus focused on humans because the ability to increase food supplies artificially reduces constraints on population growth, and he was arguing for population control. However, the same logic could be applied to nonhuman organisms. In nature, the tendency for populations to increase is continuously checked by resource availability. Thus, there is constant competition for food and other resources. In time, the extension of Malthus' principles to all organisms would be made by both Darwin and Wallace.

Charles Darwin   Charles Darwin (1809–1882) was one of six children of Dr. Robert and Susanna Darwin (Fig. 2–10). Being the grandson of wealthy Josiah Wedgwood (of Wedgwood pottery fame) as well as of Erasmus Darwin, he grew up enjoying the lifestyle of the landed gentry in rural England.

As a boy, Darwin displayed a keen interest in nature and spent his days fishing and collecting shells, birds' eggs, and rocks. However, this developing interest in natural history did not dispel the generally held view of family and friends that he was not in any way remarkable. In fact, his performance at school was no more than ordinary.

After the death of his mother when he was eight, Darwin's upbringing was guided by his rather stern father and his older sisters. Because he showed little interest in, or aptitude for, anything except hunting, shooting, and perhaps science, his father, fearing Charles would sink into dissipation, sent him to Edinburgh University to study medicine. It was at Edinburgh that Darwin first became acquainted with the evolutionary theories of Lamarck and others.

During this time (the 1820s), notions of evolution were becoming much feared in England and elsewhere. Certainly, anything identifiable with postrevolutionary France was viewed with grave suspicion by the established order in England. Lamarck, especially, was vilified by most English academicians, the majority of whom were also members of the Anglican clergy.

This was also a time of growing political unrest in Britain. The Reform Movement, which sought to undo many of the wrongs of the class system, was under way, and as with most social movements, this one contained a radical faction. Because many of the radicals were atheists and socialists who also supported Lamarck's evolutionary theory, evolution came to be associated, in the minds of many, with atheism and political subversion. Such was the growing fear of evolutionary ideas that many believed that if it were generally accepted that nature evolved unaided by God, "the Church would crash, the moral fabric of society would be torn apart, and civilized man would return to savagery" (Desmond and Moore, 1991, p. 34). It is unfortunate that some of the most outspoken early proponents of **transmutation** were so vehemently anti-Christian, because their rhetoric helped establish the entrenched suspicion and misunderstanding of evolutionary theory that persists even today.

While at Edinburgh, the young Darwin spent endless hours studying with professors who were outspoken supporters of Lamarck. Darwin's second year in Edinburgh saw him examining museum collections and attending natural history lectures. Therefore, although he hated medicine and left Edinburgh after two years, his experience there was a formative period in his intellectual development.

Subsequently, Darwin took up residence at Christ's College, Cambridge, to study theology. (Although he was rather indifferent to religion, theology was often seen as a last resort by parents who viewed their sons as having no discernible academic leanings.) It was during his Cambridge years that Darwin seriously cultivated his interests in natural science, and he often joined the field excursions of botany classes. He also was immersed in geology and was a frequent and serious participant in geological expeditions.

FIGURE 2–9

Thomas Malthus' *Essay on the Principle of Population* led both Darwin and Wallace to the principle of natural selection.

FIGURE 2–10

Charles Darwin as a young man.

Transmutation
The change of one species to another. The term *evolution* did not assume its current meaning until the late nineteenth century.

It was no wonder that following his graduation in 1831 at age 22, he was recommended to accompany a scientific expedition that would circle the globe. Thus it was, after overcoming his father's objections, that Darwin set sail aboard the HMS *Beagle* on December 17, 1831 (Fig. 2–11). The famous voyage of the *Beagle* was to last almost five years and would forever change not only the course of Darwin's life, but also the history of biological science.

Darwin went aboard the *Beagle* still believing in fixity of species. But during the voyage, he privately began to have doubts. As early as 1832, for example, he noted in his diary that a snake with rudimentary hind limbs marked "the passage by which Nature joins the lizards to the snakes." He came across fossils of ancient giant animals that looked, except for size, very much like living forms in the same vicinity, and he wondered whether the fossils were the ancestors of those living forms.

During the famous stopover at the Galápagos Islands (see Fig. 2–11), Darwin noted that the flora and fauna of South America showed striking similarities to those of the Galápagos, as well as some intriguing differences. Even more surprising, the inhabitants of the various islands differed slightly from one another.

For example, Darwin collected 13 different varieties of Galápagos finches. These varieties shared many structural similarities, and clearly they represented a closely affiliated group. But at the same time, they differed with regard to certain physical traits, particularly in the shape and size of their beaks (Fig. 2–12). Darwin also collected finches from the South American mainland, and these appeared to represent only one group, or species.

FIGURE 2–11
The route of the HMS *Beagle*.

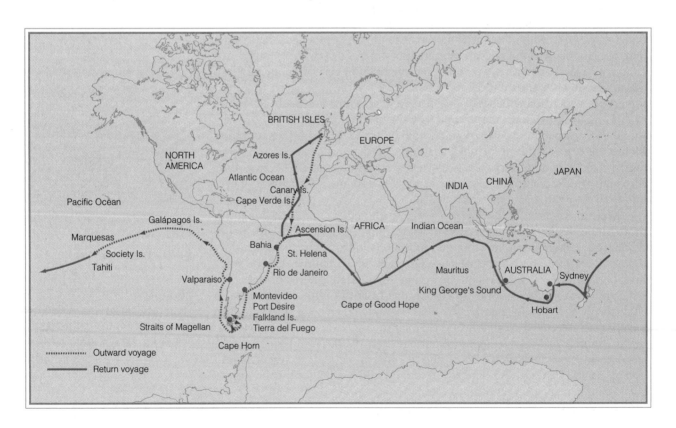

The insight that Darwin gained from the finches is legendary. He recognized that the various Galápagos finches had all descended from a common, mainland ancestor and had become modified in response to the varying island habitats and to altered dietary preferences. But actually, it was not until *after* he had returned to England that Darwin recognized the significance of the variation in beak structure. In fact, during the voyage, Darwin had paid little attention to his finches. It was only in retrospect that he considered the factors that could lead to the modification of 1 species into 13 (Gould, 1985; Desmond and Moore, 1991).

Darwin returned to England in October 1836 and almost immediately was accepted into the most eminent of scientific circles. He married his cousin Emma Wedgwood and moved to the village of Down, near London, where he spent the rest of his life writing on topics ranging from fossils to orchids (Fig. 2–13). But his overriding concern was the question of species change.

At Down, Darwin began developing his views on what he termed *natural selection.* This concept was borrowed from animal breeders, who "select" as breeding stock, those animals that exhibit specific traits they hope to emphasize in offspring. Animals with undesirable traits are "selected against," or prevented from breeding.

Darwin was keenly interested in domestic animals—pigeons, in particular—and he wanted to know how breeders could develop distinctive varieties in just a few generations. (The variations seen in domestic dog breeds may be the best example of the effects of selective breeding.) He applied his knowledge of domesticated species to naturally occurring ones, recognizing that in undomesticated organisms, the selective agent was nature, not humans.

By the late 1830s, Darwin recognized that biological variation within a species was critically important. Furthermore, he acknowledged the importance of sexual reproduction in increasing variation. Then, in 1838, Darwin read Malthus' essay, and in it he found the answer to his question of how new species came to be. He accepted from Malthus that populations increase at a faster rate than do resources, and he inferred that in nonhuman animals, increase in population size is continuously checked by limited food supplies. He also accepted Lyell's observation that in nature there is a constant "struggle for existence." The idea that in each generation more offspring were born than survived to adulthood, coupled with the notions of competition for resources and biological diversity, was all Darwin needed to develop his theory of natural selection. He wrote: "It at once struck me that under these circumstances favourable variations would tend to be preserved, and unfavourable ones to be destroyed. The result of this would be the formation of a new species" (F. Darwin, 1950, pp. 53–54). Basically, this quotation summarizes the whole of natural selection theory.

Darwin wrote a short summary of his views on natural selection in 1842 and revised it in 1844. The 1844 sketch is similar to the argument he presented 15 years later in *On the Origin of Species,* but in 1844 he did not feel he had sufficient data to support his views, so he continued his research without publishing.

Darwin had another reason for not publishing what he knew would be, to say the least, a highly controversial work. As a member of the established order, Darwin knew that many of his friends and associates were concerned with threats to the status quo, and evolutionary theory was viewed as a serious threat indeed. In addition, Darwin was a man to whom reputation was of paramount importance, and he was tormented by fears of bringing dishonor and public criticism to those he loved. Thus, he hesitated.

(a) Ground finch
Main food: seeds
Beak: heavy

(b) Tree finch
Main food: leaves, buds, blossoms, fruits
Beak: thick, short

(c) Tree finch (called woodpecker finch)
Main food: insects
Beak: stout, straight

(d) Ground finch (known as warbler finch)
Main food: insects
Beak: slender

FIGURE 2–12

Beak variation in Darwin's Galápagos finches.

An example of artificial selection is presented in Virtual Lab 2, section I, part B.

The case of Darwin's finches is presented in Virtual Lab 2, section I, part B.

FIGURE 2–13

The Darwin home, Down House, in the village of Down, as seen from the rear garden. *On the Origin of Species* was written here.

Alfred Russel Wallace   Unlike Darwin, Alfred Russel Wallace (1823–1913) was born into a family of modest means (Fig. 2–14). He went to work at the age of 14, and without any special talent and little formal education, he moved from one job to the next. He became interested in collecting plants and animals, and in 1848 he joined an expedition to the Amazon, where he acquired firsthand knowledge of natural phenomena. Then, in 1854, he sailed for Southeast Asia and the Malay Peninsula to continue his study and to collect bird and insect specimens.

In 1855, Wallace published an article suggesting that species were descended from other species and that the appearance of new species was influenced by environmental factors (Trinkaus and Shipman, 1992). The Wallace paper spurred Lyell and others to urge Darwin to publish, but still Darwin hesitated. Wallace and Darwin even corresponded briefly.

Then, in 1858, Wallace sent Darwin another paper titled "On the Tendency of Varieties to Depart Indefinitely from the Original Type." In this paper, Wallace described evolution as a process driven by competition and natural selection. Upon receipt of Wallace's paper, Darwin despaired. He feared that Wallace might be credited for a theory (natural selection) that he himself had formulated. He quickly wrote a paper presenting his ideas, and both the paper by Darwin and the one by Wallace were read before the Linnean Society of London in 1858. Neither author was present. Wallace was not in the country, and Darwin was mourning the very recent death of his young son.

The papers received little notice at the time, but at the urging of Lyell and others, Darwin completed and published his greatest work, *On the Origin of Species,** in December 1859. Upon publication, the storm broke and it has not abated even to this day. While there was much praise for the book, the gist of opinion was negative. Scientific opinion gradually came to Darwin's support, assisted by Darwin's able friend, Thomas Huxley, who for years wrote and spoke in favor of natural selection. The riddle of species was now explained: Species were mutable, not fixed; and they evolved from other species through the mechanism of natural selection.

FIGURE 2–14

Alfred Russel Wallace independently uncovered the key to the evolutionary process.

*The full title is *On the Origin of Species by Means of Natural Selection, or the Preservation of Favoured Races in the the Struggle for Life.*

Natural Selection

Early in his research, Darwin had realized that selection was the key to evolution. With the help of Malthus' ideas, he saw *how* selection in nature could be explained. In the struggle for existence, those *individuals* with favorable variations would survive and reproduce; those with unfavorable variations would not.

For Darwin, the explanation of evolution was simple. The basic processes, as he understood them, are as follows:

1. All species are capable of producing offspring at a faster rate than food supplies increase.
2. There is biological variation within all species; except for identical twins, no two individuals are exactly alike.
3. Because in each generation more individuals are produced than can survive, owing to limited resources, there is competition between individuals. (*Note:* This statement does not imply that there is constant fighting.)
4. Those individuals that possess favorable variations or traits (e.g., speed, disease resistance, protective coloration) have an advantage over individuals that do not possess them. By virtue of the favorable characteristic, these individuals are more likely to survive to produce offspring than are others.
5. The environmental context determines whether or not a trait is beneficial. That is, what is favorable in one setting may be a liability in another. In this way, which traits become most advantageous is the result of a natural process.
6. Traits are inherited and are passed on to the next generation. Because individuals possessing favorable characteristics contribute more offspring to the next generation than do others, over time, such traits become more common in the population; less favorable traits are not passed on as frequently and become less common. Those individuals that produce more offspring, compared to others, are said to have greater **reproductive success.**
7. Over long periods of geological time, successful variations accumulate in a population, so that later generations may be distinct from ancestral ones. Thus, in time, a new species may appear.
8. Geographical isolation may also lead to the formation of new species. As populations of a species become geographically isolated from one another, for whatever reasons, they begin to adapt to different environments. Over time, as populations continue to respond to different **selective pressures** (i.e., different ecological circumstances), they may become distinct species, descended from a common ancestor. The 13 species of Galápagos finches, presumably all descended from a common ancestor on the South American mainland, are an example of the role of geographical isolation.

Before Darwin, scientists thought of species as entities that could not change. Because individuals within the species did not appear to be significant, they were not the object of study; therefore, it was difficult for many scientists to imagine how change could occur. Darwin, as we have pointed out, saw that variation among individuals could explain how selection occurred. Favorable variations were selected for survival by nature; unfavorable ones were eliminated.

This emphasis on the uniqueness of the individual led Darwin to natural selection as the mechanism that made evolution work. *Natural selection operates on individuals,* favorably or unfavorably, but *it is the population that evolves.* The unit of natural selection is the individual; the unit of evolution is the population.

Reproductive success
The number of offspring an individual produces and rears to reproductive age; an individual's genetic contribution to the next generation as compared to the contributions of other individuals.

Selective pressures
Forces in the environment that influence reproductive success in individuals. In the example of the peppered moth, birds applied the selective pressure.

Virtual Lab 2, section I, provides a discussion of the concept of natural selection.

Natural Selection in Action

The best-documented case of natural selection acting in modern populations concerns changes in pigmentation among peppered moths near Manchester, England (Fig. 2–15). Before the nineteenth century, the common variety of moth was a mottled gray color. This light, mottled coloration provided extremely effective camouflage against lichen-covered tree trunks. Also present, though less common, was a dark variety of the same species. While resting on light, lichen-covered trees, the dark, uncamouflaged moths were more visible to birds and were therefore eaten more often. (In this example, birds are the *selective agent*.) Thus, in the end, the dark moths produced fewer offspring than the light, camouflaged moths. Yet, by the end of the nineteenth century, the common gray form had been almost completely replaced by the black variety.

What had brought about this rapid change? The answer lies in the swiftly changing environment of industrialized nineteenth-century England. Coal dust in the area settled on trees, killing the lichen and turning the bark a dark color. Moths continued to rest on trees, but the gray (light) variety was increasingly conspicuous as the trees became darker. Consequently, they began to be preyed on more frequently by birds and thus contributed fewer genes to the next generation. In the late twentieth century, increasing control of pollutants allowed trees to return to their lighter, lichen-covered, preindustrial condition. As would be expected, darker moths are being supplanted by gray ones.

The substance that produces pigmentation is called *melanin,* and the evolutionary shift in the peppered moth, as well as in many other moth species, is termed *industrial melanism.* Such evolutionary shifts in response to environmental change are called *adaptations.*

This example of the peppered moths provides numerous insights into the mechanism of evolutionary change by natural selection:

1. *A trait must be inherited in order to have importance in natural selection.* A characteristic that is not hereditary (such as a temporary change in hair pigmentation brought about by dye) will not be passed on to succeeding generations. In moths, pigmentation is a demonstrated hereditary trait.

2. *Natural selection cannot occur without variation in inherited characteristics.* If all the moths had initially been gray (you will recall that some dark forms were always present) and the trees had become darker, the survival and reproduction

FIGURE 2–15

Variation in the peppered moth. (a) The dark form is more visible on the light, lichen-covered tree. (b) On trees darkened by pollution, the lighter form is more visible.

(a)

(b)

of all moths could have been so low that the population might have become extinct. Such an event is not unusual and without variation would nearly always occur. *Selection can work only when variation already exists.*

3. *Fitness is a relative measure that will change as the environment changes.* Fitness is simply differential reproductive success. In the initial stage, the gray moth was the more fit variety because gray moths produced more offspring. But as the environment changed, the black moths became more fit, and a further change reversed the adaptive pattern. It should be obvious that statements regarding the "most fit" life form mean nothing without reference to specific environments.

Fitness
Pertaining to natural selection, a measure of *relative* reproductive success of individuals. Fitness can be measured by an individual's genetic contribution to the next generation compared to that of others.

The example of the peppered moths shows how different death rates influence natural selection, since moths that die early tend to leave fewer offspring. But mortality is not the entire picture. Another important aspect of natural selection is fertility, for an animal that gives birth to more young would pass its genes on at a faster rate than one that bears fewer offspring. However, fertility is not the entire picture either, for the crucial element is the number of young raised successfully to the point at which they themselves reproduce. We may state this simply as *differential net reproductive success.* The way this mechanism works can be demonstrated through another example.

In a variety of birds called swifts, data show that producing more offspring does not necessarily guarantee that more young will be successfully raised. The number of eggs hatched in a breeding season is a measure of fertility. The number of birds that mature and are eventually able to leave the nest is a measure of net reproductive success, or offspring successfully raised. The following tabulation shows the correlation between the number of eggs hatched (fertility) and the number of young that leave the nest (reproductive success) averaged over four breeding seasons (Lack, 1966):

Number of eggs hatched (fertility)	2 eggs	3 eggs	4 eggs
Average number of young raised (reproductive success)	1.92	2.54	1.76
Sample size (number of nests)	72	20	16

As the tabulation shows, the most efficient number is three eggs, since that number yields the highest reproductive success. Raising two is less beneficial to the parents, since the end result is not as successful as with three eggs. Trying to raise more than three young is actually detrimental, since the parents may not be able to provide adequate nourishment for all the offspring. An offspring that dies before reaching reproductive age is, in evolutionary terms, equivalent to never having been born in the first place. Actually, such a result may be an evolutionary minus to the parents, for this offspring will drain their resources and may inhibit their ability to raise other offspring, thereby lowering their reproductive success even further. Selection will favor those genetic traits that yield the maximum net reproductive success. If the number of eggs laid* is a genetic trait in birds (and it seems to be), natural selection in swifts should act to favor the laying of three eggs as opposed to two or four.

---

*The number of eggs hatched is directly related to the number of eggs laid.

Constraints on Nineteenth-Century Evolutionary Theory

Darwin argued eloquently for the notion of evolution in general and the role of natural selection in particular, but he did not entirely comprehend the exact mechanisms of evolutionary change.

As we have seen, natural selection acts on *variation* within species. But neither Darwin nor anyone else in the nineteenth century understood the source of this variation. Consequently, Darwin speculated about variation arising from "use"—an idea similar to Lamarck's. Darwin, however, was not as dogmatic in his views as Lamarck and most emphatically argued against inner "needs" or "effort." Darwin had to confess that when it came to explaining variation, he simply did not know: "Our ignorance of the laws of variation is profound. Not in one case out of a hundred can we pretend to assign any reason why this or that part differs, more or less, from the same part in the parents" (Darwin, 1859, pp. 167–168).

In addition to his inability to explain the origins of variation, Darwin also did not completely understand the mechanism by which parents transmitted traits to offspring. Almost without exception, nineteenth-century scholars were confused about the laws of heredity, and the popular consensus was that inheritance was *blending* by nature. In other words, offspring were expected to express intermediate traits as a result of a blending of their parents' contributions. Without any viable alternatives, Darwin accepted this popular misconception. As it turned out, a contemporary of Darwin's had systematically worked out the rules of heredity. However, the work of this Augustinian monk, Gregor Mendel (whom you will meet in Chapter 4), was not recognized until the beginning of the twentieth century.

Opposition to Evolution

The publication of *On the Origin of Species* fanned the flames of controversy over evolution into an inferno, but the question had already been debated in intellectual circles for some years, with most people vehemently opposed to evolutionary theory. The very idea that species could give rise to other species was particularly offensive to many Christians because it appeared to be in direct conflict to the special creation event depicted in Genesis. People were horrified at the notion that humans might be biologically related to other animals and especially that they might share a common ancestor with the great apes. Even to make such a claim was degrading, for it denied humanity its unique and exalted place in the universe; in the minds of many, it denied the very existence of God.

The debate has not ended even now, some 140 years later. For the majority of scientists today, evolution is fact. Indeed, the genetic evidence for it is indisputable, and anyone who appreciates and understands genetic mechanisms cannot avoid the conclusion that populations and species evolve. Moreover, the majority of Christians do not believe that biblical depictions are to be taken literally. But at the same time, surveys show that almost half of all Americans believe that evolution does not occur. There are a number of reasons for this.

The mechanisms of evolution are complex and do not lend themselves to simple explanations. To understand these mechanisms requires some familiarity with genetics and biology, a familiarity that most people unfortunately do not possess. Moreover, people who have not been exposed to scientific training want definitive answers to complicated questions. But as you learned in Chapter 1, science does not prove truths, and it frequently does not provide definitive answers.

Another fact to consider is that while all religions offer explanations for natural phenomena, and some even feature the transformation of individuals from one form to another, none really proposes biological change over time. Most people, regardless of their culture, are raised in belief systems that do not emphasize biological continuity between species or offer scientific explanations for natural phenomena.

The relationship between science and religion has never been easy. While both serve, in their own ways, to explain phenomena, scientific explanations are based in data analysis and interpretation. Religion, meanwhile, is a system of beliefs not amenable to scientific testing and falsification; it is based in faith. Religion and science concern different aspects of the human experience, and although they use different approaches in areas where they overlap, they are not inherently mutually exclusive. In fact, many people see them as two sides of the same coin. Moreover, evolutionary theories are not considered anathema by all religions (or even by all forms of Christianity). Some years ago, the Vatican hosted an international conference on human evolution, and in 1996, Pope John Paul II issued a statement to the Pontifical Academy of Sciences acknowledging that "fresh knowledge leads to recognition of the theory of evolution as more than just a hypothesis." Today, the official position of the Catholic Church is that evolutionary processes do occur but that the human soul is of divine creation and not subject to evolutionary processes. Likewise, mainstream Protestants do not generally see a conflict. Unfortunately, those who believe in a literal interpretation of the Bible (frequently termed fundamentalists) do not accept any form of compromise.

Reacting to rapid cultural changes after World War I, conservative Christians in the United States sought a revival of what they considered traditional values. In their view, one way to do this was to prevent any mention of Darwinism in public schools. The Butler Act, passed in Tennessee in 1925, was one result of this effort, and it banned the teaching of evolution in public schools in that state. To test the validity of the law, the American Civil Liberties Union persuaded John Scopes, a high school teacher, to be arrested and ultimately tried for teaching evolution.

The subsequent trial was the famous Scopes Monkey Trial, in which the well-known orator William Jennings Bryan was the prosecuting attorney. The lawyer for the defense was Clarence Darrow, a nationally known labor and criminal lawyer. The trial ended with the conviction of Scopes, who was fined $100. The case was appealed to the Tennessee Supreme Court, which upheld the law, and the teaching of evolution remained illegal in Tennessee. Eventually, several other states, mostly in the South, passed similar laws, and it was not until 1967 that the last two states (Tennessee and Arkansas) ceased to prohibit the teaching of evolution.

But the story does not end there. In the more than 70 years since the Scopes trial, religious fundamentalists have persisted in their attempts to remove evolution from public school curricula. Known as creationists because they explain the existence of the universe as a result of a sudden creation, they are determined either to eliminate the teaching of evolution or to introduce antievolutionary material into public school classes. In the past 20 years, creationists have insisted that "creation science" is just as valid a scientific endeavor as is the study of evolution. They argue that in the interest of fairness, a balanced view should be offered: If evolution is taught as science, then creationism should also be taught as science.

But "creation science" is, by definition, not science at all. Creationists assert that their view is absolute and infallible. Consequently, creationism is not a hypothesis that can be tested, nor is it amenable to falsification. Because such testing is the basis of all science, creationism, by its very nature, cannot be considered science. It is religion.

Still, creationists have been active in state legislatures, promoting the passage of laws mandating the inclusion of creationism in school curricula. To this effect, the Arkansas state legislature passed such a law in 1981, but this law was overturned in 1982. Judge William Ray Overton, in his ruling against the state, found that "a theory that is by its own terms dogmatic, absolutist and never subject to revision is not a scientific theory." And he added: "Since creation is not science, the conclusion is inescapable that the only real effect of such a law is the advancement of religion." In 1987, the United States Supreme Court struck down a similar law in Louisiana.

So far, these and related laws have been overturned because they violate the provision for separation of church and state in the First Amendment to the Constitution. But this has not stopped the creationists, who have encouraged teachers to claim "academic freedom" to teach creationism. Also, they have dropped the term *creationism* in favor of less religious sounding terms, such as *intelligent design theory.* And as recently as August 1999, the Kansas state legislature adopted a policy that will probably eliminate the teaching of evolution from standardized public school curricula. Moreover, antievolution feeling remains strong among politicians. In 1999, one U.S. congressman went so far as to say that the teaching of evolution is one of the factors behind violence in America today!

Although the courts have consistently ruled against the creationists, these religious fundamentalists have nevertheless had an impact on the teaching of evolution. Many public school teachers, seeking to avoid controversy, simply do not cover evolution, or they refer to it as "just a theory" (see p. 14). Thus, students may not be exposed to theories of evolution until they go to college—and only then if they take related courses. This consequence is ultimately to the detriment of the biological sciences (and education in general) in the United States.

Be sure to complete the exercise at the end of Virtual Lab 2, section IV.

SUMMARY

Our current understanding of evolutionary processes is directly traceable to developments in intellectual thought in western Europe over the last 300 years. In particular, the contributions of Linnaeus, Lamarck, Buffon, Lyell, and Malthus all had a significant impact on Darwin. The year 1859 marks a watershed in evolutionary theory, for in that year, the publication of Darwin's *On the Origin of Species* crystallized the understanding of the evolutionary process (particularly the crucial role of natural selection) and for the first time thrust evolutionary theory into the consciousness of the common person. Debates both inside and outside the sciences continued for several decades and, as you have seen, persist today, but the theory of evolution irrevocably changed the tide of intellectual thought. Gradually, Darwin's formulation of evolutionary principles became accepted almost universally by scientists as the very foundation of all the biological sciences, physical anthropology included. As we begin the twenty-first century, contributions from genetics allow us to demonstrate the mechanics of evolution in a way unknown to Darwin and his contemporaries.

Natural selection is the central determining factor influencing the long-term direction of evolutionary change. How natural selection works can best be explained as differential reproductive success—in other words, how successful individuals are in leaving offspring to succeeding generations.

QUESTIONS FOR REVIEW

1. Trace the history of intellectual thought immediately leading to Darwin's theory.
2. What is fixity of species? Why did it pose a problem for the development of evolutionary thinking?
3. What was John Ray's major contribution to biology and the development of evolutionary theories?
4. In what ways did Linnaeus and Buffon differ in their approach to the concept of evolution?
5. What are the bases of Lamarck's theory of acquired characteristics? Why is this theory incorrect?
6. What was Lamarck's contribution to nineteenth-century evolutionary ideas?
7. Explain Cuvier's catastrophism.
8. What did Malthus and Lyell contribute to Darwin's thinking on evolution?
9. Darwin approached the subject of species change by emphasizing individuals within populations. Why was this significant to the development of the concept of natural selection?
10. What evidence did Darwin use to strengthen his argument concerning evolution?
11. How did Darwin's explanation of evolution differ from Lamarck's?
12. What is meant by adaptation? Illustrate through the example of industrial melanism.
13. Define natural selection. What is a selective agent?
14. Explain why the changes in coloration in populations of peppered moths serve as a good example of natural selection.

SUGGESTED FURTHER READINGS

Burke, James. 1985. *The Day the Universe Changed.* Boston: Little, Brown.

Desmond, Adrian, and James Moore. 1991. *Darwin.* New York: Warner Books.

Gould, Stephen Jay. 1987. *Time's Arrow, Time's Cycle.* Cambridge, MA: Harvard University Press.

Ridley, Mark. 1993. *Evolution.* Boston: Blackwell Scientific Publications.

Scott, Eugenie C. 1997. "Antievolutionism and Creationism in the United States." *Annual Review of Anthropology* 2: 263–289.

Trinkaus, Eric, and Pat Shipman. 1993. *The Neandertals.* New York: Knopf.

Young, David. 1992. *The Discovery of Evolution.* London: Natural History Museum Publications, Cambridge University Press.

MULTIMEDIA RESOURCES

Wadsworth Anthropology Resource Center

http://anthropology.wadsworth.com

Visit Anthropology Online to obtain current updates in the field, surfing tips, career information, and more. In addition, enrich your study efforts with text-specific study aids arranged by chapter.

InfoTrac College Edition

http://www.infotrac-college.com/wadsworth

1. A subject search in InfoTrac College Edition for *natural selection* will yield at least 100 current periodical references. Explore these references, and select and read at least one article (not just the abstract) pertaining to a topic you find especially interesting. How does this article illustrate and elaborate on the basic principles of natural selection as presented in Chapter 2?

2. This chapter contains a great deal of information about Darwin and the theory of evolution through natural selection. Yet there is much information that could not be discussed in these pages. What more can you learn about Darwin and the theory of evolution by natural selection on InfoTrac College Edition?

Internet Exercises

1. As you learned in this chapter, Charles Darwin's theory of natural selection was influenced by the writings of numerous other naturalists. You can either use your search engine or go to **www.ucmp.berkeley.edu/history/evolution.html** to read more about these influential people and the development of evolutionary thought. Scroll down to "Preludes to Evolution" and click on the name of someone discussed in this chapter (perhaps Lamarck). What additional facts did you learn? Then choose someone not discussed in the textbook and write one or two paragraphs describing that person's contributions.

2. Using the same Web site or another you have discovered, read about Thomas Huxley. (In the above-mentioned Web site, he is listed under "Natural Selection and Beyond.") Although this chapter does not discuss Huxley, he was instrumental in the acceptance of Darwin's theories. Write a few paragraphs summarizing Huxley's defense of evolutionary theory. On what points was he critical?

CHAPTER
3

The Biological Basis of Life

CONTENTS

CHAPTER 3

Introduction

This textbook is about human evolution and adaptation, both of which are intimately linked to life processes that involve cells, the replication and decoding of genetic information, and the transmission of this information between generations. Thus, to present human evolution and adaptation in the broad sense, we must first examine how life is organized at the cellular and molecular levels, and this, in turn, necessitates a brief discussion of the fundamental principles of genetics.

Genetics is the study of how traits are transmitted from one generation to the next. Because physical anthropologists are concerned with human evolution, adaptation, and variation, they must have a thorough understanding of the factors that lie at the very root of these phenomena. Indeed, although many physical anthropologists do not actually specialize in genetics, it is genetics that ultimately links or influences many of the various subdisciplines of biological anthropology.

The discipline of genetics is largely a twentieth-century development, and much of our present knowledge has been acquired within the last 50 years. Today, insights into the numerous aspects of inheritance are increasing at an exponential rate, with new discoveries being made virtually every day. Moreover, as genetic technologies develop and increasingly come into use, they assume an ever greater role in the lives of us all.

It is therefore more important than ever that, as people living at the beginning of the twenty-first century, we achieve a basic understanding of the factors that influence our lives. Also, from an anthropological perspective, it is only through the further elucidation of genetic principles that we can hope to understand fully the evolutionary mechanisms that have permitted humans to become the species we are today.

Genetics
The study of gene structure and action and the patterns of inheritance of traits. Genetic mechanisms are the underlying foundation for evolutionary change.

The Cell

To discuss genetic and evolutionary principles, we must first have a fundamental understanding of cell function. Cells are the basic units of life in all living organisms. In some forms, such as bacteria, a single cell constitutes the entire organism. However, more complex *multicellular* forms, such as plants, insects, birds, and mammals, are composed of billions of cells. Indeed, an adult human is made up of perhaps as many as 1,000 billion (1,000,000,000,000) cells, all functioning in complex ways to promote the survival of the individual.

Life on earth can be traced back at least 3.7 billion years, in the form of *prokaryotic* cells. Prokaryotes are single-celled organisms, represented today by bacteria and blue-green algae. Structurally more complex cells appeared approximately 1.2 billion years ago, and these are referred to as *eukaryotic* cells. Because eukaryotic cells are found in all multicellular organisms, they are the focus of the remainder of this discussion. In spite of the numerous differences between various life forms and the cells that constitute them, it is important to understand that the cells of all living organisms share many similarities as a result of their common evolutionary past.

In general, a eukaryotic cell is a three-dimensional entity composed of *carbohydrates, lipids, nucleic acids,* and *proteins*. It contains a variety of structures called *organelles* within the *cell membrane* (Fig. 3–1). One of these organelles is the **nucleus** (*pl.*, nuclei), a discrete unit surrounded by a thin nuclear membrane.

The structure of the cell is presented in Virtual Lab 2, section II, part A.

Nucleus
A structure (organelle) found in all eukaryotic cells. The nucleus contains chromosomes (nuclear DNA).

Within the nucleus are two nucleic acids that contain the genetic information that controls the cell's functions. These two critically important **molecules** are **deoxyribonucleic acid (DNA)** and **ribonucleic acid (RNA).** (In prokaryotic cells, genetic information is not contained within a walled nucleus.) Surrounding the nucleus is the **cytoplasm,** which contains numerous other types of organelles involved in various activities, such as breaking down nutrients and converting them to other substances (*metabolism*), storing and releasing energy, eliminating waste, and manufacturing **proteins (protein synthesis).**

Two of these organelles—**mitochondria** and **ribosomes**—require further mention. The mitochondria (*sing.,* mitochondrion) are responsible for energy production in the cell and are thus the "engines" that drive the cell. Mitochondria are round or oval structures enclosed within a folded membrane, and they contain their own distinct DNA, called mitochondrial DNA (mtDNA), which directs mitochondrial activities. Mitochondrial DNA has the same molecular structure and function as nuclear DNA, but it is organized somewhat differently. In recent years, mtDNA has attracted much attention because of particular traits it influences and because it has significance for studies of certain evolutionary processes. Ribosomes are roughly spherical in shape and are the most common type of cytoplasmic organelle. They are made up partly of RNA and are essential to the synthesis of proteins (see p. 47).

There are basically two types of cells: **somatic cells** and **gametes.** Somatic cells are the cellular components of body tissues, such as muscle, bone, skin, nerve, heart, and brain. Gametes, or sex cells, are specifically involved in reproduction and are not important as structural components of the body. There are two types of gametes: *ova* (*sing.,* ovum), or egg cells, produced in the ovaries in females; and *sperm,* which develop in male testes. The sole function of a sex cell is to unite with a gamete from another individual to form a **zygote,** which has the potential of developing into a new individual. By so doing, gametes transmit genetic information from parent to offspring.

Molecules
Structures made up of two or more atoms. Molecules can combine with other molecules to form more complex structures.

Deoxyribonucleic acid (DNA)
The double-stranded molecule that contains the genetic code. DNA is a main component of chromosomes.

Ribonucleic acid (RNA)
A single-stranded molecule, similar in structure to DNA. The three forms of RNA are essential to protein synthesis.

Cytoplasm
The portion of the cell contained within the cell membrane, excluding the nucleus. The cytoplasm consists of a semifluid material and contains numerous structures involved with cell function.

Proteins
Three-dimensional molecules that serve a wide variety of functions through their ability to bind to other molecules.

Protein synthesis
The assembly of chains of amino acids into functional protein molecules. The process is directed by DNA.

Mitochondria
(*sing.,* mitochondrion) Organelles found in the cytoplasm of cells that are responsible for producing energy for cellular functions.

Ribosomes
Structures composed of a specialized form of RNA and protein. Ribosomes are found in the cell's cytoplasm and are essential to the manufacture of proteins.

Somatic cells
Basically, all the cells in the body except those involved with reproduction.

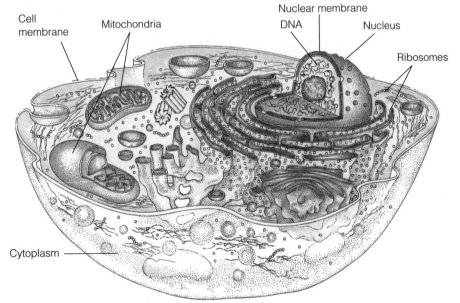

Cell membrane · Mitochondria · Nuclear membrane · DNA · Nucleus · Ribosomes · Cytoplasm

FIGURE 3–1

Structure of a generalized eukaryotic cell, illustrating the cell's three-dimensional nature. Although various organelles are shown, for the sake of simplicity only those we discuss in this text are labeled.

Gametes
Reproductive cells (eggs and sperm in animals) developed from precursor cells in ovaries and testes.

Zygote
A cell formed by the union of an egg and a sperm cell. It contains the full complement of chromosomes (in humans, 46) and has the potential of developing into an entire organism.

Nucleotides
Basic units of the DNA molecule, composed of a sugar, a phosphate, and one of four DNA bases.

Complementary
Referring to the fact that DNA bases form base pairs in a precise manner. For example, adenine can bond only to thymine. These two bases are said to be *complementary* because one requires the other to form a complete DNA base pair.

FIGURE 3–2

Part of a DNA molecule. The illustration shows the two DNA strands with the sugar and phosphate backbone and the bases extending toward the center.

DNA Structure

As already mentioned, cellular functions are directed by DNA. If we are to understand these functions and how characteristics are inherited, we must first know something about the structure and function of DNA. The exact physical and chemical properties of DNA were unknown until 1953, when at Cambridge University, an American researcher, James Watson, and three British scientists—Francis Crick, Maurice Wilkins, and Rosalind Franklin—developed a structural and functional model for DNA (Watson and Crick, 1953a, 1953b). The importance of this achievement cannot be overstated, for it completely revolutionized the fields of biology and medicine and forever altered our understanding of biological and evolutionary mechanisms.

The DNA molecule is composed of two chains of even smaller molecules called **nucleotides.** A nucleotide, in turn, is made up of three components: a sugar molecule (deoxyribose), a phosphate unit, and one of four nitrogenous bases (Fig. 3–2). In DNA, nucleotides are stacked upon one another to form a chain that is bonded along its bases to another **complementary** nucleotide chain. Together the

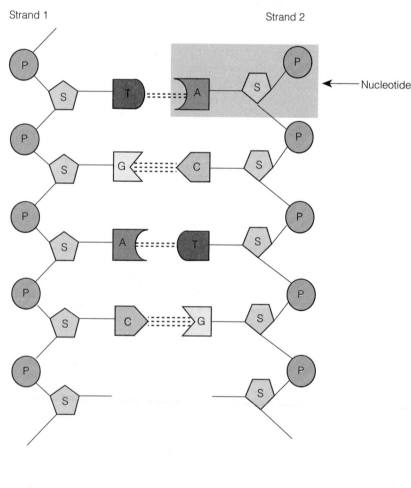

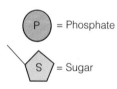
P = Phosphate

S = Sugar

BASES

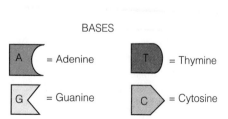
A = Adenine
T = Thymine
G = Guanine
C = Cytosine

two twist to form a spiral, or helical, shape. The resulting DNA molecule, then, is two-stranded and is described as forming a *double helix* that resembles a twisted ladder. If we follow the twisted ladder analogy, the sugars and phosphates represent the two sides, while the bases and the bonds that join them form the rungs.

The secret of how DNA functions lies within the four bases. These bases are *adenine, guanine, thymine,* and *cytosine,* and they are frequently referred to by their initial letters, A, G, T, and C. In the formation of the double helix, it is possible for one type of base to pair or bond with only one other type. Thus, base pairs can form *only* between adenine and thymine and between guanine and cytosine (see Fig. 3–2). This specificity is essential to the DNA molecule's ability to **replicate,** or make an exact copy of itself, and DNA is the only molecule known to have this capacity.

Replicate
To duplicate. The DNA molecule is able to make copies of itself.

DNA Replication

Growth and development of organisms and tissue repair following injury are among the crucial processes made possible by cell division. Cells multiply by dividing in such a way that each new cell receives a full complement of genetic material. This is a crucial point, since a cell cannot function properly without the appropriate amount of DNA. For new cells to receive the essential amount of DNA, it is first necessary for the DNA to replicate.

Discussions of DNA structure and the process of replication are presented in Virtual Lab 2, section II, parts B and C.

Prior to cell division, specific **enzymes** break the bonds between bases in the DNA molecule, leaving the two previously joined strands of nucleotides with their bases exposed (Fig. 3–3). The exposed bases attract unattached nucleotides, which are free-floating in the cell nucleus.

Enzymes
Specialized proteins that initiate and direct chemical reactions in the body.

Because one base can be joined to only one other, the attraction between bases occurs in a complementary fashion. Thus, the two previously joined parental nucleotide chains serve as models, or *templates,* for the formation of new strands of nucleotides. As each new strand is formed, its bases are joined to the bases of an original strand. When the process is completed, there are two double-stranded DNA molecules exactly like the original one, and each newly formed molecule consists of one original nucleotide chain joined to a newly formed chain (see Fig. 3–3).

Protein Synthesis

One of the most important functions of DNA is that it directs protein synthesis within the cell. Proteins are complex, three-dimensional molecules that function through their ability to bind to other molecules. For example, the protein **hemoglobin,** found in red blood cells, is able to bind to oxygen and serves to transport oxygen to cells throughout the body.

Hemoglobin
A protein molecule that occurs in red blood cells and binds to oxygen molecules.

Proteins function in myriad ways. Some are structural components of tissues. Collagen, for example, is the most common protein in the body and is a major component of all connective tissues. Aside from mineral components, it is the most abundant structural material in bone. Enzymes are also proteins, and their function is to initiate and enhance chemical reactions. An example of a digestive enzyme is *lactase,* which breaks down *lactose,* or milk sugar, into two simpler sugars. Another class of proteins includes many types of **hormones.** Specialized cells produce and release hormones into the bloodstream to circulate to other areas of

Hormones
Substances (usually proteins) that are produced by specialized cells and that travel to other parts of the body, where they influence chemical reactions and regulate various cellular functions.

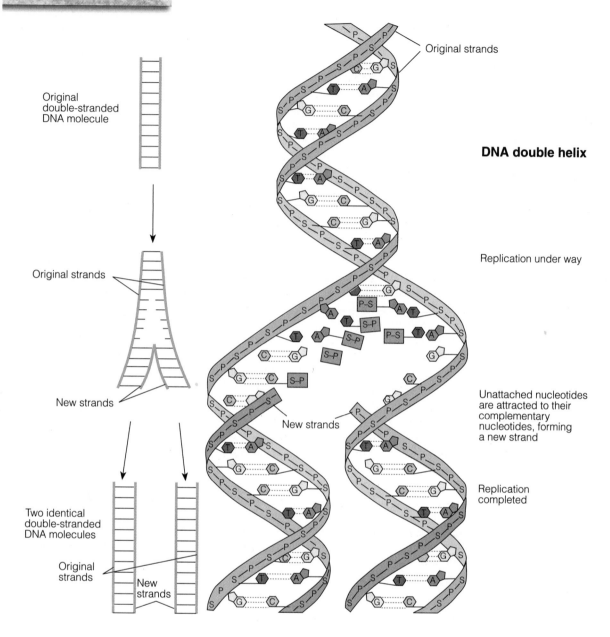

Original double-stranded DNA molecule

Original strands

New strands

Two identical double-stranded DNA molecules

Original strands

New strands

Original strands

DNA double helix

Replication under way

Unattached nucleotides are attracted to their complementary nucleotides, forming a new strand

New strands

Replication completed

FIGURE 3–3

DNA replication. During DNA replication, the two strands of the DNA molecule are separated, and each strand serves as a template for the formation of a new strand. When replication is complete, there are two DNA molecules. Each molecule consists of one new and one original DNA strand.

the body, where they produce specific effects in tissues and organs. A good example of this type of protein is *insulin*, produced by cells in the pancreas. Insulin causes cells in the liver and certain types of muscle tissue to absorb glucose (sugar) from the blood. (Enzymes and hormones will be discussed in more detail in Chapter 14.)

As you can see, proteins make us what we are. Not only are they the major constituents of all body tissues, but they also direct and perform physiological and cellular functions. It is therefore critical that protein synthesis occur accurately, for if it does not, physiological development and metabolic activities can be disrupted or even prevented.

Proteins are composed of chains of smaller molecules called **amino acids.** In all, there are 20 amino acids, which are combined in different amounts and sequences to produce potentially millions of proteins. What makes proteins different from one another is the number of amino acids involved and the *sequence* in which they are arranged. For a protein to function properly, its amino acids must be arranged in the proper sequence.

DNA serves as a recipe for making a protein, because it is the sequence of DNA bases that ultimately determines the order of amino acids in a protein molecule. In the DNA instructions, a *triplet,* or group of three bases, specifies a particular amino acid. For example, if a triplet includes the bases cytosine, guanine, and adenine (CGA), it specifies the amino acid *alanine.* If the next triplet in the chain contains guanine, thymine, and cytosine (GTC), it refers to another amino acid—*glutamine.* Therefore, a DNA recipe might look like this: AGA CGA ACA ACC TAC TTT TTC CTT AAG GTC, and so on, as it directs the cell in assembling proteins (Table 3–1).

Protein synthesis is a little more complicated than the preceding few sentences would imply. For one thing, protein synthesis occurs outside the nucleus at the specialized structures called ribosomes. A logistics problem arises because the DNA molecule is not capable of traveling outside the cell's nucleus. Thus, the first step in

Amino acids
Small molecules that are the components of proteins.

Virtual Lab 2, section II, part C, presents an example of protein synthesis.

TABLE 3–1 The Genetic Code

Amino Acid Symbol	Amino Acid	mRNA Codon	DNA Triplet
Ala	Alanine	GCU, GCC, GCA, GCG	CGA, CGG, CGT, CGC
Arg	Arginine	CGU, CGC, CGA, CGG, AGA, AGG	GCA, GCG, GCT, GCC, TCT, TCC
Asn	Asparagine	AAU, AAC	TTA, TTG
Asp	Aspartic acid	GAU, GAC	CTA, CTG
Cys	Cysteine	UGU, UGC	ACA, ACG
Gln	Glutamine	CAA, CAG	GTT, GTC
Glu	Glutamic acid	GAA, GAG	CTT, CTC
Gly	Glycine	GGU, GGC, GGA, GGG	CCA, CCG, CCT, CCC
His	Histidine	CAU, CAC	GTA, GTG
Ile	Isoleucine	AUU, AUC, AUA	TAA, TAG, TAT
Leu	Leucine	UUA, UUG, CUU, CUC, CUA, CUG	AAT, AAC, GAA, GAG, GAT, GAC
Lys	Lysine	AAA, AAG	TTT, TTC
Met	Methionine	AUG	TAC
Phe	Phenylalanine	UUU, UUC	AAA, AAG
Pro	Proline	CCU, CCC, CCA, CCG	GGA, GGG, GGT, GGC
Ser	Serine	UCU, UCC, UCA, UCG, AGU, AGC	AGA, AGG, AGT, AGC, TCA, TCG
Thr	Threonine	ACU, ACC, ACA, ACG	TGA, TGG, TGT, TGC
Trp	Tryptophan	UGG	ACC
Tyr	Tyrosine	UAU, UAC	ATA, ATG
Val	Valine	GUU, GUC, GUA, GUG	CAA, CAG, CAT, CAC
Terminating triplets		UAA, UAG, UGA	ATT, ATC, ACT

protein synthesis is to copy the DNA message into a form that can pass through the nuclear membrane into the cytoplasm. This process is accomplished through the formation of a molecule similar to DNA called ribonucleic acid, or RNA. RNA is different from DNA in three important ways:

1. It is single-stranded.
2. It contains a different type of sugar.
3. It contains the base uracil as a substitute for the DNA base thymine. (Uracil is attracted to adenine, just as thymine is.)

The RNA molecule forms on the DNA template in much the same manner as new strands of DNA are assembled during DNA replication. The new RNA nucleotide chain is a particular type of RNA called **messenger RNA (mRNA).** During its assembly on the DNA model, mRNA is transcribing the DNA code, and in fact, the formation of mRNA is called *transcription* (Fig. 3–4). Once the appropriate DNA segment has been copied, the mRNA strand peels away from the DNA

Messenger RNA (mRNA)
A form of RNA that is assembled on one sequence of DNA bases. It carries the DNA code to the ribosome during protein synthesis.

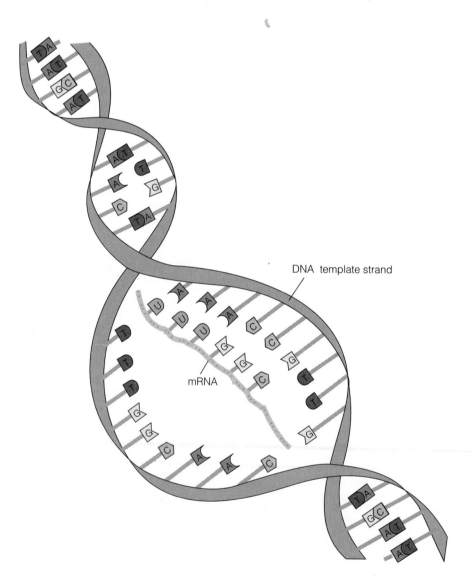

DNA template strand

mRNA

FIGURE 3–4

Transcription. The two DNA strands have partly separated. Free messenger RNA (mRNA) nucleotides have been drawn to the template strand, and a strand of mRNA is being made. Note that the mRNA strand will exactly complement the DNA template strand except that uracil (U) replaces thymine (T).

model and travels through the nuclear membrane to the ribosome. Meanwhile, the bonds between the DNA bases are reestablished, and the DNA molecule is once more intact.

As the mRNA strand arrives at the ribosome, the message it contains is translated. (This stage of the process is called *translation* because at this point, the genetic instructions are actually being decoded and implemented.) Just as each DNA triplet specifies one amino acid, mRNA triplets—called **codons**—also serve this function. Therefore, the mRNA strand is "read" in codons, or groups of three bases taken together.

One other form of RNA—**transfer RNA (tRNA)**—is essential to the actual assembly of a protein. Each molecule of tRNA has the ability to bind to one specific amino acid. A particular tRNA molecule carrying the amino acid matching the mRNA codon being translated arrives at the ribosome and deposits its amino acid (Fig. 3–5). As a second amino acid is deposited, the two are joined in the

Codons
The triplets of messenger RNA bases that refer to a specific amino acid during protein synthesis.

Transfer RNA (tRNA)
The type of RNA that binds to specific amino acids and transports them to the ribosome during protein synthesis.

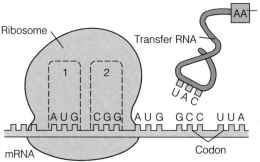

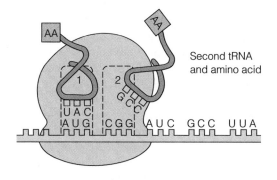

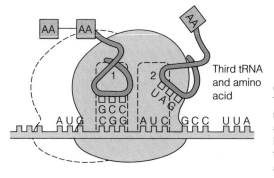

(a)
As the ribosome binds to the mRNA, tRNA brings a particular amino acid, specified by the mRNA codon, to the ribosome.

(b)
The tRNA binds to the first codon while a second tRNA–amino acid complex arrives at the ribosome.

(c)
The ribosome moves down the mRNA, allowing a third amino acid to be brought into position by another tRNA molecule. Note that the first two amino acids are now joined together.

FIGURE 3–5

Assembly of an amino acid chain in protein synthesis.

51

order dictated by the sequence of mRNA codons. In this way, series of amino acids are linked together to form a structure that will eventually function as a protein.

The entire sequence of DNA bases responsible for the synthesis (or manufacture) of a protein or, in some cases, portion of a protein is referred to as a **gene.** Or, put another way, a gene is a segment of DNA that specifies the sequence of amino acids in a particular protein. A gene may comprise only a few hundred bases, or it may be composed of thousands. If the sequence of DNA bases is altered through **mutation** (a change in the DNA), the manufacture of some proteins may not occur, and the cell (or indeed the organism) may not function properly, if it functions at all.

This definition of a gene is a functional one and is technically correct. But it is important to understand that gene action is an incredibly complex phenomenon that is only partly understood. For example, the DNA segments that are transcribed into mRNA and therefore code for specific amino acids are termed *exons.* But not all nucleotide sequences in a gene are actually expressed during protein synthesis. In fact, some sequences, called *introns,* are initially transcribed but subsequently eliminated; thus, they are not translated into amino acid sequences. But while introns are not instrumental in protein synthesis, they are indeed a part of the DNA molecule, and it is the combination of introns and exons, interspersed along a strand of DNA, that comprises the unit we call a gene.

While we usually think of genes as coding for the production of structural proteins, some genes function primarily to control the expression of other genes. Basically, these *regulatory genes* produce enzymes and other proteins that either switch on or turn off other segments of DNA. Consequently, this mechanism is critical for individual organisms and also has important evolutionary implications.

All somatic cells contain the same genetic information, but in any given cell, only a fraction of the DNA is actually involved in protein synthesis. For example, bone cells carry the same DNA that codes for the production of digestive enzymes, as do the cells of the stomach lining. But bone cells do not produce digestive enzymes. Instead, they manufacture collagen, the major organic component of bone. Bone cells produce collagen and not digestive enzymes because of the differentiation of cell lines early in embryonic development. During this process, cells undergo changes in form, their functions become specialized, and most of their DNA is permanently deactivated through the action of regulatory genes.

On a larger scale, alterations in the behavior of regulatory genes that influence the activities of the structural genes involved in growth and development may be responsible for some of the physical differences between closely related species. For example, some of the anatomical differences between humans and chimpanzees, who share 98 percent of their DNA, may be the results of evolutionary changes in regulatory genes in one or both lineages.

A final point is that the genetic code is said to be universal in that, at least on earth, DNA is the genetic material in all forms of life. Moreover, the DNA of all organisms, from bacteria to oak trees to human beings, is composed of the same molecules using the same kinds of instructions. Consequently, the DNA triplet CGA, for example, specifies the amino acid alanine, regardless of species. These similarities imply biological relationships among, and an ultimate common ancestry for, all forms of life. What makes oak trees distinct from humans is not differences in the DNA material, but differences in how that material is arranged.

Gene
A sequence of DNA bases that specifies the order of amino acids in an entire protein or, in some cases, a portion of a protein. A gene may be made up of hundreds or thousands of DNA bases.

Mutation
A change in DNA. Technically, mutation refers to changes in DNA bases as well as changes in chromosome number and/or structure.

The concept of the gene is discussed in Virtual Lab 2, section II, part B.

Cell Division: Mitosis and Meiosis

Throughout much of a cell's life, its DNA exists as an uncoiled, threadlike substance. (Incredibly, there are an estimated 6 feet of DNA in the nucleus of every one of your somatic cells!) However, at various times in the life of most types of cells, normal functions are interrupted and the cell divides. Cell division is the process that results in the production of new cells, and it is during this process that the DNA becomes tightly coiled and is visible under a light microscope as a set of discrete structures called **chromosomes** (Fig. 3–6).

A chromosome is composed of a DNA molecule and associated proteins (Fig. 3–7). During normal cell function, if chromosomes were visible, they would appear as single-stranded structures. However, during the early stages of cell division, they are made up of two strands, or two DNA molecules, joined together at a constricted area called the **centromere**. There are two strands simply because the DNA molecules have *replicated.* Therefore, one strand of a chromosome is an exact copy of the other.

Every species is characterized by a specific number of chromosomes in somatic cells. In humans there are 46. Chimpanzees and gorillas possess 48. This difference in chromosome number does not necessarily indicate that humans possess less DNA than chimpanzees and gorillas. The DNA is simply packaged differently in the three species. Chromosomes occur in pairs. Thus, human somatic cells contain 23 pairs. One member of each pair is inherited from the father (paternal), while the other member is inherited from the mother (maternal). Members of chromosomal pairs are said to be **homologous** in that they are alike in size and position of the centromere and they carry genetic information influencing the

Chromosomes
Discrete structures composed of DNA and protein found only in the nuclei of cells. Chromosomes are visible only under magnification during certain stages of cell division.

Centromere
The constricted portion of a chromosome. After replication, the two strands of a double-stranded chromosome are joined at the centromere.

Homologous
Referring to members of chromosome pairs. Homologous chromosomes carry genes that govern the same traits. During meiosis, homologous chromosomes pair and exchange segments of DNA. They are alike with regard to size and also position of the centromere.

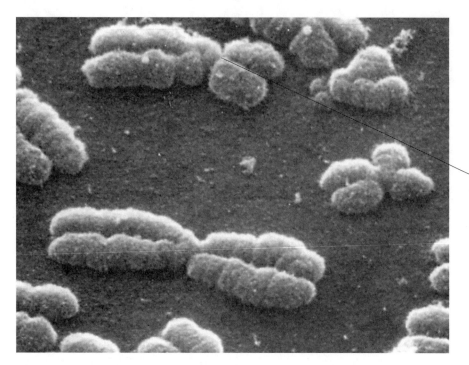

Centromere

FIGURE 3–6

Scanning electron micrograph of human chromosomes during cell division. Note that these chromosomes are composed of two strands, or two DNA molecules.

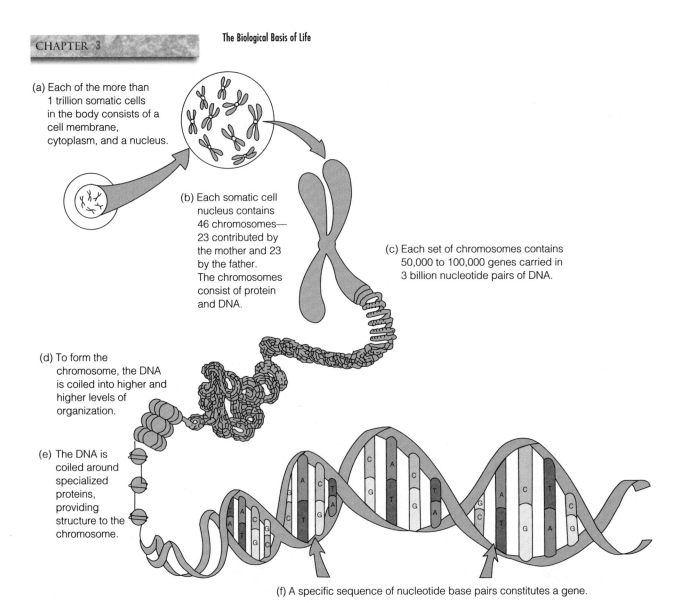

(a) Each of the more than 1 trillion somatic cells in the body consists of a cell membrane, cytoplasm, and a nucleus.

(b) Each somatic cell nucleus contains 46 chromosomes— 23 contributed by the mother and 23 by the father. The chromosomes consist of protein and DNA.

(c) Each set of chromosomes contains 50,000 to 100,000 genes carried in 3 billion nucleotide pairs of DNA.

(d) To form the chromosome, the DNA is coiled into higher and higher levels of organization.

(e) The DNA is coiled around specialized proteins, providing structure to the chromosome.

(f) A specific sequence of nucleotide base pairs constitutes a gene.

FIGURE 3–7

A model of a human chromosome, illustrating the relationship of chromosomes to DNA.

Autosomes
All chromosomes except the sex chromosomes.

Sex chromosomes
In mammals, the X and Y chromosomes.

same traits (e.g., ABO blood type). This does not imply that partner (homologous) chromosomes are genetically identical; it simply means that the traits they govern are the same. (This topic will be discussed in more detail in Chapter 4.)

There are two basic types of chromosomes: **autosomes** and **sex chromosomes.** Autosomes carry genetic information that governs all physical characteristics except primary sex determination. The two sex chromosomes are the X and Y chromosomes. The Y chromosome carries genes that are directly involved with determining maleness. The X chromosome, although termed a "sex chromosome," is larger and functions more like an autosome in that it is not actually involved in primary sex determination but does influence a number of other traits.

Among mammals, all genetically normal females have two X chromosomes (XX); they are female simply because the Y chromosome is not present. All genetically normal males have one X and one Y chromosome (XY). In other classes of animals, such as birds or insects, primary sex determination is governed by differing chromosomal mechanisms.

It is extremely important to note that *all* autosomes occur in pairs. Normal human somatic cells have 22 pairs of autosomes and one pair of sex chromosomes. It should also be noted that abnormal numbers of autosomes, with few exceptions, are fatal to the individual, usually soon after conception. Although abnormal numbers of sex chromosomes are not usually fatal, they may result in sterility and frequently have other consequences as well. Therefore, to function normally, it is essential for a human cell to possess both members of each chromosomal pair, or a total of 46 chromosomes.

Mitosis

Cell division in somatic cells is called **mitosis.** Mitosis occurs during growth of the individual. It also acts to promote healing of injured tissues and to replace older cells with newer ones. In short, it is the way somatic cells reproduce.

In the early stages of mitosis, a human somatic cell possesses 46 double-stranded chromosomes, which line up in random order along the center of the cell (Fig. 3–8). As the cell wall begins to constrict at the center, the chromosomes split apart at the centromere, so that the two strands are separated. Once the two strands are apart, they pull away from each other and move to opposite ends of the dividing cell. At this point, each strand is now a distinct chromosome, *composed of one DNA molecule.* Following the separation of chromosome strands, the cell wall pinches in and becomes sealed, so that two new cells are formed, each with a full complement of DNA, or 46 chromosomes (see Fig. 3–8).

Mitosis is referred to as "simple cell division" because a somatic cell divides one time to produce two daughter cells that are genetically identical to each other and to the original cell. In mitosis, the original cell possesses 46 chromosomes, and each new daughter cell inherits an exact copy of all 46 (Fig. 3–9a). This precise arrangement is made possible by the ability of the DNA molecule to replicate. Thus, it is DNA replication that ensures that the quantity and quality of the genetic material remain constant from one generation of cells to the next.

It should be noted that not all somatic cells undergo mitosis. Red blood cells are produced by specialized cells in bone marrow and possess no nucleus and no nuclear DNA. Moreover, it is believed that once full growth has occurred, brain and nerve cells (neurons) do not divide, although some debate currently surrounds this issue. Liver cells also do not divide after growth has ceased unless this vital organ is damaged through injury or disease. However, with these three exceptions (red blood cells, mature neurons, and liver cells), somatic cells are regularly duplicated through the process of mitosis.

Meiosis

While mitosis produces new cells, **meiosis** may lead to the development of new individuals, since it produces reproductive cells, or gametes. Although meiosis is another form of cell division and is in some ways similar to mitosis, it is a more complicated process.

During meiosis, specialized cells in male testes and female ovaries divide and develop, eventually to produce sperm or egg cells. Meiosis is characterized by *two*

Mitosis
Simple cell division; the process by which somatic cells divide to produce two identical daughter cells.

Meiosis
Cell division in specialized cells in ovaries and testes. Meiosis involves two divisions and results in four daughter cells, each containing only half the original number of chromosomes. These cells can develop into gametes.

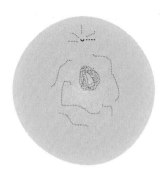

(a) The cell is involved in metabolic activities. DNA replication occurs, but chromosomes are not visible.

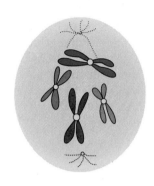

(b) The nuclear membrane disappears, and double-stranded chromosomes are visible.

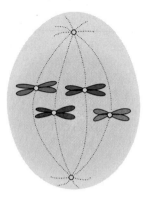

(c) The chromosomes align themselves at the center of the cell.

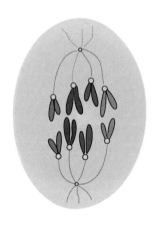

(d) The chromosomes split at the centromere, and the strands separate and move to opposite ends of the dividing cell.

(e) The cell membrane pinches in as the cell continues to divide. The chromosomes begin to uncoil (not shown here).

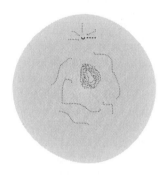

(f) After mitosis is complete, there are two identical daughter cells. The nuclear membrane is present, and chromosomes are no longer visible.

FIGURE 3–8
Mitosis.

divisions that result in *four daughter cells,* each of which contains only 23 chromosomes, or half the original number (Fig. 3–9b).

Reduction of chromosome number is a critical feature of meiosis, for the resulting gamete, with its 23 chromosomes, may ultimately unite with another gamete that also carries 23 chromosomes. The product of this union is a *zygote,* or

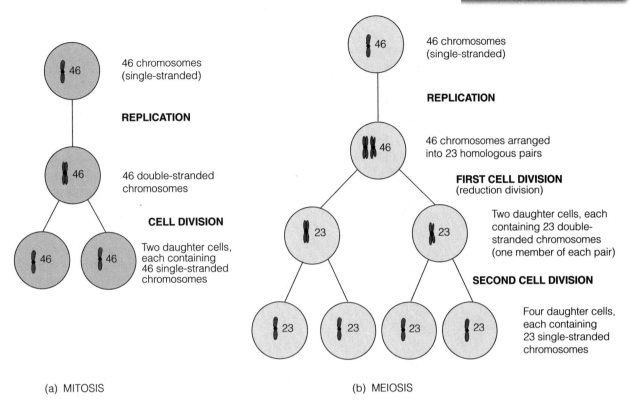

(a) MITOSIS

(b) MEIOSIS

fertilized egg, which, in humans, receives a total of 46 chromosomes. In other words, the zygote inherits the full complement of DNA it needs (half from each parent) to develop and function normally. If it were not for reduction division (the first division) in meiosis, it would not be possible to maintain the correct number of chromosomes from one generation to the next.

During the first meiotic division, chromosomes line up at the center of the cell as in mitosis, but there is a difference. In this first division, homologous chromosomes come together to form pairs of double-stranded chromosomes. In this way, then, *pairs* of chromosomes line up along the cell's equator (Fig. 3–10).

Pairing of homologous chromosomes is highly significant, for while they are together, members of pairs exchange genetic information in a critical process called **recombination** or *crossing over*. Pairing is also important because it facilitates the accurate reduction of chromosome number by ensuring that each new daughter cell will receive only one member of each pair.

As the cell begins to divide, the chromosomes themselves remain intact (i.e., double-stranded), but *members of pairs* separate and migrate to opposite ends of the cell. After the first division, there are two new daughter cells, but they are not identical to each other or to the parental cell because each contains only one member of each chromosome pair and therefore only 23 chromosomes, each of which still has two strands (see Fig. 3–10). Moreover, because of crossing over, each chromosome now contains some genetic variations it did not have previously.

FIGURE 3–9

Mitosis and meiosis compared. In mitosis, one division produces two daughter cells, each of which contains 46 chromosomes. Meiosis is characterized by two divisions. After the first, there are two cells, each containing only 23 chromosomes (one member of each original chromosome pair). Each daughter cell divides again, so that the final result is four cells, each with only half the original number of chromosomes.

Recombination
The exchange of DNA between homologous chromosomes during meiosis; also called "crossing over."

FIGURE 3–10

Meiosis.

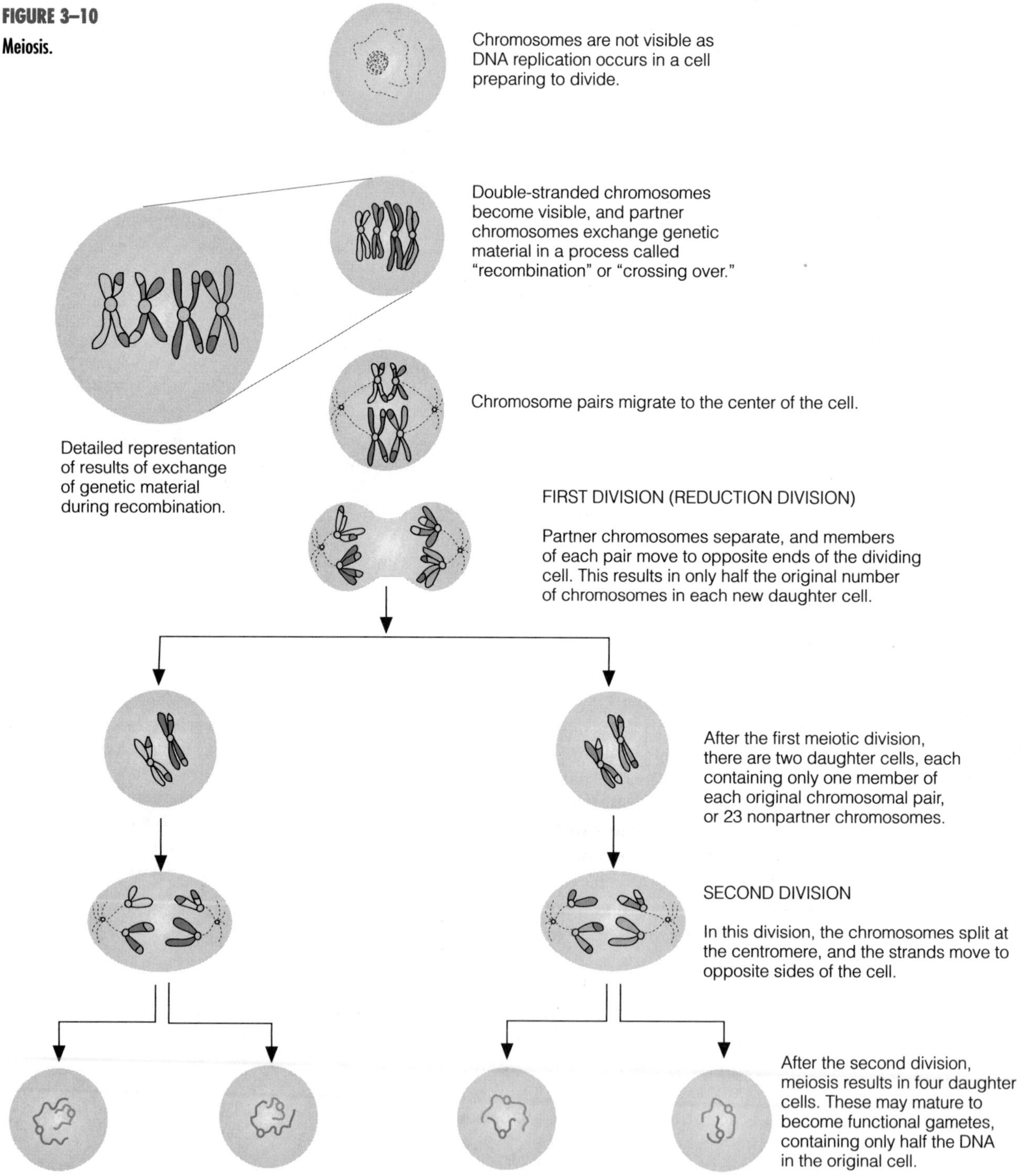

Chromosomes are not visible as DNA replication occurs in a cell preparing to divide.

Double-stranded chromosomes become visible, and partner chromosomes exchange genetic material in a process called "recombination" or "crossing over."

Detailed representation of results of exchange of genetic material during recombination.

Chromosome pairs migrate to the center of the cell.

FIRST DIVISION (REDUCTION DIVISION)

Partner chromosomes separate, and members of each pair move to opposite ends of the dividing cell. This results in only half the original number of chromosomes in each new daughter cell.

After the first meiotic division, there are two daughter cells, each containing only one member of each original chromosomal pair, or 23 nonpartner chromosomes.

SECOND DIVISION

In this division, the chromosomes split at the centromere, and the strands move to opposite sides of the cell.

After the second division, meiosis results in four daughter cells. These may mature to become functional gametes, containing only half the DNA in the original cell.

The second meiotic division proceeds in much the same way as cell division in mitosis. In the two newly formed cells, the 23 double-stranded chromosomes align themselves at the cell's center, and as in mitosis, the strands of each chromosome separate at the centromere and move apart. Once this second division is completed, there are four daughter cells, each with 23 single-stranded chromosomes, or 23 DNA molecules.

The Evolutionary Significance of Meiosis Meiosis occurs in all sexually reproducing organisms, and it is a highly important evolutionary innovation, since it increases genetic variation in populations at a faster rate than mutation alone can do in asexually reproducing species. Individual members of sexually reproducing species are not genetically identical clones of other individuals. Rather, they result from the contribution of genetic information from two parents. Therefore, each individual represents a unique combination of genes that, in all likelihood, has never occurred before and will never occur again. The genetic uniqueness of individuals is further enhanced by recombination between homologous chromosomes during meiosis, for recombination ensures that chromosomes are not transmitted intact from one generation to the next. Instead, in every generation, parental contributions are reshuffled in an almost infinite number of combinations, thus altering the genetic composition of chromosomes even before they are passed on.

Genetic diversity is therefore considerably enhanced by meiosis. As was mentioned in Chapter 2, natural selection acts on genetic variation in populations. If all individuals in a population are genetically identical over time, then natural selection (and evolution) cannot occur. Although there are other sources of variation (mutation being the only source of *new* variation), sexual reproduction and meiosis are of *major* evolutionary importance because they contribute to the role of natural selection in populations.

Problems with Meiosis For meiosis to ensure a reasonably good opportunity for the completion of normal fetal development, the process must be exact. The two-stage division must produce a viable gamete with exactly 23 chromosomes—with only one member of each chromosome pair present. Superficially, it appears that the process works quite well, since more than 98 percent of newborns have the correct number of chromosomes. However, this statistic is misleading. It has been estimated that as many as one of every two pregnancies naturally terminates early as a spontaneous abortion (miscarriage). An estimated 70 percent of these miscarriages are caused by an improper number of chromosomes (Cummings, 2000). Thus, it appears that during meiosis, there are frequent errors with quite serious consequences.

If chromosomes or chromosome strands fail to separate during either of the two meiotic divisions, serious problems can arise. This failure to separate is called **nondisjunction.** The result of nondisjunction is that one of the daughter cells receives two copies of the affected chromosome, while the other daughter cell receives none. If such an affected gamete unites with a normal gamete containing 23 chromosomes, the resulting zygote will have either 45 or 47 chromosomes.

The far-reaching effects of an abnormal number of chromosomes can be appreciated only by remembering that the zygote will reproduce itself through mitosis. Thus, every cell in the developing body will also have the abnormal chromosomal complement. Most situations of this type involving autosomes are

The importance of meiosis to random assortment and inheritance is discussed in Virtual Lab 2, section II, part E.

Virtual Lab 2, section II, parts A and E, discusses the importance of gametes in sexual reproduction and inheritance.

Nondisjunction
The failure of homologous chromosomes or chromosome strands to separate during cell division.

lethal, and the embryo is spontaneously aborted, frequently before the pregnancy is even recognized.

One example of an abnormal number of autosomes is *Down syndrome,* more properly called *trisomy 21,* where there are three copies of the twenty-first chromosome. This is the only example of an abnormal number of autosomes being compatible with life beyond infancy. Trisomy 21, which occurs in approximately 1 out of every 1,000 live births, is associated with a number of developmental and health problems. These problems include congenital heart defects (seen in about 40 percent of affected newborns), increased susceptibility to respiratory infections, and leukemia. However, the most widely recognized effect of trisomy 21 is mental retardation, which is variably expressed and ranges from mild to severe.

Nondisjunction also occurs in the X and Y chromosomes. Although these conditions do not always result in death, they frequently cause sterility and may result in other problems as well. Clearly, normal development relies on the presence of the correct number of chromosomes.

The importance of accuracy in meiosis cannot be overstated. If normal development is to occur, it is essential that the correct number of both autosomes and sex chromosomes be present.

SUMMARY

This chapter has dealt with several concepts that are fundamental to understanding human variation as well as the processes of biological evolution. These are topics that will be discussed in succeeding chapters.

It has been shown that cells are the fundamental units of life and that there are basically two types of cells. Somatic cells make up body tissues, while gametes (eggs and sperm) are reproductive cells that transmit genetic information from parent to offspring.

Genetic information is contained in the DNA molecule, found in the nuclei of cells. The DNA molecule is capable of replication, or making copies of itself, and it is the only molecule known to have this ability. Replication makes it possible for parent cells to retain a full complement of DNA while also transmitting a full complement to daughter cells.

DNA also controls protein synthesis by directing the cell to arrange amino acids in the proper sequence for each particular type of protein. Also involved in the process of protein synthesis is another, similar molecule called RNA.

Cells multiply by dividing, and during cell division DNA is visible under a microscope in the form of chromosomes. In humans, there are 46 chromosomes, or 23 pairs.

Somatic cells divide during growth or tissue repair or to replace old or damaged cells. Somatic cell division is called mitosis. During mitosis, a cell divides one time to produce two daughter cells, each possessing a full and identical set of chromosomes.

Sex cells are produced when specialized cells in the ovaries and testes divide in meiosis. Unlike mitosis, meiosis is characterized by two divisions, which produce four nonidentical daughter cells, each containing only half the amount of DNA (23 chromosomes) carried by the original cell.

QUESTIONS FOR REVIEW

1. Genetics is the study of what?
2. What components of a eukaryotic cell are discussed in this chapter?
3. What are the two basic types of cells in individuals? Give an example of each.
4. What are nucleotides?
5. Name the four DNA bases. Which pairs with which?
6. What is DNA replication, and why is it important?
7. What are proteins? Give two examples.
8. What are enzymes and what do they do?
9. What are the building blocks of protein? How many different kinds are there?
10. What is the function of DNA in protein synthesis?
11. What is the function of mRNA?
12. What is the function of tRNA?
13. Define gene.
14. Define chromosome.
15. What are homologous chromosomes?
16. How many cell divisions occur in mitosis? In humans, how many chromosomes does each new cell have?
17. How many cell divisions occur in meiosis? How many daughter cells are produced when meiosis is complete? In humans, how many chromosomes does each new cell contain?
18. Why is reduction division important?
19. What is recombination, and why is it important? When does it occur?
20. Why is the genetic code said to be universal?
21. What are the two sex chromosomes? Which two do males have? Which two do females have?
22. Why is meiosis important to the process of natural selection?
23. Why is the study of genetics important to physical anthropology?

SUGGESTED FURTHER READINGS

Brennan, James R. 1985. *Patterns of Human Heredity.* Englewood Cliffs, NJ: Prentice-Hall.

Cummings, Michael R. 2000. *Human Heredity. Principles and Issues.* 5th ed. Pacific Grove, CA: Brooks/Cole.

Gribbin, John. 1987. *In Search of the Double Helix.* New York: Bantam Books.

Ridley, Mark. 1993. *Evolution.* Cambridge, MA: Blackwell Scientific.

See entire issue of *Scientific American,* vol. 253(4), October 1985, for numerous articles pertaining to molecular genetics and evolution.

MULTIMEDIA RESOURCES

🌐 Wadsworth Anthropology Resource Center

http://anthropology.wadsworth.com

Visit Anthropology Online to obtain current updates in the field, surfing tips, career information, and more. In addition, enrich your study efforts with text-specific study aids arranged by chapter.

InfoTrac College Edition

http://www.infotrac-college.com/wadsworth

1. Conduct a subject search for *chromosomes* and go to "Encyclopedia excerpt." Read this entry. Then go back and click on all terms highlighted in blue (e.g., *mitosis, meiosis*) and read the sections concerning these terms. Also, read at least one article listed under "Periodical references." Did this material help you understand the information in Chapter 3? If so, how?

2. Conduct a subject search for *DNA*. Choose at least one article, read it, and write a short summary. In your summary, discuss some aspect of the article that pertains to one of the topics discussed in Chapter 3.

🌐 Internet Exercises

1. The subject of genetics is well represented on the Internet. Use your search engine to do a word search for *genetics*. See if you can find the original 1953 article by Watson and Crick that describes the structure of the DNA molecule. Read this very short Nobel Prize–winning article and make a list of facts that are not presented in Chapter 3. What is your overall impression of the Watson and Crick paper?

2. Again, using your search engine, search for *cell biology*. Look for a site that describes the functions of the various organelles in the cytoplasm. Choose one of these organelles (we suggest ribosomes or mitochondria) and write a two- or three-paragraph summary of the activities of these structures. How are these activities related to genetic mechanisms?

3. The Genetic Sciences Learning Center (**http://gslc.genetics.utah.edu/**) is a fun and informative site that provides several easy and inexpensive ways to explore basic genetics. We encourage you to explore the entire site, but in particular, scroll down the home page and click on "How to extract DNA from anything living." This is an exercise you can do in your kitchen with products you already have available. For your source of DNA, you can use just about anything from the produce bin in your refrigerator. As you do this exercise, keep a journal that includes a detailed record of each step.

CHAPTER
4

CONTENTS

Heredity
and Evolution

Introduction

In Chapter 3, we discussed the structure and function of DNA within the cell. In this chapter, we shift to a somewhat broader perspective and focus on the principles that guide how characteristics are passed from parent to offspring.

For at least 10,000 years, beginning with the domestication of plants and animals, people have attempted to explain how traits are passed from parents to offspring. Although most theories have been far from accurate, farmers and herders have known for millennia that they could enhance the frequency and expression of desirable attributes through selective breeding. However, exactly why desirable traits were often seen in the offspring of carefully chosen breeding stock remained a mystery. It was equally curious when offspring did not show the traits their human owners had hoped for.

From the time ancient Greek philosophers considered the problem until well into the nineteenth century, one predominant belief was that characteristics of offspring resulted from the *blending* of parental traits. Blending was supposedly accomplished by means of particles that existed in every part of the body. These so-called *pangenes* contained miniatures of the body part (limbs, organs, etc.) from which the particles derived, and they traveled through the blood to the reproductive organs and blended with particles of another individual during reproduction. There were variations on the theme of *pangenesis,* and numerous scholars, including Charles Darwin, adhered to some aspects of the theory.

The importance of sexual reproduction is discussed in Virtual Lab 2, section II, part E.

The Genetic Principles Discovered by Mendel

It was not until Gregor Mendel (1822–1884) addressed the question of heredity that it began to be resolved (Fig. 4–1). Mendel was a monk living in an Augustinian abbey at Brno in what is now the Czech Republic. At the time he began his research, he had already acquired scientific expertise in botany, physics, and mathematics at the University of Vienna and had conducted various experiments in the monastery gardens. These experiments led him to explore the various ways in which physical traits, such as color or height, could be expressed in plant **hybrids.** He hoped that by making crosses between two strains of *purebred* plants and examining their progeny, he could determine (and predict) how many different forms of hybrids there were, arrange the forms according to generation, and evaluate the proportion of each type in each generation.

Mendel chose to work with common garden peas, and unlike previous researchers, he chose to consider only one trait at a time. In all, he focused on seven traits, each of which could be expressed in two different ways (Table 4–1). Because the genetic principles Mendel discovered apply to humans as well as to peas (and all other sexually reproducing organisms), we discuss his work in some detail to illustrate the basic rules of inheritance.

FIGURE 4–1
Gregor Mendel.

Hybrids
Offspring of mixed ancestry; heterozygotes.

Segregation

Mendel began by crossing different varieties of purebred plants that differed with regard to a specific trait. For example, if he was interested in stem length, he crossed varieties that produced only tall plants with varieties that produced only short plants.

TABLE 4–1   The Seven Garden Pea Characteristics Studied by Mendel

Characteristic	Dominant Trait	Recessive Trait
1. Form of ripe seed	Smooth	Wrinkled
2. Color of seed	Yellow	Green
3. Color of seed coat	Gray	White
4. Form of ripe pods	Inflated	Constricted
5. Color of unripe pods	Green	Yellow
6. Position of flowers on stem	Along stem	End of stem
7. Length of stem	Tall	Short

 The results of these experiments are similar to the goals that are pursued by breeders during animal and plant domestication. See Virtual Lab 2, section I, part B.

The plants used in the first cross were designated the *parental,* or *P,* generation, and all were either tall or short. The hybrid offspring of the P generation were designated the F_1 (first filial) generation. As they matured, the F_1 plants were not intermediate in height, as blending theories of inheritance would have predicted. To the contrary, they were all tall (Fig. 4–2).

Next, Mendel allowed the F_1 plants to self-fertilize and produce a second generation of plants (the F_2 generation). But this time, only approximately $3/4$ of the offspring plants were tall, and the remaining $1/4$ were short. Regardless of the trait he examined, every time he performed the experiment, he obtained almost the same results. One expression of the trait completely disappeared in the F_1 generation and reappeared in the F_2 generation. Moreover, the expression that was present in the F_1 generation was more common in the F_2 plants, occurring in a ratio of approximately 3:1.

These results suggested an important fact. It appeared that different expressions of a trait were controlled by discrete *units,* which occurred in pairs, and that offspring inherited one unit from each parent. Mendel correctly concluded that the members of a pair of units controlling a trait somehow separated into different sex cells and were again united with another member during fertilization of the egg. This is Mendel's *first principle of inheritance,* known as the **principle of segregation.**

Today we know that meiosis explains Mendel's principle of segregation. You will remember that during meiosis, paired chromosomes (and the genes they carry) separate from each other and are distributed to different gametes. However, in the zygote, the full complement of chromosomes is restored, and both members of each chromosome pair are present in the offspring.

Dominance and Recessiveness

Mendel also recognized that the expression that was absent in the F_1 plants had not actually disappeared at all. It had remained present, but somehow it was masked and could not be expressed. To describe the trait that seemed to be lost, Mendel used the term **recessive;** the trait that was expressed was said to be **dominant.** Thus, the important principles of *dominance* and *recessiveness* were formulated, and they remain today as important concepts in the field of genetics.

Principle of segregation
Genes (alleles) occur in pairs (because chromosomes occur in pairs). During gamete production, the members of each gene pair separate, so that each gamete contains one member of each pair. During fertilization, the full number of chromosomes is restored, and members of gene or allele pairs are reunited.

Recessive
Describing a trait that is not expressed in heterozygotes; also refers to the allele that governs the trait. For a recessive allele to be expressed, there must be two copies of the allele (i.e., the individual must be homozygous).

Dominant
Describing a trait governed by an allele that can be expressed in the presence of another, different allele (i.e., in heterozygotes). Dominant alleles prevent the expression of recessive alleles in heterozygotes. (This is the definition of *complete* dominance.)

FIGURE 4–2

Results of crosses when only one trait at a time is considered.

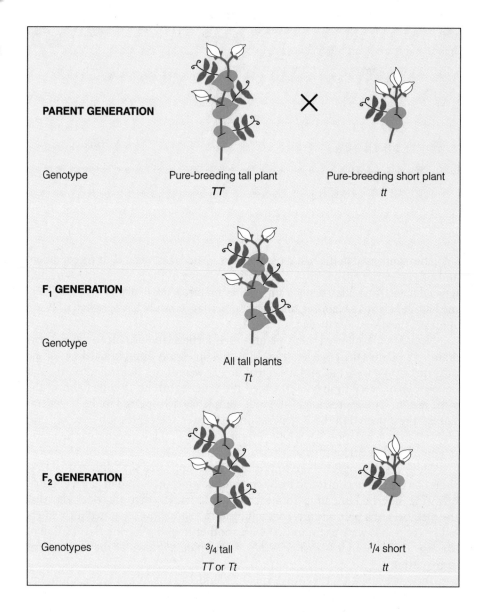

Locus (*pl.,* loci)
(lo´-kus, lo-sigh´)
The position on a chromosome where a given gene occurs. The term is sometimes used interchangeably with gene.

Alleles
Alternate forms of a gene. Alleles occur at the same locus on homologous chromosomes and thus govern the same trait. However, because they are different, their action may result in different expressions of that trait. The term is often used synonymously with *genes*.

As you already know, a *gene* is a segment of DNA that directs the production of a specific protein or part of a protein. Furthermore, the location of a gene on a chromosome is its **locus** (*pl.,* loci). At numerous genetic loci, however, there is more than one possible form of the gene, and these variations of genes at specific loci are called **alleles.** Therefore, an allele is an alternate form of a gene that can direct the cell to produce slightly different forms of the same protein and, ultimately, different expressions of traits.

As it turns out, plant height in garden peas is controlled by two different alleles at one genetic locus. The allele that determines that a plant will be tall is dominant to the allele for short. (It is worth mentioning that height is not governed in this manner in all plants.)

In Mendel's experiments, all the parent (P) plants had two copies of the same allele, either dominant or recessive, depending on whether they were tall or short. When two copies of the same allele are present, the individual is said to be **homozygous.** Thus, all the tall P plants were homozygous for the dominant allele, and all the short P plants were homozygous for the recessive allele. (This homozygosity explains why tall plants crossed with tall plants produced only tall offspring, and short plants crossed with short plants produced all short offspring; they were "pure lines" and lacked genetic variation at this locus.) However, all the F_1 plants (hybrids) had inherited one allele from each parent plant; therefore, they all possessed two different alleles at specific loci. Individuals that possess two different alleles at a locus are **heterozygous.**

Figure 4–2 illustrates the crosses that Mendel initially performed. Geneticists use standard symbols to refer to alleles. Uppercase letters refer to dominant alleles (or dominant traits), and lowercase letters refer to recessive alleles (or recessive traits). Therefore,

T = the allele for tallness
t = the allele for shortness

The same symbols are combined to describe an individual's actual genetic makeup, or **genotype.** The term *genotype* can be used to refer to an organism's entire genetic makeup or to the alleles at a specific genetic locus. Thus, the genotypes of the plants in Mendel's experiments were

TT = homozygous tall plants
Tt = heterozygous tall plants
tt = homozygous short plants

Figure 4–3 is a *Punnett square.* It represents the different ways the alleles can be combined when the F_1 plants are self-fertilized to produce an F_2 generation. In this way, the figure shows the *genotypes* that are possible in the F_2 generation, and it also demonstrates that approximately ¼ of the F_2 plants are homozygous dominant (TT); ½ are heterozygous (Tt); and the remaining ¼ are homozygous recessive (tt).

The Punnett square can also be used to show (and predict) the proportions of F_2 **phenotypes,** or the observed physical manifestations of genes. Moreover, the Punnett square also illustrates why Mendel observed three tall plants for every

Homozygous
Having the same allele at the same locus on both members of a pair of homologous chromosomes.

Heterozygous
Having different alleles at the same locus on members of a pair of homologous chromosomes.

Genotype
The genetic makeup of an individual. Genotype can refer to an organism's entire genetic makeup or to the alleles at a particular locus.

Phenotypes
The observable or detectable physical characteristics of an organism; the detectable expressions of genotypes.

FIGURE 4–3

Punnett square representing possible genotypes and phenotypes and their proportions in the F_2 generation. The circles across the top and at the left of the Punnett square represent the gametes of the F_1 parents. The four squares illustrate that ¼ of the F_2 plants will be homozygous tall (TT); another ½ also will be tall but will be heterozygous (Tt); and the remaining ¼ will be short (tt). Thus, ¾ can be expected to be tall and ¼ will be short.

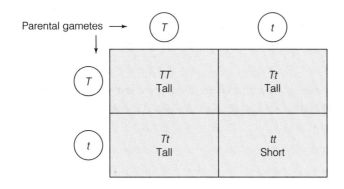

 Virtual Lab 2, section II, part E, provides a Punnett square exercise for you to complete.

Phenotypic ratio
The proportion of one phenotype to other phenotypes in a group of organisms. For example, Mendel observed that there were approximately three tall plants for every short plant in the F₂ generation. This is expressed as a phenotypic ratio of 3:1.

Mendelian traits
Characteristics that are influenced by alleles at only one genetic locus. Examples include many blood types, such as ABO. Many genetic disorders, including sickle-cell anemia and Tay-Sachs disease, are also Mendelian traits.

Principle of independent assortment
The distribution of one pair of alleles into gametes does not influence the distribution of another pair. The genes controlling different traits are inherited independently of one another.

short plant in the F_2 generation. By examining the Punnett square, you can see that $\frac{1}{4}$ of the F_2 plants are tall because they have the *TT* genotype. Furthermore, an additional $\frac{1}{2}$, which are heterozygous (*Tt*), will also be tall because *T* is dominant to *t* and will therefore be expressed in the phenotype. The remaining $\frac{1}{4}$ are homozygous recessive (*tt*), and they will be short because no dominant allele is present. It is important to note that the *only* way a recessive allele can be expressed is if it occurs with another recessive allele, that is, if the individual is homozygous recessive at the particular locus in question.

In conclusion, $\frac{3}{4}$ of the F_2 generation will express the dominant phenotype, and $\frac{1}{4}$ will show the recessive phenotype. This relationship is expressed as a **phenotypic ratio** of 3:1 and typifies all **Mendelian traits** (characteristics governed by only one genetic locus) when only two alleles are involved, one of which is completely dominant to the other.

Independent Assortment

Mendel also made crosses in which two characteristics were considered simultaneously to determine whether there was a relationship between them. Two such characteristics were plant height and seed (pea) color. Mendel's peas came in two colors: yellow (dominant) and green (recessive).

In the P generation, crosses were made between pure-breeding tall plants with yellow seeds and short plants with green seeds. As expected, the recessive expression of each trait was not seen in the F_1 generation; all these plants were tall and produced yellow seeds. However, in the next (F_2) generation, both recessive traits reappeared in a small proportion of plants. These results suggested that there is no relationship between the two traits; that is, there is nothing to dictate that a tall plant must have yellow (or green) seeds. The expression of one trait is not influenced by the expression of the other trait.

Mendel stated this, his second principle of inheritance, as the **principle of independent assortment.** The principle of independent assortment says that the units (genes) that code for different traits assort independently of each other during gamete formation. Today, we know this to be true because we know that the genetic loci controlling these two characteristics are located on different, nonhomologous chromosomes, and during meiosis, chromosomes travel to newly forming cells independently of one another. If Mendel had used just *any* two traits, his results would have been quite different. For example, if the two traits in question were influenced by genes located on the same chromosome, Mendel's ratios would have been considerably altered. The ratios came out as he predicted because the loci governing most of the traits he chose were carried on different chromosomes.

In 1866, Mendel's results were published, but the methodology and statistical nature of the research were beyond the thinking of the time, and their significance was overlooked and unappreciated. However, by the end of the nineteenth century, several investigators had made important contributions to the understanding of chromosomes and cell division. These discoveries paved the way for the acceptance of Mendel's work by 1900, when three different groups of scientists, conducting similar breeding experiments, came across his paper. Regrettably, Mendel had died 16 years earlier and thus never saw his work vindicated.

Mendelian Inheritance in Humans

Mendelian traits (also referred to as *discrete traits* or *traits of simple inheritance*) are controlled by alleles at *one* genetic locus. Currently, over 4,500 human traits are known to be inherited according to simple Mendelian principles. Examples include several blood group systems, such as ABO.

The ABO system is governed by three alleles, *A, B,* and *O,* found at the ABO locus on the ninth chromosome. Although three alleles are present in populations, each individual can possess only two. These alleles determine which ABO blood type an individual has by coding for the production of substances called **antigens** on the surface of red blood cells. If only antigen A is present, the blood type (phenotype) is A; if only B is present, the blood type is B; if both are present, the blood type is AB; and when neither is present, there is no A or B antigen and the blood type is said to be O. (The *O* allele appears to have no function; i.e., it does not code for the production of any antigen.)

Dominance and recessiveness are clearly illustrated by the ABO system. The *O* allele is recessive to both *A* and *B;* therefore, if a person has type O blood, he or she must be homozygous for (have two copies of) the *O* allele. However, since both *A* and *B* are dominant to *O,* an individual with blood type A can actually have one of two genotypes: *AA* or *AO.* The same is true of type B, which results from the genotypes *BB* and *BO* (Table 4–2). However, type AB presents a slightly different situation and is an example of **codominance.**

Codominance is seen when two different alleles occur in heterozygous condition, but instead of one having the ability to mask the expression of the other, the products of *both* are expressed in the phenotype. Therefore, when both *A* and *B* alleles are present, both A and B antigens can be detected on the surface of red blood cells.

A number of genetic disorders are inherited as dominant traits (Table 4–3). This means that if a person inherits only one copy of a harmful, dominant allele, the condition it causes will be present, regardless of the existence of a different, recessive allele on the corresponding chromosome.

Recessive conditions are commonly associated with the lack of a substance, usually an enzyme (see Table 4–3). For a person actually to have a recessive disorder, he or she must have *two* copies of the recessive allele that causes it. Heterozygotes who have only one copy of a harmful recessive allele are unaffected. Such individuals are frequently called *carriers.*

 An example of human blood groups is given in Virtual Lab 2, section II, part E.

Antigens
Large molecules found on the surface of cells. Several different loci governing antigens on red and white blood cells are known. (Foreign antigens provoke an immune response in individuals.)

Codominance
The expression of two alleles in heterozygotes. In this situation, neither allele is dominant or recessive, thus both influence the phenotype.

TABLE 4–2 ABO Genotypes and Associated Phenotypes

Genotype	Antigens on Red Blood Cells	ABO Blood Type (Phenotype)
AA, AO	A	A
BB, BO	B	B
AB	A and B	AB
OO	None	O

TABLE 4–3 Some Mendelian Disorders in Humans

Dominant Traits		Recessive Traits	
Condition	**Manifestations**	**Condition**	**Manifestations**
Achondroplasia	Dwarfism due to growth defects involving the long bones of the arms and legs; trunk and head size usually normal.	Cystic fibrosis	Among the most common genetic (Mendelian) disorders among whites in the United States; abnormal secretions of the exocrine glands, with pronounced involvement of the pancreas; most patients develop obstructive lung disease. Until the recent development of new treatments, only about half of all patients survived to early adulthood.
Brachydactyly	Shortened fingers and toes.		
Familial hyper-cholesterolemia	Elevated cholesterol levels and cholesterol plaque deposition; a leading cause of heart disease, with death frequently occurring by middle age.		
Neurofibromatosis	Symptoms range from the appearance of abnormal skin pigmentation to large tumors resulting in gross deformities; this so-called Elephant Man disease can, in extreme cases, lead to paralysis, blindness, and death.	Tay-Sachs disease	Most common among Ashkenazi Jews; degeneration of the nervous system beginning at about 6 months of age; lethal by age 2 or 3 years.
		Phenylketonuria (PKU)	Inability to metabolize the amino acid phenylalanine; results in mental retardation if left untreated during childhood; treatment involves strict dietary management and some supplementation.
Marfan syndrome	The eyes and cardiovascular and skeletal systems are affected; symptoms include greater than average height, long arms and legs, eye problems, and enlargement of the aorta; death due to rupture of the aorta is common. Abraham Lincoln may have had Marfan syndrome.	Albinism	Inability to produce normal amounts of the pigment melanin; results in very fair, untannable skin, light blond hair, and light eyes; may also be associated with vision problems. (There is more than one form of albinism.)
Huntington disease	Progressive degeneration of the nervous system accompanied by dementia and seizures. Age of onset variable but commonly between 30 and 40 years.	Sickle-cell anemia	Abnormal form of hemoglobin (Hb^s) that results in collapsed red blood cells, blockage of capillaries, reduced blood flow to organs and, without treatment, death.
Camptodactyly	Malformation of the hands whereby the fingers, usually the little finger, is permanently contracted.	Thalassemia	A group of disorders characterized by reduced or absent alpha or beta chains in the hemoglobin molecule. Results in severe anemia and, in some forms, death.

Although carriers do not actually show full-blown manifestations of the recessive allele they carry, they can pass the allele on to their children. (Remember, half their gametes will carry the recessive allele.) If their mate is also a carrier, then it is possible for them to have a child who will be homozygous for the allele, and that child will be affected. In fact, in a mating between two carriers, the risk of having an affected child is 25 percent (refer back to Fig. 4–3).

Misconceptions Regarding Dominance and Recessiveness

Traditional methods of teaching genetics have led to some misunderstanding of dominance and recessiveness. Thus, virtually all introductory students (and most people in general) have the impression that these phenomena are all-or-nothing situations. This misconception especially pertains to recessive alleles, and the general view is that when these alleles occur in heterozygotes (i.e., carriers), they have absolutely no effect on the phenotype—that is, they are completely inactivated by the presence of another (dominant) allele. Certainly, this is how it appeared to Gregor Mendel and, until the last two or three decades, to most geneticists.

However, various biochemical techniques, unavailable in the past but in wide use today, have demonstrated that recessive alleles do indeed exert some influence on phenotype, although these effects are not usually apparent through simple observation. This influence is detectable because in heterozygotes, many recessive alleles act to reduce the amount of the gene products they control. Indeed, it is now clear that our *perception* of recessive alleles greatly depends on one important factor: whether we examine them at the directly observable phenotypic level or the biochemical level.

Scientists now know of several recessive alleles that do produce detectable phenotypic effects in heterozygotes. Consider Tay-Sachs disease, a lethal condition that results from the inability to produce the enzyme hexosaminidase A (see Table 4–3). This inability, seen in people who are homozygous for a recessive allele (*ts*) on chromosome 15, invariably results in death by early childhood. Carriers do not have the disease, and practically speaking, they are unaffected. However, in 1979, it was shown that Tay-Sachs carriers, although functionally normal, have only about 40 to 60 percent of the amount of the enzyme seen in normal people. In fact, there are now voluntary tests to screen carriers in populations at risk for Tay-Sachs disease.

Similar misconceptions also relate to dominant alleles. The majority of people see dominant alleles as somehow "stronger" or "better," and there is always the mistaken notion that dominant alleles are more common in populations. These misconceptions undoubtedly stem partly from the label "dominant" and the connotations that the term carries. But in genetic usage, those connotations are somewhat misleading. If dominant alleles were always more common, then a majority of people would be affected by such conditions as achondroplasia and Marfan syndrome (see Table 4–3).

Clearly, the relationship between recessive and dominant alleles and their functions are more complicated than they would appear at first glance. (Indeed, most things are.) Previously held views of dominance and recessiveness were guided by available technologies; as genetic technologies continue to change, new theories may emerge, and if so, our perceptions will be further altered. It is just possible that one day the concepts of dominance and recessiveness, as they have traditionally been taught, will be obsolete.

Polygenic Inheritance

Mendelian traits are said to be *discrete,* or *discontinuous,* because their phenotypic expressions do not overlap, but rather fall into clearly defined categories (Fig. 4–4a). For example, Mendel's pea plants were either short or tall, but none was intermediate in height. In the ABO system, the four phenotypes are completely

Polygenic
Referring to traits that are influenced by genes at two or more loci. Examples of such traits are stature, skin color, and eye color. Many polygenic traits are also influenced by environmental factors.

FIGURE 4–4

(a) This histogram shows the discontinuous distribution of a Mendelian trait (ABO blood type) in a hypothetical population. The expression of the trait is described in terms of frequencies. (b) This histogram represents the continuous expression of a polygenic trait (height) in a large group of people. Note that the percentage of extremely short or tall individuals is low, where the majority of people are closer to the mean, or average, height, represented by the vertical line at the center of the distribution.

distinct from one another; that is, there is no intermediate form between type A and type B to represent a gradation between the two. In other words, Mendelian traits do not show *continuous* variation.

However, many traits do have a wide range of phenotypic expressions that form a graded series. These are called **polygenic,** or *continuous,* traits. While Mendelian traits are governed by only one genetic locus, polygenic characteristics are influenced by alleles at two or more loci, with each locus making a contribution to the phenotype. For example, one of the most frequently cited instances of polygenic inheritance in humans is skin color, and the single most important factor influencing skin color is the amount of the pigment melanin present.

Melanin production is believed to be influenced by between three and six genetic loci, with each locus having at least two alleles, neither of which is dominant. Individuals having only alleles for maximum melanin production (i.e., they are homozygous at all loci) have the darkest skin. Those having only alleles that code for reduced melanin production have very fair skin.

As there are perhaps six loci and at least 12 alleles, there are numerous ways in which these alleles can combine in individuals. If an individual inherits 11 alleles coding for maximum pigmentation and only 1 for reduced melanin production, skin color will be very dark. A person who inherits a higher proportion of reduced pigmentation alleles will have lighter skin color. This is because in this system, as in some other polygenic systems, there is an *additive effect.* This means that each allele that codes for melanin production makes a contribution to increased melanization (although for some characteristics the contributions of the alleles are not all equal). Likewise, each allele coding for less melanin production contributes to reduced pigmentation. Therefore, the effect of multiple alleles at several loci is to produce continuous variation from very dark to very fair skin within the species. (Skin color is also discussed in Chapter 13.)

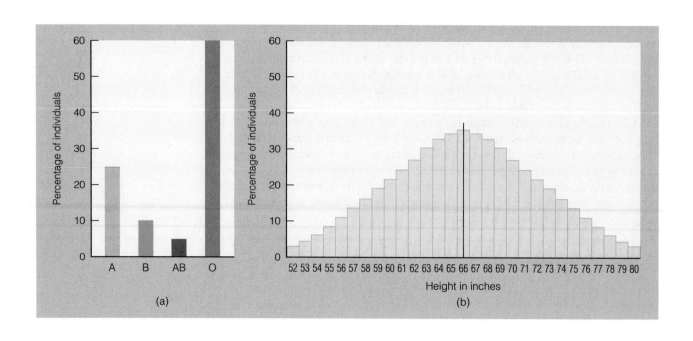

(a)

(b)

Polygenic traits actually account for most of the readily observable phenotypic variation seen in humans, and they have traditionally served as a basis for racial classification (see Chapter 13). In addition to skin color, polygenic inheritance in humans is seen in hair color, weight, stature, eye color (Fig. 4–5), shape of face, shape of nose, and fingerprint pattern. Because they exhibit continuous variation, most polygenic traits can be measured on a scale composed of equal increments (Fig. 4–4b). For example, height (stature) is measured in feet and inches (or meters and centimeters). If one were to measure height in a large number of individuals, the distribution of measurements would continue uninterrupted from the shortest extreme to the tallest. That is what is meant by the term *continuous traits.*

Because polygenic traits usually lend themselves to metric analysis, biologists, geneticists, and physical anthropologists treat them statistically. Although statistical analysis can be complicated, the use of simple summary statistics, such as the *mean* (average) or *standard deviation* (a measure of within-group variation), permits basic descriptions of, and comparisons between, populations. For example, one might be interested in average height in two different populations and whether or not differences between the two are significant, and if so, why. Or a researcher might determine that in the same geographical area, one group shows significantly more variation in skin color than another, and it would be useful to explain this variability. (You should also note that *all* physical traits measured and statistically treated in fossils are polygenic in nature.)

However, these particular statistical manipulations are not possible with Mendelian traits simply because those traits cannot be measured in the same manner. They are either present or they are not; they are expressed one way or another. But just because Mendelian traits are not amenable to the same statistical tests used to study polygenic characters does not mean that Mendelian traits are less worthy of study or less informative of genetic processes. It simply means that scientists must approach the study of these two types of inheritance from different perspectives.

Mendelian characteristics can be described in terms of frequency within populations, thus yielding between-group comparisons regarding incidence. Moreover, these characteristics can also be analyzed for mode of inheritance (dominant or recessive). Finally, for many Mendelian traits, the approximate or exact positions of genetic loci have been identified, thus making it possible to examine the mechanisms and patterns of inheritance at these loci. Because polygenic characters are influenced by several loci, they cannot, as yet, be traced to specific loci; therefore, such analysis is currently not possible.

Genetic and Environmental Factors

From the preceding discussion, it might appear that phenotype is solely the expression of the genotype, but this is not true. (Here we use the terms *genotype* and *phenotype* in a broader sense to refer to an individual's entire genetic makeup and *all* observable or detectable characteristics.) The genotype sets limits and potentials for development, but it also interacts with the environment, and many aspects of phenotype are influenced by this genetic-environmental interaction. For many traits, scientists have developed statistical methods for calculating what proportion of phenotypic variation is due to genetic or environmental

FIGURE 4–5

Examples of the continuous variation seen in human eye color.

 See the exercise in Virtual Lab 2, section IV, for a discussion of skin color in humans.

components. However, it is usually not possible to identify the *specific* environmental factors affecting the phenotype.

Many polygenic traits are quite obviously influenced by environmental conditions. Adult stature is strongly affected by the individual's nutritional status during growth and development (see Chapter 14). Other important environmental factors include exposure to sunlight, altitude, temperature, and, unfortunately, increasing levels of exposure to toxic waste and airborne pollutants. All these and many more contribute in complex ways to the continuous phenotypic variation seen in characteristics governed by multiple loci.

Mendelian traits are less likely to be influenced by environmental factors. For example, ABO blood type is determined at fertilization and remains fixed throughout the individual's lifetime, regardless of diet, exposure to ultraviolet radiation, temperature, and so forth.

Mendelian and polygenic inheritance produce different kinds of phenotypic variation. In the former, variation occurs in discrete categories, while in the latter, it is continuous. However, it is important to understand that even for polygenic characteristics, Mendelian principles still apply at individual loci. In other words, if a trait is influenced by seven loci, each one of those loci may have two or more alleles, with one perhaps being dominant to the other or with the alleles being codominant. It is the combined action of the alleles at all seven loci, interacting with the environment, that results in observable phenotypic expression.

Heredity and Evolution

In Chapters 2 and 3, we presented an overview of natural selection and we discussed the molecular and cellular bases of heredity. Thus far in this chapter, we have shown how genetic information is passed from individuals in one generation to those in the next. These different levels (molecular, cellular, individual, and populational) reflect different aspects of evolution, and they are all related and highly integrated in a way that can eventually produce evolutionary change.

For example, consider a situation where everyone in a population has the same allele (*A*) at the ABO locus. In this population, then, there is no genetic variation at the ABO locus. Consequently, without some source of new variation, evolution is not possible at this locus. But how can variation be introduced? The only source of *new* variation is *mutation,* or a change in the DNA sequence. Specifically, this example concerns chemical alterations in one or more of the DNA bases that comprise the gene. Such mutations are termed *point mutations*.

For a point mutation to have evolutionary significance, it must alter the DNA code sufficiently to change the protein product and thus the phenotype of the individual. Consider that in each generation, mutations do occur spontaneously in one or a few individuals, and some loci are more susceptible to change than others. The reasons for mutational change are only partially known, but they include size of the gene (i.e., genes with thousands of base pairs have greater opportunity to mutate than those with fewer base pairs) and environmental exposure to various forms of radiation and/or numerous chemicals.

For a mutant allele to be passed on to succeeding offspring, it must occur in the gametes, or sex cells. Once such a mutation has occurred, it will be carried by one of the individual's chromosomes, which in turn will assort during meiosis to be passed on to offspring. In other words, if the individual has a mutation in only one member of a pair of alleles on a set of homologous chromosomes, there will be a 50 percent chance of passing the allele to an offspring.

But, you may ask, what does all this have to do with evolution? One contemporary definition of evolution describes the process as a *change in the frequency of alleles in a population from one generation to the next.* The crucial point here is that it is the population that is important, and it is the population that will change genetically, and thus phenotypically, over time. But if and when the population does exhibit change, it will do so as a result of changes in **allele frequency.**

For many traits, such as ABO blood type, we can determine whether allele frequencies have changed over time by comparing the percentage of individuals with specific ABO antigens in one generation with the percentages observed in preceding and succeeding generations. If, in our hypothetical group of individuals with type A blood, we began to detect a few with type AB, we would assume that in some small proportion of people, the *A* allele had mutated to *B* and that the *B* allele had been transmitted to offspring who were heterozygous. But this change would not constitute an evolutionary one, because in a relatively large population, the alteration of one person's genes would not significantly alter allele frequencies for the entire group. For evolutionary change to occur, this new allele must spread through the population and increase in frequency.

A few factors can lead to such an increase. If the population in question happens to be small, mutation in one or a few individuals can be passed on to a high proportion of the population, simply because the group is composed of only a few people. This case is representative of what is called **genetic drift,** which acts in small populations, where random or chance factors may cause significant changes in the frequency of alleles. In a small population, there is not likely to be a balance of factors affecting individual survival or reproduction. Consequently, just by chance, some alleles may be completely removed from the group, while others may become established as the only allele present at a given locus. These alleles are said to be "fixed" in the population. It is important to remember that genetic drift is the *random* factor in evolution, and its effects are tied to population size. That is, the smaller the population, the greater the effect of genetic drift.

Another factor that can influence evolutionary change is **gene flow.** Gene flow is the movement of alleles between populations. It occurs when individuals in one population move to another population, in which allele frequencies differ, and mate with individuals in this new group, thus altering allele frequencies. As you can see, the more people who migrate and mate outside their original population, the greater the effect of gene flow.

In the course of human evolution, genetic drift and gene flow may have played a significant role at times, and it is important to remember that genetic drift and/or gene flow can (and will) produce evolutionary change, even in the absence of natural selection. However, directional evolutionary trends could only have been sustained by natural selection. The way this has worked in the past and still operates today is through differential reproduction. That is, individuals who carry a particular allele or combination of alleles produce more offspring than do others. By producing more offspring than other individuals with alternative alleles, such individuals cause the frequency of the new allele in the population to increase slowly from generation to generation. When this process is compounded over hundreds of generations for numerous loci, the result is significant evolutionary change. The levels of organization in the evolutionary process are summarized in Table 4–4.

Allele frequency
In a population, the percentage of all the alleles at a specific locus accounted for by one specific allele.

Genetic drift
Evolutionary changes—that is, changes in allele frequency—produced by random factors in small populations.

Gene flow
The exchange of genes between populations.

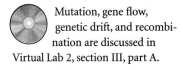
Mutation, gene flow, genetic drift, and recombination are discussed in Virtual Lab 2, section III, part A.

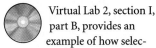
Virtual Lab 2, section I, part B, provides an example of how selection operates on variation within populations.

TABLE 4–4   Levels of Organization in the Evolutionary Process

Evolutionary Factor	Level	Evolutionary Process	Technique of Study
Mutation microscope,	DNA	Storage of genetic information; ability to replicate; influences phenotype by production of proteins	Biochemistry, electron recombinant DNA
Mutation	Chromosomes	A vehicle for packaging and transmitting genetic material (DNA)	Light or electron microscope
Recombination (sex cells only)	Cell	The basic unit of life that contains the chromosomes and divides for growth and for production of sex cells	Light or electron microscope
Natural selection	Organism	The unit, composed of cells, that reproduces and that we observe for phenotypic traits	Visual study, biochemistry
Drift, gene flow	Population	A group of interbreeding organisms; changes in allele frequencies between generations; it is the population that evolves	Statistical study

In summary, then, we have discussed four factors of evolution: natural selection, mutation, genetic drift, and gene flow. During the first four decades of the twentieth century, the contributions of Charles Darwin and Gregor Mendel were combined into a single encompassing theory of evolution called the modern synthesis. A comprehensive discussion of the modern synthesis and how the four factors of evolution interact in modern human populations will be the central topics of Chapter 12.

New Frontiers

Since the discovery of DNA structure and function in the 1950s, the field of genetics has revolutionized biological science and reshaped our understanding of inheritance, genetic disease, and evolutionary processes. For example, it is now possible to ascertain the exact sequence of nucleotides in a DNA sample, and in fact, the goal of the **Human Genome Project** is to sequence the entire human **genome.** This goal came closer to realization in December, 1999, with the publication of the DNA sequence of most of chromosome 22 (Dunham et al., 1999). Thus, chromosome 22 has the distinction of being the first human chromosome to be mapped entirely, but more is soon to follow. The announcement of the full sequence of human DNA is expected by the year 2003.

A technique developed in 1986 called **polymerase chain reaction (PCR)** enables scientists to produce multiple copies of DNA, and consequently it has made it possible to analyze segments of DNA as small as one molecule. This ability is important because samples of DNA, such as those obtained at crime scenes or from fossils, are often too small to permit reliable analysis of DNA sequences.

In PCR, the two strands of a DNA sample are separated, and an enzyme synthesizes complementary strands on the exposed bases, as in DNA replication. Because this process can be repeated many times, it is possible to produce over a million copies of the original DNA material! Thus, scientists have been able to identify nucleotide sequences in, for example, fossils (including Neandertals), Egyptian mummies, and members of the Russian royal family murdered in 1918

Human Genome Project
An international effort aimed at sequencing and mapping the entire human genome.

Genome
The entire genetic makeup of an individual or species. In humans, it is estimated that each individual possesses approximately 3 billion DNA nucleotides.

Polymerase chain reaction (PCR)
A method of producing copies of a DNA segment using the enzyme DNA polymerase.

(see p. 19). As you can imagine, PCR has limitless potential for many disciplines, including forensic science, medicine, and evolutionary biology.

Over the last two decades, using the techniques of recombinant DNA, scientists have been able to transfer genes from the cells of one species into those of another. The most common method has been to insert genes that code for the production of various proteins into bacterial cells, thus causing the altered bacteria to produce human gene products. There are numerous commercial applications for this technology, many of which are aimed at treating genetic disease in humans. For example, until the early 1980s, diabetic patients relied on insulin derived from nonhuman animals. However, this insulin was not plentiful; moreover, some patients developed allergies to it. But since 1982, abundant supplies of human insulin, produced by bacteria, have been available; and bacteria-derived insulin does not cause allergic reactions in patients.

Human genes may also be inserted into the fertilized eggs of some nonhuman animals. The eggs are then implanted into the uteri of females who subsequently give birth to genetically altered offspring. These offspring serve as a source of various substances needed in medical practice. For example, genetically altered female sheep can carry a human gene that causes them to produce an enzyme that is present in most people and which prevents a serious form of emphysema. This enzyme is produced in the sheep's milk, and once extracted and purified, it can be administered to people who do not normally produce it.

Genetic transfer techniques have also been used to improve crops in a variety of ways. For instance, genetically altered strawberries are able to withstand temperatures of 10–12°F below freezing without being damaged. Likewise, some tomatoes can be ripened on the vine before being shipped, because they carry a gene that inhibits the potentially damaging softness that normally develops during ripening.

In recent years, genetic manipulation has become increasingly controversial owing to numerous questions related to product safety, environmental concerns, and animal welfare, among others. For example, the insertion of bacterial DNA into certain crops has made them toxic to leaf-eating insects, thus reducing the need for pesticide use. Cattle and pigs are commonly treated with genetically engineered growth hormone to increase growth rates. Although there is no current evidence that humans are susceptible to the insect-repelling bacterium or adversely affected by the consumption of meat and dairy products from animals treated with growth hormone, there are concerns over the unknown effects of such long-term exposure.

But regardless of how exciting and important these new techniques may be, nothing has generated as much attention and controversy as the birth of Dolly, a **clone** of a female sheep, in 1997 (Wilmut et al., 1997). Actually, cloning is not as new as you might think. Anyone who has ever taken a cutting from a plant and rooted it to grow a new plant has produced a clone. In the 1950s, plant biologists developed methods of cloning carrots by culturing cells taken from mature plants. In the 1960s, an African toad became the first animal to be cloned, but for a number of reasons, cloning a mammal remained an elusive goal. Then, in 1981, a Swiss team of geneticists successfully produced cloned mice, and these experiments were followed by cloned cattle and sheep. So, you might ask, why was Dolly such a big deal? The furor was partly due to the fact that earlier cloning results had not been well publicized. But in the scientific community, the enthusiasm was due to the techniques that were used.

Animal cloning can be done in two ways. Traditionally, nuclei from fertilized eggs are removed and replaced with nuclei taken from embryonic cells derived

Clone
An organism that is genetically identical to another organism. The term may also be used to refer to genetically identical DNA segments and molecules.

from another organism. The altered egg is then implanted into the uterus of a surrogate (substitute) mother, where it develops into an individual that is genetically identical to the embryo donor.

The Dolly research was unique because the donor nucleus was derived from a cell of a *mature* animal. This demonstrated that DNA derived from a specialized somatic cell is capable of returning to an embryonic state where it can direct cell division and ultimately orchestrate the development of an entire organism. Until now, this ability was questioned, and it was the focus of many genetic studies. Thus, Dolly's successful development and birth solved a highly important problem in genetic investigation.

Since the original reports of the Dolly experiment were published, it has emerged that the donor cell for Dolly may inadvertently have been a fetal cell and not one taken from an adult sheep after all. But since the birth of Dolly, teams of Japanese scientists have reported cloning cattle and mice using donor cells from adult animals (Wakayama et. al, 1998). Thus, while it is possible (but not certain) that Dolly was not derived from an adult somatic cell, other animals have been. These experiments have demonstrated that DNA derived from a specialized somatic cell is capable of being "turned back on" so that it can orchestrate the development of an entire organism.

This brief discussion really only hints at the possibilities that lie in the future of genetic technology. While humans certainly have much to gain from genetic research, the emerging technologies are highly controversial, and the number of ethical and moral questions will only increase. Indeed, it is an exciting time for genetic discovery, and it is to be hoped that an informed public will be able to evaluate the issues that will increasingly become the concerns of the scientific community, the legal experts, and, ultimately, the politicians.

SUMMARY

We have seen how Gregor Mendel discovered the principles of segregation, independent assortment, and dominance and recessiveness by conducting experiments on garden peas. Although the field of genetics progressed dramatically in the twentieth century, the concepts first put forth by Gregor Mendel remain basic to our current knowledge of how traits are inherited.

Traits that are influenced by only one genetic locus are Mendelian traits. At many genetic loci, two or more alleles may interact in dominant/recessive or codominant fashion with one another. Examples of Mendelian traits in humans include ABO blood type, cystic fibrosis, and sickle-cell anemia. In contrast, many characteristics such as stature and skin color are said to be polygenic, or continuous, because they are influenced by more than one genetic locus and show a continuous range of expression.

The expression of all biological traits is, to varying degrees, under genetic control. Genes, then, can be said to set limits and potentials for human growth, development, and achievement. However, these limits and potentials are not written in stone, so to speak, because many characteristics are also very much influenced by such environmental factors as temperature, diet, and sunlight. Thus, ultimately it is the interaction between genetic and environmental factors that produces phenotypic variation in all species, including *Homo sapiens.*

Building on fundamental nineteenth-century contributions by Charles Darwin and his contemporaries and the rediscovery in 1900 of Mendel's work, further refinements later in the twentieth century added to contemporary evolutionary thought. In particular, the combination of natural selection with Mendel's principles of inheritance and experimental evidence concerning the nature of mutation have all been synthesized into a modern understanding of evolutionary change, appropriately termed the *modern synthesis*. In this, the central contemporary theory of evolution, evolutionary change is seen as a two-stage process. The first stage is the production and redistribution of variation. The second stage is the process whereby natural selection acts on the accumulated genetic variation.

Crucial to all evolutionary change is mutation, the only source of completely new genetic variation. In addition, the factors of gene flow, genetic drift, and recombination function to redistribute variation within individuals (recombination), within populations (genetic drift), and between populations (gene flow).

QUESTIONS FOR REVIEW

1. What is Mendel's principle of segregation?
2. How does meiosis explain the principle of segregation?
3. What is Mendel's principle of independent assortment?
4. Explain dominance and recessiveness.
5. Define allele.
6. What is a phenotype, and what is its relationship to a genotype?
7. Why were all of Mendel's F_1 pea plants phenotypically the same?
8. What is codominance? Give an example.
9. If two people who have blood type A (both with the *AO* genotype) have children, what proportion of their children would be expected to have the O blood type? Why?
10. In a cross between two carriers for a recessive trait, why would ³/₄ of the offspring be expected *not* to show the recessive characteristic?
11. Explain how natural selection works. Illustrate through an example in humans.
12. What is polygenic inheritance? How does it differ from Mendelian inheritance?
13. What is the modern synthesis? Explain how the major components of this theory explain evolutionary change.
14. What is genetic drift?
15. Define gene flow.
16. What role does variation play in the evolutionary process? Where does variation come from? (*Hint:* You may wish to discuss the source of variation as completely new to a species or as it is introduced into a population within a species.)
17. Discuss how evolutionary change occurs as an integrated process. Illustrate through an example.
18. Why are polygenic traits said to be continuous?

SUGGESTED FURTHER READINGS

Brennan, James R. 1985. *Patterns of Human Heredity.* Englewood Cliffs, NJ: Prentice-Hall.

Cummings, Michael R. 2000. *Human Heredity. Principles and Issues.* 5th ed. Pacific Grove, CA: Brooks/Cole.

Little, Peter. 1999 "The Book of Genes." *Nature,* 402: 467–468.

Ridley, Mark. 1993. *Evolution.* Cambridge, MA: Blackwell Scientific.

MULTIMEDIA RESOURCES

🌐 Wadsworth Anthropology Resource Center

http://anthropology.wadsworth.com

Visit Anthropology Online to obtain current updates in the field, surfing tips, career information, and more. In addition, enrich your study efforts with text-specific study aids arranged by chapter.

InfoTrac College Edition

http://www.infotrac-college.com/wadsworth

1. Use InfoTrac College Edition and search for *human genetics.* Is there any information in recent articles about dominant and recessive traits in humans? Read one of these and write a summary, indicating how this article relates to anthropological questions regarding human evolution and behavior.

2. On every can of diet soda there is a warning to phenylketonuriacs that the product contains phenylalanine. As you learned in this chapter, phenylketonuria (PKU) is an autosomal recessive condition. Go to InfoTrac College Edition to learn more about this disorder. Finally, write a paragraph or more describing *why* the can of diet soda carries such a warning.

🌐 Internet Exercises

1. Our understanding of inheritance originated with the research of Gregor Mendel. Visit MendelWeb (**http://www-hpcc.astro.washington.edu/mirrors/MendelWeb/**) to learn more about Mendel, his research, and the implications of his research. Also on MendelWeb is the text of his original paper. Click on Mendel's paper and read the first four sections. What are your overall impressions of Mendel's research? Was he thorough? What criteria did Mendel use when choosing which plants to work with? Do you think these criteria are valid today? Why? In the section entitled "The Forms of the Hybrids," Mendel introduces and defines the terms *dominant* and *recessive.* Having read the cautionary statements regarding dominant and recessive alleles in this textbook, what do you think Mendel would say today?

2. While the terminology used at this site is very technical, Online Mendelian Inheritance in Man (OMIM) is the most comprehensive Web site dealing with Mendelian and many non-Mendelian traits. To appreciate the complexity of such characteristics, go to **www3.ncbi.nlm.nih.gov/Omim/,** click on "search the OMIM database," and enter in the search field the name of one of the conditions listed in Table 4–3. We suggest albinism. Then click on #203100, the catalog number for albinism; then click on "description." Read this entry and make a list of three facts not included in the chapter. What kinds of information have you found that you think would be useful to your classmates?

CHAPTER
5

An Overview of the Living Primates

CONTENTS

Introduction

Thus far, we have presented the basic biological background for understanding human evolution. The remainder of this textbook is devoted to explaining what it is to be human—that is, the kind of animal we are and how we got to be this way.

Evolution has produced a continuum of life forms, as demonstrated genetically, anatomically, and behaviorally. To gain an understanding of any organism, it is necessary, whenever possible, to compare its anatomy and behavior with those of other, closely related forms. This comparative approach helps elucidate the significance of physiological and behavioral systems as adaptive responses to various selective pressures throughout the course of evolution. This statement applies to *Homo sapiens* just as surely as to any other species, and if we are to identify the components that have shaped hominid evolution, the starting point must be a systematic comparison between humans and our closest living relatives, the approximately 190 species of nonhuman primates (**prosimians,** monkeys, and apes). This chapter describes the physical characteristics that define the order Primates, gives a brief overview of the major groups of living nonhuman primates, and introduces some methods of comparing living primates through genetic data. (For a detailed comparison of human and nonhuman skeletons, see Appendix A.) This chapter and the one that follows concentrate on various anatomical and behavioral features that characterize nonhuman primates.

Before proceeding further, we must call attention to a few common misunderstandings about evolutionary processes. Evolution is not a goal-directed process; thus, the fact that prosimians evolved before **anthropoids** does not mean that prosimians "progressed," or "advanced," to become anthropoids. Living primate species are in no way "superior" to their evolutionary predecessors or to one another. Consequently, in discussions of major groupings of contemporary nonhuman primates, there is no implied superiority or inferiority of any of these groups. Each grouping (lineage, or species) has come to possess unique qualities that make it better suited than others to a particular habitat and lifestyle. Given that all contemporary organisms are "successful" results of the evolutionary process, it is best to avoid altogether the use of such loaded terms as "superior" and "inferior."

Finally, you should not make the mistake of thinking that contemporary primates (including humans) necessarily represent the final stage or apex of a lineage. Remember, the only species that represent final evolutionary stages of particular lineages are those that become extinct.

Primates as Mammals

The order *Primates* is a subgroup of a larger group of organisms, the mammals (technically, the class **Mammalia**). Today there are over 4,000 species of mammals, which can be further subdivided into three major subgroups: (1) the egg-laying mammals, (2) the pouched mammals (i.e., marsupials), and (3) the placental mammals. We will discuss mammalian evolution in more detail in Chapter 7. For the moment, you should recognize that primates are members of the placental subgroup, by far the most common of living mammals (and including other common orders such as rodents and carnivores). Placental mammals

Prosimians
Members of a suborder of Primates, the *Prosimii* (pronounced "pro-sim´-ee-eye"). Traditionally, the suborder includes lemurs, lorises, and tarsiers.

Anthropoids
Members of a suborder of Primates, the *Anthropoidea* (pronounced "ann-throw-poid´-ee-uh"). Traditionally, the suborder includes monkeys, apes, and humans.

Mammalia
The technical term for the formal grouping (class) of mammals.

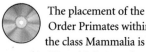 The placement of the Order Primates within the class Mammalia is discussed in Virtual Lab 1, section II.

today are distributed over most of the world in a wide variety of forms. In fact, biologists recognize more than 20 orders of mammals, including flying, swimming, and burrowing varieties and a host of other adaptations as well. Sizes range from the tiny dwarf shrews (just a few grams) to the whales, the largest animals ever to inhabit the earth.

Characteristics of Primates

All primates possess numerous characteristics they share in common with other placental mammals. Such traits include body hair; a relatively long gestation period followed by live birth; mammary glands (thus the term *mammal*); different types of teeth; the ability to maintain a constant internal body temperature through physiological means (*homeothermy*); increased brain size; and a considerable capacity for learning and behavioral flexibility. Therefore, to differentiate primates, as a group, from other mammals, we must describe those characteristics that, taken together, set primates apart from other mammalian groups.

This is not a simple task, for among mammals, primates have remained quite *generalized.* That is, primates have retained many **primitive** mammalian traits that some other mammalian species have lost over time. In response to particular selective pressures, many mammalian groups have become increasingly **specialized.** For example, through the course of evolution, horses and cattle have undergone a reduction of the number of digits (fingers and toes) from the primitive pattern of five to one and two, respectively. Moreover, these species have developed hard, protective coverings over their feet in the form of hooves. While this type of limb structure is adaptive in prey species, whose survival depends on speed and stability, it restricts the animal to only one type of locomotion. Moreover, limb function is limited entirely to support and movement, while the ability to manipulate objects is completely lost.

Primates, precisely because they are *not* so specialized, cannot be simply defined by one or even two traits they share in common. As a result, biologists (Napier and Napier, 1967; Clark, 1971) have pointed to a group of **evolutionary trends** that, to a greater or lesser degree, characterize the entire order. Keep in mind that these are a set of *general* tendencies and are not all equally expressed in all primates. Indeed, this is what we would expect in a diverse group of generalized animals. Moreover, while some of the trends are unique features found in primates, many others are retained primitive mammalian characteristics. These latter are useful in contrasting the generalized primates with the more specialized varieties of other placental mammals.

Thus, the following list is intended to give an overall structural and behavioral picture of that kind of animal we call "primate," focusing on those characteristics that tend to set primates apart from other mammals. Concentrating on certain retained (ancestral) mammalian traits, along with more specific ones, has been the traditional approach of **primatologists.** Some contemporary primatologists (Fleagle, 1999) feel that it is useful to enumerate all these features to better illustrate primate adaptations. Thus, a common evolutionary history with adaptations to similar environmental challenges is seen to be reflected in the limbs and locomotion, teeth and diet, senses, brain, and behaviors of those animals that make up the primate order.

Virtual Lab 1, section II, part A, presents a discussion of the characteristics that are typically used to define primates, while section IV, part A, provides a contrast of mammalian life history variables.

Primitive
Referring to a trait or combination of traits present in an ancestral form.

Specialized
Evolved for a particular function; usually refers to a specific trait (e.g., incisor teeth), but may also refer to the whole way of life of an organism.

Evolutionary trends
Overall characteristics of an evolving lineage, such as the primates. Such trends are useful in helping to categorize the lineage as compared to other lineages (i.e., other placental mammals).

Primatologists
Scientists who study the evolution, anatomy, and behavior of nonhuman primates. Those who study behavior in non-captive animals are usually trained as physical anthropologists.

Virtual Lab 5 provides in-depth discussions of primate diets and dental adaptations.

Morphology
The form (shape, size) of anatomical structures; can also refer to the entire organism.

Prehensility
Grasping, as by the hands and feet of primates.

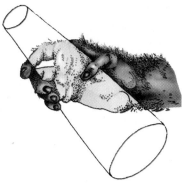

FIGURE 5–1
Primate (macaque) hand.

Omnivorous
Having a diet consisting of many food types (i.e., plant materials, meat, and insects).

Diurnal
Active during the day.

Nocturnal
Active during the night.

A. *Limbs and Locomotion*

1. *A tendency toward erect posture (especially in the upper body).* Shown to some degree in all primates, this tendency is variously associated with sitting, leaping, standing, and, occasionally, bipedal walking.

2. *A flexible, generalized limb structure, permitting most primates to engage in a number of locomotor behaviors.* Primates have retained some bones (e.g., the clavicle, or collarbone) and certain abilities, (e.g., rotation of the forearm) that have been lost in some more specialized mammals. Various aspects of hip and shoulder **morphology** also provide primates with a wide range of limb movement and function. Thus, by maintaining a generalized locomotor anatomy, primates are not restricted to one form of movement, as are many other mammals. Primate limbs are also used for activities other than locomotion.

3. *Hands and feet with a high degree of **prehensility** (grasping ability).* All primates use the hands, and frequently the feet, to grasp and manipulate objects (Fig. 5–1). This capability is variably expressed and is enhanced by a number of characteristics, including:

   a. *Retention of five digits on hands and feet.* This varies somewhat throughout the order, with some species showing marked reduction of the thumb or of the second digit.

   b. *An opposable thumb and, in most species, a divergent and partially opposable big toe.* Most primates are capable of moving the thumb so that it comes in contact (in some fashion) with the second digit or the palm of the hand.

   c. *Nails instead of claws.* This characteristic is seen in all primates except some New World monkeys. Some prosimians also possess a claw on one digit.

   d. *Tactile pads enriched with sensory nerve fibers at the ends of digits.* This trend serves to enhance the sense of touch.

B. *Diet and Teeth*

1. *Lack of dietary specialization.* This is typical of most primates, who tend to eat a wide assortment of food items.

2. *A generalized dentition.* The teeth are not specialized for processing only one type of food, a pattern correlated with the lack of dietary specialization. In general, primates are **omnivorous.**

C. *The senses and the brain.* Primates (**diurnal** ones in particular) rely heavily on the visual sense and less on the sense of smell, especially compared to many other mammals. This emphasis is reflected in evolutionary changes in the skull, eyes, and brain.

1. *Color vision.* This is characteristic of all diurnal primates. **Nocturnal** primates lack color vision.

2. *Depth perception.* **Stereoscopic vision,** or the ability to perceive objects in three dimensions, is made possible through a variety of mechanisms, including:

   a. *Eyes positioned toward the front of the face (not to the sides).* This configuration provides for overlapping visual fields, or **binocular vision** (Fig. 5–2).

b. *Visual information from each eye transmitted to visual centers in both hemispheres of the brain.* In nonprimate mammals, most optic nerve fibers cross to the opposite hemisphere through a structure at the base of the brain. In primates, about 40 percent of the fibers remain on the same side (see Fig. 5–2).

c. *Visual information organized into three-dimensional images by specialized structures in the brain itself.* The capacity for stereoscopic vision is dependent on each hemisphere of the brain having received visual information from both eyes and from overlapping visual fields.

3. *Decreased reliance on the sense of smell (olfaction).* This trend is seen in an overall reduction in the size of olfactory structures in the brain. Corresponding reduction of the entire olfactory apparatus has also resulted in decreased size of the snout (Fig. 5–3). (In some species, such as baboons, the large muzzle is not related to olfaction, but to the presence of large teeth, especially the canines.)

Stereoscopic vision
The condition whereby visual images are, to varying degrees, superimposed on one another. This provides for depth perception, or the perception of the external environment in three dimensions. Stereoscopic vision is partly a function of structures in the brain.

Binocular vision
Vision characterized by overlapping visual fields provided by forward-facing eyes; essential to depth perception.

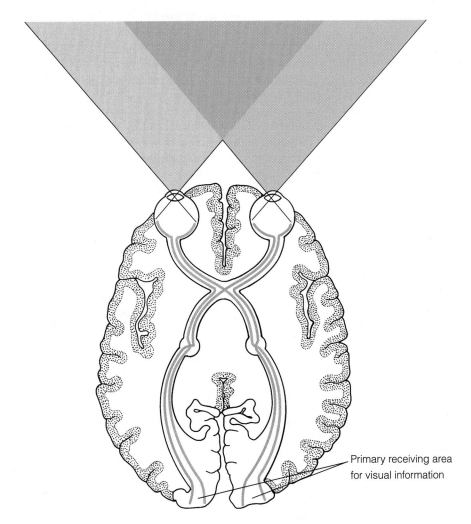

Primary receiving area for visual information

FIGURE 5–2

Simplified diagram showing overlapping visual fields (binocular vision) in primates (and some predators) with eyes positioned at the front of the face. (The green shaded area represents the area of overlap.) Stereoscopic vision (three-dimensional vision) is provided in part by binocular vision and in part by the transmission of visual stimuli from each eye to *both* hemispheres of the brain. (In nonprimate mammals, all visual information crosses over to the hemisphere opposite the eye in which it was initially received.)

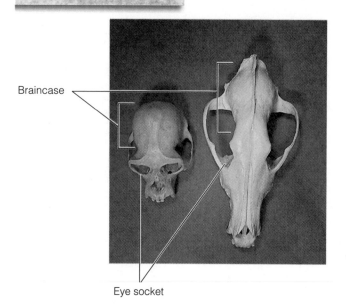

Braincase

Eye socket

FIGURE 5–3

The skull of a gibbon, a small-bodied ape (left), compared to that of a red wolf (right). Note the forward-facing eye orbits of the gibbon and the eye orbits placed more to the side in the wolf. Also, in the gibbon, the proportional size of the snout is smaller than in the wolf.

4. *Expansion and increased complexity of the brain.* This is a general trend among placental mammals, but it is especially true of primates. In primates, this expansion is most evident in the visual and association areas of the neocortex (portions of the brain where information from different sensory modalities is integrated). Expansion in regions involved with the hand (both sensory and motor) is seen in many species, particularly humans.

D. *Maturation, learning, and behavior*
   1. *A more efficient means of fetal nourishment, longer periods of gestation, reduced numbers of offspring (with single births the norm), delayed maturation, and extension of the entire life span.*
   2. *A greater dependence on flexible, learned behavior.* This trend is correlated with delayed maturation and consequently longer periods of infant and child dependency on the parent. As a result of both these trends, parental investment in each offspring is increased, so that although fewer offspring are born, they receive more intense and efficient rearing.
   3. *The tendency to live in social groups and the permanent association of adult males with the group.* Except for some nocturnal forms, primates tend to associate with other individuals. The permanent association of adult males with the group is uncommon in mammals but widespread in primates.
   4. *The tendency to diurnal activity patterns.* This is seen in most primates; only one monkey species and some prosimians are nocturnal.

Primate Adaptations

Evolutionary Factors

Arboreal
Tree-living: adapted to life in the trees.

Adaptive niche
The entire way of life of an organism: where it lives, what it eats, how it gets food, how it avoids predators, etc.

Traditionally, the suite of characteristics shared by primates has been explained as the result of adaptation to **arboreal** living. While other placental mammals were adapting to various ground-dwelling lifestyles and even marine environments, the primates found their **adaptive niche** in the trees. Indeed, some other mammals were also adapting to arboreal living, but while many of these species nested in trees, they continued to come to the ground to forage for food. But throughout the course of evolution, primates came increasingly to exploit foods (leaves, seeds, fruits, nuts, insects, and small mammals) found in the branches themselves. The exploitation of these varied foods enhanced the general trend toward *omnivory* in primates and toward the primate generalized dentition.

We can also see this adaptive process reflected in the primate reliance on vision. In a complex, three-dimensional environment with uncertain footholds, acute color vision with depth perception is extremely beneficial. The presence of grasping hands and feet is also an indicator of the adaptation to living in the trees. Climbing can be accomplished by either digging in with claws (as in many species, such as squirrels or raccoons) or grasping around branches with prehensile hands and feet. Primates adopted this latter strategy, which allowed a means of moving about, sometimes very rapidly, on small, unstable surfaces, and grasping abilities were further enhanced by the appearance of flattened nails instead of claws.

An alternative to this traditional **arboreal hypothesis,** called the *visual predation hypothesis* (Cartmill, 1972, 1992), acknowledges that forward-facing eyes are characteristic, not only of primates, but also of predators, such as cats and owls, that prey on small animals. Cartmill points out that the most significant primate trends (forward-facing eyes, grasping hands and feet, and the presence of nails instead of claws) may *not* have arisen as adaptive advantages in a purely arboreal environment. According to the visual predation hypothesis, primates may first have adapted to shrubby forest undergrowth and the lowest tiers of the forest canopy, where they exploited insects and other small prey that they captured primarily through stealth.

A third scenario (Sussman, 1991) proposes that the basic primate traits developed in conjunction with another major evolutionary occurrence, the rise of the *angiosperms* (flowering plants). Flowering plants provided numerous resources, including nectar, seeds, and fruits, and their appearance and diversification were accompanied by the appearance of ancestral forms of major groups of modern birds and mammals. Sussman argues that visual predation is not common among modern primates and that forward-facing eyes, grasping extremities, and omnivory may have arisen in response to the demand for fine visual and tactile discrimination, necessary when feeding on small food items such as fruits, berries, and seeds among branches and stems.

These hypotheses are not mutually exclusive. The complex of primate characteristics might well have begun in nonarboreal settings and certainly may have been stimulated by the new econiches provided by evolving angiosperms. But one thing is certain. At some point, the primates did take to the trees, and that is where the vast majority of nonhuman primates still live today. Whereas the basic primate structural complexes may have been adapted for visual predation and/or omnivory in shrubby undergrowth and terminal branches, they became ideally suited for the arboreal adaptation that followed. We would say, then, that the early primates were "preadapted" for arboreal living and that those early adaptations have served them long and well in the trees.

Arboreal hypothesis
The traditional view that primate characteristics can be explained as a consequence of primate diversification into arboreal habitats.

Geographical Distribution and Habitats

With just a couple of exceptions, primates are found in tropical or semitropical areas of the New and Old Worlds. In the New World, these areas include southern Mexico, Central America, and parts of South America. Old World primates are found in Africa, India, Southeast Asia (including numerous islands), and Japan (Fig. 5–4).

The majority of primates are, as we have discussed, mostly arboreal and live in forest or woodland habitats. However, some Old World monkeys (e.g., baboons) have, to varying degrees, adapted to life on the ground in areas where trees are sparsely distributed. Moreover, among the apes, gorillas and chimpanzees spend a considerable amount of time on the ground in forested and wooded habitats. Nevertheless, no nonhuman primate is adapted to a fully terrestrial lifestyle, and all spend some time in the trees.

 Interactive exercises about the global distribution and habitats of primates are provided in Virtual Lab 1, section III, parts A and B.

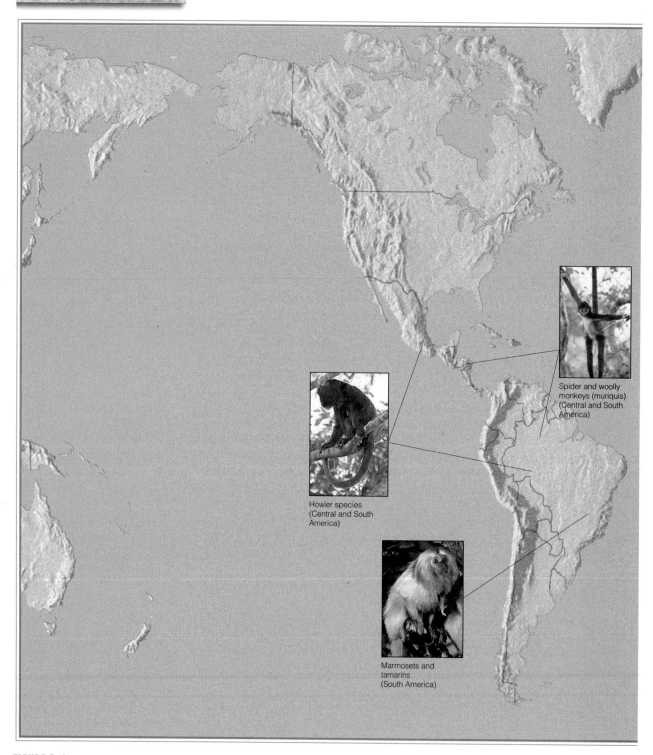

Spider and woolly
monkeys (muriquis)
(Central and South
America)

Howler species
(Central and South
America)

Marmosets and
tamarins
(South America)

FIGURE 5–4

Geographical distribution of living
nonhuman primates. Much original
habitat is now very fragmented.

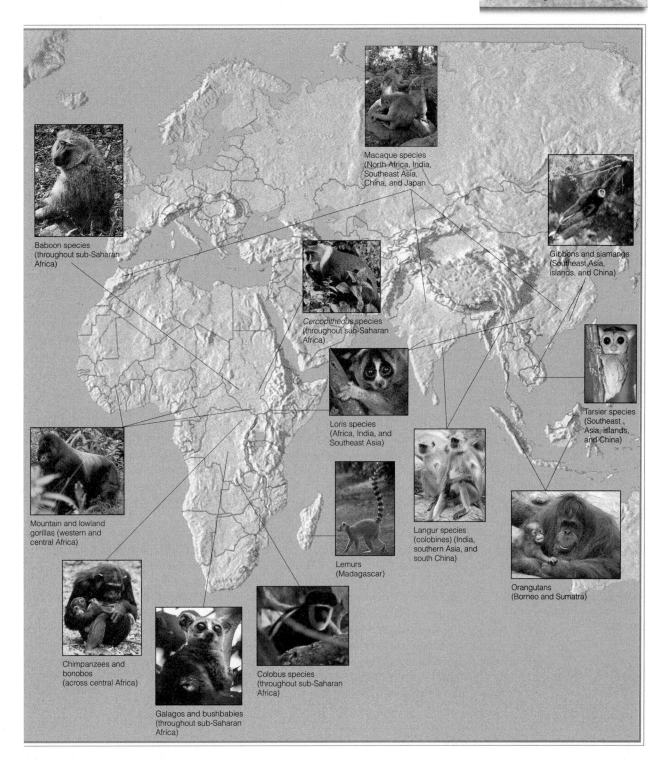

Macaque species (North Africa, India, Southeast Asia, China, and Japan

Gibbons and siamangs (Southeast Asia, islands, and China)

Baboon species (throughout sub-Saharan Africa)

Cercopithecus species (throughout sub-Saharan Africa)

Tarsier species (Southeast Asia, islands, and China)

Loris species (Africa, India, and Southeast Asia)

Mountain and lowland gorillas (western and central Africa)

Langur species (colobines) (India, southern Asia, and south China)

Lemurs (Madagascar)

Orangutans (Borneo and Sumatra)

Chimpanzees and bonobos (across central Africa)

Colobus species (throughout sub-Saharan Africa)

Galagos and bushbabies (throughout sub-Saharan Africa)

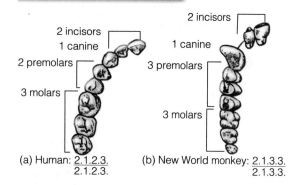

2 incisors
1 canine
2 premolars
3 molars

2 incisors
1 canine
3 premolars
3 molars

(a) Human: 2.1.2.3.
         2.1.2.3.

(b) New World monkey: 2.1.3.3.
                       2.1.3.3.

FIGURE 5–5

Dental formulae. The number of each kind of tooth is given for one-quarter of the mouth.

Midline
An anatomical term referring to a hypothetical line that divides the body into right and left halves.

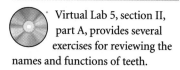

Virtual Lab 5, section II, part A, provides several exercises for reviewing the names and functions of teeth.

Cusps
The elevated portions (bumps) on the chewing surfaces of premolar and molar teeth.

Quadrupedal
Using all four limbs to support the body during locomotion; the basic mammalian (and primate) form of locomotion.

Diet and Teeth

As noted, primates are generally *omnivorous.* Indeed, the tendency toward omnivory is one example of the overall lack of specialization in primates. Although the majority of primate species tend to emphasize some food items over others, most eat a combination of fruit, leaves and other plant materials, and insects. Many obtain animal protein from birds and amphibians as well. Some (baboons and especially chimpanzees) occasionally kill and eat small mammals, including other primates. Others, such as African colobus monkeys and the leaf-eating monkeys (langurs) of India and southeast Asia, have become more specialized and subsist primarily on leaves. Such an array of choices is highly adaptive even in fairly predictable environments.

Like the majority of other mammals, most primates have four kinds of teeth: incisors and canines for biting and cutting and premolars and molars for chewing. Biologists use a device called a *dental formula* to describe the number of each type of tooth that typifies a species. A dental formula indicates the number of each tooth type in each quadrant of the mouth (Fig. 5–5). For example, all Old World *anthropoids* have two incisors, one canine, two premolars, and three molars on each side of the **midline** in both the upper and lower jaws, or a total of 32 teeth. This is represented as a dental formula of

2.1.2.3. (upper)
2.1.2.3. (lower)

The dental formula for a generalized placental mammal is 3.1.4.3. (three incisors, one canine, four premolars, and three molars). Primates have fewer teeth than this ancestral pattern because there has been a general evolutionary trend toward reduction of the number of teeth in many mammal groups. Consequently, the number of each type of tooth varies between lineages. For example, in the majority of New World monkeys, the dental formula is 2.1.3.3. (two incisors, one canine, three premolars, and three molars).

Correlated with an overall lack of dietary specialization in primates is a lack of specialization with regard to the size and shape of the teeth because tooth form is directly related to diet. For example, carnivores typically have premolars and molars with high pointed **cusps** adapted for tearing meat, while the premolars of herbivores, such as cattle and horses, have broad, flat surfaces suited to chewing tough grasses and other plant materials. Most primates possess premolars and molars that have low, rounded cusps, a molar morphology that enables them to process most types of foods. Thus, throughout their evolutionary history, the primates have developed a dentition adapted to a varied diet, and the capacity to exploit many foods has contributed to their overall success during the last 50 million years.

Locomotion

Almost all primates are, at least to some degree, **quadrupedal,** meaning they use all four limbs to support the body during locomotion. However, to describe most primate species in terms of only one or even two forms of locomotion would be to overlook the wide variety of methods they may use to move about. Many primates employ more than one form of locomotion, and they owe this important ability to their generalized structure.

Although the majority of quadrupedal primates are arboreal, terrestrial quadrupedalism is fairly common and is displayed by some lemurs, baboons, and **macaques.** Typically, the limbs of terrestrial quadrupeds are approximately of equal length, with forelimbs being 90 percent (or more) as long as hind limbs (Fig. 5–6a). In arboreal quadrupeds, forelimbs are shorter and may be only 70 to 80 percent as long as hind limbs (Fig. 5–6b).

Macaques
(muh-kaks´) Group of Old World monkeys comprising several species, including rhesus monkeys.

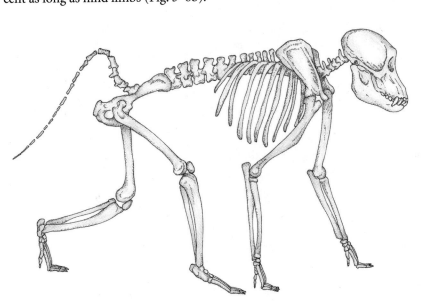

(a) Skeleton of a terrestrial quadruped (savanna baboon).

 Detailed discussions of primate locomotion are provided in Virtual Labs 3 and 4.

 Anatomical terms are presented in Virtual Lab 3. See Virtual Lab 4, sections I and II, for a discussion of relationship between relative limb lengths and locomotion patterns.

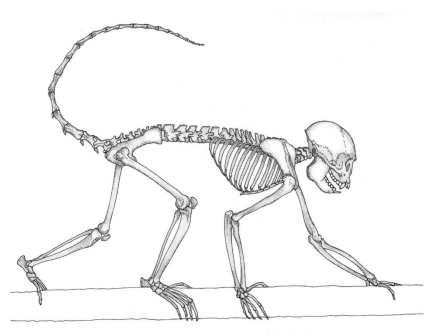

(b) Skeleton of an arboreal New World monkey (bearded saki).

FIGURE 5–6a–d (c and d on page 92)

Differences in skeletal anatomy and limb proportions reflect differences in locomotor patterns. (Redrawn from original art by Stephen Nash. In Fleagle, John G., *Primate Adaptation and Evolution,* 1988, 1998. New York: Academic Press.)

Video clips of primate quadrupedalism, bipedalism, and brachiation are given in Virtual Lab 4, section I, part D.

Brachiation
A form of locomotion in which the body is suspended beneath the hands and support is alternated from one forelimb to the other; arm swinging.

FIGURE 5.6a–d (continued)

Quadrupeds are also characterized by a relatively long and flexible *lumbar spine* (lower back). This lumbar flexibility permits the animal to bend the body during running, thus positioning the hind limbs and feet well forward under the body and enhancing their ability to propel the animal forward. (Watch for this the next time you see slow-motion footage of cheetahs or lions on television.)

Another form of locomotion is *vertical clinging and leaping,* seen in many prosimians. As the term implies, vertical clingers and leapers support themselves vertically by grasping onto trunks of trees while their knees and ankles are tightly flexed (Fig. 5–6c). Forceful extension of their long hind limbs allows them to spring powerfully away in either a forward or backward direction. Once in midair, the body rotates so that the animal lands feet first on the next vertical support.

Yet another type of primate locomotion is **brachiation,** or arm swinging, where the body is alternatively supported under either forelimb. Because of anatomical modifications at the shoulder joint, apes and humans are capable of true brachiation. However, only the small gibbons and siamangs of Southeast Asia use this form of locomotion almost exclusively (Fig. 5–6d).

Brachiation is seen in species characterized by arms longer than legs, a short stable lumbar spine, long curved fingers, and reduced thumbs. Because these are

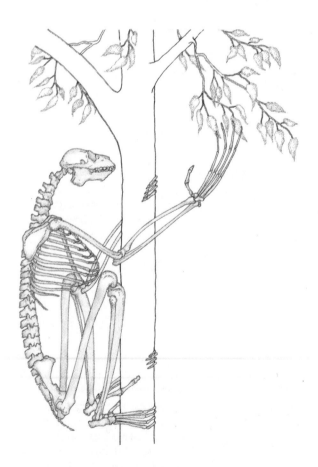

(c) Skeleton of a vertical clinger and leaper (indri).

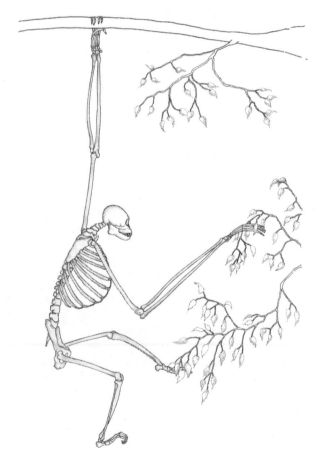

(d) Skeleton of a brachiator (gibbon).

traits seen in all the apes, it is believed that although none of the great apes (orangutans, gorillas, and chimpanzees) habitually brachiates today, they most likely inherited these characteristics from brachiating or perhaps climbing ancestors.

Some monkeys, particularly New World monkeys, are termed *semibrachiators,* as they practice a combination of leaping with some arm swinging. In a few New World species, arm swinging and other suspensory behaviors are enhanced by use of a *prehensile tail,* which in effect serves as a marvelously effective grasping fifth "hand." It should be noted that prehensile tails are strictly a New World phenomenon and are not seen in any Old World primate species.

A Survey of the Living Primates

Primate Taxonomy

The living primates are commonly categorized into their respective subgroups as shown in Figure 5–7. This taxonomy is based on the system originally established by Linnaeus. (Remember that the primate order, which includes a diverse array of approximately 190 species, belongs to a larger group, the class *Mammalia.*)

In any taxonomic system, organisms are organized into increasingly specific categories. For example, the order *Primates* includes *all* primates. However, at the next level down—the *suborder*—the primates have conventionally been divided into two large categories, Prosimii (all the prosimians: lemurs, lorises, and, customarily, the tarsiers) and Anthropoidea (all the monkeys, apes, and humans). Therefore, the suborder distinction is more specific and more precise than the order.

At the level of the suborder, the prosimians are distinct as a group from all the other primates, and this classification makes the biological and evolutionary statement that all the prosimian species are more closely related to one another than they are to any of the anthropoids. Likewise, all anthropoid species are more closely related to one another than to the prosimians.

At each succeeding level (infraorder, superfamily, family, subfamily, genus, and species), finer distinctions are made between categories until, at the species level, only those animals that can interbreed and produce viable offspring are included. In this manner, taxonomies not only organize diversity into categories; they also illustrate evolutionary and genetic relationships between species and groups of species.

The taxonomy presented in Figure 5–7 is the traditional one and is based on physical similarities between species and lineages. However, this technique can be problematic. For example, two primate species that superficially resemble each other (e.g., some New and Old World monkeys) may in fact not be closely related at all. Using external morphology alone overlooks the unknown effects of separate evolutionary history. But evidence such as biochemical data avoids these pitfalls and indeed shows Old and New World monkeys to be genetically and evolutionarily quite distinct.

This relatively new perspective has enormous potential for clarifying taxonomic problems by making between-species comparisons of chromosomes and amino acid sequences in proteins. Direct comparisons of proteins (products of DNA) are excellent indicators of shared evolutionary history. If two primate species are similar with regard to protein structure, we know that their DNA sequences are also similar. It also follows that if two species share similar DNA, it is highly probable that both inherited their blueprint from a common ancestor.

 An interactive discussion of primate taxonomy (with many examples) is presented in Virtual Lab 1, section II, part D.

FIGURE 5–7

Primate taxonomic classification. This abbreviated taxonomy illustrates how primates are grouped into increasingly specific categories. Only the more general categories are shown, except for the great apes and humans.

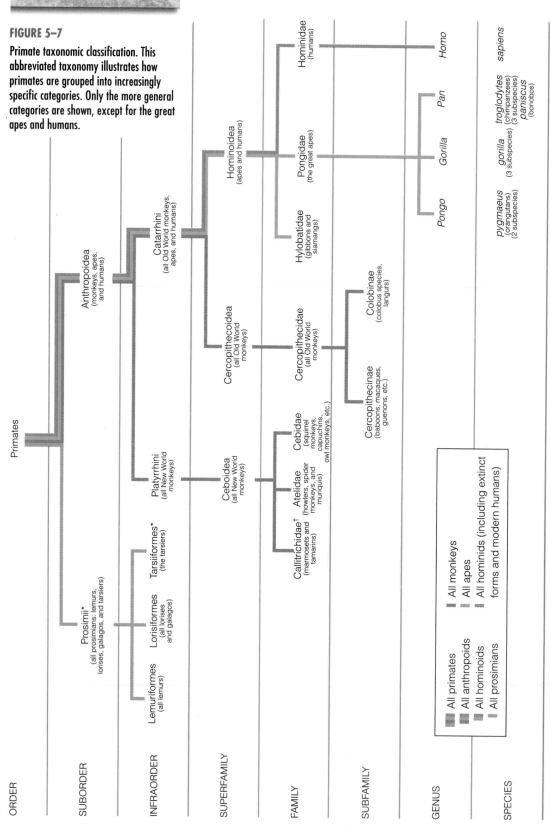

*There is some disagreement among primatologists concerning where to place tarsiers. Many researchers suggest that they more properly belong closer to the anthropoids and thus revise the primate classification to reflect this view. Here, for simplicity, we continue to use the traditional classifications.

†Fleagle (1999) and others have recently eliminated the family Callitrichidae and included marmosets and tamarins in the family Cebidae.

Detailed comparisons of protein structure can be achieved by isolating the amino acid sequences. Comparisons between humans and the African great apes for the approximately half dozen proteins analyzed in this manner show striking similarities: They are either identical or show a difference of only one or two amino acids in the entire sequence.

Another technique called DNA hybridization matches DNA strands from two species to determine what percentage of bases match. The higher the percentage, the closer the genetic relationship between the two. The results of this technique show that 98.4 percent of the human and chimpanzee DNA base sequences examined are identical.

As useful as they are, these techniques are *indirect* methods of examining the DNA code. But today there are procedures that make it possible to sequence the nucleotides *directly* from the DNA molecule. In fact, the technologies of *DNA sequencing* are being used in the Human Genome Project (see p. 76), but as yet, DNA sequencing has not been extensively used to compare the DNA of nonhuman species. Once this approach is more widely applied, it will be possible to ascertain even more clearly the precise genetic and evolutionary relationships among the primates.

At present, amino acid sequencing and DNA hybridization, as well as other techniques, have reaffirmed the basic tenets of traditional primate classification. Moreover, they have shown how close genetically humans and the African great apes are. A systematic application of DNA hybridization (Sibley and Ahlquist, 1984) demonstrated that humans and chimpanzees are closer genetically than either is to the gorilla. For that matter, chimpanzees and humans share more genetic similarities than do zebras and horses or goats and sheep. On the basis of these results, it would be entirely consistent to classify humans and chimpanzees (perhaps gorillas as well) within the *same* genus. Humans would continue to be called *Homo sapiens,* whereas chimpanzees would be classed as *Homo troglodytes.*

Virtual Lab 1, section II, part D, provides an interactive treatment of the critical issue of ape and human classification.

We have included the traditional system of primate classification here, even though we acknowledge the need for modification. At present, not all anthropologists and biologists have completely accepted the revised terminology. Until consensus is reached and new designations are formally adopted, we think it appropriate to use the standard taxonomy along with discussion of some proposed changes. It is also important to point out that while specific details and names have not yet been worked out, the vast majority of experts do accept the evolutionary implications of the revised groupings.

Another area where modifications have been suggested concerns tarsiers. Tarsiers are highly specialized animals that display several unique physical characteristics. Because they possess a number of prosimian traits, tarsiers traditionally have been classified as prosimians (with lemurs and lorises); nevertheless, they also share certain anthropoid features (see p. 98). Moreover, biochemically, tarsiers are more closely related to anthropoids than to prosimians (Dene et al., 1976); but with regard to chromosomes and several anatomical traits, they are distinct from both groups.

Today, most primatologists recognize tarsiers as more closely related to anthropoids than to prosimians. But instead of simply moving them into the suborder Anthropoidea, one proposed scheme places lemurs and lorises in a new suborder, Strepsirhini (instead of Prosimii), and includes tarsiers with monkeys, apes, and humans in another new suborder, Haplorhini (Szalay and Delson, 1979) (Fig. 5–8). Thus, in this classification, the conventionally named suborders

FIGURE 5–8

Revised partial classification of the primates. In this system, the terms *Prosimii* and *Anthropoidea* have been replaced by *Strepsirhini* and *Haplorhini*, respectively. The tarsier is included in the same suborder with monkeys, apes, and humans to reflect a closer relationship with these forms than with lemurs and lorises. (Compare with Figure 5–7.)

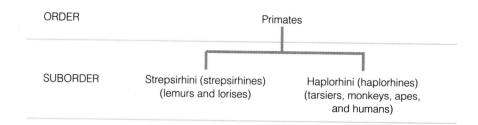

ORDER — Primates

SUBORDER — Strepsirhini (strepsirhines) (lemurs and lorises)   Haplorhini (haplorhines) (tarsiers, monkeys, apes, and humans)

Rhinarium

(rine-air´-ee-um) The moist, hairless pad at the end of the nose seen in most mammalian species. The rhinarium enhances an animal's ability to smell.

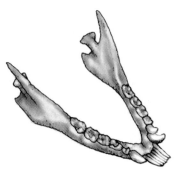

FIGURE 5–9

Prosimian dental comb, formed by forward-projecting incisors and canines.

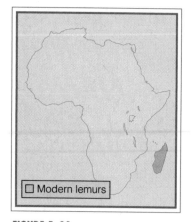

☐ Modern lemurs

FIGURE 5–10

Geographical distribution of modern lemurs.

Prosimii and Anthropoidea are replaced by Strepsirhini and Haplorhini, respectively. As yet, this designation has not been universally accepted, but the terminology is becoming common, especially in technical publications.

Prosimians (Lemurs and Lorises)

The most primitive of the primates are the lemurs and lorises. (We do not include tarsiers here, because their status is not as clear.) By "primitive" we mean that prosimians, taken as a group, are more similar anatomically to their earlier mammalian ancestors than are the other primates (monkeys, apes, and humans). Therefore, they tend to exhibit certain more ancestral characteristics, such as a more pronounced reliance on *olfaction* (sense of smell). Their greater olfactory capabilities (compared to other primates) are reflected in the presence of a moist, fleshy pad (**rhinarium**) at the end of the nose and in a relatively long snout. Moreover, prosimians mark territories with scent in a manner not seen in many other primates.

There are numerous other characteristics that distinguish lemurs and lorises from the anthropoids, including somewhat more laterally placed eyes, differences in reproductive physiology, and shorter gestation and maturation periods. Lemurs and lorises also possess a dental specialization known as the "dental comb." The dental comb is formed by forward-projecting lower incisors and canines, and together these modified teeth are used in both grooming and feeding (Fig. 5–9). One other characteristic that sets lemurs and lorises apart from anthropoids is the retention of a claw (called a "grooming claw") on the second toe.

Lemurs Lemurs are found only on the island of Madagascar and adjacent islands off the east coast of Africa (Fig. 5–10). As the only nonhuman primates on Madagascar, which comprises some 227,000 square miles, lemurs diversified into numerous and varied ecological niches without competition from monkeys and apes. Thus, while lemurs became extinct elsewhere, the 22 surviving species of Madagascar represent an evolutionary pattern that has vanished elsewhere.

Lemurs range in size from the small mouse lemur, with a body length (head and trunk) of only 5 inches, to the indri, with a body length of a little over 2 feet (Napier and Napier, 1985). While the larger lemurs are diurnal and exploit a wide variety of dietary items, such as leaves, fruit, buds, bark, and shoots, the smaller forms (mouse and dwarf lemurs) are nocturnal and insectivorous.

Lemurs display considerable variation regarding numerous other aspects of behavior. While many are primarily arboreal, others, such as the ring-tailed lemur (Fig. 5–11), are more terrestrial. Some arboreal species are quadrupeds, and others (sifakas and indris) are vertical clingers and leapers (Fig. 5–12). Socially, several species (e.g., ring-tailed lemurs and sifakas) are gregarious and live in groups of 10

FIGURE 5–11
Ring-tailed lemur.

FIGURE 5–12
Sifakas in their native habitat in Madagascar.

to 25 animals composed of males and females of all ages. Others (the indris) live in monogamous family units, and several nocturnal forms are mostly solitary.

Lorises Lorises (Fig. 5–13), which are similar in appearance to lemurs, were able to survive in mainland areas by adopting a nocturnal activity pattern at a time when most other prosimians became extinct. In this way, they were (and are) able to avoid competition with more recently evolved primates (the diurnal monkeys).

There are at least eight loris species, all of which are found in tropical forest and woodland habitats of India, Sri Lanka, Southeast Asia, and Africa. Also included in the same general category are six to nine (Bearder, 1987) galago species (Fig. 5–14), which are widely distributed throughout most of the forested and woodland savanna areas of sub-Saharan Africa.

FIGURE 5–13
Slow loris.

FIGURE 5–14
Galago, or "bush baby."

An Overview of the Living Primates

FIGURE 5–15

Tarsier.

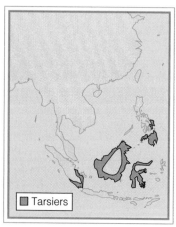

FIGURE 5–16

Geographical distribution of tarsiers.

 See Virtual Lab 1, section II, part D, for a presentation of the differences between monkeys, apes, and humans.

Locomotion in lorises is a slow, cautious climbing form of quadrupedalism, and flexible hip joints permit suspension by hind limbs while the hands are used in feeding. All galagos, however, are highly agile and active vertical clingers and leapers. Some lorises and galagos are almost entirely insectivorous; others supplement their diet with various combinations of fruits, leaves, gums, and slugs. Lorises and galagos frequently forage for food alone (females leave infants behind in nests until they are older). However, ranges overlap, and two or more females occasionally forage together or share the same sleeping nest.

Lemurs and lorises represent the same general adaptive level. Both groups exhibit good grasping and climbing abilities and a fairly well developed visual apparatus, although vision is not completely stereoscopic, and color vision may not be as well developed as in anthropoids. Most lemurs and lorises also have prolonged life spans as compared to most other small-bodied mammals, averaging about 14 years for lorises and 19 years for lemurs.

Tarsiers

There are three recognized species of tarsier (Fig. 5–15), all restricted to island areas in Southeast Asia (Fig. 5–16), where they inhabit a wide range of forest types, from tropical forest to backyard gardens. Tarsiers are nocturnal insectivores, leaping onto prey (which may also include small vertebrates) from lower branches and shrubs. They appear to form stable pair bonds, and the basic tarsier social unit is a mated pair and their young offspring (MacKinnon and MacKinnon, 1980).

As we have already discussed, tarsiers present a complex blend of characteristics not seen in other primates. Moreover, they are unique in that their enormous eyes, which dominate much of the face, are immobile within their sockets. To compensate for this inability to move the eyes, tarsiers are able to rotate their heads 180° in a decidedly owl-like manner.

Anthropoids (Monkeys, Apes, and Humans)

Although there is much variation among anthropoids, there are certain features that, when taken together, distinguish them as a group from prosimians (and other placental mammals). Here is a partial list of these traits:

1. Generally larger body size
2. Larger brain (in absolute terms and relative to body weight)
3. Reduced reliance on the sense of smell, indicated by absence of rhinarium and other structures
4. Increased reliance on vision, with forward-facing eyes placed at front of face
5. Greater degree of color vision
6. Back of eye socket formed by a bony plate
7. Blood supply to brain different from that of prosimians
8. Fusion of the two sides of the mandible at the midline to form one bone (in prosimians they are joined by fibrous tissue)
9. Less specialized dentition, as seen in absence of dental comb and some other features
10. Differences with regard to female internal reproductive anatomy
11. Longer gestation and maturation periods
12. Increased parental care
13. More mutual grooming

Approximately 70 percent of all primates (about 130 species) are monkeys. It is frequently impossible to give precise numbers of species because the taxonomic status of some primates remains in doubt, and primatologists are still making new discoveries. Monkeys are divided into two groups separated by geographical area (New World and Old World), as well as by several million years of separate evolutionary history.

New World Monkeys   The New World monkeys exhibit a wide range of size, diet, and ecological adaptation. In size, they vary from the tiny marmosets and tamarins (about 12 ounces) to the 20-pound howler monkey (Figs. 5–17 and 5–18). New World monkeys are almost exclusively arboreal, and some never come to the ground. Like Old World monkeys, all except one species (the douroucouli, or owl monkey) are diurnal. Although confined to the trees, New World monkeys can be found in a wide range of arboreal environments throughout most forested areas in southern Mexico and Central and South America (Fig. 5–19).

One of the characteristics distinguishing New World monkeys from those found in the Old World is shape of the nose. New World forms have broad noses with outward-facing nostrils. Conversely, Old World monkeys have narrower noses with downward-facing nostrils. This difference in nose form has given rise to the terms *platyrrhine* (flat-nosed) and *catarrhine* (downward-facing nose) to refer to New and Old World anthropoids, respectively.

New World monkeys have traditionally been divided into two families: **Callitrichidae** (marmosets and tamarins) and **Cebidae** (all others). Some authors have suggested that molecular data along with recently reported fossil evidence indicate that a major regrouping of New World monkeys is in order (Fleagle, 1999).*

Marmosets and tamarins are the most primitive of monkeys, retaining claws instead of nails and usually giving birth to twins instead of one infant. They are mostly insectivorous, although marmoset diet includes gums from trees, and

FIGURE 5–17
A pair of golden lion tamarins.

Callitrichidae
(kal-eh-trick´-eh-dee)

Cebidae
(see´-bid-ee)

FIGURE 5–18
Howler monkeys.

FIGURE 5–19
Geographical distribution of modern New World monkeys.

---

*One possibility is to include spider monkeys, howler monkeys, and muriquis (woolly spider monkeys) in a third family, Atelidae (see taxonomic chart, p. 94). Another is to eliminate the family Callitrichidae altogether and include marmosets and tamarins as a subfamily within the family Cebidae.

 A video clip of a spider monkey can be found in Virtual Lab 4, section I, part D.

FIGURE 5–20

Spider monkey. Note the prehensile tail.

Ischial callosities
Patches of tough, hard skin on the buttocks of Old World monkeys and chimpanzees.

tamarins also rely heavily on fruits. Locomotion is quadrupedal, and their claws aid in climbing vertical tree trunks, much in the manner of squirrels. Moreover, some tamarins employ vertical clinging and leaping as a form of travel. Socially, these small monkeys live in family groups composed usually of a mated pair, or a female and two adult males, and their offspring. Indeed, marmosets and tamarins are among the few primate species in which males are heavily involved in infant care.

There are at least 30 cebid species ranging in size from the squirrel monkey (body length 12 inches) to the howler (body length 24 inches). Diet varies, with most relying on a combination of fruit and leaves supplemented, to varying degrees, by insects. Most cebids are quadrupedal, but some—for example, the spider monkey (Fig. 5–20)—are semibrachiators. Some cebids, including the spider and howler, also possess powerful prehensile tails that are used not only in locomotion but also for suspension under branches while feeding on leaves and fruit. Socially, most cebids are found either in groups of both sexes and all age categories or in monogamous pairs with subadult offspring.

Old World Monkeys The monkeys of the Old World display much more morphological and behavioral diversity than is seen in New World monkeys. Except for humans, Old World monkeys are the most widely distributed of all living primates. They are found throughout sub-Saharan Africa and southern Asia, ranging from tropical jungle habitats to semiarid desert and even to seasonally snow-covered areas in northern Japan (Fig. 5–21).

Most Old World monkeys are quadrupedal and primarily arboreal, but some (e.g., baboons) are also adapted to life on the ground. Whether in trees or on the ground, these monkeys spend a good deal of time sleeping, feeding, and grooming while sitting with their upper bodies held erect. Usually associated with this universal sitting posture are areas of hardened skin on the buttocks (**ischial callosities**) that serve as sitting pads.

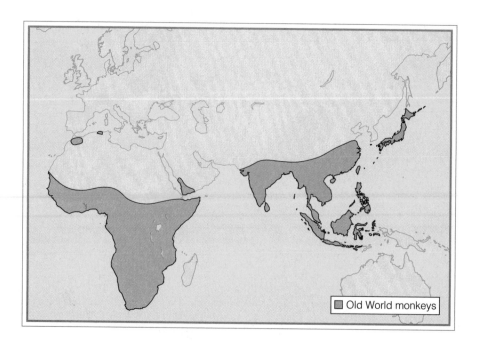

Old World monkeys

FIGURE 5–21

Geographical distribution of modern Old World monkeys.

FIGURE 5–22
Adult male sykes monkey, one of several guenon species.

Within the entire group of Old World monkeys there is only one recognized taxonomic family: **Cercopithecidae.** This family, in turn, is divided into two subfamilies: the **cercopithecines** and **colobines.**

The cercopithecines are the more generalized of the two groups, showing a more omnivorous dietary adaptation and distinctive cheek pouches for storing food. As a group, the cercopithecines eat almost anything, including fruits, seeds, leaves, grasses, tubers, roots, nuts, insects, birds' eggs, amphibians, small reptiles, and small mammals (the last seen in baboons).

The majority of cercopithecine species, such as the mostly arboreal guenons (Fig. 5–22) and the more terrestrial savanna and hamadryas baboons (Fig. 5–23) are found in Africa. However, the several species of macaque, which include the well-known rhesus monkey, are widely distributed in southern Asia and India.

Colobine species are more limited dietarily, specializing on mature leaves, a behavior that has led to their designation as "leaf-eating monkeys." The colobines are found mainly in Asia, but both the red colobus and the black-and-white colobus are exclusively African (Fig. 5–24). Other colobines include several species of Asian langur and the proboscis monkey of Borneo.

Cercopithecidae
(serk-oh-pith′-eh-sid-ee)

Cercopithecines
(serk-oh-pith′-eh-seens) The subfamily of Old World monkeys that includes baboons, macaques, and guenons.

Colobines
(kole′-uh-beans) The subfamily of Old World monkeys that includes the African colobus monkeys and Asian langurs.

 The concept of sexual dimorphism is treated in Virtual Lab 1, section IV, part B.

(a)

(b)

FIGURE 5–23
Savanna baboons. (a) Male. (b) Female.

101

FIGURE 5–24
Black-and-white colobus monkey.

Sexual dimorphism
Differences in physical characteristics between males and females of the same species. For example, humans are slightly sexually dimorphic for body size, with males being taller, on average, than females of the same population.

Estrus
(ess´-truss) Period of sexual receptivity in female mammals (except humans); correlated with ovulation. When used as an adjective, the word is spelled "estrous."

Hominoidea
The formal designation for the superfamily of anthropoids that includes apes and humans.

Hylobatidae
(high-lo-baht´-id-ee)

Pongidae
(ponj´-id-ee)

 Pronunciations of these and many other terms, as well as scientific names, are given in Virtual Lab 1, section II, and the glossary.

Locomotor behavior among Old World monkeys includes arboreal quadrupedalism in guenons, macaques, and langurs; terrestrial quadrupedalism in baboons, patas, and macaques; and semibrachiation and acrobatic leaping in colobus monkeys.

Marked differences in body size or shape between the sexes, referred to as **sexual dimorphism,** are typical of some terrestrial species and are particularly pronounced in baboons and patas. In these species, male body weight (up to 80 pounds in baboons) may be twice that of females.

Females of several species (especially baboons and some macaques) exhibit pronounced cyclical changes of the external genitalia. These changes, including swelling and redness, are associated with **estrus,** a hormonally initiated period of sexual receptivity in female nonhuman mammals correlated with ovulation.

Several types of social organization characterize Old World monkeys, and there are uncertainties among primatologists regarding some species. In general, colobines tend to live in small groups, with only one or two adult males. Savanna baboons and most macaque species are found in large social units comprising several adults of both sexes and offspring of all ages. Monogamous pairing is not common in Old World monkeys, but is seen in a few langurs and possibly one or two guenon species.

Hominoids (Apes and Humans)

The other large grouping of anthropoids, the hominoids, includes apes and humans. The superfamily **Hominoidea** includes the "lesser" apes in the family **Hylobatidae** (gibbons and siamangs); the great apes in the family **Pongidae** (orangutans, gorillas, bonobos, and chimpanzees); and humans in the family Hominidae.

Apes and humans differ from monkeys in numerous ways:

1. Generally larger body size, except for gibbons and siamangs
2. Absence of a tail
3. Shortened trunk (lumbar area relatively shorter and more stable)
4. Differences in position and musculature of the shoulder joint (adapted for suspensory locomotion)
5. More complex behavior
6. More complex brain and enhanced cognitive abilities
7. Increased period of infant development and dependency

Gibbons and Siamangs   The eight gibbon species and the closely related siamang are today found in the southeastern tropical areas of Asia (Fig. 5–25). These animals are the smallest of the apes, with a long, slender body weighing 13 pounds in the gibbon (Fig. 5–26) and 25 pounds in the larger siamang.

The most distinctive structural feature of gibbons and siamangs is related to an adaptation for brachiation. They have extremely long arms, long, permanently curved fingers, short thumbs, and powerful shoulder muscles. These highly specialized locomotor adaptations may be related to feeding behavior while hanging beneath branches. The diet of both species is largely composed of fruit. Both (especially the siamang) also eat a variety of leaves, flowers, and insects.

The basic social unit of gibbons and siamangs is the monogamous pair with dependent offspring. As in marmosets and tamarins, male gibbons and siamangs are very much involved in rearing their young. Both males and females are highly territorial and protect their territories with elaborate whoops and sirenlike "songs."

Orangutans   Orangutans (*Pongo pygmaeus*) (Fig. 5–27) are represented by two subspecies found today only in heavily forested areas on the Indonesian islands of Borneo and Sumatra (see Fig. 5–25). Due to poaching by humans and continuing habitat loss on both islands, orangutans are threatened by extinction in the wild.

FIGURE 5–25
Geographical distribution of modern Asian apes.

FIGURE 5–26
White-handed gibbon.

FIGURE 5–27
Female orangutan.

Orangutans are slow, cautious climbers whose locomotor behavior can best be described as "four-handed," referring to the tendency to use all four limbs for grasping and support. Although they are almost completely arboreal, orangutans do sometimes travel quadrupedally on the ground. Orangutans are also very large animals with pronounced sexual dimorphism (males may weigh 200 pounds or more and females less than 100 pounds).

In the wild, orangutans lead largely solitary lives, although adult females are usually accompanied by one or two dependent offspring. They are primarily **frugivorous,** but bark, leaves, insects, and meat (on rare occasions) may also be eaten.

Frugivorous
(fru-give´-or-us) Having a diet composed primarily of fruit.

Gorillas   The largest of all living primates, gorillas (*Gorilla gorilla*) are today confined to forested areas of western and eastern equatorial Africa (Fig. 5–28). There are three generally recognized subspecies, although molecular data suggest that one of these, the western lowland gorilla (Fig. 5–29), is perhaps sufficiently genetically distinct to warrant designation as a separate species (Ruvolo et al., 1994; Garner and Ryder, 1996). The western lowland gorilla is found in several countries of western central Africa and is the most numerous of the three subspecies, with a population size of perhaps 110,000 (Doran and McNeilage, 1998). The eastern lowland gorilla is found near the eastern border of the Democratic Republic of the Congo (formerly Zaire) and numbers about 12,000. Mountain gorillas (Fig. 5–30), the most extensively studied of the three subspecies, are found in the mountainous areas of central Africa in Rwanda, Democratic Republic of the Congo, and Uganda. Mountain gorillas have probably never been very numerous, and today they are among the more endangered primates, numbering only about 600.

Gorillas exhibit marked sexual dimorphism, with males weighing up to 400 pounds and females around 150 to 200 pounds. Because of their weight, adult gorillas, especially males, are primarily terrestrial and adopt a semiquadrupedal (knuckle-walking) posture on the ground.

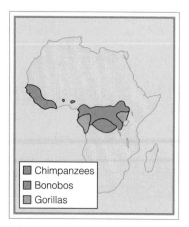

■ Chimpanzees
■ Bonobos
■ Gorillas

FIGURE 5–28
Geographical distribution of modern African apes.

(a)

(b)

Mountain gorillas live in groups consisting of one (or sometimes two) large *silverback* males, a variable number of adult females, and their subadult offspring. The term *silverback* refers to the saddle of white hair across the back of full adult (at least 12 or 13 years of age) male gorillas. Additionally, the silverback male may tolerate the presence of one or more young adult *blackback* males, probably his sons. Typically, but not always, both females and males leave their natal group as young adults. Females join other groups, and males, who appear to be less likely to emigrate, may live alone for a while, or they may join an all-male group before eventually forming their own group.

Systematic studies of free-ranging western lowland gorillas were not initiated until the mid-1980s; thus, our knowledge of their social structure and behavior is still in its infancy. In general, it appears that their social structure is similar to that of mountain gorillas, but groups are smaller and somewhat less cohesive.

FIGURE 5–29

Western lowland gorillas. (a) Male. (b) Female.

FIGURE 5–30

Mountain gorillas. (a) Male. (b) Female.

(a)

(b)

All gorillas are almost exclusively vegetarian. Mountain gorillas concentrate primarily on leaves, pith, and stalks. These foods are also important for western lowland gorillas, but they also eat considerably more fruit, depending on seasonal availability. Recent studies also report that western lowland gorillas, unlike mountain gorillas (which avoid water), frequently wade through swamps while foraging on aquatic plants.

Perhaps because of their large body size and enormous strength, gorillas have long been considered ferocious monsters; but in reality, they are shy and gentle. This is not to imply that gorillas are never aggressive. Indeed, male-male competition for females can be extremely violent. Moreover, when threatened, males will attack, and they will certainly defend their group from any perceived danger, whether it be another male gorilla or a human hunter. Still, the reputation of gorillas as murderous beasts is the result of uninformed myth making and little else.

Chimpanzees   Chimpanzees are probably the best known of all nonhuman primates (Fig. 5–31). Often misunderstood because of zoo exhibits, circus acts, television shows, and movies, the true nature of chimpanzees did not become known until years of fieldwork with wild groups provided a reliable picture. Today, chimpanzees are found in equatorial Africa, stretching in a broad belt from the Atlantic Ocean in the west to Lake Tanganyika in the east. Their range, however, is patchy within this large geographical area, and with further habitat destruction, it is becoming even more so (see Fig. 5–28).

Chimpanzees are in many ways structurally similar to gorillas, with corresponding limb proportions and upper-body shape. This similarity is due to commonalities in locomotion when on the ground (quadrupedal knuckle-walking). However, the ecological adaptations of chimpanzees and gorillas differ, with chimpanzees spending more time in the trees. Moreover, whereas gorillas are typically placid and quiet, chimpanzees are highly excitable, active, and noisy.

Chimpanzees are smaller than orangutans and gorillas, and although they are sexually dimorphic, sex differences are not as pronounced as in these other species. While male chimpanzees may weigh over 100 pounds, females may weigh at least 80.

In addition to quadrupedal knuckle-walking, chimpanzees (particularly youngsters) may brachiate while in the trees. When on the ground, they frequently walk bipedally for short distances when carrying food or other objects. One adult male at Jane Goodall's study area in Tanzania frequently walked bipedally because one arm was paralyzed by polio (Goodall, 1986).

Chimpanzees eat an amazing variety of items, including fruits, leaves, insects, nuts, birds' eggs, berries, caterpillars, and small mammals. Moreover, both males and females occasionally take part in group hunting efforts to kill such small mammals as red colobus, young baboons, bushpigs, and antelope. When hunts are successful, the prey is shared by the group members.

Chimpanzees live in large, fluid communities of as many as 50 individuals or more. At the core of a chimpanzee community is a group of bonded males. Although relationships between them are not always peaceful or stable, these males nevertheless act as a group to defend their territory and are highly intolerant of unfamiliar chimpanzees, especially nongroup males.

Even though chimpanzees are said to live in communities, there are few times, if any, when all members are together. Indeed, it is the nature of chimpanzees to come and go, so that the individuals they encounter vary from day to day. Moreover, adult females tend to forage either alone or in the company of their off-

(a)

(b)

FIGURE 5–31
Chimpanzees. (a) Male. (b) Female.

spring. The latter foraging group could comprise several chimpanzees, as females with infants sometimes accompany their own mothers and their younger siblings. A female may also leave her community, either permanently to join another community or temporarily while she is in estrus. This behavioral pattern may reduce the risk of mating with close male relatives, because males apparently never leave the group in which they were born.

Chimpanzee social behavior is complex, and individuals form lifelong attachments with friends and relatives. Indeed, the bond between mothers and infants often remains strong until one or the other dies. This may be a considerable period, because it is not unusual for some chimpanzees to live into their mid-30s and a few into their 40s.

Bonobos   Bonobos (*Pan paniscus*) are found only in an area south of the Zaire River in the Democratic Republic of the Congo (formerly Zaire) (see Fig. 5–28). Not officially recognized by European scientists until the 1920s, they remain among the least studied of the great apes. Although ongoing field studies have produced much information (Susman, 1984; Kano, 1992), research has been periodically hampered by political unrest. There are no accurate counts of bonobos, but their numbers are believed to be between 10,000 and 20,000 (IUCN, 1996), and these are threatened by human hunting, warfare, and habitat loss.

Because bonobos bear a strong resemblance to chimpanzees but are somewhat smaller, they have been called "pygmy chimpanzees." However, differences in body size are not sufficient to warrant this designation, and in fact, bonobos exhibit several anatomical and behavioral differences from chimpanzees. Physically, they have a more linear body build, longer legs relative to arms, a relatively smaller head, a dark face from birth, and tufts of hair at the side of the face (Fig. 5–32).

Bonobos are more arboreal than chimpanzees, and they appear to be less excitable and aggressive. While aggression is not unknown, it appears that physical violence both within and between groups is uncommon. Like chimpanzees, bonobos live in geographically based, fluid communities, and they exploit many of the same foods, including occasional meat derived from killing small mammals

FIGURE 5–32
Female bonobos with young.

(Badrian and Malinky, 1984). But bonobo communities are not centered around a group of closely bonded males. Rather, male-female bonding is more important than in chimpanzees (and most other nonhuman primates), and females are not as peripheral to the group (Badrian and Badrian, 1984). This may be related to bonobo sexuality, which differs in expression from that of other nonhuman primates in that copulation is frequent and occurs throughout a female's estrous cycle.

Bonobos are relatively late to arrive on the scene of primate research. But it is crucial that studies of this intriguing species be allowed to progress. Not only do bonobos have the potential of providing information about human behavior and evolution, but they are of considerable interest in their own right and they are highly endangered. In fact, without research and protection, they, like so many other nonhuman primates, are in danger of extinction.

Humans

Humans are the only living representatives of the family Hominidae (genus *Homo*, species *sapiens*). Our primate heritage is evident in our overall anatomy and genetic makeup and in many aspects of human behavior. With the exception of reduced canine size, human teeth are typical primate teeth; indeed, in overall morphology, they very much resemble ape teeth. The human dependence on vision and decreased reliance on olfaction, as well as flexible limbs and grasping hands, are rooted in our primate, arboreal past. Humans can even brachiate, and playgrounds often accommodate this ability in children.

Humans in general are omnivorous, although all societies observe certain culturally based dietary restrictions. Nevertheless, as a species with a rather generalized digestive system, we are physiologically adapted to digest an extremely wide assortment of foods. Perhaps to our detriment, given how humans tend to go to extremes, we also share with our relatives a fondness for sweets that originates from the importance of high-energy fruits in the diets of many nonhuman primates.

But quite obviously, humans are unique among primates and indeed among all animals. For example, no member of any other species has the ability to write or think about issues such as how they differ from other life forms. This ability is rooted in the fact that human evolution, during the last 800,000 years or so, has been characterized by dramatic increases in brain size and other neurological changes.

Humans are also completely dependent on culture. Without cultural innovation, it would have been impossible for us to have ever left the tropics. As it is, humans inhabit every corner of the planet with the exception of Antarctica, and we have even established outposts there. And lest we forget, a fortunate few have even walked on the moon. None of the technologies (indeed, none of the other aspects of culture) that humans have developed over the last several thousand years would have been possible without the highly developed cognitive abilities we alone possess. Nevertheless, the neurological basis for intelligence is something we share with other primates. Indeed, research has demonstrated that several nonhuman primate species—most notably chimpanzees, bonobos, and gorillas—display a level of problem solving and insight that most people would have considered impossible 25 years ago (see Chapter 6).

Humans are uniquely predisposed to use spoken language, and for the last 5,000 years or so, we have used written language as well. This ability exists because human evolution has modified certain neurological and anatomical structures in ways not observed in any other animal. But while nonhuman primates are not anatomically capable of producing speech, research has demonstrated that to varying degrees, the great apes are able to communicate through the use of symbols. And basically, that is a foundation for language that humans and the great apes (to a limited degree) have in common.

Aside from cognitive abilities, the one other trait that sets humans apart from other primates is our unique (among mammals) form of *habitual* bipedal locomotion. This particular trait appeared early in the evolution of our lineage, and over time, we have become more efficient at it because of related changes in the skeletal morphology of the pelvis, leg, and foot (see Chapter 8). But for whatever reasons, early hominids increasingly adopted bipedalism because they were already preadapted for it. That is, as primates, and especially as apelike primates, they were already behaviorally predisposed to, and anatomically capable of, at least short-term bipedal walking before they adopted it wholeheartedly.

Thus, while it is certainly true that human beings are unique intellectually and in some ways anatomically, we are still primates. In fact, it is quite reasonable to say that fundamentally, humans are exaggerated primates.

Endangered Primates

Probably the greatest challenge facing primatologists today is the urgent need to preserve in the wild what remains of free-ranging primate species. Without massive changes in public opinion and in the economics of countries with surviving rain forests, it will not be long before there are only a few nonhuman primate species left in the world. Indeed, over half of all living nonhuman primates are now in jeopardy, and some are facing almost immediate extinction in the wild.

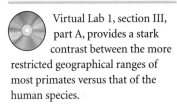

Virtual Lab 1, section III, part A, provides a stark contrast between the more restricted geographical ranges of most primates versus that of the human species.

Population estimates of free-ranging primates are difficult to obtain, but some species (hapalemur, diadem sifaka, aye-aye, lion tamarin, muriqui, red colobus subspecies, lion-tailed macaque, and mountain gorilla) now number only in the hundreds. Others are believed to be represented in the wild by a few thousand (agile mangabey, mentawi langur, red colobus subspecies, moloch gibbon, Kloss' gibbon, orangutan, lowland gorilla, chimpanzee, and bonobo).

There are three basic reasons for the worldwide depletion of nonhuman primates: habitat destruction, hunting, and live capture either for export or local trade. Underlying all three causes is one major factor: unprecedented human population growth, which is occurring at a faster rate in developing countries than in the developed world. Approximately 90 percent of all primates live in the tropical forests of Africa, Asia, and Central and South America, the same areas where most of the world's developing countries are found. Currently, these countries are cutting their forests at a rate of about 30 million acres per year. In Brazil, the Atlantic rain forest originally covered some 385,000 square miles. Today, an estimated 7 percent is all that remains of what was once home to countless New World monkeys and thousands of other species.

Much of the motivation behind the devastation of the rain forests is, of course, economic: the short-term gains from clearing forests to create immediately available (but poor) farmland or ranchland; the use of trees for lumber and paper products; and large-scale mining operations (with their necessary roads, digging, etc., all of which cause habitat destruction). We must also point out that the demand for tropical hardwoods (e.g., mahogany, teak, and rosewood) in the United States, Europe, and Japan creates an enormously profitable market for rain forest products.

Hunting of primates occurs for numerous reasons. Primates have traditionally been an important source of food for people in parts of Asia, Africa, and South America, where thousands of primates are killed annually to feed growing human populations. Moreover, in recent years, hunting of nonhuman primates, particularly in Africa, has shifted from being primarily a subsistence activity to being a commercial practice. In fact, just since the late 1980s, hunting to provide "bush meat" has become the single most serious threat to nonhuman primates in West Africa—more serious even than habitat loss! The hunting of primates (and other species) for meat has been made possible by the construction of logging roads, mainly by French, German, and Belgian logging companies. It should be pointed out that the employees of these logging companies also participate extensively in the bush meat trade. With the advent of these roads, entire forests that previously provided sanctuary to animals were opened up, and the slaughter has been unprecedented. There are no accurate numbers, but it is estimated that thousands of nonhuman primates, including gorillas and chimpanzees, are killed and sold for meat every year. Primates are also killed for commercial products, such as skins, skulls, and other body parts. Although it is illegal for tourists from the United States and several other countries to return home with such products, the trade flourishes.

Primates have also been captured live for zoos, biomedical research, and the exotic pet trade. Live capture has declined dramatically since the implementation of the Convention on Trade in Endangered Species of Wild Flora and Fauna (CITES) in 1973. Currently, 87 countries have signed this treaty, agreeing not to allow trade in species listed by CITES as being endangered. However, even some CITES members are still occasionally involved in the illegal primate trade (Japan and Belgium, among others).

Fortunately, steps are being taken to ensure the survival of some species. Many developing countries, such as Costa Rica and the Malagasy Republic (Madagascar), are designating national parks and other reserves for the protection of natural resources, including primates. It is only through such practices and through educational programs that many primate species have a chance of escaping extinction, at least in the immediate future.

If you are in your 20s or 30s, you will probably live to hear of the extinction of some of our marvelously unique and clever cousins. Many more will undoubtedly slip away unnoticed. Tragically, this will occur, in most cases, before we have even had the opportunity to get to know them.

Each species on earth is the current result of a unique set of evolutionary events that, over millions of years, has produced a finely adapted component of a diverse ecosystem. When it becomes extinct, that adaptation and that part of biodiversity is lost forever. What a tragedy it will be if, through our own mismanagement and greed, we awaken to a world without chimpanzees, mountain gorillas, or the tiny, exquisite lion tamarin. If and when this day comes, we truly will have lost a part of ourselves, and we will be the poorer for it.

SUMMARY

In this chapter, we have briefly introduced you to the primates, the mammalian order that includes humans. As a group, the primates are generalized in terms of diet and locomotor patterns, and these behavioral generalizations are reflected in the morphology of the teeth and limbs.

We have also discussed some of the anatomical similarities and differences between the major groupings of primates: prosimians, monkeys (New and Old World), and hominoids. In the next chapter, we will turn our attention to primate social behavior and cognitive abilities. These are extremely important topics, for it is through better understanding of nonhuman primate behavior that we can make more general statements about human behavior. Moreover, increasing our knowledge is essential if we are to prevent many of these uniquely adapted and marvelous relatives of ours from being lost forever.

QUESTIONS FOR REVIEW

1. Discuss why primates are said to be "generalized mammals."
2. Summarize the major evolutionary trends that characterize the primate order.
3. How does adaptation to an arboreal environment help explain primate evolution?
4. What is the geographical distribution of the nonhuman primates?
5. What are the two major subdivisions of the order Primates?
6. Which major groups of primates are included within the anthropoids?
7. What is a dental formula? What is the dental formula of all the Old World anthropoids?
8. What are quadrupedalism, vertical clinging and leaping, and brachiation? Name at least one primate species that is characterized by each of these.
9. What are the major differences between prosimians and anthropoids?
10. What are at least three anatomical differences between monkeys and apes?
11. Name the two major categories (subfamilies) of Old World monkeys. In general, what is the geographical distribution of each?
12. Explain how a taxonomic classification scheme reflects biological relationships.
13. Where are lemurs and lorises found today?
14. In general, which primates have prehensile tails?
15. What are the two family divisions of New World monkeys? Name at least one species for each.
16. In which taxonomic family are the great apes placed?
17. Define estrus.
18. Describe the type of social organization seen in chimpanzees (*Pan troglodytes*) and gorillas.
19. How do bonobos (*Pan paniscus*) differ from "common" chimpanzees (*Pan troglodytes*)?

SUGGESTED FURTHER READINGS

Fleagle, John. 1999. *Primate Adaptation and Evolution.* New York: Academic Press.

Mittermeier, Russell A., Ian Tattersall, William R. Konstant, David M. Meyers, and Roderick B. Mast. 1994. *Lemurs of Madagascar.* Washington, DC: Conservation International.

Napier, J. R., and P. H. Napier. 1985. *The Natural History of the Primates.* Cambridge, MA: MIT Press.

Sussman, Robert W. 1991. "Primate Origins and the Evolution of the Angiosperms." *American Journal of Primatology* 23: 209–223.

MULTIMEDIA RESOURCES

Wadsworth Anthropology Resource Center

http://anthropology.wadsworth.com

Visit Anthropology Online to obtain current updates in the field, surfing tips, career information, and more. In addition, enrich your study efforts with text-specific study aids arranged by chapter.

InfoTrac College Edition

http://www.infotrac-college.com/wadsworth

1. Search InfoTrac College Edition for a nonhuman primate species. You will probably find more references if you search for *chimpanzee, gorilla, orangutan,* or *baboon,* but you need not limit your search to these. Does the article you found contain much of the information presented in Chapter 5? If so, list the topics the two share. Also list those topics not included in the chapter.

2. You may also use InfoTrac College Edition to search for articles concerning endangered primates or primate conservation. Read one of the articles and write a summary of it. What information did the article present that you were previously unaware of?

Internet Exercises

1. Visit The Primate Gallery (**http://www.selu.com/~bio/PrimateGallery/main .html**) and go to the section "Primate of the Week." After reading this description and looking at the pictures, make a list of the primate characteristics and adaptations this species displays. Are there any typical primate features it does not exhibit? Next, identify this species' place in the taxonomic classification of primates. To which suborder, infraorder, superfamily, and family does it belong?

2. Because many primate species are endangered, conservation is a major topic. To learn more about conservation, visit Primate Info Net (**www.primate.wisc .edu/pin**). Click on "Resources in Primatology," then go to "Conservation," and choose one of the conservation links. Read the link and write a short summary. What species and its habitat is discussed at the link? What can we do, or what can you do, to improve the chances of survival for this species?

PHOTO ESSAY

Primate Studies: Free-Ranging and Captive Research

The study of primate behavior, as a primary component of *primatology* in the United States, has been largely the domain of physical anthropologists. Indeed, primatology is one of the major subdisciplines of physical anthropology.

While anthropologists occasionally have studied primate behavior in *captive* situations, their primary focus has been the collection of behavioral data in natural habitats. Specialized studies in a laboratory setting (such as the language studies discussed in Chapter 6) or in zoo environments are usually undertaken by psychologists. Increasingly, in the last few years, interdisciplinary research has been conducted in which methodologies developed in free-ranging contexts are applied to studies of captive animals. This type of research holds the promise of comparing behaviors seen in the wild with those observed in captivity in order to draw more general conclusions.

One such study, the ChimpanZoo project, was initiated by Jane Goodall and the Jane Goodall Institute in 1984. One of the initial goals of

FIGURE 1

Dr. Jane Goodall records a chimpanzee interaction at Gombe National Park, Tanzania.

FIGURE 2

Yahaya Alamasi, a member of the senior field staff at Gombe National Park. Dr. Goodall and other primatologists rely heavily on trained observers from neighboring villages and towns. This practice not only promotes good relations with neighboring communities but also increases interest and awareness of wildlife in African localities.

Primate Studies: Free-Ranging and Captive Research (continued)

ChimpanZoo was to establish a collaborative effort between zoo personnel and university faculty and students aimed at providing much-needed information regarding the behavior, and psychological and emotional needs of captive chimpanzees.

Ethologist Frans B. M. De Waal, of Emory University, has conducted another series of research projects involving zoo primates. Since the 1970s, Dr. De Waal has studied captive groups of chimpanzees, bonobos, and several monkey species in European and American zoos. This research has resulted in the publication of numerous books and journal articles that have contributed greatly to current understanding of complex social behaviors in these species.

FIGURE 3

The late Dian Fossey with habituated mountain gorillas.

FIGURE 4

ChimpanZoo student observer in discussion with a primate supervisor at the San Francisco Zoo.

There are numerous ways to study nonhuman animals. One method is to observe a group and describe (either by taking notes or speaking into a tape recorder) as completely as possible everything that occurs. Another technique is to "follow" one "focal" animal, describing everything it does. Still another frequently used method involves taking observations of a focal animal at precise intervals, usually on the minute. This last procedure is attractive, for it allows the data to be quantified, facilitating statistical analysis. When following this procedure, observers follow a focal animal, and using a series of behavior codes, they record whatever the animal does at precisely timed intervals.

To do this type of research, observers must know the animal well. Such familiarity facilitates interpreting sometimes difficult-to-assess behaviors. Moreover, this approach requires the development of an *ethogram* (a detailed list and description of behaviors). Many animal researchers devise a list of codes

FIGURE 5

Oakland Zoo docent records behavioral data using a specially designed software package.

FIGURE 6

Example of a traditional, nonenriched zoo habitat. Although this mangabey has access to indoor and outdoor enclosures, his environment is sterile. Moreover, keeping such highly social animals in isolation leads to boredom, depression, and often serious behavioral disorders.

Primate Studies: Free-Ranging and Captive Research (continued)

to refer to specific behaviors. These codes can then be written or keyed directly into a computer.

Because of increased awareness of the needs of nonhuman animals, including primates, habitat enrichment has become the goal of most zoos in recent years. Creating more attractive and interesting exhibits encourages public interest. Even more important, however, has been the changing role of zoos in the last 20 years. In the past, zoo animals were kept in bare cages designed for easy viewing by the public and easy cleaning for keepers. Today, zoos are increasingly seen as repositories for many endangered species, whose only hope for survival—at least in the short term—is captive breeding programs. As zoos become part of species survival plans, it is incumbent upon them to provide naturalistic habitats in which animals will breed. This approach not only has provided the viewing public with more interesting exhibits, but also has immeasurably improved the lives of captive animals.

FIGURE 7

An enriched indoor habitat for silver leaf-eating monkeys at the Bronx Zoo's Asian Jungle World exhibit in New York.

Habitats can be further enriched by applying knowledge of free-ranging behaviors to captive situations. Most especially, the animals can be kept engaged and stimulated by providing challenges in food searching and object manipulation (the latter is particularly important in chimpanzees).

Just as habitat enrichment is vitally important to captive primates, habitat protection has become critical for many free-ranging species. Consequently, in the last two decades, primatologists have increasingly directed their attention to understanding the complex ecological settings in which primates live.

FIGURE 8

A chimpanzee using a tool for removing termites, shown here at Gombe National Park.

FIGURE 9

A captive chimpanzee using the same termiting technique to obtain seeds and raisins from an artificial mound.

Primate Studies: Free-Ranging and Captive Research (continued)

One example of this relatively new emphasis is the Mountain Gorilla Project, a joint collaboration of Dieter Steklis (Dian Fossey Gorilla Fund and Rutgers University) and Scott Madry (Center for Remote Sensing and Spatial Analysis, Rutgers University) aimed at producing a digitized data base of gorilla habitats in Rwanda. This project uses imaging radar from the space shuttle *Endeavor* to generate images of gorilla habitat even in cloudy and misty conditions. In addition to space shuttle technology, Rwandan trackers use global positioning systems (GPS), which receive data from stationary satellites, to establish the precise position of, for example, gorilla groups or various types of vegetation. Ultimately, the data from these and other sources will be combined to reveal patterns of natural vegetation, gorilla ranging habits, and human use of gorilla habitat. It is hoped that this information will better enable scientists to assist local human populations in land use decisions while ensuring protection for mountain gorilla habitat.

FIGURE 10

A three-dimensional digital image of gorilla habitat in the Virunga mountains of central Africa.

New technologies have also been applied to genetic studies of primates. Phillip Morin, a biologist at the University of California, San Diego, and his colleagues compared DNA sequences at several genetic loci in free-ranging chimpanzees. To avoid capture of animals (for collection of blood or other tissues), researchers obtained DNA samples from chimpanzee hair collected from sleeping nests. So far, the results of this study have established paternity for some Gombe chimpanzees and have lent support to certain theories of chimpanzee behavior. Additionally, this type of DNA analysis may prove useful in determining the effects of genetic isolation in populations of chimpanzees and other species as habitat destruction continues to inhibit the migration of individuals from one group to another.

FIGURE 11

Biologist Phillip Morin conducting analysis of chimpanzee DNA in his laboratory.

FIGURE 12

Physical anthropologist Jim Moore collecting hair samples from a chimpanzee sleeping nest.

119

CHAPTER
6

CONTENTS

Primate Behavior

Introduction

In this chapter, discussion shifts to various aspects of nonhuman primate behavior and cognitive abilities. These are extremely important topics for anthropologists. One method of gaining a fuller understanding of human and early hominid behavior is to become more familiar with the behavior and intellectual capacities of living nonhuman primates. For that reason, as you read this chapter, you should be thinking of ways to apply some of the behavioral principles presented here to the early ancestors of *Homo sapiens.*

Because primates live in highly complex natural and social environments, they have evolved increasingly complex neurological structures. That is to say, there is a *feedback mechanism* between the biosocial environment and neurological complexity, so that over time, complex lifestyles have selected for increased neurological complexity, or intelligence. Intelligence, in turn, permits increasingly complex lifestyles. We know that all primates, including many prosimians, are extremely clever when compared to most other mammals. In this chapter, we will examine evidence that illustrates just how complex and intelligent are the other members of the order to which we ourselves belong.

Primate behavior is discussed in Virtual Lab 6.

Virtual Lab 6, section I, presents a discussion of field methods and the scientific method.

The Importance of Primate Studies

Modern African apes and humans last shared a common ancestor between 5 and 8 million years ago. Although ape behavior has undoubtedly changed since that time, the behavior of hominids, who developed culture as an adaptive strategy, has changed much more dramatically. Accordingly, if we want to know what hominid behavior was like before culture became a factor, and if we wish to speculate as to which behaviors may have led to culture, we must look for clues in nonhuman primate behavior.

One approach is to correlate specific aspects of **social structure** with elements of primate habitats, since all living organisms must adapt to their environment. Because there are limits to the ways in which adaptation can occur, it follows that all organisms are to some degree governed by the same principles. By elucidating the various environmental pressures involved and understanding how they have influenced nonhuman primate behavior, we can better comprehend those factors that led to human emergence.

In addition to studying nonhuman primates to learn more about ourselves, it is just as important to learn more about them in their own right. Only within the past four decades have they been systematically studied, and we still have much to learn about them. Indeed, many species, especially arboreal monkeys, have scarcely been studied at all. The beginning of the twenty-first century is an especially critical time for much of life on our planet. If we hope to save even some of the many threatened and endangered species from extinction, we must understand their needs (space, diet, group organization, etc.) in the wild. Without this knowledge, we can neither preserve sufficient natural habitat for their survival in the wild nor re-create it in captivity.

Social structure
The composition, size, and sex ratio of a group of animals. Social structures, in part, are the result of natural selection in specific habitats, and they function to guide individual interactions and social relationships.

Primate Socioecology

Scientists who study behavior in free-ranging primates do so within an **ecological** framework, focusing on the relationship between aspects of social behavior and the natural environment—an approach called **socioecology**. One underlying assumption of this approach is that the various components of ecological systems have evolved together. Therefore, to understand the functioning of one particular component, such as the social organization of a given species, it is necessary to determine the species' relationships with numerous environmental factors, including:

1. Quantity and quality of different kinds of foods (caloric value, digestive energy required, net value to the animal)
2. Distribution of food resources (e.g., dense, scattered, clumps, or seasonal availability)
3. Body size
4. Distribution of water
5. Distribution and types of predators
6. Distribution of sleeping sites
7. Activity patterns (nocturnal, diurnal)
8. Relationships with other (nonpredator) species, both primate and nonprimate
9. Impact of human activities

Unfortunately, the relationships among ecological variables, social organization, and behavior have not yet been thoroughly worked out, but numerous factors certainly suggest a relationship between, for example, group size and the problems of obtaining food and avoiding predators. Indeed, average group size and group composition can be viewed as adaptive responses to these problems (Pulliam and Caraco, 1984).

For example, groups composed of several adult males and females (multimale, multifemale groups) have traditionally been viewed as advantageous in areas where predation pressure is high, particularly on open savannas, where there are a number of large predators (e.g., hyenas, leopards, and lions). Where members of prey species occur in larger groups, there is increased likelihood of early predator detection and thus predator avoidance.

Savanna baboons (Fig. 6–1) have long been used as an example of these principles. They are found in semiarid grassland and broken woodland habitats throughout sub-Saharan Africa. To avoid nocturnal predators, savanna baboons sleep in trees; however, they spend much of the day on the ground foraging for food. In the presence of nonhuman predators, baboons flee to the safety of trees. (Frequently, they abandon trees at the approach of humans, for they have learned that humans shoot them from the ground.) However, if they are at some distance from safety, or if a predator is nearby, adult males may join forces to chase an intruder away. The effectiveness of male baboons in this regard should not be underestimated, for baboons have been known to kill domestic dogs and even to attack leopards and lions (Altmann and Altmann, 1970).

As you have already learned, not all primates are found in large groups. Solitary foraging is typical of many species, and it is probably related to diet and distribution of resources. In the case of the slow-moving, insectivorous loris, for example, solitary feeding reduces competition, which allows for less distance traveled (and thus less expenditure of energy) in the search for prey. Moreover, because

Ecological
Pertaining to the relationship between organisms and all aspects of their environment (temperature, predators, other animals, vegetation, availability of food and water, types of food, etc.)

Socioecology
The study of animals and their habitats; specifically, attempts to find patterns of relationship between the environment and social behavior.

 These ecological factors are discussed in Lab 5, section I.

 Virtual Lab 6 provides an in-depth investigation of the behaviors of savanna baboons.

FIGURE 6–1

Group of savanna baboons, which includes adult males and females as well as youngsters of various ages. Note adult male carrying infant in foreground.

insects usually do not occur in dense patches, they are more efficiently exploited by widely dispersed individuals rather than by groups. Solitary foraging is also related to predator avoidance, and it is particularly effective in species that rely chiefly on concealment rather than escape. Again, the loris serves as a good example.

Foraging alone or with offspring is also seen in females of some diurnal anthropoid species (e.g., orangutans, chimpanzees). These females, being relatively large-bodied, have little to fear from predators, and by feeding alone or with only one or two youngsters, they maximize their access to food, free from competition with others.

Although the exact relationships between group size and structure and the environment are not well known at this time, it is clear that certain environmental factors, such as resource availability and predation, exert strong influence. The various solutions that primate species have developed to deal with the problems of survival differ in complicated ways. Closely related species living in proximity to one another and exploiting many of the same resources can have very different types of social structure. It is only through continued research that primatologists will be able to sort out the intricate relationships between society and the natural environment.

The Evolution of Behavior

In the last two decades, the emphasis on evolutionary factors to explain various aspects of behavior has been applied to a wide variety of animals. Indeed, this concept has become a fundamental **paradigm** in animal behavior studies. For interpretations of primate behavior, an evolutionary perspective holds a central position as a theoretical framework for most contemporary researchers, and it serves as a model within which to frame discussion and interpretations of behavior.

Paradigm
A cognitive construct or framework within which we explain phenomena. Paradigms shape our world view. They can change as a result of technological and intellectual innovation.

Briefly, the cornerstone of this perspective is that *behavior has evolved through the operation of natural selection.* That is, natural selection acts on behavior in much the same way that it acts on physical characteristics. Therefore, individuals whose genotypes influence behaviors that lead to higher reproductive success will be more fit and should pass on their genes at a faster rate than others.

Superficially, such an explanation implies the existence of genes that code for specific behaviors (e.g., a gene for aggression, another for cooperation). Such conclusions result, in part, from misinterpretation, but they have caused much controversy when applied to humans. The concern partly arises out of fear that if specific human behaviors could be explained in terms of genes, and if populations varied with regard to the frequency of these genes, then such evolutionarily based theories could be used by some people to support racist and other discriminatory views.

Much of the behavior of insects and other invertebrates, as well as that of lower vertebrates, is largely under genetic control. In other words, most behavioral patterns in these forms are *innate*, not learned. However, in many vertebrates, particularly birds and mammals, the proportion of behavior that is due to *learning* is substantially increased. Accordingly, the proportion that is under genetic influence is reduced. This phenomenon is especially true of primates; and in humans, who are so much a product of culture, most behavior results from learning. Nevertheless, it is also clear that in higher organisms, some behaviors are partly influenced by certain gene products, (e.g., hormones). For example, numerous studies have shown that increased levels of testosterone increase aggressive behavior in many nonhuman species.

Behavior is a highly complex trait and must be seen not only as being influenced by specific gene products, but also as the product of *interactions between genetic and environmental factors* that are not yet fully elucidated. Indeed, the ability to learn is ultimately based in the genome inherited by individuals of any species. Between species, there is considerable variation in the limits and potentials for learning and behavioral **plasticity.** But for any given species, those limits and potentials are ultimately influenced by genetic factors that have been shaped by the evolutionary history of that species. The evolutionary history of any species is shaped by the ecological setting, not only of that species, but of ancestral species as well. Thus, behaviors are viewed as adaptations to environmental circumstances, and it is important to note that behavioral flexibility is also a form of adaptation.

A dispute arises when trying to establish the actual mechanics of behavioral evolution in complex social animals such as primates. There is a need to determine which primate behaviors have a genetic basis and how these behaviors influence reproductive success. To accomplish these goals, we must learn considerably more about genotype-phenotype interactions in complex traits, and such an understanding is probably years away. We also need accurate data on reproductive success in primate groups, and so far, such data are almost completely lacking. Thus, rather than offering precise explanations, an evolutionary approach provides a set of hypotheses for explaining primate behavior, and it remains for these hypotheses to be tested.

Obtaining conclusive data for primates and other mammals is not easy. A good starting point, however, is to frame hypotheses concerning behavioral evolution on the basis of the evidence that does exist. A good example of such a per-

Plasticity
The capacity to change; in a physiological context, the ability of systems or organisms to make alterations in order to respond to differing conditions.

spective is Sarah Blaffer Hrdy's (1977) explanation of infanticide among Hanuman langurs of India (Fig. 6–2). Hanuman langurs typically live in social groups composed of one adult male, several females, and their offspring. Other males without mates associate in "bachelor" groups. These peripheral males occasionally attack and defeat a reproductive male and drive him from his group. Sometimes, following such takeovers, the group's infants (fathered by the previous male) are attacked and killed by the new male.

It would certainly seem that such behavior is counterproductive, especially from the species' perspective. However, individuals act to maximize their *own* reproductive success, no matter what the effect may be on the population or ultimately the species. Ostensibly, that is exactly what the male langur is doing, albeit unknowingly. While a female is lactating, she does not come into estrus, and therefore she is not sexually available. But when an infant dies, its mother ceases to lactate, and within two or three months, she resumes cycling and becomes sexually receptive. Therefore, by killing the infants, the male avoids a two- to three-year wait until they are weaned. This could be especially advantageous to him, as chances are good that his tenure in the group will not even last two or three years. Moreover, he does not expend energy and put himself at risk defending infants who do not carry his genes.

Hanuman langurs are not the only primates that engage in infanticide. Indeed, infanticide has been observed (or surmised) in many primate species, such as redtail monkeys, red colobus, blue monkeys, savanna baboons, howlers, orangutans, gorillas, chimpanzees (Struhsaker and Leyland, 1987), and humans. It also occurs in numerous nonprimate species, including rodents and cats. In the majority of nonhuman primate examples, infanticide occurs in conjunction with the transfer of a new male into a group or, as in chimpanzees, an encounter with an unfamiliar female and infant.

Numerous objections to this explanation of infanticide have been raised. Alternative explanations have included competition for resources (Rudran, 1973) and aberrant behaviors related to human-induced overcrowding (Curtin and Dohlinow, 1978); and inadvertent killing during aggressive episodes, where it was not clear that the infant was actually the target animal (Bartlett et al., 1993). Sussman and colleagues (1995), as well as others, have questioned the actual prevalence of the practice, arguing that although it does occur, it is not particularly common. These authors have also postulated that if indeed male fitness is increased through the practice, such increases are negligible. Yet others (Struhsaker and Leyland, 1987; Hrdy, 1995) maintain that the incidence and patterning of infanticide by males are not only significant, but consistent with the assumptions established by theories of behavioral evolution.

Evolutionary interpretations have had a dramatic impact on the direction of behavioral studies of nonhuman animals, including primates. But even though most primatologists today use theoretical models derived from an evolutionary perspective, the approach has not gone completely uncriticized. For example, Richard and Schulman (1982, pp. 243–244) named the following limitations:

1. The lack of long-term data on the demography and social behavior of large groups of individually known animals
2. The lack of long-term, precise data on the distribution of resources in time and space

FIGURE 6–2
Hanuman langurs.

A discussion of reproductive success is presented in Virtual Lab 2, section I.

Virtual Lab 6 has many examples of the interactions between males and females and infants.

3. The nearly complete absence of information on genetic relatedness through the male line

4. The difficulty in assigning reproductive and other costs and benefits to particular behaviors (e.g., infanticide)

5. Our almost total ignorance of the genetics of primate social behavior

In spite of these obstacles, an evolutionary focus offers the best opportunity to understand how animal behavior has been shaped by natural selection. Thus, primatologists worldwide are now employing this perspective to interpret primate (including human) behavior.

Primate Social Behavior

Because primates solve their major adaptive problems in a social context, we might expect them to participate in a number of activities to reinforce the integrity of the group. The better known of these activities are described in the sections that follow.

Dominance

Many primate societies are organized into **dominance hierarchies.** Dominance hierarchies impose a certain degree of order within groups by establishing parameters of individual behavior. Although aggression is frequently a means of increasing one's status, dominance usually serves to reduce the amount of actual physical violence. Not only are lower-ranking animals unlikely to attack or even threaten a higher-ranking one, but dominant animals are also frequently able to exert control simply by making a threatening gesture.

Individual rank or status may be measured by access to resources, including food items and mating partners. Dominant individuals are given priority by others, and they usually do not give way in confrontations.

Many (but not all) primatologists postulate that the primary benefit of dominance is the increased reproductive success of the individual. This observation would be true if it could be demonstrated that dominant males compete more successfully for mates than do subordinate males. However, there is also good evidence that lower-ranking males of some species successfully mate; they just do so surreptitiously. Likewise, increased reproductive success can be postulated for high-ranking females, who have greater access to food than subordinate females. High-ranking females are provided with more energy for offspring production and care (Fedigan, 1983), and presumably their reproductive success is greater.

An individual's rank is not permanent and changes throughout life. It is influenced by many factors, including sex, age, level of aggression, amount of time spent in the group, intelligence, perhaps motivation, and sometimes the mother's social position (particularly true of macaques).

In species organized into groups containing a number of females associated with one or several adult males, the males are generally dominant to females. Within such groups, males and females have separate hierarchies, although very high ranking females can dominate the lowest-ranking males (particularly young males). There are exceptions to this pattern of male dominance. Among many lemur species, females are the dominant sex. Moreover, among species that form monogamous pairs (e.g., indris, gibbons), males and females are codominant.

The concept of an ethogram, or a catalog of behaviors, is discussed in Virtual Lab 6, section II. Various behaviors of savanna baboons are presented in section III.

Dominance hierarchies
Systems of social organization wherein individuals within a group are ranked relative to one another. Higher-ranking individuals have greater access to preferred food items and mating partners than lower-ranking individuals. Dominance hierarchies are sometimes referred to as "pecking orders."

All primates *learn* their position in the hierarchy. From birth, an infant is carried by its mother, and it observes how she responds to every member of the group. Just as importantly, it sees how others react to her. Dominance and subordination are indicated by gestures and behaviors, some of which are universal throughout the primate order (including humans), and this gestural repertoire is part of every youngster's learning experience.

Young primates also acquire social rank through play with age peers. As they spend more time with play groups, their social interactions widen. Competition and rough-and-tumble play allow them to learn the strengths and weaknesses of peers, and they carry this knowledge with them throughout their lives. Thus, through early contact with the mother and subsequent exposure to peers, young primates learn to negotiate their way through the complex web of social interactions that make up their daily lives.

Communication

Communication is universal among animals and includes scents and unintentional, **autonomic** responses and behaviors that convey meaning. Such attributes as body posture convey information about an animal's emotional state. For example, a crouched position indicates a certain degree of insecurity or fear, while a purposeful striding gait implies confidence. Moreover, autonomic responses to threatening or novel stimuli, such as raised body hair (most species) or enhanced body odor (gorillas), indicate excitement.

Many intentional behaviors also serve as communication. In primates, these include a wide variety of gestures, facial expressions, and vocalizations, some of which we humans share. Among many primates, a mild threat is indicated by an intense stare, and indeed, we humans find prolonged eye contact with strangers very uncomfortable. For this reason, people should avoid eye contact with captive primates. Other threat gestures are a quick yawn to expose canine teeth (baboons, macaques) (Fig. 6–3); bobbing back and forth in a crouched position (patas monkeys); and branch shaking (many monkey species). High-ranking baboons *mount* the hindquarters of subordinates to express dominance (Fig. 6–4). Mounting may also serve to defuse potentially tense situations by indicating something like, "It's okay, I accept your apology, I know you didn't intend to offend me."

There is also a variety of behaviors to indicate submission, reassurance, or amicable intentions. Submission is indicated by a crouched position (most primates) or presenting the hindquarters (baboons). Reassurance takes the form of touching, patting, and, in chimpanzees, hugging and holding hands. Grooming also serves in a number of situations to indicate submission or reassurance.

A wide variety of facial expressions indicating emotional states is seen in chimpanzees and bonobos (Fig. 6–5). These include the well-known play face (also seen in several other species), associated with play behavior, and the fear grin (seen in *all* primates) to indicate fear and submission.

Primates also use a wide array of vocalizations for communication. Some, such as the bark of a baboon that has just spotted a leopard, are unintentional startled reactions. Others, such as the chimpanzee food grunt, are heard only in specific contexts. Nevertheless, both serve the same function: They inform others, although not necessarily deliberately, of the possible presence of predators or food.

Primates (and other animals) also communicate through **displays,** which are more complicated, frequently elaborate combinations of behaviors. For example,

Communication
Any act that conveys information, in the form of a message, to another individual. Frequently, the result of communication is a change in the behavior of the recipient. Communication may not be deliberate but may be the result of involuntary processes or a secondary consequence of an intentional action.

Autonomic
Pertaining to physiological responses not under voluntary control. An example in chimpanzees would be the erection of body hair during excitement. An example in humans is blushing. Both convey information regarding emotional states, but neither is a deliberate behavior, and communication is not intended.

FIGURE 6–3

Adolescent male savanna baboon threatens photographer with a characteristic "yawn" that shows the canine teeth. Note also that the eyes are closed briefly to expose light, cream-colored eyelids. This has been termed the "eyelid flash."

Displays
Sequences of repetitious behaviors that serve to communicate emotional states. Nonhuman primate displays are most frequently associated with reproductive or agonistic behavior.

FIGURE 6–4

One young male savanna baboon mounts another as an expression of dominance.

FIGURE 6–5

Chimpanzee facial expressions. (Adapted with permission of the publishers from *The Chimpanzees of Gombe* by Jane Goodall, Cambridge, Mass.: Harvard University Press, © 1986 by the President and Fellows of Harvard College.)

the exaggerated courtship dances of many male birds, often enhanced by colorful plumage, are displays. Common gorilla displays are chest slapping and the tearing of vegetation to indicate threat. Likewise, an angry chimpanzee, with hair bristling, may charge an opponent while screaming, waving its arms, and tearing vegetation.

All nonhuman animals employ various vocalizations, body postures, and, to some degree, facial expressions that transmit information. However, the array of communicative devices is much richer among nonhuman primates, even though they do not use language in the manner of humans. Communication is important, for it truly is what makes social living possible. Through submissive gestures, aggression is reduced and physical violence is less likely. Likewise, friendly intentions and relationships are reinforced through physical contact and grooming. Indeed, it is in the familiar methods of nonverbal communication that we humans can see ourselves in other primate species most clearly.

Relaxed   Relaxed with dropped lip   Horizontal pout face (distress)   Fear grin (fear/excitement)   Full play face

Aggression

Within primate societies, there is an interplay between **affiliative** behaviors that promote group cohesion and aggressive behaviors that can lead to group disruption. Conflict within a group frequently develops out of competition for resources, including mating partners and food items. Instead of actual attacks or fighting, most intragroup aggression occurs in the form of various signals and displays, frequently within the context of a dominance hierarchy. Likewise, the majority of such situations are resolved through various submissive and appeasement behaviors.

But conflict is not always resolved peacefully, and it can have serious consequences. For example, high-ranking female macaques frequently intimidate, harass, and even attack lower-ranking females, particularly to restrict their access to food. High-ranking females consistently chase subordinates away from food and have even been observed to take food from their mouths; these behaviors can result in weight loss and poorer nutrition in low-ranking females.

Competition between males for mates frequently results in injury and occasionally in death. In species that have a distinct breeding season (e.g., squirrel monkeys), conflict between males is most common during that time. Male squirrel monkeys form coalitions to compete with other males, and when outright fighting occurs, injuries can be severe. In species not restricted to a mating season, competition between males can be an ongoing process.

Aggressive encounters occur *between* groups as well as within groups. Between groups, aggression occurs in the defense of **territories.** Primate groups are associated with a **home range,** where they remain permanently. Within this home range is a portion called the **core area,** which contains the highest concentration of predictable resources and where the group is most frequently found. Although portions of the home range may overlap with the home range of one or more other groups, core areas of adjacent groups do not overlap. The core area can also be said to be a group's territory, and it is the portion of the home range that is usually defended against intrusion by others. However, in some species, such as chimpanzees, other areas of the home range may also be defended. Whatever area is defended, this portion is termed the *territory.*

Beginning in 1974, Jane Goodall and her colleagues witnessed at least five unprovoked and extremely brutal attacks by groups of chimpanzees (usually, but not always, males) on lone individuals. To explain these attacks, it is necessary to point out that by 1973, the original Gombe community had divided into two distinct groups. The larger group was located in the north of the original home range. The smaller offshoot group established itself in the southern portion, effectively denying the others access to part of their former territory.

By 1977, all seven males and one female of the splinter group were either known or suspected to have been killed. All observed incidents involved several animals who attacked lone individuals. Although it is not possible to know exactly what motivated the attackers, it was clear that they intended to incapacitate their victims (Goodall, 1986).

Goodall has suggested that these attacks strongly imply that although chimpanzees do not possess language and do not wage war as we know it, they do exhibit behaviors that could be considered precursors to war:

> The chimpanzee, as a result of a unique combination of strong affiliative bonds
> between adult males on the one hand and an unusually hostile and violently

Affiliative
Pertaining to amicable associations between individuals. Affiliative behaviors, such as grooming, reinforce social bonds and promote group cohesion.

Territories
Areas that will be aggressively protected against intrusion, particularly by other members of the same species.

Home range
The entire area exploited by an animal or group of animals.

Core area
The portion of a home range containing the highest concentration of resources.

aggressive attitude toward nongroup individuals on the other, has clearly reached a stage where he stands at the very threshold of human achievement in destruction, cruelty, and planned intergroup conflict. If ever he develops the power of language—and, as we have seen, he stands close to that threshold, too—might he not push open the door and wage war with the best of us? (Goodall, 1986, p. 534)

A situation similar to that at Gombe has been reported for a group of chimpanzees in the Mahale Mountains south of Gombe. Over a 17-year period, all the males of a small community disappeared. Although no attacks were actually observed, there was circumstantial evidence that most of these males met the same fate as the Gombe attack victims (Nishida et al., 1985; Nishida et al., 1990).

In addition to territoriality, Manson and Wrangham (1991) have proposed a number of other factors that may contribute to male chimpanzee aggression, including acquisition of females from other groups. While the precise motivation of chimpanzee intergroup violence may never be fully elucidated, it is clear that a number of interrelated factors are involved. Moreover, although chimpanzees do not meet all the criteria developed for true territorial behavior (Goodall, 1986), it appears that various aspects of resource acquisition and protection are involved.

Affiliative Behaviors

Even though conflict can be destructive, a certain amount of aggression is useful in maintaining order within groups and protecting either individual or group resources. Fortunately, to minimize actual violence and to defuse potentially dangerous situations, there is an array of affiliative, or friendly, behaviors that serve to reinforce bonds between individuals and enhance group stability.

Common affiliative behaviors include reconciliation, consolation, and simple amicable interactions between friends and relatives. Most such behaviors involve various forms of physical contact, such as touching, hand holding, hugging, and, among chimpanzees, kissing (Fig. 6–6). In fact, physical contact is one of the most important factors in primate development and is crucial in promoting peaceful relationships in many primate social groups.

Grooming is one of the most important affiliative behaviors in many primate species. Although grooming occurs in other animal species, social grooming is mostly a primate activity, and it plays an important role in day-to-day life (Fig. 6–7). Because grooming involves using the fingers to pick through the fur of another individual (or one's own) to remove insects, dirt, and other materials, it serves hygienic functions. But it is also an immensely pleasurable activity that individuals of some species (especially chimpanzees) engage in for considerable periods of time.

Grooming occurs in a variety of contexts. Mothers groom infants. Males groom sexually receptive females. Subordinate animals groom dominant ones, sometimes to gain favor. Friends groom friends. In general, grooming is comforting. It restores peaceful relationships between animals who have quarreled and provides reassurance during tense situations. In short, grooming reinforces social bonds and consequently helps to maintain and strengthen the structure of the group. For this reason, it has been called "the social cement of primates from lemur to chimpanzee" (Jolly, 1985, p. 207).

Conflict resolution through reconciliation is another important aspect of primate social behavior. Following a conflict, chimpanzee opponents frequently

FIGURE 6–6
Adolescent savanna baboons holding hands.

Grooming
Picking through fur to remove dirt, parasites, and other materials that may be present. Social grooming is common among primates and reinforces social relationships.

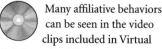
Many affiliative behaviors can be seen in the video clips included in Virtual Lab 6, section IV.

(a)

(b)

(c)

(d)

FIGURE 6–7

Grooming primates. (a) Patas monkeys; female grooming male. (b) Longtail macaques. (c) Savanna baboons. (d) Chimpanzees.

move, within minutes, to reconcile (de Waal, 1982). Reconciliation takes many forms, including hugging, kissing, and grooming. Even uninvolved individuals may take part, either grooming one or both participants or forming their own grooming parties. In addition, bonobos are unique in their use of sex to promote group cohesion, restore peace after conflicts, and relieve tension within the group (de Waal, 1987, 1989).

Relationships are crucial to nonhuman primates, and the bonds between individuals can last a lifetime. These relationships serve a variety of functions. Individuals of many species form alliances in which one supports another against a third. Alliances, or coalitions, as they are also called, can be used to enhance the status of members. For example, at Gombe, the male chimpanzee Figan achieved alpha status because of support from his brother (Goodall, 1986, p. 424). In fact, chimpanzees so heavily rely on coalitions and are so skillful politically that an entire book, appropriately titled *Chimpanzee Politics* (de Waal, 1982), is devoted to the topic.

There are other behaviors that also illustrate the importance of social relationships, some of which can perhaps be described as examples of caregiving or compassion. When discussing nonhuman animal (or indeed, human) behavior, it is impossible to know with certainty what an individual's motivation is. Thus, the use of the term *compassion* is risky, because in humans, compassion is motivated by empathy for another. Whether nonhuman primates can empathize with the suffering or misfortune of another is not really known, but certainly there are numerous examples, mostly from chimpanzee studies, of caregiving actions that resemble compassionate behavior in humans. Examples include protection of others during attacks, helping younger siblings, and staying near ill or dying relatives or friends.

Altruism

Any behavior or act that benefits another individual but poses some potential risk or cost to oneself.

Altruism, behavior that benefits another while involving some risk or sacrifice to the performer, is common in many primate species, and altruistic acts sometimes contain elements of compassion and cooperation. The most fundamental of altruistic behaviors, the protection of dependent offspring, is ubiquitous among mammals and birds, and in the majority of species, altruistic acts are confined to this context. However, among primates, recipients of altruistic acts may include individuals who are not offspring and who may not even be closely related to the performer. Chimpanzees routinely come to the aid of relatives and friends; female langurs join forces to protect infants from males; and male baboons cooperate to chase predators. In fact, the primate literature abounds with examples of altruistic acts, whereby individuals place themselves at some risk to protect others from attacks by conspecifics or predators.

Adoption of orphans is a form of altruism that has been reported for macaques and baboons and is common in chimpanzees. When chimpanzee youngsters are orphaned, they are routinely adopted, usually by older siblings who are solicitous and highly protective. Adoption is crucial to the survival of orphans, who would certainly not survive on their own. In fact, it is extremely rare for a chimpanzee orphan less than three years of age to survive even if it is adopted.

Reproduction and Reproductive Strategies

Patterns of Reproduction

A behavioral interaction between a female (who has recently mated) and a male can be seen in a video clip at the end of Virtual Lab 6, section II.

In most primate species, sexual behavior is tied to the female's reproductive cycle, with females sexually receptive to males only when they are in estrus. Estrus is characterized by behavioral changes that indicate a female is receptive. In Old World monkeys and apes that live in multimale groups, estrus is also accompanied by swelling and changes in color of the skin around the genital area. These changes serve as visual cues of a female's readiness to mate (Fig. 6–8).

Permanent bonding between males and females is not common among nonhuman primates. However, male and female savanna baboons sometimes form mating *consortships*. These temporary relationships last while the female is in estrus, and the two spend most of the time together, mating frequently. Moreover, lower-ranking baboon males often form "friendships" (Smuts, 1985) with females and occasionally may mate with them, although they may be driven away by high-ranking males when the female is most receptive.

FIGURE 6–8

Estrous swelling of genital tissues in a female chimpanzee.

Mating consortships are sometimes seen in chimpanzees and are particularly common among bonobos. In fact, a male and female bonobo may spend several weeks primarily in each other's company. During this time, they mate often, even when the female is not in estrus. These relationships of longer duration are not typical of chimpanzee (*Pan troglodytes*) males and females.

Such a male-female bond may result in increased reproductive success for both sexes. For the male, there is the increased likelihood that he will be the father of any infant the female conceives. At the same time, the female potentially gains protection from predators or others of her group and perhaps assistance in caring for offspring she may already have.

Reproductive Strategies

Reproductive strategies, and especially how they differ between the sexes, have been a primary focus of primate research. The goal of such strategies is to produce and successfully rear to adulthood as many offspring as possible.

Primates are among the most **K-selected** of mammal species. By this we mean that individuals produce only a few young, in whom they invest a tremendous amount of parental care. Contrast this pattern with **r-selected** species, where individuals produce large numbers of offspring but invest little or no energy in parental care. Good examples of r-selected species include insects, most fish, and, among mammals, mice and rabbits.

When we consider the degree of care required by young, growing primate offspring, it is clear that enormous investment by at least one parent is necessary, and it is usually the mother who carries most of the burden both before and after birth. Primates are totally helpless at birth. They develop slowly and are thus exposed to

Reproductive strategies
The complex of behavioral patterns that contributes to individual reproductive success. The behaviors need not be deliberate, and they often vary considerably between males and females.

K-selected
Pertaining to an adaptive strategy whereby individuals produce relatively few offspring, in whom they invest increased parental care. Although only a few infants are born, chances of survival are increased for each individual because of parental investments in time and energy. Examples of nonprimate K-selected species are birds and canids (e.g., wolves, coyotes, and dogs).

r-selected
Pertaining to an adaptive strategy that emphasizes relatively large numbers of offspring and reduced parental care (compared to K-selected species). (*K-selection* and *r-selection* are relative terms; e.g., mice are r-selected compared to primates but K-selected compared to many fish species.)

expanded learning opportunities within a *social* environment. This trend has been elaborated most dramatically in great apes and humans, and especially in the latter. Thus, what we see in ourselves and our close primate kin (and presumably in our more recent ancestors as well) is a strategy wherein a few "high-quality," slowly maturing offspring are produced through extraordinary investment by at least one parent, usually the mother.

Finding food and mates, avoiding predators, and caring for and protecting dependent young represent difficult challenges for nonhuman primates. Moreover, in most species, males and females employ different strategies to meet these challenges.

Female primates spend almost all their adult lives either pregnant, lactating, and/or caring for offspring, and the resulting metabolic demands are enormous. A pregnant or lactating female, although perhaps only half the size of her male counterpart, may require about the same number of calories per day. Even if these demands are met, her physical resources may be drained. For example, analysis of chimpanzee skeletons from Gombe National Park, in Tanzania, shows significant loss of bone and bone mineral in older females (Sumner et al., 1989).

Given these physiological costs, a female's best strategy is to maximize the amount of resources available to her and her offspring. Indeed, females of many primate species (gibbons, marmosets, and macaques, to name a few) are viciously competitive with other females and aggressively protect resources and territories. In other species, as we have seen, females distance themselves from others to avoid competition.

Males, however, face a separate set of challenges. Having little investment in the rearing of offspring (except in the case of monogamous pairs), it is to the male's advantage to secure as many mates and produce as many offspring as possible. By so doing, he is effectively increasing his genetic contribution to the next generation relative to other males.

One outcome of different mating strategies is **sexual selection,** a phenomenon first described by Charles Darwin. Sexual selection is a type of natural selection that operates on only one sex, usually males, whereby the selective agent is male competition for mates and, in some species, mate choice in females. The long-term effect of sexual selection is to increase the frequency of those traits that lead to greater success in acquiring mates.

In the animal kingdom there are numerous male attributes that result from sexual selection. In some bird species, for example, males are much more brightly colored than females. For various reasons, female birds find those males with more vividly colored plumage more attractive as mates; thus, selection has increased the frequency of alleles that influence brighter coloration in males.

Sexual selection in primates is most important in species characterized by multimale social groups, but it is a factor in any species where mating is polygynous and male competition for females is prominent. In these species, sexual selection produces dimorphism with regard to a number of traits, most noticeably body size. The males of many primate species are considerably larger than females (indeed, male gorillas and orangutans can be twice as large), and males also have larger canine teeth. Conversely, in species where mating is monogamous (e.g., gibbons) or where male competition is reduced, dimorphism in canine and body size is either reduced or nonexistent. For these reasons, the presence or absence of sexually dimorphic traits in a species is a reasonably good indicator of mating structure.

Sexual selection
A type of natural selection that operates on only one sex within a species. It is the result of competition for mates, and it can lead to sexual dimorphism with regard to one or more traits.

Mothers and Infants

The basic social unit among all primates is the female and her infants (Fig. 6–9). Except in those species in which monogamy or **polyandry** occurs, males do not participate greatly in the rearing of offspring. Observations both in the field and in captivity suggest that the mother-offspring core provides the social group with its stability.

The mother-infant bond, one of the most basic themes running throughout primate social relations, begins at birth. Although the exact nature of the bonding process is not fully known, there appear to be predisposing innate factors that strongly attract the female to her infant, so long as she herself has had sufficiently

Polyandry
A mating system wherein a female continuously associates with more than one male (usually two or three) with whom she mates. Among nonhuman primates, this pattern is seen only in marmosets and tamarins.

FIGURE 6–9
Primate mothers with young.
(a) Mongoose lemur. (b) Chimpanzee.
(c) Patas monkey. (d) Orangutan.
(e) Sykes monkey.

(a)

(b)

(c)

(d)

(e)

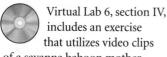

Virtual Lab 6, section IV, includes an exercise that utilizes video clips of a savanna baboon mother and infant.

FIGURE 6–10
Infant macaque clinging to cloth mother.

normal experiences with her own mother. This does not mean that primate mothers possess innate knowledge of how to care for an infant. Indeed, they do not. Monkeys and apes raised in captivity without contact with their own mothers not only do not know how to care for a newborn infant, but may also be afraid of it and attack and kill it. Even if they do not directly attack the infant, they may kill it indirectly through mishandling or improper nursing.

The crucial role of bonding between primate mothers and infants was clearly demonstrated by the Harlows (1959), who raised infant monkeys with surrogate mothers fashioned from wire or a combination of wire and cloth. Other monkeys were raised with no mothers at all. In one experiment, infants retained an attachment to their cloth-covered surrogate mother (Fig. 6–10). But those raised with no mother were incapable of forming lasting affectional ties. These deprived monkeys sat passively in their cages and stared vacantly into space. None of the motherless males ever successfully copulated, and those females who were (somewhat artificially) impregnated either paid little attention to offspring or reacted aggressively toward them (Harlow and Harlow, 1961). The point is that monkeys reared in isolation were denied opportunities to *learn* the rules of social behavior. Moreover, and just as essential, they were denied the all-important physical contact so necessary for normal primate psychological and emotional development.

The importance of a normal relationship with the mother is demonstrated by field studies as well. From birth, infant primates are able to cling to their mother's fur, and they are in more or less constant physical contact with her for several months. During this critical period, the infant develops a closeness with the mother that does not always end with weaning. This closeness is often maintained throughout life (especially among some Old World monkeys). It is reflected in grooming behavior that continues between mother and offspring even after the young reach adulthood and have infants of their own.

Nonhuman Primate Cultural Behavior

One important trait that makes primates, and especially chimpanzees and bonobos, attractive as models for behavior in early hominids may be called *cultural behavior.* Although many cultural anthropologists and others prefer to use the term *culture* to refer specifically to human activities, most biological anthropologists consider it appropriate to use the term in discussions of nonhuman primates as well (McGraw, 1992, 1998; de Waal, 1999; Whiten et al., 1999).

Undeniably, there are many aspects of culture that are uniquely human, and one must be cautious when interpreting nonhuman animal behavior. But again, since humans are products of the same evolutionary forces that have produced other species, they can be expected to exhibit some of the same *behavioral patterns* seen in other species, particularly primates. However, because of increased brain size and learning capacities, humans express many characteristics to a greater degree. We would argue that the *aptitude for culture,* as a means of adapting to the natural environment, is one such characteristic.

Among other things, cultural behavior is *learned,* and it is passed from generation to generation—not biologically, but through learning. Whereas humans deliberately teach their young, free-ranging nonhuman primates (with the exception of a few reports) do not generally appear to do so. But human children also acquire tremendous knowledge not from instruction, but through observation in the same manner as young nonhuman primates. Nonhuman primate infants, through observing their mothers and others, learn about food items, appropriate behaviors, and how to use and modify objects to achieve certain ends. In turn, their own offspring will observe their activities. What emerges is a *cultural tradition* that may eventually come to typify an entire group or even a species.

A famous example of cultural behavior was seen in a study group of Japanese macaques on Koshima Island. In 1952, Japanese researchers began provisioning the 22-member troop with sweet potatoes. The following year, a young female named Imo began washing her potatoes in a freshwater stream prior to eating them. Within three years, several monkeys had adopted the practice, but they had switched from using the stream to taking their potatoes to the ocean nearby. Perhaps they liked the salt seasoning!

The researchers proposed that dietary habits and food preferences are learned and that potato washing was an example of nonhuman culture. Because this practice arose as an innovative solution to a problem and was imitated by others until it became a tradition, it was seen as resembling human culture.

Among chimpanzees we see more elaborate examples of cultural behavior in the form of *tool use.* This point is very important, for traditionally, tool use (along with language) was said to set humans apart from other animals.

Chimpanzees insert twigs and grass blades into termite mounds in a practice called "termite fishing." When termites seize the twig, the chimpanzee withdraws it and eats the attached insects. Chimpanzees modify some of their stems and twigs by stripping the leaves—in effect, manufacturing a tool from the natural material. To some extent, chimpanzees even alter objects to a "regular and set pattern" and have been observed preparing objects for later use at another location (Goodall, 1986, p. 535). For example, a chimpanzee will very carefully select a piece of vine, bark, twig, or palm frond and modify it by removing leaves or other extraneous material, then break off portions until it is the proper length. Chimpanzees have also been seen making these tools even before the termite mound is in sight.

All this preparation has several implications. First, the chimpanzees are engaged in an activity that prepares them for a future (not immediate) task at a somewhat distant location, and this action implies planning and forethought. Second, attention to the shape and size of the raw material indicates that chimpanzee toolmakers have a preconceived idea of what the finished product needs to be in order to be useful. To produce a tool, even a simple tool, based on a concept is an extremely complex behavior. Scientists previously believed that such behavior was the exclusive domain of humans, but now we must question this very basic assumption.

Chimpanzees also crumple and chew handfuls of leaves, which they dip into the hollow of a tree where water has accumulated. Then they suck the water from their newly made "leaf sponges," water that otherwise would have been inaccessible to them. Leaves are also used to wipe substances from fur; twigs are sometimes used as toothpicks; stones may be used as weapons; and various objects, such as branches and stones, may be dragged or rolled to enhance displays. Lastly, sticks or leaves are used as aids in processing mammalian prey, but with one exception these practices appear to be incidental. The one exception, observed in chimpanzees in the Tai forest (Ivory Coast), is the frequent use of sticks to extract marrow from long bones (Boesch and Boesch, 1989).

Chimpanzees in numerous West African study groups use hammerstones with platform stones to crack nuts and hard-shelled fruits (Boesch et al, 1994).

However, it is important to note that neither the hammerstone nor the platform stone was deliberately manufactured.* Wild capuchin monkeys use leaves to extract water from cavities in trees (Phillips, 1998) and also smash objects against stones (Izawa and Mizuno, 1977), and their use of stones in captivity (both as hammers and anvils) has been reported (Visalberghi, 1990). (Stones serve as anvils when fruit or other objects are bashed against the rock surface.) In nature, chimpanzees are the only nonhuman animal to use stones both as hammers and anvils to obtain food. They are also the only nonhuman primate that consistently and habitually makes and uses tools (McGrew, 1992).

Importantly, chimpanzees exhibit regional variation regarding both the types and methods of tool use. Use of stone hammers and platforms is confined to West African groups. And at central and eastern African sites, termites are obtained by means of stems and sticks, while at some West African locations, it appears that no tools are used in this context (McGrew, 1992).

Regional dietary preferences are also noted for chimpanzees (Nishida et al., 1983; McGrew, 1992, 1998). For example, oil palms are exploited for their fruits and nuts at many locations, including Gombe, but even though they are present in the Mahale Mountains, they are not utilized by the chimpanzees there. Such regional patterns in tool use and food preferences that are not due to environmental variation are reminiscent of the cultural variations characteristic of humans.

Using sticks, twigs, and stones enhances chimpanzees' ability to exploit resources. Learning these behaviors occurs during infancy and childhood, partly as a function of prolonged contact with the mother. Also important in this regard is the continued exposure to others provided by living in social groupings. These statements also apply to early hominids. While sticks and unmodified stones do not remain to tell tales, our early ancestors surely used these same objects as tools in much the same manner as do chimpanzees.

While chimpanzees in the wild have not been observed modifying the stones they use, a male bonobo named Kanzi (see p. 142) has learned to strike two stones together to produce sharp-edged flakes. In a study conducted by Sue Savage-Rumbaugh and archaeologist Nicholas Toth, Kanzi was allowed to watch as Toth produced stone flakes, which were then used to open a transparent plastic food container (Savage-Rumbaugh and Lewin, 1994). Although bonobos apparently do not commonly use objects as tools in the wild, Kanzi readily appreciated the utility of the flakes in obtaining foods. Moreover, he was able to master the basic technique of producing flakes without having been taught the various components of the process, but for a time, his progress was slow. Eventually, Kanzi realized that he could overcome his difficulties by throwing a stone onto a hard floor, causing it to shatter, thus providing an abundance of cutting implements. Although his solution was not necessarily the one that Savage-Rumbaugh and Toth expected, it nevertheless provided an excellent example of bonobo insight and problem-solving capability. Moreover, Kanzi did eventually learn to produce flakes by striking two stones together, and these flakes were then used to obtain food. Not only is this behavior an example of tool manufacture and tool use, albeit in a captive situation; it is also a very sophisticated goal-directed activity.

---

*Observers of nonhuman primates rarely distinguish natural objects used as tools from modified objects deliberately manufactured for specific purposes. The term *tool* is usually employed in both cases.

Human culture has become the environment in which modern *Homo sapiens* lives. Quite clearly, use of sticks in termite fishing and hammerstones to crack nuts is hardly comparable to modern human technology. However, modern human technology had its beginnings in these very types of behaviors we observe in other primates. This does not mean that nonhuman primates are "on their way" to becoming human. Remember, evolution is not goal directed, and if it were, there is nothing to dictate that modern humans necessarily constitute an evolutionary goal. Such a conclusion is a purely **anthropocentric** view, and it has no validity in discussions of evolutionary processes.

Moreover, nonhuman primates have probably been capable of certain cultural behaviors for millions of years. As we have stated, the common ancestor that humans share with chimpanzees may have used sticks and stones to exploit resources, perhaps even as weapons. These behaviors are not newly developed in our close relatives simply because we have only recently discovered and documented them. Thus, we must continue to study these capabilities in nonhuman primates in their social and ecological context so that we may eventually understand more clearly how cultural traditions emerged in our own lineage.

Anthropocentric
Viewing nonhuman phenomena in terms of human experience and capabilities; emphasizing the importance of humans over everything else.

Primate Cognitive Abilities

As we have already seen, primates are extremely intelligent, as demonstrated by their complicated social interactions and problem-solving abilities. Indeed, their use of tools represents solutions to such problems as how to get termites out of their mounds or how to gain access to water in difficult places.

Although numerous studies have demonstrated the abilities of nonhuman primates, probably no research has had the impact, certainly on the general public, that the language acquisition studies have had. As previously discussed, all animals communicate through a variety of modalities, including scent, vocal expression, touch, and visual indicators (gestures, facial expressions, and body posture). However, the amount and kinds of information that nonhuman animals are able to convey are limited.

The view traditionally held by most linguists and behavioral psychologists has been that nonhuman communication consists of mostly involuntary vocalizations and actions that convey information about the emotional state of the animal (anger, fear, etc.). Nonhuman animals have not been considered capable of communicating about external events, objects, or other animals, either in close proximity or removed in space or time. For example, when a startled baboon barks, its fellow baboons know only that it is startled. What they do not know is what elicited the bark, and this they can only ascertain by looking around. In general, then, it has been assumed that nonhuman animals, including primates, use a *closed system* of communication, one in which use of vocalizations and other modalities does not include references to specific external phenomena.

In recent years, these views have been challenged (Steklis, 1985; King, 1994). Vervets (Fig. 6–11) have been shown to use specific vocalizations for particular categories of predators such as snakes, eagles, and leopards (Struhsaker, 1967; Seyfarth, Cheney, and Marler, 1980a, 1980b). When researchers made tape recordings of various vervet alarm calls and played them back within hearing distance of free-ranging vervets, they observed differing responses to various calls. In response to leopard alarm calls, the monkeys climbed trees; eagle alarm calls caused them to

FIGURE 6–11

Group of free-ranging vervets.

look upward and run into bushes; and snake alarm calls elicited looking around in the nearby grass.

These results demonstrate that vervets use distinct vocalizations to refer to specific components of the external environment. These calls are not involuntary, and they do not refer solely to the emotional state of the individual animal, although this information is also conveyed. While these significant findings dispel certain long-held misconceptions about nonhuman communication (at least for some species), they also indicate certain limitations. Vervet communication is restricted to the present; as far as we know, no vervet can communicate about a predator it saw yesterday or one it might see in the future.

Other studies have now shown that numerous other nonhuman primates, including cottontop tamarins (Cleveland and Snowdon, 1982), red colobus (Struhsaker, 1975), and gibbons (Tenaza and Tilson, 1977), also produce distinct calls that have specific references. There is also growing evidence that many birds and some nonprimate mammals use distinct predator alarm calls as well (Seyfarth, 1987).

In contrast, humans use *language,* a set of written and spoken symbols that refer to concepts, other humans, objects, and so on. This set of symbols is said to be *arbitrary* in that the symbol itself has no relationship to whatever it represents. For example, the English word *flower* when written or spoken neither looks, smells, nor feels like the thing it represents. Moreover, humans can recombine their linguistic symbols in an infinite number of ways to create new meanings, and we can use language to refer to events, places, objects, and people far removed in both space and time. For these reasons, language is described as an *open system* of communication, based on the human ability to think symbolically.

Language, as distinct from other forms of communication, has been considered a uniquely human achievement, one that sets humans apart from the rest of the animal kingdom. But work with captive apes has raised some doubts about that supposition. While many people were skeptical about the capacity of nonhuman primates to use language, reports from psychologists who work with apes, especially chimpanzees, leave little doubt that these primates can learn to interpret signs and use them to communicate with their trainers and companions in their own group.

No mammal, other than humans, has the ability to speak. However, the fact that apes cannot speak has less to do with lack of intelligence than to differences in the anatomy of the vocal tract and *language-related structures in the brain.* Quite clearly, communication became increasingly important in hominid evolution, and natural selection increasingly favored anatomical and neurological changes that enhanced our ancestors' ability to use spoken language.

Because of failed attempts at teaching young chimpanzees to speak, psychologists Beatrice and Allen Gardner designed a study to test language capabilities in chimpanzees by teaching an infant female named Washoe to use ASL (American sign language for the deaf). Beginning in 1966, the Gardners began teaching Washoe signs in the same way parents would teach a deaf human infant. In just over three years, Washoe had acquired at least 132 signs. "She asked for goods and services, and she also asked questions about the world of objects and events around her" (Gardner et al., 1989, p. 6).

Years later, an infant chimpanzee named Loulis was placed in Washoe's care. Researchers wanted to know if Loulis would acquire signing skills from Washoe and other chimpanzees in the study group. Within just eight days, Loulis began to imitate the signs of others. Moreover, Washoe also deliberately *taught* Loulis some signs. For example, teaching him to sit, "Washoe placed a small plastic chair in front of Loulis, and then signed CHAIR/SIT to him several times in succession, watching him closely throughout" (Fouts et al., 1989, p. 290).

There have been other ape language experiments. The chimpanzee Sara, for instance, was taught by Professor David Premack to recognize plastic chips as symbols for various objects. The chips did not resemble the objects they represented. For example, the chip that represented an apple was neither round nor red. Sara's ability to associate chips with concepts and objects to which they bore no visual similarity implies some degree of symbolic thought.

At the Yerkes Regional Primate Research Center in Atlanta, Georgia, another chimpanzee, Lana, worked with a specially designed computer keyboard with chips attached to keys. After six months, Lana recognized symbols for 30 words and was able to ask for food and answer questions through the machine (Rumbaugh, 1977). Also at Yerkes, two male chimpanzees, Sherman and Austin, learned to communicate using a series of lexigrams, or geometric symbols, imprinted on a computer keyboard (Savage-Rumbaugh, 1986b).

Dr. Francine Patterson, who taught ASL to Koko, a female gorilla, reports that Koko uses more than 500 signs. Furthermore, Michael, an adult male also involved in the gorilla study, has a considerable sign vocabulary, and the two gorillas communicate with each other via signs.

In the late 1970s, a male orangutan, Chantek (also at Yerkes), began to use signs after one month of training when he was two years old. Chantek eventually acquired a total of approximately 140 signs, which in some situations were used to refer to objects and persons not present. Chantek also invented signs and recombined them in novel ways, and he appeared to understand that his signs were *representations* of items, actions, and people (Miles, 1990).

Questions have been raised about this type of experimental work. Do the apes really understand the signs they learn? Are they merely imitating their trainers? Do they learn that a symbol is a name for an object or simply that executing a symbol will produce a desired object? Other unanswered questions concern the apes' use of grammar, especially when they combine more than just a few "words" to communicate.

Partly in an effort to address some of these questions and criticisms, Dr. Sue Savage-Rumbaugh taught the chimpanzees Sherman and Austin to use symbols to categorize *classes* of objects, such as "food" or "tool." This was done in recognition of the fact that in previous studies, apes had been taught symbols for *specific* items. Savage-Rumbaugh reasoned that simply using a symbol as a label is not the same thing as understanding the *representational value* of the symbol.

Sherman and Austin were taught to recognize familiar food items, for which they routinely used symbols, as belonging to a broader category referred to by yet another symbol, "food." They were then introduced to unfamiliar food items, for which they had no symbols, to see if they would place them in the food category. The fact that they both had perfect or nearly perfect scores further substantiated that they could categorize unfamiliar objects. More importantly, it was clear that they were capable of assigning to unknown objects symbols that denoted membership in a broad grouping. This ability was a strong indication that the chimpanzees understood that the symbols were being used referentially.

However, subsequent work with Lana, who had different language experiences, did not prove as successful. Although Lana was able to sort actual objects into categories, she was unable to assign generic symbols to novel items (Savage-Rumbaugh and Lewin, 1994). Thus, it became apparent that the manner in which chimpanzees are introduced to language influences their ability to understand the representational value of symbols.

Chimpanzees learn language differently than do human children in that they must be taught. Human children learn language spontaneously, through exposure, without needing to be deliberately taught. Therefore, it is significant that Savage-Rumbaugh and her colleagues reported that the infant male bonobo Kanzi (Fig. 6–12), much prior to his toolmaking days, was spontaneously acquiring and using symbols at the age of 2½ years (Savage-Rumbaugh et al., 1986a). Kanzi's younger half-sister began to use symbols spontaneously at 11 months of age. Both animals had been exposed to the use of lexigrams when they accompanied their mother to training sessions. But neither youngster had received instruction and in fact were not involved in the sessions.

The scientists involved in ape language research are convinced that apes are capable, to varying degrees, of employing symbols to communicate. It has been strongly suggested that bonobos are superior in this ability to chimpanzees and gorillas (Savage-Rumbaugh, 1986, 1994).

These statements do not mean that apes acquire and use language in the same way humans do. In general, apes must be taught to use symbols to communicate. Moreover, it appears that not all signing apes understand the referential relationship between symbol and object, person, or action. Nonetheless, there is abundant evidence that humans are not the only species capable of some degree of symbolic thought and complex communication.

FIGURE 6–12

The bonobo Kanzi, as a youngster, using lexigrams to communicate with human observers.

(Photograph by Elizabeth Pugh)

From an evolutionary perspective, the ape language experiments may suggest clues to the origins of human language. Quite possibly, the last common ancestor that hominids shared with the great apes possessed communication capabilities similar to those we see now in modern **pongids.** If so, we need to elucidate the factors that enhanced the adaptive significance of these characteristics in our own lineage. It is equally important to explore why these pressures did not operate to the same degree in gorillas, chimpanzees, and bonobos.

It would be difficult to overstate the significance of human cognitive abilities, as evidenced in our reliance on complex patterns of communication and our technological manipulations of the natural environment. But these capacities should not be used to set humankind apart from the rest of nature, as they almost universally are. In fact, the genetic and behavioral similarities we share with the great apes, as well as the apes' proficiency at symbolic communication, indicate that the very qualities we have traditionally considered unique to our species are in reality expressed in other species, too, but to a lesser degree.

The Primate Continuum

For decades, behavioral psychology taught that animal behavior represents nothing more than a series of conditioned responses to specific stimuli (Fig. 6–13). (This perspective is very convenient for those who wish to exploit nonhuman animals, for whatever purposes, and remain free of guilt.) Fortunately, this attitude has begun to change in recent years to reflect a growing awareness that humans, although in many ways unquestionably unique, are nevertheless part of a **biological continuum.**

Where do humans fit, then, in this biological continuum? Are we at the top? The answer depends on the criteria used, and we must also bear in mind that evolution is not a goal-directed process. Certainly, we are the most intelligent species, if we define intelligence in terms of problem-solving abilities and abstract thought. However, if we look more closely, we recognize that the differences between ourselves and our primate relatives, especially chimpanzees and bonobos, are primarily quantitative and not qualitative.

Although human brains are absolutely and relatively larger, neurological processes are functionally the same. The necessity of close bonding with at least one parent and the need for physical contact are essentially the same. Developmental stages and dependence on learning are strikingly similar. Indeed, even in the chimpanzee's capacity for cruelty and aggression combined with compassion, tenderness, and altruism, we see a close parallel to the dichotomy between "evil" and "good" so long recognized in ourselves. The main difference between how chimpanzees and humans express these qualities (and therefore the dichotomy) is one of degree. Humans are much more adept at both cruelty and compassion, and humans reflect on their behavior in

Pongids
Members of the family Pongidae, including orangutans, gorillas, chimpanzees, and bonobos.

Biological continuum
Referring to the fact that organisms are related through common ancestry and that behaviors and traits seen in one species are also seen in others to varying degrees. (When expressions of a phenomenon continuously grade into one another so that there are no discrete categories, they are said to exist on a continuum. Color is such a phenomenon.)

FIGURE 6–13

This unfortunate advertising display is a good example of how humans misunderstand and thus misrepresent our closest relatives.

ways that chimpanzees do not. While chimpanzees may not understand the suffering they inflict on others, humans do. Likewise, while an adult chimpanzee may sit next to and protect a dying relative or friend, it does not appear to feel intense grief and a sense of loss to the extent a human normally does.

To arrive at any understanding of what it is to be human, it is vastly important to recognize that many of our behaviors are but elaborate extensions of those of our hominid ancestors and close primate relatives. We share 98 percent of our DNA with chimpanzees. The fact that so many of us prefer to bask in the warmth of the "sun belt" with literally millions of others reflects our heritage as social animals adapted to life in the tropics. Likewise, it is no mistake that industry has invested millions of dollars in the development of low-calorie, artificial sweeteners. The "sweet tooth" which afflicts so many humans is a direct result of our earlier primate ancestors' predilection for high-energy sugar contained in desirably sweet, ripe fruit.

Be sure to complete the self-quiz at the end of Virtual Lab 6.

The fact that humans are part of an evolutionary continuum is the entire basis for animal research aimed at benefiting our species. Yet, even with our growing awareness of the similarities we share, we continue to cage nonhuman primates with little regard for the very needs they share with us. We would argue that nonhuman primates should be maintained in social groups and that habitat enrichment programs should be introduced. It would seem the very least we can do for our close relatives, from whom we continue to derive so many benefits.

SUMMARY

We have discussed many aspects of nonhuman primate behavior, such as social organization and dominance hierarchies, communication, reproduction, intra- and intergroup relationships (including mothers and infants), aggression, friendship, and culture (in the form of tool use). These behaviors have been treated, to considerable extent, from an ecological perspective; specifically, we have attempted to show what features of the environment are most likely to be important in shaping primate social behavior.

Group size and composition are influenced by such environmental components as diet, resource availability, and predators. Moreover, many behaviors are seen as the result of natural selection; that is, they promote increased likelihood of survival and reproduction. Therefore, individuals, ideally, should behave in ways that will maximize their own reproductive success relative to others. Although this does not imply that in mammals, and especially primates, there are genes for specific behaviors, it does suggest that genes may have mediating effects on behavior—perhaps through such products as hormones.

We have emphasized that humans are part of a biological continuum that includes all the primates. It is this evolutionary relationship, then, that accounts for many of the behaviors we have in common with prosimians, monkeys, and apes.

QUESTIONS FOR REVIEW

1. What factors should be considered if one approaches the study of nonhuman primate behavior from an ecological perspective?

2. What are some of the environmental factors believed to influence group size and social organization? Give two examples.

3. How could multimale, multifemale groupings be advantageous to species living in areas where predation pressure is high?

4. How may solitary foraging be advantageous to primates? Discuss two examples.

5. How may genetic factors influence behavior?

6. Discuss a primate behavior that has traditionally been used as an example of behavioral evolution.

7. What are reproductive strategies, and what is their basic goal?

8. Primates are said to be K-selected. What is meant by this? What is r-selection? Give an example of r-selection.

9. Explain male and female differences with regard to parental investment.

10. What are dominance hierarchies? What is their function in primate groups?

11. What is believed to be the primary benefit of being a high-ranking individual? What are three factors that influence an individual's rank in a group?

12. What is grooming? Why is it so important in many primate species; that is, what functions does it serve?

13. Discuss three ways nonhuman primates can communicate information to other group members. Name at least two "threat gestures."

14. Name two ways in which nonhuman primates communicate reassurance.

15. What is meant by an open system of communication? How does it differ from a closed system?

16. What is seen as the basic social unit among all primates? Why is it so important?

17. Discuss an example of between-group aggression. What is thought to have motivated the violence between two groups of chimpanzees at Gombe?

18. Discuss two examples of nonhuman primate cultural behavior. Why is our discovery of these behaviors important to studies of early human evolution?

19. Discuss the language acquisition studies using chimpanzees, bonobos, and gorillas. What are the implications of this research?

20. What do we mean when we state that humans are a part of a biological continuum? How does the view expressed in this statement differ from traditional views expressed by most people?

SUGGESTED FURTHER READINGS

Cartmill, Matt. 1990. "Human Uniqueness and Theoretical Content in Paleoanthropology." *International Journal of Primatology* 11(3): 173–192.

Cheney, Dorothy L., and Robert M. Seyfarth. 1990. *How Monkeys See the World.* Chicago: University of Chicago Press.

Goodall, Jane. 1986. *The Chimpanzees of Gombe.* Cambridge, MA: The Belknap Press of Harvard University Press.

King, Barbara J. 1994. *The Information Continuum: Social Information Transfer in Monkeys, Apes, and Hominids.* Santa Fe: SAR Press.

McGrew, W. C. 1992. *Chimpanzee Material Culture.* Cambridge, MA: Cambridge University Press.

_____. 1998. "Culture in Nonhuman Primates?" *Annual Review of Anthropology* 27: 301–328.

Napier, J. R., and P. H. Napier. 1985. *The Natural History of the Primates.* Cambridge, MA: The MIT Press.

Packer, C. and A. E. Pusey. 1997. "Divided We Fall: Cooperation among Lions." *Scientific American* 276(5): 52–59.

Savage-Rumbaugh, S., and Roger Lewin. 1994. *Kanzi: The Ape at the Brink of the Human Mind.* New York: Wiley.

Smuts, Barbara B., Dorothy L. Cheney, Robert M. Seyfarth, Richard W. Wrangham, and Thomas T. Struhsaker (eds.). 1987. *Primate Societies.* Chicago: University of Chicago Press.

MULTIMEDIA RESOURCES

🌐 Wadsworth Anthropology Resource Center

http://anthropology.wadsworth.com

Visit Anthropology Online to obtain current updates in the field, surfing tips, career information, and more. In addition, enrich your study efforts with text-specific study aids arranged by chapter.

InfoTrac College Edition

http://www.infotrac-college.com/wadsworth

1. Do a search for *primatology* and go to *primates,* then the subdivision *behavior.* Select an article from this list of references that relates to some aspect of primate behavior. Do the behaviors described in this article have any relevance for studies of human or early hominid behavior?

2. Under the subject *animal communication,* there are several articles that concern language capabilities in nonhuman primates. There are also several interesting articles that discuss communication in nonprimate species. After reading at least one of these articles, explain how it has supplemented what you learned in Chapter 6.

🌐 Internet Exercises

1. Living Links is a Web site at the Yerkes Regional Primate Research Center dedicated to research on the great apes. Visit this site at **www.emory.edu/ LIVING_LINKS/** and explore the various topics presented there. Topics include behavior, communication, and conservation, to name a few. There are also audios of some nonhuman primate vocalizations. Choose any topic, and after reading the available information, make a list of facts you have learned.

2. If you wanted to become involved with primate research, where would you begin? Where would you find more information on primates or be able to observe their behavior? There are a number of primate research centers in the United States and other countries. Use one of the Internet search engines to find some of these. Which one is closest to you? Whom would you contact at the center?

CHAPTER
7

Mammalian/ Primate Evolutionary History

CONTENTS

Introduction

In the two preceding chapters, we surveyed the structure, ecology, and social behavior of *living* primates. In this chapter, we shift our focus to primate evolution. To place primates, and more specifically, hominids, in their proper evolutionary context, we first give a brief summary of vertebrate and mammalian evolution.

In addition to the broad trends of evolutionary history, we also discuss some contemporary issues relating to evolutionary theory. In particular, we emphasize concepts that relate to large-scale evolutionary processes, that is, *macroevolution* (in contrast to the microevolutionary focus, which we will discuss in Chapter 12). The fundamental perspectives reviewed here concerning geological history, principles of classification, and modes of evolutionary change will serve as a basis for topics covered throughout the remainder of the text.

The Human Place in the Organic World

There are millions of species living today; if we were to include microorganisms, the total would surely exceed tens of millions. And if we then added in the vast multitudes of life forms that are now extinct, the total would be staggering—perhaps hundreds of millions of species!

How do biologists cope with all this diversity? As is typical for *Homo sapiens,* scientists approach complexity through simplification. Thus, biologists group life forms together; that is, they construct a **classification.** For example, today there are probably more than 15 million species of animals, most of them insects. No one knows exactly how many species there are, because more than 90 percent have yet to be scientifically described or named. Nevertheless, even with the tens of thousands of species that biologists do know something about, there is still too much diversity to handle conveniently—indeed, too many names for the human brain to remember. Thus, the solution is to organize the diversity into groups to (1) reduce the complexity and (2) indicate evolutionary relationships.

Organisms that move about and ingest food (but do not photosynthesize, as do plants) are called animals. More precisely, the multicelled animals are placed within the group called the **Metazoa.** Within the Metazoa there are more than 20 major groups termed *phyla* (*sing.,* phylum) (Fig. 7–1). One of these phyla is the **Chordata,** animals with a nerve cord, gill slits (at some stage of development), and a stiff supporting cord along the back called a *notochord.* Most chordates today are **vertebrates,** in which the notochord has become a vertebral column (which gives its name to the group); in addition, vertebrates have a developed brain and paired sensory structures for sight, smell, and balance.

The vertebrates themselves are subdivided into six classes: bony fishes, cartilaginous fishes, amphibians, reptiles, birds, and mammals. We will discuss mammal classification later in this chapter.

Taxonomy

Before we go any further, it would be useful to discuss the bases of animal classification. The field that specializes in delineating the rules of classification is called *taxonomy.* As mentioned in Chapter 5, organisms are classified first, and most traditionally, on the basis of physical similarities. Such was the basis of the

Classification
In biology, the ordering of organisms into categories, such as phyla, orders, and families, to show evolutionary relationships.

Taxonomy and classification are discussed in Virtual Lab 7, section II.

Metazoa
Multicellular animals; a major division of the animal kingdom.

Chordata (Chordates)
The phylum of the animal kingdom that includes vertebrates.

Vertebrates
Animals with bony backbones; includes fishes, amphibians, reptiles, birds, and mammals.

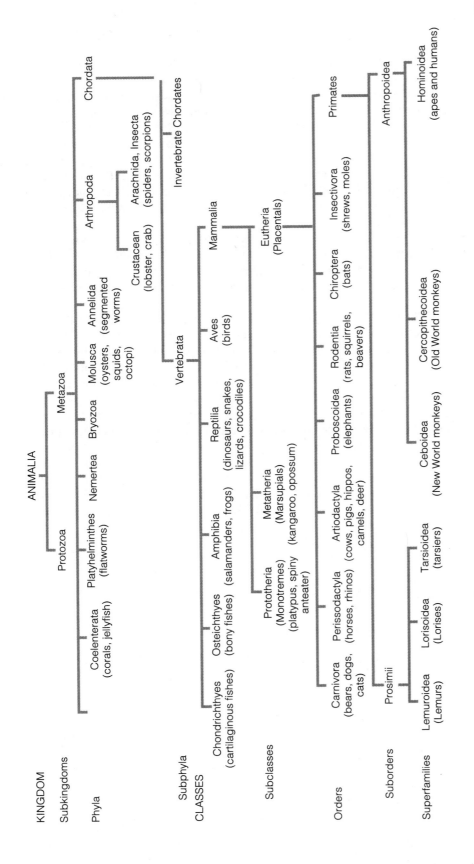

FIGURE 7–1

Classification chart, modified from Linnaeus. All animals are placed in certain categories based on structural similarities. Not all members of categories are shown. For example, there are up to 20 orders of placental mammals (8 are depicted). A more comprehensive classification of the primate order was presented in Chapter 5.

first systematic classification devised by Linnaeus in the eighteenth century (see Chapter 2).

Today, basic physical similarities are still considered a good starting point in postulating schemes of organic relationships. For similarities to be useful, however, they *must* reflect evolutionary descent. For example, the bones of the forelimb of all terrestrial air-breathing vertebrates (tetrapods) are so similar in number and form (Fig. 7–2) that the obvious explanation for the striking resemblance is that all four kinds of air-breathing vertebrates ultimately derived their forelimb structure from a common ancestor.

Structures that are shared by species on the basis of descent from a common ancestor are called **homologies.** Homologies alone are reliable indicators of evolutionary relationship. But we must be careful not to draw hasty conclusions from superficial similarities.

For example, both birds and butterflies have wings, but they should not be grouped together on the basis of this single characteristic; butterflies (as insects) differ dramatically from birds in a number of other, even more fundamental ways. (For example, birds have an internal skeleton, central nervous system, and four limbs; insects do not.).

What has happened in evolutionary history is that from quite distant ancestors, both butterflies and birds have developed wings *independently*. Thus, their (superficial) similarities are a product of separate evolutionary response to roughly similar functional demands; such similarities, based on independent functional adaptation and *not* on shared evolutionary descent, are called **analogies.** The process that leads to the development of analogies (also called analogous structures) such as wings in birds and butterflies is termed **homoplasy.** In the case of butterflies and birds, the homoplasy occurs in evolutionary lines that share only very remote ancestry. Here, homoplasy has produced analogous structures separately from any homology. In some cases, however, homoplasy can occur in lineages that are more closely related (and which thus share considerable homology as well). Examples of homoplasy in closely related lineages are evident among the primates (e.g., among New and Old World monkeys and also among the great apes; see Chapter 5).

Homologies
Similarities between organisms based on descent from a common ancestor.

Analogies
Similarities between organisms based strictly on common function with no assumed common evolutionary descent.

Homoplasy
(*homo,* meaning "same," and *plasy,* meaning "growth") The separate evolutionary development of similar characteristics in different groups of organisms.

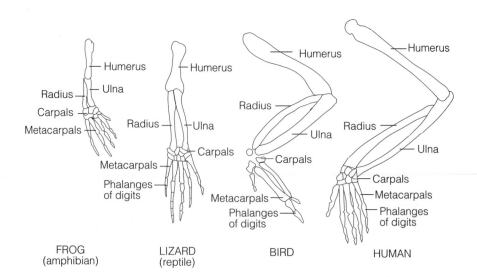

FIGURE 7–2

Homologies. The similarities in the bones of these animals can be most easily explained by descent from a common ancestor.

In making consistent evolutionary interpretations and devising classifications that reflect these interpretations, evolutionary biologists must concentrate on the homologies and treat the analogies as extraneous "noise." Nor is it sufficient simply to isolate the homologies. For certain purposes, some structural homologies are much more informative than others. As already mentioned, the forelimbs of air-breathing vertebrates are all similar in overall structure. As a result, we cannot sort birds from bats or frogs from lizards on the basis of the number of bones in the forelimb. They all possess *generally* similar structures (presumably which they all *did* inherit from a common vertebrate ancestor). We would say, therefore, that the basic forelimb structure for all tetrapods is **primitive.** The term *primitive* is not used to indicate a characteristic or type of organism that is in any way inferior. Perhaps a less confusing term would be *ancestral.* Among mammals, for example, human (and other primate) hands retain the ancestral condition of five digits, while the hooves of cattle, with only two digits, are much more **derived** (i.e., modified from the ancestral condition). Few people—perhaps because we are so *anthropocentric*—would be willing to concede that hooves are superior to hands. Of course, hooves function better to support a large grazing animal, while hands serve other functions in animals that spend time in trees (see Chapter 5). As you can see, concepts like "inferior" and "superior" are meaningless when we are comparing organisms.

Among vertebrates, *only* birds have feathers and *only* mammals have fur. In comparing mammals with other vertebrates, presence of fur is a *derived* characteristic. Similarly, in describing birds, feathers are derived only in this group.

So, how do we know which kinds of characteristics to use? The answer is determined by which group one is describing and with what it is being compared. For the most part, it is best to use those characteristics that reflect more specific evolutionary adaptations; in other words, derived characteristics are the most informative. Moreover, when grouping two forms together (say, a bat with a mouse, both as mammals), this should be done *only* when they show **shared derived** characteristics (here, both possessing fur). (See Figs. 5–10 and 7–1 for examples of classifications of animals.)

The current emphasis on identification and application of shared derived characteristics underscores a contemporary school of taxonomy called **cladistics.** Now widely used in physical anthropology and other disciplines, practitioners of this approach, called cladists, have sought to add more rigor to interpretations of evolutionary relationships. An important scientific aspect of cladistic methods is that the proposed hypothesis must be explicitly stated, detailing derived traits as contrasted to primitive traits. In this way, the scientific validity of evolutionary schemes is more easily tested, since the basic tenets are clearly presented in a falsifiable form.

Time Scale

In addition to the staggering array of living and extinct life forms, biologists must also contend with the vast amount of time that life has been evolving on earth. Again, scientists have devised simplified schemes—but in this case to organize *time,* not organic diversity.

Geologists have formulated the **geological time scale** (Fig. 7–3). Very large time spans are here organized into eras and periods. Periods, in turn, can be broken down into epochs (as we will do later in our discussion of primate evolution).

 Virtual Lab 7, section II, part A, presents a discussion of the approaches used to reconstruct and interpret evolutionary relationships.

Primitive (ancestral)
Referring to characters inherited by a group of organisms from a remote ancestor and thus not diagnostic of groups (lineages) branching subsequent to the time the character first appeared.

Derived (modified)
Referring to characters that are modified from the ancestral condition and thus *are* diagnostic of particular evolutionary lineages.

Shared derived
Relating to specific character states shared in common between two forms and considered the most useful for making evolutionary interpretations.

Cladistics
The approach to taxonomy that groups species (as well as other levels of classification) on the basis of shared derived characteristics. In this way, organisms are classified solely on the basis of presumed closeness of evolutionary relationship.

Geological time scale
The organization of earth history into eras, periods, and epochs; commonly used by geologists and paleoanthropologists.

ERA	PERIOD	(Began m.y.a.)	EPOCH	(Began m.y.a.)
CENOZOIC	Quaternary	1.8	Holocene Pleistocene	0.01 1.8
CENOZOIC	Tertiary	65	Pliocene Miocene Oligocene Eocene Paleocene	5 23 34 55 65
MESOZOIC	Cretaceous	136		
MESOZOIC	Jurassic	190		
MESOZOIC	Triassic	225		
PALEOZOIC	Permian	280		
PALEOZOIC	Carboniferous	345		
PALEOZOIC	Devonian	395		
PALEOZOIC	Silurian	430		
PALEOZOIC	Ordovician	500		
PALEOZOIC	Cambrian	570		
PRE-CAMBRIAN				

FIGURE 7–3
Geological time scale.

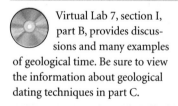 Virtual Lab 7, section I, part B, provides discussions and many examples of geological time. Be sure to view the information about geological dating techniques in part C.

Vertebrate Evolutionary History—A Brief Summary

There are three basic eras: the Paleozoic, the Mesozoic, and the Cenozoic. (For a breakdown of the major divisions of the Paleozoic and Mesozoic, refer to Fig. 7–3.) The first vertebrates are on the scene early in the Paleozoic by 500 million years ago (m.y.a.), and they probably go back considerably further. It is the vertebrate capacity to form bone that accounts for their more complete fossil record *after* 500 m.y.a.

During the Paleozoic, several varieties of fishes (including the ancestors of modern sharks and bony fishes), amphibians, and reptiles appeared. In addition, at the end of the Paleozoic, close to 250 m.y.a., several varieties of mammal-like reptiles were also diversifying. It is widely thought that some of these gave rise to the mammals (see Fig. 7–6 for a summary of major events).

During most of the Mesozoic, reptiles were the dominant land vertebrates, and they exhibited a broad expansion into a variety of **ecological niches,** which included aerial and marine habitats. Such a fairly rapid expansion marked by diversification of many new species is called an **adaptive radiation.** No doubt, the most famous of these highly successful Mesozoic reptiles were the dinosaurs, which themselves evolved into a wide array of sizes and lifestyles. Dinosaur paleontology, never a boring field, has advanced several startling notions in recent years: that many dinosaurs were warm-blooded; that some varieties were quite social and probably also showed considerable parental care; that many forms became extinct as the result of major climatic changes resulting from collisions with comets or asteroids; and finally, that not all dinosaurs became extinct, with many descendants still living and doing remarkably well (i.e., all modern birds).

The first mammals are known from fossil traces fairly early in the Mesozoic, but the first *placental* mammals cannot be positively identified until quite late in the Mesozoic, circa 70 m.y.a. This highly successful mammalian adaptive radiation is thus almost entirely within the most recent era of geological history, the Cenozoic.

The Cenozoic is divided into two periods, the Tertiary (about 63 million years duration) and the Quaternary, from about 1.8 m.y.a. up to and including the present. Because this division is rather imprecise, paleontologists more frequently refer to the next level of subdivision within the Cenozoic, the **epochs.** There are seven epochs within the Cenozoic: the Paleocene, Eocene, Oligocene, Miocene, Pliocene, Pleistocene, and Holocene (the last often referred to as the Recent) (see Fig. 7–3).

Mammalian Evolution

Following the extinction of dinosaurs and many other Mesozoic forms (at the beginning of the Cenozoic), a wide array of ecological niches opened for the rapid expansion and diversification of mammals. And indeed, in the Cenozoic, conditions were nearly ideal for mammals. Their resulting adaptive radiation was so rapid and so successful that the Cenozoic is known as the Age of Mammals. Mesozoic mammals were small animals, about the size of mice, which they superficially resembled. Romer (1959) suggested that the Mesozoic may be seen as a training period during which mammalian characters were being perfected. The mammalian adaptive radiation of the early Cenozoic saw the rise of the major lineages of all modern mammals. Mammals, along with birds, replaced reptiles as the dominant terrestrial vertebrate (Fig. 7–4).

How do we account for the rapid success of mammals? Several characteristics relating to learning and general flexibility of behavior are of prime importance. To process more information, mammals were selected for larger brains than those typically found in reptiles. In particular, the outer portion of the brain, called the **neocortex,** which controls higher brain functions, enlarged greatly (Fig. 7–5). In mammals, the neocortex expanded so much in size that it came to comprise the majority of brain volume; moreover, increased numbers of surface convolutions evolved, creating more surface area and thus providing space for even more nerve cells (neurons).

Ecological niches
Specific environmental settings to which organisms are adapted.

Adaptive radiation
The relatively rapid expansion and diversification of an evolving group of organisms as they adapt to new niches.

Epochs
A category of the geological time scale; subdivisions of periods. In the Cenozoic, epochs include the Paleocene, Eocene, Oligocene, Miocene, Pliocene (from the Tertiary period) and the Pleistocene and Holocene (from the Quaternary period).

Neocortex
The outer (cellular) portion of the cerebrum, which has expanded during the course of mammalian evolution, particularly in primates, and most especially in humans. The neocortex is associated with higher mental function.

FIGURE 7–4

Mesozoic mammal. A speculative reconstruction of what a Mesozoic mammal might have looked like.

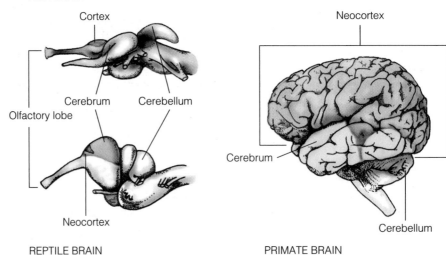

FIGURE 7–5

Lateral view of the brain. The illustration shows the increase in the neocortex of the brain. The cortex integrates sensory information and selects responses.

Viviparous
Giving birth to live young.

FIGURE 7–6

Time line of major events in early vertebrate evolution.

For an animal to develop such a large and complex organ as the mammalian brain, a longer, more intense period of growth is required. This slower development can occur during fetal development (*in utero*) as well as after birth. While internal fertilization and internal development are not unique to mammals, the latter is a major innovation among terrestrial vertebrates. Other forms (some reptiles and birds) incubate their young externally (oviparous), while mammals give birth to live young and are thus called **viviparous.** Even among mammals, however, there is considerable variation among the major groups in how mature the young are at birth. As you will see, it is in mammals like ourselves, the *placental* forms, where development *in utero* goes the furthest. (See Fig. 7–6 for a summary of major events in early vertebrate evolution.)

PALEOZOIC						MESOZOIC		
Cambrian	Ordovician	Silurian	Devonian	Carbon-iferous	Permian	Triassic	Jurassic	Cretaceous
Trilobites abundant; also brachiopods, jellyfish, worms, and other invertebrates	First fishes; trilobites still abundant; graptolites and corals become plentiful; possible land plants	Jawed fishes appear; first air-breathing animals; definite land plants	Age of fish; first amphibians; first forests	First reptiles; radiation of amphibians; modern insects diversify	Reptile radiation; mammal-like reptiles	Reptiles further radiate; first dinosaurs; egg-laying mammals	Great age of dinosaurs; flying and swimming dinosaurs; first toothed birds	Placental and marsupial mammals appear; first modern birds

Major extinction event (between Permian and Triassic)
Major extinction event (after Cretaceous)

570 m.y.a   500 m.y.a   430 m.y.a   395 m.y.a   345 m.y.a   280 m.y.a   225 m.y.a   190 m.y.a   136 m.y.a   65 m.y.a

Major Mammalian Groups

Virtual Lab 7, section II, part B, provides a presentation of placental mammalian relationships.

There are three major subgroups of living mammals: the egg-laying mammals (monotremes), the pouched mammals (marsupials), and the placental mammals. The monotremes are extremely primitive and are considered more distinct from marsupials and placentals than these latter groups are from each other.

The most notable distinction differentiating the marsupials from the placentals is the form and intensity of fetal development. In marsupials, the young are born extremely immature and must complete development in an external pouch. It has been suggested (Carrol, 1988) that such a reproductive strategy is more energetically costly than retaining the young for a longer period *in utero*. In fact, the latter more efficient mechanism is exactly what placental mammals have achieved through a more advanced placental connection (from which the group gets its popular name). But perhaps even more basic than fetal nourishment is the means to allow the mother to *tolerate* her young internally over an extended period. Marsupial young are born so quickly after conception that there is little chance for the mother's system to recognize and have a physiological (immune) rejection of the fetal "foreign" tissue. But in placental mammals, such an immune response would occur were it not for the development of a physiological mechanism that isolates fetal tissue from the mother's immune detection, thus preventing tissue rejection. Quite possibly, this innovation is the central factor in the origin and initial rapid success of placental mammals (Carrol, 1988).

In any case, with a longer gestation period, the brain and central nervous system could develop more completely in the fetus. Moreover, after birth, the "bond of milk" between mother and young also would allow more time for complex neural structures to form. It should also be emphasized that from a *biosocial* perspective, this dependency period not only allows for adequate physiological development, but also provides greater learning stimuli. That is, the young mammal brain, through observation of the mother's behavior as well as that of other adults and through play with age-mates, is a receptacle for a vast amount of learning stimuli. It is not sufficient to have evolved a brain capable of learning. Collateral evolution of mammalian social systems has ensured that young mammal brains are provided with ample learning opportunities and are thus put to good use.

Early Primate Evolution

Detailed presentations of fossil primates from the Paleocene, Eocene, and Oligocene are given in Virtual Lab 7, section III, parts A, B, and C. Animations of possible dispersal routes to the New World are given under "South American Oligocene Primates" in part C.

The roots of the primate order go back to the beginnings of the placental mammal radiation circa 65 m.y.a. Thus, the earliest primates were diverging from quite early, primitive placental mammals. We have seen (in Chapter 5) that strictly defining living primates using clear-cut derived features is not an easy task. The further back we go in the fossil record, the more primitive and, in many cases, the more generalized the fossil primates become. Such a situation makes classifying them all the more difficult.

As a case in point, the earliest identifiable primates were long thought to be a Paleocene group known as the plesiadapiforms (see the geological time scale in Fig. 7–3). You must remember, however, that much of our understanding, especially of early primates, is based on quite fragmentary evidence, mostly jaws and teeth. In just the last few years, much more complete remains of plesiadapiforms from

FIGURE 7–7
Colugo.

FIGURE 7–8a, b

Continental drift. Changes in positions of the continental plates. (a) The position of the continents during the Mesozoic (c. 125 m.y.a.) Pangea is breaking up into a northern land-mass (Laurasia) and a southern land-mass (Gondwanaland). (b) The position of continents at the beginning of the Cenozoic (c. 65 m.y.a.).

Wyoming have been discovered, including a nearly complete skull and elements of the hand and wrist.

As a result of this more complete information, the plesiadapiforms have been removed from the primate order altogether. From distinctive features (shared derived characteristics) of the skull and hands, these Paleocene mammals are now thought to be closely related to the colugo (Fig. 7–7). The colugo is sometimes called a "flying lemur," a misnomer, really, as it is not a lemur, nor does it fly (it glides). This group of unusual mammals is probably closely linked to the roots of primates, but apparently was already diverged by Paleocene times.

Given these new and major reinterpretations, we are left with extremely scarce traces of the beginnings of primates. Scholars have suggested that some other recently discovered bits and pieces from North Africa *may* be those of a primitive, very small primate. Until more evidence is found, and remembering the lesson of the plesiadapiforms, we will just have to wait and see.

A large array of fossil primates from the Eocene (55–34 m.y.a.) that display distinctive primate features has been identified. Indeed, primatologist Elwyn Simons (1972, p. 124) has called them "the first primates of modern aspect." These animals have been found primarily in sites in North America and Europe (which were then still connected). It is important to bear in mind that the continents are not fixed, but "float" on huge plates. As a result of this continental drift, the positions of the continents have shifted dramatically over the last several million years (Fig. 7–8). The landmasses that connect continents, as well as the water boundaries that separate them, have obvious impact on the geographical distribution of such terrestrially bound animals as primates.

Some interesting late Eocene forms have also been found in Asia, which was joined to Europe by the end of the Eocene epoch. Looking at the whole array of Eocene primates, it is certain that they were (1) primates, (2) widely distributed, and (3) mostly extinct by the end of the Eocene. What is less certain is how any of them might be related to the living primates. Some of these forms are probably ancestors of the *prosimians*—the lemurs and lorises. Others are probably related to the tarsier. New evidence of *anthropoid* origins has also recently been discovered in

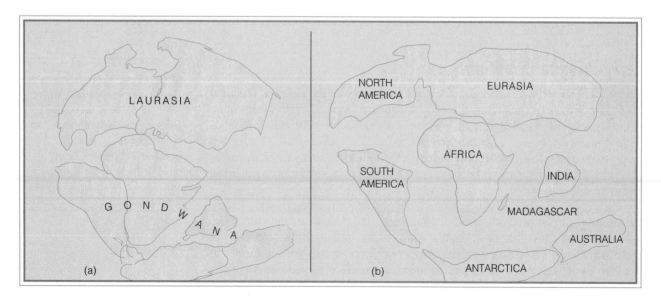

(a)   (b)

several sites from North Africa, the Persian Gulf, and China. These newly discovered fossils of late Eocene anthropoids have now shown that anthropoid origins were well established by 35 m.y.a.

The Oligocene (34–23 m.y.a.) has yielded numerous additional fossil remains of several different species of early anthropoids. Most of these forms are *Old World anthropoids,* all discovered at a single locality in Egypt, the Fayum (Fig. 7–9). In addition, from North and South America, there are a few known bits that relate only to the ancestry of New World monkeys. By the early Oligocene, continental drift had separated the New World (i.e., the Americas) from the Old World (Africa and Eurasia). Some of the earliest Fayum forms, nevertheless, *may* potentially be close to the ancestry of both Old and New World anthropoids. It has been suggested that late in the Eocene or very early in the Oligocene, the first anthropoids (primitive "monkeys") arose in Africa and later reached South America by "rafting" over the water separation on drifting chunks of vegetation. What we call "monkey," then, may have a common Old World origin, but the ancestry of New and Old World varieties remains separate after about 35 m.y.a. Our closest evolutionary affinities after this time are with other Old World anthropoids, that is, Old World monkeys and apes.

The possible roots of anthropoid evolution are illustrated by different forms from the Fayum; one is the **genus** *Apidium.* By *genus* (*pl.,* genera) we mean a group of species that are closely related. In Chapter 2, we discussed Linnaeus' binomial system for designating different organisms (e.g., *Equus callabus* for the horse, *Pan troglodytes* for the chimp, and *Homo sapiens* for humans). The first term (always capitalized—*Equus, Pan, Homo*) is the genus. In paleontological contexts, when remains are fragmentary and usually separated by long time spans, often the best that can be achieved is to make genus-level distinctions (see p. 164 for further discussion).

Apidium, well known at the Fayum, is represented by several dozen jaws or partial dentitions and more than 100 specimens from the limb and trunk skeleton. Because of its primitive dental arrangement, some paleontologists have suggested that *Apidium* may lie near or even before the evolutionary divergence of Old and New World anthropoids. As so much fossil material of teeth and limb bones of *Apidium* has been found, some informed speculation regarding diet and locomotor behavior is possible. It is thought that this small, squirrel-sized primate ate mostly fruits and some seeds and was most likely an arboreal quadruped, adept at leaping and springing (Table 7–1).

The other genus of importance from the Fayum is *Aegyptopithecus.* This genus, also well known, is represented by several well-preserved crania and abundant jaws

FIGURE 7–9

Location of the Fayum, an Oligocene primate site in Egypt.

Genus
A group of closely related species.

TABLE 7–1 Inferred General Paleobiological Aspects of Oligocene Primates

	Weight Range	Substratum	Locomotion	Diet
Apidium	850–1,600 g (2–3 lb)	Arboreal	Quadruped	Fruit, seeds
Aegyptopithecus	6,700 g (15 lb)	Arboreal	Quadruped	Fruit, some leaves?
After Fleagle, 1999.				

A phylogeny of primate evolution along with pronunciations of the names is provided under "Primate Relationships" in the glossary of Virtual Lab 7.

FIGURE 7–10

Major events in early primate evolution.

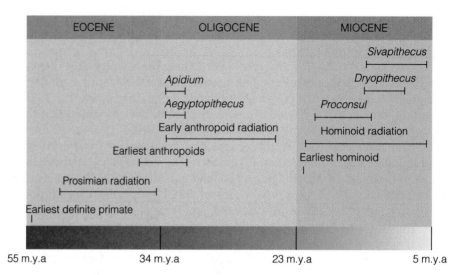

See screen 3 under "African Oligocene Primates" in Virtual Lab 7, section III, part C, to view a 3-D animation of the cranium of *Aegyptopithecus*.

and teeth. The largest of the Fayum anthropoids, *Aegyptopithecus* is roughly the size of a modern howler monkey (13 to 20 pounds) (Fleagle, 1983) and is thought to have been a short-limbed, slow-moving arboreal quadruped (see Table 7–1). *Aegyptopithecus* is important because, better than any other known form, it bridges the gap between the Eocene fossils and the succeeding Miocene hominoids.

Nevertheless, *Aegyptopithecus* is a very primitive Old World anthropoid, with a small brain and long snout and not showing any derived features of either Old World monkeys or hominoids. Thus, it may be close to the ancestry of *both* major groups of living Old World anthropoids.

Found in geological beds dating to 35–33 m.y.a., *Aegyptopithecus* further suggests that the crucial evolutionary divergence of hominoids from other Old World anthropoids occurred *after* this time (Fig. 7–10).

Miocene Fossil Hominoids

The Miocene fossil primates from the Old World are presented in Virtual Lab 7, section III, part D.

During the approximately 18 million years of the Miocene (23–5 m.y.a.), a great deal of evolutionary activity took place. In Africa, Asia, and Europe, a diverse and highly successful group of hominoids emerged (Fig. 7–11). Indeed, there were many more forms of hominoids from the Miocene than are found today (now represented by the highly restricted groups of apes and one species of humans). In fact, the Miocene could be called "the golden age of hominoids." Many thousands of fossils have been found from dozens of sites scattered in East Africa, southwest Africa, southwest Asia, into western and southern Europe, and extending into southern Asia and China.

A problem arises in any attempt to simplify this complex evolutionary situation. For example, for many years paleontologists tended to think of these fossil forms as either "apelike" or "humanlike" and used modern examples as models. But as we have just noted, there are very few hominoids remaining. We should not rashly generalize from the living forms to the much more diverse fossil forms; otherwise, we obscure the evolutionary uniqueness of these animals. In addition, we

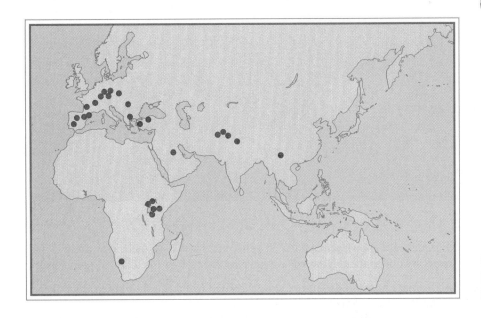

FIGURE 7–11
Miocene hominoid distribution, from fossils thus far discovered.

should not expect all fossil forms to be directly or even particularly closely related to living varieties. Indeed, we should expect the opposite; that is, most lines vanish without descendants.

Over the last three decades, the Miocene hominoid assemblage has been interpreted and reinterpreted. As more fossils are found, the evolutionary picture grows more complicated. The vast array of fossil forms has not yet been completely studied, so conclusions remain tenuous. Given this uncertainty, it is probably best, for the present, to group Miocene hominoids geographically:

1. *African forms (23–14 m.y.a.)* Known especially from western Kenya, these include quite generalized, in many ways primitive, hominoids. The best-known genus is *Proconsul* (Fig. 7–12). In addition to the well-known East African early Miocene hominoids, a recent discovery (in 1992) in Namibia has further extended by over 1,800 miles the known range of African Miocene hominoids (Conroy et al., 1992).

2. *European forms (13–11 m.y.a.)* Known from widely scattered localities in France, Spain, Italy, Greece, Austria, and Hungary, most of these forms are quite derived. However, this is a varied and not well-understood lot. The best known of the forms are placed in the genus *Dryopithecus;* the Hungarian and Greek fossils are usually assigned to other genera.

3. *Asian forms (16–7 m.y.a.)* The largest and most varied group from the Miocene fossil hominoid assemblage, geographically dispersed from Turkey through India/Pakistan and east to the highly prolific site Lufeng, in southern China, most of these forms are *highly* derived. The best-known genus is *Sivapithecus* (known from Turkey and Pakistan). The Lufeng material (now totaling more than 1,000 specimens) is usually placed in a separate genus from *Sivapithecus* and is referred to as *Lufengpithecus.*

Four points are certain concerning Miocene hominoid fossils: They are widespread geographically; they are numerous; they span a considerable portion of the

FIGURE 7–12

Proconsul africanus skull (from early Miocene deposits on Rusinga Island, Kenya).

 Virtual Lab 7, section III, part D, provides 3-D animations of many of the important fossil primates from the Miocene.

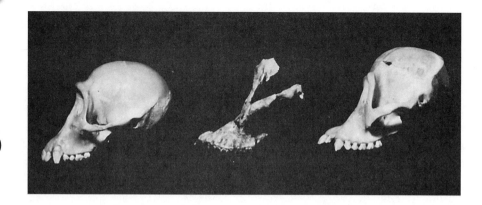

FIGURE 7–13

Comparison of *Sivapithecus* cranium (center) with that of modern chimpanzee (left) and orangutan (right). The *Sivapithecus* fossil is specimen GSP 15000 from the Potwar Plateau, Pakistan, c. 8 m.y.a.

Large-bodied hominoids

Those hominoids including "great" apes (orangutans, chimpanzees, gorillas) and hominids, as well as all ancestral forms back to the time of divergence from small-bodied hominoids (i.e., the gibbon lineage).

Hominids

Popular form of Hominidae, the family to which modern humans belong; includes all bipedal hominoids back to the divergence from African great apes.

Speciation

The process by which new species are produced from earlier ones; the most important mechanism of macroevolutionary change.

Miocene, with *known* remains dated between 23 and 6 m.y.a.; and at present, they are poorly understood. However, we can reasonably draw the following conclusions:

1. These are hominoids—more closely related to the ape-human lineage than to Old World monkeys.
2. Moreover, they are mostly **large-bodied hominoids,** that is, more akin to the lineages of orangutans, gorillas, chimpanzees, and humans than to smaller-bodied apes (i.e., gibbons).
3. Most of the Miocene forms thus far discovered are so derived as to be improbable ancestors of *any* living form.
4. One lineage that appears well established relates to *Sivapithecus* from Turkey and Pakistan. This form shows some highly derived facial features similar to the modern orangutan, suggesting a fairly close evolutionary link (Fig. 7–13).
5. There are no definite **hominids** yet discerned from any Miocene-dated locale. All the confirmed members of our family come from Pliocene beds and later. (The detailed story of hominid evolution will encompass much of the remainder of this text.)

Modes of Evolutionary Change

In this chapter, we are discussing evolutionary change from the perspective of macroevolution. The major evolutionary factor underlying macroevolutionary change is **speciation,** the process whereby new species first arise. As you will recall, we have defined a species as a group of *reproductively isolated* organisms, a characterization that follows the biological species concept (Mayr, 1970). According to this same view, the way new species are first produced involves some form of isolation. Picture a single species (baboons, for example) composed of several populations distributed over a wide geographical area. Gene exchange between populations (gene flow) will be limited if a geographical barrier such as an ocean or mountain range effectively separates these populations. This extremely important form of isolating mechanism is termed *geographical isolation.*

If one baboon population (A) is separated from another baboon population (B) by a mountain range, individual baboons of population A will not be able to mate with individuals from B (Fig. 7–14). As time passes (several generations), genetic differences will accumulate in both populations. If population size is small,

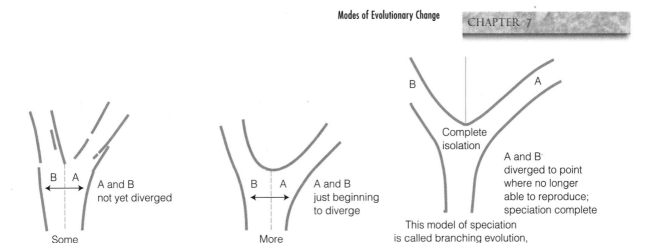

FIGURE 7–14

A speciation model.

we can predict that genetic drift will cause allele frequencies to change in both populations. Moreover, since drift is random in nature, we would not expect the effects to be the same. Consequently, the two populations will begin to diverge.

As long as gene exchange is limited, the populations can only become more genetically different with time. Moreover, further difference would be expected if the baboon groups are occupying slightly different habitats. These additional genetic differences would be incorporated through the process of natural selection. Certain individuals in population A may be most reproductively fit in their own environment, but would show less reproductive success in the environment occupied by population B. Thus, allele frequencies will shift further, and the results, again, will be divergent in the two groups.

With the cumulative effects of genetic drift and natural selection acting over many generations, the result will be two populations that—even if they were to come back into geographical contact—could no longer interbreed. More than just geographical isolation might now apply. There may, for instance, be behavioral differences interfering with courtship—what we call *behavioral isolation.* Using our *biological* definition of species, we now would recognize two distinct species, where initially only one existed.

Until recently, the general consensus among evolutionary biologists was that microevolutionary mechanisms could be translated directly into the larger-scale macroevolutionary changes, especially speciation (also called *transspecific evolution*). A smooth gradation of change was assumed to run directly from microevolution into macroevolution. A representative view was expressed by a leading synthesist, Ernst Mayr: "The proponents of the synthetic theory maintain that all evolution is due to accumulation of small genetic changes, guided by natural selection, and that transspecific evolution is nothing but an extrapolation and magnification of events that take place within populations and species" (Mayr, 1970, p. 351).

In the last two decades this view has been seriously challenged. Many theorists now believe that macroevolution cannot be explained solely in terms of accumulated microevolutionary changes. Consequently, these researchers are convinced that macroevolution is only partly understandable through microevolutionary models.

Gradualism vs. Punctuationalism

The traditional view of evolution has emphasized that change accumulates gradually in evolving lineages—the idea of phyletic gradualism. Accordingly, the complete fossil record of an evolving group (if it could be recovered) would display a series of forms with finely graded transitional differences between each ancestor and its descendant. The fact that such transitional forms are only rarely found is attributed to the incompleteness of the fossil record, or, as Darwin called it, "a history of the world, imperfectly kept, and written in changing dialect."

For more than a century, this perspective dominated evolutionary biology, but in the last 20 years, some biologists have called this notion into question. The evolutionary mechanisms operating on species over the long run are often not continuously gradual. In some cases, species persist for thousands of generations basically unchanged. Then, rather suddenly, at least in evolutionary terms, a "spurt" of speciation occurs. This uneven, nongradual process of long stasis and quick spurts has been termed **punctuated equilibrium** (Gould and Eldredge, 1977).

What the advocates of punctuated equilibrium are disputing are the tempo (rate) and mode (manner) of evolutionary change as commonly understood since Darwin's time. Rather than a slow, steady tempo, this alternate view postulates long periods of no change punctuated only occasionally by sudden bursts. From this observation, it was concluded that the mode of evolution, too, must be different from that suggested by classical Darwinists. Rather than gradual accumulation of small changes in a single lineage, advocates of punctuated equilibrium believe that an additional evolutionary mechanism is required to push the process along. They thus postulate *speciation* as the major influence in bringing about rapid evolutionary change.

How well does the paleontological record agree with the predictions of punctuated equilibrium? Indeed, considerable fossil data show long periods of stasis (on the order of 10,000 to 50,000 years) punctuated by occasional quite rapid changes. The best supporting evidence for punctuated equilibrium has come from the fossilized remains of marine invertebrates. Intermediate forms are rare, not so much because the fossil record is poor, but because the speciation events and longevity of these transitional species were so short that we should not expect to find them very often.

How well, then, does the primate fossil record fit the punctuated equilibrium model? In studies of Eocene primates, rates of evolutionary change were shown to be quite gradual (Gingerich, 1985; Brown and Rose, 1987; Rose, 1991). In another study, here of Paleocene plesiadapiforms, evolutionary changes were also quite gradual. Although no longer considered primates, these forms show a gradual tempo of change in another, closely related group of mammals. The predictions consistent with punctuated equilibrium have thus far not been substantiated in those evolving lineages of primates for which we have adequate data to test the theory.

It would, however, be a fallacy to assume that evolutionary change in primates or in any other group must therefore be of a completely gradual tempo. Such is clearly not the case. In all lineages, the pace assuredly speeds up and slows down as a result of factors that influence the size and relative isolation of populations. In addition, environmental changes that influence the pace and direction of natural selection must also be considered. Nevertheless, in general accordance with the modern synthesis, microevolution and macroevolution need not be "decoupled," as some evolutionary biologists have recently suggested.

Punctuated equilibrium
The concept that evolutionary change proceeds through long periods of stasis punctuated by rapid periods of change.

The Meaning of Genus and Species

Our discussion of fossil primates has introduced a variety of taxonomic names. We should pause at this point and ask why we use so many names like *Aegyptopithecus,* *Apidium,* and *Sivapithecus.* What do such names mean in evolutionary terms?

Our goal when applying genus, species, or other taxonomic labels to groups of organisms is to make meaningful biological statements about the variation that is present. When looking at populations of living or long-extinct animals, we are assuredly going to see variation. The situation is true of *any* sexually reproducing organism because of the factors of recombination (see Chapter 3). As a result of recombination, each individual organism is a unique combination of genetic material, and the uniqueness is usually reflected to some extent in the phenotype.

In addition to such *individual variation,* we see other kinds of systematic variation in all biological populations. *Age changes* certainly alter overall body size as well as shape in many mammals. One pertinent example for fossil hominoid studies is the great change in number, size, and shape of teeth from deciduous (milk) teeth (only 20 present) to the permanent dentition (32 present). It would be an obvious error to differentiate fossil forms solely on the basis of such age-dependent criteria. If one individual were represented just by milk teeth and another (seemingly very different) individual were represented just by adult teeth, they easily could be different-aged individuals from the *same* population. Variation due to sex also plays an important role in influencing differences among individuals observed in biological populations. Differences in structural traits between males and females of the same population are called *sexual dimorphism* and can result in marked variance in body size and proportions in adults of the same species.

Keeping in mind all the types of variation present within interbreeding groups of organisms, the minimum biological category we would like to define in fossil primate samples is the *species.* As already defined, a species is a group of interbreeding or potentially interbreeding organisms that is reproductively isolated from other such groups. In modern organisms, this concept is theoretically testable by observations of reproductive behavior. In animals long dead, such observations are obviously impossible. Therefore, to get a handle on the interpretation of variation seen in fossil groups, we must refer to living animals.

We know without doubt that variation is present. The question is, What is its biological significance? Two immediate choices occur: Either the variation is accounted for by individual, age, and sex differences seen within every biological species—**intraspecific**—or the variation represents differences between reproductively isolated groups—**interspecific.** How do we choose between the alternatives, intra- or interspecific? We clearly must refer to already defined groups where we can observe reproductive behavior—in other words, contemporary species.

If the amount of morphological variation observed in fossil samples is comparable to that seen today *within species of closely related forms,* then we should not "split" our sample into more than one species. We must, however, be careful in choosing modern analogues, for rates of morphological evolution vary widely among different groups of mammals. In interpreting past primates, we do best when comparing them with well-known species of modern primates.

Nevertheless, studies of such living groups have shown that delimiting exactly where species boundaries begin and end is often difficult. In dealing with extinct species, the uncertainties are even greater. In addition to the overlapping patterns

Intraspecific
Within species; refers to variation seen within the same species.

Interspecific
Between species; refers to variation beyond that seen within the same species to include additional aspects seen between two different species.

Paleospecies
Species defined from fossil evidence, often covering a long time span.

of variation *over space,* variation also occurs *through time.* In other words, even more variation will be seen in such **paleospecies,** since individuals may be separated by thousands or even millions of years. Applying strict Linnaean taxonomy to such a situation presents an unavoidable dilemma. Standard Linnaean classification, designed to take account of variation present at any given time, describes a static situation. However, when we deal with paleospecies, the time frame is expanded, and the situation can be dynamic (i.e., later forms might be different from earlier ones). In such a dynamic situation, taxonomic decisions (where to draw species boundaries) are ultimately going to be somewhat arbitrary.

The next level of formal taxonomic classification, the *genus,* presents another problem. To have more than one genus, we obviously must have at least two species (reproductively isolated groups), and, in addition, the species must differ in a basic way. A genus is therefore defined as a group of species composed of members more closely related to each other than they are to species from any other genus.

Grouping species together into genera is largely a subjective procedure wherein the degree of relatedness becomes a relative judgment. One possible test for contemporary animals is to check for results of hybridization between individuals of different species—rare in nature but quite common in captivity. If two normally separate species interbreed and produce live, though not necessarily fertile, offspring, they probably are not too different genetically and should therefore be grouped together in the same genus. A well-known example of such a cross is horses with donkeys (*Equus callabus* × *Equus asinus*), which normally produces live, sterile offspring (mules).

As previously mentioned, we cannot perform breeding experiments with extinct animals, but another definition of genus becomes highly relevant. Species that are members of the same genus share the same broad adaptive zone. What this represents is a general ecological lifestyle more basic than the narrower ecological niches characteristic of individual species. This ecological definition of genus can be an immense aid in interpreting fossil primates. Teeth are the most frequently preserved parts, and they often can provide excellent general ecological inferences. In addition, cladistic analysis (see p.151) of derived characteristics provides a more rigorous means of evaluating relationships. In other words, members of the *same* genus should share derived characters not seen in other genera.

As a final comment, we should point out that classification by genus is not always a straightforward decision. Indeed, the argument among primatologists over whether the chimpanzee and gorilla represent one genus (*Pan troglodytes, Pan gorilla*) or two different genera (*Pan troglodytes, Gorilla gorilla*) demonstrates that even with living, breathing animals, the choices are not always clear. For that matter, many current researchers, pointing to the very close genetic similarities between humans and chimpanzees, would place both in the same genus (*Homo sapiens, Homo troglodytes*). When it gets this close to home, it is even more difficult to maintain objectivity!

SUMMARY

This chapter has surveyed the basics of mammalian/primate evolution, emphasizing a macroevolutionary perspective. Given the huge amount of organic diversity displayed, as well as the vast time involved, two major organizing perspectives prove indispensable: schemes of formal classification to organize organic diversity and the geological time scale to organize geological time. Because primates are vertebrates and, more specifically, mammals, these broader organic groups were briefly reviewed, emphasizing major evolutionary trends. The fossil history of primates was taken up in more detail with surveys of earliest traces from the Paleocene and Eocene epochs. The beginnings of anthropoid radiation can be traced to the end of the Eocene and to the Oligocene (the Fayum in Egypt), and the broad, complex radiation of hominoids during the Miocene is even more central to understanding human evolution.

Theoretical perspectives relating to contemporary understanding of macroevolutionary processes (especially the concept of speciation) are crucial to interpreting any long-term aspect of evolutionary history, be it mammalian, primate, hominoid, or hominid. In this context, evolutionary biologists have postulated two different modes of evolutionary change: gradualism and punctuated equilibrium. At present, the available primate evolutionary record does not conform to the predictions of punctuated equilibrium, but one should not conclude that evolutionary tempo was necessarily strictly gradual (which it certainly was not). Finally, as genus and species designation is the common form of reference for both living and extinct organisms (and will be used frequently throughout the balance of this text), its biological significance was discussed in depth.

QUESTIONS FOR REVIEW

1. What are the two primary goals of organic classification?
2. What are the six major groups of vertebrates?
3. What are the major eras of geological time over which vertebrates have evolved?
4. What primary features distinguish mammals—especially placental mammals—from other vertebrates?
5. What is meant by a homology? Contrast with analogy, using examples.
6. Why do evolutionary biologists concentrate on derived features rather than primitive ones? Give an example of each.
7. What are the seven epochs of the Cenozoic?
8. Why is it difficult to identify clearly very early primates from other primitive placental mammals?
9. How diversified and geographically widespread were hominoids in the Miocene?
10. Humans are Old World anthropoids. What other groups are also Old World anthropoids?
11. Contrast the gradualist view of evolutionary change with a punctuationalist view. Give an example from primate evolution that supports one view or the other.

SUGGESTED FURTHER READINGS

Carroll, Robert L. 1988. *Vertebrate Paleontology and Evolution.* New York: Freeman.
Conroy, G. C. 1990. *Primate Evolution.* New York: Norton.

Fleagle, John. 1999. *Primate Adaptation and Evolution.* 2nd ed. New York: Academic Press.

Jones, Steve, Robert Martin, and David Pilbeam (eds.). 1992. *The Cambridge Encyclopedia of Human Evolution.* New York: Cambridge University Press.

MULTIMEDIA RESOURCES

Wadsworth Anthropology Resource Center

http://anthropology.wadsworth.com

Visit Anthropology Online to obtain current updates in the field, surfing tips, career information, and more. In addition, enrich your study efforts with text-specific study aids arranged by chapter.

InfoTrac College Edition

http://www.infotrac-college.com/wadsworth

1. On InfoTrac College Edition, search for the keywords *evolution* and *mammals.* Choose one of the articles found by this search and read through it. What does this research reveal about evolution?

2. Now do the same search for the keywords *evolution* and *primates.* Choose a recent article about primate evolution. What does it say about primate evolution that is different from the information presented in the text?

Internet Exercises

1. Visit the University of California Museum of Paleontology (**http://www.ucmp .berkeley.edu/**). This site provides extensive online exhibits on geology, phylogeny, and mammalian evolution. Explore the site and see what you can find to supplement the information in the text on mammalian evolution. When did mammals first appear? When did they begin to differentiate into the modern orders? When and where did primates first appear? What did the earliest primates look like?

2. Most of the Internet search engines provide a news search as well as a general search. Examples include Excite's Newstracker (**http://nt.excite.com**), Yahoo! News (**http://www.yahoo.com/headlines/**), and Infoseek News (**http://guide-p.infoseek.com/News**). Search recent news stories for topics related to primate evolution. What have researchers learned about primate evolution in the last few months? Are there any recently discovered fossils or new analyses of previously studied fossils? Read several of these stories and write a brief report on new discoveries in primate evolution and what they contribute to our understanding of human origins.

CHAPTER
8

Hominid Origins

CONTENTS

Introduction

In the last three chapters, we have seen how and why humans are grouped as primates, both structurally and behaviorally, and how our evolutionary history coincides with that of other primates. However, we are a unique kind of primate, and our ancestors have been adapted to a particular kind of lifestyle for several million years. Some primitive hominoid may have begun this process more than 10 m.y.a., but fossil evidence indicates much more definite hominid relationships beginning about 5 m.y.a. The hominid nature of these remains is revealed by more than the morphological structure of teeth and bones; in many cases, we know that these animals are hominids also because of the way they behaved—emphasizing once again the **biocultural** nature of human evolution.

In this chapter, we will review abundant and exciting discoveries that have come from Africa. Spanning much of the twentieth century, these discoveries have resulted from the dedication and efforts of a number of scientists and have also frequently captured the interest of the general public. Archaeological discoveries of early cultural behavior are fascinating, as they provide information concerning the behavioral and cognitive capabilities of our more immediate ancestors. Perhaps, even more so, the remains of the hominids themselves fire the imagination, since here, in these fossils, we can more easily see the roots of human emergence. In this chapter, and in the remainder of this text, we will trace more directly the beginnings of humankind.

Definition of Hominid

If any of the hominoid fossils prior to 5 m.y.a. (i.e., from the Miocene) that have been discussed thus far (see Chapter 7) represent the earliest phases of hominid emergence, our recognition of them *as hominids* must primarily be a dental one. Teeth and jaws are mostly what we have of these Miocene hominoids, but dental features are not the only way to describe the special features of hominids and are certainly not the most distinctive of the later stages of human evolution. Modern humans, as well as our most immediate hominid ancestors, are distinguished from great apes by more obvious features than tooth and jaw dimensions. For example, various scientists have pointed to such distinctive hominid characteristics as bipedal locomotion, large brain size, and toolmaking behavior as being significant (at some stage) in defining what makes a hominid a hominid.

It must be emphasized that not all these characteristics developed simultaneously or at the same pace. Indeed, over the last several million years of hominid evolution, quite a different pattern has been evident, in which each of the components (dentition, locomotion, brain size, and toolmaking) have developed at quite different rates. Such a pattern, where physiological/behavioral systems evolve at different rates, is called **mosaic evolution.** As we first pointed out in Chapter 1 and will much emphasize in this chapter, the single most important defining characteristic for the full course of hominid evolution is **bipedal locomotion.** In the earliest stages of hominid emergence, skeletal evidence indicating bipedal locomotion is the only truly reliable indicator that these fossils were indeed hominids. However, in later stages of hominid evolution, other features, especially those relating to brain development and behavior, become highly significant (see Fig. 8–1).

Biocultural
Pertaining to the concept that biology makes culture possible and that culture influences biology.

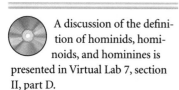
A discussion of the definition of hominids, hominoids, and hominines is presented in Virtual Lab 7, section II, part D.

Mosaic evolution
A pattern of evolution in which the rates of evolution in one functional system varies from those in other systems. For example, in hominid evolution, the dental system, locomotor system, and neurological system (especially the brain) all evolved at markedly different rates.

Bipedal locomotion
Walking on two feet. Walking habitually on two legs is the single most distinctive feature of the hominids.

	Locomotion	Brain	Dentition	Toolmaking Behavior
(Modern *Homo sapiens*) 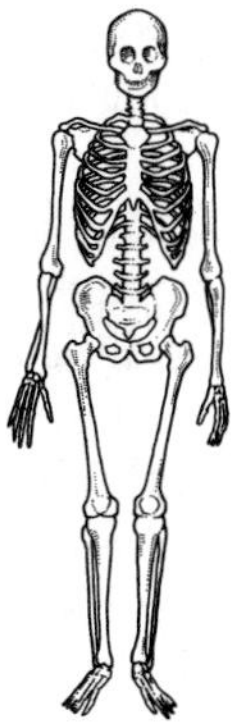	Bipedal: shortened pelvis; body size larger; legs longer; fingers and toes not as long	Greatly increased brain size—highly encephalized	Small incisors; canines further reduced; molar tooth enamel caps thick	Stone tools found after 2.5 m.y.a.; increasing trend of cultural dependency apparent in later hominids
(Early hominid) 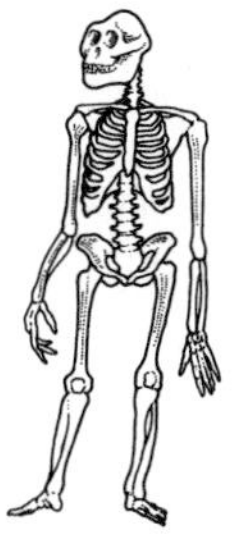	Bipedal: shortened pelvis; some differences from later hominids, showing smaller body size and long arms relative to legs; long fingers and toes; probably capable of considerable climbing	Larger than Miocene forms, but still only moderately encephalized	Moderately large front teeth (incisors); canines somewhat reduced; molar tooth enamel caps very thick	In earliest stages unknown; no stone tool use prior to 2.5 m.y.a.; probably somewhat more oriented toward tool manufacture and use than chimpanzees
(Miocene, generalized hominoid) 	Quadrupedal: long pelvis; some forms capable of considerable arm swinging, suspensory locomotion	Small compared to hominids, but large compared to other primates; a fair degree of encephalization	Large front teeth (including canines); molar teeth variable depending on species; some have thin enamel caps, others thick enamel caps	Unknown—no stone tools; probably had capabilities similar to chimpanzees

Time scale markers: 0.5 m.y.a., 1 m.y.a., 2 m.y.a., 3 m.y.a., 4 m.y.a., 20 m.y.a.

Biocultural Evolution: The Human Capacity for Culture

One of the most distinctive behavioral features of humans is our species' extraordinary elaboration of and dependence on culture. Certainly, other primates, and many other animals, for that matter, modify their environments. As we saw in Chapter 6, chimpanzees especially are known for such behaviors as using termite sticks, and some even transport rocks to crush nuts. Given such observations, it becomes tenuous to draw sharp lines between early hominid toolmaking behavior and that exhibited by other animals.

FIGURE 8–1

Mosaic evolution of hominid characteristics: a postulated time line.

Virtual Lab 11 is devoted to the archaeological record.

Another point to remember is that human culture, at least as it is defined in contemporary contexts, involves much more than toolmaking capacity. For humans, culture integrates an entire adaptive strategy involving cognitive, political, social, and economic components. The *material culture,* the tools humans use, is but a small portion of this cultural complex.

Nevertheless, when examining the archaeological record of earlier hominids, what is available for study is almost exclusively certain remains of material culture, especially residues of stone tool manufacture. Thus, it is extremely difficult to learn anything about the earliest stages of hominid cultural development prior to the regular manufacture of stone tools. As you will see, this most crucial cultural development has been traced to approximately 2.5 m.y.a. (Semaw et al., 1997). Yet, hominids were undoubtedly using other kinds of tools (made of perishable materials) and displaying a whole array of other cultural behaviors long before this time. However, without any "hard" evidence preserved in the archaeological record, our understanding of the early development of these nonmaterial cultural components remains elusive.

The fundamental basis for human cultural elaboration relates directly to cognitive abilities. Again, we are not dealing with an absolute distinction, but a relative one. Other primates, as documented in chimpanzees and bonobos, possess some of the language capabilities exhibited by humans. Nevertheless, modern humans display these abilities in a complexity several orders of magnitude beyond that of any other animal. Moreover, only humans are so completely dependent on symbolic communication and its cultural by-products that contemporary *Homo sapiens* could not survive without them.

When did the unique combination of cognitive, social, and material cultural adaptations become prominent in human evolution? We must be careful to recognize the manifold nature of culture and not expect it always to contain the same elements across species (as when compared to nonhuman primates) or through time (when trying to reconstruct ancient hominid behavior). Richard Potts (1993) has critiqued this overly simplistic perspective and suggests a more dynamic approach, one that incorporates many subcomponents (including aspects of behavior, cognition, and social interaction).

We know that the earliest hominids almost certainly did *not* regularly manufacture stone tools (at least, none that have been found!). These earliest members of the hominid lineage, dating back to approximately 7–5 m.y.a., could be referred to as **protohominids.** These protohominids may have carried objects such as naturally sharp stones or stone flakes, parts of carcasses, and pieces of wood around their home ranges. At minimum, we would expect them to have displayed these behaviors to at least the same degree as living chimpanzees.

Moreover, as you will see, by at least 4.4 m.y.a., hominids had developed one crucial advantage: They were bipedal and could therefore much more easily carry all manner of objects from place to place. Ultimately, the efficient exploitation of resources widely distributed in time and space would most likely have led to using "central" locations where key components, especially stone objects, were cached (Potts, 1991).

What is certain is that over a period of several million years, during the formative stages of hominid emergence, numerous components interacted, but not all developed simultaneously. As cognitive abilities developed, more efficient means of communication and learning resulted. Largely as a result of consequent neurological reorganization, more elaborate tools and social relationships also

Protohominids
The earliest members of the hominid lineage, as yet basically unrepresented in the fossil record; thus, their structure and behavior are reconstructed hypothetically.

emerged. These, in turn, selected for greater intelligence, which in turn selected for further neural elaboration. Quite clearly, then, these mutual dynamics are at the very heart of what we call hominid *biocultural* evolution.

Paleoanthropology as a Multidisciplinary Science

To understand human biocultural evolution adequately, a broad base of information is needed. The task of recovering and interpreting all the clues left by early hominids is the work of paleoanthropologists. Paleoanthropology is defined as the study of early humans. As such, it is a diverse **multidisciplinary** pursuit seeking to reconstruct every bit of information possible concerning the dating, structure, behavior, and ecology of our hominid ancestors. In just the last few years, the study of early hominids has marshalled the specialized skills of many diverse scientific disciplines. Included primarily in this growing and exciting adventure are geologists, archaeologists, physical anthropologists, and paleoecologists (Table 8–1).

Geologists, usually working with anthropologists (often archaeologists), do the initial survey to locate potential early hominid **sites.** Many sophisticated techniques can contribute to this search, including aerial and satellite photography. Paleontologists may also be involved in this early search, for they can help find geological beds containing **faunal** remains. (Where conditions are favorable for the preservation of such specimens as ancient pigs or baboons, conditions may also be favorable for the preservation of hominid fossils.) In addition, paleontologists can—through comparison with faunal sequences elsewhere—give quick estimates of the approximate age of sites without having to wait for the expensive and time-consuming **chronometric** analyses. In this way, fossil beds of the "right" geological ages (i.e., where hominid finds are most likely) can be identified.

Once potential early hominid localities have been identified, much more extensive surveying begins. At this point, the archaeologists take over the search for hominid traces (Fig. 8–2). We do not necessarily have to find the fossilized remains of early hominids (which will always be rare) to know that hominids consistently occupied an ancient land surface. Behavioral clues, or **artifacts,** also inform us directly and unambiguously about early hominid occupation. Modifying rocks

Multidisciplinary
Pertaining to research that involves mutual contributions and cooperation of several different experts from various scientific fields (i.e., disciplines).

Sites
Locations of discoveries. In paleontology and archaeology, a site may refer to a region where a number of discoveries have been made.

Faunal
Referring to animal remains; in archaeology, specifically refers to the fossil remains of animals.

Chronometric
Referring to a dating technique that gives an estimate in actual number of years (from *chronos,* meaning "time," and *metric,* meaning "measure").

Artifacts
Traces of hominid behavior. Very old ones are usually made of stone.

TABLE 8–1 Components of Paleoanthropology

Physical Sciences	Biological Sciences	Social Sciences
Geology	Physical anthropology	Archaeology
Stratigraphy	Ecology	Ethnoarchaeology
Petrology	Paleontology (fossil	Cultural anthropology
(rocks, minerals)	animals)	Ethnography
Pedology (soils)	Palynology (fossil pollen)	Psychology
Geomorphology	Primatology	
Geophysics		
Chemistry		
Taphonomy*		

*Taphonomy (*taphos:* dead) is the study of how bones and other materials come to be buried in the earth and preserved as fossils. A taphonomist studies such phenomena as sedimentation, the action of streams, preservation properties of bone, and carnivore disturbance factors.

 A detailed discussion of how the fossil record is generated is given in Virtual Lab 7, section I, part D.

FIGURE 8–2

Excavations in progress at Olduvai. This site is more than 1 million years old. It was located when a hominid ulna (arm bone) was found eroding out of the side of the gorge. Many artifacts and broken bones of other animals were also found at this site.

according to a consistent plan or simply carrying them over fairly long distances is a behavior exhibited by no other animal but a hominid. Therefore, when we see such behavioral evidence at a site, we know that hominids were once present there.

Dating Methods

One of the essentials of paleoanthropology is placing sites and fossils into a chronological framework. In other words, we want to know how old they are. How, then, do we date sites—or, more precisely, how do we date the geological strata in which sites are found? The question is both reasonable and important, so let us examine some of the dating techniques used by paleontologists, geologists, and paleoanthropologists.

Scientists use two basic types of dating for this purpose: relative and chronometric (also known as *absolute dating*). Relative dating methods tell you that something is older or younger than something else, but not how much. If, for example, a fossil cranium is found at a depth of 50 feet and another cranium at 70 feet at the same site, we usually assume that the cranium at 70 feet is older. We may not know the date (in years) of either one, but we would be able to infer a *relative* sequence. This method of dating is based on **stratigraphy** and is called *stratigraphic dating*. This was one of the first techniques to be used by scholars working with the vast expanses of geological time. Stratigraphic dating is based on the law of superposition, which states that a lower **stratum** (layer) is older than a higher stratum. Given the fact that much of the earth's crust has been laid down by layer after layer of sedimentary rock, stratigraphic relationships have provided a valuable tool in reconstructing the history of the earth and of life upon it.

Stratigraphic dating does, however, have a number of potential problems. Earth disturbances, such as volcanic activity, river action, and faulting, may shift the strata or materials in them, and the chronology may thus be difficult or impossible to reconstruct. Furthermore, given the widely different rates of accumulation, the elapsed time of any stratum cannot be determined with much accuracy.

Stratigraphy
Sequential layering of deposits.

Stratum (*pl.,* strata)
Geological layer.

Another method of relative dating is *fluorine analysis,* which applies only to bone. Bones in the earth are exposed to the seepage of groundwater that usually contains some fluorine. The longer a bone lies buried, the more fluorine it incorporates during fossilization. Therefore, bones deposited at the same time in the same location should contain the same amount of fluorine.

The use of this technique by Professor Oakley of the British Museum in the early 1950s exposed the famous Piltdown hoax by demonstrating that the human skull was considerably older than the jaw ostensibly found with it (Weiner, 1955). Lying in the same location, the jaw and skull should have absorbed approximately the same quantity of fluorine. But the skull contained significantly more, meaning that if it came from the same site, it had been deposited considerably earlier. The discrepancy of fluorine content led Oakley and others to a much closer examination of the bones, and they found that the jaw was not that of a hominid at all, but one of a juvenile orangutan! Clearly, then, someone had planted it at Piltdown, but who was the devious forger? Until recently, there were no firm clues, but newly discovered evidence has pointed the blame at Martin Hinton, a British zoologist (Gee, 1996).

Unfortunately, fluorine is useful only for dating bones from the same location. Because of the differing concentrations in groundwater, accumulation rates will vary from place to place. Also, some groundwater may not contain any fluorine. For these reasons, comparing fossils from different localities using fluorine analysis is not feasible.

Two other relative dating techniques, *biostratigraphy* and *paleomagnetism,* have also proved quite useful in calibrating the ages of early hominid sites. Biostratigraphy is a relative technique based on fairly regular changes seen in the dentition and other anatomical structures in such groups as pigs, rodents, and baboons. Dating of sites is based on the presence of certain fossil species that also occur elsewhere in deposits whose dates have been determined. This technique has proved helpful in cross-correlating the ages of various sites in both South and East Africa. A final type of relative dating, paleomagnetism, is based on the shifting nature of the earth's geomagnetic pole. Although now oriented northward, the geomagnetic pole is known to have shifted several times in the past and at times was oriented to the south. By examining magnetically charged particles encased in rock, geologists can determine the orientation of these ancient "compasses." One cannot derive a date in years from this particular technique, but it is used to double-check other techniques.

In all these relative dating techniques, the age of geological layers or objects within them is impossible to calibrate. To determine age as precisely as possible, scientists have developed a variety of chronometric techniques, many based on the phenomenon of radioactive decay. The theory is quite simple: Certain radioactive isotopes of elements are unstable, disintegrate, and form an isotopic variant of another element. Since the rate of disintegration follows a predictable mathematical pattern, the radioactive material serves as an accurate geological clock. By measuring the amount of disintegration in a particular sample, scientists have devised techniques for dating the immense age of the earth (and moon rocks) as well as material only a few hundred years old. Several techniques have been employed for a number of years and are now quite well known.

An important chronometric technique used in paleoanthropological research involves potassium-40 (^{40}K), which has a half-life of 1.25 billion years and produces argon-40 (^{40}Ar). That is, half the ^{40}K isotope changes to ^{40}Ar in 1.3 billion

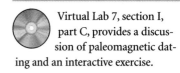

Virtual Lab 7, section I, part C, provides a discussion of geological dating methods including radioisotopic dating.

Virtual Lab 7, section I, part C, provides a discussion of paleomagnetic dating and an interactive exercise.

years. In another 1.3 billion years, half the remaining ^{40}K would be converted (i.e., only one-quarter of the original amount would still be present). Known as the K/Ar, or potassium-argon, method, this procedure has been extensively used in dating materials in the 5–1 m.y.a. range, especially in East Africa. Organic material, such as bone, cannot be measured, but the rock matrix in which the fossilized bone is found can be.

Strata that provide the best samples for K/Ar dating are those that have been heated to an extremely high temperature, such as that generated by volcanic activity. Heating drives off previously accumulated argon gas, thus "resetting" the clock to zero. As the material cools and solidifies, potassium (^{40}K) continues to break down to ^{40}Ar, but now the gas is physically trapped inside the cooling material. To date the geological material, it is reheated, and the escaping gas is then measured. Potassium-argon dating has been used to date very old events—such as the age of the earth—as well as those less than 2,000 years old.

Another well-known chronometric technique popular with archaeologists involves carbon-14 (^{14}C), with a half-life of 5,730 years. This method has been used to date material as recent as a few hundred years old and can be extended as far back as 75,000 years, although the probability of error rises rapidly after 40,000 years. The physical basis of this technique is also *radiometric;* that is, it is tied to the measurement of radioactive decay of an isotope (^{14}C) into another, more stable form. Radiocarbon dating has proved especially relevant for calibrating the latter stages of human evolution, including the Neandertals and the appearance of modern *Homo sapiens* (see Chapter 11).

Other methods have also proved useful in dating early hominid sites. For example, *fission-track dating* is a chronometric technique that works on the basis of the regular fissioning of uranium atoms. When certain types of crystalline rocks are observed microscopically, the "tracks" left by the fission events can be counted and an approximate age is thus calibrated. (Other techniques applicable to dating the later stages of human evolution are discussed briefly in Chapter 11; see Table 11–1.)

Many of the techniques just discussed are used together to provide *independent* checks for dating important early hominid sites. Each technique has a degree of error, and only by *cross-correlating* the results can paleoanthropologists feel confident regarding chronological placement of the fossil and archaeological remains they discover. This point is of the utmost importance, for a firm chronology forms the basis for making sound evolutionary interpretations (as discussed later in the chapter).

The East African Rift Valley

Stretching along a trough that extends roughly north and south for more then 1,200 miles through Ethiopia, Kenya, and Tanzania from the Red Sea in the north to the Serengeti Plain in the south is the eastern branch of the Great Rift Valley of Africa. This massive geological feature has been associated with mountain building, faulting, and volcanic activity over the last several million years.

Because of these gigantic earth movements, earlier sediments that would otherwise have remained deeply buried were literally thrown to the surface, where they became exposed to the trained eye of paleoanthropologists. Such movements have revealed Miocene beds in western Kenya, along the shores of Lake Victoria, where abundant remains of early hominoids have been found. In addition,

Pliocene and Pleistocene sediments are also exposed all along the Rift Valley, and paleoanthropologists have made the most of this unique opportunity. These remains, ranging in time from early in the Pliocene to the first half of the Pleistocene (circa 4.5–1 m.y.a.) are generally referred to as **Plio-Pleistocene.**

In addition to exposing normally hidden deposits, rifting has stimulated volcanic activity, which in turn has provided the means of chronometrically dating (by potassium-argon and fission-track methods) many sites in East Africa. Unlike the other Plio-Pleistocene sites, located in South Africa, those along the Rift Valley are *datable* and have thus yielded much crucial information relevant to the precise chronology of early hominid evolution.

Plio-Pleistocene
The time period including the Pliocene and the first half of the Pleistocene. For early hominids, this currently covers the range 4.5–1 m.y.a.

East African Hominids

Earliest Traces

Currently, there is a gap in our knowledge of the evolutionary events that occurred between 8 and 5 m.y.a. Little relevant fossil evidence has been recovered from this time period, but paleoanthropologists are well aware of two potentially productive areas in Kenya. These areas, each associated with a drainage system of a large lake within the Rift (Lake Baringo and Lake Turkana), are of the appropriate age and, in addition, have sediments that in many cases were highly favorable for fossilization (Figs. 8–3).

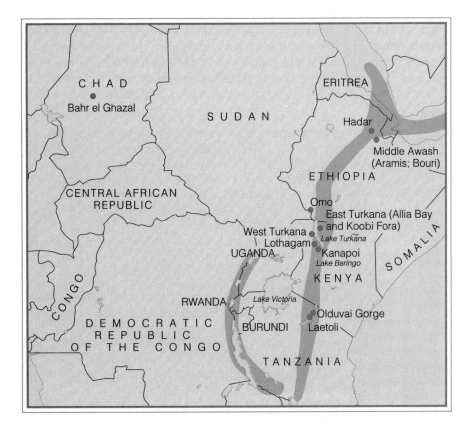

FIGURE 8–3

The East African Rift Valley system and locations of Lake Baringo and Lake Turkana and major hominid sites.

Virtual Lab 8, section I, part A, discusses the fossil evidence for the earliest hominids.

Thus far, only a very few bits and pieces of individuals have been found. Prior to 4.5 m.y.a., none of these remains can definitely be attributed to the Hominidae, but can only generally be characterized as hominoid. The one (fragmentary) specimen that several authorities identify as a *probable* hominid comes from Lothagam in northern Kenya (dated at approximately 5.7 m.y.a.). Given the reasonable likelihood of further discoveries, the search goes on. In addition to knowing the best places to look, paleoanthropologists must also rely on some good luck. And with a bit of luck, we surely will be able to begin to fill that vexing 3-million-year gap. Moreover, the Turkana Basin has proved to be the most productive region in all of Africa for yielding hominid remains from the latter part of the Plio-Pleistocene (2.5–1.0 m.y.a.).

Aramis

A comparison between the mandibles of *Ardipithecus ramidus* and *Australopithecus afarensis* is given in Virtual Lab 8, section I, part A.

One of the most exciting areas for future research in East Africa is the Afar Triangle of northeastern Ethiopia, where the Red Sea, Rift Valley, and Gulf of Aden all intersect. From this area have come many of the most important recent discoveries bearing on human origins. Several areas have yielded fossil remains in recent decades, and many potentially very rich sites are currently being explored. One of these sites just recently discovered, located in the region called the Middle Awash (along the banks of the Awash River), is called Aramis. Initial radiometric dating of the sediments places the fossil remains at 4.4 m.y.a., making this the earliest *collection* of probable hominids yet discovered.

Fossil Remains from Aramis In 1992 and 1993, up to 17 individuals were discovered at Aramis. First announced in 1994, the remains recovered from the first two field seasons include mostly jaws and teeth, but also represent parts of two crania and some upper limb bones (White et al., 1994). In addition, further important finds were made at Aramis in 1994 and 1995, including isolated teeth and mandibular fragments as well as arm, hand, and foot bones (Figs. 8–4). With these new finds,

FIGURE 8–4

New hominid discoveries from Aramis. Alemayehu Asfaw is holding his discovery of an upper arm bone (humerus). In the background, team members search for other fragments; parts of all three bones of the upper appendage of one *Ardipithecus ramidus* individual were discovered.

©1994 Tim D. White\Brill Atlanta

Milford Wolpoff (1995) of the University of Michigan suggests that now more than 40 individuals are represented in the growing Aramis collection. And most exciting of all, a 40 percent complete skeleton of an adult hominid, which preserves many cranial and **postcranial** elements, was partly excavated in late 1994 (Asfaw, 1995).

Since the fossils have been so recently discovered and to date but partially described, only provisional interpretations are possible at this time. However, some general features are apparent. If these forms *are* hominids (and they probably are), then they must be considered quite primitive. The canines are fairly large, and the upper one shears against a cutting surface on the lower first premolar (called a *sectorial* tooth, as in apes) (Fig. 8–5). In addition, the base of the cranium is quite apelike (reminiscent of a chimpanzee). With only very incomplete cranial remains available thus far, assessment of cranial capacity is not yet feasible, although the cranial capacity was probably quite small—at least as small as other early hominids. Thus, it might be asked, What makes these forms hominids? The answer lies in anatomical evidence indicative of bipedal locomotion. First, the entrance of the spine into the base of the cranium (the foramen magnum) is positioned further forward than in quadrupeds (Fig. 8–6). Second, features of the humerus suggest that the forelimb was not weight-bearing. And lastly, reports from the field suggest that the shape of the pelvis (as observed in the partial skeleton) is consistent with bipedalism.

Thus, current conclusions (which will be either unambiguously confirmed or falsified as the skeleton is fully excavated, cleaned, and studied) interpret the Aramis remains as the earliest hominids yet known. Although these individuals from Aramis were very primitive hominids, they were apparently fully bipedal.

Tim White of the University of California is supervising the excavations, and he and his colleagues have recently argued (White et al., 1995) that the fossil hominids from Aramis are so primitive and so different from other early hominids that they should be assigned to a new genus (and, necessarily, a new species as well): *Ardipithecus ramidus.* Most especially, the thin enamel caps on the molars are in dramatic contrast to all other early hominids, who show quite thick enamel caps. These other early hominid forms (all somewhat later than *Ardipithecus*) are placed in the genus ***Australopithecus.***

Postcranial
(*post,* meaning "after") Referring to that portion of the body behind the head (in a quadruped). In bipeds, *postcranial* refers to all parts of the body *beneath* the head (i.e., from the neck down).

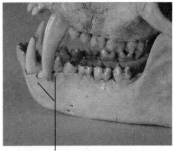

Sectorial lower first premolar

FIGURE 8–5

Left lateral view of the teeth of a male patas monkey. Note how the large upper canine shears against the elongated surface of the *sectorial* lower first premolar.

Australopithecus
An early hominid genus, known from the Plio-Pleistocene of Africa, characterized by bipedal locomotion, a relatively small brain, and large back teeth.

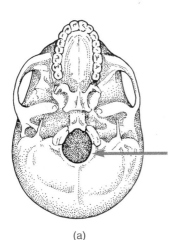

(a)

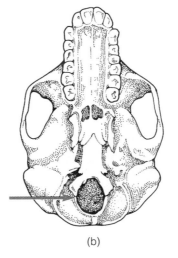

(b)

FIGURE 8–6

Position of the foramen magnum in (a) a human and (b) a chimpanzee. Note the more forward position in the human cranium.

Kanapoi and Allia Bay (East Turkana)

In northernmost Kenya, several important fossil-bearing sites have been explored, making this area the most productive in all of Africa. Two of these localities, Kanapoi (to the west of Lake Turkana) and Allia Bay (on the eastern shore) (see Fig. 8–3) have in the last few years yielded some of the earliest hominid remains yet discovered. Radiometric dates from the two sites place the hominid remains in the time range of 4.2–3.9 m.y.a. Some of the remains (a humerus discovered at Kanapoi in 1965 and a tooth found in 1982 at Allia Bay) have been known for some time, but much more abundant finds were recovered from both localities in 1994 and 1995, and the whole collection was first described in 1995 (Leakey et al., 1995).

Hominids from Kanapoi and Allia Bay   To date, a total of 9 specimens have been recovered from Kanapoi and another 12 specimens have been collected from Allia Bay. Together this collection consists mostly of teeth, but also includes six jaws and a few postcranial elements. The teeth are quite primitive, as are some suggestive facial features. However, unlike the Aramis remains (*Ardipithecus*), the enamel on the molars is thick, and in this respect, the Kanapoi and Allia Bay fossils are like other early hominids (i.e., other members of the genus *Australopithecus*). Finally, anatomical details of the leg have led researchers to be quite confident that this form was, in fact, bipedal.

From the features that are present, Meave Leakey and her colleagues have assigned the fossil material from Kanapoi and Allia Bay to the genus *Australopithecus*. Moreover, they suggest that these fossils differ significantly enough from later members of *Australopithecus* to warrant their provisional assignment to a separate species, *Australopithecus anamensis*. Whether the distinction (particularly when compared with the slightly later hominid, *Australopithecus afarensis*) justifies a separate species designation must await further discoveries and more detailed study. (A consensus will be reached after a number of other researchers have had the opportunity to study the original fossils or cast replicas.)

Laetoli

Located in northern Tanzania, Laetoli is another site that has yielded a fine collection of early hominids. With numerous volcanic sediments in the vicinity, accurate K/Ar testing is possible and provides a date of 3.7–3.5 m.y.a. for this site.

Since 1974, when systematic fossil recovery began at Laetoli, 23 fossil hominid individuals have been found, consisting almost exclusively of jaws and teeth. In February 1978, Mary Leakey announced a remarkable discovery at Laetoli: fossilized footprints pressed into an ancient volcanic bed more than 3.5 m.y.a. Literally thousands of footprints have been found at this remarkable site, representing more than 20 different animal species (Pliocene elephants, pigs, giraffes, antelopes, hyenas, and an abundance of hares). Several hominid footprints have also been found, including a trail more than 75 feet long made by at least two, and perhaps three, individuals (Leakey and Hay, 1979) (Fig. 8–7).

Such discoveries of well-preserved hominid footprints are extremely important in furthering our understanding of human evolution. For the first time, we can make *definite* statements regarding the locomotor pattern and stature of early hominids. Initial analysis of these early hominid footprints compared to

FIGURE 8–7

Hominid footprint from Laetoli, Tanzania. Note the deep impression of the heel and the large toe (arrow) in line (adducted) with the other toes.

modern humans suggests a stature of about 4 feet 9 inches for the larger individual and 4 feet 1 inch for the smaller individual (White, 1980). Studies of these impressions clearly show that the mode of locomotion of these hominids was fully bipedal and, further, *very* similar to that of modern humans (Day and Wickens, 1980). As we will discuss shortly, the development of *bipedal locomotion* is the most important defining characteristic of early hominid evolution. Some researchers, however, have concluded that these early hominids were not bipedal in quite the same way that modern humans are. From detailed comparisons with modern humans, estimates of step length, cadence, and speed of walking have been ascertained, indicating that the Laetoli hominids moved in a "strolling" fashion with a short stride (Chateris et al., 1981). There remains considerable debate regarding the locomotor pattern of these early hominids. Owen Lovejoy (1993) continues to argue strongly that the footprints (and other remains) indicate a *fully* efficient biped.

Hadar (Afar Triangle)

Also in the Afar region of Ethiopia, just north of Aramis, is the **Hadar** area. Owing to the excellent preservation conditions in the once-lakeside environment at Hadar, an extraordinary collection of fossilized bones has been discovered—6,000 specimens in the first two field seasons alone! Among the fossil remains, at least 40 hominid individuals (and possibly as many as 65) have been discovered (Johanson and Taieb, 1980). The entire time range of hominid finds at Hadar has been approximated at 3.9–2.3 m.y.a. (Kimbel et al., 1994).

    Two extraordinary discoveries at Hadar are most noteworthy. In 1974, a partial skeleton called "Lucy" was found eroding out of a hillside. This fossil is scientifically designated as Afar Locality (AL) 288-1, but is usually just called Lucy (after a popular Beatles song, "Lucy in the Sky with Diamonds"). Representing

Hadar
(ha-dar´)

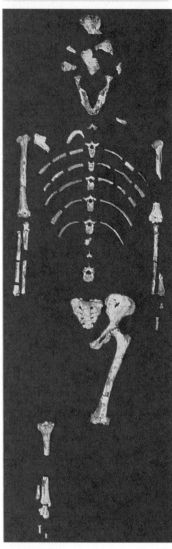

FIGURE 8–8

"Lucy," a partial hominid skeleton, discovered at Hadar in 1974.

almost 40 percent of a skeleton, this is one of the two most complete individuals from anywhere in the world for the entire period before about 100,000 years ago (Fig. 8–8).*

The second find, a phenomenal discovery, came to light in 1975 at Locality 333. Don Johanson and his amazed crew found dozens of hominid bones scattered along a hillside. These bones represented at least 13 individuals, including 4 infants. It has been argued that these individuals may have been members of one social unit and that they all died at about the same time, thus representing a "catastrophic" assemblage (White and Johanson, 1989). However, the precise deposition of the site has not been completely explained, so this assertion must be viewed as quite tentative. (In geological time, an "instant" could represent many decades or centuries.) Considerable cultural material has been found in the Hadar area—mostly washed into stream channels, but some stone tools have been reported in context at a site dated at 2.5 m.y.a., making the findings among the oldest cultural evidence yet discovered.

Unfortunately, over the last three decades, political instability in Ethiopia has caused frequent interruptions of field research at Hadar. However, in the last 10 years, considerable further surveying has been done in the Afar Triangle (and elsewhere in Ethiopia). Aided by satellite photography (from the U.S. space shuttle) that identified those geological exposures most likely to yield fossil discoveries, ground teams have recovered numerous new specimens from Hadar, including cranial fragments, mandibles, and some postcranial elements (Asfaw, 1992; Wood, 1992a). In addition, in 1992, Yoel Rak, of the Institute of Human Origins and Tel Aviv University, discovered the most complete early hominid cranium yet found at Hadar (see Fig. 8–21) (Kimbel et al., 1994). Finally, a jaw dating to 2.3 m.y.a. discovered in 1994 and announced in 1996 has been attributed to genus *Homo* and is the earliest well-dated specimen belonging to our genus. Moreover, this same individual was found associated with some stone tools, making it the earliest directly associated find of tools at the same locality as a hominid fossil (Kimbel et al., 1996).

Bouri (Middle Awash)

A significant new hominid discovery from another site in East Africa was announced in 1999 (Asfaw et al., 1999). Behane Asfaw, Tim White, and colleagues discovered several fossils, dated to 2.5 m.y.a., of what they suggest may be yet another species of *Australopithecus* (*A. garhi*, *garhi* meaning "surprise" in the Afar language). These important new finds come from the Bouri site in the Middle Awash region of Ethiopia, just south of Aramis. The hominid fossils, including an incomplete cranium and much of the limb skeleton from another individual, are in several ways quite different from any other Plio-Pleistocene hominid. For example, the cranium combines a projecting face, fairly large front teeth, and very large back teeth (Fig. 8–9). The limb proportions are also unusual, with long forelimbs (as in *A. afarensis*) but also with quite long hind limbs (as in *Homo*). Finally, the hominids at Bouri were found close to animal bones, displaying clear signs of butchering.

---

*The other is a recently discovered *H. erectus* skeleton from west of Lake Turkana, Kenya (see Chapter 9).

Koobi Fora (East Lake Turkana)

Under the direction of Richard Leakey and, for several years, the late Glynn Isaac, research in this vast arid area in northern Kenya has yielded the richest assemblage of Plio-Pleistocene hominids from the African continent. Current archaeological fieldwork is under the supervision of Offer Bar Yosef, of Harvard University. The current total exceeds 150 hominid specimens, probably representing at least 100 individuals. Among this fine sample are several complete skulls, many jaws, and an assortment of postcranial bones. Moreover, next to Olduvai Gorge (discussed shortly), sites on the east side of Lake **Turkana** have produced the most information concerning the behavior of early hominids.

For several years, the dating of the geological beds in the East Turkana area was disputed. However, after considerable testing and retesting and cross-correlation of a variety of different dating techniques, a consensus was reached: Most of the hominid-bearing levels at East Turkana are approximately 1.8 million years old. In addition, there are beds apparently considerably older that thus far have provided a few fragments of *very* early hominids dating back to 3.3 million years (Kimbel, 1988).

West Turkana

Across the lake from the fossil beds discussed above are other deposits that recently have yielded new and very exciting discoveries. In 1984, on the west side of Lake Turkana, a nearly complete skeleton of a 1.6-million-year-old *Homo erectus* adolescent was found (see Chapter 9), and the following year, a well-preserved 2.4-million-year-old skull was also found. This latter find—"the black skull"—is a most important discovery and has caused a major reevaluation of Plio-Pleistocene hominid evolution (see p. 196).

Olduvai Gorge

Located in the Serengeti Plain of northern Tanzania, **Olduvai** is a steep-sided valley resembling a miniature version of the Grand Canyon (Fig. 8–10). (Indeed, the geological processes that formed the gorge are similar to what happened in the formation of the Grand Canyon.) Following millions of years of accumulation of several hundred feet of geological strata, faulting occurred about 70,000 years ago to the east of Olduvai. As a result, a gradient was established, and a rapidly flowing river proceeded to cut the gorge.

Olduvai today is thus a deep ravine cut into the almost mile-high grassland plateau of East Africa, and it extends more than 25 miles in total length—potentially including hundreds of early hominid localities. Climatically, the semiarid pattern with scrub vegetation observable today is thought to parallel conditions over most of the last 2 million years.

Since the 1930s, when they first worked there, Olduvai came to be identified with Louis and Mary Leakey, two of the key founders of modern paleoanthropology. Louis, thanks to *National Geographic* and television, became more famous than any other paleoanthropologist of his generation. Although occupied with lecture tours, Leakey continued to make periodic trips to Olduvai up until his death in 1972. Mary Leakey, for over 40 years, was responsible for directing archaeological excavations at Olduvai (and later, Laetoli) and was instrumental in many of the most exciting discoveries. She retired from active fieldwork in 1983 and continued her writing and research until her death in 1996.

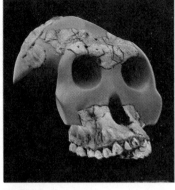

FIGURE 8–9

Reconstructed cranium of *Australopithecus garhi* from Bouri, Ethiopia. Estimated date, 2.5 m.y.a.

Turkana
(tur-kahn´-ah)

Olduvai
(ohl´-doo-vye)

FIGURE 8–10

View of the main gorge at Olduvai. Note the clear sequence of geological beds. The discontinuity to the right is a major fault line.

The greatest contribution that Olduvai has made to paleoanthropological research is the establishment of an extremely well documented and correlated *sequence* of geological, paleontological, archaeological, and hominid remains over the last 2 million years. At the very foundation of all paleoanthropological research is a well-established geological picture, and at Olduvai, owing to four decades of work, this picture is understood in minute detail. Paleontological evidence of fossilized animal bones also has been retrieved in great abundance. More than 150 species of extinct animals have been recognized, and careful analysis of these remains has yielded voluminous information concerning the ecological conditions of early hominid habitats.

The archaeological sequence at Olduvai is also extremely well documented. Due to Mary Leakey's meticulous excavations and analyses, a more complete picture of the behavior of early hominids has emerged from Olduvai than from any other locality.

Finally, fossilized remains of several hominids have been found at Olduvai, ranging in time from the earliest occupation levels (circa 1.85 m.y.a.) to fairly recent *Homo sapiens*. Of the more than 40 individuals represented, many are quite fragmentary, but a few (including four skulls and a nearly complete foot) are excellently preserved. While the center of hominid discoveries has now shifted to other areas of East Africa, it was the initial discovery by Mary Leakey in 1959 of the "Zinj" (a robust australopithecine) cranium that focused the world's attention on this remarkably rich area. This famous discovery provides an excellent example of how financial ramifications directly result from well-publicized hominid discoveries. Prior to 1959, the Leakeys had worked sporadically at Olduvai for almost three decades on a financial shoestring. During this time, they made marvelous paleontological and archaeological discoveries, but there was little support for much-needed large-scale excavation. However, following the discovery of Zinj, the National Geographic Society funded the research, and within the next year, more earth was moved than in the previous 30. Ongoing work at Olduvai has yielded yet further hominid finds, with a partial skeleton being discovered by researchers from the Institute of Human Origins in 1987.

Central Africa

In 1995, another new early hominid discovery was announced from a rather surprising location—Chad, in central Africa (Brunet et al., 1995) (see Fig. 8–3). From an area called the Bahr el Ghazal (Arabic for "River of the Gazelles"), a partial hominid mandible was discovered in association with faunal remains tentatively dated to 3.5–3.0 m.y.a. (Further confirmation will have to await radiometric dating, assuming that appropriate materials become available.) The preliminary analysis suggests that this fossil is an australopithecine with closest affinities to *A. afarensis*. What makes this find remarkable is its geographical location, more than 1,500 miles west of the previously established range of early hominids!

South African Sites

Earliest Discoveries

The first quarter of the twentieth century saw the discipline of paleoanthropology in its scientific infancy. Informed opinions considered the likely origins of the human family to be in Asia, where fossil forms of a primitive kind of *Homo* had been found in Indonesia in the 1890s. Europe was also considered a center of hominid evolution, for spectacular discoveries there of archaic *Homo sapiens* (including the famous Neandertals) and millions of stone tools had come to light, particularly in the early decades of the twentieth century.

Few scholars would have given much credence to Darwin's prediction:

> In each region of the world the living mammals are closely related to the extinct species of the same region. It is, therefore, probable that Africa was formally inhabited by extinct apes closely allied to the gorilla and chimpanzee, and as these two species are now man's nearest allies, it is somewhat more probable that our early progenitors lived on the African continent than elsewhere. (Darwin, 1871)

Moreover, it would be many more decades before the East African discoveries would come to light. It was in such an atmosphere of preconceived biases that the discoveries of a young Australian-born anatomist were to jolt the foundations of the scientific community in the 1920s. Raymond Dart (Fig. 8–11) arrived in South Africa in 1923 at the age of 30 to take up a teaching position in Johannesburg. Fresh from his evolution-oriented training in England, Dart had developed a keen interest in human evolution. Consequently, he was well prepared when startling new evidence began to appear at his very doorstep.

The first clue came in 1924, when Dart received a shipment of fossils from the commercial limeworks quarry at Taung (200 miles southwest of Johannesburg). He immediately recognized something that was quite unusual, a natural **endocast** of a higher primate. The endocast fit into another limestone block containing the fossilized front portion of the skull, face, and lower jaw (Fig. 8–12). However, these were difficult to see clearly, for the bone was hardened into a cemented limestone matrix. Dart patiently chiseled away for weeks, later describing the task:

> No diamond cutter ever worked more lovingly or with such care on a precious jewel—nor, I am sure, with such inadequate tools. But on the seventy-third day, December 23, the rock parted. I could view the face from the front, although the

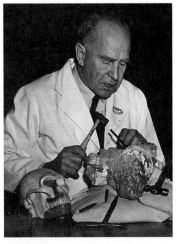

FIGURE 8-11
Raymond Dart, shown working in his laboratory.

Endocast
A solid impression of the inside of the skull, often preserving details relating to the size and surface features of the brain.

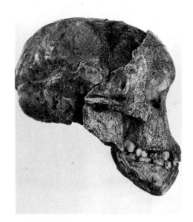

FIGURE 8–12
The Taung child discovered in 1924. The endocast is in back, with the fossilized bone mandible and face in front.

right side was still imbedded. . . . What emerged was a baby's face, an infant with a full set of milk teeth and its permanent molars just in the process of erupting. I doubt if there was any parent prouder of his offspring than I was of my Taung baby on that Christmas. (Dart, 1959, p. 10)

As indicated by the formation and eruption of teeth, the Taung child was probably about three to four years old. Interestingly, the rate of development of this and many other Plio-Pleistocene hominids was more like that of apes than of modern *Homo* (Bromage and Dean, 1985). Dart's initial impression that this form was a hominoid was confirmed when he could observe the face and teeth more clearly. However, as it turned out, it took considerably more effort before the teeth could be seen completely, since Dart worked for four years to separate the upper and lower jaws.

But Dart was convinced long before he had an unimpeded view of the dentition that this discovery was a remarkable one, an early hominoid from South Africa. The question was, What kind of hominoid? Dart realized that it was extremely improbable that this specimen could have been a forest ape, for South Africa has had a relatively dry climate for millions of years. Even though the climate at Taung may not have been as dry as Dart initially speculated (Butzer, 1974), it was still a very unlikely spot to find an ape!

If not an ape, then what was it? Features of the skull and teeth of this small child held clues that Dart seized on almost immediately. The entrance of the spinal column into the brain (the *foramen magnum* at the base of the skull; see p. 177) was further forward in the Taung skull than in modern great apes, though not as much as in modern humans. From this fact Dart concluded that the head was balanced *above* the spine, indicating erect posture. In addition, the slant of the forehead was not as receding as in apes, the milk canines were exceedingly small, and the newly erupted permanent molars were very large, broad teeth. In all these respects, the Taung fossil was more akin to hominids than to apes. There was, however, a disturbing feature that was to confuse many scientists for several years: The brain was quite small. More recent studies have estimated the Taung child's brain size at approximately 405 cm^3 (which translates to a full adult estimate of 440 cm^3), not very large (for a hominid) when compared to modern great apes (see Table 8–2, p. 195).

The estimated cranial capacity of the Taung fossil falls within the range of modern great apes, and gorillas actually average about 10 percent greater. It must, however, be remembered that gorillas are very large animals, whereas the Taung specimen derives from a population where adults may have averaged less than 80 pounds. Since brain size is partially correlated with body size, comparing such differently sized animals is unjustified. A more meaningful comparison would be with the bonobo (*Pan paniscus*), whose body weight is comparable. Bonobos have adult cranial capacities averaging 356 cm^3 for males and 329 cm^3 for females, and thus the Taung child, versus a *comparably sized* ape, displays a 25 percent increase in cranial capacity.

Despite the relatively small size of the brain, Dart saw that it was no ape. Realizing the immense importance of his findings, Dart promptly reported them in the British scientific weekly *Nature* on February 7, 1925—a bold venture, since Dart, only 32, was presumptuously proposing a whole new view of human evolution. The small-brained Taung child was christened by Dart ***Australopithecus africanus*** (southern ape of Africa), which he saw as a kind of halfway "missing

Australopithecus africanus
(os-tral-oh-pith´-e-kus) (af-ri-kan´-us)

link" between modern apes and humans. This concept of a single "missing link" was a fallacious one, but Dart correctly emphasized the hominid-like features of the fossil.

Not all scientists were ready for such a theory from such an "unlikely" place. Hence, Dart's report was received with indifference, disbelief, and even caustic scorn. Dart realized that more complete remains were needed. The skeptical world would not accept the evidence of one partial immature individual, no matter how suggestive the clues. Clearly, more fossil evidence was needed, particularly adult crania (since these would show more diagnostic features). Not an experienced fossil hunter himself, Dart sought further assistance in the search for more **australopithecines** (the colloquial name for members of the genus *Australopithecus*).

South African Hominids Aplenty

Soon after publication of his controversial theories, Dart found a strong ally in Dr. Robert Broom. A Scottish physician and part-time paleontologist, Broom's credentials as a fossil hunter had been established earlier with his highly successful paleontological work on mammal-like reptiles in South Africa.

Although interested, Broom was unable to participate actively in the search for additional australopithecines until 1936. Very soon thereafter, however, he began to meet with incredible success. From two of Dart's students, Broom learned of another commercial limeworks site called **Sterkfontein,** not far from Johannesburg (Fig. 8–13). Here, as at Taung, the quarrying involved blasting out large sections with dynamite, leaving piles of debris that often contained fossils. A limitation with such deposits, however, is that chronometric dating techniques do not apply, and the best that can be done is to extrapolate other techniques (biostratigraphy and

Australopithecines
(os-tral-oh-pith´-e-seens) The colloquial term for members of genus *Australopithecus.*

Sterkfontein
(sterk´-fon-tane)

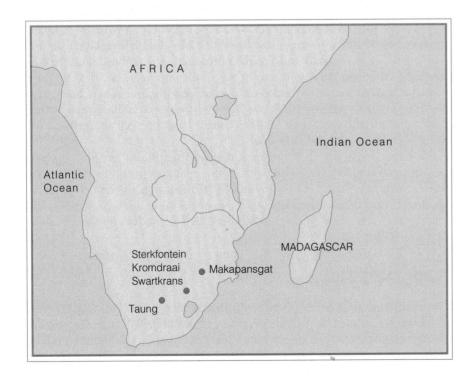

FIGURE 8-13
Australopithecine sites in South Africa.

The South African hominids are discussed in Virtual Lab 8, section I, parts D and F. These sections include several 3-D animations.

Kromdraai
(kromm´-dry)

Swartkrans
(swart´-krannz)

Makapansgat
(mack-ah-pans´-gat)

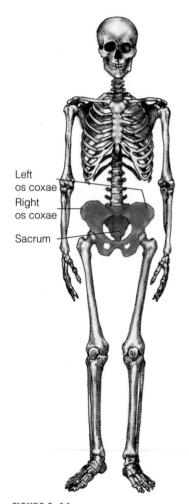

Left
os coxae
Right
os coxae

Sacrum

FIGURE 8–14

The human pelvis: various elements shown on a modern skeleton.

paleomagnetism) back to East Africa, where there is an established chronology. Indeed, it is important to remember that *all* the assigned ages for South African hominid sites are rather rough estimates, with the best current guess placing the Plio-Pleistocene hominids in the 3–1 million-year range.

Broom had found exactly what he was looking for—an adult cranium—at Sterkfontein just a few months after becoming actively involved in the search. Such remarkable fortune was not the end of Broom's luck, for in 1938 he learned of another australopithecine site at **Kromdraai,** about 1 mile from Sterkfontein. Following World War II (in 1948), Broom discovered **Swartkrans** in the same vicinity, and this site has turned out to be the most productive in southern Africa. A final australopithecine site, **Makapansgat,** was excavated in 1947 by Dart, who returned to the fossil discovery stage after an absence of over 20 years.

Numerous extremely important discoveries came from these additional sites, discoveries that would ultimately swing the tide of opinion to the thoughts that Dart first expressed in 1925. Particularly important were a nearly perfect skull and an almost complete pelvis, both discovered at Sterkfontein in 1947. As the number of discoveries accumulated, it became increasingly difficult to simply write off the australopithecines as "aberrant apes."

By the early 1950s, the path was completely cleared for the nearly unanimous acceptance of the australopithecines as early hominids. With this acceptance also came the necessary recognition that hominid brain size increased most significantly *after* earlier changes in teeth and locomotor systems. In other words, the rate of change in one functional system of the body varies from that in other systems, thus displaying the mode of change we have termed *mosaic evolution.*

Today, the search for further early hominid fossils continues in South Africa, and Sterkfontein, Kromdraai, Swartkrans, and Makapansgat have all been reopened for further excavation. Indeed, in the last few years, more than 150 additional specimens have been found at Sterkfontein alone. The most spectacular new find was made in 1998 at Sterkfontein, where the remains of a virtually complete australopithecine skeleton were found by Ron Clarke and his associates from the University of Witwatersrand. Most of the remains are still embedded in the surrounding limestone matrix and may require years for removal, cleaning, and reconstruction. In addition, numerous important new discoveries have been made at Swartkrans. The total South African Plio-Pleistocene hominid sample is thus most significant, with more than 1,500 specimens (counting isolated teeth) representing probably at least 200 individuals.

From an evolutionary point of view, the most significant remains are those from the australopithecine pelvis, which now includes portions of nine ossa coxae (hipbones) (Figs. 8–14, 8–15, and 8–16). Remains of the pelvis are so important because, better than any other area of the body, this structure displays the unique requirements of a bipedal animal, such as modern humans *and* our hominid forbears.

The Bipedal Adaptation

As we mentioned in Chapter 5, there is a general tendency in all primates for erect body posture. However, of all living primates, efficient bipedalism as the primary form of locomotion is seen *only* in hominids. Functionally, the human mode of locomotion is most clearly shown in our striding gait, where weight is alternately

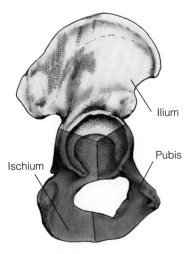

FIGURE 8–15

The human os coxa, composed of three bones (right side shown).

FIGURE 8–16

Ossa coxae. (a) *Homo sapiens*. (b) Early hominid (*Australopithecus*) from South Africa. (c) Chimpanzee. Note especially the length and breadth of the iliac blade and the line of weight transmission (shown in red).

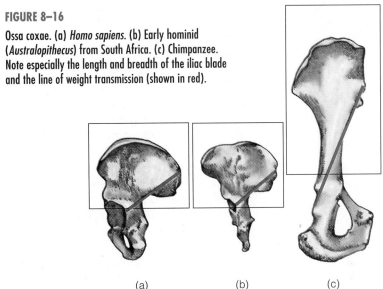

(a) (b) (c)

placed on a single fully extended hind limb. This specialized form of locomotion has developed to a point where energy levels are used to near peak efficiency. Such is not the case in nonhuman primates, who move bipedally with hips and knees bent and maintain balance in a clumsy and inefficient manner.

From a survey of our close primate relatives, it is apparent that while still in the trees, our ancestors were adapted to a fair amount of upper-body erectness. Prosimians, monkeys, and apes all spend considerable time sitting erect while feeding, grooming, or sleeping. Presumably, our early ancestors also displayed similar behavior. What caused these forms to come to the ground and embark on the unique way of life that would eventually lead to humans is still a mystery. Perhaps natural selection favored some Miocene hominoid coming occasionally to the ground to forage for food on the forest floor and forest fringe. In any case, once it was on the ground and away from the immediate safety offered by trees, bipedal locomotion could become a tremendous advantage.

First of all, bipedal locomotion freed the hands for carrying objects and for making and using tools. Such early cultural developments had an even more positive effect on speeding the development of yet more efficient bipedalism— once again emphasizing the dual role of biocultural evolution. In addition, in the bipedal stance, animals have a wider view of the surrounding countryside, and in open terrain, early spotting of predators (particularly the large cats, such as lions, leopards, and saber-tooths) would be of critical importance. We know that modern ground-living primates, such as the savanna baboon and chimpanzee, will occasionally adopt this posture to "look around" when out in open country. It has also been hypothesized that a bipedal stance would more effectively have aided in cooling early hominids while out in the open. In bipeds, less of the body is exposed directly to the sun than in quadrupeds. Moreover, a greater portion of the body is farther from the ground and thus more removed from heat radiating from the ground surface. It would perhaps have been most adaptive to favor such cooling

Virtual Lab 9 presents a detailed discussion of the evolution of bipedalism.

Hominid Origins

mechanisms if early hominids had adopted activity patterns exposing them in the open during midday. This last supposition is not really possible to test, but had hominids ranged more freely at midday, they would have avoided competition from more nocturnal predators and scavengers (such as large cats and hyenas).

Moreover, bipedal walking is an efficient means of covering long distances, and when large game hunting came into play (several million years after the initial adaptation to ground living), further refinements in the locomotor complex may have been favored. Exactly what initiated the process is difficult to say, but all these factors probably played a role in the adaptation of hominids to their special niche through a special form of locomotion.

Our mode of locomotion is indeed extraordinary, involving, as it does, a unique kind of activity in which "the body, step by step, teeters on the edge of catastrophe" (Napier, 1967, p. 56). The problem is to maintain balance on the "stance" leg while the "swing" leg is off the ground. In fact, during normal walking, both feet are simultaneously on the ground only about 25 percent of the time, and as speed of locomotion increases, this figure becomes even smaller.

To maintain a stable center of balance in this complex form of locomotion, many drastic structural and functional alterations are demanded in the basic primate quadrupedal pattern. Functionally, the foot must be altered to act as a stable support instead of a grasping limb. When we walk, our foot is used like a prop, landing on the heel and pushing off on the toes, particularly the big toe. In addition, the leg must be elongated to increase the length of the stride. The lower limb must also be remodeled to allow full extension of the knee and to allow the legs to be kept close together during walking, thereby maintaining the center of support directly under the body. Finally, significant changes must occur in the pelvis to permit stable weight transmission from the upper body to the legs and to maintain balance through pelvic rotation and altered proportions and orientations of several key muscles.

The major structural changes that are required for bipedalism are all seen in the earliest hominids from East and South Africa. In the pelvis, the blade (ilium—upper bone of the pelvis) is shortened top to bottom, which permits more stable weight support in the erect position by lowering the center of gravity (see Figs. 8–15 and 8–16). In addition, the ilium is bent backward and downward, thus altering the position of the muscles that attach along the bone. Most important, these muscles increase in size and act to stabilize the hip. One of these muscles (the *gluteus maximus*) also becomes important as an extensor, to pull the thigh back during running, jumping, and climbing.

Other structural changes shown by even the earliest definitively hominid postcranial evidence further confirm the morphological pattern seen in the pelvis. For example, the vertebral column, known from beautifully preserved specimens from Sterkfontein in South Africa and Hadar (the Lucy skeleton) in East Africa, shows the same forward curvature as in modern hominids, bringing the center of support forward. In addition, the lower limb is elongated and is apparently proportionately about as long as in modern humans. Fossil evidence of a knee fragment from South Africa and pieces from East Africa also shows that full extension of this joint was possible, thus allowing the leg to be completely straightened, as when a field goal kicker follows through.

Fossil evidence of early hominid foot structure has come from two sites in South Africa, and especially important are some recently announced new fossils from Sterkfontein coming from the same individual as the mostly complete skeleton currently being reconstructed (see p. 186) (Clarke and Tobias, 1995). These foot specimens, consisting of four articulating elements from the ankle and big toe, indicate that the heel and longitudinal arch were both well adapted for a bipedal gait. However, the paleoanthropologists (Ron Clarke and Phillip Tobias) also suggest that the large toe was *divergent* and thus unlike the hominid pattern. If the large toe really did possess this (abducted) anatomical position, it most likely would have aided the foot in grasping. In turn, this grasping ability (as in other primates) would have enabled early hominids to more effectively exploit arboreal habitats. Finally, since anatomical remodeling is always constrained by a set of complex functional compromises, a foot highly capable of grasping and climbing is less capable as a stable platform during bipedal locomotion. Some researchers therefore see early hominids as not necessarily fully as committed to bipedal locomotion as are later hominids.

Further evidence for evolutionary changes in the foot comes from Olduvai Gorge in Tanzania, where a nearly complete hominid foot is preserved, and from Hadar in Ethiopia, where numerous pedal elements have been recovered. As in the remains from South Africa, the East African fossils suggest a well-adapted bipedal gait. The arches are developed, but some differences in the ankle also imply that considerable flexibility was possible (again, suggested for continued adaptation to climbing). From this evidence, some researchers have recently concluded that many forms of early hominids spent considerable time in the trees. Nevertheless, to this point, *all* the early hominids that have been identified from Africa are thought by most investigators to have been quite well-adapted bipeds (notwithstanding the new evidence from South Africa, which will require further study). For a review of the anatomical features associated with bipedal locomotion, see Figure 8–17.

Virtual Lab 9, section IV, discusses the anatomy and function of the foot.

Plio-Pleistocene Hominids Outside Africa

For many years, it had generally been assumed that hominids not only originated in Africa, but also were confined to this continent until about 1 m.y.a. As we will discuss in more detail in Chapter 9, this view has had to be substantially modified in recent years. New fossil finds and refined dating techniques have now established that some hominids had already reached Asia by 1.8 m.y.a. and were possibly in Europe prior to 1.5 m.y.a.

Nevertheless, the *earliest* evidence of hominids (prior to 2 m.y.a.) all comes from the African continent. For a summary of the dates of the sites mentioned in the text, see Figure 8–18.

Major Groups of Plio-Pleistocene Hominids

We have already discussed the vast and complex array of early hominid material that has been discovered in South and East Africa. In just the past few years, particularly in the eastern part of the continent, a great number of new discoveries have been made. We now have Plio-Pleistocene hominid specimens representing close to 200 individuals from South Africa and more than 300 from East Africa. Given the size and often fragmentary nature of the sample, along with the fact that a good deal of it is so recently discovered, we should not be surprised that many complications arise when it comes to interpretation. In addition, both popular

During hominid evolution, several major structural features throughout the body have been reorganized (from that seen in other primates) to facilitate efficient bipedal locomotion. These are illustrated here, beginning with the head and progressing to the foot: (a) The *foramen magnum* (shown in red) is repositioned farther underneath the head, so that the head is more or less balanced on the spine (and thus requires less robust neck muscles to hold the head upright). (b) The spine has two distinctive curves—a backward (thoracic) one and a forward (lumbar) one—that keep the trunk (and weight) centered above the pelvis. (c) The pelvis is shaped more in the form of a basin to support internal

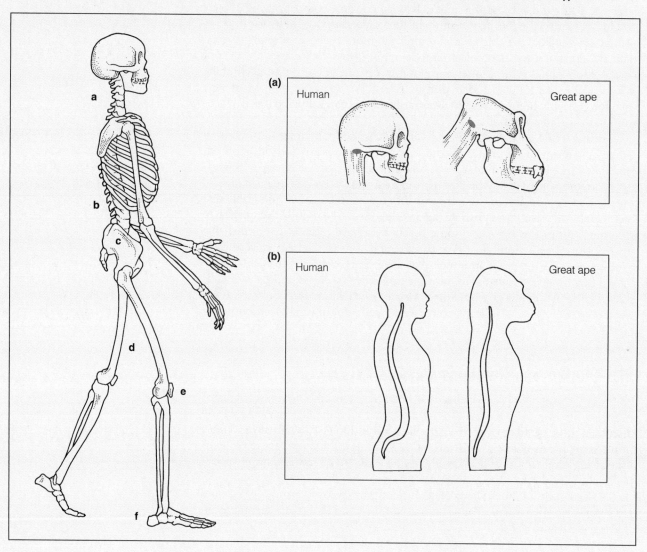

FIGURE 8–17

Major features of hominid bipedalism.

enthusiasm and strongly held views of researchers connected with fossil hominid discoveries have generated even more confusion.

In the remainder of this chapter, we will look at several hypothetical reconstructions that attempt to organize the huge amount of Plio-Pleistocene hominid material. We ask you to remember that these are hypotheses and must remain so, given the incomplete nature of the fossil record. Even considering the seemingly large number of fossils, there is a great deal of time over which they were distributed. If we estimate about 500 total individuals from all African sites recovered thus far for the period 4.4–1.0 m.y.a., we still are sampling just one individual for every 6,800 years!

organs; moreover, the ossa coxae (specifically, iliac blades) are shorter and broader, thus stabilizing weight transmission. (d) Lower limbs are elongated, as shown by the proportional lengths of various body segments (e.g., in humans the thigh comprises 20 percent of body height, while in gorillas it comprises only 11 percent). (e) The femur is angled inward, keeping the legs more directly under the body; modified knee anatomy also permits full extension of this joint. (f) The big toe is enlarged and brought in line with the other toes; in addition, a distinctive longitudinal arch forms, helping absorb shock and adding propulsive spring.

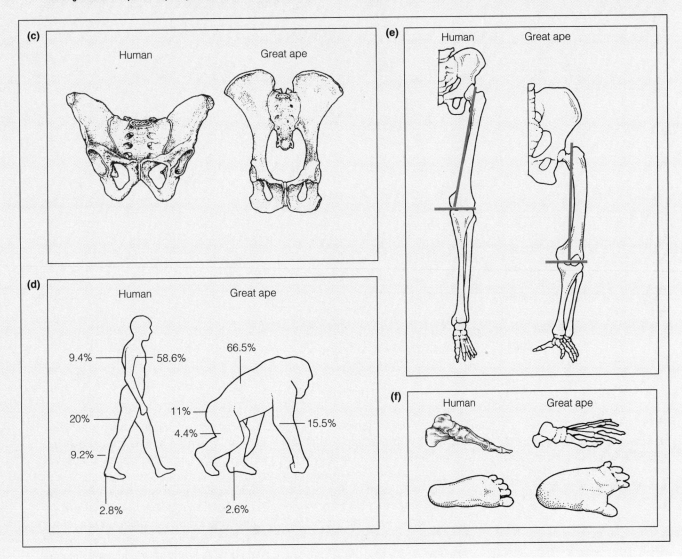

Until much of the new material from East Africa has been properly analyzed and detailed reports published, we cannot form even reasonably secure hypotheses without extreme difficulty. At the present time, only a few East African hominids have been thoroughly studied; all the rest are thus far described in preliminary reports.

It will no doubt appear that many opposing and conflicting hypotheses attempt to describe exactly what is going on in human evolution during the crucial period between about 4.5 and 1 m.y.a. And, indeed, there are many hypotheses. Hominid fossils are intriguing to both scientists and nonscientists, for some of these ancient bones and teeth are probably those of our direct ancestors. Equally

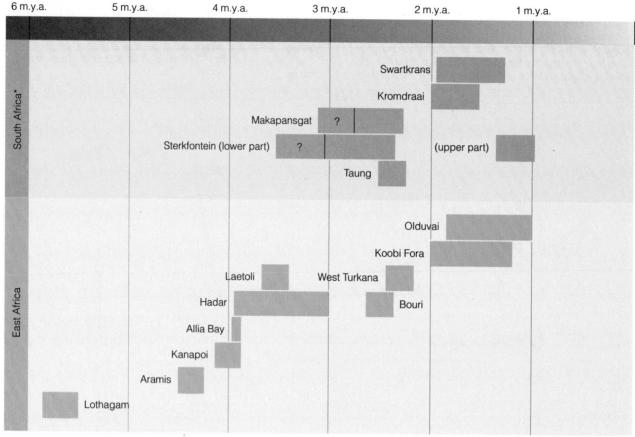

*South African dates are very approximate.

FIGURE 8–18

Time line of major Plio-Pleistocene hominid sites. Note that most dates are approximations. Question marks indicate those estimates that are most tentative.

Phylogeny

A schematic representation showing ancestor-descendant relationships, usually in a chronological framework.

intriguing, some of these fossils are representatives of populations of our close relatives that apparently met with extinction. We would like to know how they lived, what kinds of adaptations (physical and cultural) they displayed, and why some continued to evolve while others died out.

The interpretation of our paleontological past in terms of which fossils are related to other fossils and how they are all related to modern humans is usually shown diagrammatically in the form of a **phylogeny.** Such a diagram is a family tree of fossil evolution. This kind of interpretation is the eventual goal of evolutionary studies, but it is the final goal, achieved only after adequate data are available to understand what is going on.

Another, more basic way to handle these data is to divide the fossil material into subsets. This avoids (for the moment) what are still problematic phylogenetic relationships. Accordingly, for the Plio-Pleistocene hominid material from Africa, we can divide the data into four broad groupings.

Set I. Basal Hominids (4.4 m.y.a.)

The earliest (and most primitive) collection of remains that have been classified as hominids are those from Aramis (Fig. 8–19). These fossils have, for the moment, been assigned to *Ardipithecus ramidus* and are hence

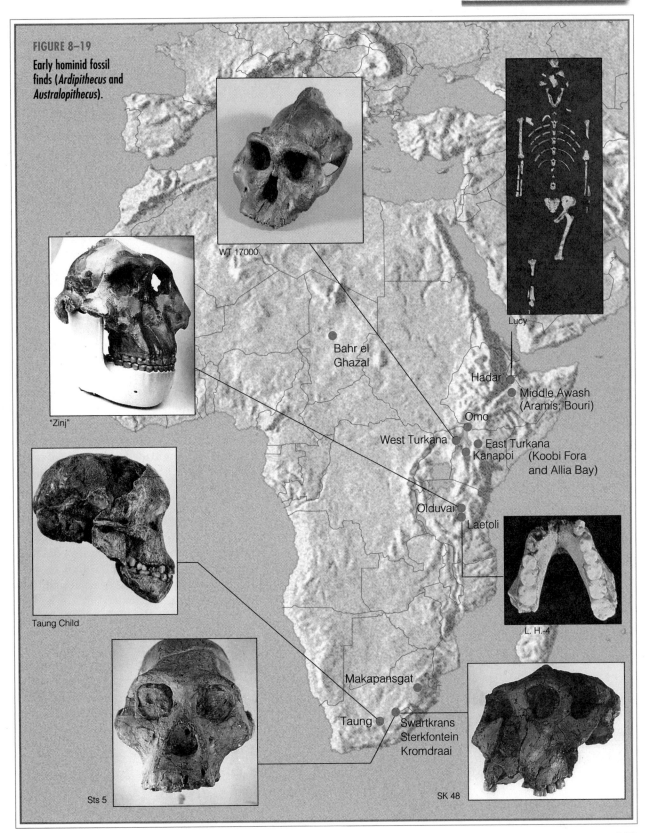

FIGURE 8–19

Early hominid fossil finds (*Ardipithecus* and *Australopithecus*).

WT 17000

Lucy

"Zinj"

Bahr el Ghazal

Hadar

Middle Awash (Aramis; Bouri)

Omo

West Turkana

East Turkana (Koobi Fora and Allia Bay)

Kanapoi

Olduvai

Laetoli

Taung Child

L. H.-4

Makapansgat

Taung

Swartkrans Sterkfontein Kromdraai

Sts 5

SK 48

Virtual Lab 8, section I, part B, provides a discussion of *Australopithecus afarensis*.

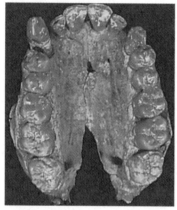

FIGURE 8–20

Australopithecus afarensis maxilla, AL 200-1a, from Hadar, Ethiopia. Note the parallel tooth rows and large canines.

FIGURE 8–21

Australopithecus afarensis cranium discovered at Hadar in 1992. This is the most complete *A. afarensis* cranium yet found.

provisionally interpreted as being in a different genus from all the other Plio-Pleistocene forms (listed in sets II–IV). Analysis thus far suggests that these forms were bipedal, but with a primitive dentition. Brain size of *A. ramidus* is not yet known, but was almost certainly quite small.

Set II. Early, Primitive *Australopithecus* (4.2–3.0 m.y.a.)

This grouping comprises one well-known species, *A. afarensis,* especially well documented at Laetoli and Hadar. Slightly earlier, closely related forms (perhaps representing a distinct second species) come from Allia Bay (East Turkana) and Kanapoi and are provisionally called *Australopithecus anamensis.* Best known from analysis of the *A. afarensis* material, these hominids are characterized by a small brain, large teeth (front and back), and a bipedal gait (probably still allowing for considerable climbing).

In many respects *A. afarensis* is less derived than later hominids; that is, this species is not as committed anatomically in any particular direction as are later forms of *Australopithecus* or *Homo.* For example, the teeth are quite primitive. The canines are often large, and the tooth rows are parallel or even slightly convergent (Fig. 8–20). In addition the back teeth have thick enamel. In fact, unlike *Ardipithecus, all* species of *Australopithecus* have quite thick enamel on their molar teeth especially. The pieces of the crania that are preserved also display several primitive hominoid characteristics. Cranial capacity estimates for *A. afarensis* show a mixed pattern when compared to later hominids. A provisional estimate for the one incomplete cranium—apparently a large individual—gives a figure of 500 cm^3, but another, even more fragmentary cranium is apparently quite a bit smaller and has been estimated at about 375 cm^3 (Holloway, 1983). The most complete cranium discovered to date (Fig. 8–21) has not yet provided an estimate of cranial capacity. Apparently, for some individuals (males?), *A. afarensis* is well within the range of other australopithecine species, but others (females?) may be significantly smaller. However, a general depiction of cranial size for this species cannot be attained at this time, owing to the poor preservation of most cranial elements. From the evidence we do have, it is clear that *A. afarensis* was small-brained, perhaps the smallest (on average) of any known hominid. (A comparison of cranial capacity estimates for early hominids is shown in Table 8–2.)

Conversely, an abundance of postcranial material has been found, most notably the Lucy skeleton from Hadar. From these remains, stature can be fairly confidently estimated: *A afarensis* was a short hominid. Lucy, for example, attained a height of only 3^1/2 feet. However, Lucy, as suggested from the pelvis, is generally thought to have been a female, and there is also evidence at Hadar and Laetoli of larger individuals. The most conservative explanation for this variation is that *A. afarensis* was quite sexually dimorphic—the larger individuals being male and the smaller, such as Lucy, being female. Estimates of male stature can be approximated from the larger footprints at Laetoli, implying a height of about 5 feet, and recently discovered fossils from Hadar conform to this estimate (Kimbel et al., 1994). In fact, for overall body size, this species may have been as dimorphic as *any* living primate (i.e., as much as gorillas, orangutans, or baboons).

What makes *A. afarensis* a hominid? The answer is revealed by its manner of locomotion. From the abundant limb bones recovered from Hadar and those beautiful footprints from Laetoli, we know unequivocally that *A. afarensis* walked

TABLE 8–2 Estimated Cranial Capacities in Early Hominids with Comparable Data for Modern Great Apes and Humans

Hominid	Cranial Capacity Range (cm³)	Cranial Capacity Average(s) (cm³)
Early Hominids		
Ardipithecus	Not presently known	Not presently known
Australopithecus anamensis	Not presently known	Not presently known
Australopithecus afarensis		420
Later australopithecines		410–530
Early members of genus *Homo*		631
Contemporary Hominoids		
Human	1150–1750	1330
Chimpanzee	285–500	395
Gorilla	340–752	506
Orangutan	276–540	411
Bonobo	—	350

The evolution of brain size in hominids is discussed in Virtual Lab 10, section IV, part B, and Virtual Lab 12, section I, part C.

bipedally. At the same time, some researchers have suggested that *A. afarensis* may still have been spending considerable time in the trees, where it found safe sleeping sites as well as some food.

Set III. Later, More Derived *Australopithecus* (2.5–1.0 m.y.a.)

This group is composed of numerous species (most experts recognize at least three; some subdivide this material into five or more species). Remains have come from several sites in both South and East Africa. All of these forms have very large back teeth and do not show appreciable brain enlargement (i.e., encephalization) compared to *A. afarensis*.

Traditionally, anthropologists have recognized two subsets of these more derived australopithecines. The first of these is a highly derived group that has popularly been called "robust" australopithecines and has been found in both South and East Africa (dating 2.5–1.0 m.y.a.). The second subset consists of the "gracile" australopithecines.

Virtual Lab 8 provides many comparisons of the craniodental features of the gracile and robust australopithecines. The laboratory exercise in section II investigates the features and diet of *Australopithecus boisei*.

Robust Australopithecines By "robust" it was meant that these forms, as compared to other australopithecines, were larger in body size. However, recent, more controlled studies (McHenry, 1992) have shown that all species of *Australopithecus* overlapped considerably in body size. Table 8–3 shows the averages of body weights for four australopithecine species as well as for early *Homo*. As can be seen, none of the species differs much from the others in *average* weight, but all show dramatic intraspecific variation, presumably due to sexual dimorphism.

As a result of these new weight estimates, many researchers have either dropped the term *robust* (along with its opposite, *gracile*) or present it in quotation marks to emphasize its conditional application. We believe that the term *robust* can be used in this latter sense, as it still emphasizes important differences in proportions of

A discussion of body mass and the methods for estimating it for fossil specimens is given in Virtual Lab 10, section III, part B.

TABLE 8–3 Estimated Body Weight and Stature in Plio-Pleistocene Hominids

	Body Weight		Stature	
	Male	Female	Male	Female
A. afarensis	45 kg (99 lb)	29 kg (64 lb)	151 cm (59 in.)	105 cm (41 in.)
A. africanus	41 kg (90 lb)	30 kg (66 lb)	138 cm (54 in.)	115 cm (45 in.)
A. robustus	40 kg (88 lb)	32 kg (70 lb)	132 cm (52 in.)	110 cm (43 in.)
A. boisei	49 kg (108 lb)	34 kg (75 lb)	137 cm (54 in.)	124 cm (49 in.)
H. habilis	52 kg (114 lb)	32 kg (70 lb)	157 cm (62 in.)	125 cm (49 in.)

Source: After McHenry, 1992.

Clade
A group of species sharing a common ancestor and distinct from other groups.

FIGURE 8–22
The "black skull," WT 17000, discovered at West Turkana in 1985. This specimen is provisionally assigned to *Australopithecus aethiopicus.*

Virtual Lab 8, section I, part C, provides a 3-D animation of WT 17000; section E provides 3-D animations of several specimens of *Australopithecus boisei.*

dental and cranial traits. In other words, even if they are not larger overall, robust forms are clearly more robust in the skull and dentition.

The earliest representative of this robust group (or **clade**) comes from northern Kenya on the west side of Lake Turkana. A complete cranium (WT 17000—the "black skull") was unearthed there in 1985 and has proved to be a most important discovery (Fig. 8–22). The skull, with a cranial capacity of only 410 cm³, has the smallest definitely determined cranial capacity of any hominid yet found. In addition, this fossil shows other primitive traits, quite reminiscent of *A. afarensis.* For example, there is a compound (joined) crest in the back of the skull, the upper face projects considerably, and the upper dental row converges in back (Kimbel, 1988).

What makes the black skull so fascinating, however, is that mixed with this array of primitive traits are a host of derived ones linking it to other members of the robust group (including a broad face, a very large palate, and a large area for back teeth). Because of this distinct morphology, the black skull has been provisionally assigned to a new species, "*Australopithecus aethiopicus.*" Some researchers, however, think that the pattern is similar enough to later East African "robust" forms to place it in the same species (thus, as an early member of *A. boisei*).

Around 2 m.y.a., different varieties of even more derived members of the robust lineage were on the scene in both East and South Africa. In East Africa, as well documented at Olduvai and Koobi Fora, robust australopithecines have relatively small cranial capacities (ranging from 510 to 530 cm³) and very large, broad faces with massive back teeth and jaws. Louis Leakey originally named the initial discovery of this form "Zinjanthropus," but paleoanthropologists now usually refer to the East African robust variety as *Australopithecus boisei.*

In addition, there are also numerous robust australopithecine finds in South Africa at Kromdraai and most especially at Swartkrans. Like their East African cousins, the South African robust forms also have small cranial capacities, large broad faces, and very large premolars and molars (though not as massive as in East Africa) (Fig. 8–23). Owing to the dental proportions, as well as important differences in facial architecture (Rak, 1983), most researchers agree that there is a species-level difference between the East African robust variety (*A. boisei*) and the South African group (*A. robustus*).

Despite these differences, all members of the robust lineage appear to be specialized for a diet of hard food items, such as seeds, nuts, and bark. Another assumption that has persisted for many years concerns the toolmaking capabilities

FIGURE 8–23

Morphology and variation of robust australopithecines. (Note both the typical features and the range of variation as shown in different specimens.)

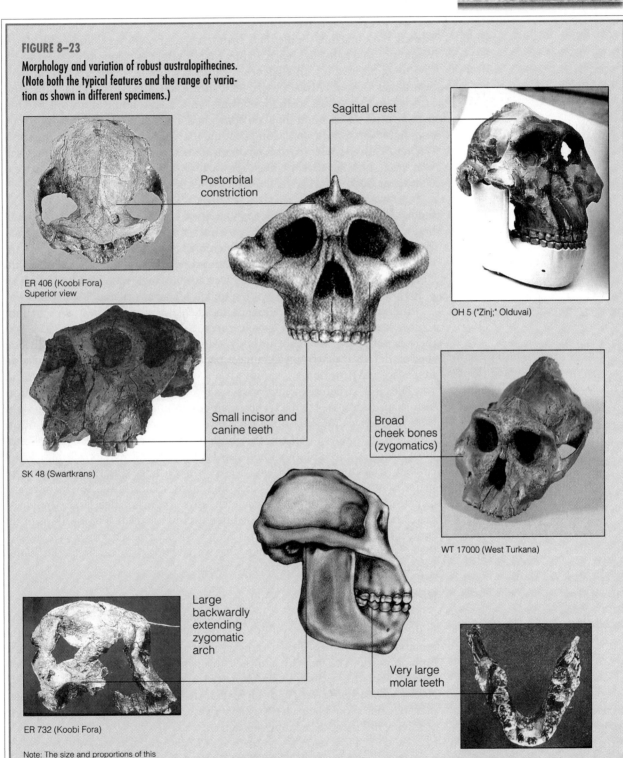

Sagittal crest

Postorbital constriction

ER 406 (Koobi Fora)
Superior view

OH 5 ("Zinj;" Olduvai)

Small incisor and canine teeth

SK 48 (Swartkrans)

Broad cheek bones (zygomatics)

WT 17000 (West Turkana)

Large backwardly extending zygomatic arch

ER 732 (Koobi Fora)

Note: The size and proportions of this specimen differ from ER 406 and OH 5 (above), and this individual has been suggested as a female A. boisei.

Very large molar teeth

ER 729 (Koobi Fora)

of robust forms. Most paleoanthropologists have depicted robust forms as quite limited in toolmaking abilities and, by inference, in cognitive skills as well. (*Note:* We do not make this inference; in any case, toolmaking alone is not necessarily *directly* indicative of intelligence.) Moreover, more recent evidence from Swartkrans, in South Africa, has led Randall Susman (1988) to conclude otherwise. He suggests that robust australopithecines (*A. robustus*) found at this site had fine manipulative abilities and thus could well have been the maker of the stone tools also found at Swartkrans. Complicating the issue further, another hominid (*Homo*) is also represented at Swartkrans (albeit in small numbers). So precisely *who* was responsible for the stone tools we find at Swartkrans (or in East Africa at Olduvai or Koobi Fora) is still largely a matter of conjecture (Klein, 1989).

Gracile Australopithecines   A second variety of australopithecine (also small-brained, but not as large-toothed as the robust varieties) is known from Africa. However, while the robust lineage is represented in both East and South Africa, the smaller-toothed form (*A. africanus*) is known only from the southern part of the continent. First named *A. africanus* by Dart for the single individual at Taung (see p. 183), this australopithecine is also found at Makapansgat and Sterkfontein.

Traditionally, it had been thought that there was significant variation in body size between the "robust" and "gracile" forms. However, as we showed in Table 8–3, there is not much difference in body size among any of the australopithecine species. In fact, most of the differences between "gracile" and "robust" are found in the face and dentition.

The facial structure of *A. africanus* is more lightly built and somewhat more dish-shaped compared to the vertical configuration seen in robust specimens. The most distinctive difference observed between the two forms is in the dentition. Compared to modern humans, they both have relatively large teeth, manifested most clearly in the posterior tooth row (premolars and molars). Robust forms emphasize this trend to an extreme degree, with the huge back teeth taking up the majority of the tooth row and possessing quite small front teeth (incisors and canines). Conversely, the gracile specimens have proportionately larger front teeth compared to their back teeth. These differences in the relative proportions of the teeth and jaws best define a gracile, as compared to a robust, form. In fact, most of the differences in face and skull shape that we have noted can be directly attributed to contrasting jaw function in the two forms.

More Australopithecines?   New discoveries from East Africa are complicating our interpretations even further. The recently announced hominid fossils from Bouri in the Middle Awash region of Ethiopia do not appear to fit neatly in any of the groups listed here (they show an unusual combination of facial/dental features and limb proportions). Tim White, of the University of California, Berkeley, and colleagues have thus provisionally suggested a new species for these hominids: *Australopithecus garhi* (see Fig. 8–9). Further study and the discovery of more complete remains should help clarify whether yet another species of *Australopithecus* was living in Africa 2.5 million years ago.

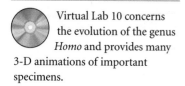

Virtual Lab 10 concerns the evolution of the genus *Homo* and provides many 3-D animations of important specimens.

Set IV. Early *Homo* (2.4–1.8 m.y.a.)

The best-known specimens are from East Africa (East Turkana and Olduvai), but early remains of *Homo* have also been found in South Africa (Sterkfontein and possibly Swartkrans) (Fig 8–24). This group is composed of possibly just

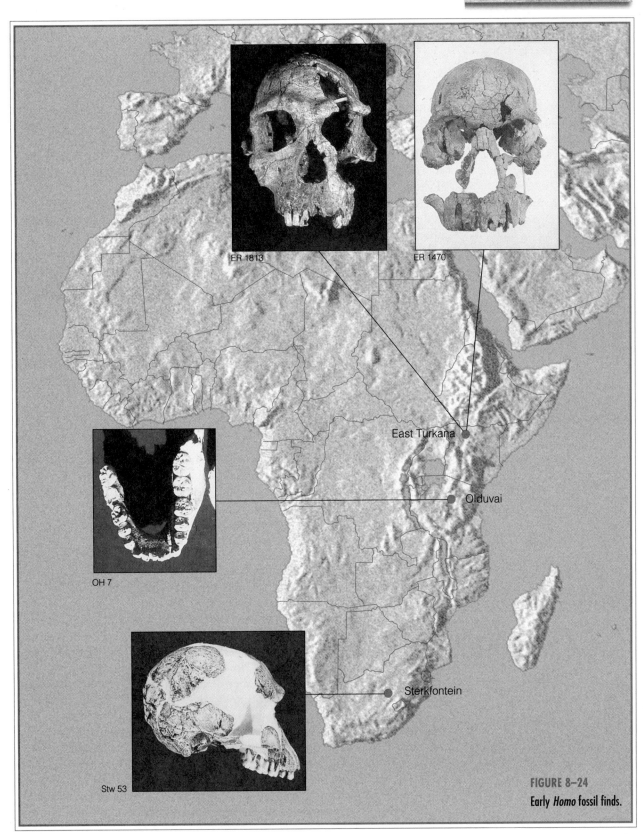

ER 1813

ER 1470

East Turkana

Olduvai

OH 7

Sterkfontein

Stw 53

FIGURE 8–24

Early *Homo* fossil finds.

A 3-D animation of ER 1470 and discussions of early *Homo* are provided in Virtual Lab 10, section I, part A.

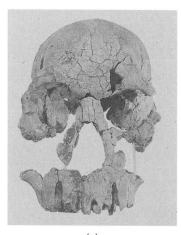

(a)

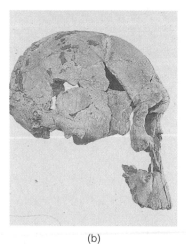

(b)

FIGURE 8–25

A nearly complete "early *Homo*" skull from East Turkana (KNM-ER 1470). One of the most important single fossil hominid discoveries from East Africa. (a) Frontal view. (b) Lateral view.

one, but probably more than one, species. Early *Homo* is characterized (compared to *Australopithecus*) by greater encephalization, altered cranial shape, and smaller (especially molars) and narrower (especially premolars) teeth.

The first hint that another hominid had been living contemporaneously in Africa with the australopithecines came at Olduvai in the early 1960s. Louis Leakey named a newly discovered form of hominid *Homo habilis*, based on remains found in beds about the same age as Zinj. Unfortunately, the fossils at Olduvai attributable to early *Homo* are all fragmentary or distorted. More complete remains, discovered later at East Turkana, would prove pivotal in establishing the validity of this species designation.

The earliest appearance of the genus *Homo* in East Africa may be as ancient as that of the robust australopithecines. As we have discussed, a robust australopithecine (the black skull from West Turkana) has been dated to approximately 2.5 m.y.a. Recent interpretations of a temporal bone fragment from the Lake Baringo region of central Kenya have suggested that early *Homo* may also be close to this same antiquity (estimated age of 2.4 m.y.a.) (Hill et al., 1992). More diagnostic remains of a lower jaw of early *Homo* have also recently been reported from Hadar, in Ethiopia, and dated to 2.3 m.y.a. (Kimbel et al., 1996). Given that the robust australopithecine lineage was already diverging at this time, it is not surprising to find the earliest representatives of the genus *Homo* also beginning to diversify.

From the beginning, the naming of this fossil material at Olduvai as *Homo habilis* (handy man) was meaningful from two perspectives. First, Leakey inferred that members of this group were the Olduvai toolmakers. You will recall, however, that some researchers have suggested that robust australopithecines could also have been making tools. Second, by calling this group *Homo,* Leakey was arguing for at least *two separate branches* of hominid evolution in the Plio-Pleistocene. Clearly, only one could then be on the line leading to modern humans, and Leakey was guessing that he had found the more likely ancestor.

The most immediately obvious feature distinguishing the early *Homo* material from the australopithecines is cranial size. For all the measurable *H. habilis* skulls, the estimated average cranial capacity is 631 cm³, compared to 520 cm³ and 442 cm³ for all measurable robust and gracile australopithecines, respectively (McHenry, 1988) (Fig. 8–25). Early *Homo* therefore shows an average increase in cranial size of 21 percent and 43 percent, respectively, over both forms of australopithecine. In addition, some researchers have pointed to differences in dental proportions and aspects of the limb skeleton.

Early members of the genus *Homo* have also been found in South Africa (see Fig. 8–24), apparently there, too, living contemporaneously with australopithecines. At both Sterkfontein and Swartkrans, fragmentary remains of an early form of *Homo* have been recognized. However, some of these remains are still controversial. While most experts agree they belong in the genus *Homo,* there is still considerable disagreement whether they should be included in the species *habilis.* In addition, a more recently discovered very partial skeleton from Olduvai Gorge (OH 62) is extremely small-statured (less than 4 feet, probably) and has several primitive aspects of limb proportions (Johanson et al., 1987).

Even more troublesome are two crania from East Turkana that do not fit neatly with other early *Homo* specimens from this site. Some experts contend that *all* of these individuals from South and East Africa can be included within one species, but one showing a high level of sexual dimorphism. Others (Lieberman et

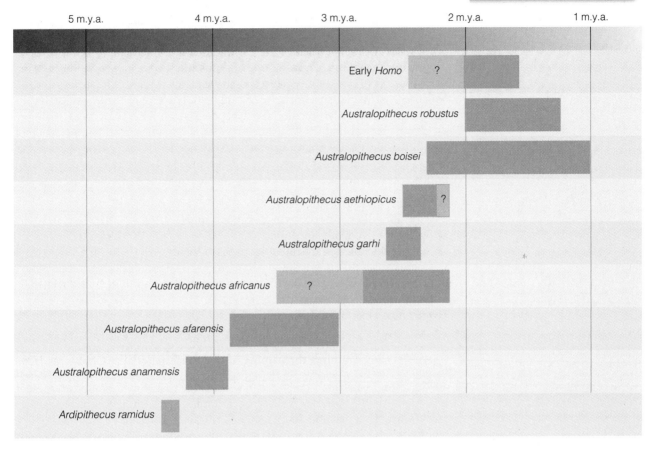

al., 1988; Wood, 1992a) are not as convinced and would thus argue for at least two species of early *Homo* (*H. habilis* and a second species, usually referred to as *H. rudolfensis*).

On the basis of current evidence, we can reasonably postulate that one or more species of early *Homo* were present in Africa by close to 2.5 m.y.a., developing in parallel with at least one australopithecine line. These two hominid lineages lived side by side for over 1 million years, after which the australopithecines disappeared forever. At the same time, one of these early *Homo* species was emerging into a later form, *Homo erectus*, which in turn developed into *Homo sapiens* (Fig. 8–26).

FIGURE 8–26

Time line of Plio-Pleistocene hominids. Note that most dates are approximations. Question marks indicate those estimates that are most tentative.

Interpretations: What Does It All Mean?

By this time, it may seem as though anthropologists have an almost perverse fascination with finding small scraps buried in the ground and then assigning them confusing numbers and taxonomic labels impossible to remember. We must remember that the collection of the basic fossil data is the foundation of human evolutionary research. Without fossils, all our theories and speculation would be completely hollow. Several ongoing paleoanthropological projects are now providing additional data in an attempt to answer some of the more perplexing questions about our evolutionary history.

The numbering of specimens is an attempt to keep the designations neutral and to make reference to each specimen as clear as possible. The formal naming of forms as *Australopithecus* or *Homo* should come much later, since it involves lengthy interpretations. The assigning of genus and species names to hominid fossils is more than just a convenience; when we attach a particular label, such as *A. boisei*, to a particular specimen, we should be fully aware of the biological implications of such an interpretation (see Chapter 7).

From the time that fossil sites are first located to the eventual interpretation of hominid evolutionary events, several steps are necessary. Ideally, they should follow a logical order, for if interpretations are made too hastily, they can confuse important issues for years. Here is a reasonable sequence:

1. Selecting and surveying sites
2. Excavating sites and recovering fossil hominids
3. Designating individual remains with specimen numbers for clear reference
4. Making a detailed study and description of fossils
5. Comparing with other fossil material, in chronological framework if possible
6. Comparing fossil material with known ranges of variation in closely related groups of living primates
7. Assigning taxonomic names to fossil material

The task of interpretation is still not complete, for what we want to know in the long run is what happened to the population(s) represented by the fossil remains. Indeed, in the process of eventually determining those populations that are our most likely antecedents, we may conclude that some hominids represent evolutionary side branches. If this conclusion is accurate, those hominids necessarily must have become extinct. It is both fascinating and relevant to us as hominids to try to determine what factors influenced some earlier members of our family to persist while others died out.

Continuing Uncertainties — Taxonomic Issues

As previously discussed, paleoanthropologists are crucially concerned with making biological interpretations of variation found in the hominid fossil record. Most especially, researchers endeavor to assign extinct forms to particular genera and species. We saw in Chapter 7 that for the diverse array of Miocene hominoids, the evolutionary picture is especially complex. As new finds accumulate, there persists continued uncertainty even as to family assignment, to say nothing of genus and species!

For the Plio-Pleistocene, the situation is considerably clearer. First of all, there is a larger fossil sample from a more restricted geographical area (South and East Africa) and from a more concentrated time period (spanning about 3.5 million years, 4.4–1 m.y.a.). Second, more complete specimens exist (e.g., Lucy), and we thus have good evidence from most parts of the body. Accordingly, there is considerable consensus on several basic aspects of evolutionary development during the Plio-Pleistocene. Researchers agree unanimously that these forms are hominids (members of the family Hominidae). And as support for this point, all these forms are seen as well-adapted bipeds. Moreover, researchers agree as to genus-level assignments for most of the forms (although some disagreement remains regarding how to group the robust australopithecines).

As for species-level designations, little consensus can be found. Indeed, as new fossils have been discovered (e.g., the black skull, OH 62, and the Bouri remains), the picture seems to be muddied further. Once again, we have a complex evolutionary process. In attempts to deal with it, we impose varying degrees of simplicity. In so doing, we hope that the evolutionary processes will become clearer—not just for introductory students, but for professional paleoanthropologists and textbook authors as well! Nevertheless, evolution is not a simple process, and disputes are bound to arise, especially in making such fine-tuned interpretations as species-level designations.

Consider the following ongoing topics of interest and occasional disagreement among paleoanthropologists dealing with Plio-Pleistocene hominids. You should realize, however, that such continued debate is at the heart of scientific endeavor; indeed, it provides a major stimulus for further research. Here, we raise questions regarding five areas of taxonomic interpretation. In general, there is still reasonably strong agreement on these points, and we follow, where possible, the current consensus as reflected in recent publications (Grine, 1988a; Klein, 1989; Fleagle, 1999):

1. *Is* Ardipithecus *a hominid? If so, is* Ardipithecus *really a distinct genus from* Australopithecus?
   Only tentative clues from the cranium and upper limb have thus far suggested that the 4.4-million-year-old fossils from Aramis were bipedal. Descriptions of the more complete skeleton (including a pelvis) have not yet been published. However, from what is known and what has been initially reported, it appears that these forms were probably bipedal and thus should be (provisionally) classified as hominids. Much more detailed analysis will need to be carried out before it can be concluded how complete was the bipedal adaptation. Equally uncertain is the genus status of these new finds. Again, from what is known, especially of the dentition (showing thin enamel on the back teeth), the Aramis finds do look quite different from *any* known *Australopithecus* species.

2. *How many species are there at Hadar and Laetoli (i.e., is* Australopithecus afarensis *one species)?*
   Some paleoanthropologists argue that what has been described as a single species (especially regarding the large Hadar sample) actually represents at least two separate species. However, it is clear that all australopithecines were highly variable, and thus the pattern seen at Hadar might well represent a single, highly dimorphic species. Most scholars accept this interpretation, and it is best, for the moment, to follow this more conservative view. As a matter of good paleontological practice, it is desirable not to overly "split" fossil samples until compelling evidence is presented.

3. *Are* Australopithecus anamensis *(from Allia Bay and Kanapoi) and* Australopithecus garhi *(from Bouri) separate species from* Australopithecus afarensis?
   The fossil discoveries of *A. anamensis* have thus far been quite fragmentary. When we compare them with the much better known *A. afarensis* materials, the anatomical differences in the Allia Bay and Kanapoi specimens are by no means striking. Likewise, the species designation for the Bouri fossils is still provisional. Thus, until more complete remains are discovered, it is best to be cautious and regard the new species designations (*Australopithecus anamensis; Australopithecus garhi*) as tentative hypotheses and ones requiring further confirmation.

 See Virtual Labs 8 and 10 for 3-D animations of these various Plio-Pleistocene hominid species.

4. *How many genera of australopithecines are there?*

Many years ago, a plethora of genera was suggested by Robert Broom and others. However, in the 1960s and 1970s, most researchers agreed to "lump" all these forms into *Australopithecus*. With the discovery of early members of the genus *Homo* in the 1960s (and its general recognition in the 1970s), most researchers also recognized the presence of our genus in the Plio-Pleistocene as well.

In the last decade, there has been an increasing tendency to resplit some of the australopithecines. Recognizing that the robust group (*aethiopicus, boisei,* and *robustus*) forms a distinct evolutionary lineage (clade), many researchers (Grine, 1988a; Howell, 1988) have argued that the generic term *Paranthropus* should be used to set these robust forms apart from *Australopithecus* (now used in the strict sense).

We agree that there are adequate grounds to make a genus-level distinction, given the evolutionary distinctiveness of the robust clade as well as its apparent adaptive uniqueness (see Fig. 8–23). However, for closely related forms, such as we are dealing with here, making this type of interpretation is largely arbitrary (see discussion, pp. 163–164). The single genus *Australopithecus* has been used for five decades in the wider sense (to include all robust forms), and because it simplifies terminology, we follow the current consensus and continue the traditional usage—*Australopithecus* for all small-brained Plio-Pleistocene hominids with large, thickly enameled teeth (particularly molars) and including all five recognized species: *A. afarensis, A. aethiopicus, A. africanus, A. robustus,* and *A. boisei* (see Fig. 8–27).

5. *How many species of early* Homo *existed?*

Here is another species-level type of interpretation that is unlikely to be resolved soon. Yet, as it strikes closer to home (our own genus) than the issue for robust australopithecines, the current debate is generating more heat.

Whether we find resolution or not, the *form* of the conflicting views is instructive. The main issue is again interpreting whether variation is *inter-* or *intra*specific. For those anthropologists who include all the early *Homo* remains from Africa within *one* species (e.g., Tobias, 1991), the considerable variation is thought to be largely due to sexual dimorphism. However, many other researchers (a growing consensus, in fact) see too much variation among the specimens to be explained as part of one species (even a highly variable one). These paleoanthropologists (Lieberman et al., 1988; Wood, 1992a) thus argue that there was *more than one species* of early *Homo*.* We agree that more than one species is probably represented, but for simplicity suggest referring to all the specimens as "early *Homo*."

FIGURE 8–27

Plio-Pleistocene hominids.

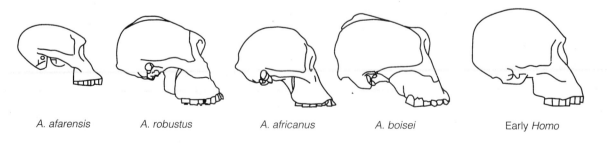

| A. afarensis | A. robustus | A. africanus | A. boisei | Early Homo |

*The species names *Homo habilis* and *Homo rudolfensis* are the ones most commonly used for two different species of early *Homo*.

Interpreting the Interpretations

Although hominid fossil evidence has accumulated in great abundance, the fact that so much of the material has been discovered so recently makes any firm judgments concerning the route of human evolution premature. However, paleoanthropologists are certainly not deterred from making their "best guesses," and diverse hypotheses have abounded in recent years. The vast majority of more than 300 fossils from East Africa are still in the descriptive and early analytical stages. At this time, the construction of phylogenies of human evolution is analogous to building a house with only a partial blueprint. We are not even sure how many rooms there are! Until the existing fossil evidence has been adequately studied, to say nothing about possible new finds, speculative hypotheses must be viewed with a critical eye.

In Figure 8–28, we present several phylogenies representing different and opposing views of hominid evolution. We suggest that you not attempt to memorize them, for they *all* could be out of date by the time you read this book. It will

FIGURE 8–28

Phylogenies of hominid evolution.

PHYLOGENY A
A. afarensis common ancestor theory
(after Johanson and White, 1979)

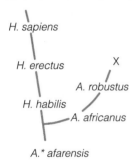

Note: Afarensis postulated as common ancestor to all Plio-Pleistocene hominids.

PHYLOGENY B
A. africanus common ancestor theory
(after Skelton et al., 1986)

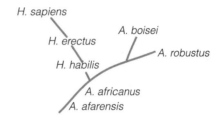

Note: Major split occurs after *A. africanus*. Therefore, *A. africanus* is seen as still in our lineage as well as that of more derived australopithecines.

PHYLOGENY C
Early robust lineage
(after Delson, 1986, 1987; Grine, 1993)

H. sapiens

A. robustus

H. erectus

A. boisei

H. habilis

A. africanus

A. aethiopicus

A. afarensis

PHYLOGENY D
Ardipithecus as probable root species for later hominids (and also incorporating other recent modifications) (after Skelton and McHenry, 1992; Wolpoff, 1999)

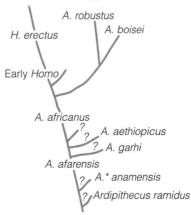

* For genus designation, the "*A*" in all phylogenies refers to *Australopithecus*.

prove more profitable to look at each one and assess the biological implications involved. Also, note which groups are on the "main line" of human evolution (the one including *Homo sapiens*) and which are placed on extinct side branches.

All the schemes in Figure 8–28 postdate 1979, when *A. afarensis* was first suggested as the most likely common ancestor of all later hominids (Johanson and White, 1979). Since the early 1980s, most paleoanthropologists have accepted this view.

We have not included evolutionary schemes prior to 1979, as they do not account for the crucial discoveries at Hadar and Laetoli of *Australopithecus afarensis*. These now-outdated models frequently postulated *A. africanus* as the common ancestor of later *Australopithecus* (robust varieties) and early *Homo*. In modified form, this view is still continued in some respects (see phylogeny B).

Indeed, probably the most intractable problems for interpretation of early hominid evolution involve what to do with *A. aethiopicus* and *A. africanus*. Carefully look at the different evolutionary reconstructions to see how various researchers deal with these complicated issues. Finally, the newest finds from Aramis (*Ardipithecus*), from Allia Bay and Kanapoi (*Australopithecus anamensis*), and from Bouri (*Australopithecus garhi*) will need to be incorporated into these schemes. Phylogeny D is an initial attempt to do so, but only points up how frequently hominid evolutionary interpretations need to be reevaluated and substantially revised.

SUMMARY

In this chapter, we have discussed the earliest known evidence of the hominid lineage. The first evidence of hominids comes from sites in East and South Africa during the Plio-Pleistocene. In East Africa, especially, the discoveries in recent years have been quite spectacular, providing scientists with a wealth of new information. From a multidisciplinary approach, paleoanthropology has attempted to correlate these remains using geological, ecological, and archaeological perspectives. Moreover, the opportunity to apply varied dating techniques, again most especially in East Africa, has proved most crucial in establishing a firm chronology for the early stages of hominid evolution.

Only very fragmentary evidence of the *earliest* stages of hominoid/hominid diversification is presently evident from localities in Kenya and Ethiopia. However, abundant evidence is now known from the period after 4.5 m.y.a. (and up to about 1 m.y.a.). From this period, nine localities in East Africa are highlighted (Aramis, Allia Bay, Kanapoi, Laetoli, Hadar, Bouri, Koobi Fora, West Turkana, and Olduvai Gorge). In addition, five other localities in South Africa (Taung, Sterkfontein, Makapansgat, Kromdraai, and Swartkrans) are also discussed.

While not providing the most complete or the most comprehensive information, South Africa (through the work of Dart and Broom) provided the *first* insights into early hominid emergence. Moreover, ongoing work in southern Africa continues to contribute to our picture of this crucial period.

Early hominids differ markedly from modern *Homo sapiens*. They are considerably smaller-brained and at the same time larger-toothed. However, they all show the distinctive hominid adaptation for *bipedal locomotion*.

After our detailed summary of hominid evolution in the Plio-Pleistocene, you may feel frustrated by what must seem to be endlessly changing and conflicting interpretations. However, after 75 years of discoveries of early hominids in Africa, there are some major points on which most researchers agree:

1. *A. afarensis* is the earliest known hominid, at present (with substantial definite supporting evidence). We can anticipate, however, that *Ardipithecus* may soon supplant *A. afarensis* for this status of earliest definite (and widely accepted) hominid.
2. *A. afarensis* is probably ancestral to all later hominids (or is very closely related to the species that is).
3. By about 2.5 m.y.a., two major lineages split from one another, one producing later, more derived australopithecines and the other producing species of the genus *Homo*.
4. All australopithecines were extinct by 1 m.y.a. (or shortly thereafter).
5. All australopithecine species (presumably early *Homo* as well) were highly variable, showing extreme sexual dimorphism.
6. All forms (*Australopithecus* and early *Homo*) were small-brained (as compared to later species of the genus *Homo*); nevertheless, all early hominids are more encephalized than apes of comparable body size.
7. Given the current state of knowledge, there are several equally supportable phylogenies. In a widely read publication a decade ago, three leading researchers (Bill Kimbel, Tim White, and Don Johanson, 1988) made this point; moreover, they noted that of four possible phylogenetic reconstructions they presented (various modifications of phylogenies C and D; see p. 205), they had not reached agreement among themselves as to which is the most likely.

As these points make clear, we have come a long way in reaching an understanding of Plio-Pleistocene hominid evolution. Nevertheless, a truly complete understanding is not at hand. Such is the stuff of science!

QUESTIONS FOR REVIEW

1. What kinds of cultural remains do archaeologists recover, and why are they important in understanding human evolution?
2. Why is paleoanthropology called a multidisciplinary science? What are its most important components?
3. Discuss what is meant by *relative* compared to *chronometric* dating.
4. Why is more than one dating technique required to establish the chronology of an early hominid locality? Use an example in your discussion.
5. Why is it so significant that the East African Plio-Pleistocene sites are all found along the Rift Valley?
6. Compare and contrast two East African Plio-Pleistocene sites for the kinds of evidence discovered.
7. What led Dart to conclude that the Taung specimen was not an ape?
8. Why is skeletal evidence of the lower limb so important in defining early hominids?
9. What are the major structural alterations (compared to a quadrupedal pattern) required for efficient bipedalism?

10. Were the australopithecines bipedal? If so, what does this imply about them?
11. Discuss the first thing you would do if you found an early hominid and were responsible for its formal description and publication. What would you include in your publication?
12. Discuss two current disputes regarding taxonomic issues concerning early hominids. Try to give support for alternative positions.
13. What is a phylogeny? Construct one for early hominids (4.4–1 m.y.a.). Make sure you can describe what conclusions your scheme makes. Also try to defend it.
14. Discuss at least two alternative ways that *A. africanus* is currently incorporated into phylogenetic schemes.
15. What are the most recently discovered of the Plio-Pleistocene hominid materials, and how are they, for the moment, incorporated into a phylogenetic scheme? How secure do you think this interpretation is?

SUGGESTED FURTHER READINGS

Binford, Lewis. 1981. *Bones: Ancient Men and Myths.* New York: Academic Press.
Conroy, Glenn C. 1997. *Reconstructing Human Origins. A Modern Synthesis.* New York: Norton.
Delson, Eric (ed.). 1985. *Ancestors: The Hard Evidence.* New York: Liss.
Grine, Fred (ed.). 1988. *Evolutionary History of the Robust Australopithecines.* New York: de Gruyter.
Johanson, Donald, and Blake Edgar. 1996. *From Lucy to Language.* New York: Simon & Schuster.
Leakey, Mary. 1984. *Disclosing the Past. An Autobiography.* Garden City, NJ: Doubleday.
Leakey, Richard. 1981. *The Making of Mankind.* New York: Dutton.
Lewin, Roger. 1998. *Principles of Human Evolution: A Core Textbook.* Boston: Blackwell Science.
Rak, Yoel. 1983. *The Australopithecine Face.* New York: Academic Press.
Rasmussen, D. T. (ed.). 1993. *The Origin and Evolution of Humans and Humaness.* Boston: Jones and Bartlett.
Wolpoff, Mulford H. 1999. *Paleoanthropology.* 2nd ed. Boston: McGraw-Hill.

MULTIMEDIA RESOURCES

Wadsworth Anthropology Resource Center

http://anthropology.wadsworth.com

Visit Anthropology Online to obtain current updates in the field, surfing tips, career information, and more. In addition, enrich your study efforts with text-specific study aids arranged by chapter.

 InfoTrac College Edition

http://www.infotrac-college.com/wadsworth

1. Search InfoTrac College Edition for *radiometric dating*. How many different methods are covered in the articles you found? If there were several techniques, make a chart showing all the different methods and the time scales they cover. Are there any major gaps in time that cannot be dated by radiometic methods? Make a list of the various applications of radiocarbon dating discussed in the articles you have found.

2. Search InfoTrac College Edition for *hominid evolution*. How many citations did you find? Read one article that deals with bipedalism, tool use, or some other aspect of early hominid locomotion or behavior and write a review of it based on what you have learned about this topic in Chapter 8.

Internet Exercises

1. Take the Lucy Test! Go to **http://www.geocities.com/CapeCanaveral/lab/8853/.** To help you learn about the differences between pongids, hominids, and humans, this site has been created to allow *you* to compare the three. Work through this comparison exercise. How did you do? Did you think that the australopithecines were more like humans or like pongids? Having done this exercise, consider how paleoanthropologists interpret such data.

2. Using your search engine, do a word search for *paleoanthropology*. How many Web sites did you find? Visit a few of these sites until you find one that has substantive articles dealing with either a specific hominid fossil or a hominid fossil site. If you read about a fossil, where was it found and who discovered it? How old is it? What are the main characteristics of this fossil species? If you read about a fossil site, where is it located and how old is it? Who has worked there, and what fossils has it produced?

CHAPTER

9

Homo erectus and Contemporaries

CONTENTS

Introduction

In Chapter 8, we traced the earliest evidence of hominid evolution by reviewing the abundant fossil material from Africa that documents the origins of *Australopithecus* and *Homo* during the Pliocene and early Pleistocene. In this chapter, we take up what might be called the next stage of hominid evolution, the appearance and dispersal of *Homo erectus.*

Homo erectus was a widely distributed species that also had a long temporal record, spanning over 1 million years. Our discussion focuses on the defining physical characteristics of *Homo erectus* compared with what came immediately before (early *Homo*) and what came immediately after (*Homo sapiens*). As we have emphasized, hominid evolution has long been characterized by a biocultural interaction. Thus, it is only through explaining the behavioral capacities of *Homo erectus* (in concert with morphological change) that we can understand the success of this hominid species. For this reason, we also highlight some of the abundant archaeological evidence and related biocultural reconstructions that have so long occupied and fascinated paleoanthropologists.

Homo erectus: Terminology and Geographical Distribution

The discoveries of fossils now referred to as *H. erectus* go back to the nineteenth century. Later in this chapter, we will discuss in some detail the historical background of these earliest discoveries in Java and the somewhat later discoveries in China. From this work, as well as presumably related finds in Europe and North Africa, a variety of taxonomic names were suggested. The most significant of these earlier terms were *Pithecanthropus* (for the Javanese remains) and *Sinanthropus* (for the fossils from northern China). In fact, you may still see these terms in older sources or occasionally used colloquially and thus placed in quotation marks (e.g., "*Pithecanthropus*").

It is important to realize that taxonomic *splitting* (which this terminology reflects) was quite common in the early years of paleoanthropology. Only after World War II and with the incorporation of the modern synthesis (see p. 74) into paleontology did more systematic biological thinking come to the fore. Following this trend, in the early 1950s all the material previously referred to as "Pithecanthropus," "Sinanthropus," and so forth, was included in a single species of genus *Homo*—*H. erectus*. This reclassification proved to be a most significant development on two counts:

1. It reflected the incorporation of modern evolutionary thinking into hominid paleontology.
2. The simplification in terminology, based as it was on sound biological principles, refocused research away from endless arguments regarding classification to broader populational, behavioral, and ecological considerations.

Discoveries in the last few decades have established *well-dated* finds of *H. erectus* in East Africa from geological contexts radiometrically dated as old as 1.8 m.y.a. In addition, new dates first published in 1994 by geologists from the Berkeley Geochronology Laboratory (Swisher et al., 1994) have suggested that two localities in Java are as old as those in East Africa (with dates of 1.8 and 1.6 m.y.a.). These early dates have come as somewhat of a surprise to many paleoanthropologists, but

 A discussion of *Homo erectus* is given in the Species Gallery in Virtual Lab 10, section I, part B. Be sure to click on the Extra Information text icon for each specimen.

Virtual Lab 10 includes an interactive map showing the distribution of *Homo erectus*. This can be accessed on every specimen screen.

FIGURE 9–1
Dmanisi mandible.

as you will see, there is now growing evidence for an early dispersal of hominids outside of Africa—that is, one *well before* 1 m.y.a.

Current interpretations thus view the first hominid dispersal out of Africa as occurring between 1.5 and 2 m.y.a. A likely route would have taken these hominids through southwestern Asia, and there are some intriguing hints from the Ubeidiya site in Israel that this route was indeed exploited quite early on. The most conclusive evidence from Ubeidiya is archaeological, including a number of stone tools dated (by paleomagnetism and faunal correlation) to 1.4–1.3 m.y.a. In addition, there are some fragmentary hominid remains, including cranial pieces and two teeth. Unfortunately, the association of these hominid remains with the tools at a date prior to 1 m.y.a. is uncertain. Consequently, there is not yet *definitive* fossil evidence of *H. erectus* (or a close relative) from Southwest Asia. Nevertheless, the Ubeidiya archaeological discoveries are highly suggestive and fit with the overall emerging pattern of an early hominid dispersal from Africa.

More than likely, these first continental migrants were members of *H. erectus* or a group very closely related to *H. erectus* (although an earlier dispersal of a more primitive member of genus *Homo* cannot be ruled out). What the current evidence most economically suggests is that *Homo erectus* migrated out of East Africa, eventually to occupy South and North Africa, southern and northeastern Asia, and perhaps Europe as well. A recent, not yet fully described hominid mandible from the Dmanisi site in the Republic of Georgia has been provisionally dated to 1.8–1.6 m.y.a. (Fig. 9–1). In other words, if this as yet unconfirmed date should prove accurate, this fossil would be as early as any *H. erectus* discovery in Java and about as old as East African remains as well! Another new find pushing back the antiquity of hominids in Europe has come from the 500,000-year-old Boxgrove site in southern England, where a hominid tibia (shinbone) was unearthed in 1994. And still another recent find (1994), from the Ceprano site in central Italy, may be the best evidence yet of *H. erectus* in Europe (Ascenzi et al., 1996). Provisional dating of a partial cranium from this important site suggests a date greater than 700,000 years ago. The primary researchers, as well as Rightmire (1998), conclude that cranial morphology places this specimen quite close to *H. erectus*.

Finally, some other fossil remains from Spain, also discovered in 1994 and announced in 1995, may well be the oldest hominids yet found in western Europe (see Fig. 9–2 for locations of these hominid sites). From the Gran Dolina site in the highly productive Atapuerca region of northern Spain, where numerous, somewhat more recent hominid fossils have also been discovered (discussed in Chapter 10), several fragments of at least four individuals have been found (Carbonell et al., 1995). The dating, based on paleomagnetic determinations (see p. 174), places the Gran Dolina hominids at approximately 780,000 y.a.* (Parés and Pérez-González, 1995). If this dating is further corroborated, these early Spanish finds would be *at least* 250,000 years older than any other hominid yet discovered in western Europe. Because all the 36 pieces thus far identified are quite fragmentary, the taxonomic assignment of these fossils still remains problematic. Initial analysis, however, suggests that they probably are *not H. erectus*, except perhaps for the Ceprano cranium. Whether any of these early European hominids belong within the species *Homo erectus* thus still remains to be determined.

The dispersal of *Homo erectus* from Africa was influenced by climate, topography, water boundaries, and access to food and other resources. Paleoenviron-

*y.a. stands for "years ago."

mental reconstructions are thus of crucial importance in understanding the expansion of *H. erectus* to so many parts of the Old World. The long temporal span of *H. erectus* begins very early in the **Pleistocene** and extends to fairly late in that geological epoch. To comprehend the world of *Homo erectus,* we must understand how environments shifted during the Pleistocene.

Pleistocene
The epoch of the Cenozoic from 1.8 m.y.a. until 10,000 y.a. Frequently referred to as the Ice Age, this epoch is associated with continental glaciations in northern latitudes.

The Pleistocene (1.8 m.y.a.–10,000 y.a.)

During much of the Pleistocene (also known as the Age of Glaciers or Ice Age), large areas of the Northern Hemisphere were covered with enormous masses of ice, which advanced and retreated as the temperature fell and rose. An early classification of glacial (and interglacial) Europe divided the Pleistocene into four major glacial periods. However, climatic conditions varied in different areas of Europe, and distinctive glacial periods are also now known for the North Sea, England, and eastern Europe, not to mention Asia and North America. New dating techniques have revealed a much more complex account of glacial advance and retreat, and the many oscillations of cold and warm temperatures during the Pleistocene affected both plants and animals: "The Pleistocene record shows that there were about 15 major cold periods and 50 minor advances during its [more than] 1.5-m.y. duration, or one major cold period every 100,000 years" (Tattersal et al., 1988, p. 230).

It is also important to emphasize that glacial advances and retreats greatly influenced hominid migrations. During periods of glacial advance, sea levels lowered, thus exposing land bridges (e.g., between Siberia and Alaska and between Southeast Asia and Java). Moreover, large expanses of continental ice sheets also served to block land migrations, especially in the northern latitudes. For example, east-west migrations across the Alps of central Europe or northerly into Scandinavia were impossible during much of the Pleistocene; and during periods of glacial advance, migration south from Alaska into the rest of North America was also mostly blocked.

The Pleistocene, which lasted more than 1.75 million years, was a significant period in hominid evolutionary history and encompassed the appearance and disappearance of *Homo erectus.* By the end of the Pleistocene, modern humans had already appeared, dependence on culture had dramatically increased, and domestication of plants and animals—one of the great cultural revolutions of human history—was either about to commence or had already begun. Given this background on the time span in which *H. erectus* evolved and lived, let us examine more closely this predecessor of *H. sapiens.*

The Morphology of *Homo erectus*

Brain Size

Homo erectus differs in several respects from both early *Homo* and *Homo sapiens.* The most obvious feature is cranial size (which, of course, is closely related to brain size). Early *Homo* had cranial capacities ranging from as small as 500 cm^3 to as large as 800 cm^3. *H. erectus,* on the other hand, shows considerable brain enlargement, with a cranial capacity of 750 to 1,250 cm^3 (with a mean of approximately 900 cm^3). However, in making such comparisons, we must bear in mind two key questions: What is the comparative sample, and what were the overall body sizes of the species being compared?

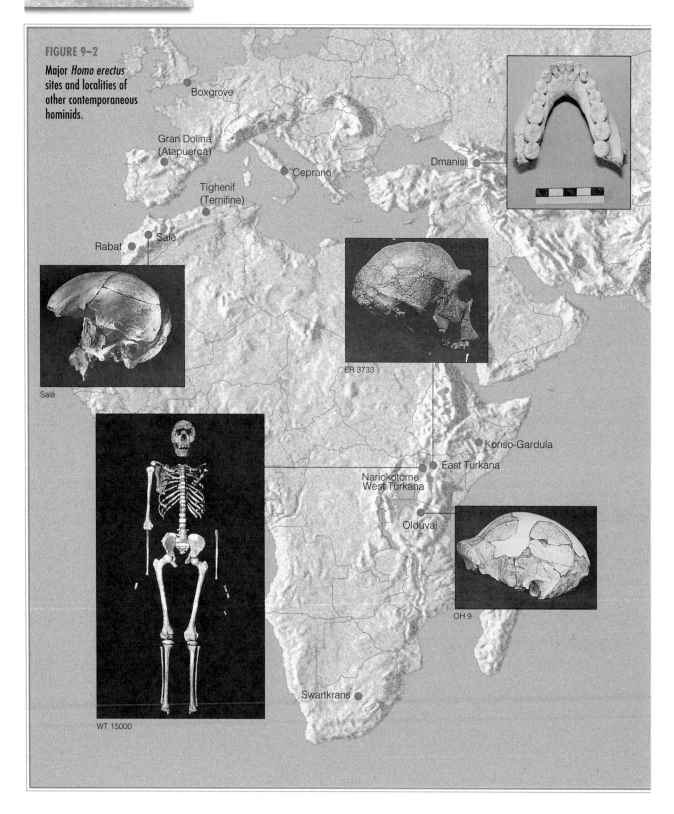

FIGURE 9–2

Major *Homo erectus* sites and localities of other contemporaneous hominids.

Boxgrove

Gran Dolina (Atapuerca)

Ceprano

Dmanisi

Tighenif (Ternifine)

Salé

Rabat

Salé

ER 3733

Konso-Gardula

East Turkana

Nariokotome West Turkana

Olduvai

OH 9

Swartkrans

WT 15000

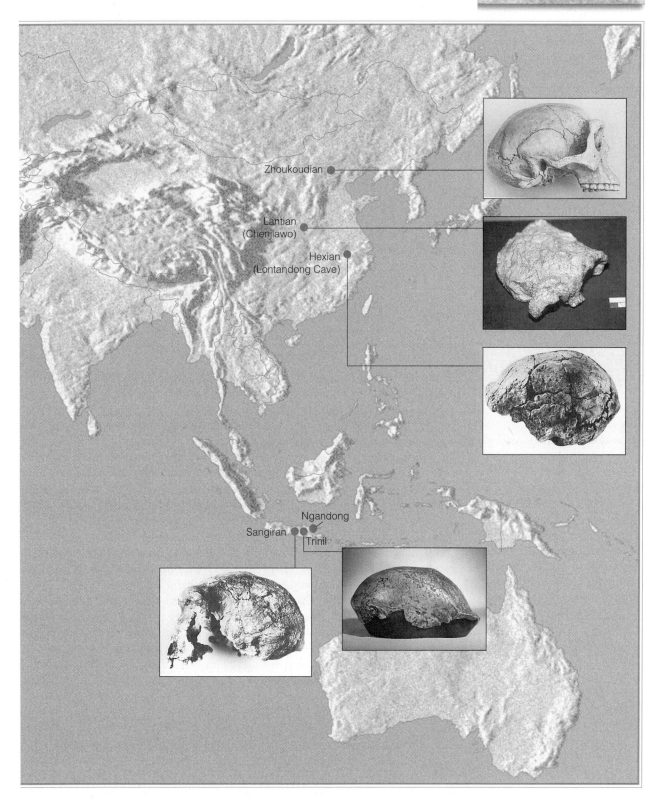

Zhoukoudian

Lantian
(Chenjiawo)

Hexian
(Lontandong Cave)

Ngandong

Sangiran

Trinil

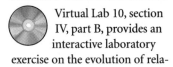

Virtual Lab 10, section IV, part B, provides an interactive laboratory exercise on the evolution of rela-

Nariokotome
(nar´-ee-oh-ko´-tow-may)

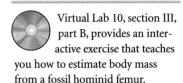

Virtual Lab 10, section III, part B, provides an interactive exercise that teaches you how to estimate body mass from a fossil hominid femur.

In relation to the first question, you should recall that many scholars are now convinced that there was more than one species of early *Homo* in East Africa around 2 m.y.a. If so, only one of these could have been ancestral to *H. erectus.* (Indeed, it is possible that neither species gave rise to *H. erectus* and that perhaps we have yet to find direct evidence of the ancestral species.) Taking a more optimistic view that at least one of these fossil groups is a likely ancestor of later hominids, the question still remains—which one? If we choose the smaller-bodied sample of early *Homo* as our presumed ancestral group, then *H. erectus* shows as much as a 40 percent increase in cranial capacity. However, if the comparative sample is the larger-bodied group of early *Homo* (as exemplified by skull 1470, from East Turkana), then *H. erectus* shows a 25 percent increase in cranial capacity.

As we previously discussed in Chapter 8, brain size is closely tied to overall body size (a relationship termed *encephalization*). We have made a point of the increase in *H. erectus* brain size; however, it must be realized that *H. erectus* was also considerably larger overall than earlier members of the genus *Homo.* In fact, when *H. erectus* is compared with the larger-bodied early *Homo* sample, *relative* brain size is about the same (Walker, 1991). Furthermore, when considering the relative brain size of *H. erectus* in comparison with *H. sapiens,* it is seen that *H. erectus* was considerably less encephalized than later members of the genus *Homo.*

Body Size

As we have just mentioned, another feature displayed by *H. erectus,* compared to earlier hominids, is a dramatic increase in body size. For several decades, little was known of the postcranial skeleton of *H. erectus.* However, with the discovery of a nearly complete skeleton in 1984 from **Nariokotome** (on the west side of Lake Turkana in Kenya) and its recent detailed analysis (Walker and Leakey, 1993), the data base is now much improved. From this specimen (and from less complete individuals at other sites), some *Homo erectus* adults are estimated to have weighed well over 100 pounds, with an average adult stature of about 5 feet 6 inches (McHenry, 1992; Ruff and Walker, 1993). Another point to keep in mind is that *Homo erectus* was quite sexually dimorphic—at least as indicated by the East African specimens. Thus, for male adult body size, weight and stature in some individuals may have been considerably greater than the average figures just mentioned. In fact, it is estimated that if the Nariokotome boy had survived, he would have attained an adult stature of over 6 feet (Walker, 1993).

Associated with the large stature (and explaining the significant increase in body weight) is also a dramatic increase in robusticity. In fact, this characteristic of very heavy body build was to dominate hominid evolution not just during *H. erectus* times, but through the long transitional era of archaic *Homo sapiens* as well. Only with the appearance of anatomically modern *H. sapiens* do we see a more gracile skeletal structure, which is still characteristic of most modern populations.

Cranial Shape

The cranium of *Homo erectus* displays a highly distinctive shape, partly as a result of increased brain size, but probably more correlated with significant body size (robusticity). The ramifications of this heavily built cranium are reflected in thick cranial bone (most notably in Asian specimens) and large browridges (supraorbital tori) in the front of the skull and a projecting **nuchal torus** at the rear (Fig. 9–3).

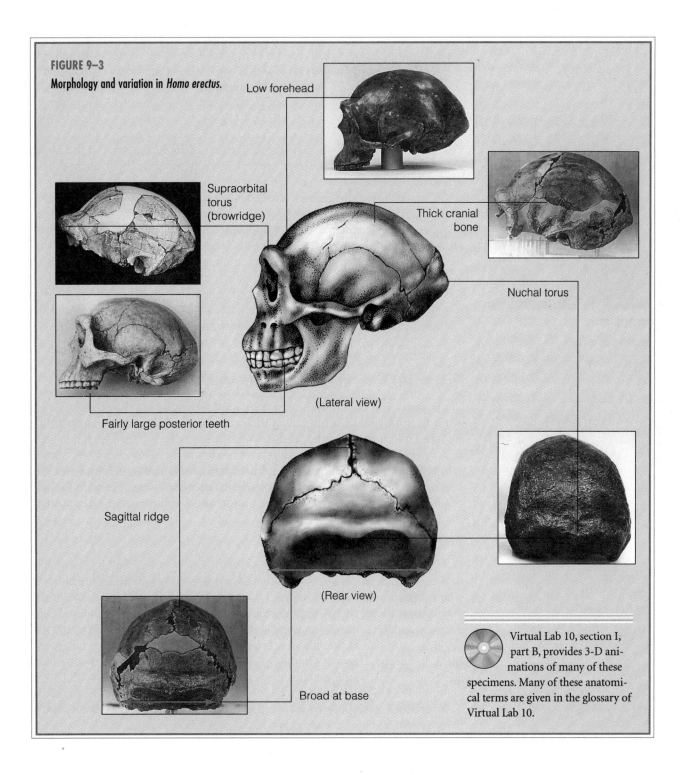

FIGURE 9–3

Morphology and variation in *Homo erectus*.

Low forehead

Supraorbital torus (browridge)

Thick cranial bone

Nuchal torus

Fairly large posterior teeth

(Lateral view)

Sagittal ridge

(Rear view)

Broad at base

Virtual Lab 10, section I, part B, provides 3-D animations of many of these specimens. Many of these anatomical terms are given in the glossary of Virtual Lab 10.

The vault is long and low, receding back from the large browridges with little forehead development. Moreover, the cranium is wider at the base compared with earlier *or* later species of genus *Homo.* The maximum breadth is below the ear opening, giving a pentagonal contour to the cranium (when viewed from behind). In contrast, both early *Homo* crania and *H. sapiens* crania have more vertical sides, and the maximum width is *above* the ear openings.

Dentition

The dentition of *Homo erectus* is much like that of *Homo sapiens,* but the earlier species exhibits somewhat larger teeth. However, compared with early *Homo,* *H. erectus* does show some dental reduction.

Another interesting feature of the dentition of some *H. erectus* specimens is seen in the incisor teeth. On the back (lingual) surfaces, the teeth are scooped out in appearance, forming a surface reminiscent of a shovel. Accordingly, such teeth are referred to as "shovel-shaped" incisors (Fig. 9–4). It has been suggested that teeth shaped in this manner are an adaptation in hunter-gatherers for processing foods, a contention not yet proved (or really even framed in a testable manner). One thing does seem likely: Shovel-shaped incisors are probably a primitive feature of the species *H. erectus,* as the phenomenon has been found not just in the Chinese specimens, but also in the early individual from Nariokotome.

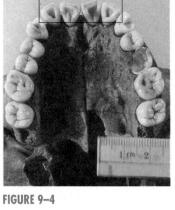

FIGURE 9–4
Shovel-shaped incisors.

Historical Overview of *Homo erectus* Discoveries

In our discussion of Plio-Pleistocene hominids, we traced the evolutionary developments in *chronological* order, that is, discussing the oldest specimens first. Here we take a different approach and discuss the finds in the order in which they were discovered. We believe that this approach is useful, as the discoveries cover a broad range of time—indeed, almost the entire history of paleoanthropology. Given this relatively long history of scientific discovery, the later finds were assessed in the light of earlier ones (and thus can still be best understood within a historical context).

Java

FIGURE 9–5
Eugene Dubois, discoverer of the first *H. erectus* fossil to be found.

Dutch anatomist Eugene Dubois (1858–1940) (Fig. 9–5) was the first scientist to deliberately design a research plan that would take him from his anatomy lab to where fossil bones might be buried. Up until this time, embryology and comparative anatomy were considered the proper methods of studying humans and their ancestry, and the research was done in the laboratory. Dubois changed all this.

The latter half of the nineteenth century was a period of intellectual excitement. In Europe, Darwin's *On the Origin of Species* (published in 1859) provoked scientists as well as educated laypeople to take opposing sides, often with heated emotion. In 1856, an unusual skull had been recovered near Düsseldorf, Germany. This specimen is now known as Neandertal, but when a description of it was published, scientific opinion was again divided, and feelings ran high.

This stimulating intellectual climate surrounded the youthful Eugene Dubois, who left Holland for Sumatra in 1887 to search for, as he phrased it, "the missing link." Dubois went to work immediately and soon unearthed a variety of animal bones, including orangutan, gibbon, and several other mammalian species.

However, his successes soon diminished, and in 1890 he switched his fieldwork to the banks of the Solo River near the town of Trinil, on the neighboring island of Java.

In October 1891, the field crew unearthed a skullcap that was to become internationally famous. The following year, a human femur was recovered about 15 yards upstream in what Dubois claimed was the same level as the skullcap. Dubois assumed that the skullcap (with a cranial capacity of slightly over 900 cm³) and the femur belonged to the same individual.

After studying these discoveries for a few years, Dubois startled the world in 1894 with a paper provocatively titled "*Pithecanthropus erectus,* A Manlike Species of Transitional Anthropoid from Java." In 1895, Dubois returned to Europe, where his paper had received strong criticism. He countered the criticism by elaborating the points briefly covered in his original paper. He also brought along the actual fossil material, which gave scientists an opportunity to examine the evidence. As a result, many opponents became more sympathetic to his views.

However, to this day, questions about the finds remain: Does the femur really belong with the skullcap? Did the field crew dig through several layers, thus mixing the remains? Moreover, some anthropologists think that the Trinil femur is relatively recent and representative of modern *H. sapiens,* not *H. erectus.*

Despite the still-unanswered questions, there is general acceptance that Dubois was correct in identifying the skull as representing a previously undescribed species; that his estimates of cranial capacity were reasonably accurate; that "*Pithecanthropus erectus,*" or *H. erectus* as we call it today, is the ancestor of *H. sapiens;* and that bipedalism preceded enlargement of the brain.

By 1930, the controversy had faded, especially in the light of important new discoveries near Peking (Beijing), China, in the late 1920s (discussed shortly). Similarities between the Beijing skulls and Dubois' "*Pithecanthropus*" were obvious, and scientists pointed out that the Java form was not an "apeman," as Dubois contended, but rather was closely related to modern *Homo sapiens.*

One might expect that Dubois would welcome the finds from China and the support they provided for the human status of "*Pithecanthropus,*" but Dubois would have none of it. He refused to recognize any connection between Beijing and Java and described the Beijing fossils as "a degenerate Neanderthaler" (von Koenigswald, 1956, p. 55). He also refused to accept the classification of "*Pithecanthropus*" in the same species with later finds from Java.

Homo erectus from Java

Six sites in eastern Java have yielded all the *H. erectus* fossil remains found to date on that island. The dating of these fossils has been hampered by the complex nature of Javanese geology. It has been generally accepted that most of the fossils belong in the Middle Pleistocene and are less than 800,000 years old. However, as we noted earlier, new dating estimates have suggested one find (from Modjokerto) to be close to 1.8 m.y.a. and another fossil from the main site of Sangiran to be approximately 1.6 m.y.a.

At Sangiran, where the remains of at least five individuals have been excavated, the cranial capacities of the fossils range from 813 cm³ to 1,059 cm³. Another site called Ngandong has also been fruitful, yielding the remains of 12 crania (Fig. 9–6). The dating here is also confusing, but the Upper Pleistocene has been suggested, which may explain the larger cranial measurements of the Ngandong individuals as well as features that are more modern than those found on other

FIGURE 9–6

Rear view of a Ngandong skull. Note that the cranial walls slope downward and outward (or upward and inward), with the widest breadth low on the cranium, giving it a pentagonal form.

 See Virtual Lab 10, section I, part B, for a 3-D animation and discussion of this specimen.

Javanese crania. Newly published dates for the Ngandong site are very recent, remarkably so, in fact. Using two specialized dating techniques (discussed in Chapter 11; see p. 277), Carl Swisher and colleagues from the Berkeley Geochronology Laboratory have determined from animal bones found at the site (and presumably associated with the hominids) a date ranging from about 50,000 years ago to as recently as 25,000 years ago (Swisher et al., 1996). If these dates are further confirmed, it would show a *very* late survival of *Homo erectus* in Java, long after they had disappeared elsewhere. They would thus be contemporary with *Homo sapiens*—which, by this time, had expanded widely in the Old World (see Chapter 11).

We cannot say much about the *H. erectus* way of life in Java. Very few artifacts have been found, and those have come mainly from river terraces, not from primary sites: "On Java there is still not a single site where artifacts can be associated with *H. erectus*" (Bartstra, 1982, p. 319).

Peking (Beijing)

The story of Peking *H. erectus* is another saga filled with excitement, hard work, luck, and misfortune. Europeans had known for a long time that "dragon bones," used by the Chinese as medicine and aphrodisiacs, were actually ancient mammal bones. In 1917, the Geological Survey of China decided to find the sites where these dragon bones were collected by local inhabitants and sold to apothecary shops. In 1921 a Swedish geologist, J. Gunnar Andersson, was told of a potentially fruitful fossil site in an abandoned quarry near the village of **Zhoukoudian.** A villager showed Andersson's team a fissure in the limestone wall, and within a few minutes they found the jaw of a pig: "That evening we went home with rosy dreams of great discoveries" (Andersson, 1934, pp. 97–98).

A young Chinese geologist, Pei Wenshong, took over the excavation in 1929 and began digging out the sediment in one branch of the lower cave, where he found one of the most remarkable fossil skulls to be recovered up to that time. One of the Chinese workers tells the story:

> We had got down about 30 meters deep. . . . It was there the skull-cap was sighted, half of it embedded in loose earth, the other in hard clay. The sun had almost set . . . . The team debated whether to take it out right away or to wait until the next day when they could see better. The agonizing suspense of a whole day was felt to be too much to bear, so they decided to go on. (Jia, 1975, pp. 12–13)

Pei brought the skull to anatomist Davidson Black (Fig 9–7). Because the fossil was embedded in hard limestone, it took Black four months of hard, steady work to free it from its tough matrix. The result was worth the labor. The skull, that of a juvenile, was thick, low, and relatively small, but in Black's mind there was no doubt it belonged to an early hominid. The response to this discovery, quite unlike that which greeted Dubois almost 40 years earlier, was immediate and enthusiastically favorable.

Franz Weidenreich (Fig 9–8), a distinguished anatomist well known for his work on European fossil hominids, succeeded Black. After Japan invaded China in 1933, Weidenreich decided to move the fossils from Beijing to prevent them from falling into the hands of the Japanese. Weidenreich left China in 1941, taking excellent prepared casts, photographs, and drawings of the Peking material with him.

Zhoukoudian
(zhoh´-koh-dee´-en)

FIGURE 9–7
Davidson Black, responsible for the first study of the Zhoukoudian fossils.

FIGURE 9–8
Franz Weidenreich.

After he left, the bones were packed, and arrangements were made for the U.S. Marine Corps in Beijing to take them to the United States. The bones never reached the United States, and they have never been found. To this day, no one knows what happened to them, and their location remains a mystery.

Zhoukoudian *Homo erectus*

In their recent book (1990), Jia and Huang list the total fossil remains of *H. erectus* unearthed at the Zhoukoudian Cave as of 1982 (Fig. 9–9):

FIGURE 9–10

H. erectus (cast of specimen from Zhoukoudian). From this view, the supraorbital torus, low vault of the skull, and nuchal torus can clearly be seen.

14 skullcaps (only 6 relatively complete) (Fig. 9–10)

6 facial bones (including maxillae, palates, and zygomatic bone fragments)

15 mandibles (mostly one side, only one nearly complete, many fragments)

122 isolated teeth

38 teeth rooted in jaws

3 humeri (upper arm bones, only 1 well preserved, the rest in fragments)

1 clavicle (both ends absent)

1 lunate (wrist bone)

7 femurs (only 1 well preserved)

1 tibia (shinbone, fragmentary)

(and over 100,000 artifacts)

These remains belong to upward of 40 male and female adults and children and constitute a considerable amount of evidence, the largest number of *H. erectus* specimens found at any one site. With the meticulous work by Weidenreich, the Zhoukoudian fossils have led to a good overall picture of the eastern *H. erectus* of China.

Peking *H. erectus,* like that from Java, possesses typical *H. erectus* features, including the supraorbital torus in front and the nuchal torus behind; also, the

A 3-D animation and discussion of this specimen from Zhoukoudian is given in Virtual Lab 10, section I, part B.

skull is keeled by a sagittal ridge, the face protrudes, the incisors are shoveled, and the molars contain large pulp cavities. Again, like the Javanese forms, the skull shows the greatest breadth near the bottom. (These similarities were recognized long ago by Black and Weidenreich.)

Cultural Remains   More than 100,000 artifacts have been recovered from this vast site that was occupied intermittently for almost 250,000 years. According to the Chinese (Wu and Lin, 1983, p.86), Zhoukoudian "is one of the sites with the longest history of habitation by man or his ancestors." The occupation of the site has been divided into three cultural stages:

> *Earliest Stage* (460,000–420,000 y.a.)*   The tools are large, close to a pound in weight, and made of soft stone, such as sandstone.

> *Middle Stage* (370,000–350,000 y.a.)   Tools become smaller and lighter (under a pound), and these smaller tools comprise approximately two-thirds of the sample.

> *Final Stage* (300,000–230,000 y.a.)   Tools are still small, and the tool materials are of better quality. The coarse quartz of the earlier periods is replaced by a finer quartz, sandstone tools have almost disappeared, and flint tools increase in frequency by as much as 30 percent.

The early tools are crude and shapeless but become more refined over time. Common tools at the site are choppers and chopping tools, but retouched flakes were fashioned into scrapers, points, burins, and awls (Fig 9–11).

Stone was not the only material used by *H. erectus* at Zhoukoudian; these hominids also utilized bone and probably horn. Found in the cave were antler fragments, which had been hacked into pieces. Antler bases might have served as hammers and the sharp tines as digging sticks. Also found in abundance were many deer skulls lacking facial bones as well as antlers, thus leaving only the braincases intact. Jia suggests that because the skulls show evidence of repeated whittling and over 100 specimens were discovered, all similarly shaped, "it is reasonable to infer they served as 'drinking bowls.'" He goes on to conjecture that the braincases

FIGURE 9–11

Chinese tools from Middle Pleistocene sites. (Adapted from Wu and Olsen, 1985.)

Quartzite chopper

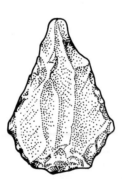

Flint point

Flint awl

Graver or burin

*These dates should be considered tentative until more precise chronometric techniques are available.

of the Beijing *H. erectus* fossils "retain similar characteristics and probably served the same purpose."

The way of life at Zhoukoudian has traditionally been described as that of hunter-gatherers who killed deer and horses as well as other animals and gathered fruits, berries, and ostrich eggs. Fragments of charred ostrich eggshells, the abundant deposits of hackberry seeds unearthed in the cave, and the flourishing plant growth surrounding the cave all suggest that meat was supplemented by the gathering of herbs, wild fruits, tubers, and eggs. Layers of ash in the cave, over 18 feet deep at one point, suggest fire and hearths, but whether Beijing hominids could actually make fire is unknown. Wu and Lin (1983, p. 94) state that "Peking Man was a cave dweller, a fire user, a deer hunter, a seed gatherer and a maker of specialized tools," but several questions about Zhoukoudian *H. erectus* remain unanswered.

Did *H. erectus* at Zhoukoudian use language? If by language we mean articulate speech, it is unlikely. Nevertheless, some scholars believe that speech originated early in hominid evolution; others argue that speech did not originate until up to 200,000 years later in the Upper Paleolithic, with the origin of anatomically modern humans (see Chapter 11). We agree with Dean Falk when she writes, "Unfortunately, what it is going to take to *settle* the debate about when language originated in hominids is a time machine. Until one becomes available, we can only speculate about this fascinating and important question" (1989, p. 141).

Did these hominids wear clothes? Almost surely clothing of some type, probably in the form of animal skins, was worn. Winters in Beijing are harsh today and appear to have been bitter during the Middle Pleistocene as well. Moreover, awls were found at Zhoukoudian, and one of the probable bone tools may be a needle.

What was the life span of *H. erectus* at Zhoukoudian? Apparently, not very long, and infant and childhood mortality was probably very high. Studies of the fossil remains reveal that almost 40 percent of the bones belong to individuals under the age of 14, and only 2.6 percent are estimated to be in the 50- to 60-year age-group (Jia, 1975).

This picture of Zhoukoudian life has been challenged by archaeologist Lewis Binford and colleagues (Binford and Ho, 1985; Binford and Stone, 1986a, 1986b). Binford and his colleagues reject the description of Beijing *H. erectus* as hunters and argue that the evidence clearly points to them as scavengers. As we saw in Chapter 8, the controversy of early hominids as hunters or scavengers has engaged the attention of paleoanthropologists, and the matter is not yet settled. Binford and his colleagues also do not accept that the Beijing hominids were clearly associated with fire, except in the later phases of occupation (about 250,000 y.a.).

Other Chinese Sites

More work has been done at Zhoukoudian than at any other Chinese site. Nevertheless, there are other hominid sites worth noting. Three of the more important sites, besides Zhoukoudian, are Chenjiawo and Gongwangling (both in Lantian County and sometimes referred to as Lantian) and Lontandong Cave in Hexian County (often referred to as the Hexian find) (Table 9–1).

At Chenjiawo, an almost complete mandible containing several teeth was found in 1963. It is quite similar to those from Zhoukoudian but has been provisionally dated at about 650,000 y.a. If the dating is correct, this specimen would be older than the Beijing material. The following year, a partial cranium was discovered at Gongwangling, not far from Chenjiawo. Provisionally dated to as

TABLE 9–1   *H. Erectus* Fossils from China

Designation	Site	Age* (Years Ago)	Material	Cranial Capacity (cm3)	Year Found	Remarks
Hexian	Longtandong Cave, Anhui	250,000	Calvarium, skull fragments, mandible fragments, isolated teeth	1,025	1980–81	First skull found in southern or southwest China
Zhoukoudian (Peking)	Zhoukoudian Cave, Beijing	500,000–200,000	5 adult crania, skull fragments, facial bones, isolated teeth, postcranial pieces (40+ individuals)	850–1,225; avg: 1,010	1927–ongoing	Most famous fossils in China and some of the most famous in the world
Yunxian	Longgudong Cave, Hubei	?500,000	Isolated teeth		1976–82	
Yunxian	Quyuanhekou	350,000	2 mostly complete (but crushed) crania	Undetermined	1989	The most complete crania from China, but still requiring much restoration
Lantian	Chenjiawo, Lantian	650,000	Mandible		1963	Old female
Lantian	Gongwangling, Lantian	1,150,000–800,000	Calvarium, facial bones	780	1964	Female over 30; most ancient *H. erectus* found so far in China

Sources: *Atlas of Primitive Man in China* (1980); Lisowski, 1984; Pope, 1984; Wu and Dong, 1985; Etler and Tianyuan, 1994.
*These are best estimates; authorities differ.

much as 1.15 m.y.a. (Etler and Tianyuan, 1994), the Gongwangling specimen may be the oldest Chinese *Homo erectus* fossil yet known.

Perhaps the most significant find was made in 1980 at Lontandong Cave, where remains of several individuals were recovered. One of the specimens is a well-preserved cranium (with a cranial capacity of about 1,025 cm^3) lacking much of its base. Dated roughly at 250,000 y.a., it is not surprising that this Hexian cranium displays several advanced features. The cranial constriction, for example, is not as pronounced as in earlier forms, and certain temporal and occipital characteristics are "best compared with the later forms of *H. erectus* at Zhoukoudian" (Wu and Dong, 1985, p. 87).

In June 1993, Li Tianyuan and Dennis Etler reported that two relatively complete skulls were discovered in 1989 at a hominid site in Yunxian County. The date given for the site is 350,000 y.a., which, if correct, would make these the most complete crania of this great antiquity in China (Fig 9–12).

The Yunxian crania are both large and robust, considerably exceeding in size those from Zhoukoudian. In general, the Yunxian individuals fit within *Homo erectus*, but in the facial region especially they also show some interesting advanced features. A few of these features suggest to some scholars "a mid-facial morphology similar to that of modern Asians" (Etler and Tianyuan, 1994, p. 668).

Unfortunately, both skulls are still covered with a hard calcareous matrix, and critics argue that until the skulls are cleaned and the crushed parts properly put together, it is too early to make accurate assessments. In any case, these Yunxian crania will ultimately provide considerable data to help clarify hominid evolution in China and perhaps elsewhere in the Old World as well.

A number of archaeological sites have been excavated in China, and early stone tools have been found in numerous locations in widely separated areas. At present, there is little reason to believe that *H. erectus* culture in these provinces differed much from that described at Zhoukoudian.

The Asian crania from both Java and China are mainly Middle Pleistocene fossils and share many similar features, which may be explained by *H. erectus* migration from Java to China about 800,000 years ago. African *H. erectus* forms are generally older than most Asian forms and are not as similar to them as Asian forms (i.e., from Java and China) are to each other.

East Africa

Olduvai   Back in 1960, Louis Leakey unearthed a fossil skull at Olduvai (OH 9) that he identified as *H. erectus*. Skull OH 9 from Upper Bed II is dated at 1.4 m.y.a. and preserves a massive cranium but is faceless except for a bit of nose below the supraorbital torus. Estimated at 1,067 cm^3, the cranial capacity of OH 9 is the largest of all the African *Homo erectus* specimens. The browridge is huge, the largest known for any hominid in both thickness and projection, but the vault walls are thin. This latter characteristic of fairly thin cranial vault bones is seen in most East African *H. erectus* specimens, and in this respect, they differ from Asian *H. erectus* (in which cranial vaults are thick).

East Turkana   Some 400 miles north of Olduvai Gorge, on the northern boundary of Kenya, is Lake Turkana. Explored by Richard Leakey and colleagues since 1969, the eastern shore of the lake has been a virtual gold mine for australopithecine, early *Homo*, and *H. erectus* fossil remains.

The most significant *H. erectus* discovery from East Turkana is ER 3733, an almost complete skull lacking a mandible (Fig. 9–13). Discovered in 1974, the specimen has been given a firm date of close to 1.8 m.y.a. The cranial capacity is estimated at 848 cm^3, at the lower end of the range for *H. erectus*, but this is not surprising considering its early date. The cranium generally resembles Asian *H. erectus* in many features (but with some important differences, discussed shortly).

Not many tools have been found at *H. erectus* sites in East Turkana. Oldowan types of flakes, cobbles, and core tools have been found, and the introduction of **Acheulian** tools about 1.4 m.y.a. replaced the Oldowan tradition.

West Turkana*   In August 1984, Kamoya Kimeu (see p. 234), a member of Richard Leakey's team further added to his reputation as an outstanding fossil hunter when he discovered a small piece of skull near the base camp on the west side of Lake Turkana. Leakey and his colleague, Alan Walker of Pennsylvania State University, excavated the site known as Nariokotome in 1984 and again in 1985.

The dig was a resounding success. The workers unearthed the most complete *H. erectus* skeleton yet found (Fig. 9–14). Known properly as WT 15000, the all but complete skeleton includes facial bones and most of the postcranial bones, a rare finding indeed for *H. erectus*, since these particular elements are scarce at other *H. erectus* sites.

---

*WT is the symbol for West Turkana, that is, the west side of Lake Turkana. The east side is designated by ER—East Rudolf. Rudolf was the former name of the lake.

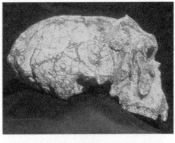

(a)

(b)

FIGURE 9–12

(a) EV 9002 (Yunxian, China). The skull is in better shape than its companion, and its lateral view clearly displays features characteristic of *H. erectus:* flattened vault, receding forehead (frontal bone), angulated occiput, and supraorbital torus. (b) EV 9001 (Yunxian). Unfortunately, the skull was crushed, but it preserves some lateral facial structures absent in EV 9002.

 Specimens from East Africa and their 3-D animations are presented in Virtual Lab 10, section I, part B.

Acheulian
(ash´-oo-lay-en) Pertaining to a stone tool industry of the Lower and Middle Pleistocene characterized by a large proportion of bifacial tools (flaked on both sides). Acheulian tool kits are very common in Africa, Southwest Asia, and western Europe, but are generally absent elsewhere. (Also spelled "Acheulean.")

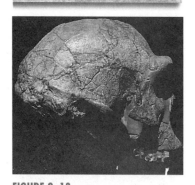

FIGURE 9–13

ER 3733, the most complete East Turkana
H. erectus cranium.

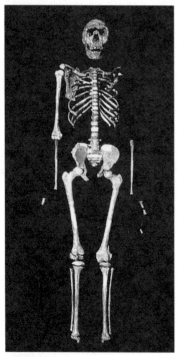

FIGURE 9–14

WT 15000 from Nariokotome, Kenya:
the most complete *H. erectus* specimen
yet found.

Be sure to consider this alternative phylogeny (with pronunciations of the species' names) that is presented in the glossary of Virtual Lab 10 under Phylogeny of *Homo*.

Another remarkable feature of the find is its age. Its dating is based on the chronometric dates of the geological formation in which the site is located and is set at about 1.6 million years. The skeleton is that of a boy about 12 years of age and 5 feet 3 inches tall. Had he grown to maturity, his height, it is estimated, would have been more than 6 feet, taller than *H. erectus* was heretofore thought to have been. The postcranial bones appear to be quite similar, though not identical, to those of modern humans. The cranial capacity of WT 15000 is estimated at 880 cm³; brain growth was nearly complete, and it is estimated that the boy's adult cranial capacity would have been approximately 909 cm³ (Begun and Walker, 1993).

Ethiopia In southern Ethiopia, the 1991 Paleoanthropological Inventory of Ethiopia team of international scientists discovered a site, Konso-Gardula (KGA), containing a remarkable abundance of Acheulian tools, a hominid upper third molar, and an almost complete mandible with several cheek teeth. Both specimens are attributed to *H. erectus* "because they lack specialized characteristics of robust *Australopithecus*" (Asfaw et al., 1992).

The mandible is robust and is dated to about 1.3 m.y.a. The Acheulian stone tools, mainly bifaces and picks, are made of quartz, quartzite, and volcanic rock.

Summary of East African *H. erectus*

The *Homo erectus* remains from East Africa show several differences from the fossil samples from Java and China. The African specimens (as exemplified by ER 3733, presumably a female, and WT 15000, presumably a male) are not as strongly buttressed in the cranium (by supraorbital or nuchal tori) and do not have such thick cranial bones as seen in Asian representatives of *H. erectus*. These differences, as well as others observed in the postcranial skeleton, have so impressed some researchers that they in fact argue for a *separate* species status for the African *H. erectus* remains (as distinct from the Asian samples). Bernard Wood, the leading proponent of this view, has suggested that the name *Homo ergaster* be used for the African remains; *H. erectus* would then be reserved solely for the Asian material (Wood, 1991). In addition, the very early dates now postulated for the dispersal of *H. erectus* into Asia (Java) would argue for a more than 1-million-year separate history for Asian and African populations.

Nevertheless, this species division has not been generally accepted, and the current consensus (reflected in this text) is to continue to refer to all these hominids as *Homo erectus* (Kramer, 1993; Conroy, 1997; Rightmire, 1998). As with the Plio-Pleistocene samples, we accordingly will have to accommodate a considerable degree of intraspecific variation within this species. Wood has concluded, regarding variation within such a broadly defined *H. erectus* species, "It is a species which manifestly embraces an unusually wide degree of variation in both the cranium and postcranial skeleton" (Wood, 1992a, p. 329).

South Africa

A mandible was found among fossil remains collected at Swartkrans in South Africa in the 1940s and 1950s. This specimen, SK 15, was originally assigned to "*Telanthropus capensis*," but is now placed within the genus *Homo* (there is, however, disagreement about its species designation). Rightmire (1990) suggests that it may be linked with *Homo erectus,* but others are not certain. If it is *H. erectus,* it would demonstrate that *H. erectus* inhabited South Africa as well as the other regions documented by other more complete fossil finds.

North Africa

With evidence from China and Java, it appears clear that *H. erectus* populations, with superior tools and weapons and presumably greater intelligence than their predecessors, had expanded their habitat beyond that of early hominids. The earliest evidence for *H. erectus,* 1.8–1.6 m.y.a., comes from East Africa and Java and about 1 million years later in China. Early dispersal of *H. erectus* to Europe (prior to 1 m.y.a.) may also have occurred. It is not surprising, therefore, that *H. erectus* migrations would have taken them to northwest Africa as well.

North African remains, consisting almost entirely of mandibles (or mandible fragments) and a partial parietal bone, have been found at Ternifine (now Tighenif), Algeria, and in Morocco, at Sidi Abderrahman and Thomas Quarries. The three Ternifine mandibles and the parietal fragment are quite robust and have been dated to about 700,000 y.a. The Moroccan material is not as robust as Ternifine and may be a bit younger, at 500,000 years. In addition, an interesting cranium was found in a quarry north of Salé, in Morocco. The walls of the skull vault are thick, and several other features resemble those of *H. erectus.* Some features suggest that Salé is *H. sapiens,* but a date of 400,000 y.a. and an estimated cranial capacity of about 900 cm^3 throw doubt on that interpretation.

Europe

The situation in Europe during the Pleistocene appears especially complex. With accumulating evidence suggesting dispersal of the first hominids to Europe in the Lower Pleistocene (i.e., prior to 700,000 y.a.), there is a growing realization that some of the earliest European hominids should perhaps be included within the species *H. erectus* (particularly the remains from Dmanisi and Ceprano, since the morphology of these specimens suggests at least a provisional assignment to *H. erectus*; see p. 212). The slightly later remains from Atapuerca, in Spain (Gran Dolina site), are not as clearly similar to *Homo erectus,* and Spanish researchers have suggested placing them in a completely different species of hominid ("*Homo antecessor*"). Clearly, such an interpretation will require considerable more evaluation (and verification) before it can become widely accepted. We should note that all of this early Pleistocene European fossil material is both fragmentary and quite recently discovered. Thus, all current interpretations are, for the moment, both tentative and controversial.

After about 400,000 y.a., the European fossil hominid record becomes increasingly abundant. Nevertheless, interpretations relating to the proper taxonomic assessment of many of these remains have been debated, in some cases for decades. In recent years, several of these somewhat later (i.e., Middle Pleistocene) specimens have been placed within a grouping of early *Homo sapiens* referred to as "archaic *Homo sapiens.*" Needless to say, not everyone agrees. These enigmatic archaic *H. sapiens* specimens are discussed in Chapter 10. A time line for the *H. erectus* discoveries discussed in this chapter as well as other finds of more uncertain status is shown in Figure 9–15.

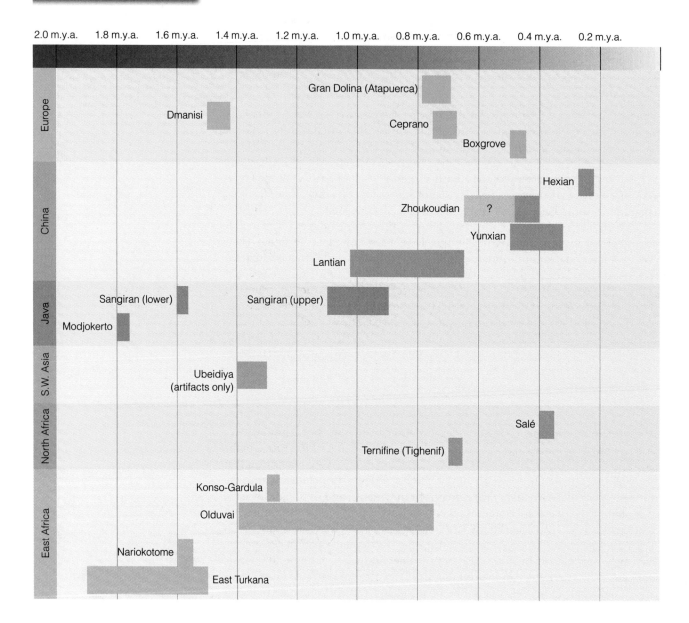

2.0 m.y.a. 1.8 m.y.a. 1.6 m.y.a. 1.4 m.y.a. 1.2 m.y.a. 1.0 m.y.a. 0.8 m.y.a. 0.6 m.y.a. 0.4 m.y.a. 0.2 m.y.a.

Europe
Gran Dolina (Atapuerca)
Dmanisi
Ceprano
Boxgrove

China
Hexian
Zhoukoudian ?
Yunxian
Lantian

Java
Sangiran (lower)
Sangiran (upper)
Modjokerto

S.W. Asia
Ubeidiya
(artifacts only)

North Africa
Salé
Ternifine (Tighenif)

East Africa
Konso-Gardula
Olduvai
Nariokotome
East Turkana

FIGURE 9–15

Time line for *Homo erectus* discoveries and other contemporary hominids. Note that most dates are approximations.

Technological and Population Trends in the Middle Pleistocene

Technological Trends

Many researchers have noted the remarkable stasis of the physical and cultural characteristics of *Homo erectus* populations, which seemed to change so little in the more than 1.5 million years of their existence. There is, however, dispute on this point. Some scholars (Rightmire, 1981) see almost no detectable changes in cranial dimensions over more than 1 million years of *H. erectus* evolution. Other paleoanthropologists (e.g., Wolpoff, 1984), who use different methodologies to date and subdivide their samples, draw a different conclusion, seeing some significant long-term morphological trends. Accepting a moderate position, we can postulate that there were some changes: The brain of later *H. erectus* was somewhat larger, the nose more protrusive, and the body not as robust as in earlier forms. Moreover, there were modifications in stone tool technology.

Expansion of the brain presumably enabled *H. erectus* to develop a more sophisticated tool kit than seen among earlier hominids. The important change in this kit was a core worked on both sides, called a *biface* (known widely as a hand axe or cleaver; Fig 9–16). The biface had a flatter core than the roundish earlier Oldowan pebble tool. And, probably even more important, this *core* tool was obviously a target design, that is, the main goal of the toolmaker. This greater focus and increased control enabled the stoneknapper to produce sharper, straighter edges, resulting in a more efficient implement. This Acheulian stone tool became standardized as the basic *H. erectus* all-purpose tool (with only minor modification) for more than a million years. It served to cut, scrape, pound, dig, and more—a most useful tool that has been found in Africa, parts of Asia, and later in western Europe.

Like populations elsewhere, *H. erectus* in China manufactured choppers and chopping tools as their core tools, and like other *H. erectus* toolmakers, fashioned scrapers and other small tools (Fig. 9–17), but they did not regularly manufacture bifaces. Interestingly, while the Acheulian is known from Africa as early as 1.4 m.y.a. and persisted there and in western Europe and southwestern Asia for over 1 million years, this industry has *never* been found in eastern Europe or East Asia. Why there was such a long period of cultural distinctiveness has never been completely explained. It has been thought that other kinds of raw materials for tools were employed (bamboo, perhaps, in China). Another possibility suggested by the redating of the early Java sites is that *H. erectus* left Africa *prior* to the development of the Acheulian, and after reaching Asia, some groups continued to remain culturally isolated in certain regions.

In early days, toolmakers employed a stone hammer (simply an ovoid-shaped stone about the size of an egg or a bit larger) to remove flakes from the core, thus leaving deep scars. Later, they used other materials, such as wood and bone. They learned to use these new materials as soft hammers, which gave them more control over flaking, thus leaving shallow scars, sharper edges, and a more symmetrical form. Toward the end of the Acheulian industry, toolmakers blocked out a core with stone hammers and then switched to wood or bone for refining the edges. This technique produced more elegant-appearing and pear-shaped implements.

Evidence of butchering is widespread at *H. erectus* sites, and in the past, such evidence has been cited in arguments for consistent hunting. For example, at the Olorgesailie site in Kenya (Fig. 9–18), dated at approximately 800,000 y.a., thousands of Acheulian hand axes have been recovered in association with remains of large animals, including giant baboons (now extinct). However, the assumption of consistent hunting has been challenged, especially by archaeologists who argue that the evidence does not prove the hunting hypothesis. Instead, they suggest that *H. erectus* was primarily a scavenger, a hypothesis that also has not yet been proved conclusively. We thus discuss *H. erectus* as a potential hunter *and* scavenger. It is crucial to remember, too, that *gathering* of wild plant foods was also practiced by *H. erectus* groups (as evidenced by the seeds at Zhoukoudian). Indeed, probably a majority of the calories they consumed came from such gathering activities.

FIGURE 9–16

Acheulian biface ("hand axe"), a basic tool of the Acheulian tradition.

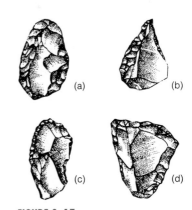

FIGURE 9–17

Small tools of the Acheulian industry. (a) Side scraper. (b) Point. (c) End scraper. (d) Burin.

(a)

(b)

FIGURE 9–18

(a) A Middle Pleistocene butchering site at Olorgesailie, Kenya, excavated by Louis and Mary Leakey, who had the catwalk built for observers. (b) A close-up of the Acheulian tools, mainly hand axes, found at the site.

Moreover, as we have seen, the mere *presence* of animal bones at archaeological sites does not prove that hominids were killing animals or even necessarily exploiting meat. Thus, in making interpretations of early hominid sites, we must consider a variety of alternatives. As Stanford University archaeologist Richard Klein has concluded regarding Middle Pleistocene sites, the interpretations are far from clear: "In sum, the available data do not allow us to isolate the relative roles of humans, carnivores, and factors such as starvation, accidents, and stream action in creating bone assemblages. . . . Certainly, as presently understood, the sites do not tell us how successful or effective *Homo erectus* was at obtaining meat" (1989, p. 221).

Population Trends

One of the fascinating qualities of *H. erectus* was a penchant for travel. From the relatively close confines of East Africa, *H. erectus* dispersed widely in the Old World. By the time *H. sapiens* appeared a million or more years later, *H. erectus* had migrated to South and North Africa. And even earlier, some groups had moved from Africa to Asia and perhaps to Europe as well.

The life of hunter-scavengers (and still, no doubt, *primarily* gatherers) was nomadic, and the woodland and savanna that covered the southern tier of Asia would have been an excellent environment for *H. erectus* (as it was similar to the econiche of their African ancestors). As the population grew, small groups budded off and moved on to find their own resource areas. This process, repeated again and again, led *H. erectus* east, crossing to Java, arriving there, it seems, as early as the most ancient known sites in East Africa itself.

Once in Java, it had been assumed that *H. erectus* would have found it impossible to venture farther south or east, since during the Pleistocene, deep water channels presumably separated Java completely from more southerly islands and Australia. However, recent reinterpretation (and firmer radiometric dates) of stone tools found on the island of Flores, 375 miles east of Java, has prompted some paleoanthropologists to reconsider this assumption (Gibbons, 1998). With a suggested date of 750,000 y.a. for these tools, it raises a most unexpected possibility: Could ancient *H. erectus* at this *very* early period construct ocean-going vessels (rafts?) that could navigate over deep, fast-moving waters?

While initial dating of the Flores stone materials appears reasonably good (using fission-track dating; see p. 174), the conclusion that the finds *prove* such seemingly advanced capabilities for *H. erectus* is not yet generally accepted. A number of troublesome issues remain to be resolved, the first being whether the lithic materials from Flores are *deliberate* tools or are simply naturally fractured rock. This latter possibility would argue against *H. erectus* (or any other hominid) having expanded south or east beyond Java at such an early date. Of course, the most unambiguous evidence would be fossil discoveries of *H. erectus* itself.

When we look back at the evolution of *H. erectus,* we realize how significant this early human's achievements were. It was *H. erectus* who increased in body size with more efficient bipedalism; who embraced culture wholeheartedly as a strategy of adaptation; whose brain was reshaped and increased in size to within *H. sapiens* range; who became a more efficient scavenger and likely hunter with greater dependence on meat; who apparently established more permanent bases; who perhaps could build vessels to cross open water; and who probably used fire and may have also controlled it. In short, it was *H. erectus,* committed to a cultural way of life, who transformed hominid evolution to human evolution; or as Foley states, "The appearance and expansion of *H. erectus* represented a major change in adaptive strategy that influenced the subsequent process and pattern of human evolution" (1991, p. 425).

SUMMARY

Homo erectus remains are found in geological contexts dating from about 1.8 million to about 200,000 years ago (and perhaps much later), a period of more than 1.5 million years. The first finds were made by Dubois in Java, and later discoveries came from China and Africa. Differences from early *Homo* are notable in *H. erectus'* larger brain, taller stature, robust build, and changes in facial structure and cranial buttressing.

The long period of *H. erectus'* existence was marked by a remarkably uniform technology over space and time. Nevertheless, compared to earlier hominids, *H. erectus* introduced more sophisticated tools and probably ate novel and/or differently processed foods, using these new tools and probably fire as well. They were also able to move into different environments and successfully adapt to new conditions.

Originating in East Africa, *H. erectus* migrated in several directions: south and northwest in Africa and east to Java and China. The evidence from China, especially Zhoukoudian, supports a *H. erectus* way of life that included gathering, scavenging, hunting, and controlled use of fire (but note that there is not complete agreement about this archaeological reconstruction).

It is generally assumed that some *H. erectus* populations evolved to *H. sapiens*, since many fossils, such as Ngandong (and others discussed in Chapter 10), display both *H. erectus* and *H. sapiens* features. There remain questions about *H. erectus* behavior (e.g., did they hunt?) and about evolution to *H. sapiens* (was it gradual or rapid, and which *H. erectus* populations contributed genes to *H. sapiens*?). The search for answers continues.

QUESTIONS FOR REVIEW

1. Describe the Pleistocene in terms of (a) relationship to glacial sequences and (b) the dating of fossil hominids.
2. Describe *Homo erectus*. How is *H. erectus* anatomically different from early *Homo*? From *H. sapiens*?
3. In what areas of the world have *Homo erectus* fossils been found?
4. In comparing *H. erectus* with earlier hominids, why is it important to specify which comparative sample is being used?
5. What was the intellectual climate in Europe in the latter half of the nineteenth century, especially concerning human evolution?
6. Why do you think there was so much opposition to Dubois' interpretation of the hominid fossils he found in Java?
7. Why do you think Zhoukoudian *H. erectus* was enthusiastically accepted, whereas the Javanese fossils were not?
8. What questions are still being asked about Dubois' finds? Explain.
9. Describe the way of life of *H. erectus* at Zhoukoudian as suggested in the text. What disagreements have been voiced about this conjecture?
10. *H. erectus* has been called the first human. Why?
11. What is the *H. erectus* evidence from Africa, and what questions of human evolution does the evidence raise?
12. Can you suggest any reason why the earliest remains of *H. erectus* have come from East Africa?
13. *H. erectus* migrated to various points in Africa and vast distances to eastern Asia and elsewhere. What does this tell you about the species?
14. What kinds of stone tools have been found at *H. erectus* sites?

SUGGESTED FURTHER READINGS

Day, Michael. 1986. *Guide to Fossil Man.* Chicago: University of Chicago Press.

Lewin, Roger. 1998. *Principles of Human Evolution: A Core Textbook.* New York: Blackwell Science Inc.

Rightmire, G.P. 1990. *The Evolution of* Homo erectus. New York: Cambridge University Press.

Shapiro, Harry L. 1980. *Peking Man.* New York: Simon & Schuster.

Walker, Alan, and Richard Leakey (eds). 1993. *The Nariokotome* Homo erectus *Skeleton.* Cambridge, MA: Harvard University Press.

Wolpoff, Milford. 1984. "Evolution in *Homo erectus:* The Question of Stasis." *Paleobiology* 10: 389–406.

MULTIMEDIA RESOURCES

 Wadsworth Anthropology Resource Center

http://anthropology.wadsworth.com

Visit Anthropology Online to obtain current updates in the field, surfing tips, career information, and more. In addition, enrich your study efforts with text-specific study aids arranged by chapter.

InfoTrac College Edition

http://www.infotrac-college.com/wadsworth

1. Using PowerTrac search InfoTrac College Edition for news on *Homo erectus*. Choose one story, read, and write a page about the contribution of this piece of research to what we know about early hominid evolution. Does this article provide any information that differs from that in the textbook? If so, write a summary of these differences.

2. Again using PowerTrac, conduct another search for *Homo erectus* and specifically look for an article that concerns the likelihood that *Homo erectus* populations coexisted with early *Homo sapiens*. Where did these two species appear to coexist, and what is the evidence to support their coexistence?

Internet Exercises

1. Visit The Evidence for Human Evolution in China (**http://www.cruzio .com/~cscp/index.htm**). There is a great deal of information on this site about *Homo erectus* and early *Homo sapiens* in China. Go to the Interactive Timeline to view summary evidence for human evolution in China. You can click on any of the individual pictures to get more information on that specimen. Choose one feature of morphology—brain size, cranial shape, facial shape, dentition, etc.—and go through the time line. Write a short paper on how that feature of the anatomy changes through time, based on the evidence presented here.

2. Go to **www.archaeology.org,** the online version of *Archaeology* magazine. This site provides brief versions of articles from past issues of the magazine covering a wide range of topics pertaining to physical anthropology and hominid evolution. Conduct a search for *Homo erectus* and, from the many references you find, choose one to read and summarize. Did this article enhance your knowledge of this species?

PHOTO ESSAY

Paleoanthropology

As we discussed in Chapter 8, paleoanthropology is a multidisciplinary science, drawing on the skills of many experts. Because sites are often found in remote, largely inaccessible locales, their discovery has traditionally been arduous and time-consuming.

In fact, sites of the appropriate age and with any likelihood of containing fossils are generally found in very restricted areas of the world (especially in Africa). In the last decade, however, sophisticated use of satellite imaging has greatly aided the search

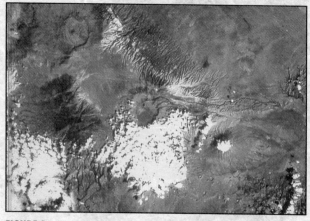

FIGURE 1

A satellite photo of geological exposures in northern Tanzania, near Olduvai Gorge. The mountainous regions are part of the escarpment of the Rift Valley. The lake has formed inside a volcanic crater.

FIGURE 2

The field camp at Hadar, in Ethiopia. A paleoanthropological project requires a large crew, all of whom must be supplied with food, water, and other basics. Members of the local Afar tribe, who serve as guards, are shown in the foreground.

FIGURE 3

The Kenyan field crew at Lake Turkana, Kenya. Kamoya Kimeu (driving) has probably been the most successful fossil discoverer in East Africa, responsible for dozens of discoveries.

FIGURE 4

Archaeologist Erella Hovers, during the 1993 field season at Hadar, carefully examines the surface of the AL 333 site. Up to 13 hominid individuals were discovered here in 1975. Work at this site is aimed at recovering more fragments of these individuals.

for likely new areas containing evidence of human origins.

After a potentially productive region has been identified, many long hours of ground surveying are required to find the fossils themselves. In most cases, and with any good fortune at all, numerous remains of nonhominid animals (such as elephant, pig, and antelope) will be found. However, the discovery of hominid fossils themselves is always a problematic undertaking. Thus, a truly successful

FIGURE 5

When large areas of geological exposures are surveyed, geological and paleontological localities are mapped.

FIGURE 6

If an area is surveyed and any fossils are seen on the surface, very precise searching is done.

FIGURE 7

It takes a well-trained eye to locate fossils eroding out of old land surfaces. Shown here is part of a hominid maxilla (upper jaw) found at Olduvai in 1987.

Paleoanthropology (continued)

paleoanthropological project (i.e., one that attracts public attention and funding) requires not just good science, but a considerable degree of luck as well.

Fossils are most often found scattered on the ground surface as they erode out from sediments (through the combined action of wind, rain, and gravity). When fossils are located, their precise position is recorded.

FIGURE 8

As fragments of a hominid find are collected, each location where a piece is discovered is marked with a flag. Here, Yoel Rak of Tel Aviv University and the Institute of Human Origins flags the precise location for each fragment of the *Australopithecus afarensis* cranium discovered at Hadar in 1992.

FIGURE 9

Even the most careful searching and hand sifting cannot locate all the fragments of a fossil. To retrieve the very small fragments, the surrounding soil is screened through a fine mesh and then sifted through again by hand.

In addition to recovering fossils, paleoanthropologists also collect various geological and pollen samples (for dating and paleoecological reconstruction).

The fossils frequently are found heavily encrusted in hard rock (called matrix) and thus require enormous effort in their cleaning and reconstruction (i.e., putting the fragments back together).

FIGURE 10

Techniques for recording the position of materials (artifacts and fossils) at a site, shown here being used at Olduvai Gorge. The grid to the left is divided into 10 cm squares to record horizontal position, and the triangular apparatus to the right is used to determine vertical position.

FIGURE 11

Geological samples are recovered along with the fossils. Here, Ethiopian field member Michael Tesfaye precisely excavates a sample of sediment to be used later for paleomagnetic analysis.

FIGURE 12

In some cases, fossils are found completely embedded in surrounding matrix, and great effort and skill are required to remove the fossil fragments from the rock. This specimen comes from Sterkfontein, in South Africa, where fossils are embedded in a limestone matrix called breccia.

Paleoanthropology (continued)

Once the field season ends, materials are brought back and distributed to various laboratories for specialized analysis. Experts in different fields study the materials in the hope of obtaining valuable data, including radiometric dating and geological context, as well as paleontological and palynological information. This painstaking work can take several years.

FIGURE 13

Dating is a key aspect of paleoanthropological interpretation. The Berkeley Geochronology Laboratory (formerly part of the Institute of Human Origins) has provided many of the radiometric dates using K/Ar or ^{39}Ar/^{40}Ar dating (e.g., the new *H. erectus* dates from Indonesia discussed in Chapter 9).

FIGURE 14

To facilitate further study and to provide precise replicas to other scholars (as well as to universities for demonstration specimens in classes), original hominid fossils are made into casts. The casting laboratory at the Kenya Museums of Natural History has provided a large number of high-quality casts to researchers and universities throughout the world.

CHAPTER
10

Neandertals and Other Archaic *Homo sapiens*

CONTENTS

Introduction

In Chapter 9, we saw that *H. erectus* was present in Africa approximately 1.8 m.y.a. and also in Java at about this same time. Except for new finds at Dmanisi, in the Republic of Georgia, and at Ceprano, in Italy, we also noted that *H. erectus* fossils thus far are very scarce in Europe, although several routes could easily have provided access. A major difficulty in accurately assessing finds is that a number of fossils from Europe—as well as Africa, China, and Java—display *both H. erectus* and *H. sapiens* features.

These particular forms, possibly representing some of the earliest members of our species, fall into the latter half of the Middle Pleistocene, from about 400,000 to 130,000 years ago, and are often referred to as **archaic *H. sapiens.*** The designation *H. sapiens* is used because the appearance of some derived sapiens traits suggests that these hominids are transitional forms. In most cases, these early archaic *H. sapiens* also retain some *H. erectus* features mixed with those derived features that distinguish them as *H. sapiens.* However, as they do not possess the full suite of derived characteristics diagnostic of **anatomically modern *H. sapiens,*** we classify them as archaic forms of our species. In general, we see in several different areas of the Old World through time a morphological trend from groups with more obvious *H. erectus* features to later populations displaying more diagnostic *H. sapiens* features.

When we speak of evolutionary trends and transitions from one species to another—for example, from *H. erectus* to *H. sapiens*—we do not wish to imply that such changes were in any way inevitable. In fact, most *H. erectus* populations never evolved into anything else. *Some* populations of *H. erectus* did apparently undergo slow evolutionary changes, and thus, some populations of what we call archaic *H. sapiens* emerge as transitional forms. In turn, *some* of these archaic *H. sapiens* populations suggest evolutionary change in the direction of anatomically modern *H. sapiens.*

In this chapter, we attempt, where the data permit, to focus on those populations that provide clues regarding patterns of hominid evolutionary change. We would like to ascertain *where* such transformations took place, *when* they occurred, and *what* the adaptive stimuli were (both cultural and biological) that urged the process along.

There are still significant gaps in the fossil data, and we certainly do not have a complete record of all the transitional stages; nor are we ever likely to possess anything approaching such a complete record. What we will do in this chapter is to paint the evolution of later hominids in fairly broad strokes to show the general trends.

Early Archaic *H. sapiens*

Many early archaic forms show morphological changes compared with *H. erectus.* These derived changes are reflected in brain expansion; increased parietal breadth (the basal portion of the skull is no longer the widest area, and therefore, the shape of the skull as seen from the rear is no longer pentagonal); some decrease in the size of the molars; and general decrease in cranial and postcranial robusticity.

A difficulty of major significance concerns exactly how to classify all this Middle Pleistocene hominid material. Here we take a conservative taxonomic approach and classify *all* of the specimens (as archaic forms) within the species

Archaic *H. sapiens*
Earlier forms of *Homo sapiens* (including Neandertals) from the Old World that differ from *H. erectus* but lack the full set of characteristics diagnostic of modern *H. sapiens.*

Anatomically modern *H. sapiens*
All modern humans and some fossil forms, perhaps dating as early as 200,000 y.a.; defined by a set of derived characteristics, including cranial architecture and lack of skeletal robusticity; usually classified at the subspecies level as *Homo sapiens sapiens.*

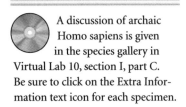

A discussion of archaic Homo sapiens is given in the species gallery in Virtual Lab 10, section I, part C. Be sure to click on the Extra Information text icon for each specimen.

Homo sapiens. However, a growing number of paleoanthropologists (e.g., Stringer, 1995; Larick and Ciochon, 1996; Rightmire, 1998) disagree with this interpretation and prefer to classify most, if not all, of the individuals into other species of the genus *Homo.* In this view, some of the earlier archaic forms could be ancestral to modern humans, but the later ones most likely would not be. As in other debates of this nature discussed in previous chapters, the essential issue concerns interpretation of intra- as compared to interspecific variation. We will return to this crucial topic at the end of this chapter.

A further complication in understanding archaic *H. sapiens* is that there is considerable variation both within and between samples of these hominids. Moreover, they are geographically very widely dispersed. In fact, archaic *H. sapiens* fossils have been found on the three continents of Africa, Asia, and Europe. In Europe, the well-known Neandertals are included in this category. (Neandertals are not found anywhere *except* Europe and western Asia.)

Africa

In Africa, archaic *H. sapiens* fossils have been found at several sites (Figs. 10–1 and 10–2). One of the best known is Broken Hill (Kabwe). At this site in Zambia, a complete cranium, together with other cranial and postcranial elements belonging to several individuals, was discovered.

In this and other African early archaic specimens, a mixture of older and more recent traits can be seen. The skull's massive supraorbital torus (one of the largest of any hominid), low vault, and prominent occipital torus recall those of *H. erectus.* On the other hand, the occipital region is less angulated, the cranial vault bones are thinner, and the cranial base is essentially modern. Dating estimates of Broken Hill and most of the other early archaic *H. sapiens* specimens from Africa have ranged throughout the Middle and Upper Pleistocene, but recent estimates have given dates for most of the localities in the range of 150,000–125,000 y.a.

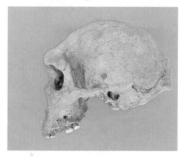

FIGURE 10–1

Broken Hill (Kabwe). Note the very heavy supraorbital torus.

A total of eight other archaic *H. sapiens* crania from South and East Africa also show a combination of *H. erectus* and *H. sapiens* characteristics, and they are all mentioned in the literature as being similar to Broken Hill. The most important of these African finds come from the sites of Florisbad and Elandsfontein in South Africa, Laetoli in Tanzania, and Bodo in Ethiopia (see Fig. 10–2). The general similarities in all these African archaic *H. sapiens* fossils may signify a fairly close genetic relationship of hominids from East and South Africa. It is also possible—although it seems most unlikely—that several populations were evolving in a somewhat similar way from *H. erectus* to a more *H. sapiens*-looking morphology.

We should point out that the evolutionary path of these hominids did not take a Neandertal turn. It seems that there were no Neandertals in Africa—nor were there any in the Far East.

Asia

China   Like their counterparts in Europe and Africa, Chinese archaic *H. sapiens*[*] specimens also display both earlier and later characteristics. Chinese paleoanthropologists suggest that archaic *H. sapiens* traits, such as a sagittal ridge (see

[*]Chinese anthropologists prefer the term "early *Homo sapiens*" instead of "archaic *H. sapiens.*"

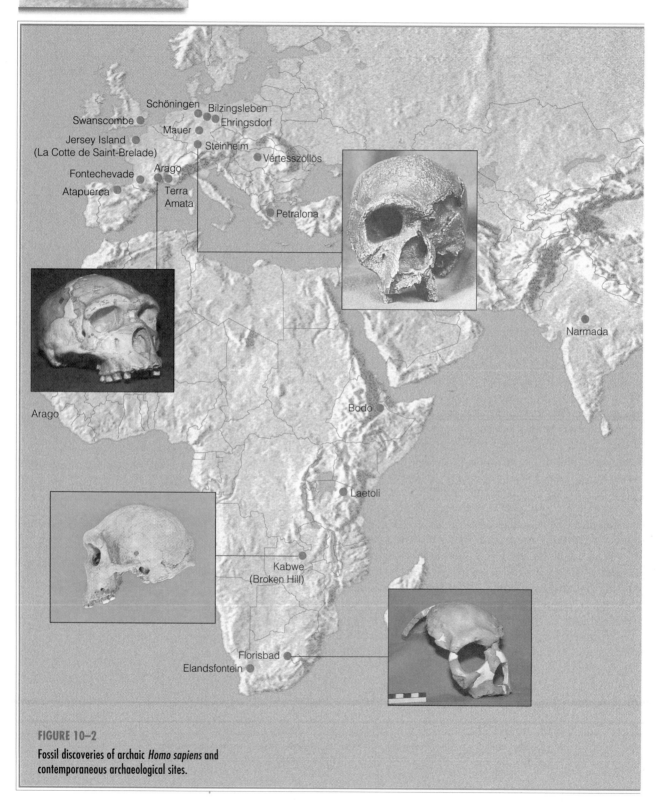

FIGURE 10–2

Fossil discoveries of archaic *Homo sapiens* and contemporaneous archaeological sites.

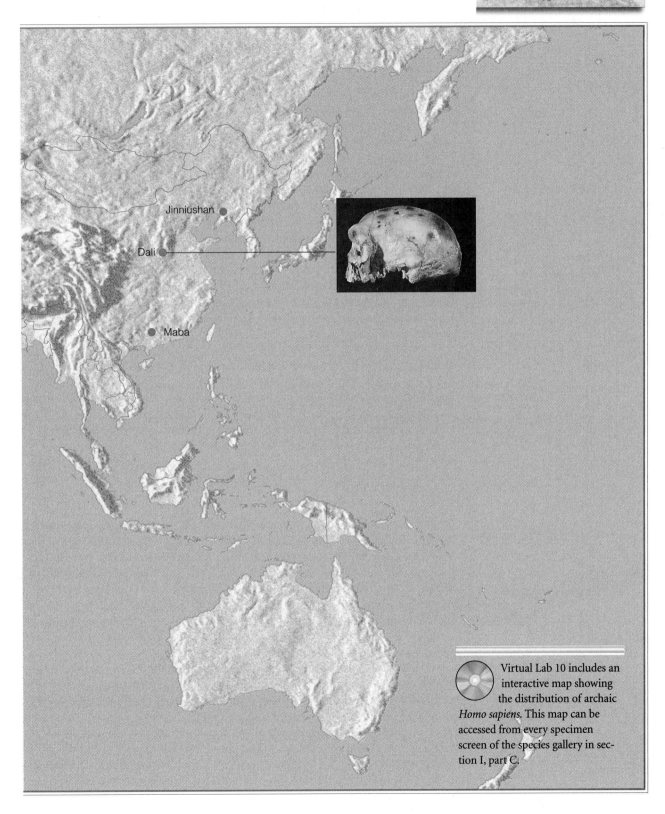

Jinniushan •

Dali •

• Maba

Virtual Lab 10 includes an interactive map showing the distribution of archaic *Homo sapiens.* This map can be accessed from every specimen screen of the species gallery in section I, part C.

p. 217) and flattened nasal bones, are shared with *H. erectus,* especially those specimens from Zhoukoudian. They also point out that some of these features can be found in modern *H. sapiens* in China today, indicating substantial genetic continuity. That is, Chinese researchers argue that anatomically modern Chinese did not evolve from *H. sapiens* in either Europe or Africa, evolving instead specifically in China from a separate *H. erectus* lineage.

That such regional evolution occurred in many areas of the world or, alternatively, that anatomically modern migrants from Africa displaced local populations is the subject of a major ongoing debate in paleoanthropology. This important controversy will be the central focus of the next chapter.

Dali, the most complete skull of the late Middle or early Upper Pleistocene fossils in China, displays *H. erectus* and *H. sapiens* traits, but it is clearly classified as early *H. sapiens* (despite its relatively small cranial capacity of 1,120 cm^3). Several other Chinese specimens also reflect both earlier and later traits and are placed in the same category as Dali. In addition, the more recently discovered (1984) partial skeleton from Jinniushan, in northeast China, has been given a provisional date of 200,000 y.a. (Tiemel et al., 1994). The cranial capacity is fairly large (approximately 1,260 cm^3), and the walls of the braincase are thin—both modern features and quite unexpected in an individual this ancient (if the dating estimate does indeed hold up).

India   In 1982, a partial skull was discovered in the Narmada Valley, in central India. Associated with this fossil were various hand axes, cleavers, flakes, and choppers. This Narmada specimen has been dated as Middle Pleistocene with a probable cranial capacity within the range of 1,155 to 1,421 cm^3. K. A. R. Kennedy (1991), who made a recent study of the fossil, suggests that Narmada should be viewed as an early example of *H. sapiens.*

Europe

Various attempts have been made to organize European archaic *H. sapiens* of the Middle and early Upper Pleistocene in the time range of 400,000–150,000 y.a. (Fig. 10–3). Because in many cases definite dates or adequate remains (or both) are lacking, it is difficult to be certain which fossils belong where in the evolutionary sequence. As already noted, what we find in Europe are fossils, such as those in Africa and China, whose features resemble both *H. erectus* and *H. sapiens.* You should further note that the earliest fossil finds from Europe (including those from Boxgrove in England and Atapuerca in Spain, discussed in Chapter 9) already show some of these transitional features.

The earliest archaic *H. sapiens* representatives from Europe show some resemblance to *H. erectus* in the robusticity of the mandible, thick cranial bones, pronounced occipital torus, heavy supraorbital torus, receding frontal bone, greatest parietal breadth near the base of the skull, and large teeth. (They, of course, also have one or more *H. sapiens* characteristics.) Examples of these early archaic forms from Europe include fossils from Steinheim, Swanscombe, and Vértesszöllös (see Fig. 10–2). Later European archaic representatives also possess some *H. erectus* characteristics, but they also have one or more of the following

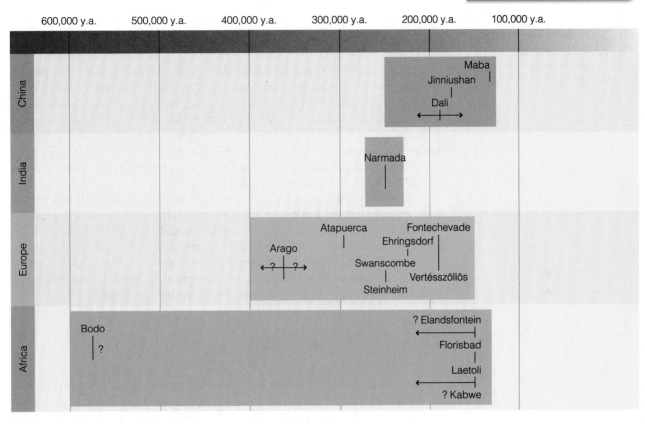

traits: larger cranial capacity, more rounded occipital area, parietal expansion, and reduced tooth size.

The later group, essentially from the latter half of the Middle Pleistocene, overlaps to some extent with the earlier group. From an evolutionary point of view, this later group may have evolved from the earlier one, and since many of these individuals display traits unique to Neandertals, they may in turn have given rise to the Neandertals. Examples of this somewhat later European transitional group include specimens from Fontechevade (France) and Ehringsdorf (Germany), as well as recent discoveries from Atapuerca, in northern Spain, in the same region as the newly discovered more ancient remains discussed in Chapter 9. This last site (called Sima de los Huesos), dated to approximately 300,000 y.a., has yielded the largest sample yet of archaic *Homo sapiens* from anywhere in the world and includes the remains of at least 32 individuals (among which are several excellently preserved crania) (Arsuaga et al., 1993, 1997; Kunzig, 1997). Excavations continue at this remarkable site, where bones have somehow accumulated within a deep chamber inside a cave. There are also large numbers of carnivore remains (bear, fox), but these fossils are generally in separate locations from where the hominids were found. From initial descriptions, the hominid morphology has been interpreted as showing several indications of an early Neandertal-like pattern (arching browridges, projecting midface, and other features) (Rightmire, 1998).

FIGURE 10–3

Time line of early archaic *Homo sapiens*. Note that most dates are approximations. Question marks indicate those estimates that are most tentative.

A time line that gives the ages for archaic *Homo sapiens* is available from every screen of the species gallery in Virtual Lab 10. Be sure to view the detailed screen.

245

Be sure to study the cranial and postcranial morphology of archaic *Homo sapiens* in Virtual Lab 10, sections II and III.

A Review of Middle Pleistocene Evolution (circa 400,000–125,000 y.a.)

Like the *erectus/sapiens* mix in Africa and China, the fossils from Europe also exhibit a mosaic of traits from both species (Fig. 10–4). However, it is important to note that the fossils from each continent differ; that is, the mosaic Chinese forms are not the same as those from Africa or Europe. Some European fossils, assumed to be earlier, are more robust and possess more similarities to *H. erectus* than to modern *H. sapiens*. The later Middle Pleistocene European fossils appear to be more Neandertal-like, but the uncertainty of dates prevents a clear scenario of the Middle Pleistocene evolutionary sequence.

The physical differences from *H. erectus* are not extraordinary. Bones remain thick, the supraorbital torus is prominent, and vault height shows little increase. There is, however, a definite increase in brain size and a change in the shape of the skull from pentagonal to globular as seen from the rear. There is also a trend, especially with the later Middle Pleistocene forms, toward less occipital angulation. It is interesting to note that in Europe, the changes move toward a Neandertal *H. sapiens* pattern, but in Africa and Asia, toward modern *H. sapiens*.

Middle Pleistocene Culture

The Acheulian technology of *H. erectus* persevered in the Middle Pleistocene with relatively little change until near the end of the period, when it became slightly more sophisticated. The hand axe, almost entirely absent in China in the Lower Pleistocene, remained rare in the Middle Pleistocene, and choppers and flake tools continued to be the basic tools. Bone, a very useful tool material, apparently went

(a)

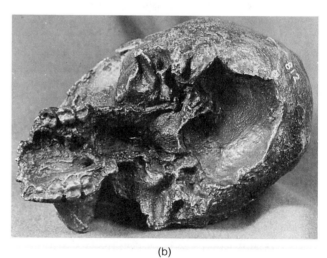

(b)

FIGURE 10–4

Cast of an archaic *Homo sapiens* skull from Germany (Steinheim). (a) Frontal view showing damaged skull. (b) Basal view showing how the foramen magnum was enlarged, apparently for removal of the brain, perhaps for dietary or ritualistic purposes.

practically unused by archaic *H. sapiens.* Stone flake tools similar to those of the earlier era persisted, perhaps in greater variety. Archaic *H. sapiens* in Africa and Europe invented a method—the Levallois technique (Fig. 10–5)—for controlling flake size and shape. Requiring several coordinated steps, this was no mean feat and suggests to many scholars increased cognitive abilities in late archaic *H. sapiens* compared to earlier archaic forms.

Interpretation of the distribution of artifacts during the later Middle Pleistocene has generated considerable discussion among archaeologists. We have noted (in Chapter 9) that there is a general geographical distribution characteristic of the Lower Pleistocene, with bifaces (mostly hand axes) found quite often at sites in Africa, but only very rarely at sites in most of Asia, and not at all among the rich assemblage at Zhoukoudian (see p. 222). Moreover, where hand axes proliferate, the stone tool industry is referred to as Acheulian, while at localities without hand axes, various other terms are used (e.g., "chopper/chopping tool"—a misnomer, since most of the tools are actually flakes).

Acheulian assemblages have been found at many African sites as well as numerous European ones (e.g., Swanscombe in England and Arago in France). Nevertheless, the broad geographical distribution of what we call Acheulian should not blind us to the considerable intraregional diversity in stone tool industries. For example, while a variety of European sites do show a typical Acheulian complex, rich in bifacial hand axes and cleavers, other contemporaneous ones—for example, Bilzingsleben in Germany and Vértesszöllös in Hungary—do not. At these latter two sites, a variety of small retouched flake tools and flaked pebbles of various sizes were found, but no hand axes.

It thus appears that different stone tool industries coexisted in some areas for long periods. Various explanations (Villa, 1983) have been offered to account for this apparent diversity: (1) The tool industries were produced by different peoples (i.e., different cultures, perhaps hominids that also differed biologically); (2) the tool industries represent different types of activities carried out at separate locales; (3) the presence (or absence) of specific tool types—bifaces—represents the availability (or unavailability) of appropriate local stone resources.

Archaic *H. sapiens* populations continued to live both in caves and in open-air sites, but may have increased their use of caves. Did archaic *H. sapiens* control fire? Klein (1989, p. 255) suggests that these hominids did. He writes that there was a "concentration of burnt bones in depressions 50–60 cm across at Vértesszöllös" and that "fossil hearths have also been identified at Bilzingsleben and in several French caves that were probably occupied by early *H. sapiens.*" Chinese archaeologists insist that many Middle Pleistocene sites in China contain evidence of human-controlled fire. However, not everyone is convinced.

That archaic *H. sapiens* built temporary structures is revealed by concentrations of bones, stones, and artifacts at several sites. Here, they manufactured artifacts and exploited the area for food. The stones may have been used to support the sides of a shelter.

In the Lazaret Cave in the city of Nice, in southern France, a shelter about 36 feet by 11 feet was built against the cave wall, and skins probably were hung over a framework of poles as walls for the shelter. The base was supported by rocks and large bones, and inside the shelter were two hearths. The hearth charcoal suggests that the hominid occupants used slow-burning oak and boxwood, which produced easy-to-rekindle embers. Very little stone waste was found inside the shelter, suggesting that they manufactured tools outside, perhaps because there was more light.

Nodule

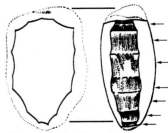

The nodule is chipped on the perimeter.

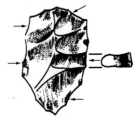

Flakes are radially removed from top surface.

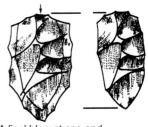

A final blow at one end removes a large flake.

FIGURE 10–5
The Levallois technique.

 Virtual Lab 11 includes 3-D animations of many stone tools and their manufacture.

Archaeological evidence clearly alludes to the utilization of many different food sources, such as fruits, vegetables, seeds, nuts, and bird eggs, each in its own season. Marine life was also exploited. From Lazaret and Orgnac (southern France) comes evidence of freshwater fishing for trout, perch, and carp. The most detailed reconstruction of Middle Pleistocene life in Europe, however, comes from evidence at Terra Amata, on the southern coast of France (de Lumley and de Lumley, 1973; Villa, 1983). From this site has come fascinating evidence relating to short-term, seasonal visits by archaic *H. sapiens* who built flimsy shelters (Fig. 10–6), gathered plants, exploited marine resources, and possibly hunted medium-sized and large mammals.

The hunting capabilities of these early members of *H. sapiens,* as for earlier hominids, remain open to dispute. What seems clear is that the evidence does not yet unambiguously establish widely practiced advanced abilities. In earlier professional discussions (as well as in earlier editions of our texts), archaeological evidence from Terra Amata (in France) and Torralba and Ambrona (in Spain) was used to argue for significantly advanced hunting skills for archaic *H. sapiens* in Europe. However, reconstruction of these sites by Richard Klein and others has now cast doubt on those prior conclusions. Once again, we see that application of scientific rigor (which is simply good critical thinking) makes us question assumptions. And in so doing, we frequently must conclude that other less dramatic (and less romantic) explanations fit the evidence as well as or better than those based on initial imaginative scenarios.

A possible exception to the current, much more conservative view of the hunting skills of archaic *H. sapiens* comes from an archaeological site excavated on the Channel Island of Jersey off the west coast of France (see Fig. 10–2). In a cave site called La Cotte de Saint-Brelade, many skeletal remains of large mammals (mammoth and woolly rhinoceros) were found in association with stone flakes. Unlike the remains from the sites mentioned earlier, the animals sampled at La Cotte de Saint-Brelade represent primarily subadults and adults in prime age (*not* what one

FIGURE 10–6

Cutaway of Terra Amata hut (reconstruction). Note the hearth (arrow), the stone scatters where people sat making tools, the poles that supported the roof, and the stones at the base of the hut supporting the sides. (Adapted from de Lumley, 1969.)

would expect in naturally occurring accumulations). Moreover, the preserved elements also exhibit the kind of damage that further suggests hominid activities. Directly killing such large animals may not have been within the capabilities of the hominids (archaic *H. sapiens*?) who occupied this site. Thus, K. Scott, who led the excavations, has suggested that these early hominids may have driven their prey off a nearby cliff, bringing certain prized parts back to the cave for further butchering (Scott, 1980).

Another recent and exceptional find is also challenging assumptions regarding hunting capabilities of archaic *H. sapiens* in Europe. From the site of Schöningen, in Germany, three remarkably well preserved wooden spears were discovered in 1995 (Thieme, 1997). As we have noted before, fragile organic remains (such as wood) can rarely be preserved more than a few hundred years; yet these beautifully crafted implements are provisionally dated to 380,000–400,000 y.a.! Beyond this surprisingly ancient date, the spears are intriguing on a variety of other counts. Firstly, they are all large (about 6 feet long), very finely made, selected from hard spruce wood, and expertly balanced. Each spear would have required considerable planning, time, and skill to manufacture. Further, the weapons were most likely used as throwing spears, presumably to hunt large animals. Of interest in this context, bones of numerous horses were also recovered at Schöningen. Archaeologist Hartmut Thieme has thus concluded that "the spears strongly suggest that systematic hunting, involving foresight, planning and the use of appropriate technology, was part of the behavioural repertoire of pre-modern hominids" (1997, p. 807). Therefore, as with the remains from La Cotte de Saint-Brelade, these extraordinary spears from Schöningen make a strong case for advanced hunting skills, practiced by at least some archaic *Homo sapiens* populations.

As documented by the fossil hominid remains as well as artifactual evidence from archaeological sites, the long period of transitional hominids in Europe was to continue well into the Upper Pleistocene (after 125,000 y.a.). However, the evolution of archaic *H. sapiens* was to take a unique turn with the appearance and expansion of the Neandertals.

Neandertals: Late Archaic *H. sapiens* (130,000–35,000 y.a.)

Since their discovery more than a century ago, the Neandertals have haunted the best-laid theories of paleoanthropologists. They fit into the general scheme of human evolution, and yet they are misfits. Classified as *H. sapiens*, they are like us and yet different. It is not an easy task to put them in their place.*

We should also point out that we emphasize Neandertals more than their contemporaries in Africa or Asia because we have more information about them. Compared with their hominid cousins elsewhere in the Old World, Neandertals have been known to scientists over a longer period of time, there are many more specimens of them (including many that are excellently preserved), and, perhaps most intriguing of all, we know so much more about their behavior (from remains

Neandertals are discussed in Virtual Lab 10, section I, part C.

Homo sapiens neanderthalensis is the subspecific designation for Neandertals, although not all paleoanthropologists agree with this terminology. (The subspecies for anatomically modern *H. sapiens* is designated as *Homo sapiens sapiens*.) *Thal*, meaning "valley," is the old spelling and is kept in the species designation (the "h" was always silent and not pronounced). The modern spelling is *tal* and is now used this way in Germany; we shall adhere to contemporary usage in the text with the spelling *Neandertal*.

of tools, preserved living sites, contexts of deliberate burials, etc.). Yet, despite all this fascinating evidence relating to Neandertals, they are most likely a side branch of later hominid evolution. Most contemporary researchers view them as fairly distinct from emerging *Homo sapiens* populations in Africa or east Asia; indeed, a growing number of paleoanthropologists now classify Neandertals as a distinct species from *Homo sapiens* (i.e., they are classified as "*Homo neanderthalensis*") (see pp. 266–267 for further discussion).

While Neandertal fossil remains have been found at dates approaching 130,000 y.a., in the following discussion of Neandertals, we refer to those populations that lived especially during the last glaciation, which began about 75,000 y.a. and ended about 10,000 y.a. (Fig. 10–7). We should also note that the evolutionary roots of Neandertals apparently reach quite far back in western Europe, as evidenced by the 300,000 y.a. remains from Sima de los Huesos, Atapuerca, in northern Spain. The majority of fossils have been found in Europe, where they have been most studied, and our description of Neandertals is based primarily on those specimens from western Europe, who are usually called *classic* Neandertals. Not all Neandertals—including others from eastern Europe and western Asia and those from the interglacial that preceded the last glacial—entirely conform to our description of the classic morphology. They tend to be less robust, perhaps because the climate in which they lived was not as cold as western Europe during the last glaciation.

One striking feature of Neandertals is brain size, which in these hominids actually was larger than that of *H. sapiens* today. The average for contemporary *H. sapiens* centers between 1,300 and 1,400 cm³, while for Neandertals it was 1,520 cm³. The larger size may be associated with the metabolic efficiency of a larger brain in cold weather. The Inuit (Eskimo) brain also averages larger than that of other modern human populations (about the size of the Neandertal brain). It should also be pointed out that the larger brain size in both archaic and contemporary *Homo sapiens* in populations adapted to *cold* climates is partially correlated with larger body size, which has also evolved among these groups (see Chapter 13).

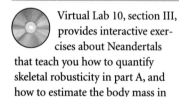 Virtual Lab 10, section III, provides interactive exercises about Neandertals that teach you how to quantify skeletal robusticity in part A, and how to estimate the body mass in part B.

The classic Neandertal cranium is large, long, low, and bulging at the sides. Viewed from the side, the posterior portion of the occipital bone is somewhat bun-shaped, but the marked occipital angle typical of many *H. erectus* crania is absent. The forehead rises more vertically than that of *H. erectus*, and the browridges arch over the orbits instead of forming a straight bar (Fig. 10–8).

Compared with anatomically modern humans, the Neandertal face stands out. It projects almost as if it were pulled forward. This feature can be seen when the distance of the nose and teeth from the eye orbits is compared with that of modern *H. sapiens*. Postcranially, Neandertals were very robust, barrel-chested, and powerfully muscled. This robust skeletal structure, in fact, dominates hominid evolution from *H. erectus* through archaic *H. sapiens*. Nevertheless, the Neandertals appear particularly robust, with shorter limbs than seen in most modern *H. sapiens* populations. Both the facial anatomy and robust postcranial structure of Neandertals have been interpreted by Erik Trinkaus (of Washington University in St. Louis) to reflect adaptation to rigorous living in a cold climate.

For about 100,000 years, Neandertals lived in Europe and western Asia (Fig. 10–9, see p. 254), and their coming and going has raised more questions and controversies than perhaps any other hominid group. Neandertal forebears date back to the later archaic *H. sapiens*. But these were transitional forms, and it is not until the last interglacial that Neandertals were fully recognizable.

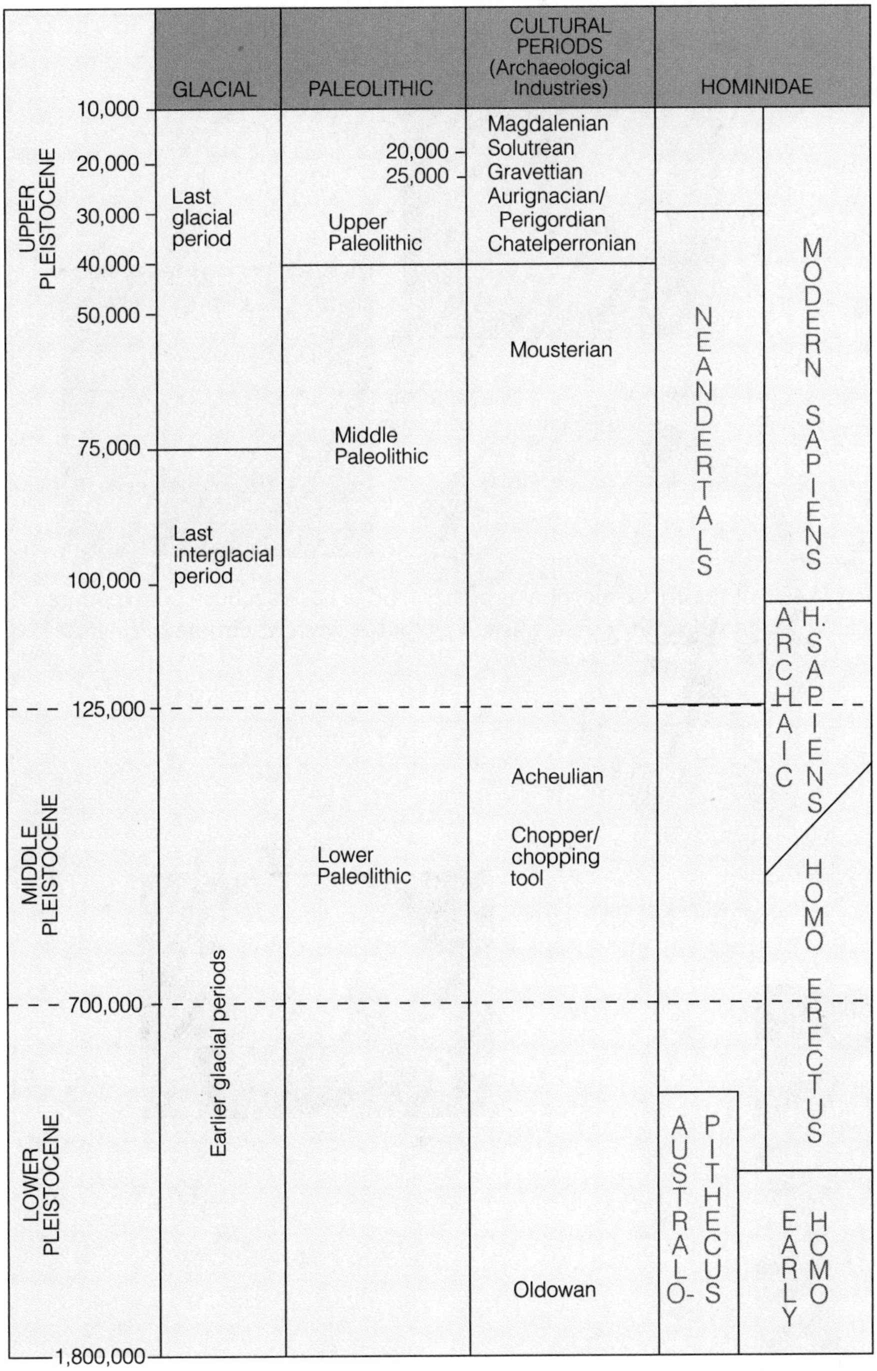

	GLACIAL	PALEOLITHIC	CULTURAL PERIODS (Archaeological Industries)	HOMINIDAE	
UPPER PLEISTOCENE	Last glacial period	Upper Paleolithic	Magdalenian / Solutrean / Gravettian / Aurignacian / Perigordian / Chatelperronian (20,000 / 25,000)	N E A N D E R T A L S	M O D E R N S A P I E N S
		Middle Paleolithic	Mousterian		
	Last interglacial period				A R C H A I C / H. S A P I E N S
MIDDLE PLEISTOCENE	Earlier glacial periods	Lower Paleolithic	Acheulian / Chopper/chopping tool		H O M O E R E C T U S
LOWER PLEISTOCENE			Oldowan	A U S T R A L O- P I T H E C U S	E A R L Y H O M O

Scale (ybp): 10,000 / 20,000 / 30,000 / 40,000 / 50,000 / 75,000 / 100,000 / 125,000 / 700,000 / 1,800,000

FIGURE 10–7

Correlation of Pleistocene subdivisions with archaeological industries and hominids. Note that the geological divisions are separate and different from the archaeological stages (e.g., Upper Pleistocene is *not* synonymous with Upper Paleolithic).

Neandertal takes its name from the Neander Valley, near Düsseldorf, Germany. In 1856, workmen quarrying limestone caves in the valley came across some fossilized bones. The owner of the quarry believed them to be bear and gave them to a natural science teacher, who realized that they were not the remains of a cave bear, but rather the remains of an ancient human. Exactly what the bones

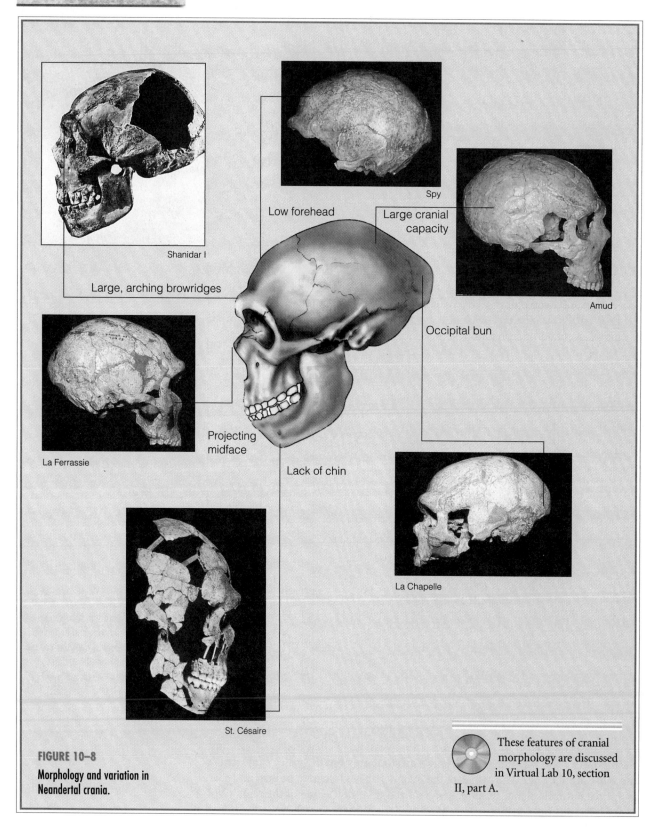

Shanidar I

Spy

Low forehead

Large cranial
capacity

Large, arching browridges

Amud

Occipital bun

La Ferrassie

Projecting
midface

Lack of chin

St. Césaire

La Chapelle

FIGURE 10–8

**Morphology and variation in
Neandertal crania.**

These features of cranial
morphology are discussed
in Virtual Lab 10, section
II, part A.

represented became a *cause célèbre* for many years, and the fate of "Neandertal Man," as the bones were named, hung in the balance until later finds provided more evidence.

What swung the balance in favor of accepting the Neander Valley specimen as a genuine hominid fossil were other nineteenth-century finds similar to it. What is more important, the additional fossil remains brought home the realization that a form of human different from nineteenth-century Europeans had in fact once existed.

France and Spain

One of the most important Neandertal discoveries was made in 1908 at La Chapelle-aux-Saints in southwestern France. A nearly complete skeleton was found buried in a shallow grave in a **flexed** position, with several fragments of nonhuman long bones placed over the head, and over them, a bison leg. Around the body were flint tools and broken animal bones.

The skeleton was turned over for study to a well-known French paleontologist, Marcellin Boule, who published his analysis in three copious volumes. Boule depicted the La Chapelle Neandertal as a brutish, bent-kneed, not fully erect biped. As a result of this exaggerated interpretation, some scholars, and certainly the general public, concluded that all Neandertals were highly primitive creatures.

Why did Boule draw these conclusions from the La Chapelle skeleton? Apparently, he misconstrued Neandertal posture owing to the presence of spinal osteoarthritis in this older male. In addition, and probably more important, Boule and his contemporaries found it difficult to accept fully as a human ancestor an individual who appeared to depart from the modern pattern.

The skull of this male, who was possibly at least 40 years of age when he died, is very large, with a cranial capacity of 1,620 cm³. As is typical for western European "classic" forms, the vault is low and long, the supraorbital ridges are immense, with the typical Neandertal arched shape, the forehead is low and retreating, and the face is long and projecting. The back of the skull is protuberant and bun-shaped (Figs. 10–8 and 10–10).

La Chapelle, however, is not a typical Neandertal, but an unusually robust male that "evidently represents an extreme in the Neandertal range of variation" (Brace et al., 1979, p. 117). Unfortunately, this skeleton, which Boule claimed did not even walk completely erect, was widely accepted as "Mr. Neandertal." But not all Neandertal materials express the suite of "classic Neandertal" traits to the degree seen in La Chapelle.

Another Neandertal site excavated recently in southern France has revealed further fascinating details relating to Neandertal behavior. From the 100,000 to 120,000-year-old Moula-Guercy cave site, Alban Defleur, Tim White, and colleagues have analyzed 78 broken hominid fragments representing probably six individuals (Defleur et al., 1999). The intriguing aspect of these remains concerns *how* they were broken. Detailed analysis of cut marks, pits, scars, and other features clearly suggests that the Neandertal individuals were *processed*—that is, they "were defleshed and disarticulated. After this the marrow cavity was exposed by a hammer-on-anvil technique" (Defleur et al., 1999, 131). Moreover, the nonhuman bones at this site, especially the deer remains, were processed in an identical fashion. In other words, the Moula-Guercy Neandertals provide the best-documented evidence thus far of Neandertal *cannibalism*.

Flexed
The position of the body in a bent orientation, with the arms and legs drawn up to the chest.

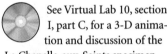

See Virtual Lab 10, section I, part C, for a 3-D animation and discussion of the La Chapelle-aux-Saints specimen.

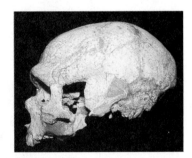

FIGURE 10–10

La Chapelle-aux-Saints. Note the occipital bun, projecting face, and low vault.

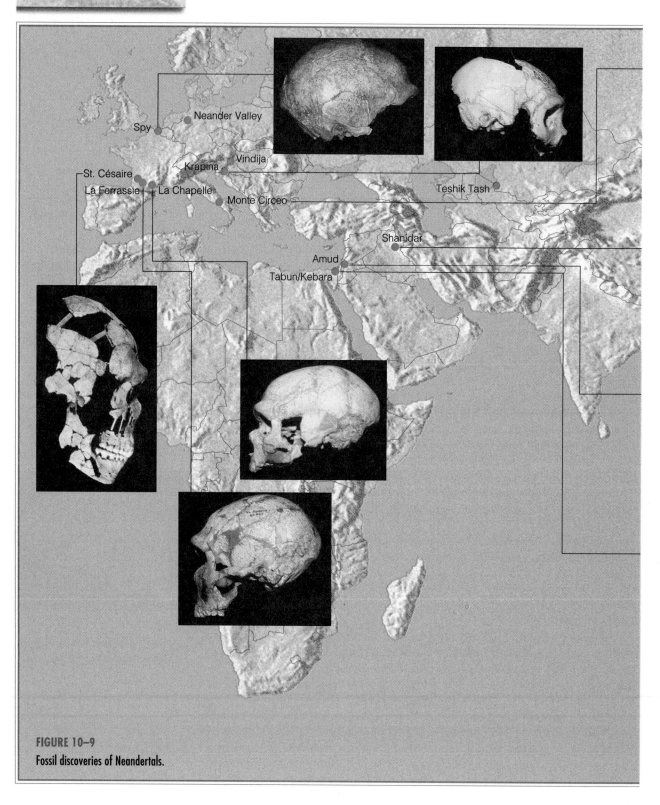

FIGURE 10–9
Fossil discoveries of Neandertals.

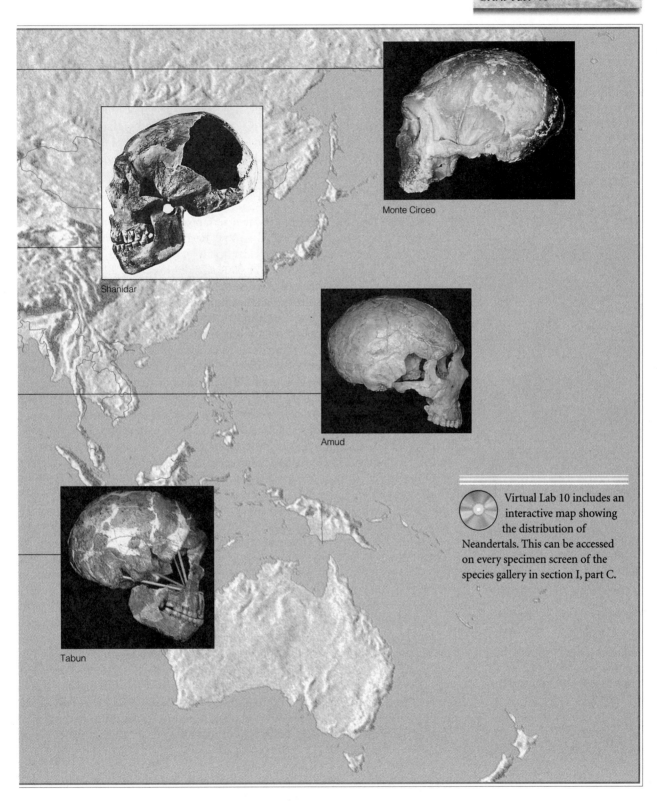

Monte Circeo

Shanidar

Amud

Tabun

Virtual Lab 10 includes an interactive map showing the distribution of Neandertals. This can be accessed on every specimen screen of the species gallery in section I, part C.

Upper Paleolithic
A cultural period usually associated with early modern humans (but also found with Neandertals) and distinguished by technological innovation in various stone tool industries. Best known from western Europe, similar industries are also known from central and eastern Europe and Africa.

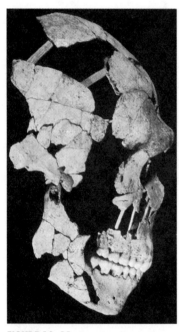

FIGURE 10–11
St. Césaire, among the "last" Neandertals.

Chatelperronian
Pertaining to an Upper Paleolithic tool industry found in France and Spain, containing blade tools and associated with Neandertals.

Some of the most recent of the western European Neandertals come from St. Césaire in southwestern France and are dated at about 35,000 y.a. (Figs. 10–11 and 10–12). The bones were recovered from a bed including discarded chipped blades, hand axes, and other stone tools of an **Upper Paleolithic** tool industry associated with Neandertals. Another site, Zafarraya Cave in southern Spain, may provide yet a more recent time range for Neandertal occupation in Europe. During the 1980s and 1990s, a few pieces of hominid individuals were found at Zafarraya that have been interpreted as Neandertal in morphology. What is most interesting, however, is the *date* (as determined by radiocarbon dating) suggested for the site. French archaeologist Jean-Jacques Hublin, who has excavated the site, asserts that the date is close to 29,000 y.a.—a full 6,000 years later than St. Césaire.

Another site, also recently redated, is apparently about the same age as Zafarraya, but it is located in central Europe. Recent recalibration by radiocarbon dating has indicated that the later Neandertal levels at Vindija, in Croatia (discussed shortly) are about 28,000 to 29,000 years old (Smith et al., 1999). If one of these dates is further confirmed, then either Zafarraya or Vindija would gain the distinction of having the most recent Neandertals thus far discovered.

Yet a more recent site in Portugal has recently been interpreted as showing hybridization between Neandertals and modern *Homo sapiens*. (We will discuss this intriguing suggestion in more detail in Chapter 11.)

The St. Césaire, Zafarraya, and Vindija sites are fascinating for several reasons. Anatomically modern humans were living in central and western Europe by about 35,000 y.a. or a bit earlier. Therefore, it is possible that Neandertals and modern *H. sapiens* were living in close proximity for several thousand years. How did these two groups interact? Evidence from a number of French sites (Harrold, 1989) indicates that Neandertals borrowed technological methods and tools (such as blades) from the anatomically modern populations and thereby modified their own tools, creating a new industry, the **Chatelperronian**. However, such an example of cultural diffusion does not specify *how* the diffusion took place. Did the Neandertals become assimilated into modern populations? Did the two groups interbreed? It would also be interesting to know more precisely how long the coexistence of Neandertals and modern *H. sapiens* lasted.* No one knows the answers to these questions, but it has been suggested that an average annual difference of 2 percent mortality between the two populations (i.e., modern *H. sapiens* lived longer than Neandertals) would have resulted in the extinction of the Neandertals in approximately 1,000 years (Zubrow, 1989).

It should be noted that not all paleoanthropologists agree with the notion of the coexistence of Neandertals and Upper Paleolithic modern humans. For example, in a recent paper, David Frayer of the University of Kansas states: "There is still *no human fossil evidence* which supports the coexistence of Neanderthal and Upper Paleolithic forms in Europe" (emphasis added) (1992, p. 9). That is, despite the indications of cultural diffusion noted here, no European site has yet produced directly associated remains of *both* types of humans.

---

*For a fictionalized account of the meeting between Neandertals and anatomically modern humans, see Bjorn Kurten's *Dance of the Tiger. A Novel of the Ice Age.* Another novel on the subject is Jean M. Auel's *Clan of the Cave Bear.* Several movies have also been made on this theme.

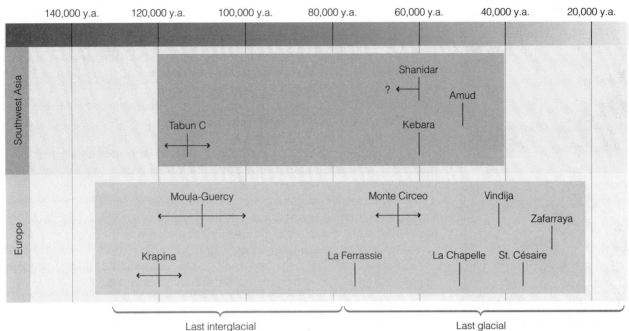

Central Europe

There are quite a few other European classic Neandertals, including significant finds in central Europe. At Krapina, Croatia, an abundance of bones (1,000 fragments representing up to 70 individuals) and 1,000 stone tools or flakes have been recovered (Trinkaus and Shipman, 1992). Krapina is an old site, perhaps the earliest showing the full "classic" Neandertal morphology, dating back to the last interglacial (estimated at 130,000–110,000 y.a.). Moreover, despite the relatively early date, the characteristic Neandertal features of the Krapina specimens (although less robust) are similar to the western European finds (Fig. 10–13). Krapina is also important as an intentional burial site, one of the oldest on record.

Another interesting site in central Europe is Vindija, about 30 miles from Krapina. The site is an excellent source of faunal, cultural, and hominid materials stratified in *sequence* throughout much of the Upper Pleistocene. Neandertal fossils consisting of some 35 specimens are dated between about 42,000 and 28,000 y.a. (the latter date would be among the most recent of all Neandertal discoveries). Even though some of their features approach the morphology of early modern south-central European *H. sapiens,* the overall pattern is definitely Neandertal. However, these modified Neandertal features, such as smaller browridges and slight chin development, may also be seen as an evolutionary trend toward modern *H. sapiens.*

Fred Smith, of Northern Illinois University, takes the view that variation in Vindija cranial features points to a trend continuing on to the later anatomically modern specimens found in the upper levels of the cave. Does Vindija support the proposition that the origin of *H. sapiens* could have occurred here in central Europe? Smith does not insist on this interpretation and suggests that anatomically modern *Homo sapiens* could have come from elsewhere. But he does believe that there is at least some morphological and genetic continuity between the samples found in the lower and upper levels of the cave.

FIGURE 10–12

Time line for Neandertal (*Homo sapiens neanderthalensis*) fossil discoveries.

257

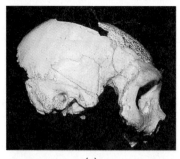

(a)

(b)

FIGURE 10–13

Krapina C. (a) Lateral view showing characteristic Neandertal traits. (b) Three-quarters view.

Western Asia

Israel   In addition to European Neandertals, there are numerous important discoveries from southwest Asia. Several specimens from Israel display some modern features and are less robust than the classic Neandertals of Europe, but again the overall pattern is Neandertal. The best known of these discoveries is from Tabun (Mugharet-et-Tabun, "Cave of the Oven") at Mt. Carmel, a short drive south from Haifa (Fig. 10–14). Tabun, excavated in the early 1930s, yielded a female skeleton, recently dated by thermoluminescence (TL) at about 120,000–110,000 y.a. If this dating proves accurate, it places the Tabun find as clearly contemporary with early modern *H. sapiens* found in nearby caves. (TL dating is discussed in Table 11–1, in Chapter 11.)

A more recent Neandertal burial, a male discovered in 1983, comes from Kebara, a neighboring cave of Tabun at Mt. Carmel. Although the skeleton is incomplete—the cranium and much of the lower limbs are missing—the pelvis, dated to 60,000 y.a., is the most complete Neandertal pelvis so far recovered. Also recovered at Kebara is a hyoid bone, the first from a Neandertal, and this find is especially important from the point of view of reconstructing language capabilities.*

Iraq   A most remarkable site is Shanidar, in the Zagros Mountains of northeastern Iraq, where partial skeletons of nine individuals—males and females, seven adults and two infants—were found, four of them deliberately buried. One of the more interesting individuals is Shanidar 1, a male who lived to be approximately 30 to 45 years old, a considerable age for a prehistoric human (Fig. 10–15). His stature is estimated at 5 feet 7 inches, with a cranial capacity of 1,600 cm^3. This individual shows several fascinating features:

---

*The Kebara hyoid is identical to that of modern humans, suggesting that Neandertals did not differ from *H. sapiens sapiens* in this key element.

FIGURE 10–14

Excavation of the Tabun Cave, Mt. Carmel, Israel.

There had been a crushing blow to the left side of the head, fracturing the eye socket, displacing the left eye, and probably causing blindness on that side. He also sustained a massive blow to the right side of the body that so badly damaged the right arm that it became withered and useless; the bones of the shoulder blade, collar bone, and upper arm are much smaller and thinner than those on the left. The right lower arm and hand are missing, probably not because of poor preservation . . . but because they either atrophied and dropped off or because they were amputated. (Trinkaus and Shipman, 1992, p. 340)

In addition to these injuries, there was damage to the lower right leg (including a healed fracture of a foot bone). The right knee and left leg show signs of pathological involvement, and these changes to the limbs and foot may have left this man with a limping gait.

How such a person could perform normal obligations and customs is difficult to imagine. However, both Ralph Solecki, who supervised the work at Shanidar Cave, and Erik Trinkaus, who has carefully studied the Shanidar remains, believe that to survive, he must have been helped by others: "A one-armed, partially blind, crippled man could have made no pretense of hunting or gathering his own food. That he survived for years after his trauma was a testament to Neandertal compassion and humanity" (Trinkaus and Shipman, 1992, p. 341).*

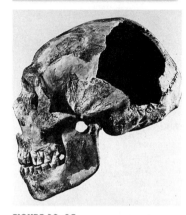

FIGURE 10–15

Shanidar 1. Does he represent an example of Neandertal compassion for the disabled?

Central Asia

Uzbekistan   About 1,600 miles east of Shanidar in Uzbekistan, in a cave at Teshik-Tash, is the easternmost Neandertal discovery. The skeleton is that of a nine-year-old boy who appears to have been deliberately buried. It was reported that he was surrounded by five pairs of wild goat horns, suggesting a burial ritual or perhaps a religious cult, but owing to inadequate published documentation of the excavation, this interpretation has been seriously questioned. The Teshik-Tash individual, like some specimens from Croatia and southwest Asia, also shows a mixture of Neandertal traits (heavy browridges and occipital bun) and modern traits (high vault and definite signs of a chin).

As noted, the Teshik-Tash site represents the easternmost location presently established for Neandertals. Thus, based on current evidence, it is clear that the geographical distribution of the Neandertals extended from France eastward to central Asia, a distance of about 4,000 miles.

Culture of Neandertals

Neandertals, who lived in the cultural period known as the Middle Paleolithic, are usually associated with the **Mousterian** industry (although the Mousterian industry is not always associated with Neandertals). In the early part of the last glacial period, Mousterian culture extended across Europe and North Africa into the former Soviet Union, Israel, Iran, and as far east as Uzbekistan and perhaps even China. Moreover, in Africa, the contemporaneous Middle Stone Age industry is broadly similar to the Mousterian.

Mousterian

Pertaining to the stone tool industry associated with Neandertals and some modern *H. sapiens* groups; also called Middle Paleolithic. This industry is characterized by a larger proportion of flake tools than is found in Acheulian tool kits.

---

*K. A. Dettwyler (1991) asserts that Shanidar 1 could have survived without assistance and that there is no solid evidence that compassion explains this individual's survival.

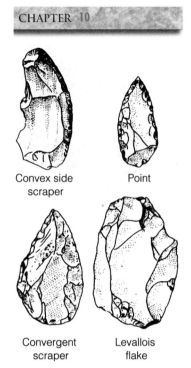

Convex side scraper

Point

Convergent scraper

Levallois flake

FIGURE 10–16

Mousterian tools. (After Bordes.)

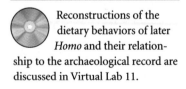

Reconstructions of the dietary behaviors of later *Homo* and their relationship to the archaeological record are discussed in Virtual Lab 11.

Technology

Neandertals improved on previous prepared-core techniques (i.e., the Levallois) by inventing a new variation. They trimmed a flint nodule around the edges to form a disk-shaped core. Each time they struck the edge, they produced a flake, continuing this way until the core became too small and was discarded. Thus, the Neandertals were able to obtain more flakes per core than their predecessors. They then trimmed (retouched) the flakes into various forms, such as scrapers, points, and knives (Fig.10–16).

Neandertal craftspeople elaborated and diversified traditional methods, and there is some indication of development in the specialization of tools used in skin and meat preparation, hunting, woodworking, and hafting. There is, however, still nearly a complete absence of bone tools, in strong contrast to the succeeding cultural period, the Upper Paleolithic. Nevertheless, Neandertals advanced their technology, which tended to be similar in basic tool types over considerable geographical distances, far beyond that of *H. erectus*. It is quite possible that their modifications in technology helped provide a basis for the remarkable changes of the Upper Paleolithic (discussed in the next chapter).

Settlements

People of the Mousterian culture lived in a variety of open sites, caves, and rock shelters. Living in the open on the cold tundra suggests the building of structures, and there is some evidence of such structures (although the last glaciation must have destroyed many open sites). At the site of Moldova, in the Ukraine (now an independent state and neighbor of Russia), archaeologists found traces of an oval ring of mammoth bones enclosing an area of about 26 by 16 feet and which may have been used to weigh down the skin walls of a temporary hut or tent. Inside the ring are traces of a number of hearths, hundreds of tools, thousands of waste flakes, and many bone fragments, quite possibly derived from animals brought back for consumption.

Evidence of life in caves is abundant. Windbreaks of poles and skin were probably erected at the cave mouth for protection against severe weather. Fire was in general use by this time and was no doubt used for cooking, warmth, light, and keeping predators at bay.

How large were Neandertal settlements, and were they permanent or temporary? These questions are not yet answered, but Binford (1981) suggests that the settlements were used repeatedly for short-term occupation.

Subsistence

Neandertals were successful hunters, as the abundant remains of animal bones at their sites demonstrate. But while it is clear that Neandertals could hunt large mammals, they may not have been as efficient at this task as were Upper Paleolithic hunters. Inferring from his detailed work in the Middle East, Harvard anthropologist Ofer Bar-Yosef (1994) has concluded that only after the beginning of the Upper Paleolithic was the spear-thrower, or atlatl (see p. 286), invented. Moreover, shortly thereafter, the bow and arrow may have greatly facilitated efficiency (and safety) in hunting large mammals. Lacking such long-distance weaponry, and thus mostly limited to close-proximity spears, Neandertals may have been more prone to serious injury—a hypothesis recently given some intriguing support by paleoanthropologists Thomas Berger and Erik Trinkaus. Berger and Trinkaus (1995) analyzed the pattern of trauma (particularly fractures) in Neandertals and compared it with that seen in contemporary human samples. Interestingly, the pattern in Neandertals—especially the relatively high proportion of head and neck injuries—matched most closely to that seen in contemporary rodeo performers. Berger and Trinkaus thus conclude, "The similarity to the rodeo distribution suggests frequent close encounters with large ungulates unkindly disposed to the humans involved" (Berger and Trinkaus, 1995, p. 841).

Meat was, of course, not the only component of Neandertal diet. Evidence (from Shanidar, for example) indicates that Neandertals gathered as well, consuming berries, nuts, and other plants.

It is assumed that in the bitter cold of the last glacial period, Neandertals wore clothing, and they probably had developed methods of curing skins. But since there is no evidence of sewing equipment, the clothing was probably of simple design, perhaps something like a poncho.

We know much more of European Middle Paleolithic culture than of any prior period, as it has been studied longer by more scholars. In recent years, however, Africa has been a target not only of physical anthropologists (as we have seen copiously documented in earlier chapters), but also of archaeologists, who have added considerably to our knowledge of African Pleistocene hominid history. In many instances, the technology and assumed cultural adaptations were similar in Africa to those in Europe and southwest Asia. We will see in the next chapter that the African technological achievements also kept pace with (or even preceded) those in western Europe.

Symbolic Behavior

There are a variety of hypotheses concerning the speech capacities of Neandertals. Many of these views are highly contradictory, with some scholars arguing that Neandertals were incapable of human speech. Nevertheless, the current consensus is that Neandertals were capable of articulate speech, even perhaps fully competent in the range of sounds produced by modern humans. However, this conclusion is not to argue that because Neandertals *could* speak, they necessarily had the same language capacities as modern *Homo sapiens*. A major contemporary focus among paleoanthropologists is the apparently sudden expansion of modern *H. sapiens* (discussed in Chapter 11) and various explanations for the success of this group. Moreover, at the same time we are explaining how and why *H. sapiens sapiens* expanded its geographical range, we are left with the further problem of explaining what happened to the Neandertals. In making these types of interpretations, a growing number of paleoanthropologists suggest that *behavioral* differences are the key.

Upper Paleolithic *H. sapiens* is hypothesized to have possessed some significant behavioral advantages that Neandertals (and other archaic *H. sapiens*) lacked. Was it some kind of new and expanded ability to symbolize, communicate, organize social activities, elaborate technology, obtain a wider range of food resources, or care for the sick or injured, or was it some other factor? Were there, compared with *H. sapiens sapiens,* neurological differences that limited the Neandertals and thus contributed to their demise?

The direct anatomical evidence derived from Neandertal fossils is not especially helpful in specifically answering these questions. Ralph Holloway (1985) has maintained that Neandertal brains (at least as far as the fossil evidence suggests) do not differ significantly from that of modern *H. sapiens.* Moreover, Neandertal vocal tracts and other morphological features, compared with our own, do not appear seriously to have limited them. Furthermore, a recent study of the size of a small opening in the base of the skull (the hypoglossal canal; see Figure A–4 in Appendix A) has shed new insight on Neandertal speech capabilities. Richard Kay, Matt Cartmill, and Michelle Balow of Duke University measured the size of this canal in a variety of fossil hominids as well as in modern humans and great apes (Kay et al., 1998). The size of the hypoglossal canal may be particularly significant to speech production, since the main nerve supply for the tongue passes through this opening. The Duke researchers found that Neandertals (and other archaic *H. sapiens*) had hypoglossal canals as large as those seen in modern humans, arguing that Neandertal speech capabilities would not have been hampered in this respect. Interestingly, however, in earlier hominids (*Australopithecus* and early *Homo*), the hypoglossal canal was much smaller—in fact, similar in size to that seen in chimpanzees.

Subsequent to this initial suggestion that size of the hypoglossal canal might reflect speech capabilities (Kay et al., 1998), the hypothesis has been further tested using a much wider sample of nonhuman primates, fossil hominids, and modern humans (DeGusta et al., 1999). These new data do *not* confirm the hypothesis and in fact seriously question it. For example, many nonhuman primates have hypoglossal canals as large as humans; similarly, some early hominids (members of *Australopithecus*) also have canals as large as contemporary humans. Perhaps even more revealing, the size of the canal, as shown in dissections of human cadavers, does not appear correlated with the size of the (hypoglossal) nerve running through it. Further studies might help resolve some of these issues, but for the moment, the initial hypothesis connecting hypoglossal canal size and speech ability has been seriously weakened.

Most of the reservations about advanced cognitive abilities in Neandertals have come from archaeological data. Interpretation of Neandertal sites, when compared with succeeding Upper Paleolithic sites (especially as documented in western Europe), have led to several intriguing contrasts, as shown in Table 10–1.

On the basis of this type of behavioral and anatomical evidence, Neandertals in recent years have increasingly been viewed as an evolutionary dead end. Whether their disappearance and ultimate replacement by anatomically modern Upper Paleolithic peoples (with their presumably "superior" culture) was solely the result of cultural differences or was also influenced by biological variation cannot at present be determined.

An intriguing possibility for future research has recently been initiated. After several years of experimentation, German researchers and their American colleagues were successfully able to extract, amplify, and sequence DNA from a Neandertal fossil (Krings et al., 1997). The investigators removed a small piece of bone from the humerus of the original Neander Valley fossil and compared the mitochondrial DNA (mtDNA) sequences with those from samples of contemporary humans. The initial results indicate that the Neandertal DNA is considerably *more* different from the contemporary human samples than these latter are from each other (on average, about three times as much). Furthermore, tentative estimates of the time of divergence of the Neandertal lineage from that of modern

TABLE 10–1 Cultural Contrasts* Between Neandertals and Upper Paleolithic *Homo sapiens sapiens*

Neandertals	Upper Paleolithic *H. sapiens sapiens*
TOOL TECHNOLOGY Numerous flake tools; few, however, apparently for highly specialized functions; use of bone, antler, or ivory very rare; relatively few tools with more than one or two parts	Many more varieties of stone tools; many apparently for specialized functions; frequent use of bone, antler, and ivory; many more tools comprised of two or more component parts
HUNTING EFFICIENCY AND WEAPONS No long-distance hunting weapons; close-proximity weapons used (thus, more likelihood of injury)	Use of spear-thrower and bow and arrow; wider range of social contacts, perhaps permitting larger, more organized hunting parties (including game drives)
STONE MATERIAL TRANSPORT Stone materials transported only short distances—just "a few kilometers" (Klein, 1989)	Stone tool raw materials transported over much longer distances, implying wider social networks and perhaps trade
ART Artwork uncommon; usually small; probably mostly of a personal nature; some items perhaps misinterpreted as "art"; others may be intrusive from overlying Upper Paleolithic contexts; cave art absent	Artwork much more common, including transportable objects as well as elaborate cave art; well executed, using a variety of materials and techniques; stylistic sophistication
BURIAL Deliberate burial at several sites; graves unelaborated; graves frequently lack artifacts	Burials much more complex, frequently including both tools and remains of animals

*The contrasts are more apparent in some areas (particularly western Europe) than others (eastern Europe, Near East). Elsewhere (Africa, eastern Asia), where there were no Neandertals, the cultural situation is quite different (see p. 292). Moreover, even in western Europe, the cultural transformations were not necessarily abrupt, but may have developed more gradually from Mousterian to Upper Paleolithic times. For example, Straus (1995) argues that many of the Upper Paleolithic features were not consistently manifested until after 20,000 y.a.

humans are put at 690,000–550,000 years ago. From these findings, the researchers support the emerging view that Neandertals did *not* contribute genetically to contemporary human populations (and may, in fact, have been a separate species from *Homo sapiens*). These results and interpretations are, however, tentative. Further DNA samples from other Neandertals as well as from early *Homo sapiens sapiens* fossils would be highly informative. At present, it is difficult to judge how "anomalous" any ancient human is, given the extremely small degree of genetic diversity seen among *all* contemporary humans (see Chapter 13).

Burials

It has been known for some time that Neandertals deliberately buried their dead. Indeed, the spectacular discoveries at La Chapelle, Shanidar, and elsewhere were the direct results of ancient burial, thus facilitating much more complete preservation.

The implications of the ancient mtDNA that was recovered from a Neandertal are discussed in Virtual Lab 10, section I, part C.

Such deliberate burial treatment extends back at least 90,000 years at Tabun. Moreover, some form of consistent "disposal" of the dead (but not necessarily below-ground burial) is evidenced at Atapuerca, Spain, where at least 32 individuals comprising more than 700 fossilized elements were found in a cave at the end of a deep vertical shaft. From the nature of the site and the accumulation of hominid remains, Spanish researchers are convinced that the site demonstrates some form of human activity involving deliberate disposal of the dead (Arsuaga et al., 1997).

The provisional 300,000-year-old age for Atapuerca suggests that Neandertals (more precisely, their immediate precursors) were, by the Middle Pleistocene, handling their dead in special ways, a behavior thought previously to have emerged only much later (in the Upper Pleistocene). And, apparently as far as current data indicate, this practice is seen in western European contexts well before it appears in Africa or in eastern Asia. For example, in the archaic *H. sapiens* sites at Laetoli, Kabwe, and Florisbad (discussed earlier), deliberate disposal of the dead is not documented. Nor is it seen in African early modern sites (e.g., Klasies River Mouth, dated at 120,000–100,000 y.a.; see p. 276).

Nevertheless, in later contexts (after 35,000 y.a.) in Europe, where anatomically modern *H. sapiens* (*H. sapiens sapiens*) remains are found in clear burial contexts, their treatment is considerably more complex than is seen in Neandertal burials. In these later (Upper Paleolithic) sites, grave goods, including bone and stone tools as well as animal bones, are found more consistently and in greater concentrations. Because many Neandertal sites were excavated in the nineteenth or early twentieth century, before the development of more rigorous archaeological methods, there are questions regarding numerous purported burials. Nevertheless, the evidence seems quite clear that deliberate burial was practiced at La Chapelle, La Ferrassie (eight graves), Tabun, Amud, Kebara, Shanidar, and Teshik-Tash (as well as at several other localities, especially in France). Moreover, in many instances, the *position* of the body was deliberately modified and placed in the grave in a flexed posture (see p. 253). Such a flexed position has been found in 16 of the 20 best-documented Neandertal burial contexts (Klein, 1989).

Finally, the placement of supposed grave goods in burials, including stone tools, animal bones (such as cave bear), and even arrangements of flowers, together with stone slabs on top of the burials, have all been postulated as further evidence of Neandertal symbolic behavior. However, in many instances, again due to poor excavation documentation, these assertions are questionable. Placement of stone tools, for example, is occasionally seen, but apparently was not done consistently. In those 33 Neandertal burials for which adequate data exist, only 14 show definite association of stone tools and/or animal bones with the deceased (Klein, 1989). It is not until the next cultural period, the Upper Paleolithic, that we see a major behavioral shift, as demonstrated in more elaborate burials and development of art.

Evolutionary Trends in the Genus *Homo*

To understand the evolution of the various forms of *Homo sapiens* discussed in this chapter, it is useful to briefly review general trends of evolution in the genus *Homo* over the last 2 million years. In doing so, we see that at least three major *transitions* have taken place. Paleoanthropologists are keenly interested in interpreting the nature of these transitions, as they inform us directly regarding human origins. In addition, such investigations contribute to a broader understanding of the mechanics of the evolutionary process—at both the micro- and macroevolutionary levels.

The first transition of note was from early *Homo* to *Homo erectus*. This transition was apparently geographically restricted to Africa and appears to have been quite rapid (lasting 200,000 years at most, perhaps considerably less). It is important to recall that such a transition by no means implies that all early *Homo* groups actually evolved into *H. erectus*. In fact, many paleoanthropologists (part of a growing consensus) suggest that there were more than one species of early *Homo*. Clearly, only one could be ancestral to *H. erectus*. Even more to the point, only *some* populations of this one species would have been part of the genetic transformation (speciation) that produced *Homo erectus*.

The second transition is more complex and is the main topic of this chapter. It is the gradual change in populations of *H. erectus* grading into early *H. sapiens* forms—what we have termed archaic *H. sapiens*. This transition was not geographically restricted, as there is evidence of archaic *H. sapiens* widespread in the Old World (in East and South Africa, in China, India, and Java, and in Europe). Moreover, the transition appears not to have been rapid, but rather quite slow and uneven in pace from area to area. The complexity of this evolutionary transition creates ambiguities for our interpretations and resulting classifications.

For example, in Chapter 9, we included the Ngandong (Solo) material from Java within *Homo erectus*. However, there are several derived features in many of these specimens that suggest, alternatively, that they could be assigned to *Homo sapiens*. The dating (just recently indicating a date of only 29,000 y.a.) would argue that if this is a *H. erectus* group, it is a *very* late remnant, probably isolated *H. erectus* population surviving in southern Asia long after archaic *H. sapiens* populations were expanding elsewhere. Whatever the interpretation of Ngandong—either as a late *H. erectus* or as a quite primitive (i.e., not particularly derived) archaic *H. sapiens*—the conclusion is actually quite arbitrary (after all, the evolutionary process is continuous). We, by the nature of our classifications, have to draw the line *somewhere*.

Another important ramification of such considerations relates to understanding the nature of the *erectus/sapiens* transition itself. In Java, the transition (with late-persisting *H. erectus* genetic components) appears to have been slower than, for example, in southern Africa or in Europe. Nowhere, however, does this transition appear to have been as rapid as that which originally produced *H. erectus*. Why should this be so? To answer this question, we must refer to basic evolutionary mechanisms. First, the environments certainly differed from one region of the Old World to another during the time period 350,000–100,000 y.a. And recall that by the beginning of this time period, *H. erectus* populations had been long established in eastern and southern Asia, in North and East Africa, and in Europe. Clearly, we would not expect the same environmental conditions in northeast China as we would in Indonesia. Accordingly, natural selection could well have played a *differential* role, influencing the frequencies of alternative alleles in different populations in a pattern similar (but more intensive) to that seen in environmental adaptations of contemporary populations (see Chapter 13).

Second, many of these populations (in Java, southernmost Africa, and glacial Europe) could have been isolated and thus probably quite small. Genetic drift, therefore, also would have played a role in influencing the pace of evolutionary change. Third, advance or retreat of barriers, such as water boundaries or glacial ice sheets, would dramatically have affected migration routes.

Thus, it should hardly come as a surprise that some populations of *H. erectus* evolved at different rates and in slightly different directions from others. Some limited migration almost certainly occurred among the various populations. With sufficient gene flow, the spread of those few genetic modifications that distinguish the earliest *H. sapiens* eventually did become incorporated into widely separated populations. This, however, was a long, slow, inherently uneven process.

What, then, of the third transition within the genus *Homo*? This is the transition from archaic *H. sapiens* to anatomically modern *H. sapiens*—and it was considerably *faster* than the transition we have just discussed. How quickly anatomically modern forms evolved and exactly *where* this happened is a subject of much contemporary debate—and is the main topic of the next chapter.

Taxonomic Issues

As we discussed in Chapter 9 (and briefly at the beginning of this chapter), there is considerable debate regarding how to classify much of the *Homo* fossil material prior to 35,000 years ago. Our view, followed throughout the discussions in Chapters 9 through 11, proposes a minimum number of species and thus interprets the evolutionary processes influencing the genus *Homo* in a fairly straightforward manner.

However, this interpretation might well be *too* simplistic, and certainly, many paleoanthropologists now suggest much more diversity and complexity in the evolution of our genus. Accordingly, several new species of *Homo* have been proposed. In this text, we have classified the *Homo* fossil materials into three recognized species: *H. habilis, H. erectus,* and *H. sapiens.* We further noted that *H. habilis* might well be only one of two species of what we collectively called "early *Homo.*" Moreover, in this chapter we made a clear distinction between archaic forms of *H. sapiens* and anatomically modern forms (*H. sapiens sapiens*). A diagrammatic phylogeny representing this interpretation is shown in Figure 10–17.

Remember, however, that this is a conservative interpretation, implying a minimum amount of species diversity. This scheme is just about as simple as most paleoanthropologists are willing to consider seriously. Yet, there is another view, proposed by Milford Wolpoff of the University of Michigan, which is even more simple. Wolpoff argues that subsequent to early *Homo,* only one species (*H. sapiens*) should be recognized (Wolpoff, 1999). In other words, Professor Wolpoff sinks *H. erectus* into *H. sapiens.* Given the significant anatomical (and probably behavioral) differences between *H. erectus* and *H. sapiens,* Wolpoff's suggestion has not received much support from other paleoanthropologists (see particularly the discussion in Rightmire, 1998).

At the other end of the spectrum are views expressed by a number of researchers who subdivide the *Homo* material into a variety of species. In fact, at every major stage of the evolution of *Homo* over the last 2 million

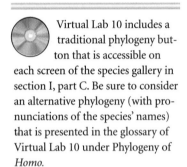

Virtual Lab 10 includes a traditional phylogeny button that is accessible on each screen of the species gallery in section I, part C. Be sure to consider an alternative phylogeny (with pronunciations of the species' names) that is presented in the glossary of Virtual Lab 10 under Phylogeny of *Homo*.

FIGURE 10–17

Phylogeny showing evolution of genus *Homo,* as discussed in the text. Only very modest species diversity is implied. (Contrast with Figure 10–18.)

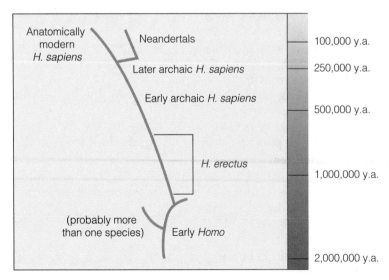

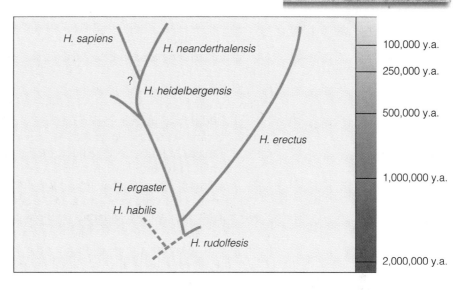

years, some professional opinion has argued seriously for more than one species. First, as noted in Chapter 8 (p. 204), early *Homo* is now frequently subdivided into two different species (usually named *H. habilis* and *H. rudolfensis*). Second, as briefly discussed in Chapter 9, what is usually called *H. erectus* is also partitioned into two species (*H. erectus* and *H. ergaster*, the latter referring solely to African specimens). And third (and most relevant to the present discussion), various forms of archaic *H. sapiens* have been assigned by other paleoanthropologists to two or three additional species of *Homo* (some researchers think even more species might be represented).

FIGURE 10–18

Phylogeny showing multiple species of genus *Homo* with considerable species diversity represented.

The major issues relating to these interpretations (and consequent classifications) of what we have termed "archaic *Homo sapiens*" are as follows:

1. The classification of individual fossils into "archaic *Homo sapiens*" is viewed by many as imprecise, since this is an ill-defined evolutionary group (and one quite geographically widespread). At minimum, many researchers have urged a more precise anatomical definition of exactly what "archaic *Homo sapiens*" means.

2. Several early archaic specimens are interpreted by paleoanthropologists as showing derived features different from *Homo sapiens*. These fossils come from Africa and Europe (e.g., Kabwe, Mauer) and are now often classified as *Homo heidelbergensis*.

3. Neandertals are also viewed by numerous researchers as representing a distinct species, what is called *Homo neanderthalensis*. In prior discussions, we have interpreted the variation as representing intraspecific differences; this alternative view argues for a greater degree of interspecific variability (with the inference that fertile interbreeding between Neandertals and *H. sapiens* would not have been possible).

Figure 10–18 shows a phylogeny incorporating these more complex, multiple-species interpretations and suggesting possible evolutionary relationships. For an introductory course, it is less important to memorize all the species names than to recognize what such interpretations imply about the evolutionary process—and what these differing views suggest about our origins.

SUMMARY

During the Middle Pleistocene, significant changes occurred in *H. erectus* morphology. The changes, especially in cranial traits, led scientists to assign a new species designation to these forms (*Homo sapiens*). Because they exhibited a

mosaic of *H. erectus* and *H. sapiens* characteristics, the name archaic *H. sapiens* is used to indicate that they were forms transitional between *H. erectus* and anatomically modern humans. Some archaic *H. sapiens* possessed more derived modern traits than others, and these populations are sometimes referred to as later archaic *H. sapiens* or early *H. sapiens sapiens*. It has been suggested that some later European archaic forms were directly ancestral to Neandertals.

In addition to morphological changes among archaic forms, there were cultural developments as well. Archaic *H. sapiens* invented new kinds of tools and toolmaking techniques, exploited new foods, built more complex shelters, probably controlled fire, and may have used some form of speech.

In western Europe, archaic *H. sapiens* developed into a unique form—classic Neandertals—who apparently migrated from Europe to the Near East and then even further into Asia. Neandertals were physically robust and muscular, different from both early archaic forms and modern *H. sapiens*. Their culture was more complex than earlier archaic cultures, and it appears that in Europe and the Near East, they lived in areas also inhabited by modern *H. sapiens*. Whether modern forms in these areas evolved directly from Neandertals or migrated from Africa (or the Near East) and ultimately replaced Neandertals is one of the important issues currently being debated by paleoanthropologists.

Finally, we would emphasize that Neandertals and all humans on earth today belong to the same species, *H. sapiens*. There are physical differences between these forms, of course, and for that reason Neandertals are assigned to the subspecies *H. sapiens neanderthalensis* and anatomically modern forms to the subspecies *H. sapiens sapiens*.

We should point out that this assignment of a *separate* subspecies for the Neandertals emphasizes some notable degrees of variation; that is, Neandertals are viewed as more different from *any* modern group of *H. sapiens* than these groups differ from one another. Some scholars would even more dramatically emphasize this variation and thus assign Neandertals to a separate species from *Homo sapiens*. In this view, Neandertals would be placed in the separate species *Homo neanderthalensis*. Likewise, many paleoanthropologists would also subdivide what we call "early archaic *H. sapiens*" into another species. The behavioral differences between Neandertals and anatomically modern *H. sapiens*, as interpreted from the archaeological record, are also discussed. These differences are emphasized by those scholars who view Neandertals as an evolutionary dead end.

QUESTIONS FOR REVIEW

1. In what respect does *H. sapiens* (broadly defined) contrast with *H. erectus*?
2. What is meant by "archaic" *H. sapiens*?
3. How does archaic *H. sapiens* contrast with anatomically modern *H. sapiens*?
4. In what areas of the world have archaic *H. sapiens* specimens been discovered? Compare and contrast the finds from two separate areas.
5. What do we mean when we say that archaic *H. sapiens* specimens are transitional?
6. Why have Neandertals been depicted (by the popular press and others) as being primitive? Do you agree with this interpretation? Why or why not?

7. In what general areas of the world have Neandertal fossil remains been discovered?

8. What evidence suggests that Neandertals deliberately buried their dead? What interpretations does such treatment of the dead suggest to you?

9. What physical characteristics distinguish the Neandertals from anatomically modern *Homo sapiens*?

10. What behavioral characteristics distinguish Neandertal culture from that of the Upper Paleolithic?

11. What two major transitions within the genus *Homo* have been discussed in this chapter and in Chapter 9? Compare these transitions for geographical distribution as well as for aspects of evolutionary pace.

12. Discuss why some paleoanthropologists subdivide the archaic *H. sapiens* material into more than one species. What does this interpretation imply biologically?

SUGGESTED FURTHER READINGS

Mellars, Paul. 1995. *The Neanderthal Legacy. An Archaeological Perspective from Western Europe.* Princeton, NJ: Princeton University Press.

Shreeve, James. 1995. *The Neandertal Enigma.* New York: Morrow.

Stiner, Mary C. 1995. *Honor Among Thieves. A Zooarchaeological Study of Neandertal Ecology.* Princeton, NJ: Princeton University Press.

Stringer, Christopher, and Clive Gamble. 1993. *In Search of the Neanderthals.* New York: Thames and Hudson.

Trinkaus, Erik, and Pat Shipman. 1993. *The Neandertals: Changing the Image of Mankind.* New York: Knopf.

MULTIMEDIA RESOURCES

 ### Wadsworth Anthropology Resource Center

http://anthropology.wadsworth.com

Visit Anthropology Online to obtain current updates in the field, surfing tips, career information, and more. In addition, enrich your study efforts with text-specific study aids arranged by chapter.

InfoTrac College Edition

http://www.infotrac-college.com/wadsworth

1. Use PowerTrac to search for *Atapuerca,* the archaic human site in Spain. Write a short paper describing the finds at Atapuerca and their importance to the study of human evolution.

2. Using PowerTrac search for the subject *Neanderthal* (InfoTrac College Edition spells Neandertal with the *h,* the older spelling—using the newer spelling will pull up fewer references). How many articles or abstracts did you find? Read at least one article and discuss how it relates to material in Chapter 10.

🌐 Internet Exercises

1. Archaic forms of *Homo sapiens* are the subject of much debate, especially those in Europe, which may have given rise to either Neandertals or more modern humans. One site that has provided many fossils of this type is Arago, or Tautavel, in France. Visit the site for this cave at **http://www.culture.fr/culture/arcnat/tautavel/en/index.htm** and read about the fossils found there and the circumstances surrounding the discovery of the site. Compare these fossils with pictures of Neandertals. Look at the section where Arago's face is reconstructed to see what it might have looked like in life. Write a paragraph or so describing how this individual looks similar to or different from anyone you might see on the street. You should also go to other topics at this Web site such as *excavation* and *dating methods.* How do these discussions add to your understanding of paleoanthropology?

2. Use your search engine to find articles pertaining to the Neandertals. Specifically, look for information regarding the evidence that Neandertals continued to exist later than previously believed. If you have difficulties finding such information, try **www.archaeology.org** but we encourage you to look for other Web sites as well.

CHAPTER
11

Homo sapiens sapiens

CONTENTS

Introduction

A discussion of modern *Homo sapiens* is given in the species gallery in Virtual Lab 12, section I, part B. Be sure to click on the Extra Information text icon for each specimen. You may wish to review the information on archaic *Homo sapiens* in section I, part A.

In this chapter, we discuss anatomically modern humans, taxonomically known as *Homo sapiens sapiens*. As we discussed in Chapter 10, in some areas evolutionary developments produced early archaic *H. sapiens* populations exhibiting a mosaic of *H. erectus* and *H. sapiens* traits. In some regions, the trend emphasizing *H. sapiens* characteristics continued, and possibly as early as 200,000 y.a., transitional forms (between early archaic and anatomically modern forms) appeared in Africa. Given the nature of the evidence and ongoing ambiguities in dating, it is not possible to say exactly when anatomically modern *H. sapiens* first appeared. However, the transition and certainly the wide dispersal of *H. sapiens sapiens* in the Old World appear to have been relatively rapid evolutionary events. Thus, we can ask several basic questions:

1. *When* (approximately) did *H. sapiens sapiens* first appear?
2. *Where* did the transition take place? Did it occur in just one region or in several?
3. *What* was the pace of evolutionary change? How quickly did the transition occur?
4. *How* did the dispersal of *H. sapiens sapiens* to other areas of the Old World (outside that of origin) take place?

These questions concerning the origins and early dispersal of *Homo sapiens sapiens* continue to fuel much controversy among paleoanthropologists. And it is no wonder, for members of early *Homo sapiens sapiens* are our *direct* kin and are thus closely related to all contemporary humans. They were much like us skeletally, genetically, and (most likely) behaviorally as well. In fact, it is the various hypotheses relating to the behavioral capacities of our most immediate predecessors that have most fired the imagination of scientists and laypeople alike. In every major respect, these are the first hominids that we can confidently refer to as "fully human."

In this chapter, we will also discuss archaeological evidence from the *Upper Paleolithic* (see p. 256). This evidence will allow us to better understand technological and social developments during the period when modern humans arose and quickly came to dominate the planet.

The evolutionary story of *Homo sapiens sapiens* is really a biological autobiography of us all. It is a story that still has many unanswered questions; but several theories have been proposed that seek to organize the diverse information that is presently available.

The Origin and Dispersal of *Homo sapiens sapiens* (Anatomically Modern Human Beings)

There are two major theories that attempt to organize and explain modern human origins: the complete replacement model and the regional continuity model. These two views are quite distinct and in some ways diametrically opposed to each other. Moreover, the popular press has further contributed to a wide and incorrect perception of irreconcilable argument on these points by "opposing" scientists. Indeed, there is a third theory, which we call the partial replacement model, that is a compromise hypothesis incorporating some aspects of the two major theories.

Because so much of our contemporary view of modern human origins is driven by the debates linked to these differing theories, let us begin by briefly reviewing each. We will then turn to the fossil evidence itself to see what it can contribute to resolving the questions we have posed.

The Complete Replacement Model (Recent African Evolution)

The complete replacement model, developed by British paleoanthropologists Christopher Stringer and Peter Andrews (1988), is based on the origin of modern humans in Africa and later replacement of populations in Europe and Asia (Fig. 11–1). In brief, this theory proposes that anatomically modern populations arose in Africa within the last 200,000 years, then migrated from Africa, completely *replacing* populations in Europe and Asia. This model does not take into account any transition from archaic *H. sapiens* to modern *H. sapiens* anywhere in the world except Africa. A critical deduction of the Stringer and Andrews theory is that it considers the appearance of anatomically modern humans as a biological speciation event. Thus, in this view there could be no admixture of migrating African modern *H. sapiens* with local populations because the African modern humans were a *biologically* different species. In a taxonomic context, all of the "archaic *H. sapiens*" populations outside Africa would, in this view, be classified as belonging to different species of *Homo* (e.g., the Neandertals would be classified as *H. neanderthalensis;* see p. 267 for further discussion). While this speciation explanation fits nicely with, and in fact helps explain, *complete* replacement, Stringer has more recently stated that he is not dogmatic regarding this issue. Thus, he suggests that there may have been potential for interbreeding, but he argues that very little apparently took place.

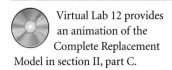 Virtual Lab 12 provides an animation of the Complete Replacement Model in section II, part C.

A crucial source of supporting evidence for the African origin hypothesis (and complete replacement elsewhere) has come from genetic data obtained from living peoples. Underlying this approach is the assumption that genetic patterning seen in contemporary populations will provide clues to relationships and origins of ancient *Homo sapiens.* However, as with numerous prior attempts to evaluate such patterning from more traditional data on human genetic traits (see Chapter 12), the obstacles are enormous.

A recent innovation uses genetic sequencing data derived directly from DNA. The most promising application has come not from the DNA within the nucleus, but from DNA found in the cytoplasm, that is, mitochondrial DNA (mtDNA; see Chapter 3). You may recall that mitochondria are organelles found in the cell, but outside the nucleus. They contain a set of DNA, dissimilar from nuclear DNA, inherited only through the mother. Thus, mtDNA does not undergo the genetic recombination that occurs in nuclear DNA during meiosis.

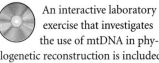 An interactive laboratory exercise that investigates the use of mtDNA in phylogenetic reconstruction is included in Virtual Lab 12 under section II, part B.

Using mtDNA gathered from a number of different populations, scientists at the University of California, Berkeley, constructed "trees" (something like a family tree) that, they claimed, demonstrated that the entire population of the world today descended from a single African lineage. However, the methodology of these molecular biologists has been faulted. Using the same mtDNA material, other scientists constructed many trees that differed from those of the Berkeley group, and some of them are *without African roots* (i.e., the same data can be used statistically to show that *H. sapiens* arose in Asia, *not* in Africa).

This question of the applicability of the mtDNA evidence continues to generate considerable disagreement. Paleoanthropologist Robert Corruccini of

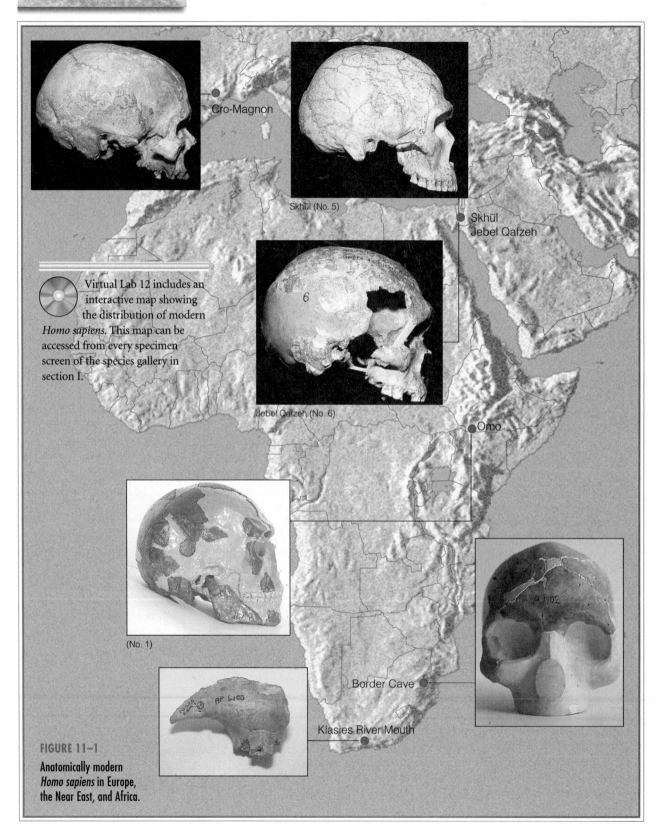

Cro-Magnon

Skhūl (No. 5)

Skhūl
Jebel Qafzeh

Virtual Lab 12 includes an interactive map showing the distribution of modern *Homo sapiens*. This map can be accessed from every specimen screen of the species gallery in section I.

Jebel Qafzeh (No. 6)

Omo

(No. 1)

Border Cave

Klasies River Mouth

FIGURE 11–1

Anatomically modern *Homo sapiens* in Europe, the Near East, and Africa.

Southern Illinois University has been unimpressed with the entire approach, stating that "critical shortcomings of molecular population genetic assumptions and of analysis . . . render any mtDNA conclusions virtually useless to ruminations about human evolution" (Corruccini, 1994, p. 698). Likewise, Glenn Conroy (1997) has critiqued many of the oversimplifications inherent in the genetic data and consequent interpretations. Problems cited with the mtDNA data include the following: (1) The estimated rate of mutation may be incorrect, thus casting doubt on the proposed date for the migration out of Africa; (2) different population sizes in various regions (greater population size in Africa) would complicate interpretation (Relethford and Harpending, 1994); (3) secondary migrations outside Africa could further complicate interpretation of the so-called direct African maternal line; and (4) inappropriate use of statistical methods in earlier publications by proponents of the complete replacement model.

However, molecular anthropologist Mark Stoneking of Pennsylvania State University (and one of the founders of this approach) remains much more confident in the general reliability of the mtDNA results, especially as they show a much greater diversity among contemporary African groups as compared to other world populations. Stoneking thus concludes: "Because non-African populations that predate the mtDNA ancestor apparently did not contribute mtDNAs to contemporary human populations, it follows that the spread of modern populations was accomplished with little or no admixture with resident non-African populations. If it were otherwise, there should be evidence of much more divergent mtDNA types in contemporary human populations" (Stoneking, 1993, pp. 66–67).

Recently, some further genetic data have helped bolster some of the main tenets of the complete replacement model. A team of Yale, Harvard, and University of Chicago researchers (Dorit et al., 1995) has investigated variation in the Y chromosome, finding *much* less variation in humans than in other primates. And another group of Yale researchers (Tishkoff et al., 1996), looking at DNA sequences on chromosome 12, again found much more variation among contemporary Africans than is seen in all the remainder of the world combined. Finally, the recent report of the distinctive nature of Neandertal mtDNA (see p. 262) also argues that substantial replacement took place. Nevertheless, some geneticists find the results unconvincing (e.g., Ayala, 1995; Templeton, 1996), and many paleoanthropologists (agreeing with the views expressed by Corruccini and Conroy) are extremely skeptical of the main conclusions derived from the genetic data.

The Partial Replacement Model

The partial replacement model also begins with African early archaic *H. sapiens*. Later, also in Africa, anatomically modern *H. sapiens* populations first evolved. This theory, proposed by Günter Bräuer of the University of Hamburg, postulates the earliest dates for African modern *Homo sapiens* at over 100,000 y.a. Bräuer sees the initial dispersal of *H. sapiens sapiens* out of South Africa as significantly influenced by shifting environmental conditions and thus as a gradual process. Moving into Eurasia, modern humans hybridized, probably to a limited degree, with resident archaic groups, and eventually replaced them. The disappearance of archaic humans was therefore due to both hybridization and replacement and was a gradual and complex process. This model includes components of regional continuity, hybridization, and replacement, with the emphasis on replacement.

Virtual Lab 12 provides an animation of the Regional Continuity Model (Multiregionalism) in section II, part D.

Polytypic
Referring to species composed of populations that differ with regard to the expression of one or more traits.

Provenience
In archaeology, the specific location of a discovery, including its geological context. (Also spelled "provenance.")

The Regional Continuity Model (Multiregional Evolution)

The regional continuity model is most closely associated with paleoanthropologist Milford Wolpoff of the University of Michigan and his associates (Thorne and Wolpoff, 1992; Wolpoff et al., 1994). These researchers suggest that local populations (not all, of course) in Europe, Asia, and Africa continued their indigenous evolutionary development from archaic *H. sapiens* to anatomically modern humans. A question immediately arises: How is it possible for different local populations around the globe to evolve with such similar morphology? In other words, how could anatomically modern humans arise separately in different continents and end up physically (and genetically) so similar? The multiregional model explains this phenomenon by (1) denying that the earliest modern *H. sapiens* populations originated *exclusively* in Africa and challenging the notion of complete replacement and (2) asserting that some gene flow (migration) between archaic populations was extremely likely, and consequently, modern humans cannot be considered a species separate from archaic forms.

Through gene flow and local selection, according to the multiregional hypothesis, local populations would *not* have evolved totally independently from one another, and such mixing would have "prevented speciation between the regional lineages and thus maintained human beings as a *single,* although obviously **polytypic** (see p. 320), species throughout the Pleistocene" (Smith et al., 1989).

The Earliest *Homo sapiens sapiens* Discoveries

Current evidence strongly indicates that the earliest modern *H. sapiens* fossils come from Africa, but not everyone agrees on the dates or designations or precisely which specimens are the modern and which are the archaic forms. With this cautionary note, we continue our discussion, but there undoubtedly will be corrections as more evidence is gathered.

Africa

In Africa, several early fossil finds have been interpreted as fully anatomically modern forms (see Fig. 11–1). These specimens come from the Klasies River Mouth on the south coast (which could be the earliest find), Border Cave slightly to the north, and Omo Kibish 1 in southern Ethiopia. With the use of relatively new techniques, all three sites have been dated to about 120,000–80,000 y.a. **Provenience** at Border Cave is uncertain, and the fossils may be younger than at the other two sites (see Table 11–1 and Fig. 11–5). Some paleoanthropologists consider these fossils to be the earliest known anatomically modern humans. Problems with dating, provenience, and differing interpretations of the evidence have led other paleoanthropologists to question whether the *earliest* modern forms (Fig. 11–2) really did evolve in Africa. Other modern *H. sapiens* individuals, possibly older than these Africans, have been found in the Near East.

The Near East

In Israel, early modern *H. sapiens* fossils (the remains of at least 10 individuals) were found in the Skhūl Cave at Mt. Carmel (Figs. 11–3 and 11–4a), very near the

TABLE 11–1   Additional Techniques for Dating Middle and Upper Pleistocene Sites

Technique	Physical Basis	Examples of Use
Uranium series dating	Radioactive decay of short-lived uranium isotopes	To date limestone formations (e.g., stalagmites) and ancient ostrich eggshells; to estimate age of Jinniushan site in China and Ngandong site in Java, both corroborated by ESR dates
Thermoluminescence (TL) dating	Accumulation of trapped electrons within certain crystals released during heating	To date ancient flint tools (either deliberately or accidentally heated); to provide key dates for the Qafzeh site
Electron spin resonance (ESR) dating	Measurement (counting) of accumulated trapped electrons	To date dental enamel; to corroborate dating of Qafzeh, Skhūl, and Tabun sites in Israel, Ngandong site in Java, and Klasies River Mouth and Border Cave sites in South Africa

Source: Cook et al., 1984; Aiken et al., 1993.

Neandertal site of Tabun. Also from Israel, the Qafzeh Cave has yielded the remains of at least 20 individuals (Fig. 11–4b). Although their overall configuration is definitely modern, some specimens show certain archaic (i.e., Neandertal) features. Skhūl has been dated to about 115,000 y.a., and Qafzeh has been placed around 100,000 y.a. (Bar-Yosef, 1993, 1994) (Fig. 11–5).

Such early dates for modern specimens pose some problems for those advocating local replacement (the multiregional model). How early do archaic *H. sapiens* populations (Neandertals) appear in the Near East? A recent chronometric calibration for the Tabun Cave suggests a date as early as 120,000 y.a. Neandertals thus may *slightly* precede modern forms in the Near East, but there would appear to be considerable overlap in the timing of occupation by these different *H. sapiens* forms. And recall, the modern site at Mt. Carmel (Skhūl) is very near the Neandertal site (Tabun). Clearly, the dynamics of *Homo sapiens* evolution in the Near East are highly complex, and no simple model may explain later hominid evolution adequately.

Central Europe

Central Europe has been a source of many fossil finds, including numerous fairly early anatomically modern *H. sapiens.* At several sites, it appears that some fossils display both Neandertal and modern features, which supports the regional continuity hypothesis (from Neandertal to modern). Some genetic continuity from earlier (Neandertal) to later (modern *Homo sapiens*) populations was perhaps the case at Vindija in Croatia, where typical Neandertals were found in earlier contexts (see p. 257).

 Be sure to study the cranial and postcranial morphology in Virtual Lab 12, section I, part C, in order to understand the dramatic changes in body mass, skeletal robusticity, and brain size that accompany the origin of modern *Homo sapiens*. This section includes several interactive exercises.

 A time line that gives the ages for modern and archaic *Homo sapiens* is available from the species gallery in Virtual Lab 12, section I. Be sure to view the detailed screen.

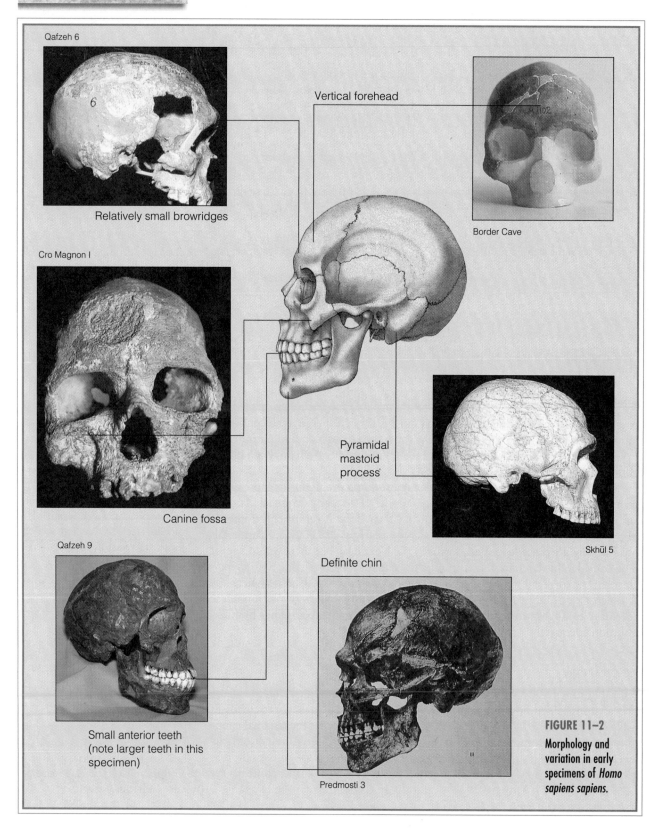

Qafzeh 6

Relatively small browridges

Cro Magnon I

Canine fossa

Qafzeh 9

Small anterior teeth
(note larger teeth in this
specimen)

Vertical forehead

Border Cave

Pyramidal
mastoid
process

Skhūl 5

Definite chin

Predmosti 3

FIGURE 11–2

Morphology and
variation in early
specimens of *Homo
sapiens sapiens.*

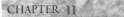

(a)

(b)

Smith (1984) offers another example of local continuity from Mladeč, in the Czech Republic. Among the earlier European modern *H. sapiens* fossils, dated to about 33,000 y.a., the Mladeč crania display a great deal of variation, probably in part due to sexual dimorphism. Although each of the crania (except for one of the females) displays a prominent supraorbital torus, it is reduced from the typical Neandertal pattern. Even though there is some suggestion of continuity from Neandertals to modern humans, Smith is certain that, given specific anatomical features, the Mladeč remains are best classified as *H. sapiens sapiens*. Reduced midfacial projection, a higher forehead, and postcranial elements "are clearly modern *H. sapiens* in morphology and not specifically Neandertal-like in a single feature" (Smith, 1984, p. 174).

FIGURE 11–3

(a) Mt. Carmel, studded with caves, was home to *H. sapiens sapiens* at Skhūl (and to Neandertals at Tabun and Kebara).
(b) Skhūl Cave.

FIGURE 11–4

(a) Skhūl 5. (b) Qafzeh 6. These specimens from Israel are thought to be representatives of early modern *Homo sapiens*. The vault height, forehead, and lack of prognathism are modern traits.

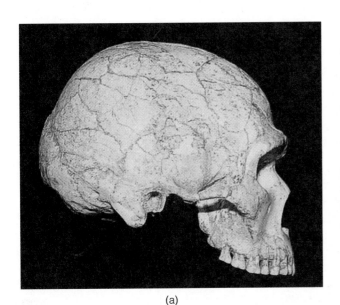

(a)

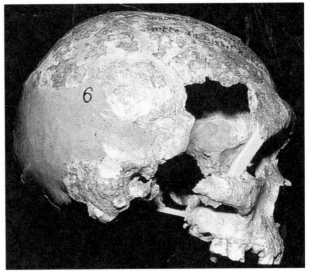

(b)

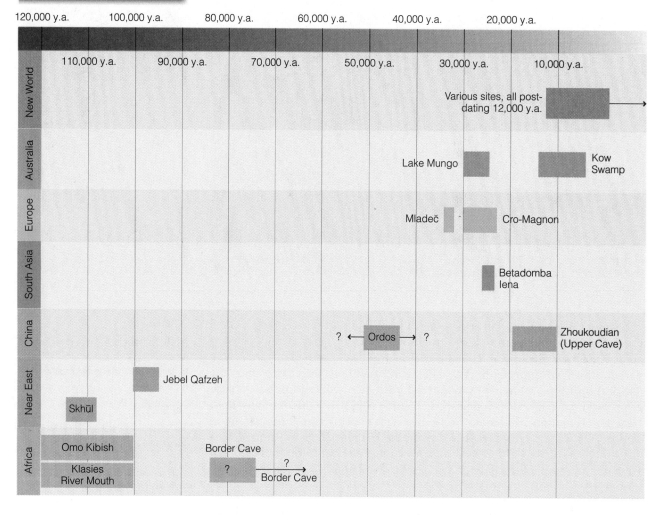

FIGURE 11–5

Time line of *Homo sapiens sapiens* discoveries. Note that most dates are approximations. Question marks indicate those estimates that are most tentative.

Western Europe

This area of the world and its fossils have received the greatest paleoanthropological attention for several reasons, one of which is probably serendipity. Over the last century and a half, many of the scholars interested in this kind of research happened to live in western Europe, and the southern region of France happened to be a fossil treasure trove. Also, early on, discovering and learning about human ancestors caught the curiosity and pride of the local population.

Because of this scholarly interest beginning back in the nineteenth century, a great deal of data accumulated, with little reliable comparative information available from elsewhere in the world. Consequently, theories of human evolution were based almost exclusively on the western European material. It has only been in recent years, with growing evidence from other areas of the world and with the application of new dating techniques, that recent human evolutionary dynamics have been seriously considered on a worldwide basis.

There are many anatomically modern human fossils from western Europe going back 40,000 years or more, but by far the best-known sample of western

European *H. sapiens* is from the **Cro-Magnon** site. A total of eight individuals were discovered in 1868 in a rock shelter in the village of Les Eyzies, in the Dordogne region of southern France (Gambier, 1989).

Associated with an **Aurignacian** tool assemblage, an Upper Paleolithic industry, the Cro-Magnon materials, dated at 30,000 y.a., represent the earliest of France's anatomically modern humans. The so-called "Old Man" (Cro-Magnon I) became the archetype for what was once termed the Cro-Magnon, or Upper Paleolithic, "race" of Europe (Fig.11–6). Actually, of course, there is no such race, and Cro-Magnon I is not typical of Upper Paleolithic western Europeans and not even all that similar to the other two male skulls that were found at the site.

Considered together, the male crania reflect a mixture of modern and archaic traits. Cro-Magnon I is the most gracile of the three—the supraorbital tori of the other two males, for example, are more robust. The most modern-looking is the female cranium, the appearance of which may be a function of sexual dimorphism.

The question of whether continuous local evolution produced anatomically modern groups directly from Neandertals in some regions of Eurasia is far from settled. From central Europe, variation seen in the Mladeč and Vindija fossils indicate a combination of both Neandertal and modern characteristics and may suggest gene flow between the two different *H. sapiens* groups. Tracing such relatively minor genetic changes—considering the ever-present problems of dating, lack of fossils, and fragmented fossil finds—has proven extremely difficult.

However, a newly discovered child's skeleton from Portugal has provided some of the best evidence yet of possible hybridization between Neandertals and anatomically modern *H. sapiens*. This important new hominid discovery from the Abrigo do Lagar Velho site in central western Portugal was excavated in late 1998 and is dated to 24,500 y.a. (i.e., at least 5,000 years *later* than the last clearly Neandertal find). Associated with an Upper Paleolithic industry (see p. 284) and interred with red ocher and pierced shell is a fairly complete skeleton of a four-year-old child (Duarte et al., 1999). Cidália Duarte, Erik Trinkaus, and colleagues, who have studied the remains, found a highly mixed set of anatomical features. Many characteristics (of the teeth, lower jaw, and pelvis) were like those seen in anatomically

Cro-Magnon
(crow mah´yon)

Aurignacian
Pertaining to an Upper Paleolithic stone tool industry in Europe beginning at about 40,000 y.a.

See Virtual Lab 12, section I, part B, for a 3-D animation and discussion of the Cro-Magnon I specimen.

FIGURE 11–6

Cro-Magnon 1 (France). In this specimen, modern traits are quite clear. (a) Lateral view. (b) Frontal view.
(Courtesy of David Frayer.)

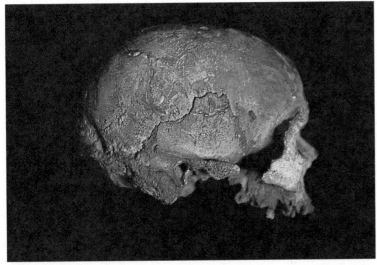

(a)

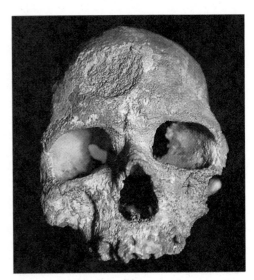

(b)

modern humans. Yet, several other features (lack of chin, limb proportions, muscle insertions) were more similar to Neandertals. The authors thus conclude, "The presence of such admixture suggests the hypothesis of variable admixture between early modern humans dispersing into Europe and local Neandertal populations" (Duarte et al., 1999, p. 7608). These researchers thus argue that this new evidence provides strong support for the partial replacement model while seriously weakening the complete replacement model. However, the evidence from one child's skeleton—while intriguing—is certainly not going to convince everyone!

Asia

There are six early anatomically modern human localities in China, the most significant of which are Upper Cave at Zhoukoudian and Ordos. The fossils from these sites are all fully modern, and most are considered to be of quite late Upper Pleistocene age. Upper Cave at Zhoukoudian has been dated to between 18,000 and 10,000 y.a. The Ordos find was discovered at Dagouwan, Inner Mongolia, and may be the oldest anatomically modern material from China, perhaps dating to 50,000 y.a. or more (Etler, personal communication) (see Fig. 11–5).

In addition, the Jinniushan skeleton discussed in Chapter 10 (see p. 244) has been suggested by some researchers (Tiemel et al., 1994) as hinting at modern features in China as early as 200,000 y.a. If this date (as early as that proposed for direct antecedents of modern *H. sapiens* in Africa) should prove accurate, it would cast doubt on the complete replacement model. Indeed, quite opposed to the complete replacement model and more in support of regional continuity, Chinese paleoanthropologists see a continuous evolution from Chinese *H. erectus* to archaic *H. sapiens* to anatomically modern humans. This view is supported by Wolpoff, who mentions that materials from Upper Cave at Zhoukoudian "have a number of features that are characteristically regional" and that these features are definitely not African (1989, p. 83).*

In addition to the well-known finds from China, anatomically modern remains have also been discovered in southern Asia. At Batadomba Iena, in southern Sri Lanka, modern *Homo sapiens* finds have been dated to 25,500 y.a. (Kennedy and Deraniyagala, 1989).

Australia

During glacial times, the Indonesian islands were joined to the Asian mainland, but Australia was not. It is likely that by 50,000 y.a., Sahul—the area including New Guinea and Australia—was inhabited by modern humans. Bamboo rafts may have been the means of crossing the sea between islands, which would not have been a simple exercise. Just where the future Australians came from is unknown, but Borneo, Java, and New Guinea have all been suggested.

Archaeological sites in Australia have been dated to at least 55,000 y.a. (Roberts et al., 1990), but the oldest human fossils themselves have been dated to about 30,000 y.a. These oldest Australians are from Lake Mungo, where the remains of two burials (one individual was first cremated) date to 25,000 y.a. and at least 30,000 y.a. (Fig. 11–7). The crania are rather gracile with, for example, only moderate development of the supraorbital torus.

*Wolpoff's statement supports his regional continuity hypothesis. His reference to Africa is a criticism of the complete replacement hypothesis.

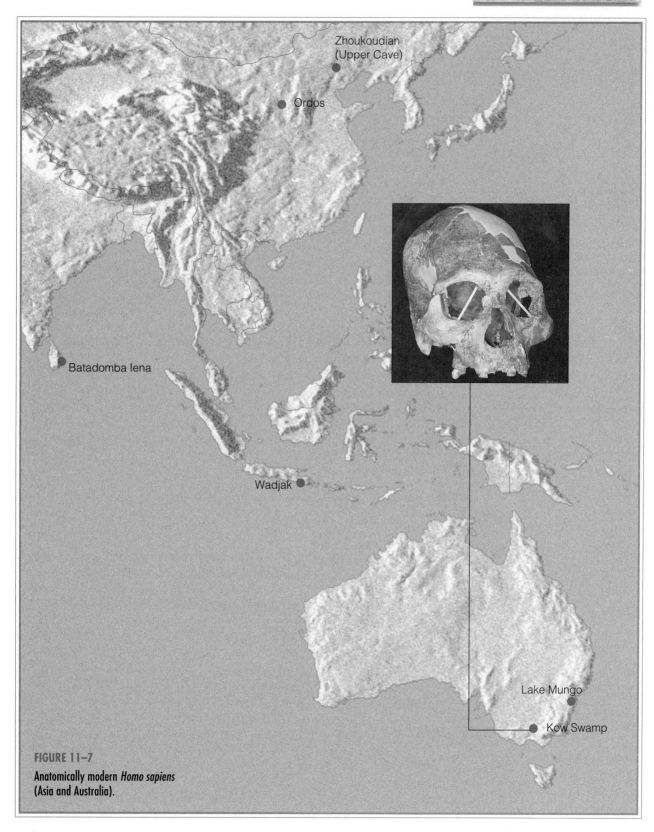

FIGURE 11–7

Anatomically modern *Homo sapiens*
(Asia and Australia).

Homo sapiens sapiens

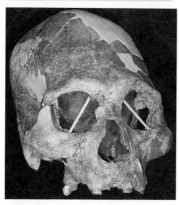

FIGURE 11-8

Kow Swamp (Australia). Note the considerable robusticity in this relatively late Australian *Homo sapiens sapiens* cranium.

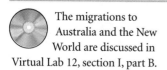

The migrations to Australia and the New World are discussed in Virtual Lab 12, section I, part B.

Unlike these more gracile early Australian forms are the Kow Swamp people, who are thought to have lived between about 14,000 and 9,000 years ago (Fig. 11–8). The presence of certain archaic traits, such as receding foreheads, heavy supraorbital tori, and thick bones, are difficult to explain, since these features contrast with the postcranial anatomy, which matches that of recent native Australians.

The New World

There have been considerable, and often heated, arguments regarding the *earliest* entry of humans into the New World. It must be remembered that the ancestors of Native Americans reached the New World through multiple migrations over the Bering Land Bridge over many millennia. Regarding the first migration, all claims of great antiquity (prior to 30,000 y.a.) have now been refuted. Nevertheless, there are still varied claims that archaeological materials (i.e., evidence of artifacts) put the date of the initial migration at prior to 15,000 y.a. Such claims have come from evidence excavated at widely scattered locales (e.g., from the Yukon, Pennsylvania, and Peru). Because of concerns about accurate dating or the nature of the artifacts (were they actually made by humans?), these reports, too, have been subjected to rigorous scrutiny. As a result, these claims are not considered well established at this time.

The most indisputable proof would, of course, be actual hominid finds in clear, datable contexts. As with the earliest confirmed archaeological discoveries, direct evidence indicating the greatest antiquity for hominids anywhere in the New World goes back only about 12,000 years. From the broader perspective of human evolution, we must emphasize that all the hominid material found thus far is obviously fully modern *Homo sapiens*. This fact should come as no surprise, given the relatively late entry of *Homo sapiens* into the Americas, perhaps as much as 40,000 years after hominids had reached Australia.

Technology and Art in the Upper Paleolithic

Europe

The cultural period known as the Upper Paleolithic began in western Europe approximately 40,000 years ago. Upper Paleolithic cultures are usually divided into five different industries based on stone tool technologies: (1) Chatelperronian, (2) Aurignacian, (3) Gravettian, (4) Solutrean, and (5) Magdalenian (Fig. 11–9). Major environmental shifts were also apparent during this period. During the last glacial period, at about 30,000 y.a., a warming trend lasting several thousand years partially melted the glacial ice. The result was that much of Eurasia was covered by tundra and steppe, a vast area of treeless country dotted with lakes and marshes. In many areas in the north, permafrost prevented the growth of trees but permitted the growth, in the short summers, of flowering plants, mosses, and other kinds of vegetation. This vegetation served as an enormous pasture for herbivorous animals, large and small, and carnivorous animals fed off the herbivores. It was a hunter's paradise, with millions of animals dispersed across expanses of tundra and grassland, from Spain through Europe and into the Russian steppes.

Large herds of reindeer roamed the tundra and steppes along with mammoths, bison, horses, and a host of smaller animals that served as a bountiful source of food. In addition, humans exploited fish and fowl systematically for the

GLACIAL	UPPER PALEOLITHIC (beginnings)	CULTURAL PERIODS
W Ü R M	17,000 – 21,000 – 27,000 – 33,000 –	Magdalenian Solutrean Gravettian Aurignacian Chatelperronian
	Middle Paleolithic	Mousterian

FIGURE 11–9

Cultural periods of the European Upper Paleolithic and their approximate beginning dates.

first time, especially along the southern tier of Europe. It was a time of relative affluence, and ultimately Upper Paleolithic people spread out over Europe, living in caves and open-air camps and building large shelters. Large dwellings with storage pits have been excavated in the former Soviet Union, with archaeological evidence of social status distinctions (Soffer, 1985). During this period, either western Europe or perhaps portions of Africa achieved the highest population density in human history up to that time.

In Eurasia, cultural innovations allowed humans for the first time to occupy easternmost Europe and northern Asia. In these areas, even during glacial warming stages, winters would have been long and harsh. Human groups were able to tolerate these environments probably because of better constructed structures as well as warmer, better fitting *sewn* clothing. The evidence for wide use of such tailored clothing comes from many sites and includes pointed stone tools such as awls and (by at least 19,000 y.a.) bone needles as well. Especially noteworthy is the clear evidence of the residues of clothing (including what has been interpreted as a cap, a shirt, a jacket, trousers, and moccasins) in graves at the 22,000-year-old Sungir site, located not far from Moscow (Klein, 1989).

Humans and other animals in the midlatitudes of Eurasia had to cope with shifts in climatic conditions, some of which were quite rapid. For example, at 20,000 y.a. another climatic "pulse" caused the weather to become noticeably colder in Europe and Asia as the continental glaciations reached their maximum extent for this entire glacial period (called the Würm in Eurasia). Meanwhile, the southern continents, too, experienced widespread climatic effects. Notably, in Africa around 20,000 y.a. it became significantly wetter, thus permitting re-occupation of areas in the north and south that had previously been abandoned.

As a variety of organisms attempted to adapt to these changing conditions, *Homo sapiens* had a major advantage: the elaboration of an increasingly sophisticated technology (and probably other components of culture as well). Indeed, probably one of the greatest challenges facing numerous late Pleistocene mammals was the ever more dangerously equipped humans—a trend that has continued to modern times.

The Upper Paleolithic was an age of technological innovation and can be compared to the past few hundred years in our recent history of amazing technological change after centuries of relative inertia. Anatomically modern humans of the Upper Paleolithic not only invented new and specialized tools (Fig. 11–10), but, as we have seen, also greatly increased the use of, and probably experimented with, new materials, such as bone, ivory, and antler.

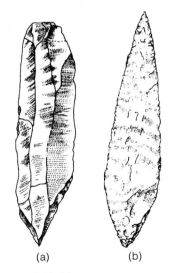

(a)   (b)

FIGURE 11–10

(a) Burin. A very common Upper Paleolithic tool. (b) Solutrean blade. This is the best-known work of the Solutrean tradition. Solutrean stonework is considered the most highly developed of any Upper Paleolithic industry.

Homo sapiens sapiens

FIGURE 11–11
Spear-thrower (atlatl). Note the carving.

Solutrean tools are good examples of Upper Paleolithic skill and perhaps aesthetic appreciation as well (Fig. 11–10b). In this lithic (stone) tradition, stone-knapping developed to the finest degree ever known. Using a pressure-flaking technique, the artist/technicians made beautiful parallel-sided lance heads, expertly flaked on both surfaces, with such delicate points that they can be considered works of art that quite possibly never served, or were intended to serve, a utilitarian purpose.

The last stage of the Upper Paleolithic, known as the **Magdalenian,** saw even more advances in technology. The spear-thrower (Fig. 11–11), a wooden or bone hooked rod (called an *atlatl*), acted to extend the hunter's arm, thus enhancing the force and distance of a spear throw. For catching salmon and other fish, the barbed harpoon is a clever example of the craftsperson's skill. There is also evidence that the bow and arrow may have been used for the first time during this period. The introduction of the punch technique (Fig. 11–12) provided an abundance of stan-

Magdalenian
Pertaining to the final phase (stone tool industry) of the Upper Paleolithic in Europe.

FIGURE 11–12
The punch blade technique.

(a) A large core is selected and the top portion is removed by use of a hammerstone.

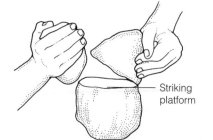

(b) The objective is to create a flat surface called a striking platform.

Striking platform

(c) Next, the core is struck by use of a hammer and punch (made of bone or antler) to remove the long narrow flakes (called blades).

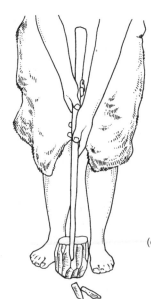

(d) Or the blades can be removed by pressure flaking.

(e) The result is the production of highly consistent sharp blades, which can be used, as is, as knives; or they can be further modified (retouched) to make a variety of other tools (such as burins, scrapers, and awls).

dardized blank stone flakes that could be fashioned into **burins** (see Fig. 11–10a) for working wood, bone, and antler; borers for drilling holes in skins, bones, and shells; and blades for knives with serrated or notched edges for scraping wooden shafts into a variety of tools.

The elaboration of many more specialized tools by Upper Paleolithic peoples probably made more resources available to them and may also have had an impact on the biology of these populations. C. Loring Brace of the University of Michigan has suggested that with more efficient tools used for food processing, anatomically modern *H. sapiens* would not have required the large front teeth (incisors) seen in earlier populations. With relaxed selection pressures (no longer favoring large anterior teeth), incorporation of random mutations would through time lead to reduction of dental size and accompanying facial features. In particular, the lower face became less prognathic (as compared to archaic specimens) and thus produced the concavity of the cheekbones called a *canine fossa* (see Fig. 11–2). Moreover, as the dental-bearing portion of the lower jaw regressed, the buttressing below would have become modified into a *chin,* that distinctive feature seen in anatomically modern *H. sapiens.*

In addition to their reputation as hunters, western Europeans of the Upper Paleolithic are even better known for their symbolic representation, what has commonly been called "art." Certainly, in the famous caves of France and Spain (discussed below), we easily relate to an aesthetic property of the images—one that *may* have been intended by the people who created them. But here we cannot be certain. Our own cultural perspective creates labels (and categories) such as "art," which in itself *assumes* aesthetic intent. While such a cultural orientation is obviously a recognizable part of Western culture, many other contemporary peoples would not relate to this concept within their own cultural context. Furthermore, prehistoric peoples during the Upper Paleolithic did not necessarily create their symbols as true artistic representations. Rather, these representations may have served a variety of quite utilitarian and/or social functions—as do contemporary highway signs or logos on a company's letterhead. Would we call these symbols art?

Given these uncertainties, archaeologist Margaret Conkey of the University of California, Berkeley, refers to Upper Paleolithic cave paintings, sculptures, engravings, and so forth, as "visual and material imagery" (Conkey, 1987, p. 423). We will continue to use the term *art* to describe many of these prehistoric representations, but you should recognize that we do so mainly as a cultural convention—and perhaps a limiting one.

Moreover, the time depth for these prehistoric forms of symbolic imagery is quite long, encompassing the entire Upper Paleolithic (from at least 35,000 to 10,000 y.a.). Over this time span there is considerable variability in style, medium, content, and no doubt meaning as well. In addition, there is an extremely wide geographical distribution of symbolic images, best known from many parts of Europe, but now also well documented from Siberia, North Africa, South Africa, and Australia. Given the 25,000-year time depth of what we call "Paleolithic art" and its nearly worldwide distribution, there is indeed marked variability in expression.

In addition to cave art, there are numerous examples of small sculptures excavated from sites in western, central, and eastern Europe. Beyond these quite well known figurines, there are numerous other examples of what is frequently termed "portable art," including elaborate engravings on tools and tool handles (Fig. 11–13). Such symbolism can be found in many parts of Europe and was already well established early in the Aurignacian (by 33,000 y.a.). Innovations in symbolic

Burins
Small, chisel-like tools (with a pointed end) thought to have been used to engrave bone, antler, ivory, or wood.

Virtual Lab 11, section IV, part B, provides a 3-D animation of blade production.

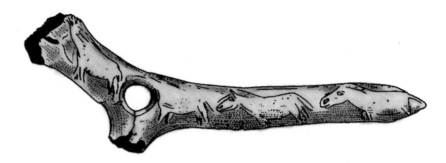

FIGURE 11–13

Magdalenian bone artifact. Note the realistic animal engraving on this object, the precise function of which is unknown.

representations also benefited from, and probably further stimulated, technological advances. New methods of mixing pigments and applying them were important in rendering painted or drawn images. Bone and ivory carving and engraving were made easier with the use of special stone tools (see Fig. 11–10). At two sites in the Czech Republic, Dolni Vestonice and Predmosti (both dated at 27,000 y.a.), small animal figures were fashioned from fired clay—the first documented use of ceramic technology anywhere (and preceding later pottery invention by more than 15,000 years!).

Female figurines, popularly know as Venuses, were sculpted not only in western Europe, but in central and eastern Europe and Siberia as well. Some of these figures were realistically carved, and the faces appear to be modeled after actual women (Fig. 11–14). Other figurines may seem grotesque, with sexual characteristics exaggerated, perhaps for fertility or other ritual purposes (Fig. 11–15).

It is, however, during the final phases of the Upper Paleolithic, particularly during the Magdalenian, that European prehistoric art reached its climax. Cave art

(a)

(b)

FIGURE 11–14

Venus of Brassempouy. Upper Paleolithic artists were capable of portraying human realism (shown here) as well as symbolism (depicted in Fig 11–15). (a) Frontal view. (b) Lateral view.

FIGURE 11–15

Venus of Willendorf, Austria.

is now known from more than 150 separate sites, the vast majority from southwestern France and northern Spain. Apparently, in other areas the rendering of such images did not take place in deep caves. Peoples in central Europe, China, Africa, and elsewhere certainly may have painted or carved representations on rockfaces in the open, but these images long since would have eroded. Thus, it is fortuitous that the people of at least one of the many sophisticated cultures of the Upper Paleolithic chose to journey belowground to create their artwork, preserving it not just for their immediate descendants, but for us as well.

In Lascaux Cave of southern France, immense wild bulls dominate what is called the Great Hall of Bulls, and horses, deer, and other animals adorn the walls in black, red, and yellow, drawn with remarkable skill. In addition to the famous cave of Lascaux, there is equally exemplary art from Altamira Cave in Spain. Indeed, discovered in 1879, Altamira was the first example of advanced cave art recorded in Europe. Filling the walls and ceiling of the cave are superb portrayals of bison in red and black, the "artist" taking advantage of bulges to give a sense of relief to the paintings. The cave is a treasure of beautiful art whose meaning has never been satisfactorily explained. It could have been religious or magical, a form of visual communication, or art for the sake of beauty.

Yet another spectacular example of cave art from western Europe was discovered in late 1994. On December 24, a team of three French cave explorers chanced upon a fabulous discovery in the valley of the Ardèche at Combe d'Arc (Fig. 11–16). Inside the cave, called the Grotte Chauvet after one of its discoverers, preserved unseen for perhaps 30,000 years are many hundreds of images, including stylized dots, stenciled human handprints, and, most dramatically, hundreds of animal representations. Included are depictions of such typical Paleolithic subjects as bison, horse, ibex, auroch, deer, and mammoth. But quite surprisingly, there are also numerous images of animals rarely portrayed elsewhere—such as rhino, lion, and bear (Fig. 11–17). Three animals seen at Grotte Chauvet—a panther, a hyena, and an owl—have never before been documented at cave sites. The artwork, at least after provisional study, seems to consistently repeat several stylistic conventions, causing French researchers to suggest that the images all may have been produced by the same artist. Provisional dating has placed the paintings during the Aurignacian (perhaps more than 30,000 y.a.), and thus Grotte Chauvet may be considerably earlier than the Magdalenian sites of Lascaux and Altamira. The cave was found as Paleolithic peoples had left it, and the initial discoverers, as well as archaeologists, have been careful not to disturb the remains. Among the archaeological traces already noted are dozens of footprints on the cave floor, produced by bears as well as by humans. We do not know yet how far the cave extends or what crucial artifactual remains lie along the floor.

A familiar motif seen at Grotte Chauvet and elsewhere is the representation of human hands, usually in the form of outlines. Apparently, the technique used was to liquefy the pigment and blow it onto a hand held flat against the cave wall. At one site in France, at least 159 such hand outlines were found (Leroi-Gourhan, 1986). Another stylistic innovation was the partial sculpting of a rock face—in what is called bas-relief (a technique used much later, for example, by the ancient Greeks at the Parthenon). Attaining depths up to 6 inches, some of the Paleolithic sculptures were quite dramatic and were attempted on a fairly grand scale. In one rock shelter in southwest France, several animals (including mountain goats, bison, reindeer, and horses) and one human figure were depicted in bas-relief. Interestingly, these representations were carved in an area also used as a living

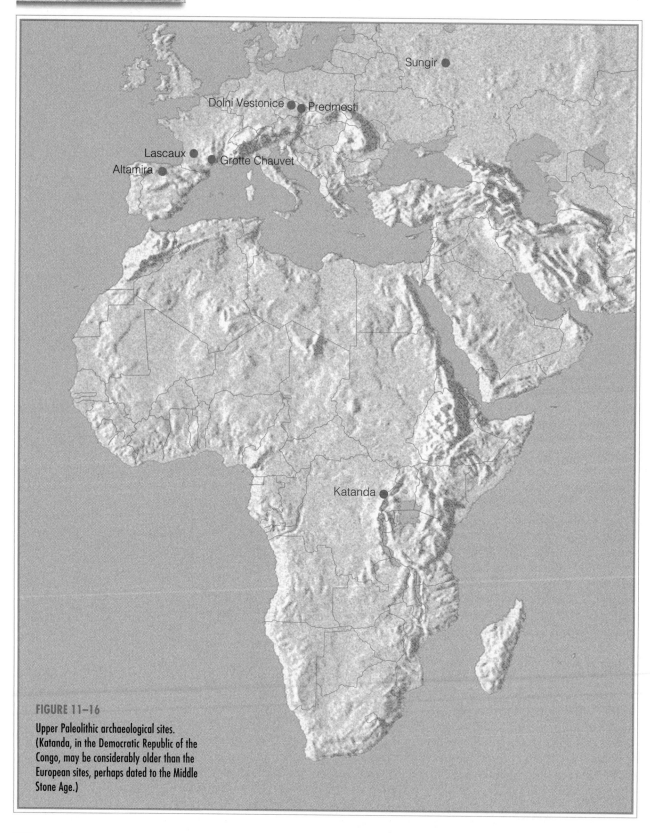

FIGURE 11–16

Upper Paleolithic archaeological sites. (Katanda, in the Democratic Republic of the Congo, may be considerably older than the European sites, perhaps dated to the Middle Stone Age.)

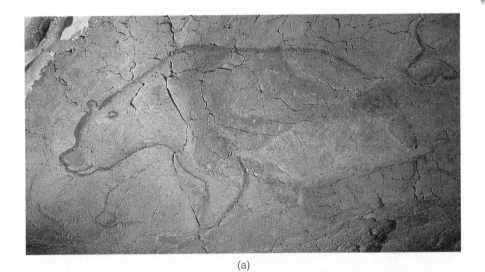

(a)

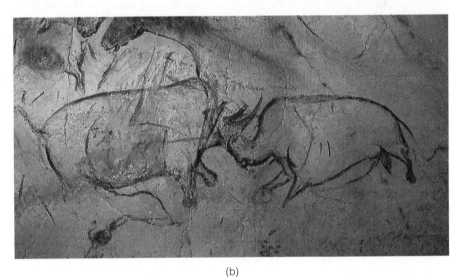

(b)

FIGURE 11–17

Cave art. (a) Bear. Grotte Chauvet, France. (b) Aurochs and rhinoceros, Grotte Chauvet.

site—quite distinct from the special-purpose contexts in the deep cave locations. These bas-reliefs were executed throughout the Magdalenian, always in areas immediately adjacent to those of human habitation.

Strikingly, subject matter seems to differ by location and type of art motif. In portable art, common themes are horses and reindeer as well as stylized human figures; rarely are bison represented. However, in cave contexts, bison and horses are frequently seen, but almost never do we see reindeer (although in Europe, reindeer were probably the most common meat source). Cave artists were thought heretofore to have depicted carnivores only rarely, but the new finds at Grotte Chauvet give us a further perspective on the richness *and* diversity of Paleolithic art.

Ever since ancient art was discovered, attempts have been made to interpret the sculptures, paintings, and other graphic material found in caves or on rocks and tools at open-air archaeological sites. One of the early explanations of Upper Paleolithic art emphasized the relationship of paintings to hunting. Hunting rituals were viewed as a kind of imitative magic that would increase prey animal populations or help hunters successfully find and kill their quarry. As new hypotheses were published, their applicability and deficiencies were discussed. When many of these new hypotheses faded, others were expounded, and the cycle of new hypotheses followed by critiques continued.

Among these hypotheses, the association of religious ritual and magic is still considered viable because of the importance of hunting in the Upper Paleolithic. Nevertheless, other ideas about these graphics have been widely discussed, including the viewing of Upper Paleolithic art from a male/female perspective and the consideration of a prevalent dots-and-lines motif as a notational system associated with language, writing, or a calendar (Marshack, 1972). Other perspectives and ongoing questions include why certain areas of caves were used for painting, but not other, similar areas; why certain animals were painted, but not others; why males were painted singly or in groups, but women only in groups; why males were painted near animals, but women never were; and why groups of animals were painted in the most acoustically resonant areas. (Were rituals perhaps performed in areas of the cave with the best acoustic properties?) It should be noted that given the time depth, different contexts, and variable styles of symbolic representations, no *single* explanation regarding their meaning is likely to prove adequate. As one expert has concluded, "It is clear that there can no longer be a single 'meaning' to account for the thousands of images, media, contexts, and uses of what we lump under the term 'paleolithic art'" (Conkey, 1987, p. 414).

A recent explanation for the florescence of cave art in certain areas has been suggested by archaeologists Clive Gamble (1991) and Lawrence Straus (1993), who point to the severe climatic conditions during the maximum (coldest interval) of the last glacial, around 20,000–18,000 y.a. It was during this period in southwestern France and northern Spain that most of the cave art was created. Straus notes that wherever there are clusters of living sites, there are cave art sanctuaries and residential sites with abundant mobile art objects. The caves could have been meeting places for local bands of people and locations for group activities. Bands could share hunting techniques and knowledge, and paintings and engravings served as "encoded information" that could be passed on across generations. Such information, Straus argues, would have been crucial for dealing with the severe conditions of the last glacial period.

Africa

Early accomplishments in rock art, perhaps as early as in Europe, are seen in southern Africa (Namibia), where a site containing such art is dated between 28,000 and 19,000 y.a. In addition, evidence of portable personal adornment is seen as early as 38,000 y.a. in the form of beads fashioned from ostrich eggshells.

In terms of stone tool technology, microliths (thumbnail-sized stone flakes hafted to make knives, saws, etc.) and blades characterize Late Stone Age* African industries. There was also considerable use of bone and antler in central Africa, perhaps some of it quite early. Recent excavations in the Katanda area of the eastern portion of the Democratic Republic of the Congo have shown remarkable development of bone craftsmanship. In fact, preliminary reports by Alison Brooks of George Washington University and John Yellen of the National Science

---

*The Late Stone Age in Africa is equivalent to the Upper Paleolithic in Eurasia.

Foundation have demonstrated that these technological achievements rival those of the more renowned European Upper Paleolithic (Yellen et al., 1995).

The most important artifacts discovered at Katanda are a dozen intricately made bone tools excavated from three sites along the Semiliki River (not far from Lake Rutanzige—formerly, Lake Edward) (see Fig. 11–16). These tools, made from the ribs or long bone splinters of large mammals, apparently were first ground to flatten and sharpen them, and then some were apparently precisely pressure-flaked to produce a row of barbs. In form these tools are similar to what have been called "harpoons" from the later Upper Paleolithic of Europe (Magdalenian, circa 15,000 y.a.). Their function in Africa, as well, is thought to have been for spearing fish, which archaeological remains indicate were quite large (catfish weighing up to 150 pounds!). In addition, a few carved bone rings with no barbs were also discovered, but their intended function (if indeed they were meant to have a utilitarian function at all) remains elusive.

The dating of the Katanda sites is crucial for drawing useful comparisons with the European Upper Paleolithic. However, the bone used for the tools retained no measurable nitrogen and thus proved unsuitable for radiocarbon dating (perhaps it was too old and beyond the range of this technique). As a result, the other techniques now used for this time range—thermoluminescence, electron spin resonance, and uranium series dating (see p. 277)—were all applied. The results proved consistent, indicating dates between 180,000 and 75,000 y.a.[*]

However, there remain some difficulties in establishing the clear association of the bone implements with the materials that have supplied the chronometric age estimates. Indeed, Richard Klein, a coauthor of one of the initial reports (Brooks et al., 1995), does not accept the suggested great antiquity for these finds and believes they may be much younger. Nevertheless, if the early age estimates should hold up, we once again will look *first* to Africa as the crucial source area for human origins—not just for biological aspects, but for cultural aspects as well.

 You may wish to review these dating techniques in Virtual Lab 12, section II, part A.

Summary of Upper Paleolithic Culture

As we look back at the Upper Paleolithic, we can see it as the culmination of 2 million years of cultural development. Change proceeded incredibly slowly for most of the Pleistocene, but as cultural traditions and materials accumulated, and the brain (and, we assume, intelligence) expanded and reorganized, the rate of change quickened.

Cultural evolution continued with the appearance of early archaic *H. sapiens* and moved a bit faster with later archaic *H. sapiens*. Neandertals in Eurasia and their contemporaries elsewhere added deliberate burials, technological innovations, and much more.

Building on existing cultures, late Pleistocene populations attained sophisticated cultural and material heights in a seemingly short (by previous standards) burst of exciting activity. In Europe and central Africa particularly, there seem to have been dramatic cultural innovations that saw big game hunting, potent new weapons (including harpoons, spear-throwers, and possibly the bow and arrow), body ornaments, needles, "tailored" clothing, and burials with elaborate grave goods (the latter might indicate some sort of status hierarchy).

---

[*]If these dates prove accurate, Katanda would actually be earlier than Late Stone Age (and thus be referrable to the Middle Stone Age).

This dynamic age was doomed, or so it appears, by the climatic changes of about 10,000 y.a. As the temperature slowly rose and the glaciers retreated, animal and plant species were seriously impacted, and humans were thus affected as well. As traditional prey animals were depleted or disappeared altogether, other means of obtaining food were sought.

Grinding hard seeds or roots became important, and as familiarity with plant propagation increased, domestication of plants and animals developed. Dependence on domestication became critical, and with it came permanent settlements, new technology, and more complex social organization.

The long road from hominid origins, from those remarkable footprints engraved into the African savanna, has now led by millions of chance evolutionary turnings to ourselves, anatomically modern human beings. But this road is not yet finished. We are the inheritors, both biologically and culturally, of our hominid forebears. Now, for the first time in human evolution, perhaps we have some choice in the direction our species may take. The continuing story of human evolution and the ways we study contemporary population diversity will be the topics of the remainder of this text.

SUMMARY

The date and location of the origin of anatomically modern human beings have been the subjects of a fierce debate for the past decade, and the end is not in sight. One hypothesis (complete replacement) claims that anatomically modern forms first evolved in Africa more than 100,000 y.a. and then, migrating out of Africa, completely replaced archaic *H. sapiens* in the rest of the world. Another school (regional continuity) takes a diametrically different view and maintains that in various geographical regions of the world, local groups of archaic *H. sapiens* evolved directly to anatomically modern humans. A third hypothesis (partial replacement) takes a somewhat middle position, suggesting an African origin but also accepting some later hybridization outside of Africa.

The Upper Paleolithic was an age of extraordinary innovation and achievement in technology and art. Many new and complex tools were introduced, and their production indicates fine skill in working wood, bone, and antler. It was a period that might be compared, for its time, to the past few hundred years of our own technological advances.

Cave art in France and Spain displays the masterful ability of Upper Paleolithic painters, and beautiful sculptures have been found at many European sites. Sophisticated symbolic representations have also been found in Africa and elsewhere. Upper Paleolithic *Homo sapiens* displayed amazing development in a relatively short period of time. The culture produced during this period led the way to still newer and more complex cultural techniques and methods.

QUESTIONS FOR REVIEW

1. What characteristics define anatomically modern *H. sapiens?*
2. How do the characteristics of modern *H. sapiens* compare with those of archaic *H. sapiens?*

3. What are the three major theories that seek to explain the origin and dispersal of *Homo sapiens sapiens?* Compare and critically discuss these three views.

4. How have data from mitochondrial DNA been used to support an African origin of *H. sapiens sapiens?* What other genetic data have recently been analyzed, and how do they accord with the mtDNA results?

5. Discuss (and compare) the early evidence of anatomically modern humans from two different regions.

6. It is said that the Upper Paleolithic was a time of technological innovation. Support this statement with specific evidence, and compare the Upper Paleolithic with cultural data from earlier in the Pleistocene.

7. From which regions has cave art, dating to the Upper Pleistocene, been discovered? Particularly for the cave art of Europe, what explanations of its meaning have been proposed?

SUGGESTED FURTHER READINGS

Aitken, M. J., C. B. Stringer, and P. A. Mellars (eds.). 1993. *The Origin of Modern Humans and the Impact of Chronometric Dating.* Princeton, NJ: Princeton University Press.

Klein, Richard. 1989. *The Human Career: Human Biological and Cultural Origins.* Chicago: University of Chicago Press.

Nitecki, Matthew H., and Doris V. Nitecki (eds.). 1994. *Origins of Anatomically Modern Humans.* New York: Plenum.

Smith, Fred, and Frank Spencer (eds.). 1984. *The Origin of Modern Humans.* New York: Liss.

Wolpoff, Milford. 1999. *Paleoanthropology.* 2nd ed. New York: McGraw-Hill.

MULTIMEDIA RESOURCES

Wadsworth Anthropology Resource Center

http://anthropology.wadsworth.com

Visit Anthropology Online to obtain current updates in the field, surfing tips, career information, and more. In addition, enrich your study efforts with text-specific study aids arranged by chapter.

InfoTrac College Edition

http://www.infotrac-college.com/wadsworth

1. Use PowerTrac to search for *Upper Paleolithic.* This should pull up several references from which you should choose at least two that deal with topics not covered in detail in Chapter 11. After reading these articles, make a list of facts you found particularly interesting. Did these articles change your views of how humans lived during the Upper Paleolithic? If so, how?

2. Again, in the same subject are (*Upper Paleolithic*), look specifically for articles on New World cultures. Read at least one and write one or two pages comparing the cultures of the earliest human inhabitants of North America with the Upper Paleolithic peoples of the Old World. You might also want to make a list of the journals in which these articles appear.

🌐 Internet Exercises

1. Some of the most recently discovered cave paintings are those at Grotte Chauvet in France. These paintings were completed between 30,000 and 32,000 years ago. Visit the site on the Web at **http://www.culture.fr/culture/arcnat/ chauvet/en/index.htm,** or use your search engine to find sites for either Grotte *Chauvet* or *Laxcaux Cave.* Another suggestion is: *Prehistoric France.* Examine the photographs of the cave paintings and read the text. What is portrayed in the pictures? What do you think might have motivated the people to make the images? What do you think they were trying to communicate? In your own words, describe one painting you especially like.

2. Go to **www.archaeology.org** and search for *Cro-Magnon.* What were you able to find regarding human populations living in western Europe during the Upper Paleolithic?

CHAPTER
12

CONTENTS

Microevolution in Modern Human Populations

Introduction

In the last chapter, we completed our overview of hominid evolution. The dispersal of *Homo sapiens sapiens* was the last major event in our lineage relating to what we have termed **macroevolution.** However, the evolution of our species did not conclude at this point, but has in fact continued over the last several thousand years. This ongoing process of evolutionary change is part of what is referred to as **microevolution.**

How is microevolution evaluated and measured in contemporary species? In earlier chapters, we discussed the mechanisms of inheritance and the manner in which heritable characteristics influence evolutionary change. In this chapter, we will demonstrate how these genetic processes produce evolutionary change in contemporary human populations. As with all other organisms, the variation exhibited by *Homo sapiens* can be understood within an evolutionary framework. Evolutionary change not only characterizes the human past, but also continues as a major factor shaping human beings today. In this explicit evolutionary context, physical anthropologists are able to assess broad patterns of human population diversity.

The Modern Theory of Evolution

By the beginning of the twentieth century, the two essential foundations of modern evolutionary theory were in place. Darwin and Wallace had articulated the crucial role of natural selection 40 years earlier, and in 1900, Mendel's pioneering work was rediscovered, clearly establishing the mechanisms for inheritance.

We might expect that the two basic contributions would have been joined rather quickly into one consistent theory of evolution. However, such was not the case. For the next 30 years, rival "camps" advocated what seemed to be opposing viewpoints. One, supported by experimental biologists working with such organisms as fruit flies, emphasized the central role of mutation. The other school of thought continued with the more traditional Darwinian view, pointing to the key role of natural selection.

A combination of these two views, in what is called the *modern synthesis,* was not achieved until the mid-1930s, and we owe much of our current understanding of evolutionary change to this important intellectual breakthrough. Biologists working primarily on mathematical models came to realize that mutation and selection processes were not opposing themes, but that a comprehensive explanation of organic evolution required *both.* Small changes in the genetic material (i.e., mutations) are transmitted from parent to child according to the rules first discovered by Mendel. Mutations do not usually, by themselves, produce evolutionary change, but are selected for (or against) in particular environments. Indeed, mutation is the origin of variation, and it is the only original source of "fuel" for natural selection.

Using such a perspective, evolution is described by the modern synthesis as a two-stage process:

1. Production and redistribution of **variation** (inherited differences between individuals)
2. **Natural selection** (whereby genetic differences in some individuals lead to their higher reproductive success)

Macroevolution
Large-scale evolutionary changes (especially speciation) that may require many hundreds of generations and are usually only detectable paleontologically (in the fossil record).

Microevolution
Small-scale evolutionary changes that occur over the span of a few generations and can therefore be detected in living populations.

Variation
Inherited (i.e., genetically influenced) differences between individuals.

Natural selection
The differential reproductive success of certain phenotypes (and their underlying genotypes) relative to others in a population.

Definition of Evolution

Darwin saw evolution as the gradual emergence of new life forms derived from earlier ones. Such a depiction is in accordance with the common understanding of evolutionary change and indeed is one result of the evolutionary process. However, such long-term effects (what we call *macroevolution*) can only come about by the accumulation of the many small evolutionary changes (*microevolution*) that unfold every generation. To understand how the process of evolution works, we must study the short-term events. Using such a modern *population genetics* perspective, we have defined evolution as a change in *allele frequency* from one generation to the next. This concept is really very simple. As we have seen, *alleles* are alternative forms of genes that occur at the same locus. For example, the ABO blood type in humans is governed by a single locus on chromosome 9. As such, it is a good example of a *Mendelian* trait in humans. As we have seen in Chapter 4, this locus has three alternative forms (alleles): *A, B,* or *O.*

Allele frequencies are simply the proportions of alleles in a population. If 70 percent of all alleles at the ABO locus are *O,* the frequency of the *O* allele is .70. If *A* and *B* constitute, respectively, 10 percent and 20 percent of alleles at this locus, their frequencies are .10 and .20. In any genetic system, the total of allele frequencies for a locus must equal 1.0 (100 percent).

Evolution, then, is a *change* in these proportions. For example, if the allele frequencies noted above were to shift, over a few generations, to $O = .50$, $A = .30$, and $B = .20$, then we would say that evolution had occurred (*O* had decreased in frequency, *A* had increased, and *B* had stayed the same).

What causes allele frequencies to change in human populations? In the following section, you will find the answer to this question.

Population Genetics

What do we mean by "population"? A **population** is a group of interbreeding individuals. More precisely, a population is the group within which one is most likely to find a mate. As such, a population is marked by a degree of genetic relatedness, and its members share a common **gene pool**.

In theory, this is a straightforward concept. In every generation, the genes (alleles) are mixed by recombination and rejoined through mating. What emerges in the next generation is a direct product of the genes going into the pool, which in turn is a product of who is mating with whom.

In practice, however, describing human populations is difficult. The largest population of *Homo sapiens* that could be described is the entire **species**. All members of a species are *potentially* capable of interbreeding, but are incapable of mating and producing fertile offspring with members of other species. Our species is thus a *genetically closed system*. The problem arises not in describing who potentially can interbreed, but in isolating exactly the pattern of those individuals who are doing so.

Factors that determine mate choice are geographical, ecological, and social. If individuals are isolated on a remote island in the middle of the Pacific, there is not much chance of their finding a mate outside the immediate vicinity. Such **breeding isolates** are fairly easily defined and are a favorite target of microevolutionary studies. Geography plays a dominant role in producing these isolates by rather

The central importance of the concept of a population is discussed in Virtual Lab 2, section I, part A.

Population
Within a species, the community of individuals where mates are usually found.

Gene pool
The total complement of genes shared by reproductive members of a population.

Species
A group of organisms that can interbreed to produce fertile offspring. Members of one species are reproductively isolated from all other species.

Breeding isolates
Populations that are clearly isolated geographically and/or socially from other breeding groups.

strictly determining the range of available mates. But even within these limits, cultural rules strongly influence the choice of partners among those who are potentially available.

Human population segments within the species are defined as groups with relative degrees of **endogamy** (marrying/mating within the group). These are, however, not totally closed systems. Migration often occurs between groups, and individuals may choose mates from distant localities. With the modern advent of rapid transportation, greatly accelerated rates of **exogamy** (marrying/mating outside the group) have emerged.

Most humans today are not so clearly identified as members of particular populations as they would be if they belonged to a breeding isolate. Inhabitants of large cities may appear to be members of a single population, but within the city borders, social, ethnic, and religious boundaries crosscut in a complex fashion to form smaller population segments. In addition to being members of these highly open local population groupings, we are simultaneously members of overlapping gradations of larger populations—the immediate geographical region (a metropolitan area or perhaps an entire state), a section of the country, the whole nation, and ultimately, again, the whole species.

Once specific human populations have been identified, the next step is to ascertain what evolutionary forces, if any, are operating on this group. To determine whether evolution is taking place at a given locus, we measure allele frequencies for specific traits and compare these observed frequencies with a set predicted by a mathematical model: the **Hardy-Weinberg equilibrium** equation. The approach used by physical anthropologists to measure evolution using this model is called *population genetics*. Just how the equation is used is illustrated in Appendix B.

The Hardy-Weinberg formula provides the tool to establish whether allele frequencies in a human population are indeed changing. What factors initiate changes in allele frequencies? There are a number of such factors, including those that

1. Produce new variation (i.e., *mutation*)
2. Redistribute variation through *gene flow*
3. Redistribute variation through *genetic drift*
4. Select "advantageous" allele combinations that promote reproductive success—that is, *natural selection*

Note that factors 1, 2, and 3 constitute the first stage of the evolutionary process, as emphasized by the modern synthesis, while factor 4 is the second stage.

Mutation

In Chapter 3, we defined mutation as a change in DNA that can occur either as a single base substitution or at a larger, chromosomal level. From an evolutionary perspective, mutation is the only way totally *new* variation can be produced. Effects on any one gene should be minor, however, since mutation rates for any given locus are quite low (estimated at about 1 per 10,000 gametes per generation). In fact, because mutation occurs so infrequently at any particular locus, it would rarely have any significant effect on allele frequencies. Certainly, mutation occurs every generation, but unless we sample a huge number of subjects, we are unlikely to detect any noticeable effect.

Endogamy
Mating with others from the same group.

Exogamy
Mating with individuals from other groups.

Hardy-Weinberg equilibrium
The mathematical relationship expressing—under ideal conditions—the predicted distribution of genes in populations; the central theorem of population genetics.

 Virtual Lab 2, section III, part A, provides a virtual exercise on the Hardy-Weinberg equation.

However, because we each have many loci (estimated at about 100,000), we all possess numerous mutations that have accumulated over recent generations. Most of these are not expressed in the phenotype, but are "hidden" as recessive alleles (see Chapter 4 for a discussion of recessive inheritance). An example of such a recessive mutation is the allele for PKU (phenylketonuria). About 1 in 12,000 babies born in the United States carry this allele in homozygous form and thus are affected phenotypically. Without early detection and treatment, this condition leads to severe mental retardation.

Several dominant alleles that produce phenotypic effects are also well known. An example of such a condition is a type of dwarfism called achondroplasia. Individuals with one copy of the responsible mutant allele have abnormally shortened limbs but normal-sized head and trunk. The incidence of achondroplasia among newborns in the United States is about 1 in 10,000. (See Chapter 4 for further examples.)

 Mutation, gene flow, genetic drift, and recombination are discussed in Virtual Lab 2, section III, part A.

Gene Flow

Gene flow is the movement of alleles between populations. The term *migration* is frequently used synonymously with gene flow; however, migration, strictly defined, means movement of people, whereas gene flow refers to the exchange of *genes*— which can occur only if the migrants interbreed. In the last 500 years especially, population movements have reached enormous proportions, and few breeding isolates remain. It should not, however, be assumed that significant population movements did not occur prior to modern times. Our hunting and gathering ancestors probably lived in small groups that were mobile as well as flexible in membership. Early farmers may well have been fairly mobile, moving from area to area as the land wore out. Intensive, highly sedentary agricultural communities came later, but even then, significant migration was still possible. From the Near East, one of the early farming centers, populations spread gradually in a "creeping occupation of Europe, India, and northern and eastern Africa" (Bodmer and Cavalli-Sforza, 1976, p. 563).

An interesting application of how gene flow influences microevolutionary change in modern human populations is seen in the population history of African Americans over the last three centuries. In the United States, African Americans are largely of West African descent, but there has also been considerable influx of alleles from non-African populations. By measuring allele frequencies for specific genetic loci (such as those influencing the Rh blood group), we can estimate the amount of gene flow of non-African alleles being incorporated into an African American gene pool. By using different methods, the percentage of gene flow from one population to another has been estimated, and with strikingly varied results. Data from northern and western U.S. cities (including New York, Detroit, and Oakland) have shown the admixture rate (i.e., the proportion of *non*-African genes in the African American gene pool) at 20 to 25 percent (Cummings, 1997). However, more restricted data from the southern United States (Charleston and rural Georgia) have suggested a lower degree of gene flow (4 to 11 percent). The more consistent of these studies employ new genetic techniques, especially those involving direct DNA comparisons (discussed later in this chapter).

It would be a misconception to conclude that human gene flow can occur only through large-scale movements of groups. In fact, significant alterations in allele frequencies can come about through long-term patterns of mate selection. If exchanges

Gene flow
The exchange of genes between populations (also called migration).

of mates are consistently in one direction over a long period of time, allele frequencies will ultimately be altered. Due to demographic, social, or economic pressures, an individual may choose a mate from outside the immediate vicinity.

Transportation plays an obvious role in determining the manageable geographical distance for finding available mates. When people were limited to walking or using the horse, transportation ranges were typically limited to about a 10-mile radius. With the spread of affordable railway transportation through rural England in the nineteenth century, a dramatic increase in the mean marital distance* of 20 to 30 miles was seen. Today, with even more efficient means of transportation, the potential range has become worldwide. Actual patterns are, however, somewhat more restricted. For example, data from Ann Arbor, Michigan, indicate a mean marital distance of close to 160 miles—not worldwide by any means, but still including a tremendous number of potential marriage partners.

Genetic Drift

Genetic drift is the chance factor in evolution and is tied directly to population size. The term *drift* is used because, as a completely random process, the allele frequencies can change in any direction. A particular kind of drift seen in modern populations is called **founder effect**. Founder effect operates when an unusually small number of individuals contributes genes to the next generation, making for a kind of genetic bottleneck. This phenomenon can occur when a small migrant band of "founders" colonizes a new and separate area away from the parent group. Small founding populations may also be left as remnants when famine, plague, or war ravages a normally larger group. Actually, each generation is the founder of all succeeding generations in any population.

The cases of founder effect producing evolutionary change in human populations are necessarily seen in small groups. For example, an island in the South Atlantic, Tristan da Cunha, has unusually high frequencies of a hereditary eye disorder (retinitis pigmentosa). First settled in 1817 by one Scottish family, this isolated island's indigenous inhabitants include only descendants of this one family and a few other individuals. All in all, only about two dozen founders established this population. A fortuitous opportunity to study the descendants occurred in 1961 when, owing to an imminent volcanic eruption, all 294 residents were evacuated to England. There, extensive medical tests were performed that revealed four individuals with retinitis pigmentosa. The allele frequency for the mutant allele was unusually high in this population, and no doubt, a high proportion of individuals were carriers.

How did this circumstance come about? Apparently, just by chance, one of the initial founders carried the allele and later passed it on to descendants who, with some inbreeding, occasionally produced affected offspring. The fact that so few individuals founded this population allowed the one person who carried the retinitis pigmentosa allele to make a disproportionate contribution to the incidence of this condition in future generations. An important point to keep in mind is that the larger the population, the smaller the effect of drift. Drift can exert influence *only* when the population is relatively small.

Genetic drift has probably played an important role in human evolution, influencing genetic changes in small groups. From studies of recent hunter-

Genetic drift
Evolutionary changes—that is, changes in allele frequencies—produced by random factors. Genetic drift is a result of small population size.

Founder effect
Also called the *Sewall-Wright effect,* a type of genetic drift in which allele frequencies are altered in small populations that are taken from, or are remnants of, larger populations.

*The average distance between husband's and wife's birthplace.

gatherers in Australia, we know that the range of available mates was restricted to within the linguistic tribe, usually consisting of about 500 individuals. In groups of this size, drift can have significant effects, particularly if drought, disease, and so on, should temporarily reduce the population still further.

While drift has been a factor over the long term, the effects have been irregular and nondirectional (for drift is *random* in nature). Certainly, the pace of evolutionary change could have been accelerated if many small populations were isolated and thus subject to drift.

It is important to emphasize that natural selection need not be the inevitable and *only* prime mover of evolutionary change. As we have seen, both gene flow and genetic drift can produce some evolutionary changes by themselves. However, these changes are usually *microevolutionary* ones; that is, they produce changes within species over the short term. To yield the kind of evolutionary changes that ultimately result in entire new groups (e.g., the diversification of the first primates, the appearance of the hominids), natural selection most likely would play the major role. Remember, however, that natural selection does not and cannot operate independently of the other evolutionary factors—mutation, gene flow, and genetic drift. All four factors (sometimes called the "four forces of evolution") work interactively.

Additional insight concerning the relative influences of the different evolutionary factors has emerged in recent studies of the early dispersal of modern *Homo sapiens* (discussed in Chapter 11). New evidence suggests that in the last 100,000 to 200,000 years, our species experienced a genetic bottleneck, which considerably influenced the pattern of genetic variation seen in all human populations today. In this sense, modern humans can be seen as the fairly recent product of a form of genetic drift (founder effect) acting on a somewhat grand scale. Such evolutionary changes could be potentially significant over tens of thousands of years and could cause substantial genetic shifts within species.

Natural Selection

In the long run, the most important factor influencing the course of evolutionary change is natural selection. As you will recall, we have defined natural selection as differential net reproductive success (see p. 35). Controlled observations of laboratory animals or natural populations of quickly reproducing organisms, such as moths (see Chapter 2), have demonstrated how differential reproductive success eventually leads to adaptive shifts within populations.

Human beings are neither quickly reproducing nor amenable to controlled laboratory manipulations. Therefore, unambiguous examples of natural selection in action among contemporary humans are extremely difficult to find.

The best-documented case concerns the *sickle-cell allele,* which is the result of a single amino acid substitution in the hemoglobin molecule. If inherited in homozygous form, this gene causes severe anemia and frequently early death. Even with aggressive medical treatment, life expectancy in the United States today is less than 45 years for victims of the severe recessive disease, sickle-cell anemia. Worldwide, sickle-cell anemia is estimated to cause 100,000 deaths each year.

 Virtual Lab 2, section I, part B, provides an example of how selection operates on variation within populations.

With such obviously harmful effects, it is surprising to find the sickle-cell allele so frequent in some populations (Fig. 12–1). The highest allele frequencies are found in western and central African populations, reaching levels close to 20 percent; values are also moderately high in some Greek and Asiatic Indian populations.

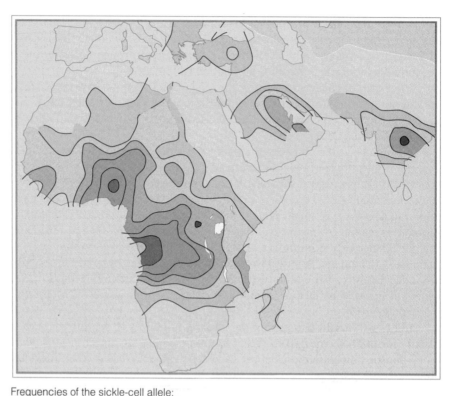

Frequencies of the sickle-cell allele:

Greater than .14

.12–.14

.10–.12

.08–.10

.06–.08

.04–.06

.02–.04

.00–.02

FIGURE 12–1

Map of the sickle-cell allele distribution in the Old World.

Endemically (endemic)
Continuously present in a population. With regard to disease, refers to populations in which there will always be some infected individuals.

How do we explain such a phenomenon? Obviously, the allele originated from a simple mutation, but why did it increase in frequency?

The answer lies in yet another kind of disease, one that exerts enormous selective pressure. In those areas of the world where the sickle-cell allele is found in highest frequency, *malaria* is also found (Fig. 12–2). Caused by a single-celled parasite, this debilitating infectious disease is transmitted to humans by mosquitoes. In areas that are **endemically** infected, many individuals suffer sharply lower reproductive success, owing to high infant mortality rates or to lowered vitality as adults.

Such a geographical correlation between malarial incidence and distribution of the sickle-cell allele is indirect evidence of a biological correlation. Further confirmation was provided by British biologist A. C. Allison in the 1950s. Volunteers from the Luo tribe of eastern Africa with known genotypes were injected with the malarial parasite. The ethics concerning human subjects would preclude such experimentation today; even when the original study was conducted, its justification was questionable. A short time following infection, results showed that heterozygous carriers of the sickle-cell allele were much more resistant to malarial infection than the homozygous "normals." Apparently, carriers resist infection because their red blood cells provide a less conducive environment for the malarial parasite to reproduce itself. As a result, the parasite often dies before widely

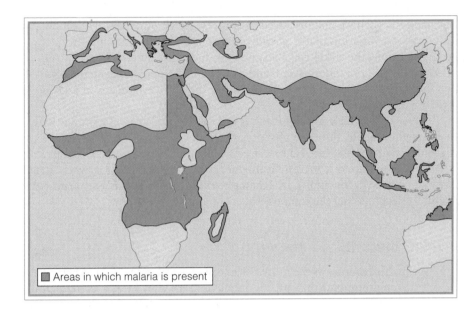

FIGURE 12–2
Malaria distribution in the Old World.

infecting the body of a carrier. But for the homozygous "normals," the infection usually persists.

A genetic trait (such as sickle-cell trait) that provides a reproductive advantage in certain environments is a clear example of natural selection in action among human populations. The precise evolutionary mechanism in the sickle-cell example is termed a **balanced polymorphism**.

A genetic trait is called a **polymorphism** "when two or more alleles at a given genetic locus occur with appreciable frequencies in a population" (Bodmer and Cavalli-Sforza, 1976, p. 308). How much is "appreciable" is a fairly arbitrary judgment, but it is usually placed at 1 percent. In other words, if a population is sampled for a particular trait, and frequencies for more than one allele are higher than 1 percent, the trait (more precisely, the locus that governs the trait) is polymorphic.

The limit of 1 percent is an attempt by population geneticists to control for mutation effects, which normally add new alleles at rates far below our 1 percent level. So when an allele like that for the sickle-cell trait is found in a population in frequencies approaching 10 percent, this is clearly polymorphic. It is higher than can be accounted for by mutation *alone* and thus demands a fuller evolutionary explanation. In this case, the additional mechanism is natural selection.

This brings us back to the other part of the term *balanced polymorphism.* By "balanced," we are referring to the interaction of selective pressures operating in a malarial environment. Some individuals (mainly homozygous normals) will be removed by the infectious disease malaria, and some (homozygous recessives) will die of the inherited disease sickle-cell anemia. Those with the highest reproductive success are the heterozygous carriers. But what alleles do they carry? Clearly, they are passing *both* the "normal" allele as well as the sickle-cell allele to offspring, thus maintaining both alleles at fairly high frequencies (*above* the minimum level for polymorphism). Since one allele in this population will not significantly increase in frequency over the other allele, this situation will reach a balance and persist, at least as long as malaria continues to be a selective factor.

Because students frequently misunderstand how natural selection operates, it is useful to reiterate what natural selection does and does not do. As we explained

Balanced polymorphism
The maintenance of two or more alleles in a population due to the selective advantage of the heterozygote.

Polymorphism
A genetic trait (the locus governing the trait) with more than one allele in appreciable frequency (i.e., greater than 1 percent).

 The relationship between malaria and the sickle-cell trait is provided in a virtual exercise in Virtual Lab 2, section III, part B.

in Chapter 2 when we first discussed the process (see p. 36), natural selection can only work on variation that is *already present* in a population. Thus, in the preceding example, the sickle-cell allele was produced by mutation (*not* by natural selection). This is a random event, and in fact, many populations might not have any individuals with this mutation. Whether the allele ever arises in a group is strictly a matter of *chance*.

The way natural selection functions is to deal with available variation, and in different environments, different phenotypes will be "selected" (i.e., they will have higher reproductive success). Natural selection did not "cause" the sickle-cell allele to appear; it merely acted to increase its frequency in some populations (where it had already appeared by mutation). This example reinforces the evolutionary axiom that "natural selection is not the composer of evolution, it is the editor."

Human Biocultural Evolution

We have defined culture as the human strategy of adaptation. Human beings live in cultural environments that are continually modified by human activity; thus, evolutionary processes are understandable only within this *cultural* context. You will recall that natural selection pressures operate within specific environmental settings. For humans and many of our hominid ancestors, this means an environment dominated by culture. For example, the sickle-cell allele has not always been an important genetic factor in human populations. In fact, human cultural modification of the environment apparently provided the initial stimulus. Before the development of agriculture, humans rarely, if ever, lived close to mosquito breeding areas. With the development and spread to Africa of **slash-and-burn agriculture,** perhaps in just the last 2,000 years, penetration and clearing of tropical rain forests occurred. As a result of deforestation, open, stagnant pools provided prime mosquito breeding areas in close proximity to human settlements.

Malaria, for the first time, now struck human populations with its full impact, and as a selective force it was powerful indeed. No doubt, humans attempted to adjust culturally to these circumstances, and numerous biological adaptations also probably came into play. The sickle-cell trait is one of these biological (genetic) adaptations. However, there is a definite cost involved with such an adaptation. Carriers have increased resistance to malaria and presumably higher reproductive success, but some of their offspring may be lost through the genetic disease sickle-cell anemia. So there is a counterbalancing of selective forces with an advantage for carriers *only* in malarial environments. The genetic patterns of recessive traits such as sickle-cell anemia are discussed in Chapter 4.

Following World War II, extensive DDT spraying by the World Health Organization began systematically to wipe out mosquito breeding areas in the tropics. As would be expected, malaria decreased sharply, and also as would be expected, the frequency of the sickle-cell allele also seemed on the decline. The intertwined story of human cultural practices, mosquitoes, malarial parasites, and the sickle-cell allele is still not finished. Forty years of DDT spraying killed many mosquitoes, but natural selection is also acting on these insect populations. Because of the tremendous amount of genetic diversity among insects, as well as their short generation span, several DDT-resistant strains have arisen and spread in the last few years (Fig. 12–3). Accordingly, malaria is again on the rise, with several hundred thousand new cases reported in India, Africa, and Central America.

Slash-and-burn agriculture
A traditional land-clearing practice whereby trees and vegetation are cut and burned. In many areas, fields were abandoned after a few years and clearing occurred elsewhere.

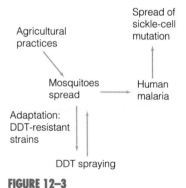

FIGURE 12–3

Evolutionary interactions affecting the frequency of the sickle-cell allele.

Two other traits that may also be influenced by the selective agent of malaria are G-6-PD deficiency* and the thalassemias (results of several different mutations that block hemoglobin production). However, in both these cases, evidence of natural selection is not as strong as with the sickle-cell allele. The primary evidence suggesting a link with malaria is the geographical concordance of increased frequency of these traits with areas (especially around the Mediterranean) that historically have had a high incidence of malarial infection.

Another example of human biocultural evolution concerns the ability to digest milk. In all human populations, infants and young children can digest milk, an obvious necessity for any young mammal. A major ingredient of milk is the sugar *lactose*, which is broken down by humans and other mammals by the enzyme *lactase*. In most mammals, including humans, the gene coding for lactase production "switches off" by adolescence. If too much milk is then ingested, it ferments in the large intestine, leading to diarrhea and severe gastrointestinal upset. Among many African and Asian populations—a majority of humankind today—most adults are intolerant of milk (Table 12–1).

Recent evidence has suggested a simple dominant mode of inheritance for **lactose intolerance.** The environment also plays a role in expression of the trait—that is, whether a person will be lactose-intolerant—since intestinal bacteria can somewhat buffer the adverse effects. Because these bacteria will increase with previous exposure, some tolerance can be acquired, even in individuals who genetically have become lactase-deficient.

Why do we see variation in lactose tolerance among human populations? Throughout most of hominid evolution, no milk was available after weaning. Perhaps, in such circumstances, continued action of an unnecessary enzyme might inhibit digestion of other foods. Therefore, there *may* be a selective advantage for the gene coding for lactase production to switch off. The question can then be asked: Why can some adults (the majority in some populations) tolerate milk? The distribution of lactose-tolerant populations is very interesting, revealing the probable influence of cultural factors on this trait.

European groups, who are generally lactose-tolerant, are partially descended from groups of the Middle East. Often economically dependent on pastoralism, these groups raised cows and/or goats and no doubt drank considerable quantities of milk. In such a cultural environment, strong selection pressures would act to shift allele frequencies in the direction of more lactose tolerance. Modern European descendants of these populations apparently retain this ancient ability.

Even more informative is the distribution of lactose tolerance in Africa. For example, groups such as the Fulani and Tutsi, who have been pastoralists probably for thousands of years, have much higher rates of lactose tolerance than nonpastoralists.

As we have seen, the geographical distribution of lactose tolerance is related to a history of cultural dependence on milk products. There are, however, some populations that rely on dairying but are not characterized by high rates of lactose tolerance. It has been suggested that such populations traditionally have consumed their milk produce as cheese and other derivatives in which the lactose has been broken down by bacterial action (Durham, 1981).

TABLE 12–1 Frequencies of Lactose Intolerance

Population Group	Percent
U.S. whites	2–19
Finnish	18
Swiss	12
Swedish	4
U.S. blacks	70–77
Ibos	99
Bantu	90
Fulani	22
Thais	99
Asian Americans	95–100
Native Australians	85

Source: Lerner and Libby, 1976, p. 327.

Lactose intolerance
The inability to digest fresh milk products; caused by the discontinued production of lactase, the enzyme that breaks down lactose (milk sugar).

---

*G-6 PD is an abbreviation for the enzyme glucose-6-phosphate dehydrogenase. Individuals affected with G-6-PD deficiency are homozygous for the recessive allele and do not produce the enzyme.

The interaction of human cultural environments and changes in lactose tolerance among human populations is another example of biocultural evolution. In the last few thousand years, cultural factors have influenced specific evolutionary changes in human groups. Such cultural factors have probably influenced the course of human evolution for at least 3 million years, and today they are of paramount importance.

Human Polymorphisms

Differences in hemoglobin and the production of the enzyme lactase are both *Mendelian* traits. That is, the phenotype of each of these traits can unambiguously be linked to the action of a single locus. These simple genetic mechanisms are much more straightforward than the polygenic traits usually associated with studies of human **racial** variation (discussed in Chapter 13). In fact, the difficulty in tracing the genetic influence on such characteristics as skin color or face shape has led some human biologists to avoid investigations of such polygenic traits. Although physical anthropologists, by tradition, have been keenly interested in explaining such variation, we have seen a trend toward greater concentration on those traits with a clearly demonstrated genetic mechanism (i.e., Mendelian characteristics).

Racial
In biology, pertaining to populations of a species that differ from other populations of the same species with regard to some aspects of outwardly expressed phenotype. Such phenotypic variation within a species is usually associated with differences in geographical location.

Simple Polymorphisms

Of greatest use in contemporary studies of human variation are those traits that can be used to document genetic differences among various populations. Such genetic traits are what we have defined as polymorphisms, which, as noted, must have more than one allele in appreciable frequency. To explain this pattern of variation beyond mutation, some *additional* evolutionary factor (gene flow, drift, natural selection) must also have been at work.

Clearly, then, the understanding of human genetic polymorphisms demands evolutionary explanations. As students of human evolution, physical anthropologists use these polymorphisms as their principal tool to understand the dynamics of evolution in modern populations. Moreover, by utilizing these simple polymorphisms and comparing allele frequencies in different populations, we can begin to reconstruct the evolutionary events that link human populations with one another.

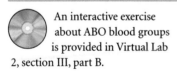
An interactive exercise about ABO blood groups is provided in Virtual Lab 2, section III, part B.

ABO   In addition to some components of hemoglobin, there are many other polymorphisms known in human blood. Because samples can easily be obtained and transported, blood has long been a favorite tissue for studying human polymorphisms. Consequently, we know a great deal regarding genetic traits found in red blood cells, white blood cells, and blood serum. The first of these to be described, and certainly the best known, is the ABO blood group system. As we have seen, ABO is expressed phenotypically in individuals as molecules called antigens on the surface of red blood cells. A person's blood group (i.e., which antigens are on the red blood cells) is directly determined by his or her genotype at the ABO locus. The complications that result from mismatched blood transfusions are the result of antigen-antibody reactions. The body has a finely tuned capacity to recognize foreign antigens and to produce antibodies to deactivate them. Such an immune response is normally beneficial (indeed, indispensable), as it allows the body to fight infections—especially those caused by viruses or bacteria.

Usually, antibodies are produced only after foreign antigens have been introduced and recognized. However, in the case of ABO, antibodies are already present in the blood serum at birth, having been stimulated in fetal life. (Some of the relationships within the ABO system are shown in Table 4–2, p. 69.)

The ABO system is interesting from an anthropological perspective because the frequencies of the three alleles *(A, B, O)* vary tremendously among human populations. In most groups, *A* and *B* are only rarely found in frequencies greater than 50 percent; usually, frequencies for these two alleles are considerably below this figure (Fig. 12–4). Most human groups, however, are polymorphic for all three alleles. Occasionally, as in native South American Indians, frequencies of *O* reach 100 percent, and this allele is said to be "fixed" in this population. Indeed, in most native New World populations, the frequency of *O* is at least 80 percent and is usually considerably higher. Unusually high frequencies of *O* are also found in northern Australia, and some islands off the Australian coast show frequencies exceeding 90 percent. Since these figures are higher than presumably closely related mainland populations, genetic drift (founder effect) is probably the evolutionary factor responsible.

HLA Another important polymorphic system is found on the surface of certain white blood cells. Called HLA, this genetic system influences histocompatibility (i.e., tissue type) and is the reason that organ transplants are usually rejected if not properly matched. Genetically, the HLA system is exceedingly complex, and researchers are still discovering more details about it. There are four major and

Virtual Lab 2, section III, part A, provides a discussion of the critical factors underlying population genetics including genetic drift.

FIGURE 12–4

Distribution of the *B* allele in the indigenous populations of the world. (After Mourant et al., 1976.)

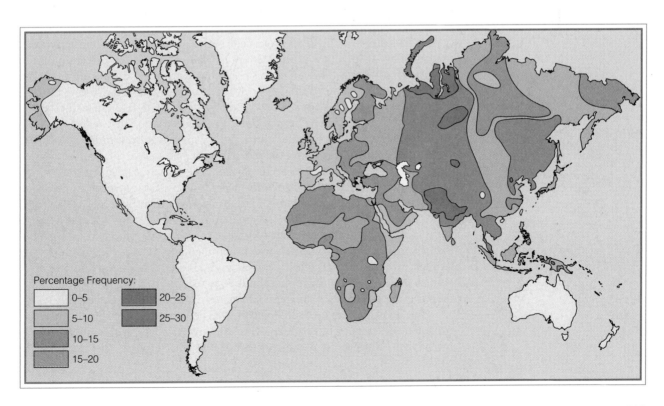

Percentage Frequency:

0–5	20–25
5–10	25–30
10–15	
15–20	

several associated loci on chromosome 6 that make up the HLA system. Taken together, there are already well over 100 antigens known within the system, with a potential of at least 30 million different genotypes (Williams, 1985; Bodmer, 1995). By far, this is the most polymorphic of any known human genetic system.

Since the system has only fairly recently been discovered, the geographical distribution of many of the alleles is still not well known. Some interesting patterns, however, are apparent. For example, Lapps, Sardinians, and Basques show differences in frequencies of some HLA alleles from those seen in other European populations, paralleling evidence from ABO. In addition, many areas of New Guinea and Australia are quite divergent, possibly resulting from past effects of genetic drift. It is imperative, however, that care be taken in postulating genetic relatedness on the basis of very restricted polymorphic data; otherwise, such ridiculous links as some proposed for HLA (e.g., Tibetans with native Australians; Inuit with some New Guineans) would confound our attempts to understand human microevolution (Livingstone, 1980). Because HLA is involved in the superfine detection of foreign antigens, selection relative to infectious disease, especially viruses, may also play a significant role in the distribution (and past evolution) of HLA alleles. The further understanding of these processes promises to be among the most exciting frontiers of medical and evolutionary biology.

Miscellaneous Polymorphisms   An interesting genetically controlled variation in human populations was discovered by accident in 1931. When the artificially synthesized chemical phenylthiocarbamide (PTC) was dropped in a laboratory, some researchers were able to smell it, while others could not. It was later established that there is a dichotomy among humans regarding those who can versus those who cannot taste PTC. Although tasters vary considerably in sensitivity, most report a very bitter, unpleasant sensation. The pattern of inheritance follows a Mendelian model, with the inability to taste behaving as a simple recessive. In most populations, a majority of individuals are tasters, but the frequency of nontasters varies dramatically—from as low as 5 percent in Africa to as high as 40 percent in India.

The evolutionary function of this polymorphism is not known, although the fact that it is also seen in some other primates argues that it has a long history. Obviously, evolution has not acted to produce discrimination for an artificial substance recently concocted by humans. The observed variation *may* reflect selection for taste discrimination of other, more significant substances. Indeed, taste discrimination, which may allow the avoidance of many toxic plants (which frequently are bitter), may well be an important evolutionary consideration.

Another puzzling human polymorphism is the variability seen in earwax, or cerumen. Earwax is found in human groups in two basic varieties: (1) yellow and sticky with a good deal of lipids (fats and fatlike substances) and (2) gray and dry with fewer lipids. Cerumen variation appears also to be inherited as a simple Mendelian trait with two alleles (sticky is dominant; dry is recessive). Interestingly, frequencies of the two varieties of earwax vary considerably among human populations. In European populations, about 90 percent of individuals typically have the sticky variety, while in northern China, only about 4 percent are of this type.

How do we explain these differences? Even between very large groups there are consistent differences in cerumen type, arguing that drift is an unlikely causal mechanism. However, it is difficult to imagine what kind of selective pressure would act directly on earwax. Perhaps, as previously suggested for PTC discrimination, earwax variation is an incidental expression of a gene controlling something more adaptively significant. Suggestions along these lines have pointed to the relation of cerumen to other body secretions, especially those affecting odor. Certainly, other mammals, including nonhuman primates, pay considerable attention to smell stimuli. Although the sense of smell is not as well developed in humans as in other mammals, humans still process and utilize olfactory (smell) stimuli. Thus, it is not impossible that during the course of human evolution, genes affecting bodily secretions (including earwax) came under selective influence.

Polymorphisms at the DNA Level

Geneticists and physical anthropologists over the last 50 years have used somewhat indirect techniques to study human polymorphisms, observing some *phenotypic* product. For example, the ABO antigens are phenotypic products (quite immediate ones) of the DNA locus coding for them. In the last decade, with the revolution in DNA technology, much more *direct* means have become available by which to study human genetic variation.

mtDNA   In addition to the DNA found in the nucleus (nuclear DNA), human (and other eukaryotic) cells contain another kind of DNA. This DNA, found in the cytoplasm, is contained within the organelles called mitochondria and is thus called **mitochondrial DNA (mtDNA)**. While the nuclear DNA is extraordinarily long, containing an estimated 3 billion nucleotides, the mtDNA is much shorter, containing only 16,500 nucleotides. Using special enzymes (restriction enzymes, derived from bacteria) that cut the DNA in specific locations, researchers have been able to sequence much of the mtDNA **genome**. Thus, it has become possible to compare variation among individuals and among populations. Ongoing work is establishing that some mtDNA regions are more variable than others but that for the *total* mtDNA genome, variation within *Homo sapiens* is apparently much less pronounced than in other species (e.g., chimpanzees). The possible evolutionary reasons for this surprising finding might relate to a quite recent origin of all modern *Homo sapiens* from a restricted ancestral population base (thus producing, as noted earlier, genetic drift/founder effect; see Chapter 11).

Mitochondrial DNA (mtDNA)
DNA found in the mitochondria (structures found within the cytoplasm of the cell) and inherited through the maternal line.

Genome
The full genetic complement of an individual (or of a species). In humans, it is estimated that each individual possesses approximately 3 billion nucleotides in his or her nuclear DNA.

Nuclear DNA   As with mtDNA analysis, the use of restriction enzymes has permitted much greater precision in direct study of the DNA contained within human chromosomes, that is, nuclear DNA. This work has been greatly facilitated as part of the continuing intense research of the *Human Genome Project* (see Chapter 4). Untangling the entire human genetic complement is obviously an enormous undertaking, but to date, considerable insight has been gained regarding human variation *directly at the DNA level*. By cutting the DNA of different individuals and comparing the results, researchers have observed great variation in the length of the DNA fragments at numerous DNA sites. Accordingly, these genetic differences (caused by variable DNA sequences) are referred to as **restriction fragment length polymorphisms (RFLPs)**. In addition to providing direct evidence of human genetic variation, the RFLPs are also of vital importance in mapping other loci (e.g., that for cystic fibrosis) to specific regions of specific chromosomes.

Restriction Fragment Length Polymorphisms (RFLPs)
Variation among individuals in the length of DNA fragments produced by enzymes that break the DNA at specific sites.

Patterns of Human Population Diversity

A fairly simple approach to help understand human genetic diversity is to look at the pattern of allele frequencies over space for *one* polymorphic trait at a time. Here, allele frequencies are shown geographically on a map in what is called a **cline**. Although we did not label it as such in our previous discussion, the distribution of the *B* allele in Eurasia (see Fig. 12–4) is a good example of a cline.

Utilizing single traits can be informative regarding potential influences of natural selection or gene flow, but this approach has limitations when we try to sort out population relationships. As noted in our discussion of the HLA polymorphisms, single traits *by themselves* often can yield confusing interpretations regarding likely population relationships. What is needed, then, is a method to analyze a larger, more consistent body of data—that is, to look at several traits simultaneously. Such a *multivariate* approach makes ready use of digital computers. (In the next chapter, we will discuss the more traditional approach using polygenic characteristics and some of the controversies surrounding "racial" classification.)

An excellent example of the contemporary multivariate approach to human diversity was undertaken by Harvard population geneticist R. D. Lewontin (1972), and his results are most informative. Lewontin calculated population differences in allele frequency for 17 polymorphic traits. In his analysis, Lewontin immediately faced a dilemma: Which groups (populations) should he contrast and how should they be weighted? That is, should larger population segments, such as Arabs, carry the same weight in the analysis as small populations, such as the one from the island Tristan da Cunha? After considerable deliberation, Lewontin decided to break down his sample into seven geographical areas, and he included several equally weighted population samples within each (Table 12–2). He then calculated how much of the total genetic variability within our species could be accounted for by these population subdivisions.

The results are surprising. Only 6.3 percent of the total genetic variation is explained by differences among major "races" (Lewontin's seven geographical units). In other words, close to 94 percent of human genetic diversity occurs *within* these very large groups. The larger population subdivisions within the geographical clusters (e.g., within Caucasians: Arabs, Basques, Welsh) account for another 8.3 percent. Thus, geographical and local "races" together account for just 15 percent of all human genetic variation, leaving the remaining 85 percent unaccounted for.

Cline
A gradient of genotypes (usually measured as allele frequencies) over geographical space; more exactly, the depiction of allele distribution produced by connecting points of equal frequency (as on a temperature map).

TABLE 12–2 Population Groupings Used by Lewontin in Population Genetics Study (1972)

Geographical Group	Examples of Populations Included
Caucasians	Arabs, Armenians, Tristan da Cunhans
Black Africans	Bantu, San, U.S. blacks
Asians	Ainu, Chinese, Turks
South Asians	Andamanese, Tamils
Amerinds	Aleuts, Navaho, Yanomama
Oceanians	Easter Islanders, "Micronesians"
Australians	All treated as a single group

The vast majority of genetic differences among human beings is explicable in terms of differences from one village to another, one family to another, and, to a very significant degree, one person to another—even within the same family. Of course, when you recall the high degree of genetic polymorphism (discussed in this chapter) combined with the vast number of combinations resulting from recombination during meiosis (discussed in Chapter 3), all this individual variation should not be that surprising.

Our visual perceptions superficially suggest to us that race does exist. But the visible phenotypic traits most frequently used to make racial distinctions (skin color, hair form, nose shape, etc.) may very well produce a highly biased sample, not giving an accurate picture of the actual pattern of *genetic variation*. The simple polymorphic traits discussed in this chapter (many of the same used by Lewontin) are a more objective basis for accurate biological comparisons of human groups, and they indicate that the traditional concept of race is very limited. Indeed, Lewontin concludes his analysis with a ringing condemnation of traditional studies: "Human racial classification is of no social value and is positively destructive of social and human relations. Since such racial classification is now seen to be of virtually no genetic or taxonomic significance either, no justification can be offered for its continuance" (Lewontin, 1972, p. 397).

If one feels compelled to continue to classify humankind into large geographical segments, population genetics offers some aid in isolating consistent patterns of genetic variation. Following and expanding on the approach used by Lewontin, population geneticist L. L. Cavalli-Sforza, of Stanford University, and colleagues evaluated 44 different polymorphic traits ascertained in 42 different human sample populations. From the results, these researchers constructed a "tree" (technically called a dendrogram) depicting the relationships of these samples as part of larger populations (Cavalli-Sforza et al., 1988) (Fig. 12–5). Analysis of mitochondrial DNA has produced similar results, especially showing greater genetic diversity among African populations than among other groups (Stoneking, 1993). Because mtDNA is passed solely through the maternal line (and thus does not undergo recombination), it has certain advantages in reconstructing population relationships. Nevertheless, as a single genetic component, it acts like one large locus; thus, mtDNA results must be supplemented by other genetic data.

Comparative data from nuclear DNA studies (RFLPs) in conjunction with the studies discussed here are thus potentially illuminating. Initial analysis comparing 80 RFLPs in eight different groups (Mountain et al., 1993) again produced patterns quite similar to those established for the traditional polymorphisms and for mtDNA. However, another recent large-scale study (Jia and Chakraborty, 1993) of DNA markers among 59 different groups (and including about 12,000 individuals) found the vast majority of variation (up to 98.5 percent) occurring *within* populations at the *individual* level. These latest data dramatize even further the results obtained by Lewontin, leading one geneticist to conclude, "These results indicate that individual variation in DNA profiles overwhelm any interpopulational differences, no matter how the populations are ethnically or racially classified" (Cummings, 1994, p. 500). And while not quite as overwhelming, *all* the genetically based studies cited here support Lewontin's initial results, strongly indicating that the great majority of human variation does occur within human populations—not between them. How, then, do these genetic data compare and articulate with the traditional concept of race? We turn to this topic in the next chapter.

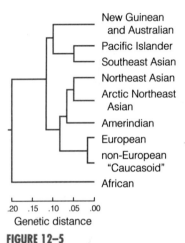

.20   .15   .10   .05   .00
Genetic distance

FIGURE 12–5

Genetic tree (dendrogram) showing population relationships. This dendrogram was constructed by population geneticists (Cavalli-Sforza et al., 1988) using 44 polymorphic traits.

SUMMARY

In this chapter, we have discussed human variation from an evolutionary perspective. Modern evolutionary theory views evolutionary change as a two-stage process in what has come to be known as the modern synthesis. In this theory, the factors of mutation, gene flow, and genetic drift, acting in concert with natural selection, come together to produce evolutionary change.

We have focused on the contemporary trend to describe simple genetic polymorphisms that can be measured for allele frequencies as well as emphasizing genetic data obtained directly from analysis of mitochondrial and nuclear DNA. Data on such polymorphic traits can then be used to understand aspects of human microevolution. For humans, of course, culture also plays a crucial evolutionary role, and the sickle-cell trait and lactose intolerance are thus discussed from an explicit biocultural perspective.

Finally, data derived from population genetics analysis of genetic polymorphisms and DNA variation are employed to measure human population diversity. From such studies, continued classification of the world's peoples into large population groups (analogous to race) is shown to be of limited utility, since the vast majority of genetic variation in *Homo sapiens* occurs between individuals.

QUESTIONS FOR REVIEW

1. How is a population defined? Discuss why, in human groups, defining particular populations can be very difficult.
2. What are the two stages of the evolutionary process as postulated by the modern synthesis?
3. What role does variation play in natural selection?
4. Give a concise *genetic* definition of evolution. Discuss an example in human populations.
5. What is meant by gene flow? Discuss an example derived from human population studies.
6. How has the sickle-cell allele come to be common in some parts of the world? Why is it thought to be a good example of natural selection?
7. What biocultural interactions have occurred that help explain the distribution of lactose intolerance?
8. Discuss how genetic drift may have influenced the geographical distribution of the *A, B,* and *O* alleles.
9. Discuss how population genetics data can be used to assess the genetic diversity among different populations. How well do the varied data from simple polymorphisms, mtDNA, and nuclear DNA agree with one another?

SUGGESTED FURTHER READINGS

Bodmer, W. F., and L. L. Cavalli-Sforza. 1976. *Genetics, Evolution and Man.* San Francisco: Freeman.

Cummings, Michael. 2000. *Human Heredity: Principles and Issues.* 5th ed. Pacific Grove: Brooks/Cole.

Durham, W. 1991. *Coevolution: Genes, Culture and Human Diversity.* Stanford: Stanford University Press.

Lewontin, R. 1974. *The Genetic Basis of Evolutionary Change.* New York: Columbia University Press.

MULTIMEDIA RESOURCES

🌐 Wadsworth Anthropology Resource Center

http://anthropology.wadsworth.com

Visit Anthropology Online to obtain current updates in the field, surfing tips, career information, and more. In addition, enrich your study efforts with text-specific study aids arranged by chapter.

InfoTrac College Edition

http://www.infotrac-college.com/wadsworth

1. On InfoTrac College Edition, search for human population genetics. What does this search find? Choose one article and report on the gene(s) studied and the distribution of that gene in the population investigated. Is an explanation offered for the distribution seen?

2. Just as you searched the Internet at large for information regarding the sickle-cell trait, research this trait on InfoTrac College Edition. Go especially to the subdivision of the sickle-cell subject, *genetic aspects.* Were you able to learn yet more about the trait?

3. A subject search for *gene frequencies* should produce several references to articles that deal with the genetic structure of various populations. Read at least one article and make a list of historic, geographic, and cultural factors that have been proposed to explain genetic differences between large populations and/or the subgroups within them. You might want to focus on those articles from the journal *Human Biology.*

🌐 Internet Exercises

1. Natural selection and genetic drift can both change the frequencies of different alleles in a population over a short period of time. This site, designed at the University of Tennessee at Martin, **http://fmc.utm.edu/~rirwin/NatSelMod Intro.htm,** allows you to experiment with evolutionary mechanisms. Try this exercise with each of the different animals offered. Does evolution proceed differently with the different animals?

2. Visit Online Mendelian Inheritance in Man (OMIM—**http://www3.ncbi.nlm .nih.gov/Omim/**) and search for one of the Mendelian traits discussed in Chapter 12, such as sickle-cell anemia, thalassemia, G-6-PD, or lactase deficiency (lactose intolerance). Read part of the discussion and note how complicated the genetic effects of the relevant alleles are. Make a list of facts you learned from this site.

CHAPTER
13

Human Variation and Adaptation

CONTENTS

Introduction

In Chapters 3 and 4, we saw how physical characteristics are influenced by the DNA in our cells. Furthermore, we discussed how individuals inherit genes from parents and how variations in genes (alleles) can produce different expressions of phenotypic traits. In Chapter 12, we emphasized the study of Mendelian traits in our discussion of evolutionary factors in human populations.

In this chapter, our focus shifts to polygenic traits, or traits that express continuous variation. In particular, we examine how these traits have been used as a basis for traditional racial classification, and we look at some of the issues that currently surround the topic of race in physical anthropology.

Following the discussion of historical attempts at racial classification, we look at more recent explanations of certain polygenic traits; but instead of emphasizing their utility as "racial markers," we focus on their adaptive value in specific environmental contexts. We also examine how populations and individuals differ in their adaptive responses to such environmental factors as heat, cold, and high altitude. Finally, we consider the role of infectious disease in human evolution and adaptation.

Historical Views of Human Variation

The first step toward human understanding of natural phenomena is the ordering of variation into categories that can then be named, discussed, and perhaps studied. Historically, when different groups of people came into contact with one another, they offered explanations for the phenotypic variations they saw. Because skin color was so noticeable, it was one of the more frequently explained traits, and most systems of racial classification were based on it.

As early as 1350 B.C., the ancient Egyptians had classified humans on the basis of skin color: red for Egyptian, yellow for people to the east, white for those to the north, and black for Africans from the south (Gossett, 1963, p. 4). In the sixteenth century, after the discovery of the New World, Europe embarked on a period of intense exploration and colonization in both the New and Old Worlds. Resulting from this contact was an increased awareness of human diversity.

As you learned in Chapter 2, the discovery of the New World was of major importance in altering the views of Europeans who had perceived the world as static and nonchanging. One of the most influential discoveries of the early European explorers was that the Americas were inhabited by people, some of whom were dark-skinned (compared to most Europeans). Furthermore, these people were not Christian and, because of this and numerous other cultural differences, they were not considered "civilized" by Europeans. At first, Native Americans were thought to be Asian, and since Columbus believed that he had discovered a new route to India, he called them "Indians." This term was later applied to indigenous, dark-skinned populations of Australia as well.

By the late eighteenth century, Europeans and European Americans were asking questions that challenged traditional Christian beliefs. They wanted to know if other groups belonged to the same species as themselves; that is, were Native Americans and other indigenous peoples indeed human? Were they descendants of Adam and Eve, or had there been separate creations of non-Europeans? If the latter were true, then Native Americans had to represent different species, or else the Genesis account of creation could not be taken literally.

Monogenism
The theory that all human races were descended from one pair (Adam and Eve), but they differed from one another because they occupied different habitats. This concept was an attempt to explain phenotypic variation between populations, but did not imply evolutionary change.

Polygenism
A theory, opposed to monogenism, that stated that human races were not all descended from Adam and Eve. Instead, there had been several original human pairs, each giving rise to a different group. Thus, human races were considered to be separate species.

Plasticity
The capacity to change; in a physiological context, the ability of systems or organisms to make alterations in order to respond to differing conditions.

Two schools of thought, known as **monogenism** and **polygenism**, devised responses. In the monogenist view, all humans were descended from a single, original pair (Adam and Eve). Insisting on the **plasticity** of human structure, monogenists contended that local environmental conditions, such as climate and terrain, could modify the original form, resulting in observable phenotypic differences between populations. Monogenist views were initially attractive to many because they did not conflict with the Genesis version of creation.

The polygenist view, on the other hand, argued that all populations did not descend from a single, original pair, but from a number of pairs. Also, polygenists saw such a wide gap in the physical, mental, and moral attributes between themselves and other peoples that they were sure that outsiders belonged to different species. Furthermore, polygenists did not accept the monogenist notion of plasticity of physical traits, and they rejected the proposition that climate and environment were modifying influences.

Throughout the eighteenth and nineteenth centuries, European and American scientists concentrated primarily on describing and classifying the biological variation in humans as well as in nonhuman species. The first scientific attempt to describe the newly discovered variation between human populations was Linnaeus' taxonomic classification, which placed humans into four separate categories (Linnaeus, 1758) (Table 13–1). Linnaeus assigned behavioral and intellectual qualities to each group, with the least complimentary descriptions going to African blacks. This ranking was typical of the period and reflected the almost universal European view that Europeans were superior to all other peoples.

TABLE 13–1   Racial Classification Schemes

Linnaeus, 1758	Stanley M. Garn, 1965
Homo europaeus *Homo afer* (Africans) *Homo asiaticus* *Homo americanus* (Native Americans)	GEOGRAPHICAL RACES: "a collection of race populations, separated from other such collections by major geographical barriers."

Linnaeus, 1758

Homo europaeus
Homo afer (Africans)
Homo asiaticus
Homo americanus (Native Americans)

Blumenbach, 1781

Caucasoid   Ethiopian
Mongoloid   American
Malay

E. A. Hooton, 1926

PRIMARY RACE

White   Mongoloid
  Mediterranean   Classic Mongoloid
  Ainu   Arctic Mongoloid
  Keltic   Malay-Mongoloid
  Nordic   Indonesian
  Alpine
  East Baltic
Negroid
  African Negro
  Nilotic Negro
  Negrito

Stanley M. Garn, 1965

GEOGRAPHICAL RACES: "a collection of race populations, separated from other such collections by major geographical barriers."

Amerindian	Melanesian-Papuan	Indian
Polynesian	Australian	European
Micronesian	Asiatic	African

LOCAL RACE: "a breeding population adapted to local selection pressures and maintained by either natural or social barriers to gene interchange."

These are some examples of local races; there are many others:

Northwest European	East African	North Chinese
Northeast European	Bantu	Extreme Mongoloid
Alpine	Tibetan	Hindu
Mediterranean		

MICRORACES: Not well defined but apparently refers to neighborhoods within a city or a city itself, since "marriage or mating is a mathematical function of distance. With millions of potential mates, the male ordinarily chooses one near at hand."

Johann Friedrich Blumenbach (1752–1840), a German anatomist, classified humans into five races (see Table 13–1). Although Blumenbach's categories came to be described simply as white, yellow, red, black, and brown, he also used criteria other than skin color. Moreover, Blumenbach emphasized that racial categories based on skin color were arbitrary and that many traits, including skin color, were not discrete phenomena. Blumenbach pointed out that to attempt to classify all humans using such a system would be to omit completely all those who did not neatly fall into a specific category. Furthermore, it was recognized by Blumenbach and others that traits such as skin color showed overlapping expression between groups. At the time, it was thought that racial taxonomies should be based on characteristics unique to particular groups and uniformly expressed within them. Some scientists, taking the polygenist view, began attempting to identify certain physical traits that were thought to be stable or that did not appear to be influenced by external environmental factors. Therefore, these so-called *nonadaptive* traits should exhibit only minimal within-group variation and could thus be used to typify entire populations. Shape of the skull was incorrectly believed to be one such characteristic, and the fallacy of this assumption was not demonstrated until the early twentieth century (Boas, 1912).

In 1842, Anders Retzius, a Swedish anatomist, developed the *cephalic index* as a method of describing the shape of the head. The cephalic index, derived by dividing maximum head breadth by maximum length and multiplying by 100, gives the ratio of head breadth to length. (It is important to note that the cephalic index does not measure head size.) Compared to the statistical methods in use today, the cephalic index seems rather simplistic, but in the nineteenth century it was seen as an important scientific tool. Furthermore, because people could be neatly categorized by a single number, it provided an extremely efficient method for describing variation. Individuals with an index of less than 75 had long, narrow heads and were termed **dolichocephalic**. **Brachycephalic** individuals, with broad heads, had an index of over 80; and those whose indices were between 75 and 80 were *mesocephalic*.

Northern Europeans tended to be dolichocephalic, while southern Europeans were brachycephalic. Not surprisingly, these results led to heated and nationalistic debate over whether one group was superior to another. Furthermore, when it was shown that northern Europeans shared their tendency to long, narrow heads with several African populations, the cephalic index ceased to be considered a reliable indicator of race.

By the mid-nineteenth century, monogenists were beginning to reject their somewhat egalitarian concept of race in favor of a more hierarchical view. Populations were ranked essentially on a scale based on skin color (along with size and shape of the head), with Africans at the bottom. Moreover, Europeans themselves were ranked so that northern, light-skinned populations were considered superior to their southern, more olive-skinned neighbors.

The fact that non-Europeans were viewed as "uncivilized" implied an inferiority of character and intellect. This view was based in a concept now termed **biological determinism**, which in part holds that there is an association between physical characteristics and such attributes as intelligence, morals, values, abilities, and even social and economic differences between groups. In other words, cultural variations are *inherited* in the same manner as biological variations. It follows, then, that there are inherent behavioral and cognitive differences between groups, and therefore, some groups are *by nature* superior to others. Following this logic, it is a

Dolichocephalic
Having a long, narrow head in which the width measures less than 75 percent of the length.

Brachycephalic
Having a broad head in which the width measures more than 80 percent of the length.

Biological determinism
The concept that various attributes and behaviors (e.g., intelligence, values, morals) are governed by biological (genetic) factors; the inaccurate association of various behavioral attributes with certain biological traits, such as skin color.

simple matter to justify the persecution and even enslavement of other peoples simply because their appearance differs from what is familiar.

After 1850, biological determinism was a constant theme underlying common thinking as well as scientific research in Europe and the United States. Deterministic (and what we today would call racist) views were held to some extent by most people, including such notable figures as Thomas Jefferson, Georges Cuvier, Benjamin Franklin, Charles Lyell, Abraham Lincoln, Charles Darwin, and Oliver Wendell Holmes. Commenting on this usually deemphasized characteristic of notable historical figures, Stephen J. Gould (1981, p. 32), of Harvard University, emphasizes that "all American culture heroes embraced racial attitudes that would embarrass public-school mythmakers."

Francis Galton (1822–1911), a cousin of Charles Darwin, shared the increasingly common fear among Europeans that "civilized society" was being weakened by the failure of natural selection to completely eliminate unfit and inferior members (Greene, 1981, p. 107). Galton wrote and lectured on the necessity of "race improvement" and suggested governmental regulation of marriage and family size, an approach he called **eugenics**.

Galton's writings attracted a considerable following in both Europe and the United States, and a number of eugenics societies were formed. The eugenics movement had a great deal of snob appeal, for fitness was deemed to be embodied in the upper classes, while the lower classes were associated with criminality, illness, and mental retardation. Moreover, many eugenics groups sought to rid society of crime and poverty through mandatory sterilization programs of the poorer classes.

Although eugenics had its share of critics, its popularity flourished throughout the 1930s, but nowhere was it more attractive than in Germany, where the viewpoint took a disastrous turn. The false idea of pure races was increasingly extolled as a means of reestablishing a strong and prosperous state. Eugenics was seen as scientific justification for purging Germany of its "unfit," and many of Germany's scientists continued to support the policies of racial purity and eugenics during the Nazi period (Proctor, 1988, p. 143), when they served as justification for condemning millions of people to death.

But at the same time, many were turning away from racial typologies and classification in favor of a more evolutionary approach. No doubt for some, this shift in direction was motivated by their growing concerns over the goals of the eugenics movement. Probably more important, however, was the synthesis of Mendelian genetics and Darwin's theories of natural selection during the 1930s. This breakthrough influenced all the biological sciences, and some physical anthropologists began to apply evolutionary principles to the study of human variation.

The Concept of Race

All contemporary humans are members of the same **polytypic** species, *Homo sapiens*. A polytypic species is one composed of local populations that differ from one another with regard to the expression of one or more traits. Moreover, *within* local populations there is a great deal of phenotypic and genotypic variation between individuals. Many species are polytypic.

In discussions of human variation, people have traditionally clumped together various attributes such as skin color, shape of the face, shape of the nose, hair color,

Eugenics
The philosophy of "race improvement" through the forced sterilization of members of some groups and encouraged reproduction among others; an overly simplified, often racist view that is now discredited.

Polytypic
Referring to species composed of populations that differ with regard to the expression of one or more traits.

hair form (curly, straight), and eye color. People possessing particular *combinations* of these and other traits have been placed together into categories associated with specific geographical localities. Such categories are called *races.*

We all think we know what we mean by the word *race,* but in reality, the term has had a number of meanings since it gained common usage in English in the 1500s. It has been used synonymously with *species,* as in "the human race," or to refer to a more limited grouping of individuals all descended from a single individual (e.g., "the race of Abraham").

Since the 1600s, race has also referred to various culturally defined groups, and this meaning still enjoys popular usage. For example, one hears "the English race" or "the Japanese race," where the reference is actually to nationality. Another often-heard phrase is "the Jewish race," when the speaker is really talking about a particular ethnic and religious identity.

Thus, while *race* is usually used as a biological term, or at least one with biological connotations, it is also one with enormous social significance. Moreover, there is still a widespread perception that there is an association between certain physical traits (skin color, in particular) and numerous cultural attributes (such as language, occupational preferences, or even morality). Therefore, in many cultural contexts, a person's social identity is strongly influenced by the manner in which he or she expresses those physical traits traditionally used to define "racial groups." Characteristics such as skin color are highly visible, and they facilitate an immediate and superficial designation of individuals into socially defined categories. However, so-called racial traits are not the only phenotypic expressions that contribute to social identity. Sex and age are also critically important. But aside from these two variables, an individual's racial and/or *ethnic* background is still inevitably a factor that influences how he or she is initially perceived and judged by others, especially in diverse societies.

The use of expressions of national origin (e.g., African, Asian) or the terms *ethnic* or *ethnicity* as substitutes for racial labels has become more common in recent years, both within and outside anthropology. Within anthropology, *ethnicity* was proposed in the early 1950s as a means of avoiding the more emotionally charged term *race.* Strictly speaking, *ethnicity* refers to cultural factors, and for this reason, some have objected to its use in discussions that also include biological characteristics. However, the fact that the words *ethnicity* and *race* are used interchangeably reflects the social importance of phenotypic expression and demonstrates once again how phenotype is associated with culturally defined variables.

In its most common biological usage, race refers to geographically patterned phenotypic variation within a species. By the seventeenth century, naturalists began to describe races in plants and nonhuman animals, because they recognized that when populations of a species occupied different regions, they sometimes differed from one another in the expression of one or more traits. But even today, there are no established criteria by which races of plants and animals are to be assessed. To a biologist studying nonhuman forms, the degree of genetic difference necessary for racial distinctions is a subjective issue, determined in part by the investigator. However, if we are to apply the term to humans, we must elucidate the degree of genetic difference that exists between individuals *within* populations as well as *between* populations.

Prior to World War II, most studies of human variation focused on observable phenotypic variation between large, geographically defined populations, and these studies were largely descriptive. Since that time, the emphasis has shifted to the examination of differences in allele frequencies within and between populations as well as the adaptive significance of phenotypic and genotypic variation. This shift in focus occurred partly as the outcome of historical trends in biological science in general and physical anthropology in particular. Especially crucial to this shift was the emergence of the modern synthesis in biology (see p. 298), which was based on the recognition of the fundamental importance of the *interaction* of natural selection and other factors, such as gene flow, mutation, and drift, to the process of evolution.

Application of evolutionary principles to the study of modern human variation replaced the superficial nineteenth-century view of race *based solely on observed phenotype.* Additionally, the genetic emphasis dispelled previously held misconceptions that races were fixed biological units that did not change over time and that were composed of individuals who all conformed to a particular *type.*

Clearly, there are phenotypic differences between humans, and some of these differences roughly correspond to particular geographical locations. It is unlikely that anyone would mistake a person of Asian descent for one of northern European ancestry. But certain questions must be asked. Is there any adaptive significance attached to observed phenotypic variation? What is the degree of underlying genetic variation that influences it? What is the role of such factors as genetic drift? These questions place considerations of human variation within a contemporary evolutionary framework.

Although, in part, physical anthropology has its roots in attempts to explain human diversity, anthropologists have never been in complete agreement on the topic of race. Even attempts to reach a consensus in defining the term have consistently failed. Among physical anthropologists there is still sometimes heated debate over whether it is justifiable to apply racial concepts to humans at all.

Today, some anthropologists recognize population patterning corresponding to at least three major racial groups, each composed of several subgroupings. However, no contemporary scholar subscribes to pre-Darwinian and pre–modern synthesis concepts of races (human and nonhuman) as fixed biological entities, the members of which all conform to specific types. Among those who accept the validity of the race concept, there are various viewpoints. Many who continue to use broad racial categories do not view them as particularly important, especially from a genetic perspective, because the amount of genetic variation accounted for by differences *between* groups is vastly exceeded by the variation that exists *within* groups (see p. 312). But given these considerations, there are those who see variation in outwardly expressed phenotype, because of its potential adaptive value, as worthy of investigation and explanation within the framework of evolutionary principles (Brues, 1991).

Forensic anthropologists in particular find the phenotypic criteria associated with race to have practical applications because they are frequently called on by law enforcement agencies to assist in the identification of human skeletal remains. Inasmuch as unidentified human remains are often those of crime victims, and forensic analysis may lead to courtroom testimony, identification must be as accurate as possible. The most important variables in such identification are the individual's sex, age, stature, and "racial" or "ethnic" background. Using metric and nonmetric criteria, forensic anthropologists employ a number of techniques for establishing broad population affinity, and they are generally able to do so with about 80 percent accuracy.

On the other side of the issue, there are numerous physical anthropologists who argue that race is a meaningless concept when applied to humans. Race is an outdated creation of the human mind that attempts to simplify biological complexity by organizing it into categories. Thus, human races are a product of the human tendency to superimpose order on complex natural phenomena. While classification may have been an acceptable approach some 150 years ago, it is viewed as no longer valid given the current state of genetic and evolutionary science.

Objections to racial taxonomies have also been raised because classification schemes are *typological* in nature, meaning that categories are discrete and based on stereotypes or ideals that comprise a specific set of traits. Thus, in general, typologies are inherently misleading, because there are always many individuals in any grouping who do not conform to all aspects of a particular type.

In any "racial" group, there will be individuals who fall into the normal range of variation for another group with regard to one or several characteristics. For example, two people of different ancestry might vary with regard to skin color, but they could share any number of other traits, such as height, shape of head, hair color, eye color, or ABO blood type. In fact, they could easily share more similarities with each other than they do with many members of their own populations. (Remember, at most, only about 6 percent of genetic difference among humans has been shown to be due to differences between large geographical groups.)

Moreover, as we have stressed, because the characteristics that have traditionally been used to define races are polygenic, they exhibit a continuous range of expression. It thus becomes difficult, if not impossible, to draw discrete boundaries between races with regard to many traits. This limitation becomes clear if you ask yourself, "At what point is hair color no longer dark brown, but medium brown; or no longer light brown, but blond?"

The scientific controversy over race is not likely to disappear. It has received considerable attention outside academia in popular publications such as *Newsweek* and *Discover*. But in spite of all the scientific discussion that has ensued, among the general public, variations on the theme of race will undoubtedly continue to be the most common view toward human biological and cultural variation. Given this fact, it falls to anthropologists and biologists to continue to explore the issue so that, to the best of our abilities, accurate information regarding human variation is available for anyone who seeks informed explanations of complex phenomena.

Racism

The most detrimental outcome of biological determinism is racism. Racism is based on the false belief that such factors as intellect and various cultural attributes are inherited along with physical characteristics. Such beliefs also commonly rest on the assumption that one's own group is superior to other groups.

Because we have already alluded to certain aspects of racism, such as the eugenics movement, notions of racial purity, and persecution of people based on racial or ethnic misconceptions, we will not belabor the point here. However, it is important to point out that racism is hardly a thing of the past, nor is it restricted to European and American whites. Racism is a cultural, not a biological, phenomenon, and it is found worldwide.

Ultimately, racism is one of the more dangerous aspects of human behavior. We have seen recent manifestations of racism in many cities in the United States. The rioting that occurred in Los Angeles in 1992 after the acquittal of white police officers accused of beating Rodney King, an African American suspect, was a clear example of the tensions among the diverse populations of large urban centers. In the past few years, there has been an increase in racial slurs and hate speech on radio talk shows and on the Internet. Sadly, the twentieth century provided numerous examples of ethnic/racial conflict, and it is crucial to point out that most of these conflicts were due to cultural, not biological, differences between the participants. The unspeakable genocidal events of the Holocaust during World War II, in Cambodia in the 1970s, and in Rwanda in 1994 as well as the tragedies of Bosnia, Croatia, and Kosovo, all bespeak the outcomes of intolerance of groups we call "others," however we define the term.

We end this brief discussion of racism with an excerpt from an article, "The Study of Race," by Sherwood Washburn, a well-known physical anthropologist at the University of California, Berkeley. Although written some years ago, the statement is as fresh and applicable today as it was when it was written:

> Races are products of the past. They are relics of times and conditions which have long ceased to exist.
>
> Racism is equally a relic supported by no phase of modern science. We may not know how to interpret the form of the Mongoloid face, or why Rh is of high incidence in Africa, but we do know the benefits of education and of economic progress. We . . . know that the roots of happiness lie in the biology of the whole species and that the potential of the species can only be realized in a culture, in a social system. It is knowledge and the social system which give life or take it away, and in so doing change the gene frequencies and continue the million-year-old interaction of culture and biology. Human biology finds its realization in a culturally determined way of life, and the infinite variety of genetic combinations can only express themselves efficiently in a free and open society. (Washburn, 1963, p. 531)

Intelligence

As we have shown, belief in the relationship between race and specific behavioral attributes is popular even today, but evidence is lacking that personality or any other behavioral trait differs genetically *between* human groups. Most scientists would agree with this last statement, but one question that has produced controversy both inside scientific circles and among laypeople is whether population affinity and **intelligence** are associated.

Both genetic and environmental factors contribute to intelligence, although it is not yet possible to measure accurately the percentage each contributes. What can be said is that IQ scores and intelligence are not the same thing. IQ scores can change during a person's lifetime, and average IQ scores of different populations overlap. Such differences in IQ scores as do exist between groups are difficult to interpret, given the problems inherent in the design of the IQ tests. Moreover, complex cognitive abilities, however measured, are influenced by multiple loci and are thus strikingly polygenic.

Innate factors set limits and define potentials for behavior and cognitive ability in any species. In humans, the limits are broad and the potentials are not fully known. Individual abilities result from complex interactions between genetic and environmental factors. One product of this interaction is learning, and the ability to learn is influenced by genetic and other biological components. Undeniably,

Intelligence
Mental capacity; ability to learn, reason, or comprehend and interpret information, facts, relationships, meanings, etc.; the capacity to solve problems, whether through the application of previously acquired knowledge or through insight.

there are differences between individuals regarding these biological components. However, elucidating what proportion of the variation in test scores is due to biological factors probably is not possible. Moreover, innate differences in abilities reflect individual variation *within* populations, not inherent differences *between* groups. Comparing populations on the basis of IQ test results is a misuse of testing procedures, and there is no convincing evidence *whatsoever* that populations vary with regard to cognitive abilities, regardless of the assertions in some popular books. Unfortunately, it appears that no matter what is said about the lack of evidence of the mental inferiority of some populations (and the mental superiority of others) and the questionable validity of intelligence tests, racist attitudes toward the topic continue to flourish.

The Adaptive Significance of Human Variation

Today, physical anthropologists view human variation as the result of such evolutionary factors as genetic drift, founder effect, gene flow, and adaptations to environmental conditions, both past and present. Cultural adaptations have also played an important role in the evolution of *Homo sapiens,* and although in this discussion we are primarily concerned with biological issues, we must still consider the influence of cultural practices on human adaptive response.

All organisms must maintain the normal functions of internal organs, tissues, and cells in order to survive, and this task must be accomplished within the context of an ever-changing environment. Even during the course of a single, seemingly uneventful day, there are numerous fluctuations in temperature, wind, solar radiation, humidity, and so on. Physical activity also places **stress** on physiological mechanisms. The body must accommodate all these changes by compensating in some manner to maintain internal constancy, or **homeostasis**, and all life forms have evolved physiological mechanisms that, within limits, achieve this goal.

Physiological response to environmental change is, to some degree, influenced by genetic factors. We have already defined adaptation as a functional response to environmental conditions in populations and individuals. In a narrower sense, adaptation refers to *long-term* evolutionary (i.e., genetic) changes that characterize all individuals within a population or species.

Examples of long-term adaptations in *Homo sapiens* include some physiological responses to heat (sweating) and deeply pigmented skin in tropical regions. Such characteristics are the results of evolutionary change in species or populations, and they do not vary as the result of short-term environmental change. For example, the ability to sweat is not lost in people who spend their entire lives in predominantly cool areas. Likewise, individuals born with deeply pigmented skin will not become pale, even if never exposed to intense sunlight.

Short-term physiological response to environmental change, which occurs in all people, is called **acclimatization**. Tanning, which occurs in all people, is a form of acclimatization. Another example is the very rapid increase in hemoglobin production that occurs when lowland natives travel to higher elevations. This increase provides the body with more oxygen in an environment where oxygen is less available. In both these examples, the physiological change is temporary. Tans fade once exposure to sunlight is reduced; and hemoglobin production drops to original levels following a return to lower altitudes.

Stress
In a physiological context, any factor that acts to disrupt homeostasis; more precisely, the body's response to any factor that threatens its ability to maintain homeostasis.

Homeostasis
A condition of balance or stability within a biological system, maintained by the interaction of physiological mechanisms that compensate for changes (both external and internal).

Acclimatization
Physiological response to changes in the environment that occurs during an individual's lifetime. Such responses may be short-term. The capacity for acclimatization may typify an entire population or species. This capacity is under genetic influence and thus is subject to evolutionary factors such as natural selection.

In the following discussion, we present some examples of how humans respond to environmental challenges. Some of these examples illustrate adaptations that characterize the entire species. Others illustrate adaptations seen in only some populations. And still others illustrate the process of acclimatization.

Solar Radiation, Vitamin D, and Skin Color

Skin color is often cited as an example of adaptation and natural selection in human populations. In general, skin color in populations, prior to European contact, follows a particular geographical distribution, especially in the Old World. Figure 13–1 illustrates that populations with the greatest amount of pigmentation are found in the tropics, while lighter skin color is associated with more northern latitudes, particularly the inhabitants of northwestern Europe.

Skin color is influenced by three substances: hemoglobin, carotene, and most important, the pigment *melanin*. Melanin is a granular substance produced by specialized cells (*melanocytes*) found in the epidermis. All humans appear to have approximately the same number of melanocytes. It is the amount of melanin and the size of the melanin granules that vary.

Melanin has the capacity to absorb potentially dangerous ultraviolet (UV) rays present (although not visible) in sunlight. Therefore, melanin provides protection from overexposure to ultraviolet radiation, which can cause genetic mutations in skin cells. These mutations may ultimately lead to skin cancer, which, if left untreated, can eventually spread to other organs and result in death.

As already mentioned, exposure to sunlight triggers a protective mechanism in the form of tanning, which results from temporarily increased melanin production (acclimatization). This protective response occurs in all humans except

FIGURE 13–1

Geographical distribution of skin color among the indigenous populations of the world. (After Biasutti, 1959.)

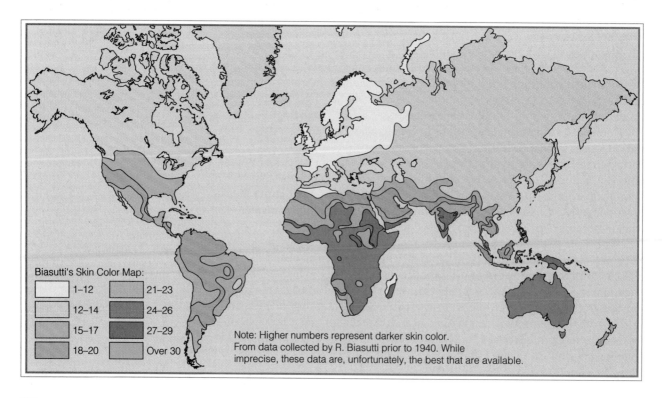

Biasutti's Skin Color Map:
1–12
12–14
15–17
18–20
21–23
24–26
27–29
Over 30

Note: Higher numbers represent darker skin color. From data collected by R. Biasutti prior to 1940. While imprecise, these data are, unfortunately, the best that are available.

albinos, who carry a genetic mutation that prevents their melanocytes from producing melanin (Fig. 13–2). Moreover, tanning is limited in many fair-complexioned people of northern European descent who do produce small amounts of melanin but have a reduced capacity for temporary increases in melanin production.

Natural selection appears to have favored dark skin in areas nearest the equator, where the sun's rays are most direct and thus where exposure to UV light is most intense. However, as hominids migrated out of Africa into Europe and Asia, selective pressures changed. Not only were these populations moving away from the tropics, where ultraviolet rays were most direct, but they were also moving into areas where it was cold and cloudy during winter. Bear in mind, too, that physiological adaptations were not sufficient to meet the demands of living in colder climates. Therefore, we must assume that these populations had adopted certain cultural practices, such as wearing animal skins or other types of clothing. Although clothing would have added necessary warmth, it also would have effectively blocked exposure to sunlight. Consequently, the advantages provided by deeply pigmented skin in the tropics were no longer important, and selection for melanin production may have been relaxed (Brace and Montagu, 1977).

However, relaxed selection favoring dark skin may not be adequate to explain the very depigmented skin seen especially in some northern Europeans. Perhaps another factor, the need for adequate amounts of vitamin D, was also critical. The theory concerning the possible role of vitamin D, known as the *vitamin D hypothesis*, offers the following explanation.

Vitamin D is produced in the body partly as a result of the interaction between ultraviolet radiation and a substance similar to cholesterol. It is also available in some foods, including liver, fish oils, egg yolk, butter, and cream. Vitamin D is necessary for normal bone growth and mineralization, and some exposure to ultraviolet radiation is therefore essential. Insufficient amounts of vitamin D during childhood result in *rickets*, which often leads to bowing of the long bones of the legs and deformation of the pelvis. Pelvic deformities are of particular concern for women, for they can lead to a narrowing of the birth canal, which, in the absence of surgical intervention, frequently results in the death of both mother and fetus during childbirth.

This example illustrates the potential for rickets as a significant selective factor favoring less pigmented skin in regions where climate and other factors operate to reduce exposure to UV radiation. It is obvious how reduced exposure to sunlight due to climate and increased use of clothing could have been detrimental to dark-skinned individuals in more northern latitudes. In these individuals, melanin would have blocked absorption of the already reduced amounts of available ultraviolet radiation required for vitamin D synthesis. Therefore, selection pressures would have shifted over time to favor individuals with lighter skin. There is substantial evidence, both historically and in contemporary populations, to support this theory.

During the latter decades of the nineteenth century in the United States, black inhabitants of northern cities suffered a higher incidence of rickets than whites. Northern blacks were also more commonly affected than blacks living in the South, where exposure to sunlight is greater. (The supplementation of milk with vitamin D was initiated to alleviate this problem.) Another example is seen in Britain, where darker-skinned East Indians and Pakistanis show a higher incidence of rickets than people with lighter skin (Molnar, 1983).

FIGURE 13–2
An African albino.

 The adaptive significance of skin color is presented as a virtual exercise in Virtual Lab 2, section IV.

Perhaps more social importance has been attached to variation in skin color than to any other single human biological trait. But aside from its probable adaptive significance relative to UV radiation, skin color is no more important physiologically than many other biological characteristics. Still, from an evolutionary perspective, skin color provides a good example of how the forces of natural selection have produced geographically patterned variation as the consequence of two conflicting selective forces: the need for protection from overexposure to UV radiation, on the one hand, and the need for adequate UV exposure for vitamin D synthesis on the other.

The Thermal Environment

Mammals and birds have evolved complex mechanisms to maintain a constant internal body temperature. While reptiles must rely on exposure to external heat sources to raise body temperature and energy levels, mammals and birds possess physiological mechanisms that, within certain limits, increase or reduce the loss of body heat. The optimum internal body temperature for normal cellular functions is species-specific, and for humans it is approximately 98.6° F.

Homo sapiens is found in a wide variety of habitats, with thermal environments ranging from exceedingly hot (in excess of 120° F) to bitter cold (less than −60° F). In such extremes, particularly cold, human life would not be possible without cultural innovations. But even accounting for the artificial environments in which we live, such external conditions place the human body under enormous stress.

Response to Heat   All available evidence suggests that the earliest hominids evolved in the warm-to-hot savannas of East Africa. The fact that humans cope better with heat than they do with cold is testimony to the long-term adaptations to heat that evolved in our ancestors.

In humans, as well as certain other species, such as horses, sweat glands are distributed throughout the skin. This wide distribution of sweat glands makes possible the loss of heat at the body surface through evaporative cooling, a mechanism that has evolved to the greatest degree in humans.

The capacity to dissipate heat by sweating is seen in all humans to an almost equal degree, with the average number of sweat glands per individual (approximately 1.6 million) being fairly constant. However, there is variation in that persons not generally exposed to hot conditions do experience a period of acclimatization that initially involves significantly increased perspiration rates (Frisancho, 1993). An additional factor that enhances the cooling effects of sweating is increased exposure of the skin through reduced amounts of body hair. We do not know when in our evolutionary history loss of body hair began, but it represents a species-wide adaptation.

Heat reduction through evaporation can be expensive, and indeed dangerous, in terms of water and sodium loss. Up to 3 liters of water can be lost by a human engaged in heavy work in high heat. The importance of this fact can be appreciated if you consider that the loss of 1 liter of water is approximately equivalent to losing 1.5 percent of total body weight, and loss of 10 percent of body weight can be life threatening.

Another mechanism for radiating body heat is **vasodilation**, whereby capillaries near the skin's surface widen to permit increased blood flow to the skin. The

Vasodilation
Expansion of blood vessels, permitting increased blood flow to the skin. Vasodilation permits warming of the skin and also facilitates radiation of warmth as a means of cooling. Vasodilation is an involuntary response to warm temperatures, various drugs, and even emotional states (blushing).

visible effect of vasodilation is flushing, or increased redness of the skin, particularly of the face, accompanied by warmth. But the physiological effect is to permit heat, carried by the blood from the interior of the body, to be emitted from the skin's surface to the surrounding air. (Some drugs, including alcohol, also produce vasodilation, which accounts for the increased redness and warmth of the face in some people.)

Body size and proportions are also important in regulating body temperature. Indeed, there seems to be a general relationship between climate and body size and shape in birds and mammals. In general, within a species, body size (weight) increases as distance from the equator increases. In humans, this relationship holds up fairly well, but there are numerous exceptions.

Two rules that pertain to the relationship between body size, body proportions, and climate are *Bergmann's rule* and *Allen's rule.*

1. *Bergmann's rule (concerns the relationship of body mass or volume to surface area):* In mammalian species, body size tends to be greater in populations that live in colder climates. This is because as mass increases, the relative amount of surface area decreases proportionately. Because heat is lost at the surface, it follows that increased mass allows for greater heat retention and reduced heat loss.

2. *Allen's rule (concerns shape of the body, especially appendages):* In colder climates, shorter appendages, with increased mass-to-surface ratios, are adaptive because they are more effective at preventing heat loss. Conversely, longer appendages, with increased surface area relative to mass, are more adaptive in warmer climates because they promote heat loss.

According to these rules, the most suitable body shape in hot climates is linear with long arms and legs. In a cold climate, a more suitable body type is stocky with shorter limbs. Considerable data gathered from several human populations generally conform to these principles. In colder climates, body mass tends, on average, to be greater and characterized by a larger trunk relative to arms and legs (Roberts, 1973). People living in the Arctic tend to be short and stocky, while many sub-Saharan Africans, especially East African pastoralists, are tall and linear (Fig. 13–3). But there is much human variability regarding body proportions, and not all populations conform so readily to Bergmann's and Allen's rules.

Response to Cold   Human physiological responses to cold combine factors that increase heat retention with those that enhance heat production. Of the two, heat retention is more efficient because it requires less energy. This is an important point because energy is derived from dietary sources. Unless food resources are abundant, and in winter they frequently are not, any factor that conserves energy can have adaptive value.

Short-term responses to cold include increased metabolic rate and shivering, both of which generate body heat, at least for a short time. **Vasoconstriction**, another short-term response, restricts heat loss and conserves energy. In addition, humans possess a subcutaneous (beneath the skin) fat layer that provides an insulative layer throughout the body. Behavioral modifications include increased activity, wearing warmer clothing, increased food consumption, and assuming a curled-up position.

Increases in metabolic rate (the rate at which cells break up nutrients into their components) release energy in the form of heat. Shivering also generates muscle heat, as does voluntary exercise. But these methods of heat production are

Vasoconstriction
Narrowing of blood vessels to reduce blood flow to the skin. Vasoconstriction is an involuntary response to cold and reduces heat loss at the skin's surface.

(a)   (b)

FIGURE 13–3

(a) This African woman has the linear proportions characteristic of many inhabitants of sub-Saharan Africa. (b) By comparison, the Inuit woman is short and stocky. These two individuals serve as good examples of Bergmann's and Allen's rules.

expensive, because they require an increased intake of nutrients to provide energy. (Perhaps this explains why we tend to have a heartier appetite during the winter and why we also tend to increase our intake of fats and carbohydrates, the very sources of energy our bodies require.)

In general, people exposed to chronic cold (meaning much or most of the year) maintain higher metabolic rates than those living in warmer climates. The Inuit (Eskimo) people living in the Arctic maintain metabolic rates between 13 and 45 percent higher than observed in non-Inuit control subjects (Frisancho, 1993). Moreover, the highest metabolic rates are seen in inland Inuit, who are exposed to even greater cold stress than coastal populations. Traditionally, the Inuit had the highest animal protein and fat diet of any human population in the world. Such a diet, necessitated by the available resource base, served to maintain the high metabolic rates required by exposure to chronic cold.

Vasoconstriction restricts capillary blood flow to the surface of the skin, thus reducing heat loss at the body surface. Because retaining body heat is more economical than creating it, vasoconstriction is very efficient, provided temperatures do not drop below freezing. However, if temperatures do fall below freezing, continued vasoconstriction can allow the skin temperature to decline to the point of frostbite or worse.

Long-term responses to cold vary among human groups. For example, in the past, desert-dwelling native Australian populations were subjected to wide temperature fluctuations from day to night. As they wore no clothing and did not build shelters, their only protection from temperatures that hovered only a few degrees above freezing was provided by sleeping fires. They experienced continuous vasoconstriction throughout the night, and this permitted a degree of skin cooling most people would find extremely uncomfortable. But there was no threat of frostbite, and continued vasoconstriction helped to prevent excessive internal heat loss.

By contrast, the Inuit experience intermittent periods of vasoconstriction and vasodilation. This compromise provides periodic warmth to the skin that helps prevent frostbite in below-freezing temperatures. At the same time, because vasodilation is intermittent, energy loss is restricted, with more heat retained at the body's core.

The preceding examples illustrate but two of the many ways in which human populations vary with regard to adaptation to cold. Although all humans respond to cold stress in much the same manner, there is variation in how adaptation and acclimatization are manifested.

High Altitude

Today, perhaps as many as 25 million people live at altitudes above 10,000 feet. In Tibet, permanent settlements exist above 15,000 feet, and in the Andes, they can be found as high as 17,000 feet (Fig. 13–4).

At such altitudes, multiple factors produce stress on the human body. These include **hypoxia** (reduced available oxygen), more intense solar radiation, cold, low humidity, wind (which amplifies cold stress), a reduced nutritional base, and rough terrain. Of these, hypoxia exerts the greatest amount of stress on human physiological systems, especially the heart, lungs, and brain.

Hypoxia results from reduced barometric pressure. It is not that there is less oxygen in the atmosphere at high altitudes; rather, it is less concentrated. Therefore, to obtain the same amount of oxygen at 9,000 feet as at sea level, people must make certain physiological alterations aimed at increasing the body's ability to transport and utilize efficiently the oxygen that is available.

People who reside at higher elevations, especially recent immigrants, display a number of manifestations of their hypoxic environment. Reproduction, in

Hypoxia
Lack of oxygen. Hypoxia can refer to reduced amounts of available oxygen in the atmosphere (due to lowered barometric pressure) or to insufficient amounts of oxygen in the body.

FIGURE 13–4

(a) La Paz, Bolivia, at just over 12,000 feet above sea level, is home to 1 million people. (b) A household in northern Tibet, situated at an elevation of over 15,000 feet above sea level.

(a)

(b)

particular, is affected through increased rates of infant mortality, miscarriage, and prematurity. Low birth weight is also more common and is attributed to decreased fetal growth due to impaired maternal-fetal transport of oxygen (Moore and Regensteiner, 1983). But there is also some evidence to suggest that low birth weight may actually have some adaptive value in high-altitude natives.

Compared to populations at lower elevations, lifelong residents of high altitude display slowed growth and maturation. Other differences include larger chest size, associated, in turn, with greater lung volume and larger hearts.

Compared to high-altitude natives, nonnatives exhibit some differences in acclimatization and adaptation to hypoxia. Frisancho (1993) terms these different responses "adult acclimatization" and "developmental acclimatization." *Adult acclimatization* occurs upon exposure to high altitude in people born at low elevation. The responses may be short-term modifications, depending on duration of stay, but they begin within hours of the altitude change. These changes include an increase in respiration rate, heart rate, and production of red blood cells. (Red blood cells contain hemoglobin, the protein responsible for transporting oxygen to organs and tissues.)

Developmental acclimatization occurs in high-altitude natives whose adaptations are acquired during growth and development. (Note that this type of acclimatization is present only in people who grow up in high-altitude areas, not in those who moved there as adults.) In addition to greater lung capacity, people born at high altitudes are more efficient than migrants at diffusing oxygen from the blood to bodily tissues. Hence, they do not rely as heavily on increased red cell formation as do newcomers. Developmental acclimatization serves as a good example of physiological plasticity by illustrating how, within the limits set by genetic factors, development can be influenced by environment.

There is evidence that some populations have adapted to high altitudes. Indigenous peoples of Tibet who have inhabited regions higher than 12,000 feet for around 25,000 years may have made genetic (i.e., evolutionary) accommodations to hypoxia. Altitude does not appear to affect reproduction in these people to the degree it does in other populations. Infants have birth weights as high as those of lowland Tibetan groups and higher than those of recent (20 to 30 years) Chinese immigrants. This fact may be the result of alterations in maternal blood flow to the uterus during pregnancy (Moore et al., 1994).

Another line of evidence concerns the utilization of glucose (blood sugar). Glucose is critical in that it is the only source of energy used by the brain, and it is also utilized, although not exclusively, by the heart. Both highland Tibetans and the Quechua (inhabitants of high-altitude regions of the Peruvian Andes) burn glucose in a way that permits more efficient use of oxygen. This implies the presence of genetic mutations in the mitochondrial DNA that directs how cells use glucose. It also implies that natural selection has acted to increase the frequency of these advantageous mutations in these groups.

There is no certain evidence that Tibetans and Quechua have made evolutionary changes to accommodate high-altitude hypoxia. Moreover, the genetic mechanisms that underlie these populations' unique abilities have not been identified. The data are intriguing, however, and they strongly suggest that selection has operated to produce evolutionary change in these two groups. If further study supports these findings, we will have an excellent example of evolution in action producing long-term adaptation at the population level.

Infectious Disease

Infection, as opposed to other disease categories, such as degenerative or genetic disease, is a category that includes those pathological conditions caused by microorganisms (viruses, bacteria, or fungi). Throughout the course of human evolution, infectious disease has exerted enormous selective pressures on populations and thus has influenced the frequency of certain alleles that affect the immune response. But as important as infectious disease has been as an agent of natural selection in human populations, its role in this regard is not very well documented.

Malaria provides perhaps the best-documented example of the evolutionary role of disease. In Chapter 12, you saw how malaria has operated in some African and Mediterranean populations to alter allele frequencies at the locus governing hemoglobin formation. In spite of extensive long-term eradication programs, malaria still poses a serious threat to human health. Indeed, the World Health Organization estimates the number of people currently infected with malaria to be between 300 and 500 million worldwide. This number is increasing, too, as drug-resistant strains of the disease-causing microorganism become more common (Olliaro et al., 1995).

Another example of the selective role of infectious disease is indirectly provided by AIDS (acquired immune deficiency syndrome). In the United States, the first cases of AIDS were reported in 1981. Since that time, perhaps as many as 1.5 million have been infected by HIV (human immunodeficiency virus), the agent that causes AIDS. As of June 30, 1999, 420,000 had died in the United States, but worldwide, 16 million had died and another 34 million were infected.

HIV is transmitted from person to person through the exchange of bodily fluids, usually blood or semen. It is not spread through casual contact. Within six months of infection, most persons test positive for anti-HIV antibodies, meaning that their immune system has recognized the presence of foreign antigens and has responded by producing antibodies. However, serious HIV-related symptoms may not appear in infected people for years, and in the United States, the average "latency period" is over 11 years.

Like all viruses, HIV must invade certain types of cells and alter the functions of those cells to produce more virus particles in a process that eventually leads to cell destruction. (The manner in which HIV accomplishes this task is different from that of many other viruses.) HIV can attack various types of cells, but it especially targets so-called T4 helper cells, which are major components of the immune system. As HIV infection spreads and T4 cells are destroyed, the patient's immune system begins to fail. Consequently, he or she begins to exhibit symptoms caused by various **pathogens** that are commonly present but usually kept in check by a normal immune response. When an HIV-infected person's T cell count drops to a level that indicates immune suppression, and when symptoms of "opportunistic" infections appear, the patient is said to have AIDS.

By the early 1990s, scientists were aware of a number of patients who had been HIV positive for 10 to 15 years, but continued to show few if any symptoms. Awareness of these patients led researchers to suspect that some individuals possess a natural immunity or resistance to HIV infection. This was shown to be true in late 1996 with the publication of two different studies (Dean et al., 1996; Samson et al., 1996) that demonstrated a mechanism for resistance to HIV.

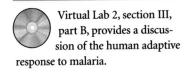

Virtual Lab 2, section III, part B, provides a discussion of the human adaptive response to malaria.

Pathogens
Substances or microorganisms, such as bacteria, fungi, or viruses, that cause disease.

These two reports describe a genetic mutation that concerns a major protein "receptor site" on the surface of certain immune cells, including T4 cells. (Receptor sites are protein molecules that enable HIV and other viruses to invade cells.) In this particular situation, the mutant allele results in a malfunctioning receptor site, and current evidence now strongly suggests that individuals who are homozygous for this allele may be completely resistant to many types of HIV infection. In heterozygotes, infection may still occur, but the course of HIV disease is markedly slowed.

Interestingly, and for unknown reasons, the mutant allele occurs mainly in people of European descent, among whom its frequency is about 10 percent. Samson and colleagues (1996) reported that in the Japanese and West African samples they studied, the mutation was absent, but Dean and colleagues (1996) reported an allele frequency of about 2 percent among African Americans. These researchers speculate that the presence of the allele in African Americans may be entirely due to genetic admixture (gene flow) with American whites. Moreover, they suggest that this polymorphism exists in Europeans as a result of selective pressures favoring an allele that originally occurred as a rare mutation. But it is critical to note that the original selective agent was *not* HIV. Instead, it was some other, as yet unidentified pathogen that requires the same receptor site as HIV. Researchers may be close to identifying which pathogen, or group of pathogens, it was. In December, 1999, a group of scientists reported that the myxoma poxvirus, which is related to the virus that causes smallpox, can use the same receptor site as does HIV. These authors (Lalani, et al., 1999) suggest that the agent that selected for the altered form of the receptor site may have been smallpox. While this conclusion has not yet been proven, or even really investigated, it offers a most exciting avenue of research with the possibility of revealing how a mutation that has been favored by selection because it provides protection against one disease can be shown to increase resistance to another malady (AIDS) as well.

Examples such as sickle-cell anemia and AIDS are continuously revealing new insights into the complex interactions between disease organisms and their host populations. These insights in turn provide a growing basis for understanding the many variations between individuals and populations that have arisen as adaptive responses to infectious disease.

Smallpox, once a deadly viral disease, may provide a good example of how exposure to infectious agents can produce polymorphisms in host populations. During the eighteenth century, smallpox is estimated to have accounted for 10 to 15 percent of all deaths in parts of Europe. But today, this once devastating killer is the only condition to have been successfully eliminated by modern medical technology. By 1977, through massive vaccination programs, the World Health Organization was able to declare the smallpox virus to be extinct.

Smallpox had a higher incidence in persons with either blood type A or AB than in type O individuals, a fact that has been explained by the presence of an antigen on the smallpox virus that is similar to the A antigen. It follows that when some type A individuals were exposed to smallpox, their immune systems failed to recognize the virus as foreign and thus did not mount an adequate immune response. Consequently, in regions where smallpox was common in the past, it could have altered allele frequencies at the ABO locus by selecting against the *A* allele.

The best-known epidemic in history was that of the Black Death (bubonic plague) in the mid-fourteenth century. Bubonic plague is caused by a bacterium and is transmitted from rodents to humans by fleas. In just a few years, this deadly disease had spread (following trade routes and facilitated by rodent-infested ship cargoes) from the Caspian Sea throughout the Mediterranean area to northern Europe. During the initial exposure to this disease, as many as one-third of the inhabitants of Europe died.

A lesser-known but even more devastating example was the influenza **pandemic** that broke out in 1918 at the end of World War I. This was actually one of a series of influenza outbreaks, but it has remained notable for its still unexplained virulence and the fact that it accounted for the deaths of over 21 million people worldwide.

While we have no clear-cut evidence of a selective role for bubonic plague or influenza, this does not mean that one does not exist. The tremendous mortality that these diseases (and others) are capable of producing certainly increases the likelihood that they influenced the development of human adaptive responses in ways we have not yet discovered.

The effects of infectious disease on humans are mediated culturally as well as biologically. Innumerable cultural factors, such as architectural styles, subsistence techniques, exposure to domesticated animals, and even religious practices, all affect how infectious disease develops and persists within and between populations.

Until about 10,000 to 12,000 years ago, all humans lived in small nomadic hunting and gathering groups. As these groups rarely remained in one location more than a few days at a time, they had minimal contact with refuse heaps that housed disease **vectors**. But with the domestication of plants and animals, people became more sedentary and began living in small villages. Gradually, villages became towns, and towns, in turn, developed into densely crowded, unsanitary cities.

As long as humans lived in small bands, there was little opportunity for infectious disease to have much of an impact on large numbers of people. Even if an entire local group or band were wiped out, the effect on the overall population in a given area would have been negligible. Moreover, for a disease to become **endemic** in a population, sufficient numbers of people must be present. Therefore, small bands of hunter-gatherers were not faced with continuous exposure to endemic disease.

But with the advent of settled living and association with domesticated animals, opportunities for disease increased. As sedentary life permitted larger group size, it became possible for some diseases to become permanently established in some populations. Moreover, exposure to domestic animals, such as cattle, provided an opportune environment for the spread of such maladies as tuberculosis. The crowded, unsanitary conditions that characterized parts of all cities until the late nineteenth century, and that persist in much of the world today, further added to the disease burden borne by human inhabitants.

Pandemic
An extensive outbreak of disease affecting large numbers of people over a wide area; potentially, a worldwide phenomenon.

Vectors
Agents that serve to transmit disease from one carrier to another. Mosquitoes are vectors for malaria, just as fleas are vectors for bubonic plague.

Endemic
Continuously present in a population.

The Continuing Impact of Infectious Disease

Until the twentieth century, infectious disease was the number one cause of death in all human populations. Even today, in many developing countries, as much as half the mortality is due to infectious disease, compared to about 10 percent in the United States. In the United States and other developed nations, with improved living conditions and sanitation, and especially with the widespread use of antibiotics beginning in the late 1940s, infectious disease gave way to heart disease and cancer as the leading causes of death.

Optimistic predictions held that infectious disease would be a thing of the past in developed countries and, with the introduction of antibiotics and improved living standards, in developing nations as well. But by the mid-1980s, such predictions were increasingly seen to be wrong. Between 1980 and 1992, the number of deaths in the United States in which infectious disease was the underlying cause rose from 41 to 65 per 100,000, an increase of 58 percent (Pinner et al., 1996). During that same period, there was a 25 percent increase in infectious disease mortality among people aged 65 and older, from 271 to 338 per 100,000. And deaths due to respiratory tract infections rose from 25 to 30 deaths per 100,000.

Additionally, AIDS contributed substantially to the increase in mortality due to infectious disease in the United States between 1980 and 1992. By 1992, AIDS was the leading cause of death in men aged 25 to 44 years. As of 1998, mortality due to AIDS had decreased significantly, but even when subtracting the effect of AIDS in mortality rates, there was still a 22 percent increase in mortality rates due to infectious disease between 1980 and 1992 (Pinner et al., 1996).

Increase in the prevalence of infectious disease is perhaps partly due to the overuse of antibiotics. It is estimated that half of all antibiotics prescribed in the United States are used to treat viral conditions such as colds and flu. Because antibiotics are completely ineffective against viruses, such therapy not only is useless, it may also have dangerous long-term consequences. There is a growing concern in the biomedical community over the effects of antibiotic and pesticide use, practices that have flourished since the 1950s. Antibiotics have exerted selective pressures on bacterial species that have, over time, developed antibiotic-resistant strains (an excellent example of natural selection). Consequently, the past few years have seen the *reemergence* of many bacterial diseases, including influenza, pneumonia, tuberculosis, and cholera, in forms that are less responsive to treatment.

Tuberculosis is now listed as the world's leading killer of adults by the World Health Organization (Colwell, 1996). In fact, the number of tuberculosis cases has risen 28 percent since the mid-1980s worldwide, with an estimated 10 million infected in the United States alone. Although not all infected persons develop active disease, an estimated 30 million are believed to have died from TB in the 1990s worldwide. One very troubling aspect of the increase in tuberculosis infection is that newly developed strains of *Mycobacterium tuberculosis*, the bacterium that causes TB, are resistant to antibiotics and other treatments.

Cholera, a dangerous and often fatal gastrointestinal disease caused by *Vibrio cholerae*, a bacterium found in sewage-contaminated water, has periodically occurred in epidemic proportions throughout history, including outbreaks in the nineteenth century in New York, Philadelphia, and London. Currently, cholera claims about 100,000 lives annually in Asia alone, and an antibiotic-resistant strain, first identified in India in 1992, is spreading throughout Southeast Asia. Recent cholera outbreaks throughout much of South America, India, Bangladesh, China, and parts of Southeast Asia have been partly attributed to rising ocean temperatures, lack of sanitation, and overcrowding.

Various treatments for nonbacterial conditions have also become ineffective. One such example is the appearance of chloroquin-resistant malaria, which has rendered chloroquin (the traditional preventive medication) virtually useless in some parts of Africa. And many insect species have developed resistance to commonly used pesticides.

In addition to threats posed by resistant strains of pathogens, there are other factors that may contribute to the emergence (or reemergence) of infectious disease. Scientists are becoming increasingly concerned over the potential for global warming to expand the geographical range of numerous tropical disease vectors, such as mosquitoes. And the destruction of natural environments not only contributes to global warming, but also has the potential of allowing disease vectors formerly restricted to local areas to spread to new habitats.

One other factor associated with the rapid spread of disease and directly related to technological change is the mixing of people at an unprecedented rate. Indeed, an estimated 1 million people per day cross national borders by air (Lederberg, 1996)! In addition, new road construction and wider availability of motor-driven vehicles allow more people (armies, refugees, truck drivers, etc.) to travel farther and faster than ever before.

Fundamental to all these factors is human population size (see p. 378), which, as it continues to soar, causes more environmental disturbance and, through additional human activity, adds further to global warming. Moreover, in developing countries, where as much as 50 percent of mortality is due to infectious disease, overcrowding and unsanitary conditions increasingly contribute to increased rates of communicable illness. One could scarcely conceive of a better set of circumstances for the appearance and spread of communicable disease, and it remains to be seen if scientific innovation and medical technology are able to meet the challenge.

It is still not clear what the long-term consequences of twentieth-century antibiotic therapy, environmental change, and human population growth will be on disease patterns. But there are many scientists who fear that we may not be able to develop new antibiotics and treatments fast enough to keep pace with the appearance of potentially deadly new bacteria and other pathogens. Thus, we have radically altered the course of evolution in some microbial species, just as they have altered our own evolutionary course in the past and clearly continue to do so in the present.

SUMMARY

In this chapter, we have investigated some of the ways in which humans differ from one another, both within and between populations. We explored how this variation has been approached in terms of racial typologies and as a function of adaptation to a number of environmental factors, including solar radiation, heat, cold, and high altitude. We have also considered infectious disease, with particular emphasis on AIDS, and the dynamic relationship between pathogens and human hosts.

The topic of human variation is very complicated, and the biological and cultural factors that have contributed to that variation and that continue to influence it are manifold. But from an explicitly evolutionary perspective, it is through the investigation of changes in allele frequencies in response to environmental conditions that we will continue to elucidate the diverse adaptive potential that characterizes our species.

QUESTIONS FOR REVIEW

1. What is a polytypic species?
2. What is a biological definition of race? Why is race socially important?
3. What is biological determinism?
4. What was the eugenics movement, and what were its goals?
5. How did eighteenth- and nineteenth-century European scientists deal with phenotypic variation?
6. What is homeostasis?
7. Under what conditions might light skin color be adaptive? Under what conditions might dark skin color be adaptive?
8. What physiological adjustments do humans show in coping with cold stress?
9. What physiological adjustments do humans show in coping with heat stress?
10. What do body size and shape have to do with adaptation to climate?
11. What are Bergmann's and Allen's rules?
12. How has infectious disease influenced human evolution?
13. How has susceptibility to HIV been shown to vary between populations? What genetic and biological factors have led to this variation?
14. What is a cline, and how does a clinal approach to human phenotypic variation differ from a racial approach?
15. What components of high-altitude environments are most challenging to humans?
16. What are two effects of exposure to high altitude?
17. Discuss current culturally mediated factors that may contribute to the spread of infectious disease. Provide examples.

SUGGESTED FURTHER READINGS

Bodmer, W. F., and L. L. Cavalli-Sforza. 1976. *Genetics, Evolution, and Man.* San Francisco: Freeman.

Discover. 1994. Special Issue: The Science of Race. 15 (November).

Gould, Stephen Jay. 1981. *The Mismeasure of Man.* New York: Norton.

Jacoby, R., and N. Glauberman (eds). 1995. *The Bell Curve Debate.* New York: Times Books.

Journal of the American Medical Association. 1996. Entire issue. 275 (January 17). (Numerous articles pertaining to climate change and reemergence of infectious diseases.)

Leffell, David J., and Douglas E. Brash. 1996. "Sunlight and Skin Cancer." *Scientific American* 275(1): 52–59.

Nesse, Randolph M., and George C. Williams. 1998. "Evolution and the Origins of Disease." *Scientific American* 279(5): 86–93.

O'Brien, Stephen J., and Michael Dean. 1997. "In Search of AIDS-Resistance Genes." *Scientific American* 277(3): 44–51.

Ramenofsky, Ann F. 1992. "Death by Disease." *Archaeology* 45(2): 47–49.

MULTIMEDIA RESOURCES

 Wadsworth Anthropology Resource Center

http://anthropology.wadsworth.com

Visit Anthropology Online to obtain current updates in the field, surfing tips, career information, and more. In addition, enrich your study efforts with text-specific study aids arranged by chapter.

InfoTrac College Edition

http://www.infotrac-college.com/wadsworth

1. Search InfoTrac College Edition for *smallpox.* Among the numerous articles your search brings up, look for one that deals with smallpox as a factor in natural selection. What is the topic of the article? Does it pertain to anything discussed in Chapter 13?

2. InfoTrac College Edition provides many articles about eugenics and its effects on public policy. Search for *eugenics,* and read at least one article. A number of issues are raised by these articles. Write a one-page discussion of these issues. You should also address how eugenics has affected politics and public policy.

Internet Exercises

1. Using Yahoo or another search engine, search for *acclimatization.* Read one or two articles on high altitude acclimatization. What are the causes and symptoms of high altitude sickness? What steps can you take to prevent high altitude sickness?

2. Both the American Anthropological Association (AAA) and the American Association of Physical Anthropologists (AAPA) have issued policy statements on the subject of *race.* Go the AAA home page (**http://www.aaanet.org/**) and, on the side bar, click on the search option, and conduct a search for *race.* Read the AAA statement, then go to the AAPA Web site at (**http://www.physanth.org/**) and read the statement entitled, *Biological Aspects of Race.* Write a short summary of the two statements showing how they are similar and also how they differ.

Paleopathology: Diseases and Injuries of Bone

In Chapter 12, we discussed microevolutionary processes acting on contemporary humans. An important component of such studies relates to an understanding of the role of *disease* as it has influenced adaptations in *Homo sapiens*. This topic will also be a major focus of our discussion in the next chapter. Indeed, in the last few thousand years especially, infectious disease has likely been the single most important selective influence on recent human populations.

Some of the most significant biocultural adaptive shifts occurred with the development of agriculture. We have already noted in Chapter 12 some of the biocultural dynamics that influenced the spread of the sickle-cell allele over the last 2,000 years.

In the study of human disease, how do we obtain some time depth, thus extending our perspective back from strictly contemporary contexts? The primary source of information relating to the relative recent history of disease (i.e., over the last few thousand years) comes from skeletons. Archaeological skeletal material provides evidence on a variety of pathological conditions, making it possible to expand our knowledge both *through time* and *across space* to include a wide array of different human populations. In this way, physical anthropologists and archaeologists working together maximize the clear advantages of an anthropological perspective.

The branch of physical anthropology that studies injury and disease in earlier populations is called *paleopathology.* Within this subdiscipline anthropologists, often working with medical specialists, contribute to our knowledge of the history and geographical distribution of human diseases such as rheumatoid arthritis, tuberculosis, and syphilis. In addition, patterns of disease and trauma in specific groups can further illuminate how these peoples were affected by various environmental and cultural factors.

In most cases, paleopathologists work exclusively with dry, skeletonized specimens. Occasionally, however, under unusual circumstances, soft tissues—such as skin, hair, cartilage, or even internal organs—may also be preserved. For example, artificial mummification was practiced in ancient Egypt and Chile, and natural mummification may also occur in extremely dry climates (such as in the American Southwest and parts of North Africa).

FIGURE 1

Naturally mummified tissue on a cranium from Nubia (part of the modern country of the Sudan; c. A.D. 700–1400).

In addition, in permanently wet environments such as bogs, where bacterial action is forestalled, soft tissues can endure. For example, there are the famous bog bodies discovered in Denmark and England. In such circumstances, preservation may be quite extraordinary.

One major category of pathological process that leaves its mark on bone is trauma. Injuries in ancient human populations may be manifested in the skeleton as fractures (which frequently are well healed), dislocations, or wounds (e.g., from projectile points).

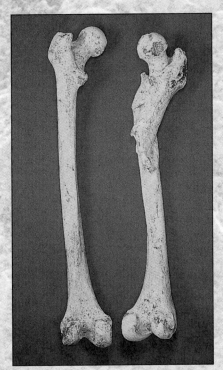

FIGURE 2

Fracture of a right femur (thigh bone) seen from the rear. (The normal left femur is shown for comparison.) Such an injury is extremely severe, even life threatening, but in this individual the bone healed remarkably well.

FIGURE 3

Embedded piece of obsidian projectile point in a lumbar vertebra from a central California male, 25 to 40 years old. The portion being held was found with the burial and may have been retained during life in soft tissue (muscle?). The injury shows some healing.

FIGURE 4

Unfused portion along the midline of a sacrum from a central California male, 16 to 18 years old. This condition, called "spina bifida occulta," is a fairly common, genetically influenced, asymptomatic condition.

Paleopathology: Diseases and Injuries of Bone (continued)

Other categories of skeletal abnormality include those that are *congenital* (present at birth) and *hereditary* (genetically determined). Rarely in skeletal collections are severe hereditary maladies (such as dwarfism) clearly diagnostic. More commonly, modifications are subtle and probably asymptomatic (i.e., not producing symptoms).

Tumors are another category of bone pathology, and, very rarely, malignant, life-threatening conditions can reliably be diagnosed from skeletal remains. (Usually, conditions such as lung or colon cancer kill the person *before* the skeleton becomes involved.)

A very common condition seen in all skeletal populations is degenerative arthritis. Bone changes

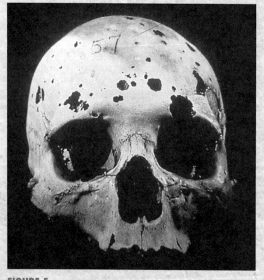

FIGURE 5

Numerous lesions of the cranium (such erosive lesions were also found in other bones), probably the result of a disseminated (metastasized) cancer, possibly originating from the breast, shown here in an Inuit female.

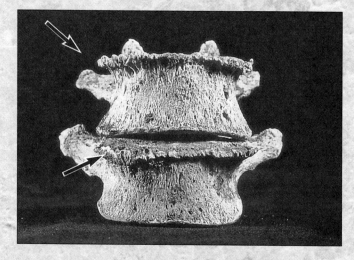

FIGURE 6

Bony lipping around the margins of two lumbar vertebrae (see arrows).

are most visible around the margins of vertebral body surfaces or are either peripheral to the margins or on the articular surfaces of appendicular joints (such as the knee).

In common conditions such as arthritis (seen in all human groups), the most informative approach is to compare *frequencies* of involvement in different populations. Such an approach is called *paleoepi-*

demiology and is best controlled when the study samples are partitioned by sex and age (the latter is especially important in age-related diseases, such as arthritis).

Because infectious disease has been such an important selective factor in human evolution and adaptation, it is an important disease category for paleopathological inquiry. Unfortunately, many

FIGURE 7

Extreme degenerative arthritis of a knee joint in an adult female from Nubia.

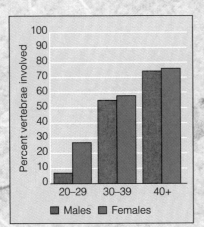

FIGURE 8

Bar graph showing incidence of vertebral body arthritis (osteophytosis) controlling for age and sex. The frequencies shown here are for a medieval Nubian population, and such information can be compared with data from other groups.

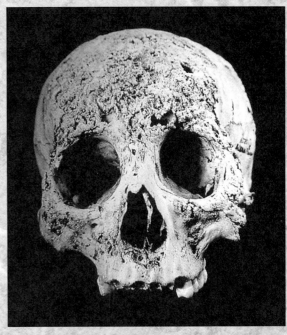

FIGURE 9

Extreme reaction in a cranium from an Alaskan Inuit (Eskimo), diagnostic of syphilis (although other possibilities must be considered).

Paleopathology: Diseases and Injuries of Bone (continued)

infectious processes do not leave evidence in bone, because affected individuals either recover or die before bone tissue becomes involved. But, some conditions such as syphilis or tuberculosis occasionally produce bone reaction. Interpretation of such processes in skeletons from varied geographical and chronological contexts provides some of the best bio-

logical data regarding the history of significant human diseases.

In recent years, the techniques of DNA fingerprinting have been added to the arsenal of tools to be used in the identification of infectious disease in archaeological populations. Perhaps the most successful of these investigations to date has

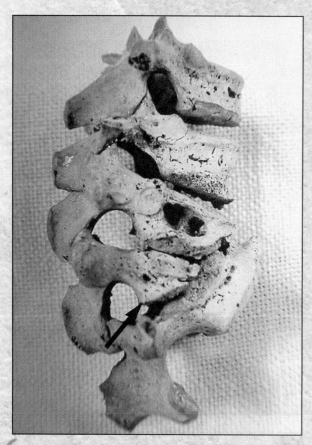

FIGURE 11

Dr. Arthur Aufderheide (right) and Dr. Wilmar Salo (left) examine DNA fingerprints obtained by PCR. From this analysis these researchers were the first to obtain such clear molecular evidence of tuberculosis in the pre-Columbian New World.

FIGURE 10

Probable case of tuberculosis, as seen in the thoracic vertebrae of an individual from Pueblo Bonito, New Mexico. As the disease progresses, one or more vertebrae can collapse (see arrow), producing a severe forward angulation of the spine.

been the recovery of a segment of DNA that is unique to *Mycobacterium tuberculosis,* the bacterium that causes tuberculosis, from a 1,000 year old mummy from Peru. This discovery, which would have been impossible without the use of PCR amplification techniques, has provided the most definitive evidence to date for the existence of tuberculosis in the New World prior to European contact.

Probably the most common conditions seen in ancient human groups are those that affect the teeth. In some groups, abrasive diets (and perhaps use of the teeth as tools) resulted in severe wear throughout the dentition.

Other types of dental lesions include caries (popularly called "cavities"), abscesses, loss of teeth (with resorbed sockets and loss of bone in the jaws), and improperly erupted teeth.

FIGURE 12
Lung tissue from which *Mycobacterium tuberculosis* DNA samples were taken.

FIGURE 13
Severe dental wear in the upper jaw (maxilla) of a central California male, 30+ years old. There is almost no enamel left on most of the teeth.

FIGURE 14
Severe abscess in the maxilla of a California Indian male, 31 to 40 years old. Despite the degree of bone reaction, such lesions can be asymptomatic.

CHAPTER
14

The Anthropological Perspective on the Human Life Course

CONTENTS

Introduction

Throughout this book, we have emphasized the importance of the anthropological perspective for understanding human beings through time and space. As defined in the first chapter, anthropology is the study of humankind. Unlike most other fields that have humans as their focus, the anthropological approach to humankind draws on and integrates research about people from all parts of the earth and from both past and contemporary cultures. An anthropological perspective on the life course will serve as a way of further illustrating the breadth of this approach.

Because this is a physical anthropology text, we have placed primary emphasis on human biological evolution and adaptation. We have learned that our biology is the result of millions of years of evolutionary history: 225 million years of mammalian evolution, 65 million years of primate evolution, 5 million years of hominid evolution, 2 million years of evolution of the genus *Homo*. But are we just another mammal, just another primate? In some ways, of course, we are like other mammals and other primates. But as emphasized throughout the text, modern human beings are the result of *biocultural evolution*. In other words, human biology and behavior today have been shaped by the biological and cultural forces that operated on our ancestors. In fact, it would be fruitless to attempt an understanding of modern human biology and diversity without considering that humans have evolved in the context of culture. It would be like trying to understand the biology of fish without considering that they live in water.

A good place to explore the interaction of biology and culture is the human life course. If we consider how a human develops from an embryo into an adult and examine the forces that operate on that process, then we will have a better perspective of how both biology and culture influence our own lives. Throughout this book, we have focused on the primate order (Chapters 5 and 6), the evolution of the family Hominidae (Chapters 8 through 10), and populations of modern *Homo sapiens* (Chapters 11 through 13). We continue the focus on modern humans in this chapter, but our interest shifts to the life course to understand how past and present evolutionary and cultural forces operate on our own lives. Another name for this chapter might be "Anthropology of the Individual."

There is, of course, much variation in the extent to which cultural factors interact with genetically based biological characteristics; these variable interactions influence how characteristics are expressed in individuals. Some genetically based characteristics will be exhibited no matter what the cultural context of growth and development happen to be. If a person inherits two alleles for albinism, for example (see Chapter 4), he or she will be deficient in production of the pigment melanin, resulting in lightly colored skin, hair, and eyes. This phenotype will emerge regardless of the cultural environment in which the person lives.

Other characteristics, such as intelligence, body shape, and growth will reflect the interaction of environment and genes. We know, for example, that each of us is born with a genetic makeup that influences the maximum stature we can achieve in adulthood. But to reach that maximum stature, we must be properly nourished during our growing years and avoid many childhood diseases and other stresses that inhibit growth. What factors determine whether we are well fed and receive good medical care? In the United States, socioeconomic status is probably the primary determinant of nutrition and health. Thus, socioeconomic status is an example of a cultural factor that affects growth.

Fundamentals of Growth and Development

The terms *growth* and *development* are often used interchangeably, but they actually refer to different processes. **Growth** refers to an increase in mass or number of cells, whereas **development** refers to the differentiation of cells into different types of tissues and their subsequent maturation. Increase in cell number is referred to as *hyperplasia,* and increase in cell size, or mass, is called *hypertrophy.* Some cells are manufactured only once and are usually not replaced if damaged (e.g., some nerve and muscle cells); some cells are continuously dying and being replaced (skin and red blood cells); and some can be regenerated if damaged (cells in the liver, kidneys, and most glands). (See Chapter 3 for discussions of cell division.)

Stature

Increased stature is a common indicator of health status in children because it is easy to assess under most circumstances. Growth spurts occur in early infancy and at puberty. Typically, well-nourished humans grow fairly rapidly during the first two trimesters (6 months) of fetal development, but growth slows during the third trimester. After birth, the rate of development increases and remains fairly rapid for about four years, at which time it decreases again to a relatively slow, steady level that is maintained until puberty. At puberty, there is once again a very pronounced increase in growth. During this so-called **adolescent growth spurt,** Western teenagers typically grow 9 to 10 cm per year. Subsequent to the adolescent growth spurt, the rate of development declines again and remains slower until adult stature is achieved by the late teens (Fig. 14–1).

Growth curves for boys and girls are significantly different, with the adolescent growth spurt occurring approximately two years earlier in girls than in boys. At birth, there is slight **sexual dimorphism** in many body measures (e.g., height, weight, head circumference, and body fat), but the major divergence in these characteristics does not occur until puberty. Table 14–1 shows the differences between body measurements for boys and girls at birth and at age 18. Boys are slightly

Growth
Increase in mass or number of cells.

Development
Differentiation of cells into different types of tissues and their maturation.

Adolescent growth spurt
The period during adolescence in which well-nourished teens typically increase in stature at greater rates than at other points in the life cycle.

Sexual dimorphism
Differences in physical characteristics between males and females of the same species. For example, humans are slightly sexually dimorphic for body size, with males being taller, on average, than females of the same population.

FIGURE 14–1

Distance and velocity curves of growth in height for a healthy American girl. (a) The distance curve shows the height attained in a given year. (b) The velocity curve plots the amount gained in a given year.

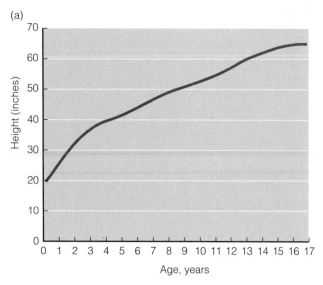

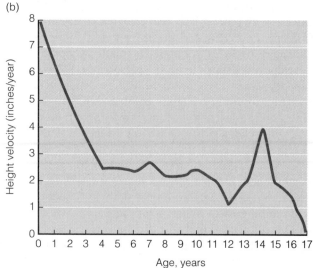

TABLE 14–1   Some Measurements of Size at Birth and at Age 18 for Children Born in the United States

	Boys		Girls	
	Birth	18	Birth	18
Body length (cm)*	49.9	181.1	49.3	166.7
Weight (kg)*	3.4	69.9	3.3	55.6
Head circumference (cm)[†]	34.8	55.9	34.1	54.9
Triceps skinfold (mm)	3.8[††]	8.5[§]	4.1[††]	17.5[§]
Subscapular skinfold (mm)	3.5[††]	10.0[§]	3.8[††]	12.0[§]

*Hamill et al., 1977
[†]Nellhaus, 1968.
[††]Johnston and Beller, 1976.
[§]Johnson et al., 1981.

Source: From Bogin, 1988, p. 22.

larger than girls at birth and are even more so at age 18, except in the last two measurements, triceps skinfold and subscapular skinfold. These two variables give information on body fat content and are determined by a special skinfold-measuring caliper. The triceps skinfold measure is taken by gently pinching the skin and fat underneath the upper arm, and the subscapular measurement is taken by gently pinching the skin and fat below the shoulder blade. These measurements reflect differences not only in the more obvious characteristics of height and weight, but also in body composition, with girls generally having more body fat than boys at all ages.

An individual's adult stature is influenced by genetics, health, and nutrition. In other words, children who experience good health and adequate nutrition during their growing years are much more likely to reach their genetic potential for height. On the other hand, children who are malnourished or experience prolonged periods of ill health may not reach that potential. In general, members of higher socioeconomic groups in a given population have taller average stature than members of lower socioeconomic groups, reflecting the impact of culture and economic status on the processes of growth and development (Bogin, 1998). This, then, is a good example of how growth is a result of biocultural processes.

Brain Growth

The head is a relatively large part of the body at birth. The continued growth of the brain after birth occurs at a rate far greater than that of any other part of the body, with the exception of the eyeball. At birth, the human brain is about 25 percent of its adult size. By 6 months of age, the brain has doubled in size, reaching 50 percent of adult size. It reaches 75 percent of adult size at age $2^1/_2$ years, 90 percent at age 5 years, and 95 percent by age 10 years. There is only a very small spurt at adolescence, making the brain an exception to the growth curves characteristic of most other parts of the body. As we will see later in this chapter, this pattern of brain growth, including the relatively small amount of growth before birth, is unusual among primates and other mammals. By contrast, the typical picture for most mammalian species is that at least 50 percent of adult brain size has been attained prior to birth. For humans, however, the narrow pelvis necessary for walking

bipedally provides limits on the size of the fetal head that can be delivered through it. That limitation, in addition to the value of having most brain growth occur in the more stimulating environment outside the womb, has resulted in human infants being born with far less of their total adult brain size than most other mammals. (As we saw in Chapter 9, this pattern of delayed maturation was probably already established in hominid evolution by 1.5 m.y.a.)

Nutritional Effects on Growth and Development

Nutrition has an impact on human growth at every stage of the life cycle. During pregnancy, for example, a woman's diet can have a profound effect on the development of her fetus and the eventual health of the child. Moreover, the effects are transgenerational, because a woman's own supply of eggs is developed while she herself is *in utero* (see Chapter 3). Thus, if a woman is malnourished during pregnancy, the eggs that develop in her female fetus may be damaged in a way that will impact the health of her future grandchildren.

Basic Nutrients for Growth and Development

Nutrients needed for growth, development, and body maintenance are organized into five major categories: proteins, carbohydrates, lipids (fats), vitamins, and minerals. As you learned in Chapter 3, *proteins,* composed of amino acids (see p. 49), are the major structural components of such structures as muscles, skin, hair, and most of the organs of the body. Antibodies and enzymes are proteins, as are most hormones. When you eat a meal, stomach and pancreatic enzymes break the protein down into the 20 amino acids described in Chapter 3. The amino acids are then absorbed into the bloodstream through the walls of the small intestine and are transported to other cells in the body, where they will be used in the synthesis of new proteins (the process by which this occurs is described in Chapter 3).

Carbohydrates are important sources of energy needed to run the body. Good sources of carbohydrates are potatoes, beans, and grains. Carbohydrate digestion begins in the mouth and continues in the small intestine, where simple sugars are absorbed into the bloodstream through the walls of the small intestine in a manner similar to that for amino acids. From there they are transported to the liver, where all are converted into glucose, the primary source of energy for the body. Indeed, glucose is the only source of energy utilized by the brain. The hormone insulin is responsible for regulating glucose levels in the blood and tissues. The condition in which insufficient amounts of insulin are produced or the cells are unable to respond to the insulin that is available is referred to as *diabetes.* We shall see later that diabetes, a leading cause of death in the United States, is a disorder of relatively recent origin (Eaton, Shostak, and Konner, 1988).

Lipids comprise the third major nutrient category and include fats and oils. Fats are broken down into fatty acids and are absorbed into the bloodstream through the walls of the small intestine. These fatty acids are then further broken down and stored until needed for energy.

Vitamins are another category of nutrients needed for growth and for a healthy, functioning body. Vitamins serve as components of enzymes, and enzymes speed up chemical reactions. There are two categories of vitamins: those that are water-soluble (the B vitamins and vitamin C) and those that, like fats, are not soluble in water but are soluble in fat (vitamins A, D, E, and K). The fat-soluble vitamins can be stored, so a deficiency of any of them is slow to develop. Because water-soluble vitamins are excreted in urine, very little is stored; these vitamins must be consumed almost daily in order to maintain health.

Unlike other nutrients, minerals are not organic, but they, too, contribute to normal functioning and health. The minerals needed in the greatest quantity include calcium (this mineral alone makes up 2 percent of our body weight, mostly in the skeleton and teeth), phosphorus, potassium, sulfur, sodium, chlorine, and magnesium. Our requirements for iron are comparatively low, but this mineral plays a critical role in oxygen transport. Iron-deficiency anemia is one of the most common nutritional deficiency diseases worldwide, especially in women of reproductive age, whose iron needs are greater than those of men. Other essential minerals include iodine, zinc, manganese, copper, cobalt, fluoride, molybdenum, selenium, and chromium.

Evolution of Nutritional Requirements

Our nutritional requirements have coevolved with the types of food that were available to human ancestors throughout our evolutionary history. Because the earliest mammals and the first primates were probably insect eaters, humans have inherited the ability to digest and process animal protein. Early primates also evolved the ability to process most vegetable material. Our more immediate ape-like ancestors were primarily fruit eaters, so we are able to process fruits. Furthermore, human needs for specific vitamins and minerals reflect these ancestral nutritional adaptations. A good example is our requirement for vitamin C, also known as ascorbic acid. Vitamin C plays an important role in the metabolism of all foods and in the production of energy. It is a crucial organic compound for all animals—so crucial, in fact, that most animals are able to manufacture, or *synthesize*, it internally and need not depend on dietary sources. It is likely that most of the early primates were able to make their own vitamin C. As the monkeys evolved, however, they began to eat more leaves and fruits and less animal protein; thus, they were getting adequate amounts of vitamin C in their diets. At some point in early primate evolution (about 35 m.y.a.; see Chapter 7), it is hypothesized that some individuals "lost" the ability to synthesize vitamin C, perhaps through a genetic mutation. This loss would not have been disadvantageous as long as dietary sources of vitamin C were regularly available. In fact, it may have been selectively advantageous to conserve the energy required for the manufacture of vitamin C, so that natural selection favored those individuals in a species who were unable to synthesize it. Eventually, all descendants of these early higher primates (i.e., modern monkeys, apes, and humans) were unable to synthesize vitamin C and became dependent entirely on external (food) sources.

Through much of the course of human evolution, the inability to manufacture vitamin C was never a problem because of the abundance of the vitamin in the human diet. It has been estimated that the average daily intake of vitamin C for preagricultural people was 440 mg, compared to an approximate 90 mg in the current American diet (Eaton and Konner, 1985). When people get insufficient amounts of vitamin C, they often develop **scurvy,** a disease that was probably extremely rare or absent in preagricultural populations (agriculture arose approximately 10,000 to 12,000 years ago). Symptoms of scurvy include abnormal

Scurvy
Disease resulting from a dietary deficiency of vitamin C. It may result in anemia, poor bone growth, abnormal bleeding and bruising, and muscle pain.

bleeding of gums, slowed healing of wounds, loss of energy, anemia, and abnormal formation of bones and teeth. Scurvy was probably not very common in the past except in extreme northern regions. Today, the condition occasionally appears in infants who are fed exclusively on powdered or canned milk that does not have added vitamin C.

Humans also lack the ability to synthesize some of the amino acids that are necessary for growth and maintenance of the body. As noted in Chapter 3, there are 20 amino acids that make up the proteins of all living things. Plants synthesize all the amino acids, but animals must get some or all from the foods they consume. *Lactobacillus*, for example, is a bacterium that lives in milk; since it can get all 20 amino acids from the milk it consumes, it is unable to synthesize any of them. Because adult humans cannot synthesize eight of the amino acids in sufficient quantities, we must get them from the foods we eat ; they are thus referred to as the eight **essential amino acids** (for infants, there are nine). Interestingly, the amounts of each of the amino acids we need parallel the amounts present in animal protein, suggesting that food from animal sources may have been an important component of ancestral hominid diets when our specific nutrient requirements were evolving. Biologically, most humans can best meet their requirements for protein from animal sources, but meat consumption is expensive, in both ecological and economic terms. By combining vegetables such as legumes and grains, humans can obtain the eight essential amino acids in the correct proportions (Fig. 14–2). Thus, most contemporary populations meet their need for protein by eating enough variety of vegetable foods so that adequate proportions of amino acids are achieved. Examples of familiar cuisines that reflect these combinations include beans and corn in Mexico, beans and rice in Caribbean cultures, rice and lentils in India, and black-eyed peas and cornbread in the southern United States.

Essential amino acids
The eight (nine for infants) amino acids that must be ingested by humans for normal growth and body maintenance; include tryptophan, leucine, lysine, methionine, phenylalanine, isoleucine, valine, and threonine (plus histidine for infants).

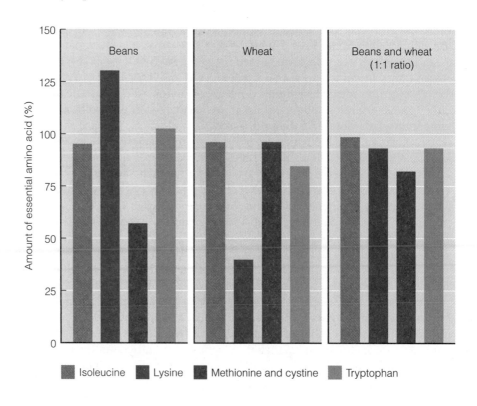

FIGURE 14–2

Complementarity of beans and wheat.
(Adapted from *Scientific American,* 1976.)

An example of biological and cultural interaction in meeting nutritional requirements is seen in the traditional methods for processing corn into tortillas or hominy. Wherever corn is a major part of the diet, it is usually associated with a high incidence of the disease **pellagra,** which results from a deficiency of the vitamin niacin (vitamin B_3). The exception to this pattern is the Americas, where corn was originally domesticated and where pellagra is not common. The reason for the lower prevalence of pellagra appears to be the practice of adding lime or ashes to the cornmeal when making tortillas or hominy. These additives increase the availability of niacin in the corn so that it can be absorbed by the body (Katz et al., 1974). Unfortunately, when corn was exported to the rest of the world, this particular technology was not exported with it.

Because humans can use cultural responses to adapt to environmental challenges, does that mean that culture has enabled us as a species to transcend the limitations placed on us by our biology? At this stage of human history, it seems that we are still constrained by our evolved nutritional requirements. These requirements reflect adaptation to a food base that included a great deal of variety. Not only did we evolve against a background of variety, we are now "stuck with" requirements for variety. As agriculture has evolved and population size expanded, however, the human food base has become narrower, leading to the appearance of nutritional deficiency disease, which, like scurvy and pellagra, probably did not exist in the evolutionary past (i.e., prior to the development of agriculture).

Diets of Humans Before Agriculture

The preagricultural diet, while perhaps high in animal protein, was low in fats, particularly saturated fats (Table 14–2). The diet was also high in complex carbohydrates (including fiber), low in salt, and high in calcium. We do not need to be reminded that the contemporary American diet has the opposite configuration of the one just described. It is high in saturated fats and salt and low in complex carbohydrates, fiber, and calcium (Table 14–3). There is very good evidence that many of today's diseases in industrialized countries are related to the lack of fit between our diet today and the one with which we evolved (Eaton, Shostak, and Konner, 1988).

Many of our biological and behavioral characteristics evolved because in the past they contributed to adaptation; but today these same characteristics may be maladaptive. An example is our ability to store fat. This capability was an advantage in the past, when food availability often alternated between abundance and scarcity. Those who could store fat during the times of abundance could draw on those stores during times of scarcity and remain healthy, resist disease, and, for women, maintain the ability to reproduce. Today, people with adequate economic resources spend much of their lives with a relative abundance of foods. Considering the number of disorders associated with obesity, the formerly positive ability to store extra fat has now turned into a liability. Our "feast or famine" biology is now incompatible with the constant feast many of us indulge in today.

It is clear that both deficiencies and excesses of nutrients can cause health problems and interfere with growth and development. Certainly, many people in all parts of the world, both industrialized and developing, suffer from inadequate supplies of food of any quality. We read daily of thousands dying from starvation due to drought, warfare, or political instability. We have noted that the agricultural revolution is partly responsible for some of the problems with food and health we

Pellagra
Disease resulting from a dietary deficiency of niacin (vitamin B_3). Symptoms include dermatitis, diarrhea, dementia, and death (the "four Ds").

353

TABLE 14–2   Selected Meats in Agricultural and Preagricultural Diets

	Meat (100 g portion)	Protein (g)	Fat (g)
Domestic meat	Prime lamb loin	14.7	32.0
	Ham	15.2	29.1
	Regular hamburger	17.9	21.2
	Choice sirloin steak	16.9	26.7
	Pork loin	16.4	28.0
Wild game	Goat	20.6	3.8
	Cape buffalo	—	2.8
	Warthog	—	4.2
	Horse	20.5	3.7
	Wild boar	16.8	8.3
	Beaver	30.0	5.1
	Muskrat	27.2	4.1
	Caribou	—	2.4
	Moose	—	1.5
	Kangaroo	—	1.2
	Turtle	26.8	3.9
	Opossum	33.6	4.5
	Wildebeest	—	5.4
	Thomson's gazelle	—	1.6
	Kob (waterbuck)	—	3.1
	Pheasant	24.3	5.2
	Rabbit	21.0	5.0
	Impala	—	2.6
	Topi	—	2.2
	Deer	21.0	4.0
	Bison	25.0	3.8

Note: Dashes indicate that data are not available.
Source: From Eaton, Shostak, and Konner, 1988.

see today. The blame must be placed not only on the narrowed food base that resulted from the emergence of agriculture, but also on the increase in human population that occurred when people began to settle in permanent villages and have more children. Today, the crush of billions of humans almost completely dependent on cereal grains means that millions face undernutrition, malnutrition, and even starvation. (See Chapter 15 for a further discussion of world population growth and related problems.)

Undernutrition and Malnutrition

Undernutrition
A diet insufficient in quantity (calories) to support normal health.

By **undernutrition,** we mean an inadequate quantity of food; in other words, not enough calories are consumed to support normal health. There is, of course, a great deal of variation in what constitutes an "adequate" diet (factors such as age, health, and activity levels all affect this determination), but it has been estimated that between 16 and 63 percent of the world's population is undernourished.

TABLE 14–3 Preagricultural, Contemporary American, and Recently Recommended Dietary Composition

	Preagricultural Diet	Contemporary Diet	Recent Recommendations
Total dietary energy (%)			
Protein	33	12	12
Carbohydrate	46	46	58
Fat	21	42	30
Alcohol	~0	(7–10)	—
P:S ratio*	1.41	0.44	1
Cholesterol (mg)	520	300–500	300
Fiber (g)	100–150	19.7	30–60
Sodium (mg)	690	2,300–6,900	1,000–3,300
Calcium (mg)	1,500–2,000	740	800–1,500
Ascorbic acid (mg)	440	90	60

*Polyunsaturated: saturated fat ratio.

Malnutrition refers to an inadequate amount of some key element in the diet, such as proteins, minerals, or vitamins. In underdeveloped countries, protein malnutrition is the most common variety. The hallmark of severe protein malnutrition is *kwashiorkor,* a disease manifested by tissue swelling (especially in the abdominal area, giving its victims the typical "swollen belly" profile), anemia, loss or discoloration of hair, and apathy.

More than causing discomfort, malnutrition greatly affects reproduction and infant survival. Malnourished mothers have difficult labor, more premature births, more children born with birth defects, higher prenatal mortality, and generally lower birth weights of newborns. Given all these potential physiological difficulties, it is surprising that overall **fertility** among malnourished mothers is not disrupted more than it is. Moderate chronic malnutrition (unless malnutrition becomes exceedingly severe, approaching starvation) has only a small effect on the number of live births (Bongaarts, 1980).

Children born to malnourished mothers are at a disadvantage even at birth. They are smaller and behind in most aspects of physical development. After birth, if malnutrition persists, such children fall further behind because of their mothers' generally poor **lactation.** Growth processes are often greatly slowed when environmental insults are severe (malnutrition and/or disease). Later on, a period of accelerated growth (called the **catch-up period**) can make up some of the deficit. There are certain critical periods, however, in which growth in certain tissues is normally very rapid. If a severe interruption occurs during one of these periods, the individual may never catch up completely. For example, malnutrition during the last trimester of fetal life or during the first year of infancy can have marked effects on brain development. Autopsies of children who have died from complications of severe malnutrition have shown reduced brain size and weight, as well as fewer numbers of brain cells (Frisancho, 1978).

In summary, our nutritional adaptations were shaped in an environment that included times of scarcity alternating with times of abundance. The variety of foods consumed was so great that nutritional deficiency diseases were rare. Small

Malnutrition
A diet insufficient in quality (i.e., lacking some essential component) to support normal health.

Fertility
Actual production of offspring; distinguished from fecundity, which is the (potential) ability to produce children. For example, a woman in her early 20s is probably fecund, but she is not actually fertile unless she has had children.

Lactation
The production of milk in mammals.

Catch-up period
A period of time during which a child who has experienced delayed growth because of malnutrition, undernutrition, or disease can increase in height to the point of his or her genetic potential.

amounts of animal foods were probably an important part of the diet in many parts of the world. In northern latitudes, subsequent to approximately 1 million years ago, meat was an important part of the diet, but because meat was low in fats, the negative effects of high meat intake that we see today did not occur. Our diet today is often incompatible with the adaptations that evolved in the millions of years preceding the development of agriculture, and the consequences of that incompatibility include both starvation and obesity.

Other Factors Influencing Growth and Development

Genetics

No matter how much you eat in your lifetime or how excellent your health is, you will not be able to exceed your genetic potential for stature and a number of other physiological parameters. Genetic factors set the underlying limitations and potentialities for growth and development, but the life experience and environment of the organism determine how the body grows within those parameters. How do we assess the relative contributions of genes and the environment in their effects on growth? Much of our information comes from studies of monozygotic and dizygotic twins. Monozygotic ("identical") twins come from the union of a single sperm and ovum and share 100 percent of their genes. Dizygotic ("fraternal") twins come from separate ova and sperm and share only 50 percent of their genes, just as any other siblings from the same parents. If monozygotic twins with identical genes but different growth environments are exactly the same in stature at various ages (i.e., show perfect correlation or *concordance* for stature), then we can conclude that genes are the primary, if not the only, determinants of stature. Most studies of twins reveal that under normal circumstances, stature is "highly correlated" for monozygotic twins, leading to the conclusion that stature is under fairly strong genetic control (Table 14–4). Weight, on the other hand, seems to be more strongly influenced by diet, environment, and individual experiences than by genes.

TABLE 14–4 Correlation Coefficients for Height Between Monozygotic (MZ) and Dizygotic (DZ) Twin Pairs from Birth to Age 8.

Age	Total N	MZ	DZ Same sex	DZ Different Sex
Birth	629	0.62	0.79	0.67
3 months	764	0.78	0.72	0.65
6 months	819	0.80	0.67	0.62
12 months	827	0.86	0.66	0.58
24 months	687	0.89	0.54	0.61
3 years	699	0.93	0.56	0.60
5 years	606	0.94	0.51	.068
8 years	444	0.94	0.49	0.65

Source: From Wilson, 1979, after Bogin, 1988, p. 163.

Hormones

One of the primary ways in which genes have an effect on growth and development is through their effects on hormones. Hormones are substances produced in one cell that have an effect on another cell (see p. 47). Most hormones are produced by *endocrine* glands; they are transported in the bloodstream, and almost all have an effect on growth. The hypothalamus (located at the base of the forebrain) can be considered the relay station, control center, or central clearinghouse for most hormonal action. This control center receives messages from the brain and other glands and sends out messages that stimulate hormonal action. Most of the hormonal messages transmitted from the hypothalamus result in the inhibition or release of other hormones.

We can use the hormone thyroxine, produced by the thyroid gland in the neck, to illustrate the action of hormones and the communication system among the endocrine glands (Fig. 14–3) (Crapo, 1985). Thyroxine regulates metabolism and aids in body heat production. When thyroxine levels fall too low for normal metabolism, the brain senses this and sends a message to the hypothalamus. The hypothalamus reacts by releasing TRH, or thyrotropin-releasing hormone. TRH goes to the anterior pituitary, where it stimulates the release of TSH, or thyroid-stimulating hormone. TSH then goes to the thyroid gland, stimulating it to release thyroxine. When the brain senses that the levels of thyroxine are adequate, it sends signals that inhibit the further release of TRH and TSH. In many ways, this process is similar to what your household thermostat does: When it senses that the temperature has dropped too low for comfort, it sends a message to the furnace to begin producing more heat; when the temperature reaches or exceeds the preset level, the thermostat sends another message to turn the furnace off.

Two other hormones that are important in growth include growth hormone and insulin. Growth hormone, secreted by the anterior pituitary, promotes growth and has an effect on just about every cell in the body. Tumors and other disorders can result in excessive or insufficient amounts of growth hormone secretion, which in turn can result in gigantism or dwarfism. One group of people who have notably short stature are African Efe pygmies. Recent research suggests that altered levels of growth hormone and its controlling factors interact with nutritional factors and infectious diseases to produce the relatively short adult stature of these people (Shea and Bailey, 1996), providing another example of the interaction of biological and cultural forces.

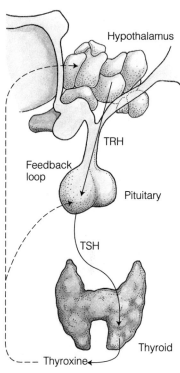

FIGURE 14–3

Example of a feedback loop. When thyroxine levels in the blood fall too low, the hypothalamus releases TRH (thyrotropin-releasing hormone), which goes to the anterior pituitary, triggering the release of TSH (thyroid-stimulating hormone). TSH causes thyroxine to be released from the thyroid gland. Release of TRH and TSH is then inhibited.

Environmental Factors

Environmental factors, such as altitude and climate, have effects on growth and development. Perhaps the primary influence of such external factors comes from their effects on nutrition, but there is evidence of independent effects as well. For example, as noted in Chapter 13, infant birth weight is lower at high altitude, and this is so even when such factors as nutrition, smoking, and socioeconomic status are taken into consideration. In the United States, the percentage of low-birth-rate (LBW) infants (those weighing less than 2,500 g, or 5.7 pounds) is about 6.5 percent at sea level, rising to 10.4 percent at 5,000 feet and almost 24 percent above 10,000 feet. In a Bolivian study, the mean birth weight was 3,415 g (7.8 pounds) at low elevations and 3,133 g (7.1 pounds) at high elevations (Haas et al., 1980). Most studies of children have found that those at high elevations are shorter and lighter than those at low elevations.

In general, populations in cold climates tend to be heavier and have longer trunks and shorter extremities than populations in tropical areas. This reflects Bergmann's and Allen's rules, discussed in Chapter 13. Exposure to sunlight also appears to have an effect on growth, most likely through its effects on vitamin D production. Children tend to grow more rapidly in times of high sunlight concentration (i.e., in the summer in temperate regions and in the dry season in monsoonal tropical regions). Vitamin D, necessary for skeletal growth, requires sunlight for its synthesis (see p. 327).

Among the most significant environmental factors having an effect on growth and development is infectious disease, such as malaria, influenza, cholera, and tuberculosis (see pp. 333–337). These diseases have their greatest impact during childhood and can delay growth, particularly when coupled with malnutrition. In fact, the effects of infectious disease and malnutrition are said to be *synergistic;* that is, each worsens the effect of the other so that in combination their effects are potentially more damaging than either is acting alone. Unfortunately, they often occur together because chronic malnutrition lowers resistance to disease organisms that are present in the environment.

The Human Life Cycle

Many of the following variables are discussed within a comparative mammalian context in Virtual Lab 1, section IV, part A.

As noted in earlier chapters, primatologists and other physical anthropologists view primate and human growth and development from an evolutionary perspective, with an interest in how natural selection has operated on the life cycle from conception to death, a perspective known as *life history theory.* Why, for example, do humans have longer periods of infancy and childhood compared with other primates? What accounts for differences seen in the life cycles of such closely related species as humans and chimpanzees? Life history research seeks to answer such questions.

Not all animals have clearly demarcated phases in their lives; moreover, among mammals, humans have more such phases than do other species (Fig. 14–4). Protozoa, among the simplest of animals, have only one phase; many invertebrates have two: larval and adult. Almost all mammals have at least three phases: prenatal, infancy, and adulthood. Most primates have four phases: prenatal, infancy,

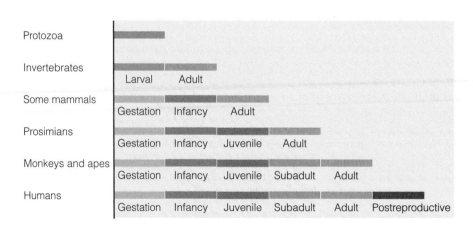

FIGURE 14–4

Life cycle stages for various animal species.

juvenile (usually called childhood in humans), and adult. Monkeys, apes, and humans add a phase between the juvenile phase and adulthood that is referred to as the subadult period (adolescence, or teenage, in humans). Finally, for humans there is the addition of a sixth phase in women, the postreproductive years following menopause. One could argue that during the course of primate evolution, more recently evolved forms have longer life spans and more divisions of the life span into phases, or stages.

Most of these life cycle stages are well marked by biological transitions. The prenatal phase begins with conception and ends with birth; infancy is the period of nursing; childhood, or the juvenile phase, is the period from weaning to sexual maturity (puberty in humans); adolescence is the period from puberty to the end of growth; adulthood is marked by the birth of the first child and/or the completion of growth; and menopause is recognized as having occurred one full year after the last menstrual cycle. These biological markers are similar among higher primates, but for humans, there is an added complexity: They occur in cultural contexts that define and characterize them. Puberty, for example, has very different meanings in different cultures. A girl's first menstruation (menarche) is often marked with ritual and celebration, and a change in social status typically occurs with this biological transition. Likewise, menopause is often associated with a rise in status for women in non-Western societies, whereas it is commonly seen as a negative transition for women in many Western societies. As we shall see, collective and individual attitudes toward these life cycle transitions have an effect on growth and development.

Pregnancy, Birth, and Infancy

The biological aspects of conception and gestation can be discussed in a fairly straightforward way, drawing information from what is known about reproductive biology at the present time: A sperm fertilizes an egg; the resulting zygote travels through a uterine (fallopian) tube to become implanted in the uterine lining; and the embryo develops until it is mature enough to survive outside the womb, at which time birth occurs. But this is clearly not all there is to human pregnancy and birth. Female biology may be similar the world over, but cultural rules and practices are the primary determinants of who will get pregnant, as well as when, where, how, and by whom.

Once pregnancy has occurred, there is much variation in how a woman should behave, what she should eat, where she should and should not go, and how she should interact with other people. Almost every culture known, including our own, imposes dietary restrictions on pregnant women. Many of these appear to serve an important biological function, particularly that of keeping the woman from ingesting toxins that would be dangerous for the fetus. (Alcohol is a good example of a potential toxin whose consumption in pregnancy is discouraged in the United States.) The food aversions to coffee, alcohol, and other bitter substances that many women experience during pregnancy may be evolved adaptations to protect the embryo from toxins. The nausea of early pregnancy may also function to limit the intake of foods potentially harmful to the embryo at a critical stage of development (Profet, 1988; Williams and Nesse 1991).

Birth is an event that is celebrated with ritual in almost every culture studied. In fact, the relatively little fanfare associated with childbirth in the United States is unusual by world standards. Because risk of death for both mother and child is so great at birth, it is not surprising that it is surrounded with ritual significance. Perhaps because of the high risk of death, we tend to think that birth is far more difficult in humans than it is in other mammals. But since almost all primate infants have large heads relative to body size, birth is challenging to many primates (Fig. 14–5).

An undeveloped brain seems necessary for birth to occur through a narrow pelvis, but it may also be advantageous for other reasons. For a species as dependent on learning as we are for survival, it may be adaptive for most of our brain growth to take place in the presence of environmental stimuli rather than in the relatively unstimulating uterus. This may be particularly true for a species dependent on language. The language centers of the brain develop in the first three years of life, when the brain is undergoing its rapid expansion; these three years are considered a critical period for the development of language in the human child.

Infancy is defined as the period during which nursing takes place, typically lasting about four years in humans. When we consider how unusual it is for a mother to nurse her child for even a year in the United States or Canada, this figure may surprise us. But considering that four or five years of nursing is the norm for chimpanzees, gorillas, orangutans, and for women in foraging societies, most anthropologists conclude that four years was the norm for most humans in the

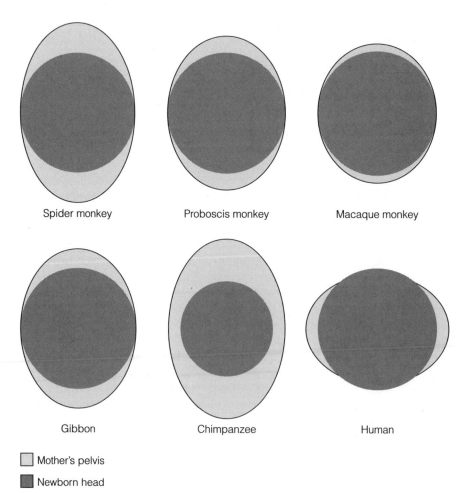

FIGURE 14–5

The relation between the average diameter of the birth canal of adult females and average head length and breadth of newborns of the same species. (After Jolly, 1985.)

Spider monkey   Proboscis monkey   Macaque monkey

Gibbon   Chimpanzee   Human

☐ Mother's pelvis

■ Newborn head

evolutionary past (Eaton, Shostak, and Konner, 1988). Other lines of evidence confirm this pattern, including the lack of other foods that infants could consume until the origin of agriculture and the domestication of milk-producing animals. In fact, if the mother died during childbirth in preagricultural populations, it is very likely that the child died also, unless there was another woman available who could nurse the child. Jane Goodall has noted that this is also true for chimpanzees: Infants who are orphaned before they are weaned do not usually survive (see also Chapter 6). Even those orphaned after weaning are still emotionally dependent on their mothers and exhibit clinical signs of depression for a few months or years after the mother's death, assuming they survive the trauma (Goodall, 1986).

Human milk, like that of other primates, is extremely low in fats and protein (Fig. 14–6). Such a low nutrient content is typical for species in which mothers are seldom or never separated from their infants and nurse in short, frequent bouts. Not coincidentally, prolonged, frequent nursing suppresses ovulation (Konner and Worthman, 1980); this behavior helps to maintain a four-year birth interval, during which infants have no nutritional competition from siblings. Thus, nursing served as a natural birth control mechanism in the evolutionary past, as it does in some populations today.

Breast milk also provides important antibodies that contribute to infant survival. Throughout the world, breast-fed infants have far greater survival rates than those who are not breast-fed or who are weaned too early. The only exception is in societies where scientifically developed milk substitutes are readily available

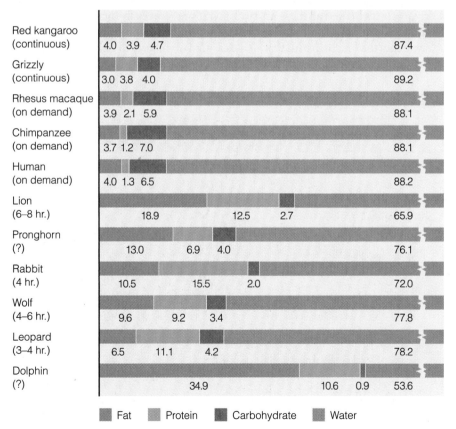

FIGURE 14–6

Carbohydrate, protein, and fat composition of milk of selected mammals (indicated in percent). Terms in parentheses indicate nursing frequency. (From Ben Shaul, 1962.)

and appropriately used. The importance of adequate nutrients during this period of rapid brain growth cannot be overestimated. Thus, it is not surprising that there are many cultural practices designed to ensure successful nursing.

Childhood

Humans have unusually long childhoods, reflecting the importance of learning for our species. *Childhood* is that time between weaning and puberty when the brain is completing its growth and acquisition of technical and social skills is taking place. For most other mammals, once weaning has occurred, getting food is left to individual effort. Humans may be unique in the practice of providing food for children or juveniles (Lancaster and Lancaster, 1983). Such sustained care requires much extra effort by parents, but the survival rate of offspring is a great deal higher than in other primates (Table 14–5). During childhood, the roles of fathers and older siblings become very significant. While mothers are highly involved with caring for new infants, the socialization and child care of other children often fall to other family or community members. Clearly, family environment, stress, and other biosocial factors have a major impact on children's health (Flinn, 1999).

Adolescence

A number of biological events mark the transition to adolescence for both males and females. These include increase in body size, change in body shape, and the development of testes and penes in boys, and breasts in girls. Hormonal changes are the driving forces behind all these physical alterations, especially increased testosterone production in boys and increased estrogen production in girls. As already noted, menarche (the first menstruation) is a clear sign of puberty in girls and is usually the marker of this transition in cultures where the event is ritually celebrated.

TABLE 14–5   Providing for Juveniles

| | Percent of Those Who Survive | |
	Weaning	Adolescence
Lion	28	15
Baboon	45	33
Macaque	42	13
Chimpanzee	48	38
Provisioned macaques	82	58
Human Populations		
!Kung*	80	58
Yanomamo †	73	50
Paleoindian ††	86	50

* A hunting and gathering population of southern Africa.
† Horticultural population of South America.
†† Preagricultural people of the Americas.

Source: Adapted from Lancaster and Lancaster, 1983.

A number of factors affect the onset of puberty in humans, including genetics, gestational experience, nutrition, disease, activity levels, and stress. In humans and other primates, females reach sexual maturity before males do. An illustration of the effect of diet and other lifestyle factors on puberty is seen in the trend toward a lower age of menarche that has been noted in human populations in the last hundred years and the tendency for girls who are very active and thin to mature later than those who are heavier and less active. Socioeconomic factors are also implicated in this "secular trend": In less developed nations, girls from higher social classes tend to mature earlier than girls from lower social classes. In general, physical development has accelerated in the past several decades along with worldwide improvements in public health and nutrition (Worthman, 1999).

Adolescence is the time between puberty and the completion of physical growth or the social recognition of adulthood. This social recognition may result from marriage, bearing a child, or a particular accomplishment. In nonhuman primates, the equivalent stage is defined in males as the time from which they are capable of fertilization to the time when physical growth is complete. At this point, they have male-specific features and size and are recognized as adults by other members of the social group. Females begin to engage in sexual behavior, exhibiting signs of sexual receptivity before they are capable of bearing young. These early cycles are usually not ovulatory and define the period of adolescence for them. Adulthood comes with the first pregnancy.

Adulthood

Pregnancy and child care occupy much of a woman's adult life in most cultures, as they likely did throughout hominid evolution. For most women, the years from menarche to menopause are marked by monthly menstruation, except when they are pregnant or nursing. A normal menstrual cycle has two phases: the follicular phase, in which the egg is preparing for ovulation, marked by high estrogen production; and the luteal phase, during which the uterus is preparing for implantation, marked by high progesterone production. If the egg is not fertilized, progesterone production drops off and menstruation, the shedding of the uterine lining, occurs. A woman who never becomes pregnant may have as many as 400 cycles between menarche and menopause. Because reliable contraceptives were unavailable in the past, this high number of menstrual cycles is probably a relatively recent phenomenon. It has been suggested, in fact, that highly frequent menstrual cycling may be implicated in several cancers of the female reproductive organs, especially of the breast, uterus, and ovaries (Eaton et al., 1994). During the course of human evolution, females may have had as few as 60 menstrual cycles in their entire lives, unless they were sterile or not sexually active.

At the social level, adulthood for women in the majority of world cultures means, in addition to caring for children, participation in economic activities. Adulthood for men typically includes activities related to subsistence, religion, politics, and family. Women may be equally or less involved in these activities, depending on the culture.

During adulthood, the status of an individual may change as new skills are acquired or new achievements made. Where such records are kept, status may be defined by chronological age, as seen in the common pattern of retirement at age 65 or 70 in the United States.

For women, menopause, or the end of menstruation, is a sign of entry into a new phase of the life cycle. Estrogen and progesterone production begin to decline toward the end of the reproductive years until ovulation (and thus menstruation) ceases altogether. This occurs at approximately age 50 in all parts of the world. Throughout human evolution, the majority of females (and males) did not survive to age 50; thus, few women lived much past menopause. But today, this event occurs when women have as much as one-third of their active and healthy lives ahead of them. As already noted, such a long postreproductive period is not found in other primates. Female chimpanzees and monkeys experience decreased fertility in their later years, but most continue to have monthly cycles until their deaths. Occasional reports of menopause in apes and monkeys have been noted, but it is far from a routine and expected event.

Why do human females have such a long period during which they can no longer reproduce? One theory relates to parenting. Because it takes about 12 to 15 years before a child becomes independent, it has been argued that females are biologically "programmed" to live 12 to 15 years beyond the birth of their last child (Mayer, 1982). This hypothesis assumes that the maximum human life span for preagricultural humans was about 65 years, a figure that corresponds to what is known for contemporary hunter-gatherers and for prehistoric populations. Another theory that has been gaining attention is known as the "grandmother hypothesis." This proposes that women who lived several years beyond the independence of their last children would be freed to provide food and other resources to their children and grandchildren. Because these practices would likely increase the survival of grandchildren, productive postmenopausal years would be favored by natural selection (Hawkes et al., 1997). A third theory regarding menopause suggests that it was not itself favored by natural selection; rather it is an artifact of the extension of the human life span that has occurred in the last several centuries.

Aging

Postreproductive years are physiologically somewhat well defined for women, but "old age" is a very ambiguous concept. In the United States, we tend to associate old age with physical ailments and decreased activity. Thus, a person who is vigorous and active at age 70 might not be regarded as "old," whereas another who is frail and debilitated at age 55 may be considered old.

One reason we are concerned with this definition is that old age is generally regarded negatively and is typically unwelcome in the United States, a culture noted for its emphasis on youth. This attitude is quite different from that of many other societies, where old age brings with it wealth, higher status, and new freedoms, particularly for women. This is because high status is often correlated with knowledge, experience, and wisdom, which are themselves associated with greater age in most societies. Such has been the case throughout most of history, but today, in technologically developed countries, knowledge is changing so rapidly that the old may no longer control the most relevant knowledge.

By and large, people today are living longer than they did in the past because, in part, they are not dying from infectious diseases. Currently, the top five killers in the United States, for example, are heart disease, cancer, stroke, accidents, and chronic obstructive lung disease. Together these account for 75 percent of deaths (Eaton, Shostak, and Konner, 1988). All these conditions are considered "diseases of civilization" in that most can be accounted for by conditions in the modern environment that were not present in the past. Examples include cigarette smoke, air and water pollution, alcohol, automobiles, high-fat diets, and environmental carcinogens. It should be noted, however, that the high incidence of these diseases is also a result of people living to older ages because of factors such as improved hygiene, regular medical care, and new medical technologies.

Relative to most other animals, humans have a long life span. The maximum life span potential, estimated to be about 120 years, has probably not changed in the last several thousand years, although life expectancy at birth (the average length of life) has increased significantly in the last 100 years, probably due to the decreased influence of infectious diseases, which typically take their toll on the young (Crews and Harper, 1998). Clearly, advances in medicine, public health, and technology have contributed to the increase in life expectancy among most human populations. Can we assume that further advances will lead to an increase in the life span? Will scientific advances eventually mean that humans can live 150, 200, even 300 years? Most scholars think not.

The final phase of the life cycle, if we can call it that, is death. Humans all over the world celebrate this transition, often with great fanfare and expense. Some people interpret evidence from Neandertal remains to mean that ritual treatment of the dead may go back as far as 125,000 years in human history (see Chapter 10). Death is a less ambiguous transition than any of the others previously described, although there is great variation in what is believed to happen to the individual after death. There is also variability in mortuary practices surrounding the disposal of the physical remains. Most common are cremation and burial.

SUMMARY

This chapter has reviewed the fundamental concepts of growth and development and how those processes occur within the contexts of both biology and culture. Diet has an important effect on growth, and human nutritional requirements themselves result from biocultural evolution. The preagricultural human diet was reviewed, with the suggestion that many of our contemporary ills may result from incompatibilities between our evolved nutritional requirements and the foods that are currently consumed. In particular, the preagricultural diet was probably high in complex carbohydrates and fiber and low in fat and sodium. Diets for many contemporary people are low in complex carbohydrates and fiber and high in fat and sodium. This type of diet has been implicated in many current health problems.

The human life cycle can be divided into six phases: prenatal, infancy, juvenile, subadult, adult, and postreproductive. Each is fairly well defined by biological markers. Pregnancy lasts about nine months in humans, and infants are born with only about 25 percent of their adult brain size. This means that human infants are helpless at birth and therefore dependent on their parents for a long time. Birth is somewhat more challenging for humans than for other mammals because of the very close correspondence between maternal pelvic size (narrow because of bipedalism) and fetal head size (large, even though the brain is relatively undeveloped). Infancy is the period of nursing, approximately four years for most humans and apes. The unusually long period of childhood in humans is important as the time in which social and technological skills are acquired. Sexual maturation is

apparent at puberty, but full adult status is not achieved until growth has been completed and childbearing capabilities are reached. The last phase of the human life cycle, the postreproductive period, is marked in women by menopause, the cessation of menstruation and ovulation.

QUESTIONS FOR REVIEW

1. What is meant by the analogy "Water is to fish as culture is to humans"?
2. What is sexual dimorphism? List some examples in humans.
3. Briefly describe human brain growth.
4. What are essential amino acids? Develop a scenario for how our requirements for these amino acids might have evolved.
5. What were the characteristics of the preagricultural human diet? What are the major differences today?
6. Why is nursing important for infant health? What is the proposed relationship between nursing and ovulation?
7. What is the proposed significance of providing food for children beyond the age of weaning?
8. What biological changes occur in males and females at puberty? What role do lifestyle factors appear to play in determining the onset of puberty in girls?
9. How have attitudes toward the elderly changed in modern, high-tech cultures?
10. Why are humans living longer today than they did in the past?

SUGGESTED FURTHER READINGS

Bogin, Barry. 1988. *Patterns of Human Growth.* Cambridge, England: Cambridge University Press.

Cohen, Mark Nathan. 1989. *Health and the Rise of Civilization.* New Haven: Yale University Press.

Crews, D. E., and R. M. Garutto (eds.). *Biological Anthropology and Aging: An Emerging Synthesis.* New York: Oxford University Press.

Diamond, Jared. 1992. *The Third Chimpanzee: The Evolution and Future of the Human Animal.* New York: Harper Collins.

Eaton, S. Boyd, Marjorie Shostak, and Melvin Konner. 1988. *The Paleolithic Prescription.* New York: Harper & Row.

Panter-Brick, C., and C. M. Worthman (eds.). 1999. *Hormones, Health and Behavior: A Socio-Ecological and Lifespan Perspective.* Cambridge, England: Cambridge University Press.

Sinclair, D. 1989. *Human Growth After Birth.* New York: Oxford University Press.

Tanner, James M. 1990. *Foetus into Man: Physical Growth from Conception to Maturity.* 2nd ed., Cambridge, MA: Harvard University Press.

Trevathan, Wenda R. 1987. *Human Birth: An Evolutionary Perspective.* Hawthorne, NY: Aldine de Gruyter.

Trevathan, W. R., E. O. Smith, and J. J. McKenna (eds.). 1999. *Evolutionary Medicine.* New York: Oxford University Press.

Ulijaszek, S. J., F. E. Johnston, and M. A. Preece (eds.). 1998. *The Cambridge Encyclopedia of Human Growth and Development.* Cambridge, England: Cambridge University Press.

MULTIMEDIA RESOURCES

Wadsworth Anthropology Resource Center

http://anthropology.wadsworth.com

Visit Anthropology Online to obtain current updates in the field, surfing tips, career information, and more. In addition, enrich your study efforts with text-specific study aids arranged by chapter.

InfoTrac College Edition

http://www.infotrac-college.com/wadsworth

1. How do social factors such as war, population growth, weaning practices, and food production techniques influence the prevalence of malnutrition and undernutrition in developing countries. What are the long-term effects of malnutrition and undernutrition in children. Using Infotrac College Edition, do a subject search for *malnutrition, nutritional disorders,* and/or *malnutrition in children* to retrieve references that address these and related questions. Read two or three of these articles and write a short summary that discusses the types of nutritional disorders you read about. What causes them? What do you think could be done to remedy these problems? Also, you should go to *Related Subjects* to discover what other information on this topic is available.

2. As populations, particularly in developed countries, continue to age, more and more attention is being paid to problems associated with aging. These include, care of the elderly; treatment and prevention of age-related conditions such as heart disease, memory loss and other neurological changes, and osteoporosis; and rising health care costs. A subject search in InfoTrac College Edition on *aging* will pull up many references on a wide range of topics related to this issue. Read a few of these articles. Make a list of the issues and concerns facing the elderly that you had not considered before. How are they being addressed? How do you think they will be addressed when you begin to be affected by them?

Internet Exercises

1. Visit the American Museum of Natural History's Electronic Newspaper's Story on Aging at: **www.amnh.org/enews/aging/a43.html**. How does human longevity vary around the world? What are some of the factors that lead to regional and national differences? Follow the link to *evolution*. What was life expectancy for early hominids?

2. The World Health Organization Web site (**www.who.org**) provides current information for a wide range of topics pertaining to global health and nutrition. Browse this site or go directly to **www.who.org/nut** and choose from a list of topics a subject such as *protein-calorie malnutrition, iodine deficiency disorders, vitamin A deficiency, intrauterine growth deficiency,* or *iron deficiency anemia*. How do these nutritional disorders affect growth, development, and longevity? How does prevalence vary from country to country? In general, how do developing countries compare to developed nations such as the United States? What kinds of nutritional disorders are more common in the developed world?

CHAPTER

15

CONTENTS

Lessons from the Past, Lessons for the Future

Introduction

Homo sapiens is but one of approximately 1.4 million living species thus far known to science. All of these organisms, including bacteria and plants, ultimately are the contemporary result of the same basic evolutionary processes, and all share the same DNA material. But more than any other life form, humans, through cultural innovation and ever-expanding numbers, have come to dominate the planet, now to the detriment of thousands of species, including ourselves.

The preceding chapters have traced the evolutionary history of *Homo sapiens*. In our discussion of such topics as evolution and adaptation, we have emphasized the importance of culture in the development of our species. Such investigations of human evolution and the interplay between biology and culture can provide useful information about why humans behave the way they do. Moreover, they help us understand how a medium-sized bipedal primate came to occupy a position of dominance over many other forms of life on earth.

In this chapter, we briefly discuss some of the challenges that face humanity today, challenges that have emerged as a result of our own doing. In this discussion, we emphasize our place in nature and focus on how, since the domestication of plants and animals, we have altered the face of our planet, at the same time shaping the destiny of thousands of species, including *Homo sapiens*.

Although anthropology texts do not usually dwell on the topics included here, we feel that it is important to consider them, however brief and simplified our treatment must be. We are living during a critical period in the earth's history. Indeed, the future of much of life as we know it will be decided forever in the next few decades. It is crucial that we, as individuals, cities, and nations, make wise decisions, and to do this we must be well informed. The importance of acquiring knowledge cannot be overstated, for our decisions will be irrevocable.

It is valid to ask such questions as, What is the future of *Homo sapiens*? Will we continue to thrive? What kind of world will our descendants inherit? What is the future of the millions of other species? Perhaps we, as anthropologists, are in a position to address these and many other questions of immediate concern. The study of human biological and cultural evolution, coupled with an examination of the results of early human activities, can provide some insights from the past that may help illuminate the future. At the very least, we can provide students with an anthropological perspective on the serious problems that face us today.

How Successful Are We?

As we have emphasized, humans are animals and, more specifically, primates. Like all life forms on earth, our very existence is based in the molecule DNA. As all living forms share this same genetic foundation, it can be strongly argued that all life has evolved from a common ancestor and that human beings are part of a continuum made up of biologically related species.

Yet, we humans have come to regard our species as the masters of the planet. In Western cultures, this view has been reinforced by the conventionally held Old Testament assertion that humans shall have *dominion* over the nonhuman animals. The teachings of Islam and certain other religions and philosophies can also be interpreted in a similar manner. (The Old Testament, in Genesis, actually presents two separate versions; the second conveys a quite different meaning: that humans are to have "stewardship" over other animals.) Moreover, there is the prevailing view that nature represents an array of resources that exists primarily to be exploited for the betterment of humankind. This view is as widely held today, unfortunately, as ever before. More than merely being anthropocentric, such a perspective reveals a misplaced, unjustified arrogance.

By most standards, *Homo sapiens* is a successful species. There are currently more than 6 billion human beings living on this planet. Each one of these 6,000,000,000 individuals comprises upwards of 20 trillion cells. Nevertheless, we and all other multicellular organisms contribute but a small fraction of all the cells on the planet—the vast majority of which are bacteria. Thus, if we see life ultimately as a competition among reproducing organisms, bacteria are the winners, hands down.

Bacteria, then, could be viewed as the dominant life form on earth. However, even when only considering multicellular animals, there are additional lessons in evolutionary humility. As mammals, we are members of a group that includes about 4,000 species—a group of animals that has been on the decline over the last several million years. Looking even more specifically, as primates, we see ourselves belonging to a grouping that today numbers not even 200 species (and is also probably declining since its peak several million years ago). Compare these species numbers with those estimated for insects. Over 750,000 insect species have been identified, and estimates are as high as 30 million (Wilson, 1992)! Number of species (as an indicator of biological diversity) is as good a barometer of evolutionary success as any other. By this standard, humans (and our close relatives) could hardly be seen as the most successful of species.

Evolutionary success can also be gauged by species longevity. As we have seen, fossil evidence indicates that *Homo sapiens* has been on the scene for at least 200,000 years and perhaps as long as 400,000 years. Such time spans, seen through the perspective of a human lifetime, may seem enormous. But consider this: Our immediate predecessor, *Homo erectus*, had a species longevity of about 1.5 million years. In other words, we as a species would need to exist another million years simply to match *Homo erectus!* If such considerations as these are not humbling enough, remember that some sharks and turtles have thrived basically unchanged structurally for 400 million years (although many of these species are now seriously threatened).

Humans and the Impact of Culture

As you have learned, because humans increasingly came to use culture as a means of adapting to the natural environment, physical anthropologists view culture as an adaptive strategy. Stone tools, temporary shelters, animal products (including animal skin clothing), and the use of fire all permitted earlier populations to expand from the tropics and exploit resources in regions previously unavailable to them. In fact, it was culture that enabled humans to become increasingly successful as time passed.

For most of human history, technology remained simple, and the rate of culture change was slow. Indeed, humans enjoyed what could be termed a "comfortable" relationship with this unique adaptive strategy. However, as technologies became more complex, and especially when humans began to adopt an agricultural lifestyle, their relationship with culture became more complicated and, over time, less and less comfortable.

From the archaeological record, it appears that around 15,000 years ago, influenced in part by climate change and the extinction of many large-bodied prey species, some human groups began to settle down, abandoning their nomadic lives. Moreover, by about 10,000 years ago (and probably earlier), some peoples had learned that by keeping domestic animals and growing crops, they had more abundant and reliable food supplies. The domestication of plants and animals is seen as one of the most significant events in human history, one that was to have far-reaching consequences for the entire planet.

Keeping domesticated plants and animals requires a settled way of life, and increased sedentism, combined with more reliable food sources, led to increased population growth. Viewed from the perspective of twenty-first-century humans living in industrialized societies, it might seem that adopting a settled lifestyle would lead to better health and nutrition. Yet, scientists believe that health and nutrition among hunter-gatherers was, in fact, quite good compared to that of humans living in early settlements, for, as you learned in Chapter 13, with settled lifestyle comes increased exposure to infectious disease. Thus, it can justifiably be said that increased exposure to infectious disease was one of the earliest alterations in the harmonious relationship between humans and cultural innovation. Furthermore, as you have learned, infectious disease has been and continues to be a powerful selective force acting upon human populations.

Early agriculturalists, for whom we have only crude population estimates, probably numbered a few million worldwide. At this level, population density was still quite low, but human activity was already beginning to have an impact on the natural environment. In truth, it would be erroneous to assume that human activities have only recently come to have environmental consequences. Indeed, human impact on local environments increased dramatically as soon as people began to live in permanent settlements. (Furthermore, people themselves suffered harmful results of this shift in subsistence strategies.) Consequently, many of the earth's features we think of as natural actually came about as the result of human activities. For example, prior to the **Neolithic,** when people began to live in permanent settlements, much of Britain and continental Europe was blanketed with forests and woodlands. The moorlands and, to some extent, the peat bogs that have provided evocative settings for so many English mysteries and romantic novels are the result of deforestation that commenced over 5,000 years ago (Fig. 15–1). In Britain, local woodland clearing by hunter-gatherers began during the late **Mesolithic,** and it accelerated around 5,000 years ago with the adoption of farming. Late Bronze Age peoples (circa 4,000–3,500 y.a.) continued the process on an even larger scale, so that by 2,500 years ago, many of England's forests were disappearing (Bell and Walker, 1992). Today, the majority of European woodlands exist as discontinuous patches—the result of processes that continued until fairly recent times but that originated with prehistoric farmers.

Neolithic
The period during which humans began to domesticate plants and animals. The Neolithic is also associated with increased sedentism. Dates for the Neolithic vary from region to region, depending on when domestication occurred.

Mesolithic
The period preceding the Neolithic, during which humans increasingly exploited smaller animals (including fish), increased the variety of tools they used, and became somewhat less nomadic.

FIGURE 15–1

The moorland in the foreground is the result of woodland clearing some 2,000 years ago in southwest England.

FIGURE 15–2
Deforestation and erosion in Madagascar.

FIGURE 15–3
Map of deforestation.

Unfortunately, humans began to exploit, and increasingly depend on, non-renewable resources. Forests can be viewed as renewable resources, provided they are given the opportunity for regrowth. However, in many areas, forest clearing was virtually complete and was inevitably followed by soil erosion, frequent overgrazing, and overcultivation, which led to further soil erosion (Fig. 15–2). Therefore, in those areas, trees became a nonrenewable resource, perhaps the first resource to have this distinction.

It would not be in error to state that since the advent of settled life, and to some extent prior to it, humans have virtually waged war on trees. Early European explorers and settlers recorded extensive burning of woodlands and forests by indigenous groups of hunter-gatherers in North America and Australia, practiced presumably to clear undergrowth and drive animals from cover. The effect of such burning was not inconsequential, and as people began to live in agricultural communities and later in towns and even cities, the impact on forests became devastating. In fact, as shown in Fig. 15–3, only about one-fifth of the earth's original forests remain intact today, and much of the clearing occurred centuries and even millennia ago.

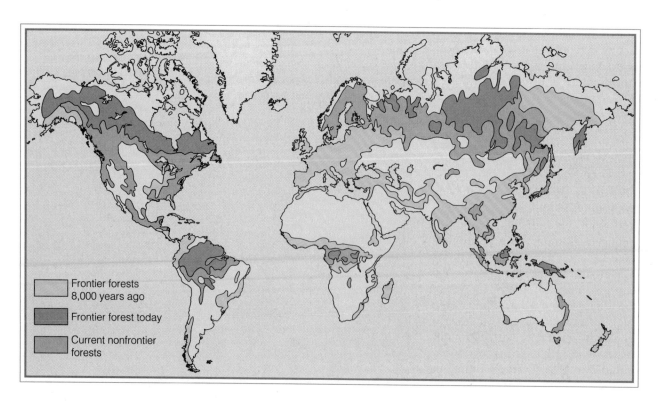

Frontier forests
8,000 years ago

Frontier forest today

Current nonfrontier
forests

There are many reasons for cutting forests, and the earliest of these were to clear the land for cultivation and grazing and to provide firewood and lumber for construction. As small communities grew into towns and cities, wood came to be used for shipbuilding, fortifications, and even the construction of temples and palaces. In short, the human experience over the last 10,000 to 15,000 years would not have been possible without the exploitation of woodlands and forests.

One of the earliest documented examples of humankind's appetite for lumber is the cutting of the famous cedars of Lebanon. Over 3,000 years ago, the eastern Mediterranean (modern-day Israel, Jordan, Lebanon, and Syria), southern Turkey, and Mesopotamia (in present-day Iraq) had become major sources of valuable cedar, fir, cypress, and other woods. But by far the most highly prized wood was Lebanese cedar, which was cut and shipped throughout the eastern Mediterranean, where it was used in the construction of buildings and ships (Fig. 15–4). The Old Testament tells us that King Solomon's temple was made of cedar from Lebanon, and numerous other texts, written over several centuries, document the extensive use and desirability of this precious wood. Not surprisingly, the deforestation of the mountains of Lebanon was eventually so complete that what "forest" remains today is but small patches and stands of trees.

Just to prove the old adage that, "The more things change, the more they are the same," it is informative to note that classical scholars (most notably Plato and Aristotle) bemoaned the effects of deforestation and other forms of environmental degradation in Greece and other areas of the Mediterranean basin. They warned that the cutting of forests and overuse of land led to soil erosion, disturbed water supplies, agricultural decline, and even climate change. Their views, expressed some 2,400 years ago, are verified by combined archaeological and geological data that show sequences of soil accumulation followed by intense human occupation, then soil erosion, and finally, abandonment of archaeological sites throughout Greece. Furthermore, this sequence of episodes dates to around 5,000 years ago. But, given the relatively small size of human populations, even by the time of the ancient Greeks and Romans, the human impact on ecosystems mostly remained a localized, not global, phenomenon. Nevertheless, these impacts were in some cases significant. The barren (but enchanting) landscape of Greece and much of what is now desert in the Middle East and the Sahara Desert in Africa are the direct legacy of overgrazing (mostly by goats) and subsequent erosion over the last few thousand years.

Destruction of natural resources in the past has also had severe consequences for people living today. The 1990 typhoon and severe flooding that killed over 100,000 people in Bangladesh were partly due to previous deforestation of regions in the Himalayas of northern India. There is also evidence that continued erosion and flooding in China are partly the result of deforestation that occurred in the past. Lastly, many scientists have long speculated that the collapse of the Maya civilization of southern Mexico around 1,000 years ago was at least partly due to over-cultivation of land and depletion of nutrient-poor tropical soils.

FIGURE 15-4

This eighth-century B.C. Assyrian panel depicts the transport of cedar logs from Lebanon to Assyria.

Archaeologists can provide many examples of what humans have done wrong in the past. But just as importantly, they are also able to provide us with positive examples from earlier cultures, innovative techniques that, for all our modern wisdom, we still have yet to match. For example, in the Andean highlands of South America, soil is very poor and subject to erosion. Agricultural peoples living in the region today (in Bolivia and Peru), even with considerable input from modern technology, still can barely scrape together a meager existence. Yet, such unrelenting poverty was not always the case in this part of the world. Five hundred years ago, the Inca ancestors of these peoples reaped enormous wealth from this same land and built from it one of the largest, best-organized empires in the world. How did they do it?

Archaeologist Craig Erickson sought an answer. By examining Inca agricultural fields, terracing, and irrigation, he was able to extrapolate the ancient techniques and duplicate many of the same methods. This was no mere academic exercise, however, for the next step was to teach these methods to the modern farmers. As a result, crop yields have vastly improved, with less environmental damage, with less use of fertilizer, and at less cost than before!

The Loss of Biodiversity

Although the term *biodiversity* is currently a popular one, many people do not really understand what it means. Biodiversity is basically the totality of all living things, from bacteria and fungi to trees and humans. The term refers not only to species, but to individuals and the various genetic combinations they represent, as well as to entire ecosystems. The fact that we are currently losing biodiversity is indisputable. What we are not certain of is the exact rate of loss or what its impact will be.

The geological record indicates that in the past 570 million years, there have been at least 15 mass extinctions, two of which altered all of the earth's ecosystems (Ward, 1994). The first of these major extinction events took place some 250 million years ago and resulted from climatic change subsequent to the joining of all the earth's landmasses into one supercontinent.

The second event occurred around 65 million years ago and ended 150 million years of evolutionary processes that, among other things, had produced the dinosaurs. This mass extinction is believed by many researchers to have resulted from climatic changes following the impact of an asteroid.

A third major extinction event, perhaps of the same magnitude, is occurring now, and according to some scientists, may have begun in the late Pleistocene or early **Holocene** (Ward, 1994). Unlike all other mass extinctions, the current one has not been caused by continental drift, climate change (so far), or collisions with asteroids. Rather, these recent and ongoing extinctions are due to the activities of a single species—*Homo sapiens.*

Many scientists, in fact, believe that several large mammalian species were pushed toward extinction by overhunting by earlier human populations, particularly near the end of the Pleistocene, some 10,000 years ago. In North America, at least 57 mammalian species became extinct, including the mammoth, mastodon, giant ground sloth, saber-toothed cat, several large rodents, and numerous ungulates (hooved mammals) or grazing animals (Lewin, 1986; Simmons, 1989). Although climate change (warming) was undoubtedly a factor in these Pleistocene extinctions, hunting and other human activities may also have been important. Although there is some dispute as to when humans first entered North America

Holocene
The most recent epoch of the Cenozoic. Following the Pleistocene, it is estimated to have begun 10,000 years ago.

from Asia, it is certain that they were firmly established by at least 12,000 years ago (and probably earlier).

We have no direct evidence that early American big game hunters contributed to extinctions; but we do have evidence of what can happen to indigenous species when new areas are colonized by humans for the first time. Within just a few centuries of human occupation of New Zealand, the moa, a large flightless bird, was exterminated. Madagascar serves as a similar example. In the last one thousand years, after the arrival of permanent human settlement, 14 species of lemurs, in addition to other mammalian and bird species, have become extinct (Jolly, 1985; Napier and Napier, 1985). One such species was *Megaladapis*, a lemur that weighed an estimated 300 pounds (Fleagle, 1999)! Lastly, scientists have debated for years whether the extinction of all large-bodied animals (some 60 species) in Australia during the late Pleistocene was due to human hunting and other activities, or to climate change. Recently, Miller, et al. (1999), using four different techniques, were able to date the rapid extinction of a large flightless bird, *Genyornis newtoni,* to about 50,000 years ago, a date that roughly coincides with the arrival of humans in Australia. This study suggests that the simultaneous extinction of this species in a number of localities, occurred during a period of relative climatic stability and therefore is best explained as a consequence of human activities, especially the widespread burning of large areas and subsequent changes in vegetation. Previous studies have suggested that the incidence of fires increased substantially in Australia after the arrival of humans, and ethnographic reports indicate that the practice was common among indigenous Australians.

Hunter-gatherers, for whom we have some ethnographic evidence, differed in their views regarding conservation of prey species. Some groups believed that overhunting would anger deities. Others (some Great Basin Indians, for example) killed large numbers only every several years, allowing populations of game species, such as antelope, time to replenish. Still others avoided killing pregnant females or were conscientious about using all parts of the body to avoid waste. Nevertheless, there were some groups, such as the Hadza of the Pacific Northwest Coast, who appear not to have been especially concerned with conservation.

Moreover, hunting techniques were frequently incompatible with conservation. Prior to domestication of the horse (or its availability in the New World), the only effective way to hunt large herd animals was to organize game drives. In some cases, fire was used to drive stampeding animals into blind canyons or human-made "corrals." Other times, bison were driven over cliffs or into *arroyos* (narrow, deep gullies). Unfortunately, this practice often led to unavoidable waste, as more animals might be killed than could be utilized (even though it was common practice to store dried meats for future use). Moreover, there might be so many animals that it was impossible to retrieve those at the bottom of the pile.

The Olsen-Chubbuck site in eastern Colorado is a bison kill site where, in one hunt some 10,000 years ago, 190 bison *(Bison occidentalis)* were driven into an arroyo. (This species, approximately 25 percent larger than the familiar *Bison bison*, is believed to have become extinct approximately 7,000 years ago.) Of the 190 animals killed, 170 (90 percent) were partially or completely butchered (Wheat, 1972). The 20 complete skeletons of those left unbutchered were found at the bottom of the arroyo, where they would have been virtually inaccessible.

The evidence at Olsen-Chubbuck suggests a certain degree of overkill. In addition to the 20 untouched animals, many of those that were partially butchered appear to have remained mostly intact. As the Olsen-Chubbuck scenario was played out thousands of times over the course of many centuries, it is likely that such game drives contributed to the demise of at least some of the large-bodied prey species of the New World.

Since the end of the Pleistocene, human activities have continued to take their toll on nonhuman species. Today, however, species are disappearing at an unprecedented rate. Hunting, which occurs for a number of reasons other than acquisition of food, continues to be a factor. Competition with introduced nonnative species, such as pigs, goats, and rats, has also contributed to the problem. But in most cases, the most important single cause of extinction is habitat reduction.

Habitat reduction is a direct result of the burgeoning human population and the resulting need for building materials, grazing and agricultural land, and living areas. We are all aware of the risk to such visible species as the elephant, panda, rhinoceros, tiger, and mountain gorilla, to name a few. These risks are real, and within your lifetime some of these will certainly become extinct, at least in the wild. But the greatest threat to biodiversity is to the countless unknown species that live in the world's rain forests (Fig. 15–5).

It is estimated that over half of all plants and animals on earth live in rain forests. By 1989, these habitats had been reduced to a little less than half their original size—that is, down to about 3 million square miles. The annual net loss between 1980 and 1995 was almost 67,000 square miles. As Harvard biologist E. O. Wilson puts it: "The loss is equal to the area of a football field every second. Put another way, in 1989 the surviving rain forests occupied an area about that of the continuous forty-eight states of the United States, and they were being reduced by an amount equivalent to the size of Florida every year" (Wilson, 1992, p. 275). By the year 2022, half the world's remaining rain forests will be gone if destruction continues at its present rate. This will result in a loss of between 10 and 22 percent of all rain forest species, or 5 to 10 percent of all plant and animal species on earth (Wilson, 1992).

Should we care about the loss of biodiversity? If so, why? In fact, there are many people who do not show much concern. Moreover, reasons as to why we should care are usually stated in terms of the benefits (known and unknown) that humans may derive from rain forest species. An example of such a benefit is the chemical taxol (derived from the Pacific yew tree), which may be an effective treatment for ovarian and breast cancer.

It is undeniable that humans stand to benefit from continued research into potentially useful rain forest products. However, such anthropocentric reasons are not the sole justification for preserving the earth's biodiversity. Each species that is lost is the product of millions of years of evolution, and each fills a specific econiche. Quite simply, the destruction of so much of the planet's biota is within our power. But ethically, we must ask ourselves, is it within our rights?

FIGURE 15–5

Stumps of recently felled forest trees are still visible in this newly cleared field in Rwanda. The haze is wood smoke from household fires.

Could the Human Species Become Extinct?

An obvious answer to this question is yes. After all, eventually (in a few billion years) there will be no sun, and ultimately no earth, so all life here will cease to exist. Of course, science fiction writers have long envisioned wide-ranging colonization of the galaxy by interstellar voyagers from earth. Perhaps such a circumstance will come about. Certainly, on this planet, we are the only species with the ability to envision our possible fate, and we alone have the capacity to do something about it.

However, it is only through such cultural and technological means that we as a species have a chance to endure. There are no biological guarantees. Most species that have existed on this planet have long since died out. Such could be the expected fate for all living forms.

Evolution, as commonly rendered in nature programs on television and in popular books, presents a misleading picture. We often are told that *species* are adapting to survive. But an understanding of evolutionary processes shows such statements to be nonsense. Life forms, through the central process of natural selection, compete as *individuals.* Their success in such competition is measured solely by their individual abilities to reproduce. Life forms, in following this biological imperative, may indeed prove to be individually successful, but at the same time may be contributing to a situation highly detrimental to the species. For example, it is through such maximization of individual reproductive success that overpopulation occurs. Severe overexploitation of resources, a population "crash," and even complete extinction may then ensue. But, the individual organism obviously cannot foresee such a calamity and will, accordingly, act to maximize its own success—regardless of the ultimate effects on the species.

Humans, as we will discuss shortly, are in the midst of an explosive population increase. An increase of this magnitude is by no means unique, although it is probably unprecedented in such a large animal (and in one so environmentally "hungry"). Another biological lesson shows that we are but part of an integrated ecological system. As we expand so rapidly (and appear so successful in the short term), we cannot predict the potential negative effects of this very "success" for the long term.

It is clear, then, that all life forms *can* become extinct, even hominids. Robust australopithecines are sometimes depicted as overly specialized, rather dimwitted vegetarians. Yet, they were highly successful hominids in their own right and may have had significant cognitive and cultural capacities. One thing we know for certain: They endured for at least 1.5 million years; in the end, however, they vanished. As hominids, we can learn from such evolutionary history—if we choose to. To ignore the past might well condemn us to repeat it.

The Present Crisis: Our Cultural Heritage?

It would be difficult to escape the media attention given today to environmental problems. At some level, everyone is aware that problems exist. Unfortunately, it seems that few are aware of how serious the situation is, and even fewer still are prepared to do anything about it.

Overpopulation

If we had to point to one single challenge facing humanity, a problem to which virtually all others are tied, it would have to be population growth. We currently are trapped in a destructive cycle of our own making. Population size has skyrocketed in our own species as we have increased our ability to produce food surpluses. As population size increases, more and more land is converted to crops, pasture, and construction, providing more opportunities for yet more humans. Additionally, through the medical advances of the twentieth century, we have reduced mortality at both ends of the life cycle. Thus, fewer people die in childhood, and having survived to adulthood, they live longer than ever before. Although these medical advances are unquestionably beneficial to individuals (who has not benefited from medical technology?), it is also clear that there are significant detrimental consequences to the species and to the planet.

Population size, if left unchecked, increases exponentially, that is, as a function of some percent, like compound interest in a bank account. Currently, human population increases worldwide at an annual rate of about 1.8 percent. Although this figure may not seem too startling at first, it deserves some examination. In addition, it is useful to discuss doubling time, or the amount of time it takes for a population to double in size.

Scientists estimate that around 10,000 years ago, only about 5 million people inhabited the earth (not even half as many as live in Los Angeles County or New York City today). By A.D. 1650, there were perhaps 500 million, and by 1800, 1 billion. In other words, between 10,000 years ago and A.D. 1650 (a period of 9,650 years), population size doubled seven and a half times. On average, then, the doubling time between 10,000 years ago and 1650 was about 1,287 years. But from 1650 to 1800 it doubled again, which means that doubling time had been reduced to 150 years (Ehrlich and Ehrlich, 1990). And in the 37 years between 1950 and 1987, world population doubled from 2 billion to 4 billion.

Dates and associated population estimates up to the present are as follows: mid-1800s, 1 billion; 1930s, 2 billion; mid-1960s, 3 billion; mid-1980s, 4 billion; present, 6 billion (Fig. 15–6). To state this problem in terms we can appreciate, we add 1 billion people to the world's population approximately every 11 years. That comes out to 90 to 95 million every year and roughly a quarter of a million every day!

The rate of growth is not equally distributed among all nations. Although the world's rate of increase has ranged from 1.7 to 2.1 percent since the 1950s (Ehrlich and Ehrlich, 1990), it is the developing countries that share most of the burden (not to be interpreted as blame). During the 1980s, the population of Kenya grew at a rate of a little over 4 percent per year, while India added a million per month, and 36,000 babies were born every day in Latin America.

The most recent United Nations International Conference on Population and Development set as its goal the development of a plan to contain the world's population to about 7.3 billion by the year 2015 and to prevent future growth. Otherwise, by the year 2050, human numbers will approach 10 billion. The United Nations plan emphasizes women's education, health, and rights throughout the world, but has met with stiff resistance from religious groups opposed to abortion and contraception.

The United Nations goal is an admirable but ambitious one, and achieving it will be a formidable task. Although the average number of live births per woman

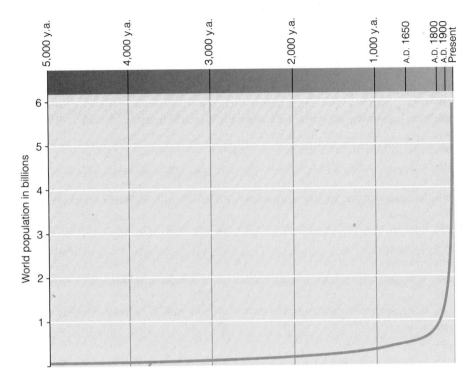

FIGURE 15–6

Line graph depicting exponential growth of human population. Note that for almost all of the last 5,000 years, the number of humans increased very slowly. It was not until 1650 that population size was even half a billion (500 million). The rapid increase to 1 billion by about 1850 is, in part, attributable to the Industrial Revolution. Population increase occurs as a function of some percent (in some developing countries, the annual rate is over 3 percent). With advances in food production and medical technologies, humans are now undergoing a population explosion, as this graph illustrates.

declined in developing nations from 5 in 1955 to 3 by the 1990s, it will still be next to impossible to prevent huge population increases in the next century. Bear in mind that *approximately half of all people currently living in the developing world are less than 15 years old.* These young people have not yet reproduced, but they will.

You might logically ask, Can we not make technological changes sufficient to feed all these people? Certainly this and similar questions are being asked more frequently today than in the past. There surely are methods that would more efficiently utilize agricultural lands already available. Clearly, there are better ways to distribute the food surpluses already produced (in the United States in particular). But can we continue forever to make technological changes sufficient to feed ever-growing numbers of humans? Is there enough land to support an endless demand for housing, crop cultivation, and grazing? Is there enough water? We probably can develop technologies to meet our species' increasing needs for a while. But can we do so and still meet the requirements of thousands of undomesticated species? The answer for the immediate future is: Probably not. For the long term, without major changes in human population growth, the answer is: Certainly not.

The Greenhouse Effect and Global Warming

With increases in numbers comes greater consumption of nonrenewable resources. At the same time, activities involved in the production of goods and services produce waste and pollution, all of which leads to further environmental degradation.

Consider for a moment the fact that much of the energy used for human activities is derived from the burning of fossil fuels such as oil and coal (non-renewable resources). The burning of fossil fuels increases the amount of carbon dioxide emitted into the atmosphere, and this, in turn, traps heat. Increased production of carbon dioxide and other "greenhouse gases," such as methane and chlorofluorocarbons (CFCs), is of growing concern to many in the scientific community who anticipate potentially dramatic climate change in the form of global warming. Deforestation, both in the tropics and North America, also has the potential to contribute to global warming, for we are reducing the number of trees available to absorb carbon dioxide. Moreover, in the tropics, trees are burned as land is cleared, a practice that releases carbon dioxide contained within vegetation into the atmosphere. In fact, an estimated 20 percent of all carbon dioxide emissions are accounted for by the burning of the Amazon rain forest alone (Ehrlich and Ehrlich, 1990). As a sobering note, Friends of the Earth, an environmental organization, estimated that between 50,000 and 80,000 fires were burning in the forests of Brazil at any given time during October 1991. And in Indonesia, an estimated 370,000 to 740,000 acres of forest were burned in 1997 alone (European Union GIS/Remote Sensing Expert Group, 1997).

The scientific community is now in almost complete agreement that we are seeing the effects of global warming. But, while there is no doubt that greenhouse gases are building up in the atmosphere, there are still uncertainties as to the extent of the role played by human agricultural and industrial activities. (We would comment here that most of this uncertainty comes from politicians and others who do not wish to assume the political and financial costs associated with the enormous changes to business and industrial practices that would be necessary just to mitigate the effects and pace of climate change.) Uncertainty also surrounds the issue of the myriad ways climate change will be manifested. What is certain is that, since records began being kept in 1860, the 1990s were the hottest decade, followed closely by the 1980s. The year 1998 has the distinction of being the warmest year on record. It is also accepted that the surface temperature of the earth has increased between 0.3 and 0.6 degrees centigrade (0.54 to 1.1 degrees F). The need for concern cannot be overstated. An increase in the mean annual temperature worldwide of even 0.5 to 1 degree centigrade (1 to 2 degrees F) could result in some melting of the polar caps with subsequent flooding of coastal areas.

Global warming is the result of the interactions of many factors and the consequences of these interactions are not possible to predict with accuracy. But, the consensus among scientists from many disciplines is that in general we can anticipate dramatic fluctuations in weather patterns with alterations in precipitation levels. The results of changing temperatures and rainfall include loss of agricultural lands due to desertification in some regions and flooding in others; increased human hunger and undernutrition; extinction of numerous plant and animal species; and altered patterns of infectious disease. Regarding the latter, health officials are particularly concerned about the spread of mosquito-borne diseases such as malaria, dengue fever and yellow fever, as warmer temperatures increase the geographic range of those species that serve as vectors for these potentially fatal conditions. And, in addition to altering the geographic distribution of insect and vertebrate disease vectors, changing climate conditions can also increase the range and reproductive rates of the very microbes that cause infectious disease.

Depletion of the Ozone Layer

Another major concern is the depletion of the earth's stratospheric ozone layer. Ozone is a form of oxygen, and the ozone layer filters out ultraviolet radiation, protecting the earth from the ultraviolet B (UV-B) radiation that damages DNA and leads to skin cancer. Scientists believe that the well-publicized hole in the ozone layer above Antarctica has been caused primarily by CFCs used as aerosol propellants, solvents, refrigerants, and components of styrofoam products. (CFCs release chlorine into the atmosphere, and the chlorine binds to oxygen molecules, thus breaking down atmospheric ozone.)

Unfortunately, scientists do not know the full extent of damage to the ozone layer, but estimates place the loss above the United States at approximately 2 to 3 percent (Ehrlich and Ehrlich, 1990). What is known is that with ozone depletion, skin cancer rates will increase, as will associated mortality. Currently there are approximately 600,000 cases of skin cancer per year in the United States, with 9,000 deaths. With continued ozone depletion, the U.S. Environmental Protection Agency estimates that these figures could double in the next 40 years. Even more sobering, it is also suspected that terrestrial life on earth is not possible without an ozone layer.

Looking for Solutions

Steps are being taken to correct some of the almost insurmountable problems facing humankind. Automobile manufacturers are working to develop more fuel-efficient automobiles. In fact, one Japanese company has begun to market a car that is said to get 60 to 65 miles per gallon of gasoline. Alternative fuels using alcohol for automobiles are also being used with success in the United States, and manufacturers continue to experiment with electrically powered cars. Additionally, as of 1997, all air-conditioned automobiles sold in the United States were required to be free of CFCs. Several manufacturers met this requirement even prior to 1997.

The automobile industry's rapid shift away from CFCs was, in part, a response to the 1987 Montreal Protocol, an international treaty designed to protect the ozone layer. This treaty established guidelines for the elimination of CFCs and other ozone-depleting substances. Since then, the use of these chemicals has declined worldwide by more than 70 percent, but many problems still exist. For example, most developed countries, where CFC use was most widespread, were able to cease CFC manufacture by 1996, but they can continue production until 2006 in order to help developing nations meet basic domestic needs. Moreover, the still substantial demand for CFCs has led to a thriving black market trade, and, in rapidly developing nations, there has been a dramatic increase in the use of CFCs and other ozone-damaging substances. But, if developed nations can assist developing countries in cutting CFC consumption while continuing to decrease their own, perhaps the goals of the Montreal Protocol can still be achieved. Briefly, it is now hoped that stratospheric levels of CFC-breakdown products peaked by 1999, and that they have now begun to decline. If this reduction has occurred, ozone loss will diminish and previous levels will eventually be restored. Certainly, the Montreal Protocol and subsequent meetings and amendments have been landmark achievements in international efforts to combat one serious aspect of environmental degradation.

FIGURE 15–7

Air pollution, increasingly a factor in human respiratory disease, is caused by human activities.

The massive problems facing our planet reflect an adaptive strategy gone awry. Indeed, it would seem that we no longer enjoy a harmonious relationship with culture. Instead, culture has become the environment in which we live, and every day that environment becomes increasingly hostile. All we need do is examine the very air we breathe to realize that we have overstepped our limits (Fig. 15–7).

What can be done? Are the problems we have created amenable to human solution? Perhaps, but any objective assessment of the future offers little optimism. The declining quality of the air, depletion of the ozone layer, the greenhouse effect, reduced amounts of arable land, and the accumulation of refuse already seem catastrophic problems in a world of 6 billion people. How well does the world *now* cope with feeding, housing, and educating its inhabitants? What quality of life do the majority of the world's people enjoy right now? What kind of world have we wrought for the other organisms that share our planet as many are steadily isolated into fragments of what were once large habitats? If these concerns are not currently overwhelming enough, what kind of world will we see in 30 years, when the world's population numbers perhaps 8 billion?

In recent years, environmental concerns have been more widely discussed. Some world leaders now frequently pay lip service to preserving the environment. All this is well and good, but the real test of any policy will be the willingness of the world's population to sacrifice *now* for rewards that will not become apparent for perhaps several decades.

If there is any real chance of reversing current trends, *everyone* will have to sacrifice. In the developing world, family planning must universally be adopted to halt population expansion. Most cultures are so constructed, however, as to make such behavioral change very difficult. And sacrifice on the part of the developing world alone would not be adequate to stem the tide. It is entirely too convenient for someone from North America to point at residents of Bangladesh and demand that they control their rate of reproduction (it runs two to three times that of the United States). But consider this: The average American uses an estimated 400 times the resources consumed by a resident of Bangladesh (Ehrlich and Ehrlich, 1990)! The United States *alone* produces 25 to 30 percent of all carbon dioxide emissions into the atmosphere. Clearly, much of the responsibility for current problems rests squarely on the shoulders of the industrialized West.

In addition to population containment, the developed nations (most especially, the United States) must get along with far fewer resources. To accomplish any meaningful reduction in our wasteful habits, major behavioral changes and personal sacrifice will be required. For example, private automobile transportation (especially with only one passenger) and large, single-family dwellings are luxuries we enjoy, but they are luxuries the planet can ill afford. In addition, the dogs, cats, horses, and other pets we so prize are enormously costly in terms of resources. Must we then give up our pets as well? We could also ask, Wouldn't it be less costly to reduce our dietary intake of meat and grow grain to feed people directly?

Who is prepared to make the sacrifices that are required? Whence will the leadership come? The planet already faces serious problems, and there is little time left for indecision. Either we, as members of the species *Homo sapiens*, find the courage to make dramatic personal sacrifices, or we are doomed to suffer the consequences of our own folly.

SUMMARY

Studies of human evolution have much to contribute to our understanding of how we, as a single species, came to exert such control over the destiny of our planet. It is a truly phenomenal story of how a small apelike creature walking on two feet across the African savanna challenged nature by learning to make stone tools. From these humble beginnings came large-brained humans who, instead of stone tools, have telecommunications satellites, computers, and nuclear arsenals at their fingertips. The human story is indeed unique and wonderful. Our two feet have carried us not only across the plains of Africa, but onto the polar caps, the ocean floor, and even across the surface of the moon! Surely, if we can accomplish so much in so short a time, we can act responsibly to preserve our home and the wondrous creatures who share it with us.

QUESTIONS FOR REVIEW

1. How is human culture related to environmental degradation and over-population?
2. How are loss of biodiversity, environmental degradation, and human population growth related?
3. What is the current estimate of human population worldwide?
4. Are humans the most successful of all species? Why? How is success defined?
5. As early as the Mesolithic and Neolithic, human activities began to alter the landscape. Give two examples.
6. Human activities may have influenced extinction in the past as well as today. Give two examples.
7. Why do we say that culture, as an adaptive strategy, has gone awry?

SUGGESTED FURTHER READINGS

Bell, Martin, and Michael J. C. Walker. 1992. *Late Quaternary Environmental Change.* New York: Wiley.

Gore, Al. 1992. *Earth in the Balance.* Boston: Houghton Mifflin.

Karl, Thomas R., Neville Nicholls, and Jonathan Gregory. 1997. "The Coming Climate." *Scientific American* 276(5): 78–83.

Monastersky, Richard. 1996. "Health in the Hot Zone." *Science News* 149(14): 218–219.

Runnels, Curtis N. 1995. "Environmental Degradation in Ancient Greece." *Scientific American* 272(3): 96–99.

Ward, Peter. 1994. *The End of Evolution.* New York: Bantam Books.

Wilson, Edward O. 1992. *The Diversity of Life.* Cambridge, MA: Harvard University Press.

World Resources. 1996–97. *A Guide to the Global Environment.* A joint publication by The World Resources Institute, the United Nations Environment Programme, the United Nations Development Programme, and the World Bank.

MULTIMEDIA RESOURCES

Wadsworth Anthropology Resource Center

http://anthropology.wadsworth.com

Visit Anthropology Online to obtain current updates in the field, surfing tips, career information, and more. In addition, enrich your study efforts with text-specific study aids arranged by chapter.

InfoTrac College Edition

http://www.infotrac-college.com/wadsworth

1. Search InfoTrac College Edition for *biological diversity.* There are over 100 references to this topic. From them select two, read them, and write an essay on the importance of maintaining biological diversity and the steps that government agencies and other organizations are taking to mitigate the loss of plant and animal species.

2. InfoTrac College Edition also has numerous references to the topic *global warming.* Do a subject search for this topic and read a few of the articles that come up. What is the evidence for global warming? What are the possible outcomes, especially in terms of economic effects and changes in the incidence and patterning of infectious disease? What about the extinction of plants and animals? Make a list of the various lines of evidence that have been investigated by scientists. Make a separate list of suggested changes in governmental policies and human behaviors that might slow the effect of global warming.

Internet Exercises

1. Go to the World Resources Institute Web site (www.wri.org) and, on the side-bar menu, click on forests. Read the discussions of deforestation and answer the following questions. How much of the estimated worldwide original forest cover has been destroyed? What are the many detrimental consequences of continued destruction? Why do we continue to cut forests? What plans are being implemented to save at least some of what remains of the world's forests?

2. Again, go to the World Resources Institute Web site and proceed to *Index,* then proceed to *Index by Topic* and click on "P" for *population.* Or, you can go directly to **www.wri.org/topicndx.html#P**. Read all of *Chapter 8.* Write a short essay on how such factors as population growth, environmental change, women's rights, and changing patterns of infectious disease are all interrelated.

Appendix A
Atlas of Primate Skeletal Anatomy

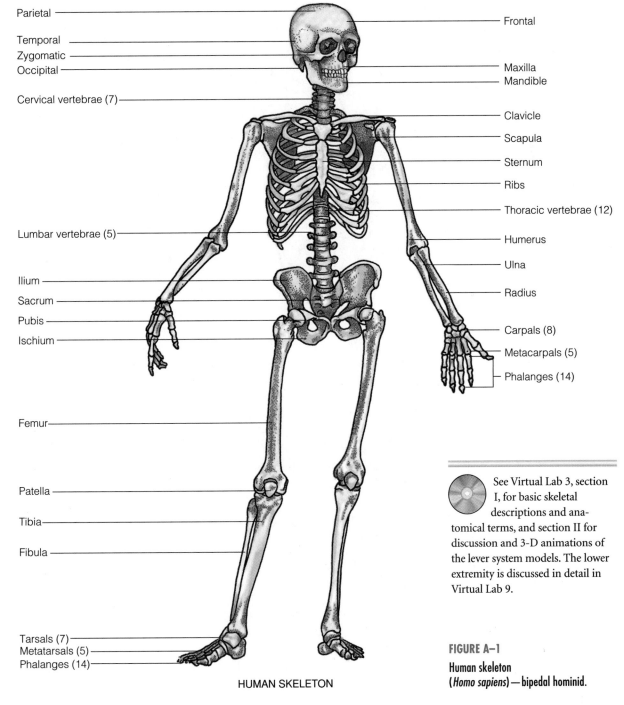

Parietal

Temporal
Zygomatic
Occipital

Cervical vertebrae (7)

Lumbar vertebrae (5)

Ilium
Sacrum
Pubis
Ischium

Femur

Patella

Tibia

Fibula

Tarsals (7)
Metatarsals (5)
Phalanges (14)

Frontal

Maxilla
Mandible

Clavicle

Scapula

Sternum

Ribs

Thoracic vertebrae (12)

Humerus

Ulna

Radius

Carpals (8)

Metacarpals (5)

Phalanges (14)

HUMAN SKELETON

See Virtual Lab 3, section I, for basic skeletal descriptions and anatomical terms, and section II for discussion and 3-D animations of the lever system models. The lower extremity is discussed in detail in Virtual Lab 9.

FIGURE A–1

Human skeleton
(*Homo sapiens*) — bipedal hominid.

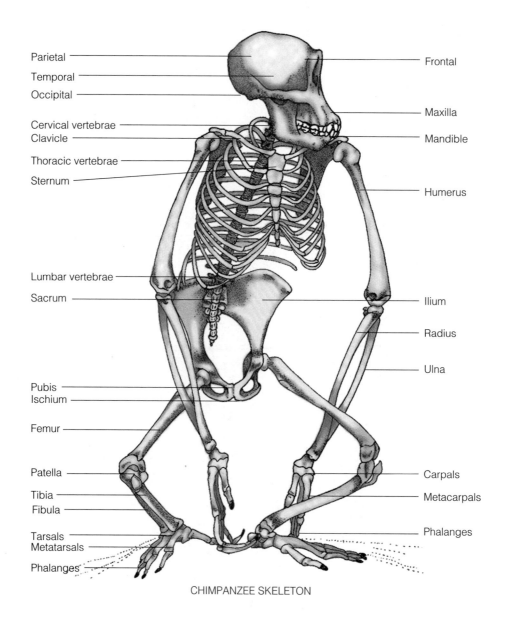

Parietal

Temporal

Occipital

Cervical vertebrae

Clavicle

Thoracic vertebrae

Sternum

Lumbar vertebrae

Sacrum

Pubis

Ischium

Femur

Patella

Tibia

Fibula

Tarsals

Metatarsals

Phalanges

Frontal

Maxilla

Mandible

Humerus

Ilium

Radius

Ulna

Carpals

Metacarpals

Phalanges

CHIMPANZEE SKELETON

FIGURE A–2

Chimpanzee skeleton (*Pan troglodytes*) — knuckle-walking pongid.

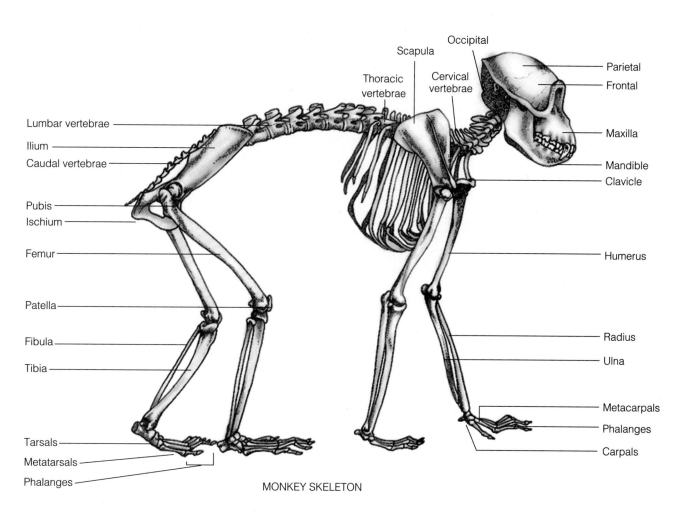

Lumbar vertebrae

Ilium

Caudal vertebrae

Pubis

Ischium

Femur

Patella

Fibula

Tibia

Tarsals

Metatarsals

Phalanges

Thoracic vertebrae

Scapula

Cervical vertebrae

Occipital

Parietal

Frontal

Maxilla

Mandible

Clavicle

Humerus

Radius

Ulna

Metacarpals

Phalanges

Carpals

MONKEY SKELETON

FIGURE A–3

Monkey skeleton (rhesus macaque; *Macaca mulatta*) — a typical quadrupedal primate.

See Virtual Lab 3 for a detailed discussion and virtual exercise on the role of the forelimb in locomotion, and Virtual Lab 4 for a virtual exercise on relative limb lengths

FIGURE A–4

Human cranium.
(continued on next page)

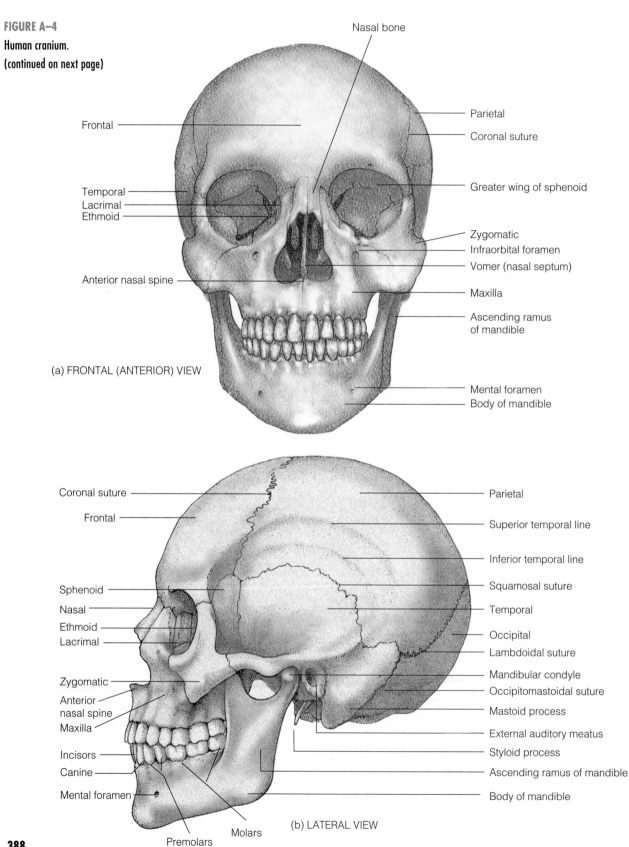

Nasal bone

Frontal

Parietal

Coronal suture

Temporal

Greater wing of sphenoid

Lacrimal

Ethmoid

Zygomatic

Infraorbital foramen

Vomer (nasal septum)

Anterior nasal spine

Maxilla

Ascending ramus
of mandible

(a) FRONTAL (ANTERIOR) VIEW

Mental foramen

Body of mandible

Coronal suture

Parietal

Frontal

Superior temporal line

Inferior temporal line

Sphenoid

Squamosal suture

Nasal

Temporal

Ethmoid

Occipital

Lacrimal

Lambdoidal suture

Zygomatic

Mandibular condyle

Anterior
nasal spine

Occipitomastoidal suture

Maxilla

Mastoid process

External auditory meatus

Incisors

Styloid process

Canine

Ascending ramus of mandible

Mental foramen

Body of mandible

(b) LATERAL VIEW

Molars

Premolars

388

FIGURE A–4
Human cranium. (continued)

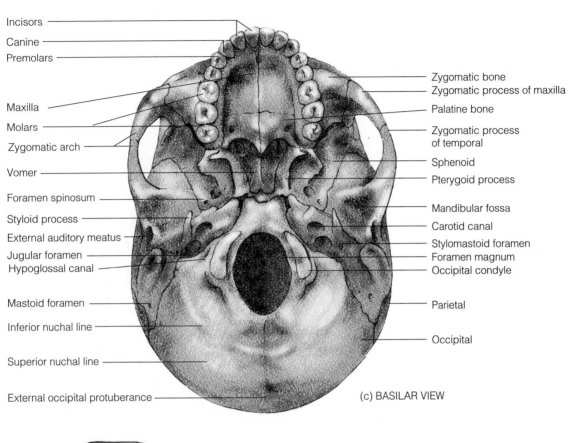

Incisors
Canine
Premolars

Maxilla
Molars
Zygomatic arch
Vomer
Foramen spinosum
Styloid process
External auditory meatus
Jugular foramen
Hypoglossal canal
Mastoid foramen
Inferior nuchal line
Superior nuchal line
External occipital protuberance

Zygomatic bone
Zygomatic process of maxilla
Palatine bone
Zygomatic process of temporal
Sphenoid
Pterygoid process
Mandibular fossa
Carotid canal
Stylomastoid foramen
Foramen magnum
Occipital condyle
Parietal
Occipital

(c) BASILAR VIEW

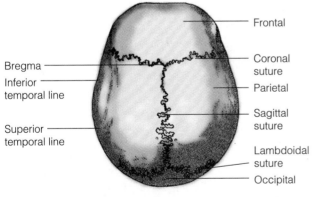

Bregma
Inferior temporal line
Superior temporal line

Frontal
Coronal suture
Parietal
Sagittal suture
Lambdoidal suture
Occipital

(d) SUPERIOR VIEW

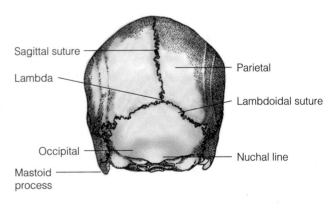

Sagittal suture
Lambda
Occipital
Mastoid process

Parietal
Lambdoidal suture
Nuchal line

(e) REAR VIEW

Cranial, mandibular, and dental anatomy are covered in Virtual Lab 5, section II. You can test your knowledge with the virtual exercise in section III.

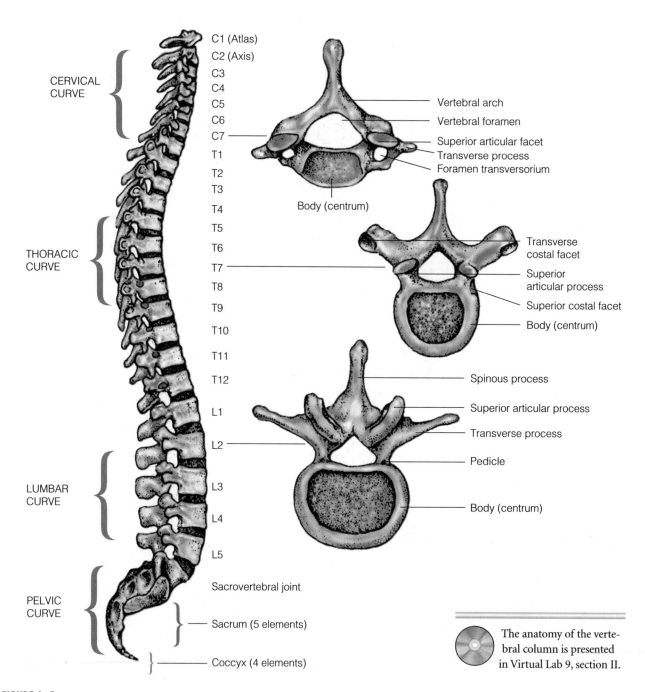

C1 (Atlas)
C2 (Axis)
C3
C4
C5
C6
C7
T1
T2
T3
T4
T5
T6
T7
T8
T9
T10
T11
T12
L1
L2
L3
L4
L5

CERVICAL CURVE

THORACIC CURVE

LUMBAR CURVE

PELVIC CURVE

Vertebral arch
Vertebral foramen
Superior articular facet
Transverse process
Foramen transversorium
Body (centrum)

Transverse costal facet
Superior articular process
Superior costal facet
Body (centrum)

Spinous process
Superior articular process
Transverse process
Pedicle
Body (centrum)

Sacrovertebral joint
Sacrum (5 elements)
Coccyx (4 elements)

The anatomy of the vertebral column is presented in Virtual Lab 9, section II.

FIGURE A–5

Human vertebral column (lateral view) and representative cervical, thoracic, and lumbar vertebrae (superior views).

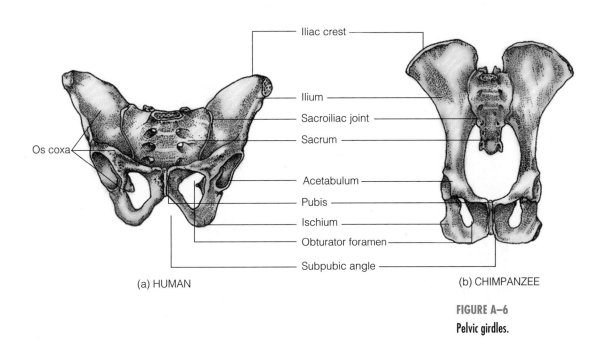

(a) HUMAN

(b) CHIMPANZEE

FIGURE A–6
Pelvic girdles.

The anatomy of the pelvis is presented in Virtual Lab 9, section I.

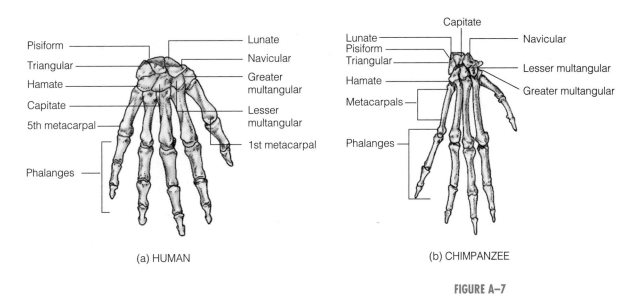

(a) HUMAN

(b) CHIMPANZEE

FIGURE A–7
Hand anatomy.

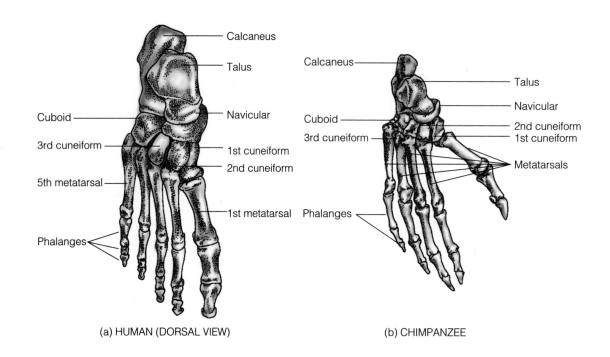

(a) HUMAN (DORSAL VIEW)

(b) CHIMPANZEE

The anatomy and function of the foot is presented in Virtual Lab 9, section IV.

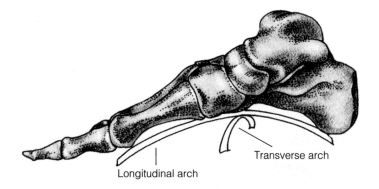

(c) HUMAN (MEDIAL VIEW)

FIGURE A–8

Foot (pedal) anatomy.

Appendix B
Population Genetics

As noted in Chapter 12, the basic approach in population genetics makes use of a mathematical model called the Hardy-Weinberg equilibrium equation. The Hardy-Weinberg theory of genetic equilibrium postulates a set of conditions in a population where *no* evolution occurs. In other words, none of the forces of evolution are acting, and all genes have an equal chance of recombining in each generation (i.e., there is random mating of individuals). More precisely, the hypothetical conditions that such a population would be *assumed* to meet are as follows:

1. The population is infinitely large. This condition eliminates the possibility of random genetic drift or changes in allele frequencies due to chance.
2. There is no mutation. Thus, no new alleles are being added by molecular changes in gametes.
3. There is no gene flow. There is no exchange of genes with other populations that can alter allele frequencies.
4. Natural selection is not operating. Specific alleles confer no advantage over others that might influence reproductive success.
5. Mating is random. There are no factors that influence who mates with whom. Thus, any female is assumed to have an equal chance of mating with any male.

If all these conditions are satisfied, allele frequencies will not change from one generation to the next (i.e., no evolution will take place), and a permanent equilibrium will be maintained as long as these conditions prevail. An evolutionary "barometer" is thus provided that may be used as a standard against which actual circumstances are compared. Similar to the way a typical barometer is standardized under known temperature and altitude conditions, the Hardy-Weinberg equilibrium is standardized under known evolutionary conditions.

Note that the idealized conditions that define the Hardy-Weinberg equilibrium are just that: an idealized, *hypothetical* state. In the real world, no actual population would fully meet any of these conditions. But do not be confused by this distinction. By explicitly defining the genetic distribution that would be *expected* if *no* evolutionary change were occurring (i.e., in equilibrium), we can compare the *observed* genetic distribution obtained from actual human populations. The evolutionary barometer is thus evaluated through comparison of these observed allele and genotype frequencies with those expected in the predefined equilibrium situation.

If the observed frequencies differ from those of the expected model, then we can say that evolution is taking place at the locus in question. The alternative, of course, is that the observed and expected frequencies do not differ sufficiently to state unambiguously that evolution is occurring at a locus in a population. Indeed, frequently this is the result that is obtained, and in such cases, population geneticists are unable to delineate evolutionary changes at the particular locus under study. Put another way, geneticists are unable to reject what statisticians call the *null hypothesis* (where "null" means nothing, a statistical condition of randomness).

The simplest situation applicable to a microevolutionary study is a genetic trait that follows a simple Mendelian pattern and has only two alleles (*A, a*). As you recall from earlier discussions, there are then only three possible genotypes: *AA, Aa, aa*. Proportions of these genotypes (*AA:Aa:aa*) are a function of the *allele frequencies* themselves (percentage of *A* and percentage of *a*). To provide uniformity for all genetic loci, a standard notation is employed to refer to these frequencies:

Frequency of dominant allele (A) = p
Frequency of recessive allele (a) = q

Since in this case there are only two alleles, their combined total frequency must represent all possibilities. In other words, the sum of their separate frequencies must be 1:

$$p \quad + \quad q = 1 \text{ (100\% of alleles at the locus in question)}$$
(Frequency   Frequency
of *A* alleles)   of *a* alleles)

To ascertain the expected proportions of genotypes, we compute the chances of the alleles combining with one another into all possible combinations. Remember, they all have an equal chance of combining, and no new alleles are being added.

These probabilities are a direct function of the frequency of the two alleles. The chances of all possible combinations occurring randomly can be simply shown as

$$
\begin{array}{r}
p + q \\
\times\ p + q \\
\hline
pq + q^2 \\
p^2 + pq \\
\hline
p^2 + 2pq + q^2
\end{array}
$$

Mathematically, this is known as a binomial expansion and can also be shown as

$$(p + q)(p + q) = p^2 + 2pq + q^2$$

What we have just calculated is simply:

Allele Combination	Genotype Produced	Expected Proportion in Population
Chances of A combining with A	AA	$p \times p = p^2$
Chances of A combining with a;	Aa	$p \times q$
a combining with A	aA	$p \times q$ = 2 pq
Chances of a combining with a	aa	$q \times q = q^2$

Thus, p^2 is the frequency of the AA genotype, $2pq$ is the frequency of the Aa genotype, and q^2 is the frequency of the aa genotype, where p is the frequency of the dominant allele and q is the frequency of the recessive allele in a population.

Calculating Allele Frequencies: An Example

How geneticists use the Hardy-Weinberg formula is best demonstrated through an example. Let us assume that a population contains 200 individuals, and we will use the MN blood group locus as the gene to be measured. This gene produces a blood group antigen—similar to ABO—located on red blood cells. Because the M and N alleles are codominant, we can ascertain everyone's phenotype by taking blood samples and observing reactions with specially prepared antisera. From the phenotypes, we can then directly calculate the *observed* allele frequencies. So let us proceed.

All 200 individuals are tested, and the results are shown in Table B–1. Although the match between observed and expected frequencies is not perfect, it is close enough statistically to satisfy equilibrium conditions. Since our population is not a large one, sampling may easily account for the small observed deviations. Our population is therefore probably in equilibrium (i.e., at this locus, it is not evolving). At the minimum, what we can say scientifically is that we cannot reject the *null hypothesis*.

TABLE B–1   Calculating Allele Frequencies in a Hypothetical Population

Observed Data

Genotype	Number of individuals*	Percent	Number of Alleles M	N			
MM	80	(40%)	160	0			
MN	80	(40%)	80	80			
NN	40	(20%)	0	80			
Totals	200	(100%)	240	+	160	=	400
		Proportion:	.6	+	.4	=	1

*Each individual has two alleles. Thus, a person who is MM contributes two M alleles to the total gene pool. A person who is MN contributes one M and one N. Two hundred individuals, then, have 400 alleles for the MN locus.

Observed Allele Frequencies

$M = .6(p)$
$N = .4(q)$ ($p + q$ should equal 1, and they do)

Expected Frequencies

What are the predicted genotypic proportions if genetic equilibrium (no evolution) applies to our population? We simply apply the Hardy-Weinberg formula: $p^2 + 2pq + q^2$.

$p2$	=	(.6)(.6)	=	.36
$2pq$	=	2(.6)(.4) = 2(.24)	=	.48
q^2	=	(.4)(.4)	=	.16
Total				1.00

There are only three possible genotypes (MM:MN:NN), so the total of the relative proportions should equal 1; as you can see, they do.

Comparing Frequencies

How do the expected frequencies compare with the observed frequencies in our population?

	Expected Frequency	Expected Number of Individuals	Observed Frequency	Actual Number of Individuals with Each Genotype
MM	.36	72	.40	80
MN	.48	96	.40	80
NN	.16	32	.20	40

Appendix C
Sexing and Aging the Skeleton

The field of physical anthropology that is directly concerned with the analysis of skeletal remains is called *osteology*. Using an osteological perspective allows researchers to study skeletons of both human and nonhuman primates to understand the ways in which hominids are similar to, and distinct from, other primates. Moreover, paleoanthropologists also use many of the same techniques to analyze the remains of fossil hominids (which mostly consist of teeth and bones). In more recent contexts, encompassing the last few thousand years, skeletal remains of *Homo sapiens* have been investigated by osteologists to learn about the size, nutritional status, and diseases present in prior human populations.

Two very important questions that osteologists ask when analyzing a skeleton are the sex and age of the individual. Such basic demographic variables as sex and age are crucial in any comprehensive osteological analysis, especially of human remains.

Sexing the Skeleton

During infancy and childhood, male and female skeletons do not differ much. Consequently, osteologists usually cannot determine the sex of a skeleton of someone who died before 13 to 15 years of age. However, during development, *sexual dimorphism* is increasingly manifested in the skeleton, making sex determination feasible in adult remains, provided enough of the skeleton is present.

The differences between male and female skeletons are most clearly expressed in the pelvis (*pl.,* pelves), and this variation is due to the requirements of childbirth in females. In particular, during hominid evolution, the dual influences of bipedal locomotion and relatively large-brained newborns placed adaptive constraints on pelvic anatomy. As a result, in females the pelvis is generally broader and more splayed out than in males. The most useful criteria for sex determination are listed in Table C–1 and illustrated in Figure C–1. While these criteria, taken together, are good indicators of sex, you should be aware that none, taken in isolation, is true in all cases. Moreover, this is not a complete listing of all traits used in sexing skeletons, although it does include those most commonly used.

There are also sex differences in cranial dimensions, most especially relating to facial proportions. However, these differences are not as consistent as those in the pelvis. Therefore, it is important to recognize patterns of cranial variation as they

TABLE C–1   Differences Between the Male and Female Pelvis

Pelvic Characteristic	Female	Male
General	Muscle attachments less robust; overall appearance sometimes less massive	Muscle attachments more robust; overall appearance sometimes more massive
Subpubic angle	Wider (more than 90°)	Narrower (less than 90°)
Greater sciatic notch	Wider—more open (more than 68°)	Narrower—more closed (less than 68°)
Ischiopubic ramus (medial view)	Thinner	Thicker
Ventral arc (elevated ridge on ventral surface of pubis)	Frequently present	Absent
Sacrum	Wider and straighter	Narrower and more curved

FIGURE C–1

Male and female pelves compared.

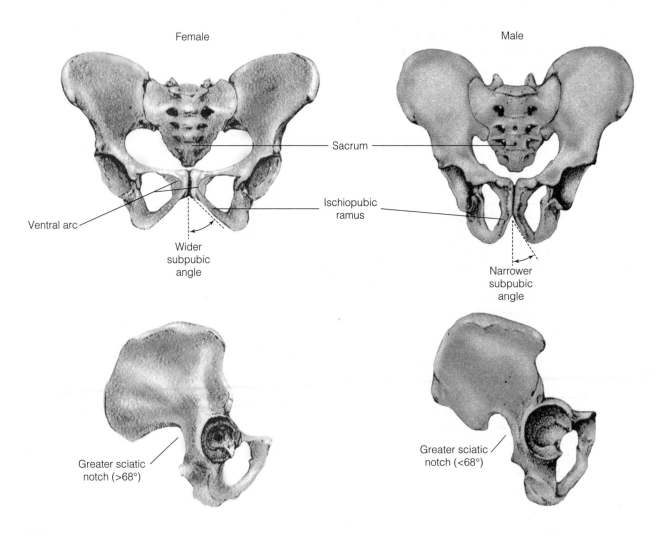

TABLE C–2 Cranial Variation Between Males and Females

Cranial Feature	Females	Males
Points of muscle attachment (e.g., mastoid process)	Less pronounced	Larger, more pronounced
Supraorbital torus (browridge)	Less pronounced or absent	More pronounced
Supraorbital rim (upper margin of eye orbit)	Sharper	More rounded
Palate	More shallow	Deeper

are expressed in different populations. The cranial features most commonly used for sex determination are listed in Table C–2 (see also Fig. C–2). These differences reflect the fact that in males, the skeleton is larger than in females. The bones are denser, and areas of muscle attachment are frequently more robust. However, such differences are not consistently expressed across various populations, and knowledge of relevant population variation is thus important in drawing reasonable determinations of sex.

Determining Age

During growth, the skeleton and dentition undergo developmental changes that occur within known age ranges. Thus, estimating age in individuals who were younger than 20 when they died is based primarily on the presence of deciduous (baby) and permanent teeth, the appearance of ossification centers of bones, and the fusion of the ends of long bones to bone shafts.

FIGURE C–2
Cranium and mandible.

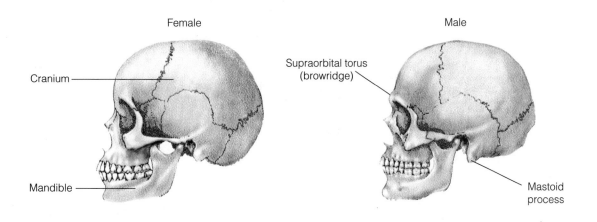

Female

Male

Cranium

Mandible

Supraorbital torus (browridge)

Mastoid process

Dental Eruption

Age estimation based on dental eruption is useful in individuals up to approximately 15 years of age. The third molar (wisdom tooth) erupts after this time, but the age of eruption of this tooth (if it forms at all) is highly variable. Thus, the third molar is not a very reliable indicator of age except that its presence indicates that the individual was at least a young adult (Fig. C–3).

Bone Growth

The size of long bones, the development of secondary ossification centers (epiphyses), and the degree of fusion of epiphyses to bone shafts are just as important as dental eruption. Postcranial bones are preceded by a cartilage model that is gradually replaced by bone, both in the diaphyses (shafts) and the secondary centers (the ends of the bones, or epiphyses). In children and adolescents, bones continue to grow until the epiphyses fuse to the diaphyses. Because this fusion occurs within different age ranges in different bones, the age of an individual can be estimated by determining which epiphyses have fused and which have not (Fig. C–4). The characteristic undulating appearance of the unfused surfaces helps differentiate immature elements from the broken end of a mature bone.

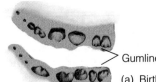

Gumline

(a) Birth: The crowns for all the deciduous teeth (shown in color) are present; no roots, however, have yet formed.

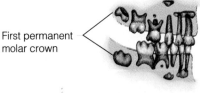

First permanent molar crown

(b) 2 years: All deciduous teeth (shown in color) are erupted; the first permanent molar and permanent incisors have crowns (unerupted) formed, but no roots.

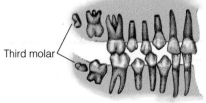

Third molar

(c) 12 years: All permanent teeth are erupted except the third molar (wisdom tooth).

FIGURE C–3
Dental development.

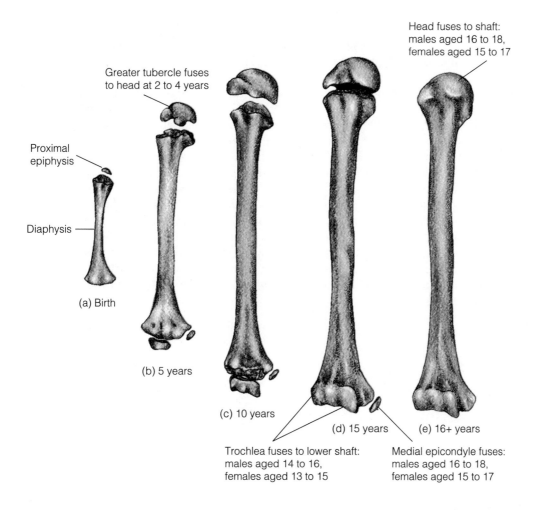

Head fuses to shaft:
males aged 16 to 18,
females aged 15 to 17

Greater tubercle fuses
to head at 2 to 4 years

Proximal
epiphysis

Diaphysis

(a) Birth

(b) 5 years

(c) 10 years

(d) 15 years

(e) 16+ years

Trochlea fuses to lower shaft:
males aged 14 to 16,
females aged 13 to 15

Medial epicondyle fuses:
males aged 16 to 18,
females aged 15 to 17

Other Skeletal Changes

Once a person has reached physiological maturity (by the early 20s), determinations of age become more difficult and less precise. Several techniques are used, and these are based on the occurrence of progressive, regular changes in the face of the pubic symphysis (the most common technique), in the sternal ends of the ribs, and in the auricular surface of the ilium (where the ilium articulates with the sacrum). Other indicators are closure of the cranial sutures and cellular changes that are determined by microscopic examination of cross sections of long bones. Degenerative changes, such as arthritis, osteoporosis, and wear of dental enamel, can also aid in the determination of relative age (older versus younger), but they provide imprecise estimates. In fact, it is very difficult to age accurately the skeletons of adults. For example, the presence of severe tooth wear would imply that the individual was not young, but enamel attrition varies between populations and depends on many factors, including diet. Moreover, the appearance of many degenerative changes is influenced by disease, trauma, and the biological makeup of individuals. Thus, at present, osteologists must be content to use broad age ranges when estimating age at death in mature skeletons.

FIGURE C–4

Skeletal age: epiphyseal union in the humerus. Some regions of the humerus exhibit some of the earliest fusion centers in the body, while others are among the latest to complete fusion (not until late adolescence).

Pubic Symphyseal Face   The face of the pubic symphysis in young individuals is characterized by a billowing surface (with ridges and furrows) such as that seen on the surface of an epiphysis (Fig. C–5). The symphyseal face undergoes regular age-related changes from the age of about 18 onward.

The first aging technique based on the alterations of the pubic symphysis was developed by T. W. Todd (1920, 1921) utilizing dissection room cadavers. McKern and Stewart (1957) developed a technique by analyzing a sample of American males killed in the Korean War. Both of the samples from which these systems were derived, however, have limitations. The dissection room sample used by Todd contained some individuals of uncertain age, and the Korean War sample was predominantly made up of young white males, with few being older than 35.

More recently, a system has been developed by Katz and Suchey (1986), based on an autopsy sample of 739 males for whom documentation of age was provided by death certificates. This sample has proved to be more representative of the general population than the earlier samples. Because this technique is derived from data collected from a large sample of people of known age at death, it is currently the most accurate method available for estimating age in adult human skeletal remains.

FIGURE C–5

Skeletal age: remodeling of the pubic symphysis.

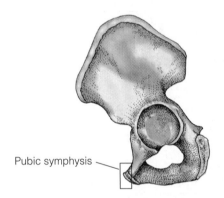

Pubic symphysis

(a) Position of the pubic symphysis. This area of the pelvis shows systematic changes progressively throughout adult life. Two of these stages are shown in (b) and (c).

(b) Age: 21. The face of the symphysis shows the typical "billowed" appearance of a young joint; no rim present.

(c) Age: mid-50s. The face is mostly flat, with a distinct rim formed around most of the periphery.

Glossary

Acheulian (ash´-oo-lay-en) Pertaining to a stone tool industry of the Lower and Middle Pleistocene characterized by a large proportion of bifacial tools (flaked on both sides). Acheulian tool kits are very common in Africa, Southwest Asia, and western Europe, but are generally absent elsewhere. (Also spelled "Acheulean.")

Acclimatization Physiological response to changes in the environment that occurs during an individual's lifetime. Such responses may be short-term. The capacity for acclimatization may typify an entire population or species. This capacity is under genetic influence and thus is subject to evolutionary factors such as natural selection.

Adaptations Physiological and/or behavioral adjustments made by organisms in response to environmental circumstances. Adaptations may be short-term or long-term, and strictly defined, they are the results of evolutionary factors.

Adaptive niche The entire way of life of an organism: where it lives, what it eats, how it gets food, how it avoids predators, etc.

Adaptive radiation The relatively rapid expansion and diversification of an evolving group of organisms as they adapt to new niches.

Adolescent growth spurt The period during adolescence in which well-nourished teens typically increase in stature at greater rates than at other points in the life cycle.

Affiliative Pertaining to amicable associations between individuals. Affiliative behaviors, such as grooming, reinforce social bonds and promote group cohesion.

Allele frequency In a population, the percentage of all the alleles at a specific locus accounted for by one specific allele.

Alleles Alternate forms of a gene. Alleles occur at the same locus on homologous chromosomes and thus govern the same trait. However, because they are different, their action may result in different expressions of that trait. The term is often used synonymously with *genes.*

Altruism Any behavior or act that benefits another individual but poses some potential risk or cost to oneself.

Amino acids Small molecules that are the components of proteins.

Analogies Similarities between organisms based strictly on common function with no assumed common evolutionary descent.

Anatomically modern *H. sapiens* All modern humans and some fossil forms, perhaps dating as early as 200,000 y.a.; defined by a set of derived characteristics, including cranial architecture and lack of skeletal robusticity; usually classified at the subspecies level as *Homo sapiens sapiens.*

Anthropoids Members of a suborder of Primates, the *Anthropoidea* (pronounced "ann-throw-poid´-ee-uh"). Traditionally, the suborder includes monkeys, apes, and humans.

Anthropology The field of inquiry that studies human culture and evolutionary aspects of human biology; includes cultural anthropology, archaeology, linguistics, and physical anthropology.

Anthropocentric   Viewing nonhuman phenomena in terms of human experience and capabilities; emphasizing the importance of humans over everything else.

Anthropometry   Measurement of human body parts. When osteologists measure skeletal elements, the term *osteometry* is often used.

Antigens   Large molecules found on the surface of cells. Several different loci governing antigens on red and white blood cells are known. (Foreign antigens provoke an immune response in individuals.)

Arboreal   Tree-living: adapted to life in the trees.

Arboreal hypothesis   The traditional view that primate characteristics can be explained as a consequence of primate diversification into arboreal habitats.

Archaic *H. sapiens*   Earlier forms of *Homo sapiens* (including Neandertals) from the Old World that differ from *H. erectus* but lack the full set of characteristics diagnostic of modern *H. sapiens*.

Artifacts   Objects or materials made or modified for use by hominids. The earliest artifacts tend to be tools made of stone or, occasionally, bone.

Aurignacian   Pertaining to an Upper Paleolithic stone tool industry in Europe beginning at about 40,000 y.a.

Australopithecines   (os-tral-oh-pith´-e-seens) The colloquial term for members of genus *Australopithecus*.

Australopithecus   An early hominid genus, known from the Plio-Pleistocene of Africa, characterized by bipedal locomotion, a relatively small brain, and large back teeth.

Autonomic   Pertaining to physiological responses not under voluntary control. An example in chimpanzees would be the erection of body hair during excitement. An example in humans is blushing. Both convey information regarding emotional states, but neither is a deliberate behavior, and communication is not intended.

Autosomes   All chromosomes except the sex chromosomes.

Balanced polymorphism   The maintenance of two or more alleles in a population due to the selective advantage of the heterozygote.

Binocular vision   Vision characterized by overlapping visual fields provided by forward-facing eyes; essential to depth perception.

Binomial nomenclature   (*Binomial* means "two names.") In taxonomy, the convention established by Carolus Linnaeus whereby genus and species names are used to refer to species. For example, *Homo sapiens* refers to human beings.

Biocultural   Pertaining to the concept that biology makes culture possible and that culture influences biology.

Biocultural evolution   The mutual, interactive evolution of human biology and culture; the concept that biology makes culture possible and that developing culture further influences the direction of biological evolution; a basic concept in understanding the unique components of human evolution.

Biological continuum   Referring to the fact that organisms are related through common ancestry and that behaviors and traits seen in one species are also seen in others to varying degrees. (When expressions of a phenomenon continuously grade into one another so that there are no discrete categories, they are said to exist on a continuum. Color is such a phenomenon.)

Biological determinism   The concept that various attributes and behaviors (e.g., intelligence, values, morals) are governed by biological (genetic) factors; the inaccurate association of various behavioral attributes with certain biological traits, such as skin color.

Bipedal locomotion   Walking on two feet. Walking habitually on two legs is the single most distinctive feature of the hominids.

Bipedally   On two feet. Walking habitually on two legs is the single most distinctive feature of the Hominidae.

Brachiation   A form of locomotion in which the body is suspended beneath the hands and support is alternated from one forelimb to the other; arm swinging.

Brachycephalic   Having a broad head in which the width measures more than 80 percent of the length.

Breeding isolates   Populations that are clearly isolated geographically and/or socially from other breeding groups.

Burins   Small, chisel-like tools (with a pointed end) thought to have been used to engrave bone, antler, ivory, or wood.

Catastrophism   The view that the earth's geological landscape is the result of violent cataclysmic events. This view was promoted by Cuvier, especially in opposition to Lamarck.

Catch-up period   A period of time during which a child who has experienced delayed growth because of malnutrition, undernutrition, or disease can increase in height to the point of his or her genetic potential.

Centromere   The constricted portion of a chromosome. After replication, the two strands of a double-stranded chromosome are joined at the centromere.

Cercopithecines   (serk-oh-pith'-eh-seens) The subfamily of Old World monkeys that includes baboons, macaques, and guenons.

Chatelperronian   Pertaining to an Upper Paleolithic tool industry found in France and Spain, containing blade tools and associated with Neandertals.

Chordata (Chordates)   The phylum of the animal kingdom that includes vertebrates.

Chromosomes   Discrete structures composed of DNA and protein found only in the nuclei of cells. Chromosomes are visible only under magnification during certain stages of cell division.

Chronometric   Referring to a dating technique that gives an estimate in actual number of years (from *chronos,* meaning "time," and *metric,* meaning "measure").

Clade   A group of species sharing a common ancestor and distinct from other groups.

Cladistics   The approach to taxonomy that groups species (as well as other levels of classification) on the basis of shared derived characteristics. In this way, organisms are classified solely on the basis of presumed closeness of evolutionary relationship.

Classification   In biology, the ordering of organisms into categories, such as phyla, orders, and families, to show evolutionary relationships.

Cline   A gradient of genotypes (usually measured as allele frequencies) over geographical space; more

exactly, the depiction of allele distribution produced by connecting points of equal frequency (as on a temperature map).

Clone   An organism that is genetically identical to another organism. The term may also be used to refer to genetically identical DNA segments and molecules.

Codominance   The expression of two alleles in heterozygotes. In this situation, neither allele is dominant or recessive, thus both influence the phenotype.

Codons   The triplets of messenger RNA bases that refer to a specific amino acid during protein synthesis.

Colobines   (kole'-uh-beans) The subfamily of Old World monkeys that includes the African colobus monkeys and Asian langurs.

Communication   Any act that conveys information, in the form of a message, to another individual. Frequently, the result of communication is a change in the behavior of the recipient. Communication may not be deliberate but may be the result of involuntary processes or a secondary consequence of an intentional action.

Complementary   Referring to the fact that DNA bases form base pairs in a precise manner. For example, adenine can bond only to thymine. These two bases are said to be *complementary* because one requires the other to form a complete DNA base pair.

Continuum   A set of relationships in which all components fall along a single integrated spectrum. All life reflects a single *biological* continuum.

Core area   The portion of a home range containing the highest concentration of resources.

Culture   All aspects of human adaptation, including technology, traditions, language, and social roles. Culture is learned and transmitted from one generation to the next by nonbiological means.

Cusps   The elevated portions (bumps) on the chewing surfaces of premolar and molar teeth.

Cytoplasm   The portion of the cell contained within the cell membrane, excluding the nucleus. The cytoplasm consists of a semifluid material and contains numerous structures involved with cell function.

Data (*sing.,* **datum**)   Facts from which conclusions can be drawn; scientific information.

Deoxyribonucleic acid (DNA)   The double-stranded molecule that contains the genetic code. DNA is a main component of chromosomes.

Derived (modified)   Referring to characters that are modified from the ancestral condition and thus *are* diagnostic of particular evolutionary lineages.

Development   Differentiation of cells into different types of tissues and their maturation.

Displays   Sequences of repetitious behaviors that serve to communicate emotional states. Nonhuman primate displays are most frequently associated with reproductive or agonistic behavior.

Diurnal   Active during the day.

Dolichocephalic   Having a long, narrow head in which the width measures less than 75 percent of the length.

Dominance hierarchies   Systems of social organization wherein individuals within a group are ranked relative to one another. Higher-ranking individuals have greater access to preferred food items and mating partners than lower-ranking individuals. Dominance hierarchies are sometimes referred to as "pecking orders."

Dominant   Describing a trait governed by an allele that can be expressed in the presence of another, different allele (i.e., in heterozygotes). Dominant alleles prevent the expression of recessive alleles in heterozygotes. (This is the definition of *complete* dominance.)

Ecological   Pertaining to the relationship between organisms and all aspects of their environment (temperature, predators, other animals, vegetation, availability of food and water, types of food, etc.)

Ecological niches   Specific environmental settings to which organisms are adapted.

Empirical   Relying on experiment or observation; from the Latin *empiricus,* meaning "experienced."

Endemic   Continuously present in a population.

Endemically (endemic)   Continuously present in a population. With regard to disease, refers to populations in which there will always be some infected individuals.

Endocast   A solid impression of the inside of the skull, often preserving details relating to the size and surface features of the brain.

Endogamy   Mating with others from the same group.

Enzymes   Specialized proteins that initiate and direct chemical reactions in the body.

Epochs   A category of the geological time scale; subdivisions of periods. In the Cenozoic, epochs include the Paleocene, Eocene, Oligocene, Miocene, Pliocene (from the Tertiary period) and the Pleistocene and Holocene (from the Quaternary period).

Essential amino acids   The eight (nine for infants) amino acids that must be ingested by humans for normal growth and body maintenance; include tryptophan, leucine, lysine, methionine, phenylalanine, isoleucine, valine, and threonine (plus histidine for infants).

Estrus   (ess´-truss) Period of sexual receptivity in female mammals (except humans); correlated with ovulation. When used as an adjective, the word is spelled "estrous."

Ethnocentric   Viewing other cultures from the inherently biased perspective of one's own culture. Ethnocentrism usually results in cultures being seen as inferior to one's own.

Ethnographies   Detailed descriptive studies of human societies. In cultural anthropology, an ethnography is traditionally the study of a non-Western society.

Eugenics   The philosophy of "race improvement" through the forced sterilization of members of some groups and encouraged reproduction among others; an overly simplified, often racist view that is now discredited.

Evolution   A change in the genetic structure of a population. The term is also frequently used to refer to the appearance of a new species.

Evolutionary trends   Overall characteristics of an evolving lineage, such as the primates. Such trends are useful in helping to categorize the lineage as compared to other lineages (i.e., other placental mammals).

Exogamy   Mating with individuals from other groups.

Faunal   Referring to animal remains; in archaeology, specifically refers to the fossil remains of animals.

Fertility Actual production of offspring; distinguished from fecundity, which is the (potential) ability to produce children. For example, a woman in her early 20s is probably fecund, but she is not actually fertile unless she has had children.

Fitness Pertaining to natural selection, a measure of *relative* reproductive success of individuals. Fitness can be measured by an individual's genetic contribution to the next generation compared to that of others.

Fixity of species The notion that species, once created, can never change; an idea diametrically opposed to theories of biological evolution.

Flexed The position of the body in a bent orientation, with the arms and legs drawn up to the chest.

Forensic anthropology An applied anthropological approach dealing with legal matters. Forensic anthropologists work with coroners and others in the analysis and identification of human remains.

Founder effect Also called the *Sewall-Wright effect,* a type of genetic drift in which allele frequencies are altered in small populations that are taken from, or are remnants of, larger populations.

Frugivorous (fru-give´-or-us) Having a diet composed primarily of fruit.

Gametes Reproductive cells (eggs and sperm in animals) developed from precursor cells in ovaries and testes.

Gene A sequence of DNA bases that specifies the order of amino acids in an entire protein or, in some cases, a portion of a protein. A gene may be made up of hundreds or thousands of DNA bases.

Gene flow The exchange of genes between populations (also called migration).

Gene pool The total complement of genes shared by reproductive members of a population.

Genetic drift Evolutionary changes—that is, changes in allele frequencies—produced by random factors. Genetic drift is a result of small population size.

Genetics The study of gene structure and action and the patterns of inheritance of traits. Genetic mechanisms are the underlying foundation for evolutionary change.

Genome The full genetic complement of an individual (or of a species). In humans, it is estimated that each individual possesses approximately 3 billion nucleotides in his or her nuclear DNA.

Genotype The genetic makeup of an individual. Genotype can refer to an organism's entire genetic makeup or to the alleles at a particular locus.

Genus A group of closely related species.

Geological time scale The organization of earth history into eras, periods, and epochs; commonly used by geologists and paleoanthropologists.

Grooming Picking through fur to remove dirt, parasites, and other materials that may be present. Social grooming is common among primates and reinforces social relationships.

Growth Increase in mass or number of cells.

Hardy-Weinberg equilibrium The mathematical relationship expressing—under ideal conditions—the predicted distribution of genes in populations; the central theorem of population genetics.

Hemoglobin A protein molecule that occurs in red blood cells and binds to oxygen molecules.

Heterozygous Having different alleles at the same locus on members of a pair of homologous chromosomes.

Holocene The most recent epoch of the Cenozoic. Following the Pleistocene, it is estimated to have begun 10,000 years ago.

Home range The entire area exploited by an animal or group of animals.

Homeostasis A condition of balance or stability within a biological system, maintained by the interaction of physiological mechanisms that compensate for changes (both external and internal).

Hominidae The taxonomic family to which humans belong; also includes other, now extinct, bipedal relatives.

Hominids Popular form of Hominidae; includes all bipedal hominoids back to the divergence from African great apes.

Hominoidea The formal designation for the superfamily of anthropoids that includes apes and humans.

Homologies   Similarities between organisms based on descent from a common ancestor.

Homologous   Referring to members of chromosome pairs. Homologous chromosomes carry genes that govern the same traits. During meiosis, homologous chromosomes pair and exchange segments of DNA. They are alike with regard to size and also position of the centromere.

Homoplasy   (*homo,* meaning "same," and *plasy,* meaning "growth") The separate evolutionary development of similar characteristics in different groups of organisms.

Homozygous   Having the same allele at the same locus on both members of a pair of homologous chromosomes.

Hormones   Substances (usually proteins) that are produced by specialized cells and that travel to other parts of the body, where they influence chemical reactions and regulate various cellular functions.

Human Genome Project   An international effort aimed at sequencing and mapping the entire human genome.

Hybrids   Offspring of mixed ancestry; heterozygotes.

Hypothesis (*pl.,* hypotheses)   A provisional explanation of a phenomenon. Hypotheses require verification.

Hypoxia   Lack of oxygen. Hypoxia can refer to reduced amounts of available oxygen in the atmosphere (due to lowered barometric pressure) or to insufficient amounts of oxygen in the body.

Intelligence   Mental capacity; ability to learn, reason, or comprehend and interpret information, facts, relationships, meanings, etc.; the capacity to solve problems, whether through the application of previously acquired knowledge or through insight.

Interspecific   Between species; refers to variation beyond that seen within the same species to include additional aspects seen between two different species.

Intraspecific   Within species; refers to variation seen within the same species.

Ischial callosities   Patches of tough, hard skin on the buttocks of Old World monkeys and chimpanzees.

K-selected   Pertaining to an adaptive strategy whereby individuals produce relatively few offspring, in whom they invest increased parental care. Although only a few infants are born, chances of survival are increased for each individual because of parental investments in time and energy. Examples of nonprimate K-selected species are birds and canids (e.g., wolves, coyotes, and dogs).

Lactation   The production of milk in mammals.

Lactose intolerance   The inability to digest fresh milk products; caused by the discontinued production of lactase, the enzyme that breaks down lactose (milk sugar).

Large-bodied hominoids   Those hominoids including "great" apes (orangutans, chimpanzees, gorillas) and hominids, as well as all ancestral forms back to the time of divergence from small-bodied hominoids (i.e., the gibbon lineage).

Locus (*pl.,* loci) (lo´-kus, lo-sigh´)   The position on a chromosome where a given gene occurs. The term is sometimes used interchangeably with gene.

Macaques   (muh-kaks´) Group of Old World monkeys comprising several species, including rhesus monkeys.

Macroevolution   Large-scale evolutionary changes (especially speciation) that may require many hundreds of generations and are usually only detectable paleontologically (in the fossil record).

Magdalenian   Pertaining to the final phase (stone tool industry) of the Upper Paleolithic in Europe.

Malnutrition   A diet insufficient in quality (i.e., lacking some essential component) to support normal health.

Mammalia   The technical term for the formal grouping (class) of mammals.

Material culture   The physical manifestations of human activities; includes tools, art, and structures. As the most durable aspects of culture, material remains make up the majority of archaeological evidence of past societies.

Meiosis   Cell division in specialized cells in ovaries and testes. Meiosis involves two divisions and results in four daughter cells, each containing only half the original number of chromosomes. These cells can develop into gametes.

Mendelian traits   Characteristics that are influenced by alleles at only one genetic locus. Examples include many blood types, such as ABO. Many genetic disorders, including sickle-cell anemia and Tay-Sachs disease, are also Mendelian traits.

Mesolithic   The period preceding the Neolithic, during which humans increasingly exploited smaller animals (including fish), increased the variety of tools they used, and became somewhat less nomadic.

Messenger RNA (mRNA)   A form of RNA that is assembled on one sequence of DNA bases. It carries the DNA code to the ribosome during protein synthesis.

Metazoa   Multicellular animals; a major division of the animal kingdom.

Microevolution   Small-scale evolutionary changes that occur over the span of a few generations and can therefore be detected in living populations.

Midline   An anatomical term referring to a hypothetical line that divides the body into right and left halves.

Mitochondria   (*sing.*, mitochondrion) Organelles found in the cytoplasm of cells that are responsible for producing energy for cellular functions.

Mitochondrial DNA (mtDNA)   DNA found in the mitochondria (structures found within the cytoplasm of the cell) and inherited through the maternal line.

Mitosis   Simple cell division; the process by which somatic cells divide to produce two identical daughter cells.

Molecules   Structures made up of two or more atoms. Molecules can combine with other molecules to form more complex structures.

Monogenism   The theory that all human races were descended from one pair (Adam and Eve), but they differed from one another because they occupied different habitats. This concept was an attempt to explain phenotypic variation between populations, but did not imply evolutionary change.

Morphology   The form (shape, size) of anatomical structures; can also refer to the entire organism.

Mosaic evolution   A pattern of evolution in which the rates of evolution in one functional system varies from those in other systems. For example, in hominid evolution, the dental system, locomotor system, and neurological system (especially the brain) all evolved at markedly different rates.

Mousterian   Pertaining to the stone tool industry associated with Neandertals and some modern *H. sapiens* groups; also called Middle Paleolithic. This industry is characterized by a larger proportion of flake tools than is found in Acheulian tool kits.

Multidisciplinary   Pertaining to research that involves mutual contributions and cooperation of several different experts from various scientific fields (i.e., disciplines).

Mutation   A change in DNA. Technically, mutation refers to changes in DNA bases as well as changes in chromosome number and/or structure.

Natural selection   The mechanism of evolutionary change first articulated by Charles Darwin. Refers to genetic change, or to changes in the frequencies of certain traits in populations due to differential reproductive success between individuals.

Neocortex   The outer (cellular) portion of the cerebrum, which has expanded during the course of mammalian evolution, particularly in primates, and most especially in humans. The neocortex is associated with higher mental function.

Neolithic   The period during which humans began to domesticate plants and animals. The Neolithic is also associated with increased sedentism. Dates for the Neolithic vary from region to region, depending on when domestication occurred.

Nocturnal   Active during the night.

Nondisjunction   The failure of homologous chromosomes or chromosome strands to separate during cell division.

Nuchal torus   (nuke´-ul, pertaining to the neck) A projection of bone in the back of the cranium where neck muscles attach, used to hold up the head. The nuchal torus is a distinctive feature of *H. erectus*.

Nucleotides   Basic units of the DNA molecule, composed of a sugar, a phosphate, and one of four DNA bases.

Nucleus   A structure (organelle) found in all eukaryotic cells. The nucleus contains chromosomes (nuclear DNA).

Omnivorous   Having a diet consisting of many food types (i.e., plant materials, meat, and insects).

Osteology   The study of skeletons. Human osteology often focuses on the interpretation of the skeletal remains of past groups. The same techniques are used in paleoanthropology to study early hominids.

Paleoanthropology   The interdisciplinary approach to the study of earlier hominids—their chronology, physical structure, archaeological remains, habitats, etc.

Paleopathology   The branch of osteology that studies the traces of disease and injury in human skeletal (or, occasionally, mummified) remains.

Paleospecies   Species defined from fossil evidence, often covering a long time span.

Pandemic   An extensive outbreak of disease affecting large numbers of people over a wide area; potentially, a worldwide phenomenon.

Paradigm   A cognitive construct or framework within which we explain phenomena. Paradigms shape our world view. They can change as a result of technological and intellectual innovation.

Pathogens   Substances or microorganisms, such as bacteria, fungi, or viruses, that cause disease.

Pellagra   Disease resulting from a dietary deficiency of niacin (vitamin B_3). Symptoms include dermatitis, diarrhea, dementia, and death (the "four Ds").

Phenotypes   The observable or detectable physical characteristics of an organism; the detectable expressions of genotypes.

Phenotypic ratio   The proportion of one phenotype to other phenotypes in a group of organisms. For example, Mendel observed that there were approximately three tall plants for every short plant in the F_2 generation. This is expressed as a phenotypic ratio of 3:1.

Phylogeny   A schematic representation showing ancestor-descendant relationships, usually in a chronological framework.

Plasticity   The capacity to change; in a physiological context, the ability of systems or organisms to make alterations in order to respond to differing conditions.

Pleistocene   The epoch of the Cenozoic from 1.8 m.y.a. until 10,000 y.a. Frequently referred to as the Ice Age, this epoch is associated with continental glaciations in northern latitudes.

Plio-Pleistocene   The time period including the Pliocene and the first half of the Pleistocene. For early hominids, this currently covers the range 4.5–1 m.y.a.

Polyandry   A mating system wherein a female continuously associates with more than one male (usually two or three) with whom she mates. Among nonhuman primates, this pattern is seen only in marmosets and tamarins.

Polygenic   Referring to traits that are influenced by genes at two or more loci. Examples of such traits are stature, skin color, and eye color. Many polygenic traits are also influenced by environmental factors.

Polygenism   A theory, opposed to monogenism, that stated that human races were not all descended from Adam and Eve. Instead, there had been several original human pairs, each giving rise to a different group. Thus, human races were considered to be separate species.

Polymerase chain reaction (PCR)   A method of producing copies of a DNA segment using the enzyme DNA polymerase.

Polymorphism   A genetic trait (the locus governing the trait) with more than one allele in appreciable frequency (i.e., greater than 1 percent).

Polytypic   Referring to species composed of populations that differ with regard to the expression of one or more traits.

Pongids   Members of the family Pongidae, including orangutans, gorillas, chimpanzees, and bonobos.

Population   Within a species, the community of individuals where mates are usually found.

Postcranial   (*post*, meaning "after") Referring to that portion of the body behind the head (in a quadruped). In bipeds, *postcranial* refers to all parts of the body *beneath* the head (i.e., from the neck down).

Prehensility   Grasping, as by the hands and feet of primates.

Primate   A member of the mammalian order Primates (pronounced "pry-may-tees"), which includes prosimians, monkeys, apes, and humans.

Primatologists   Scientists who study the evolution, anatomy, and behavior of nonhuman primates. Those who study behavior in noncaptive animals are usually trained as physical anthropologists.

Primatology   The study of the biology and behavior of nonhuman primates (prosimians, monkeys, and apes).

Primitive   Referring to a trait or combination of traits present in an ancestral form. Characters inherited by a group of organisms from a remote ancestor and thus not diagnostic of groups (lineages) branching subsequent to the time the character first appeared.

Principle of independent assortment   The distribution of one pair of alleles into gametes does not influence the distribution of another pair. The genes controlling different traits are inherited independently of one another.

Principle of segregation   Genes (alleles) occur in pairs (because chromosomes occur in pairs). During gamete production, the members of each gene pair separate, so that each gamete contains one member of each pair. During fertilization, the full number of chromosomes is restored, and members of gene or allele pairs are reunited.

Prosimians   Members of a suborder of Primates, the *Prosimii* (pronounced "pro-sim´-ee-eye"). Traditionally, the suborder includes lemurs, lorises, and tarsiers.

Protein synthesis   The assembly of chains of amino acids into functional protein molecules. The process is directed by DNA.

Proteins   Three-dimensional molecules that serve a wide variety of functions through their ability to bind to other molecules.

Protohominids   The earliest members of the hominid lineage, as yet basically unrepresented in the fossil record; thus, their structure and behavior are reconstructed hypothetically.

Provenience   In archaeology, the specific location of a discovery, including its geological context. (Also spelled "provenance.")

Punctuated equilibrium   The concept that evolutionary change proceeds through long periods of stasis punctuated by rapid periods of change.

Quadrupedal   Using all four limbs to support the body during locomotion; the basic mammalian (and primate) form of locomotion.

Quantitatively (quantitative)   Pertaining to measurements of quantity and including such properties as size, number, and capacity. When data are quantified, they are expressed numerically and are capable of being tested statistically.

r-selected   Pertaining to an adaptive strategy that emphasizes relatively large numbers of offspring and reduced parental care (compared to K-selected species). (*K-selection* and *r-selection* are relative terms; e.g., mice are r-selected compared to primates but K-selected compared to many fish species.)

Racial   In biology, pertaining to populations of a species that differ from other populations of the same species with regard to some aspects of outwardly expressed phenotype. Such phenotypic variation within a species is usually associated with differences in geographical location.

Recessive   Describing a trait that is not expressed in heterozygotes; also refers to the allele that governs the trait. For a recessive allele to be expressed, there must be two copies of the allele (i.e., the individual must be homozygous).

Recombination   The exchange of DNA between homologous chromosomes during meiosis; also called "crossing over."

Replicate   To duplicate. The DNA molecule is able to make copies of itself.

Reproductive strategies   The complex of behavioral patterns that contributes to individual reproductive success. The behaviors need not be deliberate, and they often vary considerably between males and females.

Reproductive success   The number of offspring an individual produces and rears to reproductive age; an individual's genetic contribution to the next generation as compared to the contributions of other individuals.

Restriction Fragment Length Polymorphisms (RFLPs)   Variation among individuals in the length of

DNA fragments produced by enzymes that break the DNA at specific sites.

Rhinarium   (rine-air′-ee-um) The moist, hairless pad at the end of the nose seen in most mammalian species. The rhinarium enhances an animal's ability to smell.

Ribonucleic acid (RNA)   A single-stranded molecule, similar in structure to DNA. The three forms of RNA are essential to protein synthesis.

Ribosomes   Structures composed of a specialized form of RNA and protein. Ribosomes are found in the cell's cytoplasm and are essential to the manufacture of proteins.

Science   A body of knowledge gained through observation and experimentation; from the Latin *scientia*, meaning "knowledge."

Scientific method   A research method whereby a problem is identified, a hypothesis (or hypothetical explanation) is stated, and that hypothesis is tested through the collection and analysis of data. If the hypothesis is verified, it becomes a theory.

Scientific testing   The precise repetition of an experiment or expansion of observed data to provide verification; the procedure by which hypotheses and theories are verified, modified, or discarded.

Scurvy   Disease resulting from a dietary deficiency of vitamin C. It may result in anemia, poor bone growth, abnormal bleeding and bruising, and muscle pain.

Selective pressures   Forces in the environment that influence reproductive success in individuals. In the example of the peppered moth, birds applied the selective pressure.

Sex chromosomes   In mammals, the X and Y chromosomes.

Sexual dimorphism   Differences in physical characteristics between males and females of the same species. For example, humans are slightly sexually dimorphic for body size, with males being taller, on average, than females of the same population.

Sexual selection   A type of natural selection that operates on only one sex within a species. It is the result of competition for mates, and it can lead to sexual dimorphism with regard to one or more traits.

Shared derived   Relating to specific character states shared in common between two forms and considered the most useful for making evolutionary interpretations.

Sites   Locations of discoveries. In paleontology and archaeology, a site may refer to a region where a number of discoveries have been made.

Slash-and-burn agriculture   A traditional land-clearing practice whereby trees and vegetation are cut and burned. In many areas, fields were abandoned after a few years and clearing occurred elsewhere.

Social structure   The composition, size, and sex ratio of a group of animals. Social structures, in part, are the result of natural selection in specific habitats, and they function to guide individual interactions and social relationships.

Socioecology   The study of animals and their habitats; specifically, attempts to find patterns of relationship between the environment and social behavior.

Somatic cells   Basically, all the cells in the body except those involved with reproduction.

Specialized   Evolved for a particular function; usually refers to a specific trait (e.g., incisor teeth), but may also refer to the whole way of life of an organism.

Speciation   The process by which new species are produced from earlier ones; the most important mechanism of macroevolutionary change.

Species   A group of organisms that can interbreed to produce fertile offspring. Members of one species are reproductively isolated from members of all other species (i.e., they cannot mate with them to produce fertile offspring).

Stereoscopic vision   The condition whereby visual images are, to varying degrees, superimposed on one another. This provides for depth perception, or the perception of the external environment in three dimensions. Stereoscopic vision is partly a function of structures in the brain.

Stratigraphy   Sequential layering of deposits.

Stratum (*pl.,* strata)   Geological layer.

Stress   In a physiological context, any factor that acts to disrupt homeostasis; more precisely, the body's response to any factor that threatens its ability to maintain homeostasis.

Taxonomy The branch of science concerned with the rules of classifying organisms on the basis of evolutionary relationships.

Territories Areas that will be aggressively protected against intrusion, particularly by other members of the same species.

Theory A broad statement of scientific relationships or underlying principles that has been at least partially verified.

Transfer RNA (tRNA) The type of RNA that binds to specific amino acids and transports them to the ribosome during protein synthesis.

Transmutation The change of one species to another. The term *evolution* did not assume its current meaning until the late nineteenth century.

Undernutrition A diet insufficient in quantity (calories) to support normal health.

Uniformitarianism The theory that the earth's features are the result of long-term processes that continue to operate in the present as they did in the past. Elaborated on by Lyell, this theory opposed catastrophism and provided for immense geological time.

Upper Paleolithic A cultural period usually associated with early modern humans (but also found with Neandertals) and distinguished by technological innovation in various stone tool industries. Best known from western Europe, similar industries are also known from central and eastern Europe and Africa.

Variation Inherited (i.e., genetically influenced) differences between individuals.

Vasoconstriction Narrowing of blood vessels to reduce blood flow to the skin. Vasoconstriction is an involuntary response to cold and reduces heat loss at the skin's surface.

Vasodilation Expansion of blood vessels, permitting increased blood flow to the skin. Vasodilation permits warming of the skin and also facilitates radiation of warmth as a means of cooling. Vasodilation is an involuntary response to warm temperatures, various drugs, and even emotional states (blushing).

Vectors Agents that serve to transmit disease from one carrier to another. Mosquitoes are vectors for malaria, just as fleas are vectors for bubonic plague.

Vertebrates Animals with bony backbones; includes fishes, amphibians, reptiles, birds, and mammals.

Viviparous Giving birth to live young.

World view General cultural orientation or perspective shared by members of a society.

Zygote A cell formed by the union of an egg and a sperm cell. It contains the full complement of chromosomes (in humans, 46) and has the potential of developing into an entire organism

Bibliography

Aiello, L. C. and B. A. Wood
  1994 Cranial Variables as Predictors of Hominine
        Body Mass. *American Journal of Physical
        Anthropology,* **95**:409–426.
Aitken, M. J., C. B. Stringer, and P. A. Mellars (eds.)
  1993 *The Origin of Modern Humans and the
        Impact of Chronometric Dating.* Princeton,
        NJ: Princeton University Press.
Altmann, Stuart A. and Jeanne Altmann
  1970 *Baboon Ecology.* Chicago: University of
        Chicago Press.
Andersson, J. Gunnar
  1934 *Children of the Yellow Earth.* New York:
        Macmillan.
Arensburg, B., A. M. Tillier, et al.
  1989 "A Middle Paleolithic Human Hyoid Bone."
        Nature, **338**:758–760.
Aronson, J. L., R. C. Walter, and M. Taieb
  1983 "Correlation of Tulu Bor Tuff at Koobi Fora
        with the Sidi Hakoma Tuff at Hadar." *Nature,*
        306:209–210.
Arsuaga, Juan-Luis, et al.
  1993 "Three New Human Skulls from the Sima de
        los Huesos Middle Pleistocene Site in Sierra
        de Atapuerca, Spain." *Nature,* **362**:534–537.
Arsuaga, J. L., I. Martinez, A. Garcia, et al.
  1997 "Sima de los Huesos (Sierra de Atapuerca,
        Spain). The Site." *Journal of Human
        Evolution,* **33**:109–127.
Ascenzi, A., I. Bidditu, P. F. Cassoli, et al.
  1996 "A Calvarium of Late *Homo erectus* from
        Ceprano, Italy." *Journal of Human Evolution,*
        31:409–423.

Asfaw, Berhane
  1992 "New Fossil Hominids from the Ethiopian
        Rift Valley and the Afar." Paper presented at
        the Annual Meeting, American Association of
        Physical Anthropologists.
Asfaw, Berhane, et al.
  1992 "The Earliest Acheulian from Konso-
        Gardula." *Nature,* **360**:732–735.

———————
  1995 Three Seasons of Hominid Paleontology at
        Aramis, Ethiopia. Paper presented at
        Paleoanthropology Society meetings,
        Oakland, Ca., March 1995.
Asfaw, Berhane, Tim White, Owen Lovejoy, et al.
  1999 "*Australopithecus garhi*: A New Species of
        Early Hominid from Ethiopia." *Science,*
        284:629–635.
Avery, O. T., MacLeod, C. M., and McCarty, M.
  1944 "Studies on the Chemical Nature of the
        Substance Inducing Transformation in
        Pneumococcal Types." *Journal of
        Experimental Medicine,* **79**:137–158.
Ayala, Francisco
  1995 "The Myth of Eve: Molecular Biology and
        Human Origins." *Science,* **270**:1930–1936.

Badrian, Alison and Noel Badrian
  1984 "Social Organization of *Pan paniscus* in the
        Lomako Forest, Zaire." *In: The Pygmy
        Chimpanzee,* Randall L. Susman (ed.), New
        York: Plenum Press, pp. 325–346.

Badrian, Noel and Richard K. Malenky
1984 "Feeding Ecology of *Pan paniscus* in the Lomako Forest, Zaire." *In: The Pygmy Chimpanzee,* Randall L. Susman (ed.), New York: Plenum Press, pp. 275–299.

Balter, Michael
1996 "Cave Structure Boosts Neandertal Image." *Science,* **271**:449.

Bartlett, Thad. Q., Robert W. Sussman, and James M. Cheverud
1993 "Infant Killing in Primates: A Review of Observed Cases with Specific References to the Sexual Selection Hypothesis." *American Anthropologist,* **95**(4):958–990.

Bartstra, Gert-Jan
1982 "*Homo erectus erectus:* The Search for Artifacts." *Current Anthropology,* **23**(3):318–320.

Bar-Yosef, O.
1993 "The Role of Western Asia in Modern Human Origins." *In:* M. J. Aitken, et al. (eds.), q.v., pp. 132–147.

_____
1994 "The Contributions of Southwest Asia to the Study of the Origin of Modern Humans." *In: Origins of Anatomically Modern Humans,* M.H. Nitecki and D. V. Nitecki (eds.), New York: Plenum Press, pp. 23–66.

Bearder, Simon K.
1987 "Lorises, Bushbabies & Tarsiers: Diverse Societies in Solitary Foragers." *In:* Smuts, et al., q.v., pp. 11–24.

Begun, D. and A. Walker
1993 "The Endocast." *In:* A. Walker and R. E. Leakey (eds), q.v., pp. 326–358.

Bell, Martin and Michael J. C. Walker
1992 *Late Quaternary Environmental Change.* New York: John Wiley and Sons.

Ben Shaul, D. M.
1962 "The Composition of the Milk of Wild Animals." *International Zoo Yearbook,* **4**:333–342.

Berger, Thomas and Erik Trinkaus
1995 "Patterns of Trauma Among the Neandertals." *Journal of Archaeological Science,* **22**:841–852.

Biasutti, R.
1951 *Rassa e Popoli della Terra.* Torino: Unione Tipografico Editria Torinese.

Binford, Lewis R.
1981 *Bones. Ancient Men and Modern Myths.* New York: Academic Press.

Binford, Lewis R. and Chuan Kun Ho
1985 "Taphonomy at a Distance: Zhoukoudian, 'The Cave Home of Beijing Man'?" *Current Anthropology,* **26**:413–442.

Binford, Lewis R. and Nancy M. Stone
1986a "The Chinese Paleolithic: An Outsider's View." *AnthroQuest,* Fall 1986(1):14–20.

_____
1986b "Zhoukoudian: A Closer Look." *Current Anthropology,* **27**(5):453–475.

Birdsell, Joseph B.
1981 *Human Evolution* (3d Ed.). Boston: Houghton Mifflin.

Boas, F.
1910 "Changes in the Bodily Form of Descendants of Immigrants." *American Anthropologist,* **14**:530–562.

Boaz, N. T., F. C. Howell, and M. L. McCrossin
1982 "Faunal Age of the Usno, Shungura B and Hadar Formation, Ethiopia." *Nature,* **300**:633–635.

Bodmer, W. F.
1995 "Evolution and Function of the HLA Region." *Clinical Surveys,* **22**:5–16.

Bodmer, W. F. and L. L. Cavalli-Sforza
1976 *Genetics, Evolution, and Man.* San Francisco: W. H. Freeman and Company.

Boesch, C.
1994 "Hunting Strategies of Gombe and Tai Chimpanzees." *In:* Wrangham, R. W., C. McGrew, Frans B. M. de Waal, and Paul G. Heltne (eds.). *Chimpanzee Cultures.* Cambridge: Harvard University Press, pp. 77–91.

Boesch, Christophe and H. Boesch
1989 "Hunting Behavior of Wild Chimpanzees in the Tai National Park." *American Journal of Physical Anthropology,* **78**:547–573.

_____
1990 "Tool Use and Tool Making in Wild Chimpanzees." *Folia Primatologica,* **54**:86–99.

Boesch, Christophe, Paul Marchesi, Nathalie Marchesi, Barbara Fruth, and Frédéric Joulian
1994 "Is Nut Cracking in Wild Chimpanzees a Cultural Behaviour?" *Journal of Human Evolution,* **26**:325–338.

Bogin, Barry
1988   *Patterns of Human Growth.* Cambridge: Cambridge University Press.
Bongaarts, John
1980   Does Malnutrition Affect Fecundity? A Summary of Evidence. *Science,* **208**:564–569.
Brace, C. L. and Ashley Montagu
1977   *Human Evolution* (2nd Ed.). New York: Macmillan.
Brace, C. Loring, H. Nelson, and N. Korn
1979   *Atlas of Human Evolution* (2nd Ed.). New York: Holt, Rinehart & Winston.
Bromage, Timothy G. and Christopher Dean
1985   "Re-evaluation of the Age at Death of Immature Fossil Hominids." *Nature,* **317**:525–527.
Brooks, Alison, et al.
1995   "Dating and Context of Three Middle Stone Age Sites with Bone Points in the Upper Semliki Valley, Zaire." *Science,* **268**:548–553.
Brown, F. H.
1982   "Tulu Bor Tuff at Koobi Fora Correlated with the Sidi Hakoma Tuff at Hadar." *Nature,* **300**:631–632.
Brown, T. M. and K. D. Rose
1987   "Patterns of Dental Evolution in Early Eocene Anaptomorphine Primates Comomyidael from the Bighorn Basin, Wyoming." *Journal of Paleontology,* **61**:1–62.
Brues, Alice M.
1990   *People and Races* (2nd Ed.). Prospect Heights, IL: Waveland Press.

_____

1991   "The Objective View of Race." Paper presented at American Anthropological Association 90th Annual Meeting, Chicago, Nov.
Brunet, Michel, et al.
1995   "The First Australopithecine 2,500 Kilometers West of the Rift Valley (Chad)." *Nature,* **378**:273–274.
Butzer, Karl W.
1974   "Paleoecology of South African Australopithecines: Taung Revisited." *Current Anthropology,* **15**:367–382.

Carbonell, E., et al.
1995   Lower Pleistocene Hominids and Artifacts from Atapuerca-TDG (Spain)." *Science,* **269**:826–830.

Carrol, Robert L.
1988   *Vertebrate Paleontology and Evolution.* New York: W. H. Freeman and Co.
Cartmill, Matt
1972   "Arboreal Adaptations and the Origin of the Order Primates." *In: The Functional and Evolutionary Biology of Primates,* R. H. Tuttle (ed.), Chicago: Aldine-Atherton, pp. 97–122.

_____

1974   "Rethinking Primate Origins." *Science,* **184**:436–443.

_____

1992   "New Views on Primate Origins." *Evolutionary Anthropology,* **1**:105–111.
Cavalli-Sforza, L. L., A. Piazza, P. Menozzi, and J. Mountain
1988   "Reconstruction of Human Evolution: Bringing Together Genetic, Archaeological, and Linguistic Data." *Proceedings of the National Academy of Sciences,* **85**:6002–6006.
Censky, E. J., K. Hodge and J. Dudley
1998   "Over-water Dispersal of Lizards due to Hurricanes." *Nature,* **395** (6702):556.
Charteris, J., J. C. Wali, and J. W. Nottrodt
1981   "Functional Reconstruction of Gait from Pliocene Hominid Footprints at Laetoli, Northern Tanzania." *Nature,* **290**:496–498.
Ciochon, Russell L. and Robert S. Corruccini (eds.)
1983   *New Interpretations of Ape and Human Ancestry.* New York: Plenum Press.
Clark, W. E. LeGros
1971   *The Antecedents of Man* (3rd Ed.). New York: The New York Times Books.
Clarke, Ronald J. and Phillip V. Tobias
1995   "Sterkfontein Member 2 Foot Bones of the Oldest South African Hominid." *Science,* **269**:521–524.
Cleveland, J. and C. T. Snowdon
1982   "The Complex Vocal Repertoire of the Adult Cotton-top Tamarin (*Saguinus oedipus oedipus*)." *Zeitschrift Tierpsychologie,* **58**:231–270.
Colwell, Rita R.
1996   "Global Climate and Infectious Disease: The Cholera Paradigm." *Science,* **274**(5295): 2025–2031.
Conkey, M.
1987   New Approaches in the Search for Meaning? A Review of the Research in "Paleolithic Art." *Journal of Field Archaeology,* **14**:413–430.

Conroy, Glenn C.
1997 *Reconstructing Human Origins. A Modern Synthesis.* New York: Norton.

Conroy, G. C., M. Pickford, B. Senut, J. van Couvering, and P. Mein
1992 "*Otavipithecus namibiensis*, First Miocene Hominoid from Southern Africa." *Nature*, **356**:144–148.

Cook, J., C. B. Stringer, A. Currant, H. P. Schwarcz, and A. G. Wintle
1982 "A Review of the Chronology of the European Middle Pleistocene Record." *Yearbook of Physical Anthropology*, **25**:19–65.

Coon, Carleton
1962 *The Origin of Races.* New York: Alfred A. Knopf.

Corruccini, Robert S.
1994 "Reaganomics and the Fate of the Progressive Neandertals." *In:* R. Corruccini and R. Ciochon (eds.), q.v., pp. 697–708.

Corruccini, R. S. and R. L. Ciochon (eds.)
1994 *Integrative Paths to the Past; Paleoanthropological Advances in Honor of F. Clark Howell.* Englewood Cliffs, NJ: Prentice-Hall.

Crapo, Lawrence
1985 *Hormones: The Messengers of Life.* New York: W. H. Freeman and Company.

Cummings, Michael
1994 *Human Heredity. Principles and Issues* (3rd Ed.). St Paul: Wadsworth/West Publishing Co.

Curtin, R. and P. Dolhinow
1978 "Primate Social Behavior in a Changing World." *American Scientist*, **66**:468–475.

Dalrymple, G. B.
1972 "Geomagnetic Reversals and North American Glaciations." *In: Calibration of Hominoid Evolution*, W. W. Bishop and J. A. Miller (eds.), Edinburgh: Scottish Academic Press, pp. 303–329.

Dart, Raymond
1959 *Adventures with the Missing Link.* New York: Harper & Brothers.

Darwin, Charles
1859 *On the Origin of Species.* A Facsimile of the First Edition, Cambridge, MA: Harvard University Press (1964).

———
1871 *The Descent of Man and Selection in Relation to Sex.* Republished, 1981, Princeton: Princeton University Press.

Darwin, Francis (ed.)
1950 *The Life and Letters of Charles Darwin.* New York: Henry Schuman.

Day, M. H. and E. H. Wickens
1980 "Laetoli Pliocene Hominid Footprints and Bipedalism." *Nature*, **286**:385–387.

Dean, M., M. Carring, C. Winkler, et al.
1996 "Genetic Restriction of HIV-1 Infection and Progression to AIDS by a Deletion Allele of the CKR5 Structural Gene." *Science*, **273**:1856–1862.

Defleur, A, T. White, P. Valensi, et al.
1999 "Neanderthal Cannibalism at Moula-Guercy, Ardeche, France." *Science*, **286**:128–131.

DeGusta, D., W. H. Gilbert, and S. P. Turner
1999 "Hypoglossal Canal Size and Hominid Speech." *Proceedings of the National Academy of Sciences*, **96**:1800–1804.

de Lumley, Henry and M. de Lumley
1973 "Pre-Neanderthal Human Remains from Arago Cave in Southeastern France." *Yearbook of Physical Anthropology*, **16**:162–168.

Delson, Eric
1987 "Evolution and Palaeobiology of Robust *Australopithecus.*" *Nature*, **327**:654–655.

Dene, H. T., M. Goodman, and W. Prychodko
1976 "Immunodiffusion Evidence on the Phylogeny of the Primates." *In: Molecular Anthropology*, M. Goodman, R. E. Tashian, and J. H. Tashian (eds.), New York: Plenum Press, pp. 171–195.

Desmond, Adrian and James Moore
1991 *Darwin.* New York: Warner Books.

Dettwyler, K. A.
1991 "Can Paleopathology Provide Evidence for Compassion?" *American Journal of Physical Anthropology*, **84**:375–384.

de Waal, Frans
1982 *Chimpanzee Politics.* London: Jonathan Cape.

———
1987 "Tension Regulation and Nonreproductive Functions of Sex in Captive Bonobos (*Pan paniscus*)." *National Geographic Research*, **3**:318–335.

1989   *Peacemaking among Primates.* Cambridge: Harvard University Press.

1999   "Cultural Primatology Comes of Age." *Nature,* **399**:635–636.

Doran, D. M. and A. McNeilage
1998   "Gorilla Ecology and Behavior." *Evolutionary Anthropology,* **6**(4):120–131.

Dorit, R. L., H. Akashi, and W. Gilbert
1995   Absence of Polymorphism at the Zfy Locus on the Human Y Chromosome. *Science,* **268**:1183–1185.

Duarte, C., J. Mauricio, P. B. Pettitt, et al.
1999   "The Early Upper Paleolithic Human Skeleton from the Abrigo do Lagar Velho (Portugal) and Modern Human Emergence in Iberia." *Proceedings of the National Academy of Sciences,* **96**:7604–7609.

Dunham, I., et al.
1999   "The DNA Sequence of Human Chromosome 22." *Nature,* **402**:489–495.

Dunn, Frederick L.
1993   Malaria. *In: The Cambridge World History of Human Disease,* Kenneth F. Kiple (ed.), Cambridge: Cambridge University Press, pp. 855–862.

Durham, William
1981   Paper presented to the Annual Meeting of the American Anthropological Association, Washington, D.C., Dec. 1980. Reported in *Science,* **211**:40.

Eaton, S. Boyd and Melvin Konner
1985   "Paleolithic Nutrition: A Consideration of Its Nature and Current Implications." *New England Journal of Medicine,* **312**:283–289.

Eaton, S. Boyd, Marjorie Shostak, and Melvin Konner.
1988   *The Paleolithic Prescription.* New York: Harper and Row.

Eaton, S. B., M. C. Pike, R. V. Short, et al.
1994   "Women's Reproductive Cancers in Evolutionary Context." *The Quarterly Review of Biology,* **69**:353–367.

Ehrlich, Paul R. and Anne H. Ehrlich
1990   *The Population Explosion.* New York: Simon & Schuster.

Etler, Dennis A. and Li-Tianyuan
1994   "New Archaic Human Fossil Discoveries in China and Their Bearing on Hominid Species Definition During the Middle Pleistocene." *In:* R. Corruccini and R. Ciochon (eds.), q.v., pp. 639–675.

European Union GIS/Remote Sensing Expert Group
1997   Fires in Indonesia, September 1997, a Report to the European Union. Brussels, European Union.

Falk, Dean
1980   "A Reanalysis of the South African Australopithecine Natural Endocasts." *American Journal of Physical Anthropology,* **53**:525–539.

1983   "The Taung Endocast: A Reply to Holloway." *American Journal of Physical Anthropology,* **60**:479–489.

1989   "Comments." *Current Anthropology,* **30**:141.

Fedigan, Linda M.
1983   "Dominance and Reproductive Success in Primates." *Yearbook of Physical Anthropology,* **26**:91–129.

Fleagle, John
1983   "Locomotor Adaptations of Oligocene and Mioecene Hominoids and their Phyletic Implications." *In:* R. L. Ciochon and R. S. Corruccini (eds.), q.v., pp. 301–324.

1988/   *Primate Adaptation and Evolution.* New
1999   York: Academic Press. 2nd ed., 1999.

1994   "Anthropoid Origins." *In:* R. S. Corruccini and R. L. Ciochon (eds.), q.v., pp. 17–35.

Flinn, Mark V.
1999   "Family Environment, Stress, and Health During Childhood." *In:* Panter-Brick, C. and C. M. Worthman (eds.), *Hormones, Health, and Behavior: A Socio-ecological and Lifespan Perspective.* Cambridge: Cambridge University Press, pp. 105–138.

Foley, R. A.
1991   "How Many Species of Hominid Should There Be?" *Journal of Human Evolution,* **30**: 413–427.

Foley, R. A. and M. M. Lahr
1992   "Beyond 'Out of Africa.'" *Journal of Human Evolution*, **22**:523–529.

Fossey, Dian
1983   *Gorillas in the Mist*. Boston: Houghton Mifflin.

Fouts, Roger S., D. H. Fouts, and T. T. van Cantfort
1989   "The Infant Loulis Learns Signs from Cross-Fostered Chimpanzees." *In:* R. A. Gardner, et al., q.v., pp. 280–292.

Frayer, David
1992   "Evolution at the European Edge: Neanderthal and Upper Paleolithic Relationships." *Préhistoire Européenne*, **2**:9–69.

Frisancho, A. Roberto
1978   "Nutritional Influences on Human Growth and Maturation." *Yearbook of Physical Anthropology*, **21**:174–191.

———
1993   *Human Adaptation and Accommodation*. Ann Arbor: University of Michigan Press.

Froelich, J. W.
1970   "Migration and Plasticity of Physique in the Japanese-Americans of Hawaii." *American Journal of Physical Anthropology*, **32**:429.

Gambier, Dominique
1989   "Fossil Hominids from the Early Upper Palaeolithic (Aurignacian) of France." *In:* P. Mellars and C. Stringer (eds.), q.v., pp. 194–211.

Gamble, C.
1991   "The Social Context for European Palaeolithic Art." *Proceedings of the Prehistoric Society*, **57**:3–15.

Gao, Feng, Elizabeth Bailes, David L. Robertson, et al.
1999   "Origin of HIV-1 in the Chimpanzee *Pan troglodytes troglodytes*." *Nature*, **397**: 436–441.

Gardner, R. Allen, B. T. Gardner, and T. T. van Cantfort (eds.)
1989   *Teaching Sign Language to Chimpanzees*. Albany: State University of New York Press.

Garner, K. J. and O. A. Ryder
1996   "Mitochondrial DNA Diversity in Gorillas." *Mol. Phylogenet. Evol.*, **6**:39–48.

Gates, R. R.
1948   *Human Ancestry*. Cambridge: Harvard Univ. Press, p. 367.

Gee, Henry
1996   "Box of Bones 'Clinches' Identity of Piltdown Palaeontology Hoaxer." *Nature*, **381**:261–262.

Gibbons, Anne
1998   "Ancient Tools Suggest *Homo erectus* was a Seafarer." Research News, *Science*, **279**:1635–1637.

Gingerich, Phillip D.
1985   "Species in the Fossil Record: Concepts, Trends, and Transitions." *Paleobiology*, **11**:27–41.

Goodall, Jane
1986   *The Chimpanzees of Gombe*. Cambridge: Harvard University Press.

Gossett, Thomas F.
1963   *Race, the History of an Idea in America*. Dallas: Southern Methodist University Press.

Gould, Stephen Jay
1981   *The Mismeasures of Man*. New York: W. W. Norton.

———
1985   "Darwin at Sea—and the Virtues of Port." *In:* Stephen Jay Gould, *The Flamingo's Smile. Reflections in Natural History*. New York: W. W. Norton, pp. 347–359.

———
1987   *Time's Arrow, Time's Cycle*. Cambridge: Harvard University Press.

Gould, S. J. and N. Eldredge
1977   "Punctuated Equilibria: The Tempo and Mode of Evolution Reconsidered." *Paleobiology*, **3**:115–151.

Gould, S. J. and R. Lewontin
1979   "The Spandrels of San Marco and the Panglossian Paradigm: A Critique of the Adaptionist Programme." *Proceedings of the Royal Society of London*, **205**:581–598.

Greene, John C.
1981   *Science, Ideology, and World View*. Berkeley: University of California Press.

Grine, Frederick E. (ed.)
1988a   *Evolutionary History of the "Robust" Australopithecines*. New York: Aldine de Gruyter.

———
1988b   "New Craniodental Fossils of *Paranthropus* from the Swartkrans Formation and Their Significance in "Robust" Australopithecine Evolution." *In:* F. E. Grine (ed.), q.v., pp. 223–243.

———
1993 "Australopithecine Taxonomy and Phylogeny: Historical Background and Recent Interpretation." *In: The Human Evolution Source Book,* R. L. Ciochon and J. G. Fleagle (eds.), Englewood Cliffs, N.J.: Prentice Hall, pp. 198–210.

Harlow, Harry F.
1959 "Love in Infant Monkeys." *Scientific American,* **200**:68–74.

Harlow, Harry F. and Margaret K. Harlow
1961 "A Study of Animal Affection." *Natural History,* **70**:48–55.

Harrold, Francis R.
1989 "Mousterian, Chatelperronian and Early Aurignacian in Western Europe: Continuity or Discontinuity." *In: The Human Revolution,* P. Mellars and C. Stringer (eds.), Princeton, NJ: Princeton University Press, pp. 212–231.

Hartl, Daniel
1983 *Human Genetics.* New York: Harper and Row.

Hass, J. D., E. A. Frongillo, Jr., C. D. Stepick, et al.
1980 "Altitude, Ethnic and Sex Difference in Birth Weight and Length in Bolivia." *Human Biology,* **52**:459–477.

Hawkes, K., J. F. O'Connell, and N. G. Blurton Jones
1997 Hadza Women's Time Allocation, Offspring Provisioning, and the Evolution of Long Postmenopausal Life spans. *Current Anthropology,* **38**:551–577.

Hill, A., S. Ward, A. Deino, G. Curtis, and R. Drake
1992 "Earliest *Homo.*" *Nature,* **355**:719–722.

Hirsch, V. M., R. A. Olmsted, M. Murphey-Corb, R. H. Purcell, and P. R. Johnson
1989 "An African Primate Lentivirus (SIVsm) Closely Related to HIV-2." *Nature,* **339**:389–392.

Holloway, Ralph L.
1983 "Cerebral Brain Endocast Pattern of *Australopithecus afarensis* Hominid." *Nature,* **303**:420–422.

———
1985 The Poor Brain of *Homo sapiens neanderthalensis. In: Ancestors, The Hard Evidence,* E. Delson (ed.). New York: Alan R. Liss, pp. 319–324.

Howell, F. Clark
1988 "Forward." *In:* F. E. Grine (ed.), q.v., pp. xi–xv.

Hrdy, Sarah Blaffer
1977 *The Langurs of Abu.* Cambridge, Mass.: Harvard University Press.

Hublin, Jean-Jacques, F. Spoor, M. Braun, et al.
1996 "A Late Neanderthal Associated with Upper Palaeolithic Artifacts." *Nature,* **38**:224–226.

Humphries, Rolfe
1973 *Ovid Metamorphoses.* Bloomington: Indiana Univ. Press.

Izawa, K. and A. Mizuno
1977 "Palm-Fruit Cracking Behaviour of Wild Black-Capped Capuchin (*Cebus apella*)." *Primates,* **18**:773–793.

Jerison, H. J.
1973 *Evolution of the Brain and Behavior.* New York: Academic Press.

Jia, L. and R. Chakraborty
1993 "Extent of Within Versus Between Population Variations of VNTR Polymorphisms in Five Major Human Groups." *American Journal of Human Genetics,* **53** (Abstract #75).

Jia, L. and Huang Weiwen
1990 *The Story of Peking Man.* New York: Oxford University Press.

Jia, Lan-po
1975 *The Cave Home of Peking Man.* Peking: Foreign Language Press.

Johanson, Donald and Maitland Edey
1981 *Lucy: The Beginnings of Humankind.* New York: Simon & Schuster.

Johanson, Donald, F. T. Masao, et al.
1987 "New Partial Skeleton of *Homo habilis* from Olduvai Gorge, Tanzania." *Nature,* **327**:205–209.

Johanson, Donald C. and Maurice Taieb
1980 "New Discoveries of Pliocene Hominids and Artifacts in Hadar." International Afar Research Expedition to Ethiopia (Fourth and Fifth Field Seasons, 1975–77). *Journal of Human Evolution,* **9**:582.

Johanson, D. C. and T. D. White
1979 "A Systematic Assessment of Early African Hominids." *Science,* **202**:321–330.

Jolly, Alison
1985 *The Evolution of Primate Behavior* (2nd Ed.), New York: Macmillan.

Kano, T.
1992 *The Last Ape. Pygmy Chimpanzee Behavior and Ecology.* Stanford: Stanford University Press.

Kappleman, John
1996 "The Evolution of Body Mass and Relative Brain Size in Fossil Hominids." *Journal of Human Evolution,* **30**:243–276.

Katz, D. and J. M. Suchey
1986 "Age Determination of the Male *Os Pubis.*" *American Journal of Physical Anthropology,* **69**:427–435.

Katz, S. H., M. L. Hediger, and L. A. Valleroy
1974 "Traditional Maize Processing Techniques in the New World." *Science,* **184**:765–773.

Kay, R., M. Cartmill, and M. Balow
1998 "The Hypoglossal Canal and the Origins of Human Vocal Behavior (abstract)." *American Journal of Physical Anthropology, Supplement,* **26**:137.

Kennedy, K. A. R.
1991 "Is the Narmada Hominid an Indian *Homo erectus?*" *American Journal of Physical Anthropology,* **86**:475–496.

Kennedy, Kenneth A. R. and S. U. Deraniyagala
1989 "Fossil Remains of 28,000-Year-Old Hominids from Sri Lanka." *Current Anthropology,* **30**:397–399.

Kimbel, William H.
1988 "Identification of a Partial Cranium of *Australopithecus afarensis* from the Koobi Fora Formation, Kenya." *Journal of Human Evolution,* **17**:647–656.

Kimbel, William H., Donald C. Johanson, and Yoel Rak
1994 "The First Skull and Other New Discoveries of *Australopithecus afarensis* at Hadar, Ethiopia." *Nature,* **368**:449–451.

Kimbel, W. H., R. C. Walter, D. C. Johanson, et al.
1996 Late Pliocene *Homo* and Oldowan Tools from the Hadar Formation (Kada Hadar Member), Ethiopia. *Journal of Human Evolution,* **31**:549–561.

Kimbel, William H., Tim D. White, and Donald C. Johanson
1988 "Implications of KNM-WT-17000 for the Evolution of 'Robust' *Australopithecus.*" *In:* F. E. Grine (ed.), q.v., pp. 259–268.

Klein, R. G.
1989/ *The Human Career. Human Biological and*
1999 *Cultural Origins.* Chicago: University of Chicago Press. 2nd ed., 1999.

Konner, Melvin and Carol Worthman
1980 "Nursing Frequency, Gonadal Function, and Birth Spacing among !Kung Hunter-Gatherers." *Science,* **207**:788–791.

Kramer, Andrew
1993 "Human Taxonomic Diversity in the Pleistocene: Does *Homo erectus* Represent Multiple Hominid Species?" *American Journal of Physical Anthropology,* **91**:161–171.

Krause, D. W. and M. Maas
1990 "The Biogeographic Origins of the Late Paleocene-Early Eocene Mammalian Immigrants to the Western Interior of North America." *In: Dawn of the Age of Mammals in the Northern Part of the Rocky Mountain Interior of North America,* T. M. Brown and K. D. Rose (eds.), Boulder, CO: Geological Society of America, pp. 71–105.

Krings, Matthias, Anne Stone, Ralf W. Schmitz, et al.
1997 "Neandertal DNA Sequences and the origin of Modern Humans." *Cell,* **90**:19–30.

Kunzig, Robert
1997 "Atapuerca. The Face of and Ancestral Child." *Discover,* **18**:88–101.

Lack, David
1966 *Population Studies of Birds.* Oxford: Clarendon.

Lancaster, J. B. and C. S. Lancaster
1983 "Prenatal Investment: The Hominid Adaptation." *In:* Ortner, D. J. (ed.), *How Human Adapt. A Biocultural Odyssey.* Washington DC: Smithsonian Institution Press.

Larick, Roy and Russell L. Ciochon
1996 "The African Emergence and Early Asian Dispersals of the Genus *Homo.*" *American Scientist,* **84**:538–551.

Leakey, M. D., and R. L. Hay
1979 "Pliocene Footprints in Laetolil Beds at Laetoli, Northern Tanzania." *Nature,* **278**:317–323.

Leakey, Meave G., et al.
1995 "New Four-Million-Year-Old Hominid Species from Kanapoi and Allia Bay, Kenya." *Nature,* **376**:565–571.

Lerner, I. M. and W. J. Libby
1976 *Heredity, Evolution, and Society.* San Francisco: W. H. Freeman and Company.

Leroi-Gourhan, André
1986 "The Hands of Gargas." *October* **37**:18–34.

Lewin, Roger
1986 "Damage to Tropical Forests, or Why Were There So Many Kinds of Animals?" *Science,* **234**:149–150.

Lewontin, R. C.
1972 "The Apportionment of Human Diversity." *In: Evolutionary Biology* (Vol. 6), T. Dobzhansky, et al. (eds.), New York: Plenum, pp. 381–398.

Lieberman, Daniel, David R. Pilbeam, and Bernard A. Wood
1988 "A Probalistic Approach to the Problem of Sexual Dimorphism in *Homo habilis:* A Comparison of KNM-ER-1470 and KNM-ER-1813." *Journal of Human Evolution,* **17**:503–511.

Linnaeus, C.
1758 *Systema Naturae.*

Lisowski, F. P.
1984 "Introduction." *In: The Evolution of the East African Environment.* Centre of Asian Studies Occasional Papers and Monographs, No. 59, R. O. Whyte (ed.), Hong Kong: University of Hong Kong, pp. 777–786.

Livingstone, Frank B.
1980 "Natural Selection and the Origin and Maintenance of Standard Genetic Marker Systems." *Yearbook of Physical Anthropology,* **23**:25–42.

Lovejoy, C. O.
1993 "Modeling Human Origins: Are We Sexy Because We're Smart, or Smart Because We're Sexy?" *In:* D. T. Rasmussen (ed.), q.v., pp. 1–28.

MacKinnon, J. and K. MacKinnon
1980 "The Behavior of Wild Spectral Tarsiers." *International Journal of Primatology,* **1**:361–379.

Manson, J. H. and R. Wrangham
1991 "Intergroup Aggression in Chimpanzees and Humans." *Current Anthropology,* **32**:369–390.

Marshack, A.
1972 *The Roots of Civilization.* New York: McGraw-Hill Publishing Co.

1989 "Evolution of the Human Capacity: The Symbolic Evidence." *Yearbook of Physical Anthropology,* **32**:1–34.

Mayer, Peter
1982 "Evolutionary Advantages of Menopause." *Human Ecology,* **10**:477–494.

Mayr, Ernst
1970 *Population, Species, and Evolution.* Cambridge: Harvard University Press.

McGrew, W. C.
1992 *Chimpanzee Material Culture. Implications for Human Evolution.* Cambridge: Cambridge University Press.

1998 "Culture in Nonhuman Primates?" *Annual Review of Anthropology,* **27**:301–328.

McHenry, Henry
1988 "New Estimates of Body Weight in Early Hominids and Their Significance to Encephalization and Megadontia in 'Robust' Australopithecines." *In:* F. E. Grine (ed.), q.v., pp. 133–148.

1992 "Body Size and Proportions in Early Hominids." *American Journal of Physical Anthropology,* **87**:407–431.

1992 "How Big Were Early Hominids?" *Evolutionary Anthropology,* **1**:15–20.

McKern, T. W. and T. D. Stewart
1957 "Age Changes in Young American Males, Technical Report EP-45." Natick, MA: U.S. Army Quartermaster Research and Development Center.

Mellars, P. and C. Stringer (eds.)
1989 *The Human Revolution.* Princeton, NJ: Princeton University Press.

Miles, H. Lyn White
1990 "The Cognitive Foundations for Reference in a Signing Orangutan. *In: "Language" and Intelligence in Monkeys and Apes. Comparative Developmental Perspectives.* Sue Taylor Parker and Kathleen Rita Gibson (eds.), New York: Cambridge University Press, pp. 511–539.

Mittermeir, R. A.
1982 "The World's Endangered Primates: An Introduction and a Case Study—The Monkeys of Brazil's Atlantic Forests." *In:*

Primates and the Tropical Rain Forest, Proceedings, California Institute of Technology, and World Wildlife Fund—U.S., pp. 11–22.

Mittermeir, R. A. and D. Cheney
1987 "Conservation of Primates in Their Habitats." *In:* B. B. Smuts, et al., q.v., pp. 477–496.

Molnar, Stephen
1983 *Human Variation. Races, Types, and Ethnic Groups* (2nd Ed.). Englewood Cliffs: Prentice-Hall.

Montagu, A.
1961 "Neonatal and Infant Immaturity in Man." *Journal of the American Medical Association,* **178**:56–57.

Moore, Lorna G. and Judith G. Regensteiner
1983 "Adaptation to High Altitude." *Annual Reviews of Anthropology,* **12**:285–304.

Moore, Lorna G., et al.
1994 "Genetic Adaptation to High Altitude." *In:* Stephen C. Wood and Robert C. Roach (eds.), *Sports and Exercise Medicine.* New York: Marcel Dekker, Inc., pp. 225–262.

Morin, Phillip A., James J. Moore, Ranajit Chakraborty, et al.
1994 "Kin Selection, Social Structure, Gene Flow, and the Evolution of Chimpanzees." *Science,* **265**: 1145–1332.

Mountain, Joanna L., Alice A. Lin, Anne M. Bowcock, and L. L. Cavalli-Sforza
1993 "Evolution of Modern Humans: Evidence From Nuclear DNA Polymorphisms." *In:* M. J. Aitken, et al. (eds.), q.v., pp. 69–83.

Napier, John
1967 "The Antiquity of Human Walking." *Scientific American,* **216**:56–66.

Napier, J. R. and P. H. Napier
1967 *A Handbook of Living Primates.* New York: Academic Press.

———
1985 *The Natural History of the Primates.* London: British Museum (Natural History).

Nishida, T., M. Hiraiwa-Hasegawa, T. Hasegawa, and Y. Takahata
1985 "Group Extinction and Female Transfer in Wild Chimpanzees in the Mahale National Park, Tanzania." *Zeitschrift Tierpsychologie,* **67**:284–301.

Nishida, T., H. Takasaki, and Y. Takahata
1990 "Demography and Reproductive Profiles." *In: The Chimpanzees of the Mahale Mountains,* T. Nishida (ed.), Tokyo: University of Tokyo Press, pp. 63–97.

Nishida, T., R. W. Wrangham, J. Goodall, and S. Uehara
1983 "Local Differences in Plant-feeding Habits of Chimpanzees between the Mahale Mountains and Gombe National Park, Tanzania. *Journal of Human Evolution,* **12**:467–480.

Noe, R. and R. Bshary
1997 "The Formation of Red Colobus-Diana Monkey Associations under Predation Pressure from Chimpanzees." *Proceedings of the Royal Society of London (B) Biological Science,* **264**(1379):253–259.

Oates, John F. (compiler)
1996 *African Primates. Status Survey and Conservation Action Plan.* Cambridge, U.K.: International Union for Conservation of Nature and Natural Resources (IUCN).

Oates, John F.
1999 "Are African Primates in Crisis from the Bushmeat Trade—If so, Which Are Being Affected, Where, and By How Much?" Paper presented at the ASP African Bushmeat Crisis Workshop, New Orleans, 14 August, 1999.

Olliaro, Piero
1996 "Malaria, the Submerged Disease." *Journal of the American Medical Association,* **275**(3): 230–233.

Parés, Josef M. and Alfredo Pérez-González
1995 "Paleomagnetic Age for Hominid Fossils at Atapuerca Archaeological Site, Spain." *Science,* **269**:830–832.

Phillips, K. A.
1998 "Tool Use in Wild Capuchin Monkeys." *American Journal of Primatology,* **46**(3):259–261.

Pinner, Robert W., Steven M. Teutsch, Lone Simonson, et al.
1996 "Trends in Infectious Diseases Mortality in the United States." *Journal of the American Medical Association,* **275**(3):189–193.

Pope, G. G.
1984   "The Antiquity and Paleoenvironment of the Asian Hominidae." *In: The Evolution of the East Asian Environment.* Center of Asian Studies Occasional Papers and Monographs, No. 59, R. O. Whyte (ed.), Hong Kong: University of Hong Kong, pp. 822–847.

Potts, Richard
1991   "Why the Oldowan? Plio-Pleistocene Toolmaking and the Transport of Resources." *Journal of Anthropological Research,* **47**:153–176.

———   1993   "Archeological Interpretations of Early Hominid Behavior and Ecology." *In:* D. T. Rasmussen (ed.), q.v., pp. 49–74.

Proctor, Robert
1988   "From Anthropologie to Rassenkunde." *In: Bones, Bodies, Behavior. History of Anthropology* (Vol. 5), W. Stocking, Jr. (ed.), Madison: University of Wisconsin Press, pp. 138–179.

Profet, M.
1988   "The Evolution of Pregnancy Sickness as a Protection to the Embryo Against Pleistocene Teratogens." *Evolutionary Theory,* **8**:177–190.

Pulliam, H. R. and T. Caraco
1984   "Living in Groups: Is There an Optimal Size?" *In: Behavioral Ecology: An Evolutionary Approach* (2nd ed.), J. R. Krebs and N. B. Davies (eds.), Sunderland, Mass.: Sinauer Associates.

Rak, Y.
1983   *The Australopithecine Face.* New York: Academic Press.

Rasmussen, D. T. (ed.)
1993   "The Origin and Evolution of Humans and Humaness." Boston: Jones and Bartlett.

Relethford, John H. and Henry C. Harpending
1994   "Craniometric Variation, Genetic theory, and Modern Human Origins." *American Journal of Physical Anthropology,* 95:249–270.

Richard, A. F. and S. R. Schulman
1982   "Sociobiology: Primate Field Studies." *Annual Reviews of Anthropology,* **11**:231–255.

Rightmire, G. P.
1981   "Patterns in the Evolution of *Homo erectus.*" *Paleobiology,* 7:241–246.

———   1990   *The Evolution of* Homo erectus. New York: Cambridge University Press.

———   1998   "Human Evolution in the Middle Pleistocene: The Role of *Homo heidelbergensis.*" *Evolutionary Anthropology,* **6**:218–227.

Roberts, D. F.
1973   *Climate and Human Variability.* An Addison-Wesley Module in Anthropology, No. 34. Reading, MA: Addison-Wesley.

Roberts, Richard, Rhys Jones, and M. A. Smith
1990   "Thermoluminescence Dating of a 50,000-Year-Old Human Occupation Site in Northern Australia," *Nature,* **345**:153–156.

Romer, Alfred S.
1959   *The Vertebrate Story.* Chicago: University of Chicago Press.

Rose, M. D.
1991   "Species Recognition in Eocene Primates." *American Journal of Physical Anthropology,* Supplement 12, p. 153.

Ruben, John A., Christina Dal Sasso, Nicholas Geist, et al.
1999   "Pulmonary Function and Metabolic Physiology of Theropod Dinosaurs." *Science,* **283**:514–516.

Rudran, R.
1973   "Adult Male Replacement in One-Male Troops of Purple-Faced Langurs (*Presbytis senex senex*) and its Effect on Population Structure." *Folia Primatologica,* **19**:166–192.

Ruff, C. B. and Alan Walker
1993   "Body Size and Body Shape." *In:* A. Walker and R. Leakey (eds.), q.v., pp. 234–265.

Rumbaugh, D. M.
1977   *Language Learning by a Chimpanzee: The Lana Project.* New York: Academic Press.

Ruvolo, M., D. Pan, S. Zehr, T. Goldberg, et al.
1994   "Gene Trees and Hominoid Phylogeny." *Proceedings of the National Academy of Sciences,* **91**:8900–8904.

Samson, M., F. Libert, B. J. Doranz, et al.
1996   "Resistance to HIV-1 Infection in Caucasian Individuals Bearing Mutant Alleles of the CCR-5 Chemokine Receptor Gene." *Nature* **382**(22):722–725.

Savage-Rumbaugh, E. S.
1986 *Ape Language: From Conditioned Responses to Symbols.* New York: Columbia University Press.

Savage-Rumbaugh, S., K. McDonald, R. A. Sevic, W. D. Hopkins, and E. Rupert
1986 "Spontaneous Symbol Acquisition and Communicative Use by Pygmy Chimpanzees (*Pan paniscus*)." *Journal of Experimental Psychology: General,* **115**(3):211–235.

Savage-Rumbaugh, S. and R. Lewin
1994 *Kanzi. The Ape at the Brink of the Human Mind.* New York: John Wiley and Sons.

Schaller, George B.
1963 *The Mountain Gorilla.* Chicago: University of Chicago Press.

Schwartzman, Stephen
1997 "Fires in the Amazon: An Analysis of NOAA-12 Satellite Data, 1996–1997." Washington D.C.: Environmental Defense Fund.

Scott, K.
1980 "Two Hunting Episodes of Middle Paleolithic Age at La Cotte Sainte-Brelade, Jersey (Channel Islands)." *World Archaeology,* **12**:137–152.

Semaw, S., P. Renne, W. K. Harris, et al.
1997 "2.5-million-year-old Stone Tools from Gona, Ethiopia." *Nature,* **385**:333–336.

Senut, Brigette and Christine Tardieu
1985 "Functional Aspects of Plio-Pleistocene Hominid Limb Bones: Implications for Taxonomy and Phylogeny." *In: Ancestors: The Hard Evidence,* E. Delson (ed.), New York: Alan R. Liss, pp. 193–201.

Seyfarth, Robert M.
1987 "Vocal Communication and Its Relation to Language." *In:* Smuts, et al., *Primate Societies.* Chicago: University of Chicago Press, pp. 440–451.

Seyfarth, Robert M., Dorothy L. Cheney, and Peter Marler
1980a "Monkey Responses to Three Different Alarm Calls." *Science,* **210**:801–803.

———
1980b "Ververt Monkey Alarm Calls." *Animal Behavior,* **28**:1070–1094.

Shea, Brian T. and Robert C. Baily
1996 "Allometry and Adaptation of Body Proportions and Stature in African Pygmies." *American Journal of Physical Anthropology,* **100**:311–340.

Sibley, Charles and Jon E. Ahlquist
1984 "The Phylogeny of the Hominoid Primates as Indicated by DNA-DNA Hybridization." *Journal of Molecular Evolution,* **20**:2–15.

Simmons, J. G.
1989 *Changing the Face of the Earth.* Oxford: Basil Blackwell Ltd.

Simons, E. L.
1972 *Primate Evolution.* New York: Macmillan.

———
1992 "Diversity in the Early Tertiary Anthropoidean Radiation in Africa." *Proc. Natl. Acad. Sci., U.S.A.,* **89**:10743–10747.

Skelton, R. R., H. M. McHenry, and G. M. Drawhorn
1986 "Phylogenetic Analysis of Early Hominids." *Current Anthropology,* **27**:1–43; 361–365.

Smith, Fred H.
1984 "Fossil Hominids from the Upper Pleistocene of Central Europe and the Origin of Modern Europeans." *In:* F. H. Smith and F. Spencer (eds.), *The Origins of Modern Humans.* New York: Alan R. Liss, pp. 187–209.

Smith, Fred H., A. B. Falsetti, and S. M. Donnelly
1989 "Modern Human Origins." *Yearbook of Physical Anthropology,* **32**:35–68.

Smith, Fred H., Erik Trinkaus, Paul B. Pettitt, et al.
1999 "Direct Radiocarbon Dates for Vindija G_1 and Velika Pécina Late Pleistocene Hominid Remains." *Proceedings of the National Academy of Sciences,* **96**:12281–12286.

Smuts, B., et al. (eds.)
1987 *Primate Societies.* Chicago: University of Chicago Press.

Soffer, Olga
1985 *The Upper Paleolithic of the Central Russian Plain.* New York: Academic Press.

Stanford, C. B., J. Wallis, H. Matama, and J. Goodall
1994 "Patterns of Predation by Chimpanzees on Red Colobus Monkeys in Gombe National Park." *American Journal of Physical Anthropology,* **94**(2):213–228.

Stoneking, Mark
1993 "DNA and Recent Human Evolution." *Evolutionary Anthropology,* **2**:60–73.

Straus, Lawrence Guy
1993 "Southwestern Europe at the Last Glacial Maximum." *Current Anthropology,* **32**:189–199.

——— 1995 "The Upper Paleolithic of Europe: An Overview." *Evolutionary Anthropology,* **4**:4–16.

Stringer, C. B. and P. Andrews
1988 "Genetic and Fossil Evidence for the Origin of Modern Humans." *Science,* **239**:1263–1268.

Struhsaker, T. T.
1967 "Auditory Communication among Vervet Monkeys (*Cercopithecus aethiops*)." *In: Social Communication Among Primates,* S. A. Altmann (ed.), Chicago: University of Chicago Press.

——— 1975 *The Red Colobus Monkey.* Chicago: University of Chicago Press.

Struhsaker, Thomas T. and Lysa Leland
1979 "Socioecology of Five Sympatric Monkey Species in the Kibale Forest, Uganda." *Advances in the Study of Behavior,* Vol. 9, New York: Academic Press, pp. 159–229.

——— 1987 "Colobines: Infanticide by Adult Males." *In:* B. Smuts, et al. (eds.), q.v., pp. 83–97.

Sugiyama, Y. and J. Koman
1979 "Tool-using and -making Behavior in Wild Chimpanzees at Bossou, Guinea." *Primates,* **20**:513–524.

Sumner, D. R., M. E. Morbeck, and J. Lobick
1989 "Age-Related Bone Loss in Female Gombe Chimpanzees." *American Journal of Physical Anthropology,* **72**:259.

Susman, Randall L. (ed.)
1984 *The Pygmy Chimpanzee. Evolutionary Biology and Behavior.* New York: Plenum.

Susman, Randall L.
1988 "New Postcranial Remains from Swartkrans and Their Bearing on the Functional Morphology and Behavior of *Paranthropus robustus*." *In:* F. E. Grine (ed.), q.v., pp. 149–172.

Susman, Randall L., Jack T. Stern and William L. Jungers
1985 "Locomotor Adaptations in the Hadar Hominids." *In: Ancestors: The Hard Evidence,* E. Delson (ed.), New York: Alan R. Liss, pp. 184–192.

Sussman, Robert W.
1991 "Primate Origins and the Evolution of Angiosperms." *American Journal of Primatology,* **23**:209–223.

Sussman, Robert W., James M. Cheverud and Thad Q. Bartlett
1995 Infant Killing as an Evolutionary Strategy: Reality or Myth?" *Evolutionary Anthropology,* **3**(5):149–151.

Swisher, C. C. III, G. H. Curtis, T. Jacob, et al.
1994 "Age of the Earliest Known Hominids in Java, Indonesia." *Science,* **263**:1118–1121.

Swisher, C. C., W. J. Rink, S. C. Anton, et al.
1996 "Latest *Homo erectus* of Java: Potential Contemporaneity with *Homo sapiens* in Southwest Java." *Science,* **274**:1870–1874.

Szalay, Frederick S. and Eric Delson
1979 *Evolutionary History of the Primates.* New York: Academic Press.

Tattersal, Ian, Eric Delson, and John Van Couvering
1988 *Encyclopedia of Human Evolution and Prehistory.* New York: Garland Publishing.

Teleki, G.
1986 "Chimpanzee Conservation in Sierra Leone—A Case Study of a Continent-wide Problem." Paper presented at Understanding Chimpanzees Symposium, Chicago Academy of Sciences, Chicago, Nov. 7–10, 1987.

Templeton, Alan R.
1996 "Gene Lineages and Human Evolution." *Science,* **272**:1363–1364.

Tenaza, R. and R. Tilson
1977 "Evolution of Long-Distance Alarm Calls in Kloss' Gibbon." *Nature,* **268**:233–235.

Thieme, Hartmut
1997 "Lower Palaeolithic Hunting Spears from Germany." *Nature,* **385**:807–810.

Thorne, A. G. and M. H. Wolpoff
1992 "The Multiregional Evolution of Humans." *Scientific American,* **266**:76–83.

Tiemel, Chen, Yang Quan, and Wu En
1994 "Antiquity of *Homo sapiens* in China." *Nature,* **368**:55–56.

Tishkoft, S. A., E. Dietzsch, W. Speed, et al.
1996 "Global Patterns of Linkage Disequilibrium at the CD4 Locus and Modern Human Origins." *Science,* **271**:1380–1387.

Tobias, Phillip
    1971   *The Brain in Hominid Evolution.* New York: Columbia University Press.

—————
    1983   "Recent Advances in the Evolution of the Hominids with Especial Reference to Brain and Speech." Pontifical Academy of Sciences, *Scrita Varia,* **50**:85–140.

—————
    1991   *Olduvai Gorge, Volume IV. The Skulls, Endocasts and Teeth of* Homo habilis. Cambridge: Cambridge University Press.

Todd, T. W.
    1920,   "Age Changes in the Pubic Bone." *American*
    1921   *Journal of Physical Anthropology,* **3**:285–334; **4**:1–70.

Trinkaus, Erik and Pat Shipman
    1992   *The Neandertals.* New York: Alfred A. Knopf.

Tuttle, Russell H.
    1990   "Apes of the World." *American Scientist,* **78**:115–125.

United Nations Economic Commission for Europe/European Commission (EC-UN/ECE),
    1996   Forest Conditions in Europe. Results of the 1995 Survey (EC-UN/ECE). Brussels.

Villa, Paola
    1983   *Terra Amata and the Middle Pleistocene Archaeological Record of Southern France.* University of California Publications in Anthropology, Vol. 13. Berkeley: University of California Press.

Visalberghi, E.
    1990   "Tool Use in Cebus." *Folia Primatologica,* **54**:146–154.

Von Koenigswald, G. H. R.
    1956   *Meeting Prehistoric Man.* New York: Harper & Brothers.

Vrba, E. S.
    1988   "Late Pliocene Climatic Events and Hominid Evolution." *In:* F. Grine (ed.), q.v., pp. 405–426.

Wakayama, T., A. C. F. Perry, M. Zucotti, K. R. Johnson and R. Yanagimachi
    1998   "Full-term Development of Mice from Enucleated Oocytes Injected with Cumulus Cell Nuclei." *Nature,* **394**:369–374.

Walker, A.
    1991   "The Origin of the Genus *Homo.*" *In:* S. Osawa and T. Honjo (eds.), *Evolution of Life.* Tokyo: Springer-Verlag, pp. 379–389.

—————
    1993   "The Origin of the Genus *Homo.*" *In:* D. T. Rasmussen (ed.), *The Origin and Evolution of Humans and Humaness.* Boston: Jones and Bartlett, pp. 29–47.

Walker, Alan and R. E. Leakey
    1993   *The Nariokotome* Homo erectus *Skeleton.* Cambridge: Harvard University Press.

Wanpo, Huang, Russell Ciochon, et al.
    1995   "Early *Homo* and Associated Artifacts from Asia." *Nature,* **378**:275–278.

Ward, Peter
    1994   *The End of Evolution.* New York: Bantam.

Washburn, S. L.
    1963   "The Study of Race." *American Anthropologist,* **65**:521–531.

Watson, J. B., and F. H. C. Crick
    1953a "Genetical Implications of the Structure of the Deoxyribonucleic Acid." *Nature,* **171**:964–967.

—————
    1953b "A Structure for Deoxyribonucleic Acid." *Nature,* **171**:737–738.

Weiner, J. S.
    1955   *The Piltdown Forgery.* London: Oxford University Press.

Weiss, Robin A. and Richard W. Wrangham
    1999   "From Pan to Pandemic." *Nature,* **397**:385–386.

Wheat, Joe Ben
    1972   "The Olsen-Chubbuck Site; A Paleo-Indian Bison Kill." *American Antiquity,* **37**:1–180.

White, T. D.
    1980   "Evolutionary Implications of Pliocene Hominid Footprints." *Science,* **208**:175–176.

—————
    1983   Comment Made at Institute of Human Origins Conference on the Evolution of Human Locomotion (Berkeley, Ca.).

White, Tim D. and Donald C. Johanson
    1989   "The Hominid Composition of Afar Locality 333: Some Preliminary Observations." *Hominidae,* Proceedings of the 2nd International Congress of Human Paleontology, Milan: Editoriale Jaca Book, pp. 97–101.

White, Tim D., Gen Suwa, and Berhane Asfaw
1994 "*Australopithecus ramidus,* a New Species of Early Hominid from Aramis, Ethiopia." *Nature,* **371**:306–312.

———
1995 Corrigendum (White, et al., 1994). *Nature,* **375**:88.

Whiten, A., J. Goodall, W. C. McGrew, et al.
1999 "Cultures in Chimpanzees." *Nature,* **399**:682–685.

Williams, George C. and Randolph M. Nesse
1991 "The Dawn of Darwinian Medicine." *The Quarterly Review of Biology,* **66**:1–22.

Williams, Robert C.
1985 "HLA II: The Emergence of the Molecular Model for the Major Histocompatibility Complex." *Yearbook of Physical Anthropology,* 1985, **28**:79–95.

Wilmut, I., A. E. Schnieke, et al.
1997 "Viable Offspring Derived from Fetal and Adult Mammalian Cells." *Nature,* **385**:810–813.

Wilson, Edward O.
1992 *The Diversity of Life,* Cambridge, MA: The Belknap Press of Harvard University Press.

Wolpoff, Milford H.
1984 "Evolution in *Homo erectus:* The Question of Stasis." *Paleobiology,* **10**:389–406.

———
1989 "Multiregional Evolution: The Fossil Alternative to Eden." *In:* P. Mellars and C. Stringer, (eds.) q.v., pp. 62–108.

———
1995 *Human Evolution* 1996 Edition. New York: McGraw-Hill Inc., College Custom Series.

———
1999 *Paleoanthropology.* (2nd Ed.) New York: McGraw-Hill.

Wolpoff, M., Wu Xin Chi, and Alan G. Thorne
1984 "Modern *Homo sapiens* Origins." *In:* Smith and Spencer (eds.), q.v., pp. 411–483.

Wolpoff, M., et al.
1994 "Multiregional Evolutions: A World-Wide Source for Modern Human Populations." *In:* M. H. Nitecki and D. V. Nitecki (eds.), q.v., pp. 175–199.

Wood, Bernard
1991 *Koobi Fora Research Project IV: Hominid Cranial Remains from Koobi Fora.* Oxford: Clarendon Press.

———
1992a "Origin and Evolution of the Genus *Homo.*" *Nature,* **355**:783–790.

———
1992b "A Remote Sense for Fossils." *Nature,* **355**:397–398.

Worthman, Carol
1999 "Evolutionary Perspectives on the Onset of Puberty." *In:* Trevethan, W. R., E. O. Smith, and J. J. McKenna (eds.), *Evolutionary Medicine.* New York: Oxford University Press.

Wu, Rukang and Xingren Dong
1985 "*Homo erectus* in China." *In: Palaeoanthropology and Palaeolithic Archaeology in the People's Republic of China,* R. Wu and J. W. Olsen (eds.), New York: Academic Press, pp. 79–89.

Wu, Rukang, and S. Lin
1983 "Peking Man." *Scientific American,* **248**:(6)86–94.

Yellen, John E., et al.
1995 "A Middle Stone Age Worked Bone Industry from Katanda, Upper Semliki Valley, Zaire." *Science,* **268**:553–556.

Yi, Seonbok and G. A. Clark
1983 "Observations on the Lower Palaeolithic of Northeast Asia." *Current Anthropology,* **24**:181–202.

Young, David.
1992 *The Discovery of Evolution.* Cambridge: Natural History Museum Publications, Cambridge University Press.

Zubrow, Ezra
1989 "The Demographic Modeling of Neanderthal Extinction." *In:* P. Mellars and C. Stringer (eds.), q.v., pp. 212–231.

Photo Credits

Index

Page numbers in *italics* indicate illustrations. Page numbers in **bold** indicate definitions.

A

A allele, distribution of, 309
ABO system, 21, *72*
  as example of allele frequency change, 299
  genotypes and associated phenotypes, *69*, 71–72
  Mendelian inheritance illustrated by, 69, 74
Abrigo do Lagar Velho site, 281–282
absolute dating, 174
acclimatization, **325**
Acheulian tool industry, **225**, 226, 228–229, *229*, 246–247, *251*
achondroplasia, *70*, 301
acquired characteristics, inheritance of, 28
adaptations, **11**
adaptive niche, **86**
adaptive radiation, **153**
additive effect, 72
adenine, *46*, 47, *49*
adolescence, 359, 362–363
adolescent growth spurt, **348**
adult acclimatization, 332
adulthood, 363–364
Aegyptopithecus, 157–158
affiliative, **129**
affiliative behaviors, among primates, 130–132
Africa
  archaic *H. sapiens* fossils in, 241, *242*
  Central, hominid discoveries in, 183

East African Rift Valley, 174–175, *175*
East African sites
  early *Homo*, 198, *199*
  H. erectus, 211–212, 225–226, *228*
  hominids, 175–182, 196, 205–206
  H. sapiens sapiens discoveries in, 276
  North, *H. erectus* finds in, 227, *228*
  South
    early *Homo*, 198, *199*
    H. erectus finds in, 226–227
    hominid discoveries, 183–186, 196
African Americans
  incidence of rickets among, 327
  population history of, 301
African origin hypothesis of evolution of *H. sapiens sapiens*, 273, 275
aggression, in primates, 129–130
aging, 364–365
agriculture, effect of on environment, 373–374
AIDS, 333–334
Alamasi, Yahaya, *113*
albinism, *70*
albinos, 326–327, *327*
allele frequency, **75**, 299
  in humans, 312, *312*, 322
alleles, **66**–67, 69
  recessive and dominant, 71, 301
Allen's rule of body shape, 329, *330*, 358
Allia Bay, hominid discoveries in, 178, *192*, *193*, 203
Allison, A. C., 304
Altamira Cave, 289, *290*
altruism, **132**
American Civil Liberties Union, 39

amino acid sequencing, 95
amino acids, **49**
  essential, **352**
Amud, Neandertal remains in, *254*, *257*, 264
Amud skull, *252*, *255*
analogies, **150**
anatomical studies, 13
Andersson, J. Gunnar, 220
Andrews, Peter, 273
angiosperms, 87
animals, domestication of, 371
Antarctica, depletion of ozone layer over, 381
anthropocentric, **139**
anthropoids, **82**, 98–99, 156–157
  Aegyptopithecus, 157–158
  dental formula in, 90
  New World monkeys, 99–100
  Old World, 157
  Old World monkeys, 100–102
anthropological perspective, 14–15
anthropology, **6**
  applied, 7
  cultural, 6–7
  economic, 7
  forensic, **12**
  linguistic, 9
  medical, 7
  physical, 9–13
anthropometry, **11**
antibiotics, overuse of, 336
antigens, **69**
Apidium, 157
applied anthropology, 7
Arago, archaic *H. sapiens* fossils found at, *242*, 245

431

World Political Map

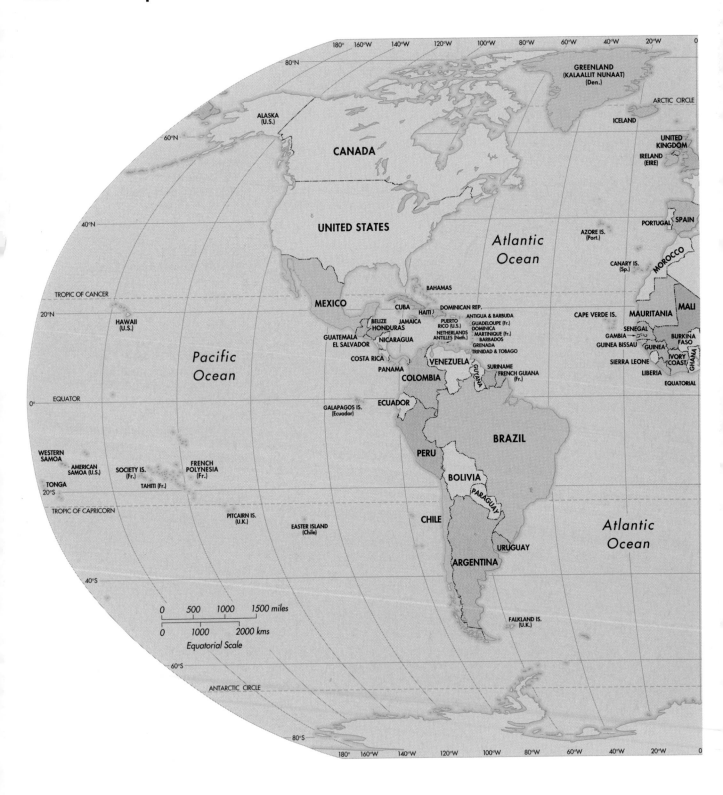